AN · ALBERTA · ART
CHRONICLE

AN · ALBERTA · ART
CHRONICLE

adventures in recent
&
contemporary art

MARY-BETH LAVIOLETTE

ALTITUDE PUBLISHING

Published by Altitude Publishing Canada Ltd.
1500 Railway Avenue, Canmore, Alberta T1W 1P6
www.altitudepublishing.com
1-800-957-6888

PUBLISHER: Stephen Hutchings ❧ EDITORS: Sebastian Hutchings, Jennifer Groundwater, Joanna Kadi, Leslie Strudwick ❧ INDEXER: Elizabeth Bell
JACKET DESIGN AND TYPESETTING: Bryan Pezzi

Alberta Foundation for the Arts

We acknowledge the financial support of the Government of Canada through the Book Publishing Industry Development Program (BPIDP) for our publishing activities. ❧ We acknowledge the financial support of the Alberta Foundation for the Arts

Altitude GreenTree Program – Altitude Publishing will plant twice as many trees as were used in the manufacturing of this product.

An Alberta Art Chronicle is comprised of two components. The first is a 544 page hardcover book; the second is a CD that contains approximately 200 colour images that illustrate the text. The CD can be found attached to the inside front cover of the book. Please note: additional or replacement copies of this CD may be purchased directly from the Publisher for $12.95 plus shipping and handling.

Library and Archives Canada Cataloguing in Publication
Laviolette, Mary-Beth
An Alberta art chronicle : adventures in recent and contemporary art/ Mary-Beth Laviolette. Includes index.
ISBN 1-55153-940-3
1. Art, Canadian--Alberta--21st century--History. I. Title.
N6546.A4L38 2005 709´.7123´09045 C2005-906648-2

An Alberta Art Chronicle CD ISBN 1-55153-941-1

Printed and bound in Canada by Friesens ❧ CD manufactured in Canada
2 4 6 8 9 7 5 3 1

To Douglas MacLean who likes the art adventure as much as I do.

TABLE OF CONTENTS

ALBERTA ART TO THE END OF CENTURY

introduction

A Chronicle of Recent and Contemporary Art in Alberta: 1970 to End of Century

THIS BOOK, ITS WRITING AND RESEARCH, began as a project for Alberta's 2005 Centennial. It was undertaken in the spirit of casting some light on Alberta's artistic landscape and in particular, the most recent one that energetically took shape post-1970. Taking nearly ten years to complete (as a part-time endeavour), this book is part history but more importantly, a narrative with several thematic areas explored and developed from one art writer's point of view. This means it has a certain bias and does not try to obscure the fact that a strong spotlight is shone on Calgary where I resided for nearly twenty years. Home to one of Canada's largest art colleges, a university with a bachelor's and master's degree in visual art, five public art galleries (including the art programming of the Glenbow Museum), five artist-run centres and an incredibly vibrant commercial art gallery scene, Calgary possesses a critical mass like no other centre in the province.

In trying to create a picture of nearly 175 artists, areas of artmaking, and certain communities, this book relies substantially on the opinions, observations and comments of other writers, critics, curators and the artists themselves. In a selective but still wide-ranging survey such as this, I cannot pretend to have personally seen all of the art covered nor is it especially fruitful to overlook some very fine, insightful writing by others in exhibition brochures and catalogues (especially), newspaper and magazine reviews and letters. In addition, there was material culled from interviews I conducted, and to fill out the picture, my own extensive background as a writer/researcher/arts journalist in Ottawa, Toronto and Calgary.

Books about Alberta art are infrequent, and as far as more recent art is concerned, there were only a small number to consult: Bente Roed Cochrane's *Printmaking in Alberta 1945–1985* (The University of Alberta Press); Jetske Ironside's *Spaces and Places Eight Decades of Landscape Painting in Alberta* (Alberta Art Foundation); Kathy E. Zimon's *Alberta Society of Artists: The First Seventy Years* (University of Calgary Press) and Suzanne Devonshire Baker's *Artists of Alberta* (The University of Alberta Press).

It might be useful to ask at this point: why bother with a book about recent and contemporary art in Alberta? To which the reply is – because of the adventure. Almost as soon as I returned to the province in 1982, there seemed to be something different about visual art activity; a spirited buzz, an energy I had not sensed anywhere after living in Ontario for nearly a decade. It's not that all of the art I was seeing was terrific or wonderful, but there was enough of it to say something is happening here and some of it is very good. It is that adventure (along with a more factual accounting of who, what, where and when) that I hope I have been able to convey.

As mentioned, there are nearly 175 artists accounted for in this chronicle, of which the great majority have training and led active lives as professional artists. (There are, of course, the exceptions, including folk artists who will have not had much of either in the way of training or a substantial history of exhibiting.) In general, most of the professionals covered trained in the late 1960s, 1970s and 1980s, and they have at least ten years of work under their belts. This still means that not every professional artist is included as it was not the intent to survey everyone, and ultimately, my own biases, base of knowledge, interests and so on played a role in the selection. In some cases, only a snapshot of an artist's practice is provided, focusing on a particular series of work; in others a more in-depth treatment is given. It will be noted, too, that the issue of reception or how an artist's work is received is of interest because, as in many fields of creative endeavour, the cream does not always rise to the top. In the mercurial world of visual arts, there is no such thing as a level playing field, with timing and place sometimes having a large influence on how an artist's work is received or not received.

In documenting the artists covered, the book also has two sides to it, beginning with a focus on art made about the region or reflective about this "place" called Alberta. In the second section and onward, the slant changes to encompass art that has other kinds of concerns or content that may or may not have anything to do with where it is made. From my perspective, there are definitely two streams of art in the province that at certain points or with certain artists intermingle with each other.

A word should also be said about why the names of certain institutions are not always the same throughout the book. For instance, until 1960, the art college in Calgary is known as the Provincial Institute of Technology and Art (The Tech). Then, for several decades, it's the Alberta College of Art (ACA) before another change in 1995 to Alberta College of Art and Design (ACAD). In keeping with the time or era discussed an effort was made to use the name then in use.

Finally, there are many thank-you's and acknowledgements to be made, of which only a small selection can be noted here. A warm thank-you to Nancy Townshend, whose own passion for Alberta art history got the ball rolling many years ago with the marshalling of a research grant from the Alberta 2005 Centennial History Society. Thank-you to Douglas MacLean, a knowledgeable and dedicated supporter of the arts who stepped in to provide much-needed funds for a portion of the writing, and personally put up with all of the unending work (along with son Duncan). At one point, too, the Alberta Foundation for the Arts provided a writer's grant but more importantly, through its art collection, made available many of the images for this book free of charge. A big thank-you to the AFA's Gail Lint and Barbara Johnston for staying on top of all of my requests. Not to be forgotten, of course, are also the many, many images and other sorts of information provided by the artists themselves or their representatives. I couldn't have done it without the cooperation of these many inspired and committed individuals.

Other forms of assistance came from Anne Severson who tirelessly condensed and assembled many artist biographies; Alberta College of Art and Design instructor Monique Westra who made available two ACAD students to do valuable research (my thanks to them as well), and Virgil Hammock who provided me with a gold mine of early reviews. Finally, big thanks must also go to Stephen Hutchings and Altitude Publishing for editing and taking this chronicle to its final destination at their own expense.

Mary-Beth Laviolette, Canmore AB, 2005

PLACE, LANDSCAPE AND ART ABOUT NATURE

chapter one

A Troubled Genre: Post-1970 Landscape Art

IN HIS 1989 LANDMARK BOOK, *Images of the West: Changing Perceptions of the Prairies, 1690–1960,* historian R. Douglas Francis explores how image and perception have shaped the Prairies more profoundly than either the surveyor's stake or the farmer's plough.

"Throughout its history, the Canadian West has evoked strong images in the minds of those who visited, settled in, or sometimes simply wrote about the region. These people saw in the West what they wanted, or were conditioned by their cultural milieu, to see. At different times, they perceived a West that was a wasteland, a pristine wilderness, a source of national greatness and imperial grandeur, a utopia, a harsh and cruel land, or a mythical region shaped by the attitudes and beliefs of its people. Each of these images held sway for a period of time and then gave way to a new image, resulting in changing images of the Canadian West." [1]

Relying on fur trader accounts, travelogues, expedition reports, literary works and landscape art, Francis undertook his unique study because he believed that "these images have been more than passing commentaries on the region; they have greatly influenced – and sometimes dictated – policies toward the area, and thus profoundly affected the historical evolution of the West." [2]

Francis completed his analysis in the post-war period with pictures and text created by prairie landscape artists, writers and historians. He optimistically concluded: "a western Canadian historical, literary and artistic tradition has emerged that has produced some of the finest expressions of a regional culture and some of the most vivid images of the West for a national and indeed, an international audience." [3]

It all sounds like a happy ending. Yet while it may be true that prairie writers have reached, and continue to reach, a national audience, landscape painting, including Alberta's rich and varied output, has all but taken a nosedive into oblivion. As the *Globe and Mail* art critic John Bentley Mays noted in a 1995 review, prairie landscape has "a complex history of art, about which gallery-goers both east and west of the vast Canadian midlands know too little." [4] This is especially true in regards to recent practitioners of landscape art in the Prairies. With a few exceptions, such as Saskatchewan's Dorothy Knowles and David Thauberger, Manitoba's Ivan Eyre, and Alberta's Ted Godwin and Takao Tanabe (who worked in the province in the '70s), contemporary landscape painting rarely registers anything more than a blip in national art circles, despite involving what Mays describes as "a mighty host" [5] of practitioners. Landscape painting may be still visible within the Canadian art market, and within a certain network of regional public galleries and collections, but within a *national* or international context, prairie-based landscape – either abstract or representational – is not what Canadian art specialists of recent art have cared to investigate or represent in the later decades of the twentieth century. (It is, for instance, largely absent in Joan Murray's book *Canadian Art in the Twentieth Century* and in other surveys produced at the time.[6])

On the few occasions when such art has reached a wider, non-Western Canadian audience, such as the 1986 exhibition *Spaces and Places: Eight Decades of Landscape Painting in Alberta,* it is a legacy *but* also a liability.[7] As critic Liz Wylie commented for the Toronto-based magazine *Canadian Art*, "Since it is touring nationally, it is a shame that *Spaces and Places* was restricted to only landscape paintings, since most of Alberta's top contemporary artists do not work in this genre. Because of its emphasis on the traditional, this exhibition serves to reinforce the national image of Alberta as a non-intellectual, unpeopled vacationland."[8]

In general, unless the subject of landscape is used to address a contemporary art issue, like deconstructing or analysing its representation in historical art and western culture, or how the developed world treats nature as a resource for exploitation, contemporary works inspired by or representing the Canadian terrain are largely viewed as passé, even problematic. As the Banff-based publication *The Cairn* informed its readership in 1994: "Landscape painting has fallen out of vogue in the mainstream of contemporary Canadian art."[9]

In addition, according to the maverick curator, Jeffrey Spalding: "The prairies and the mountains are simply overwhelming, their effect upon the human spirit unparalleled.... Yet, over the past two decades, the art world has been preoccuppied by deconstructive, combative and contrary artworks, examining human and societal folly. Art expressing optimistic life views and spiritually uplifting images is clearly out of favour. It is as if the curatorial community cannot even fathom what to do with a work that expresses joy or acknowledges surrender to the primacy of spirit over human intellect and discourse. Regardless of the root case or reason, neither the distinctive physical landforms of Alberta, nor its western/ranch heritage, figure very prominently within the contemporary practice of the province."[10]

Of course, not all art dealing with the physical landforms, or, to a lesser extent, the western/ranch heritage of Alberta expresses an optimistic point of view, but Spalding is right in pointing out how marginal these topics are to what is commonly defined as a contemporary practice. In Canada, it seems, art recognized as relevant or contemporary is usually about something else. This is not to suggest that this other art is wrong-headed, or that *all living* landscape painters have received the proverbial brush-off, but fixed within the Canadian contemporary art scene is a strangely warped glass ceiling that confines such activity to the lower echelons.

That such attitudes exist in the so-called *postmodern* era is ironic. After the restrictive, increasingly formalist doctrine of post-war modernism, this new era was supposed to be, above all, *pluralistic* – embracing a broader spectrum of approaches and subject matter than had ever been possible before. But by the 1990s there seemed to be a new set of critical do's and don'ts that, in effect, excluded most landscape painting.

Postmodern practice, for one thing, rejected modern art's fixation

– particularly since World War II – on aesthetic matters (i.e. colour, surface, composition, light, shape and so on). Postmodernism stressed content over style and meaning over form; it encouraged subject matter dealing with cultural and social issues and scorned romantic notions about art being primarily an expression of personal vision. In general, landscape painting is perceived as containing too much of the former, and too little of the latter. As the *Georgia Straight* critic Paula Gustafson put it in 1994: "Landscape painting doesn't have the subtext or awareness of critical theory that is de rigueur in today's art-world doctrines. Painting landscape is viewed as a passive art form, an irrelevant, purely descriptive activity that has become wearied with overtones of conventionalism and nostalgia." [11]

Worse, even the word landscape can now be construed to have certain negative connotations. Here is how curator and critic Annette Hurtig defined the word in *The Culture of Nature* exhibition: "The compound term – land + scape – has come to mean not only an expanse of land awaiting the imprint of ownership, but also a certain kind of composition that represents nature as the raw material upon which technology imposes its will. It signifies a particular worldview." [12]

A worldview that, from a postcolonial perspective, is interpreted as exploitative and colonial, and therefore perfect fodder for contemporary art makers to investigate and critique. Absent from this postmodern criticality, however, is any recognition of how the continuing tradition of prairie landscape is in itself considered a postcolonial marker of western identity. "The only barrier that has stood in the way of having the western self totally defined or absorbed by the [East] has been the land," writes George Melnyk about the landscape art of Edmonton's Norman Yates.[13]

Compounding landscape's troubled status in this post-1970 period is the fact that the medium of painting itself has had its own difficulties as a credible postmodern practice. For instance, in 1995 it was possible to read the following observation about the country's largest anglophone art centre and the behaviour of its publicly supported visual arts institutions: "To hear some young Toronto painters talk, as I did this week, you'd think our streets are patrolled by robocops programmed to blast the heads off people caught with tubes of oil paint on their persons. If this picture is something of a cartoon, it's got more than a grain of truth in it. Local painting is steadily, almost aggressively ignored by the Art Gallery of Ontario, the Power Plant, and even the city's established artist-run centres." [14]

In contrast, the same critic wrote a year later: "When the book of *fin-de-siecle* painting gets written, you can expect to find Alberta artists hogging an outsized number of pages. They're just that good, and that prolific – and numerous as prairie dogs, as well. And they've been fortunate, insofar as the current, corrosive distrust of painting appears to have skipped clear over their heads, from New York and Toronto right to Vancouver." [15]

It is true: painting of all kinds has survived and flourished in Alberta. But given what many in the influential public sector of the visual arts have focused their attention on across Canada, it can be said that what will have been thoroughly documented into the next century is art that is interdisciplinary, and whose strategies are conceptual and critical. Painting will be considered only when it addresses the same kind of social and cultural concerns that have preoccupied interdisciplinary work, including installation, video, mixed media, performance and photo-based art.

Thus, to sum up more broadly: in the early days of Canada's contemporary art period (1960s), there thrived the very novel, ecologically aware perspective of an artist, such as the Calgary-raised Iain Baxter and his witty mixed media work, *Bagged Landscape with W Water* (1966).[16] This work consists of a vacuum-formed vinyl bag filled with air and water, and it suggests that landscape in modern-day Canada has become simply another commodity to be packaged, marketed and sold. This and other works by Baxter are part of a surge of new ideas from that period, redefining what constitutes a work of art, and it remains a breath of fresh air. But closer to the end of the century, Willard Holmes makes the remarkably exclusionary observation, that "the terms 'conceptual, language-based painting and photo-based work' are broad enough to encompass most contemporary work purchased by the [Vancouver Art] gallery, and also *to define most art produced in the 20th century [my emphasis].*" [17]

In this book, a much broader definition of contemporary art making is entertained in order to include the continuing tradition of landscape painting in Alberta. In this chapter, I will examine the problem of its regional status, as well as suggest – with further elaboration later on – that this art practice has never been about just one thing, as it is in the highly touted landscape associated with Saskatchewan's Emma Lake Artists' Workshops.

Much has been written about the influence of Emma Lake and its reputation for cultivating a type of landscape painting sympathetic to the aims of late American modernist art in Alberta and Saskatchewan, particularly the use of colour field painting. Using this technique, the formal qualities of painting are considered more important than what is represented. On a certain level, Emma Lake became the modernist definition of how to paint a landscape on the Canadian prairies, and it continues to have its devotees.

In the eyes of its critics, though, who came to be at least as influential, Emma Lake is a Canadian dilemma, largely due to its legendary association with New York critic Clement Greenberg and other so-called "modernist grandees." [18] The art Emma Lake helped to spawn has been written off as "a minor colonial school of abstract expressionism," [19] and its workshops dismissed as "either a long-playing event of rather limited regional interest, or a shoddy chapter in American cultural adventurism." [20]

However, not every painter who abstracts or simplifies the landscape – like Edmonton's Harry Savage or Robert Sinclair – is an Emma Lake affiliate. Savage, for instance, is both a critic of Greenberg's impact on modern prairie art *and* a painter of large non-representational watercolours that respond to the flatness of the terrain and the sweep of land and sky. He attributes his sparse, horizontal view of the prairies to the day he stepped out his back door as a young child growing up on the fringe of the prairies.[21] A similar source can be found in Robert Sinclair's spartan prairie-scapes with winding road. For a survey exhibition of his art from 1969–76, in a style as simplified as his paintings, he wrote:

Many years ago
From the window
A road went by our farm and
I followed it...
Through.[22]

But regardless of what an artist's sources are, an even bigger obstacle for prairie landscape painting has been its regional label. In certain contexts, regional can have positive connotations, but in the art world, with its long-standing hierarchy of international, national and regional art, the latter often implies something that is parochial, derivative and of limited interest. To be sure, there have been attempts to recast regional art in a more positive light, or to at least acknowledge that "regionalism is an expression of difference." [23] As Calgary art critic Nancy Tousley articulated: "Regionalism in art is not, and never has been, so simple as paintings of lonesome pines, grain elevators or prairie roads. Within such images lies a political stance opposing the marginalization of the region and the dominance of established centres, whether they be Paris, New York or Toronto."[24]

Still, in the Canadian art world, where publicly supported institutions like the National Gallery of Canada and The Canada Council are geared to supporting artists of national consequence, there is a glass ceiling facing any practice designated regional. Even when such art is acknowledged as very good, a regional tag implies that "very good" is as far as it's going to go. As for determining what is regional and what is national, many times it seems to be based on nothing more than location. As curator and artist Jeffrey Spalding observed, "An important thing in Edmonton or Winnipeg is regional. In Toronto or Ottawa, it's national."[25] In Canada, it seems, geography can determine destiny.

Another difficulty with the notion of regional art is addressing such work on its own terms. Often, such labelling carries with it the implication that something else more significant is going on somewhere else more important. It's fine to acknowledge regional differences but for a real outstanding report card, conformity with the art centres is key. In this respect, the Canadian hinterland usually gets a failing grade but not through any fault of its own: "If the rest of Canada has seemed to lag behind Montreal, Toronto and Vancouver, it is because art in the modern era became so urban as to preclude much else. It has been next to impossible for the solitary, serious talent to emerge full-blown away from the influence of the larger cities."[26]

The above observation was made in the early '80s by Vancouver curator and historian Alvin Balkind. But by the end of that decade, the *Globe and Mail* arts writer Stephen Godfrey suggested a new reality had emerged in Canada. "Canadian artists in particular stopped any pretence of conforming to a 'national' vision.... If the eighties brought anything forward, it was a belated lesson in survival: small is beautiful, you don't have to leave home, creativity knows no geographical limits."[27] But lest this should sound like a glowing recommendation for regionalism, Godfrey concludes: "It was great for the art – but lousy for the country. This was the decade of the failure of our cultural nation-builders."[28]

Godfrey's lament underlines how regional voices can be viewed with misgivings and suspicion. Thus, the regional label becomes a way of putting difference in its place; to be regional in Canada means to be marginalized.

One other factor pertinent to keeping prairie landscape art neatly slotted away as a footnote is the problematic legacy of the Group of Seven. It's remarkable to think that seventy-five years after the Group's inaugural show in Toronto, their impressive work is still considered the defining, national moment in Canadian landscape art. As John Bentley Mays wrote in the *Globe and Mail* in 1995: "In a dozen years on either side of 1920, Thomson and Group artists painted the most boldly inventive and resonantly beautiful modern landscapes ever made in this country until that time, and possibly ever." [29]

In the same year, Robert Fulford observed in *Canadian Art:* "Their landscapes made such a deep appeal to the Canadian spirit, and became so firmly embedded in the national consciousness, that they obliterated just about everything else on the scene. The painters who followed the Group became a lost generation, and the painters who preceded them vanished from sight." [30]

Both Fulford and Mays were writing in response to the National Gallery of Canada's landmark exhibition, *The Group of Seven: Art for a Nation.* Curated by Charles Hill, the 1995 exhibition marked the seventy-fifth anniversary of the Group's first show. Its magisterial exhibition name and subsequent media coverage clearly reinforces the continuing rhetoric that what this one inspired, talented group of central Canadians accomplished is somehow the apotheosis of landscape art in Canada, period. That their efforts are quintessentially "Canadian" while everyone else's can be neatly slotted away into the regional cubby-hole.

As far as Alberta landscape art is concerned, Jeffrey Spalding spells out the consequences of such a prize: "From the 1920s through the 1960s, a number of English-born artists, each in turn, served as head of Alberta's art colleges: A.C. Leighton, Walter Phillips and H.G. Glyde. Their landscape art was, generally speaking, adjudged during their day by national agencies as being altogether too faithful a record of the land, too accepting of the splendours and grandeur of nature and thus, conservative rather than avant-garde. The latter distinction fell to the Group of Seven.... To this day, it irks enthusiasts of western Canadian historical art that the vision of the West as presented by Phillips, Leighton, and Glyde is excluded from the standard Canadian art histories." [31]

One Albertan artist who sought to turn the tables on how the Group is perceived, without taking away from their cultural achievement, is Robert Sinclair. His *Great Canadian Landscape* series (1969–72), consisting of sculptures made out of cut and folded plastic sheets, was motivated by his realization that the Group of Seven landscapes *were* regional, and perhaps irrelevant to prairie people.[32]

Later in the century, Chris Carson produced his mixed media *Great Canadian Hero* (1994). Comments about Carson's work echo Sinclair's observations: "The Edmonton artist's cheeky remake of Thomson's masterpiece is as much homage as lampoon, and suggests that three-quarters of a century after *The Jack Pine* was painted, it continues to cast long shadows. For years, the images made famous by Thomson and the Group of Seven decorated school hallways and bank lobbies across the country. They are stuck in our collective memory because they came to represent ... Canadian art, even though the terrain they depict doesn't necessarily speak to the hearts of those raised on the Prairies."[33]

In Douglas Francis's *Images of the West,* the post-war period is described as "the mythic west": "The West became a 'mental construct' that took shape in the mind of the beholder, based on his or her own perception of the region, often independently of the physical environment itself."[34] As an example, he quotes the Alberta author Robert Kroetsch: "The western landscape is one without boundaries quite often. So you have the experience within a kind of chaos, yet you have to order it somehow to survive. I'm particularly interested in the kinds of orderings we do on that landscape."[35]

What follows in the next three chapters is a discussion of some of the responses (or orderings, as Kroetsch defines it) created by Alberta-based artists. In the last chapter of this thematic section is art more specifically informed by nature and the environment.

chapter two

A Modernizing Perspective: Second Generation Landscape Painting

By the advent of the 1970s, Alberta's first generation of landscape artists – Illingworth Kerr, A.C. Leighton, Margaret Shelton, Maxwell Bates, W.J. Phillips, Euphemia McNaught, Roland Gissing, W.L. Stevenson, H.G. Glyde, Catharine and Peter Whyte – have been a dominant presence in the province for nearly four decades. Although their efforts would later be compared to seeds on rocky ground,[1] there is a more generous view that argues many of these pioneers generated a diverse legacy of landscape art. It encompasses the English landscape tradition of A.C. Leighton and W.J. Phillips, the rhythmic Group of Seven–inspired art of Illingworth Kerr and Euphemia McNaught and the darker, more European expressionist landscape of W.L. Stevenson and Maxwell Bates.

Part of this diverse legacy also includes certain pioneering women artists, such as Marion Nicoll, Thelma Manarey and Janet Mitchell. In the context of first generation landscape, their response is more idiosyncratic than their mostly male colleagues. Rather than simply describing the landscape, Nicoll's abstract, symbolic works, Manarey's freely worked etchings, and Mitchell's figurative-landscape images are more personal and intuitive, derived more from the imagination, and less concerned with describing the land's physical presence than with its emotional and spiritual dimensions. In a telling comment, A.C. Leighton once told Nicoll, a student of his, that as a 'visitor' he will never be as close to the western landscape as those who are from the area and that the task of painting it well will have to involve its own inhabitants.[2]

Besides being a dominant presence in landscape art up to the 1970s, this first generation has also established landscape as a primary subject matter for art in Alberta – the overwhelming presence of the environment perhaps making it almost inevitable. But given the quickening pace of avant-garde developments in western art, this elder generation is swimming against the tide. In the international art world, landscape has become a minor genre – a regional practice that can't quite shake its associations with the nineteenth century.

Abstraction has also become the prevailing language of post-war art and although some first-generation artists are willing to experiment with it, few are able to adapt to it with the vigour or success of a Marion Nicoll or Jack Taylor. Still, even with the introduction of an abstract approach, the subject of landscape guarantees its reception will most often be limited to the region in which it is produced. Worse, it will sometimes be dismissed as an unworthy subject.

In the early 1970s, for instance, art critic and curator Barry Lord coins the phrase "empty landscape," arguing that such art, like abstract painting, is uncommitted to dealing with the social realities of Canada.[3] More recently, postmodernists will dismiss the genre as a form of "cover-up art," because it often portrays the land as pristine, conveniently empty of First Nations people, and undisturbed by the environmental impact of white society.[4]

Nonetheless, by the early 70s, there were still many young Albertans willing to expend their energies on the genre; understanding that the western land still holds great meaning and resonance to those who have long lived in its presence. Maybe it has to do with what you *know,* or with a larger notion of identity including one's sense of self and one's place in the larger world. But in many cases, the following words of a second-generation artist like Norman Yates will still fall on indifferent ears: "Western history and western landscape are bound inextricably. The land is part and parcel of our history and our history has to do absolutely with the land. For me the land is a metaphor."[5]

Whatever their motives, by the 1970s, second-generation landscape painters in Alberta are adding their own voices with increasing frequency. Many like Frank Vervoort, Ken Christopher, Ted Godwin and Joice Hall have graduated from the Alberta College of Art, mostly within a ten-year period stretching from the mid 50s to the mid 60s. Others like Robert Sinclair, John McKee and Dulcie Foo Fat train elsewhere but later make their home in Alberta. Like two streams feeding into a larger current, landscape practice in Alberta is ready to flourish with this new generation.

One landscapist, who emerges somewhat earlier but can be considered within this time frame, is **O.N. (RICK) GRANDMAISON** (1932–1985, Calgary, Alberta). The son of the renowned portrait painter Nicholas and sculptor Sonia de Grandmaison Sr., the Calgary-born artist will later say that the purpose of his impressionistic oil paintings is to record the colour, mood and motion of the Canadian landscape,[6] which in his case will often be the foothills west and south of Calgary. Grandmaison's work is known for its tonal colour, rich texture and attention to the mercurial climate of the high plains. Because of his interest in capturing western sunsets and sunrises at their cranberry-coloured zenith, such occurrences are sometimes referred to as a *Grandmaison sky.*[7]

Like the elder Grandmaison, the painter also has a passion for western life, particularly ranching and what he perceives as its spirit of individualism.[8] His ranch scenes with cowboys are especially popular, and they've become his signature pieces. In 1975, he produces one of his most well-known works, entitled *The First Drive of Range Cattle*. The 5 × 10-foot canvas depicts the dusty drama of the first cattle drive in Alberta, complete with a Grandmaison sky. Related to this work, but perhaps even more important, is a series begun in 1961 documenting historic ranches and homesteads in their often compelling surroundings. He depicts these subjects as small outposts amidst a painterly landscape, surrounded by a sea of grasses and dramatic skies. According to the artist, the work investigates both art and history without compromising either.[9]

Grandmaison's representations of western life and his conservative style make him somewhat of an outsider in the local visual art community. On one hand: he "is not one who has become caught up in the New York trendy dicta,"[10] while on the other, "he [isn't] everyone's idea of an artist."[11] Despite this ambivalence, Grandmaison does share views similar with other younger artists of his generation about making art, and will make comments like: "Subject is really incidental to the expression of my ideas about it."[12] For Grandmaison it is the process of painting that matters and is similar in spirit to what curator Kate Davis observes about a younger colleague of Grandmaison's, Ken Christopher. "The real challenge is when we begin to appreciate the picture beyond illustration. We can experience the pleasure not only of recognition, but of discovery: the discovery that the canvas is not a window but a flat, two-dimensional surface; and that the green is not a tree but a gesture of paint; the discovery that the manipulation of paint upon that flat surface is the 'stuff' of art; the discovery of not only what is told, but *how* it is told."[13]

The how of what is being told becomes a major preoccupation of many second-generation Alberta landscape artists, some of the most notable being the so-called prairie modernists.[14] Influenced by New York abstraction, in particular Colour-Field painting, this group – active through the 1970s and into the 1980s – receives considerable attention from the local media, the art market and regional institutions, such as the Edmonton Art Gallery and Regina's the Norman McKenzie Art Gallery. This group consists of a loose collection of artists working in Alberta and Saskatchewan who also frequent the Emma Lake Artists' Workshops in the summer. The prairie modernists apply many of the practices of 1960s abstract painting to create what one significant exhibition in 1981 aptly calls: *The Big Picture.*[15] The characteristics of this landscape can be summed up in three words: flat – as in little or no illusion of depth; fields – as in uninterrupted fields of paint; and colour. In his commentary on the exhibition, curator Russell Bingham describes the relationship between the two genres: "On the Prairies today, abstraction and landscape painting coexist with equal vitality. The best painting generally takes the form of one or the other, and in some ways the two have become intimately related."[16]

Two Albertans working within this tradition but who achieve very different results are **KEN CHRISTOPHER** (1942, Swift Current, Saskatchewan) and **JOHN MCKEE** (1942, Sudbury, Ontario). Christopher's highly interpretative panoramas are a stark contrast to McKee's detailed representations of Albertan countryside under huge skies. Yet despite these very different stylistic results, the overall agenda is similar in that both artists are concerned with the application of paint, rather than the subject matter. In reference to this approach, McKee states, "I never see the subject, just paint the marks,"[17] and from Ken Christopher it's "the strokes of paint brushed on in a casual and yet vigorous manner that causes the work to walk a fine line between landscape and [abstract] gesture painting." [18]

According to Bingham, both artists are colour painters, "involved with formulating ways of representing the prairie landscape that will support their colouristic inventions." [19] In McKee's case, the paintings are rendered using a cool, subtle palette bathed in brilliant light, while Christopher uses lively, Fauve-like colours,[20] opaque but generously applied to create a surface of "calligraphic paint markings." [21] Both see landscape as a rich optical experience, what McKee articulates as "the freedom, independence, and limitless possibilities created by the vastness of the prairie space." [22]

Another approach to landscape still seen in the 1970s is the Group of Seven–inspired work of first-generation artists Euphemia McNaught and Illingworth Kerr, Kerr's former student and plein aire painting partner William Duma, and McNaught's younger neighbour, Robert Guest. The 1970s are particularly productive years for **EUPHEMIA MCNAUGHT** (1901–2002, Glenmorris, Ontario) and **ILLINGWORTH KERR** (1905–1989, Lumsden, Saskatchewan), both in terms of work and wider recognition. They have been around, it seems, forever, and yet as artists it is only after 1967, when Kerr retires from his position as head of the Alberta College of Art and McNaught lightens her regimen of teaching and community work in the Beaverlodge area, that painting becomes a full-time occupation for both artists. (A growing visual arts infrastructure in the province also makes it possible for their art to receive greater circulation.)

In this period, McNaught intensifies her efforts to depict the pioneer landmarks of the Peace River country, its mountains, lakes and broad valleys, utilizing her technique of strong brush strokes and clear colours "to bind the picture together like a tapestry." [23] She also taps into her life-long relationship with horses and other animals to represent their postures and personalities in watercolour and reed pen and ink. Also, through artistic acts of recollection, such as in *The Night Camp on Nose Mountain* (1981), McNaught underlines the role that an artist can play in giving a community a strong sense of belonging.

With his new freedom, Kerr "[paints] some of his biggest and best pictures." [24] Focusing on the undulating views of the foothills west of Calgary, his oils and acrylics become more atmospheric and at times hazy through

Kerr's "treatment of form, light and distance in terms of tonal values rather than colour."[25] In the 1970s, both Kerr and McNaught develop something of a passion for painting nocturnes. With its "differences in colour, fading of forms and poetic mood,"[26] both artists find something symbolic about this time of the day. Kerr's nocturnes are dark yet serene, while McNaught's are luminous and even mystical, less typical of what she has done before. In her paintings, the country is wild and unsettled; in his, the scenes are never far from a country road. The evening is Kerr's time for contemplation, and McNaught's time for dreaming.

While Kerr identifies with the Group of Seven's nationalistic spirit of painting the land "to make us at home in our own country,"[27] the motivations of a second-generation artist like **WILLIAM DUMA** (1936, Calgary, Alberta) are more inward looking. In Duma's case, his seven years as a noted stained-glass artist with a fascination for design, light and simplified form influence his painting. One reviewer remarks: "Duma's landscapes give the impression of a mosaic."[28] Duma himself writes that his painting is an attempt to capture the numerous moods of nature so that the viewer can be stimulated "to look deeper within, where intimate moments with nature cause an inner awareness."[29] In pursuit of this goal, Duma concentrates on the foothills around Calgary and south to the Crowsnest Pass, favouring those times of year when the contrasts of light and shadow are the greatest. (Robert Guest can be found in Chapter 7.)

One artist who straddles the previous two styles – the more representational Group of Seven–inspired painting and the more abstract prairie modernist style – is **TED GODWIN** (1933, Calgary, Alberta). In a sense, his paintings and watercolours are a synthesis of the two: dense brushwork laid in textured patterns on an abstract field of stained colour. In addition, rather than interpreting nature realistically, he renders a recognizable image that recreates nature as an abstract, two-dimensional entity.[30] This approach to landscape stems from Godwin's earlier work in Regina, where he spent fifteen years as a celebrated abstract painter of the Regina Five.

Once described as "the prototype of the honest western Canadian painter,"[31] Godwin's story mirrors many of the clichés connected to the introduction of post-war modernist art on the Prairies. It is a narrative that begins with the "isolated provincial"[32] who, like Godwin, blossoms as an artist when enlightened by the Wise Men of the East. In Godwin's case, the Wise

Men are New York's Barnett Newman, Jules Olitski and John Cage. Then, at a later date, his enlightenment becomes almost a liability because he is interpreted as practising art according to someone else's "canons, not his own." [33] It turns out to be another example of the "damned if you didn't and then damned if you did" theme that eventually plagues many prairie modernists as the Canadian art world turns its attention to more postmodern concerns.

Finally, in his mature years, Godwin returns to Calgary (1975) and settles on a path that neither refutes his past nor suppresses his own evolving instincts, remaining instead "his own man." [34] Having just completed his most original and compelling series of abstracts, *Tartan* paintings (1967–1976) – not fully exhibited until 1999 [35] – he surprises all by displaying his first set of landscape paintings and lithographs at the Moose Jaw Art Museum. From then on, it is landscape in a manner that is not only rich in colour and surface but also decorative: ironically, the very thing that used to draw criticism about his abstract work because it was considered not "tough enough" or "uncompromising."[36]

Godwin also has the artistic nerve to integrate his fishing hobby with the serious business of making art and makes no bones about it, subtitling one exhibition, *A Celebration of Wilderness, Art and Fishing.* It is in this vein that he produces a very significant body of landscapes, the seventy-eight-painting *Lower Bow* series, which encompasses the fabled fishing waters and shoreline of the Bow River between Calgary and Carseland. First exhibited in 1991 at Regina's Norman MacKenzie Art Gallery, the series is stylistically characteristic of much of his later landscape art.

Instead of looking towards the horizon as so many prairie painters do, Godwin picks up (it seems) a magnifying glass to illuminate the surface reflections of water and the kaleidoscopic textures and colours of the dense and tangled shoreline. His paintings make a nod to the work of Group of Seven painter J.E.H. MacDonald and his painting *The Tangled Garden,* which is a favourite of Godwin's. In addition, from the interweave [37] of his *Tartan* paintings, there is now the organic interweave of the underbrush along the river that is also linked to his study of Celtic Art, in particular its zoomorphic interlace.

With the *Lower Bow* series, Godwin makes a strong comment about the continuing efforts by the provincial government to dam every last strand of southern Albertan water, like the Old Man River. By focusing on the flowing and still waters of the foothills and plains, Godwin marries his passion for fishing and conservation with a little-known, and often little-respected, aspect of the prairie environment. Prairie rivers and creeks were an important lifeline for Aboriginal and, later, European peoples. What's different about Godwin's enduring view is the sharp contrast between it and a long-held attitude, best expressed by prairie pioneer George Spence: "It must be nothing less than a sin to allow needed water to be lost to join the ocean."[38] For Godwin, the sin is to not leave it alone.

As for those artists who look towards the horizon in a fresh way, interpreting the vast western expanse under what Kerr once described as "the great dome of sky,"[39] four individuals stand out: Harry Savage, Robert Sinclair, Takao (Tak) Tanabe and Norman Yates. In many ways, these artists are well suited to the task, because they, perhaps more than the first generation, accept the Prairies for what it is, including its sometimes uninspiring, flat, featureless terrain. Rather than focusing on the foothills or the mountains favoured by their elders, all four willingly plunge across the open plains to find the source material for their art. They also emerge during a time (post-1970) when it is possible to take a less literal, more non-objective approach, thanks to the practice of abstract art, which, by the 1960s, has become pervasive throughout the Western world. Instead of being a foreign language, as abstraction had been for the first-generation landscapists, abstraction is second nature to these younger artists and an invaluable aid in dealing with a spacious environment already pared down to three basic elements: land, horizon and sky.[40]

In this regard, on a fateful trip back to the Prairies from Ontario in 1954, **NORMAN YATES** (1923, Calgary, Alberta) is also influenced by a simple observation. "[It struck me how much] the Group of Seven were completely concerned with the 'surface' of things – light reflecting off facets of rock, the shapes of leaves. Even the clouds were solid forms modelled in a painted sky. Crossing the Prairies (in a car called Mayflower), I was struck by the ambience: not the surfaces but the space."

This ineffable impression never leaves Yates, although it is not until the early 1970s, after buying property outside of Edmonton, that he begins to make art based on this revelation. Through drawing and painting, Yates eventually develops several methods to evoke the concept of limitless space. In a nice twist, he coins the term landspace to describe his new approach. Rather than working within the conventional boundaries of a painting surrounded by a frame, he frees up the image by adding panels, allowing the picture to expand in all directions. As well, uninterested in depicting "a preconceived slice of landscape,"[41] he incorporates images of the terrain seen from different points of view and in different climatic states. The result is a type of nuance-laden, multi-view landscape, strikingly different in surface from either the Kerr-McNaught approach or the Emma Lake colour field sensibility. Instead, Yates's acrylics of prairie and mountain terrain seem to be surface-less; a composition that seems to flow with no real end in sight; reinforcing his interpretation of the land as ephemeral and ever-changing, there but not quite there, evoking the intangible western space.

ROBERT SINCLAIR (1939, Saltcoats, Saskatchewan) also takes into account the limitations of the Group of Seven's style of dealing with prairie space. Like Norman Yates – his older colleague at the University of Alberta's Department of Art and Design – Sinclair begins his journey from figurative to landscape art in the late 1960s. A decade later, he has emerged as one of Alberta's most well-known landscape artists. What makes his work so distinctive is the way the artist turns the seemingly endless prairie road stretching to the horizon into an iconic image. Commenting on Sinclair's early stain watercolours, drawings and paintings, John Allison Forbes observes: "[Sinclair] feels that the mobility granted by the automobile determines to a large extent our way of seeing the landscape. His own attitude is neither positive nor negative. Some of the roads rise and fall merrily through a bright landscape and finally meet a radiant sky at the horizon. Others turn ominous corners on mountain highways and disappear into an unknown world with a lowering sky. There is stillness as well as an emptiness to his world and a feeling that it is always late afternoon."[42]

The stillness and vastness Sinclair alludes to is partly derived from his own experience as a Saskatchewan farm boy, anxious to take the road to "somewhere." In his art, "somewhere" is never defined but with the road always present in the image it is left instead to our imagination. In more recent work, the road is no longer a standard motif but the landscape does continue to flow effortlessly in the composition, suggesting perhaps a metaphorical journey is underway. To achieve this, Sinclair employs subtle means: land forms simplified to a few fine lines and the contrast between areas of unpainted canvas with areas of colour judiciously applied in thin washes and stains. Distilled to their essence, his lyrical landscapes of prairie and mountains are noted for having a Zen-like quality: "a pure expression of [the] abstract frontier."[43] (Besides his two-dimensional work on paper and canvas,

Sinclair also incorporated the road theme into hand-cut, hand-formed acrylic and plexi-glass sculptures, one being the *Great Canadian Landscape* series mentioned in the previous chapter. When these works first emerged in the early 70s, their forms were considered unique in Canadian art.[44] "[They] respect the linear style of his paintings and can be viewed as witty, abstracted, three-dimensional drawings."[45]

Overall, Sinclair's images with a towering canopy of sky tended to emphasize the western terrain whereas for **TAKAO (TAK) TANABE**, (1926, Prince Rupert, British Columbia) his view became entirely horizontal. From 1973 to 1980, Tanabe is in charge of visual arts programming at the Banff School of Fine Arts; while there, he reinforces his national reputation with a series of beautiful minimalist paintings and works on paper depicting what he simply calls *The Land.*

A knowledgeable traveller of Alberta's backcountry roads, Tanabe is identified in 1979 by art critic Nancy Tousley as lying between the "two polarities"[46] of contemporary prairie landscape: the more factual renderings of specific places à la Kerr and Colour-Field abstraction with its colour and surface-oriented allusions to the land: "[Tanabe's paintings] are specific to the prairie region without being descriptive of specific places and, although abstracted by the reduction of landscape to its most basic elements, are firmly tied to the experience of nature."[47]

Despite his West Coast rainforest roots, the prairie and Tanabe seem made for each other. His training as an abstract artist, plus his study of Japanese techniques like Sumi-e painting and calligraphy,[48] enable him to respond in a very disciplined fashion to the tonal subtleties of the prairie environment with its powerful mood. As Nancy Tousley observes, "What is felt as much as what is seen gives form to Tanabe's conception of the land."[49] With little more than thin washes of muted colour to denote sky, horizon and land, Tanabe's elongated acrylic paintings emphasize the horizontal, almost ocean-like expanse of the Prairies and give new meaning to the word "panoramic." Another adjective that also comes to mind is "transparent," because the brushwork seems all but absent, suggesting that maybe the Prairies are nothing but a mirage, a creation of the mind rather than nature.

Interestingly, near the end of his sojourn in Alberta, Tanabe produced his own series of nocturne paintings and drawings, where layer after layer of graphite is laboriously applied. But whether of night or day, Tanabe's carefully balanced and contemplative compositions, according to Jeffrey Spalding, defy the customary attitude of the Canadian public of the time, which was "to remark on what wasn't here,"[50] as if the prairies' lack of trees and other features was somehow an aesthetic deficiency. It wouldn't be the first time a non-prairie-born artist responded so sensitively to the environment, but what is so remarkable is the lasting and vivid impression he created: his paintings a visual trademark of the Prairies.

At about the same time that Tak Tanabe is venturing out from his mountain home to explore the plains of central and southern Alberta, **HARRY SAVAGE** (1938, Camrose, Alberta) in Edmonton is adding watercolour landscape to his already lengthy repertoire. An active member of the city's cultural community since his arrival in 1962, by the early 1970s Savage has worked in photography, painting and printmaking, especially serigraphy. In fact, in the latter media, Savage produces what are probably the first examples in Alberta of environmental art or art that makes a statement about the destruction of the natural environment. There is also his social commentary on such timely concerns as the Vietnam War and his involvement in the early development of an alternative, artist-run gallery space: Latitude 53.

By the end of 1973, though, his interest in printmaking is waning, and like fellow Edmontonians Robert Sinclair and Norman Yates, he starts to consider landscape as his primary work. For an artist deeply in love with the land and concerned with conservation, the evolution to painting landscape full-time would seem like a perfectly natural step considering how even since the mid-1960s, he had also been creating acrylic, highly detailed miniature landscapes no bigger than 5 × 7 inches. These miniature landscapes would continue. But, after the technical demands of printmaking, Savage turns to watercolour for its spontaneity and his desire to react more directly to the mood of the environment.

Disregarding past landscape traditions in Alberta, Savage develops an approach that, like Tak Tanabe's, emphasizes the horizontal composition of land, horizon and sky. But instead of appearing like a mirage à la Tanabe, Savage's simplified prairie is a fluid, timeless entity defined by horizontal bands of colour that sweep-and-course across the paper. Light and colour are sometimes strong – challenging the notion that the prairie is a subtle terrain. Palpable too, in a Savage, are the atmospheric conditions.

Savage likes to think of his watercolours in terms of poetry, something that glides freely;[51] alluding to the country's wide, open space. But there is also the suggestion in both Savage's and Tanabe's work that the land is the overwhelming dominant force, and that, whatever its mood, whether dramatic or serene, it never lets go.

Many of the artists examined up to this point have taken an abstract approach, with the most baroque results coming from Ted Godwin and the most minimalist from Tak Tanabe. One landscapist who stayed well away, labouring instead as a realist, is **SYLVAIN VOYER** (1939, Edmonton, Alberta). Voyer's detailed depictions have been compared to the crisp and high-colour brilliance of a William Kurelek.[52] His paintings, though, are neither folkish in appearance, nor are they overwhelmed with many of the clichés that tend to mar so much realistic landscape. Voyer's compositions, for one thing, are often painted from unusual perspectives such as a canola field seen close up and from the height of a child. Also characteristic is his intensely coloured palette: fields that couldn't be more green or skies more blue. He achieves this effect by applying several layers of white base paint and then many more layers of acrylic colour. The result is a luminous type of landscape whose colour and radiance stems partly from the Technicolor theatrics of 1960s Op Art that once interested the artist.

A close colleague of Harry Savage, Voyer worked as a noted printmaker for more than fifteen years (1961–1979), including a stint as an experimental artist who recycled art posters and other printed reproductions into mixed media art. Since the age of eighteen, he also painted plein aire, a challenge that never lost its appeal and became integral to his practice when, in the late 1970s, he turned to landscape art full-time. But rather than searching for the essence of a place, or attempting to simplify the land into a few meaningful elements, Voyer attempts to approximate what he sees, replicating the rural environment in all of its wondrous detail.

Voyer is best known for his acrylics of Alberta's parkland region around Edmonton, in particular its brilliant canola fields. His landscapes have been compared to "old Dutch still lives, only here, instead of a bunch of flowers in the glass, we see a meadow full of flowers or wheat." [53] Rather than focusing on the ephemeral aspects of nature as Norman Yates or Tak Tanabe might, it is the "materialistic reality of the world," [54] or "the concreteness of a light and shadow, the texture of soil and stone, trees and their leaves," [55] that resonate with Voyer.

Another artist who chooses representational methods rather than abstract ones to interpret the land, and who also prefers to paint on-site, is **FRANK KARL VERVOORT** (1930–1983, Antwerp, Belgium). Raised in the Lethbridge area, his artistic blossoming comes late in the 1970s and lasts for five short years until his tragic death in 1983. Unlike many of the previous artists discussed, the Belgium-born Vervoort was never indebted to the Group of Seven aesthetic or the many-sided influences of post-war American abstract art. Instead, his affinities are with German expressionism and, more locally, with William Leroy Stevenson.[56]

This kind of artistic lineage brings a different, more northern sensibility to Alberta landscape painting. Instead of responding to the bright blue skies, panoramic space and shimmering colours that have captivated so many, Vervoort observes the less-endearing aspects of the western environment: the dour browns of a depressing fall day and the frozen roadside slush of a chilly spring. In his art, the prairie is not so much a promised land as it is a daunting place. An observation curator Chris Varley makes about John Snow's early woodcuts and W.L. Stevenson's landscapes can also be applied to Vervoort: "It was as if they saw only the winter bleakness, not the effervescent summertime beauty of their surroundings."[57]

Important to his last five years was exposure to the "perceptual method" of teaching colleague Jean Detheux and a sabbatical break (1979) from his duties as a popular instructor at the Alberta College of Art.[58] Leaving behind the fussy technique of an academically inclined painter, Vervoort adopts a more fluid, gestural approach in which the nuances of light and its effects on space and colour are carefully observed. In his case, no drama is needed: the experience itself is sufficient. Because of his teaching, in particular, Vervoort is a link between an older generation represented by Stevenson and a younger generation of such artists as Shirley Hard and Peter von Tiesenhausen. In the opinion of von Tiesenhausen, a former student who himself will achieve wide recognition, Vervoort's interpretations should be considered quite accurate.[59]

JOICE M. HALL (1943, Edmonton, Alberta), **DULCIE FOO FAT** (1946, London, England), and **MAUREEN ENNS** (1949, Chilliwack, B.C.) will close this chapter and, although their paintings from the 1970s are discussed within the context of second-generation landscape, their contemporary interpretations actually straddle the divide between the second and upcoming third generation. In Alberta, after several decades of representational or realistic landscape, followed by more abstracted treatments, the segmented skyscapes of Enns, the earthly close-ups of Foo Fat and the sensually fecund flora of Hall will broaden this regional genre both stylistically and conceptually.

They are also realists at a time when abstraction is still a prevailing attitude. As John Hall, another fellow realist, remembers it: "A graduate student in painting, Dulcie was, like myself and others, attempting to find a way of returning to a rigorous approach to representational art. Given the nearly 100-year reign of abstract and semi-abstract imagery, most members of the art community viewed our objective with only mild interest, some with outright hostility." [60]

Instead of dwelling on the unique physical characteristics of the western environment, Joice Hall and Foo Fat pursue more nature-based imagery that is "intricate, abundant and organic." [61] In effect, they bring to the easel a very personal, even proto-feminist perspective that finds echoes in the semi-abstract symbolic paintings of Marion Nicoll. They draw, though, on entirely different periods of art history for their style – late nineteenth-century figurative art for Hall,[62] and new realism for Foo Fat.[63] But things do get altered and adapted, as Foo Fat notes about her own work. "Unlike some new realists of the late 1960s and 1970s, I do not have a disinterested attitude to my subject matter.... I believe my ambition is consistent with a figurative tradition in which paintings have both formal and representational significance." [64] Working with colour photographs whose imagery is transferred to the canvas with the help of a grid, it is the minute details of the land: its pebbles, flakes of lichen and moss, clumps of grass, clay-coloured earth and patches of small wildflowers that attract her, all signifying how "a universe can be found in a plot of earth no bigger than a placemat." [65]

Hall's *Celebration Landscapes* (1972–77) are so sexually suggestive – a palm tree as a penis, a flower as a vagina[66] – that many, no doubt, have been left shaking their heads. In what can only be an understatement, curator Carol Phillips comments: "[the paintings have a] joyful physicality." [67] As landscapes, Hall's oil paintings, including her cropped, close-up views of flowers and segments of the landscape, were so far outside of the Alberta mainstream that nearly twenty-five years later they still look radical for their time. In the 80s and 90s, both artists continue to work with landscape and also other subject matter. Hall, especially, pursues subject matter (male nudes, Mexican religious icons and so on) that seem totally unrelated except for their "juxtaposition of the sensual with the spiritual," [68] a feature identified as characteristic of her art.

While Foo Fat and Hall turned downwards toward the verdant earth for their subject matter, Maureen Enns looked up to the sky. In a way, she couldn't help it, living as she does on a hilltop near Cochrane where the heavens are always in view and in motion. Her desire, though, was to look through the sky:[69] to speak about its mutability and its seemingly infinite space. Writing about her acrylics (1975–77), which are composed of horizontal or vertical bands of sky scenery, the artist observed: "These paintings represent slices of sky-time with one cloudy moment set against another cloudy moment. The resulting space is dream-like."[70] While some bands or squares are painted in a highly realistic fashion, the "slices of sky-time" seem abstract. The result is striking. This juxtaposition between realism and abstraction, between deep and shallow space is partly attributable to Enns being a self-described "rebellious representational artist"[71] at a time when the art community was still largely absorbed with the practice of abstraction.

Near the end of the decade, Enn's continued to gaze heavenward, painting a suite of acrylics featuring the image of a mirrored cube in the sky. Inspired by her student sculptural work in which mirrored cubes were installed out-of-doors, each side reflecting a segment of the land or sky, Enns photographed a cube held up by a friend outdoors in the country. In highly realistic works such as *Free Fall* (1980) and *Down to Earth* (1979), the reflective prop is a provocative instrument, revealing patches of a subtle but lively environment: airy sky, panoramic terrain and a rich groundcover of grasses and wildflowers.

Within the context of international art of the 1970s, the cube also makes sly references to sculptural minimalism and its polar opposite: decorative art (evoked by the lush vegetation). And, finally, there is Enns's linking of the sky to the spiritual. Enns believes her sky works of the 1970s brought her spiritually in touch with the environment and with nature.[72] By the late 1980s, this development would coalesce in an ongoing series of paintings, videos, catalogues and books about endangered wildlife.

In describing the development of second-generation Alberta landscape artists, it is evident that it is a story made up of several layers with no one layer dominating or defining what might be called an Albertan style or school. The reason for this diversity, according to artist **LES GRAFF** (1936, Camrose, Alberta), is that Alberta is *not,* as he puts it, a place of isolation.[73] Instead, its affluence and opportunity attract people to the area, while at the same time, its inhabitants travel to other parts of Canada and the world. Artists do this especially to exhibit, teach and educate themselves. Rather than being "a place of isolation," he believes the province is historically "a place of migration"[74] with this phenomena stretching back at least 12,000 years to the migrations of prehistoric peoples, such as the Clovis.[75] With regard to the visual arts, Graff believes this condition of flux is especially pertinent, coalescing into a multi-layered scene that locally is a plus but nationally can be perceived as a disadvantage. "Alberta doesn't present a collective, cohesive picture to the nation, and as a result, it's been easy to overlook."[76]

John Bentley Mays, though, believes that insularity *is* a defining factor in Alberta's art history. In a 1980 review of *Painting in Alberta: An Historical Survey,* he notes that in prairie culture there is a "deep sensibility of isolation," which has fostered in Alberta a strange "otherness" or a freedom to pursue "what's been shown to work well in the local environment, regardless of what is being done and said outside, and regardless of from where it came."[77] Integral to this state of "otherness" is certainly the persistence of landscape, although it is found in other kinds of Albertan art as well, such as the formalist compositions of some of Edmonton's abstract painters and sculptors, or the *individualists* of southern Alberta – John Will, Billy McCarroll, Mary Shannon Will, John Chalke, Annemarie Schmid Esler, Chris Cran and others.

Even Les Graff's own artwork can be considered within this context. A former director of the Visual Arts Branch, Graff considers himself an oddball in that he doesn't belong to any one group, does not want to produce "landscape like everyone else's"[78] and has never had any desire to be a steady producer of art objects. In all three instances, Graff has remained faithful; his paintings and drawings are indeed very different from anyone else in the province. Abstract, and with little relation to even the prairie modernists and their references to horizon, earth and sky, Graff's unstructured landscapes are the result of instinct and intuition rather than perception and detached observation. Not interested in treating the landscape "like a still-life,"[79] his drawings and paintings, compositionally, are an amalgam of multiple views that come from his connections with a particular place, such as St. Albert's Sturgeon River – Graff's "constant companion."[80] With this kind of stream-of-consciousness approach, landscape becomes a "state of mind rather than a state of being."[81] It is the sum total of all the impressions left by experiencing, for instance, a flowing stream of water near nightfall – its colour, light, smell, sound and movement.

Graff describes the development of his art as a "fight to develop form."[82]

Whether making marks on paper or applying oil colour to canvas, he feels his best work comes when he is "winging it," [83] with no particular plan in mind. A progeny of the 50s, Graff's improvisational approach is indebted to abstract expressionism which, as American critic Robert Atkins has noted, was less about style than attitude.[84] It was also more about the process than the end product, about the act of creating, about self-expression and about drawing on feelings and state of mind. The artist once titled an exhibition *Reality is Irrelevant*,[85] indicating how internalized his landscape actually is, stemming "from an inner world." [86]

chapter three

Evoking New Meanings: Third Generation Landscape Painting

A NEW GENERATION OF LANDSCAPE PAINTERS emerge in the 1980s, who, in many respects, are significantly different from the last. Part of the Baby Boom generation[1], several of these artists come to Alberta as adults, notably from southern Ontario – Jeffrey Spalding, Barbara Milne, Stephen Hutchings, Jim Davies and Alice Saltiel-Marshall. And, just as the second generation of landscapists have broadened and enriched the practice, the third will also bring new orderings (to use Kroetsch's word) or themes to the genre. This point is particularly important, because for the previous generation the overriding theme was "how" – how to represent, depict and interpret the challenging and sometimes elusive prairie landscape. On one level, it could be said that their concerns were more formal and even impressionistic, focusing on such issues as composition, form, colour, texture, light and space, aspects which fit neatly within the perimeters of post-war modern art.

But the older artists are also working at a time when so-called postmodern attitudes towards the role of art were overtaking the once revered goals of modernist art, such as truth to materials. The pendulum is swinging back in favour of the subject's content – its meanings, connotations and associations, including related social and political issues. By the time the younger crop is beginning to make its presence felt, an artistic sea change is underway in Canada and elsewhere in the Western art world, summed up by the following Duchampian echo: "Postmodernism is tough love. To see is to think, not just to look." [2]

No longer preoccupied with the "how," many of the third generation examine more closely the content of their subject matter and what they want to say about it. Rather than dwelling on the physically unique or special qualities of the Alberta landscape, some of the newcomers concentrate on its symbolic or emotional content. Others react to the romantic traditions of nineteenth-century landscape art and its idealized image of nature; while still others, in reaction to the growing environmental movement, are swayed to make art about the ecological issues. Also noteworthy is the contribution of First Nations artists, who are doing much to dispel "the illusion of a nature outside of history," [3] or a virgin landscape devoid of non-European cultures.

The swing of the art-world pendulum away from abstraction and back to so-called figurative art in the late 70s, also affects Alberta landscape art greatly. Rather than looking like an anomaly, as the contemporary realism of Joice M. Hall, Dulcie Foo Fat and Maureen Enns must have initially appeared in the 1970s, representational approaches are taken up again without much ado. Indicative, perhaps, of what American art writer Kay Larson suggests is a lack of concern by Boomer artists about which has a higher moral ground: [4] abstraction or figuration. "They know that all abstract art is figurative to some degree, in that it presents an image to the mind. And all figurative art is abstract, in that it involves a leap into the imagination." [5]

The younger generation also must share the public spotlight with artists working in other media. Whether it is through printmaking, installation, ceramics, photography, fibre or some other means, by the beginning of the 80s the pluralistic spirit of the 1970s international art scene is making serious inroads in Alberta. By the end of the 1980s, some of the most memorable artwork concerning this vastly broadened topic is being generated not only by painters, but also by other creative minds such as Bart Habermiller, Peter von Tiesenhausen and Lyndal Osborne.

Still, within this new generation, there are some who will continue the modernist project of how, and produce results considered "fresh and original."[6] From the early 1980s, two who stand out are **BARBARA BALLACHEY** (1949, Edmonton, Alberta) and **DAVID PUGH** (1946–1994, Saskatoon, Saskatchewan). Many of their Emma Lake elders have relied on abstraction almost exclusively but not Ballachey or Pugh. As late modernists, they will, without blinking an eye, paint more representational images that are still abstract up to a point but recognizable nonetheless. It's not necessarily where they started as young artists but it's the road they will travel down, with Ballachey eventually earning a national reputation for her lyrical landscapes in oil, acrylic and watercolour. Bold in their brushwork and colour with the shapes of nature flattened and reduced to their essentials, Ballachey's foothills of the early 1980s are a vivid, spontaneous blend of description and abstraction.

David Pugh's neo-cubist acrylics and oils of the Rocky Mountains are also vivid, but for more than just their strong fractured shapes and deep rich colours. Attentive to the geological structure of these primal land masses, Pugh's representational treatment is direct and unsentimental: "sidestepping," according to some, "the traditionally sublime associations of the Rockies."[7] Considered self-taught and with strong sympathies to Picasso and Cézanne, Pugh is able to emphasize the massive, rugged monumentality of the mountains with a jagged-edged decorativeness appealing to the eye. Emerging as he did in the early 1980s, Pugh presented a striking alternative to Rocky Mountain landscapes, which, aside from the inspired treatment they received at the hands of a few like Edmonton's J.B. (Jack) Taylor (1917–1970), had seen far better days when Henry Glyde and Walter Phillips were around.

ALICE SALTIEL-MARSHALL (1948, Toronto, Ontario) also makes the Rockies her prime focus, and like Pugh, manages to rise above the merely prosaic with a series of sparkling on-site and studio oils and watercolours beginning in the mid-1990s. Her style, though, is completely different from Pugh's modernism, rooted in realism and the accurate description of the terrain. Trained at Toronto's Central Technical School with Doris McCarthy as a teacher in still-life, the Canmore-based artist takes what is generally treated as a remote and grand subject and makes it unusually intimate and immediate, with close-up views of the high alpine country, its snow patches, glaciers, tarns and icy turquoise lakes. She writes of that experience: "Duality at its finest, beauty and bleakness, peaceful and raging, take me to the Ice."[8]

In 1993, Saltiel-Marshall is one of ten painters invited by the Whyte

Museum of the Canadian Rockies to paint the popular Columbia Icefields in Banff National Park.[9] Following in the footsteps of other like-minded projects, such as the Oldman River Expedition[10] (1990) and the historic McIntyre Ranch (1991), the result of the weeklong event is *Reframing the Landscape: The Columbia Icefield Expedition* (1994). "It seems essential to examine the validity and artistic relevance of landscape as a subject in contemporary art,"[11] the museum explains. Consisting of paintings, watercolours and mixed media, the exhibition, like that of the Oldman and the McIntyre, reveals that Alberta's landscape is not an exhausted subject matter.

BRENT R. LAYCOCK (1947, Lethbridge, Alberta) is another example of a landscape artist who, like Saltiel-Marshal, develops a professional practice in the province in spite of being, as Ted Godwin once told him "from out of left field."[12] (A comment in reference to Laycock's lack of time spent either as a student or an instructor with an educational art institution in the province.) Instead, Laycock studied watercolour with his great aunt Jessie Ursenbach of Leftbridge (an accomplished watercolourist in her own right), was acquainted with the early Lethbridge modernist Bart Pragnell and later received formal training at Utah's Brigham Young University.

Like Barbara Ballachey, Laycock's acrylics and watercolours of open prairie, panoramic mountain-scapes and flowers, dance back and forth between the recognizable and the abstract, with a strong interplay of lines, heightened colours and shapes. Also aiding the artist is his avid interest in an even more abstract art form, music, "where the elements derive their meaning from the dynamics of their interaction."[13] This painting-music connection imparts in Laycock's fluid landscapes a certain movement and directness, an unstarched quality far removed from the older, more restrained style of watercolour as practiced by A.C. Leighton and H.G. Glyde. Some of his commissioned work includes paintings of Waterton Lakes National Park (1982) and Glacier National Park (1984) for Canada Post stamps.

JAMES CORRIGAN (1955, Red Deer, Alberta) can also be considered "out of left field," but not because of a lack of connection to any of Alberta's art schools. (He graduates with an MVA from the University of Alberta in 1981.) Instead, as art critic Liz Wylie observes about him, "Jim Corrigan is a rarity in Edmonton because he is a painter working with an abstract vocabulary that is not part of the city's abstract mainstream."[14] Using fragments of landscape imagery, Corrigan creates mixed-media acrylics that are very open-ended in how they can be interpreted, yet adhere to the more recent art maxim of saying as much as you can with as little as possible. This philosophy leads Corrigan to produce some of the most idiosyncratic abstract landscape in the province, unrelated to either Emma Lake or those of a Harry Savage or Takao Tanabe. In fact, many of his ambiguous paintings have as little in common with the actual landscape as Les Graff's do. Corrigan's paintings, though, are far more analytical and as cool and spare as Graff's are emotional and entangled. Influenced by the geometric abstraction of British modernist Ben Nicholson and the art of Japanese-American Kenzo Okada, the artist's earlier work mingles elements of the land – often vegetation and water – with geometric forms and vague references to suburban life, such as garages and patios. More recently, in the 1990s, he singles out the tree as a motif by which to explore such formal concerns as distance and drawing.

From the mid-1970s to the early 1980s, the winds of migration are blowing chinook-strength through the province, thanks to its much-publicized oil boom. As new wealth pours into people's pockets and into government coffers, the visual arts, in particular its educational, governmental and exhibition infrastructure, undergo their most significant expansion to date. The winds also bring new creative blood, like **BARBARA MILNE** (1956, Windsor, Ontario) and **JIM DAVIES** (1950, Toronto, Ontario). Arriving in 1979 and 1977 respectively, these two young artists develop (to use Doug Francis's term from Chapter 1) "mental constructs" of the western terrain that are quite unlike anything seen since Maxwell Bate's and H.G. Glyde's prairie figurative narratives of the 1940s and 50s[15]. But it is not a one-way street: it is living in Alberta that inspires them to take on landscape in the first place. As Milne later reflected, her art education at York University and life in Toronto had given her "a restrictive view of art and art practice."[16] Coming to Alberta opened her eyes.

More a product or distillation of memory and imagination, their evocative paintings of the 1980s are concerned less with the physical appearance of the land than with its possible emotional, spiritual and narrative connotations. Fresh territory is being mined where it is no longer just a case of rendering the mood and atmosphere of a place. In Davies's case, the nocturnal countryside becomes a setting for unexplained human activity as in *Arrival* (1984), where a car and figure are parked in a tilled field. It is from his background as a figurative artist that Davies's inclusion of figurative elements – lone individuals, animals and cars – are novel and something that most second-generation artists will have studiously avoided. But by relying on the rural environs as an existentialist springboard, Davies writes about conveying "a sense of isolation or aloneness which is embedded in civilization."[17] Milne's oil paintings and works in charcoal on paper are less literal but just as dramatic in that the land is a place where unspoken but powerful things happen. Ethereal and dream-like, her simplified landscapes are, as critic Nancy Tousley observes, "a vehicle for visualizing forces of that larger presence, beyond everyday appearances, that we speak of as nature."[18] Richly coloured, there is often a simmering tension in her oils between places wild and tame, agitated and serene, dark and light, small and large: allusions, according to the artist, to the ambivalent relationship between nature and man.[19]

Another third-generation artist who has much to do with putting nature as a subject back into landscape painting is **JEFFREY SPALDING** (1951, Edinburgh, Scotland), who moves to the province in 1978. His concerns, though, are far less personal than Milne's, more connected to art history and, in particular, the tradition of nineteenth-century romantic landscape art. With this focus, the Toronto-raised Spalding introduces a type of artistic content novel to Alberta landscape art. At the same time, the province's striking physicality contributes to transforming his artwork from being "entirely intellectual, theoretical and abstract,"[20] towards representations of his personal surroundings and, in particular, nature that is rich in allusion and emotional meaning.

He participates in three groundbreaking Canadian exhibitions in the late 1980s about contemporary landscape art,[21] where he and the other participating artists are identified as "painting not nature, but nature as culture has defined it for them. Culture's nature."[22] Spalding does this by rendering atmospherically intense, luminous landscapes that echo the earlier romantic art of the American Frederic Church (Hudson River School), the German Casper David Friedrich and the American luminists – for whom light suggested the divine in nature. But Spalding is also reconsidering these influentially sublime and grand views of nature (i.e. the untouched virgin wilderness) from a late twentieth-century perspective: one that is still full of awe and wonder, but at the same time can't help but evoke a darker, more ominous feeling about nature's fate in a technological world. A sense that, as Nancy Tousley observes, "its beauty masks a poison."[23]

In one instance, this approach taken by Spalding translates into a beautiful yet eerie series of images of Niagara Falls (1979–1986), a mythic subject that was inspiring to the nineteenth-century romantic imagination.

Consisting of more than a dozen works, the effect of these paintings is interpreted by Tousley as the following: "The pull is between our still strong desire to believe in the ideal of untouched nature and how damaged by reality that ideal has become."[24]

Another aspect to Spalding's art of this period is whether landscape can inspire contemplation and awareness of life outside of the narrow confines of the self; in other words, how nature takes us far beyond the chaos of contemporary culture and its obsession with self-fulfilment. Also, during a period when much advanced art making is oriented in the direction of addressing "issues," Spalding aspires to the modest goal of "trying to see if art in this day and age can still be moving,"[25] in a sense reckoning with the much-quoted advice that Friedrich once gave to a fellow artist: "Close your physical eye so that you may first see your picture with the spiritual eye."[26]

Seeing and creating a picture of nature that is romantic in its aspirations but tempered by a late twentieth–century perspective continues to be a strong theme throughout the late 1980s and early 1990s. Four painters who add their own voices to this trend are Dan Bagan, Shirley Hard, David More and Peter von Tiesenhausen. Westerners in upbringing, educated as artists in Alberta, all four fit comfortably within what John Bentley Mays identified in 1994 as, "Alberta's new romanticism.... Everywhere one can sense the longing of intelligent, youthful artists for renewed contact with earth and sky, unburdened by the suspicions and polemics that have weighed down too many recent exhibitions of contemporary landscape painting."[27]

Certainly there are no "suspicions and polemics" in the art of these four artists, such as the kind represented in the 1991 group show of Canadian and international artists *Lost Illusions* (Vancouver Art Gallery) in which landscape is identified, somewhat clinically, as "a product of specific social contexts."[28] But, neither is their point of view oblivious to the environmental realities of Alberta. As **SHIRLEY HARD** (1957, Assinboia, Saskatchewan) discerns about her studio-produced oils: "Possibly the terrains that I am observing are not the way they 'should' be but are the way they are changing both naturally and unnaturally."[29]

Using a loose, expressive style that is compared to W.L. Stevenson and Frank Vervoort (an instructor of Hard's at the Alberta College of Art), Hard's monochromatic forest and river landscapes of the early 1990s are typically un-scenic, untidy places, painted in such a way that no natural feature stands out to attract the eye. This lack of focal point and the fact that her paintings "teeter on the edge between image and abstraction,"[30] adds to the tension already present in her quiet and unsettling landscapes that depict nothing really special. Nothing, that is, except the very certain presence of the natural world, which, whatever shape it takes in Alberta, reminds Hard of another living realm.

Less muted are DAN BAGAN's (1956, Terrace, British Columbia), which depict in a more realistic manner the visual beauty of the land. The artist uses this technique as a way of speaking about what he strongly feels cannot be taken for granted. A plein aire painter with Group of Seven influences, Bagan views the subject matter of nature as "neutral in content ... the artist can make it what he or she wishes."[31] In a continuing series *Unjiga,* begun in 1987, his impetus was to produce "a reportage of a disappearing landscape,"[32] specifically the boreal realms of the Peace River country, which has experienced extensive clear-cutting by pulp and paper companies. Part of the series involves a group of panoramic nocturnes whose deep velvety blacks, blues and purples, and rich celestial activity are meant to elevate what might be seen as monotonous bush to transcendental levels, valuable for more intrinsic reasons than just pulp.

Primarily a landscape painter in oil, Bagan has ventured more recently into mixed-media works that refer more specifically to issues such as clear-cutting. A participant of the Edmonton-based alternative art collective The Coyotes, Bagan, in a 1993 work *Allowable Cut* creates a triptych consisting of, from right to left, a photo-aerial map, an oil landscape and cross-sections of tree branches attached to a panel. The map and woodcuttings refer to what Bagan feels are two popular views of Alberta's northern forests: one scientific, the other industrial. Whichever view is taken, both, according to the artist, reinforce humankind's apartness from nature.[33]

Environmental concerns and a fascination with "humankind's placement upon and interaction with [the Earth]"[34] come into even sharper focus in the paintings and drawings of DAVID MORE (1947, Aberdeen, Scotland). The oldest of the four, More's landscape art straddles the second and third generation. Born shortly after the war in Scotland, formally trained in Alberta in the late 1960s to the mid-70s, More begins to develop two different streams: the *Garden Ceremony* series and his so-called "direct" landscape paintings, out of which comes the national touring exhibition *Forest-Fade to Silence* (1990).[35]

Dealing with the effects of acid rain on New Brunswick forests, the eerie, discordant landscapes of *Forest-Fade to Silence* play off the Group of Seven style and their celebratory depiction of the Canadian wilderness in its idyllic form.[36] For instance, rather than the bold orange-red autumn forests of a Tom Thomson, or the appealing blue skies of a Lawren Harris, the withered trees in More's *Sky with Amber Edge* "glow hot pink; the lake is painted in murky, bilious greens."[37] As Whyte Museum curator Katherine Lipsett notes: "These are not comfortable paintings."[38]

Moving from on-site sketching to much larger works done in the studio, More also continues to explore the range of moods in places often known only to the locals, like the Medicine River near his Red Deer area home. "To understand and respect even the smallest segment of it can unveil a great deal of our nation's psyche. The landscape continues to be a critical part of that enigma called Canadian."[39]

The *Garden Ceremony* is a more autobiographical, more international project, inspired by visits to gardens of the United States, England, Scotland, Canada, France and India. Initially semi-abstract and less site specific, the imagery becomes increasingly representational and symbolic as he develops a repertoire of visual elements, including steps, passageways, reflecting pools and rake marks, which he likens to "a recording of the brief passage of the human hand across a tiny portion of the world."[40] According to the artist, the connection between his direct landscape and his more conceptualized garden oils and acrylics resides in the human interaction with each one. "The *Garden Ceremony* is a metaphoric reference to humankind's desire (some may say 'need') to be in ritualistic control of some miniscule corner of their world."[41]

If being inter-connected or intimate with the environment is an aspiration for some Alberta artists, and a desire that the highly urbanized contemporary art world can barely grasp or only view as a ploy to produce a commercially marketable art, then the career of **PETER VON TIESENHAUSEN** (1959, New Westminister, British Columbia) is particularly illuminating. A native of the same Peace River district as Euphemia McNaught and Robert Guest, a student of Frank Vervoort (Alberta College of Art) and a participant in three Emma Lake Artist Workshops and two Prairie North Artist Workshops, von Tiesenhausen has had all the right pedigree to make a successful landscape painter. But instead, his short but intense stint at oil painting on canvas (1990–1993) becomes a springboard into gallery installations, large-scale drawings, outdoor land works, sculpture in wood and bronze, paintings on charred wood, and more recently, videos that continue to be an expression of what he cares about most deeply. As curator Michael Bell noted: "His style of life, his land art and his attitudes are romantic, not as nostalgic recollection of some past and distant state, but as a qualified lived experience now." [42]

Part of that experience includes working directly with wood and fire, as well as using his own 300-acre home near Demmit as a site for his much-discussed large-scale outdoor structures made of plaited twigs and branches. Situated on a broad open field and in the surrounding forest, these impressive, willow-woven land works "require the interactions of the sky and the earth, the flora and the weather to make them complete." [43] This kind of back-to-the-land art made from the very stuff of nature finds earlier precedents in the work of international artists like Richard Long and Andy Goldsworthy of Great Britian. But von Tiesenhausen's work has its own strong personal flavour in that many of the plaited willow objects – like his ship, boat, vessels, pods, huts and tower – relate symbolically to his own life in the bush.

Usually, such environmental work is brought to public attention through elegantly made photographs, and while the artist does photographically document his structures, what von Tiesenhausen chooses to exhibit publicly in the mid-90s is not only site-specific works but also large-scale charcoal drawings and small rugged paintings on burnt, scarred wood planks. Independent works of art, the drawings and paintings depict expressively the objects he has made, the landscape they are contained within, and representations of fire, flame and smoke.

One of the most organic and instinctively visceral of Alberta's third-generation landscape painters, von Tiesenhausen speaks about "communicating nature as nature does, directly through the senses." [44] This desire to create a more tactile, more elemental and more heightened art positions von Tisenhausen between the older tradition of landscape painting and the dozens of other methods and media used by Alberta artists to engage with the landscape and the natural world around them. Not surprisingly, many of them are not painters – Annemarie Schmid Esler, Lyndal Osborne and Bill Morton – and of the ones who do paint – Gary Olson and Carroll (Moppett) Taylor-Lindoe – the subject is not so much the landscape per se but nature in its many manifestations.

chapter four

Art About Nature and the Environment

GIVEN THAT CLAY IS THE VERY STUFF OF NATURE, it's not hard to imagine why some Alberta ceramic art is ripe with such references. These references, while sometimes understated, are found consistently throughout the fifty-year career of LUKE LINDOE (1913–2000, Bashaw, Alberta). Responding to a 1992 retrospective of his clay art, oils, watercolours and other media, Lindoe writes: "Art is *not* the most important undertaking of my life. That priority goes to the maintaining of my relationship with the natural world."[1] Such a remark challenges a popular cliché in the media about artists being single-minded individuals who care only about their art. But that's Luke Lindoe for you. He seemed to spar with all of the labels attached to him: "I'm known internationally as a potter," he recalled curtly, "that's a lot of BS. I'm not a potter."[2]

He was, rather, a sculptor and a painter whose work, he says, is a "product"[3] of what he calls "walking on the land."[4] In conjunction, he also pursued a lifetime profession as a clay geologist, which, like his art practice, requires an incredibly discerning eye: "By nature I am an observer...[5] [My art is] a simple, direct response to my life."[6] Stylistically, Lindoe is an early modernist shaped by the rich, austere landscape of southeastern Alberta. This landscape appears in the pared-down imagery of his paintings and in the strong, simplified forms and restrained surface decoration of his ceramics. In describing Lindoe's "clay aesthetic," Les Graff observes: "[His clay aesthetic] is an appreciation of the inherent qualities of clay: limited colour – like the prairie, compact form, natural textures."[7]

Like Illingworth Kerr and Euphemia McNaught, the 1970s mark a turning point in Lindoe's career. As a ceramic artist, his international reputation is already well-established, but as a painter, he has taken a long hiatus (1952–64) and then, after that, spends a number of years developing a new body of two-dimensional work. In 1978, Lindoe is ready to reintroduce himself and does so with a one-person show, *Come Walk With Me.* Displayed at Medicine Hat's National Exhibition Centre, the exhibit of oils, watercolours, drawing, pottery and sculpture underlines Lindoe's knowledge and interest in a wide variety of media. "None of these is more important than the others,"[8] he later commented. His subject matter included the local landscape and surrounding natural world, as displayed in his stoneware pots elegantly incised with the image of fish or reeds. The show also includes freestanding stoneware works of the human figure.

In 1992, the Medicine Hat Museum and Art Gallery organizes a touring exhibition entitled *Come Walk With Me: A Luke Lindoe Retrospective,* which surveys his work during a fifty-year span, 1941–92. This exhibition provides a broader picture of his career as a full-time artist. Commenting about Lindoe's painting, Nancy Tousley writes, "Of special note is the seventy-nine-year-old artist's unique vision of space in.... near abstractions of the landscape."[9] To this assessment the artist adds, "If location reflects anything to me, I seldom see it as realistic subject matter. I see shapes, colours and ideas."[10] He also sees an overall design and, in some images, employs strong lines to organize the composition into planes of colour that create an almost prismatic effect. Entirely subjective, Lindoe's romantic interpretations in paint suggest the spiritual and purifying power of the environment.

Although Lindoe considered himself a conservative artist with post-impressionist leanings ("...my art education came out of six bound volumes of *Studio Magazine* from 1918–1924 that my father had."[11]), his early example as a multi-disciplinary practitioner aids in broadening the definition of fine art in Alberta.[12] Through his work and the work of other Alberta ceramics artists, this medium comes to be considered a creative equal to painting and sculpture. This is especially true in Calgary and southern Alberta. (Notably, such acceptance of this medium is not the norm in many other art centres in the country). In 1990, the Alberta College of Art names the Luke Lindoe Library in honour of his contribution to the school, where he established a ceramics program in 1946.

Later in the decade, another retrospective follows, this time at the University of Calgary's Nickle Arts Museum (1998). This exhibition includes a section on his public commissions, the best-known works being *Virgin Mary and Christ Child* (1957, St. Mary's Cathedral, Calgary) and the outstanding *Petroglyph Mural* (1966–67, Provincial Museum and Archives, Edmonton). In his writing about the show, curator Les Graff highlights just how compelling the natural environment is to Lindoe, "In the 1950s, when artists were retreating to cities to find opportunities in the supportive, collective situations of the urban environment, Luke – true to his nature – headed in the other direction, ready to pound a living and lifestyle out of the bleak openness of the prairies. And as he has aged, that southern Albertan environment has become even that much more of a necessity to maintain his sense of balance and proportion. Luke has been known to drive non-stop for six hundred kilometres to make an appearance, to be part of something he felt he should support. Then, finding himself ill at ease – unable to become part of a collective event – he has announced in his booming voice, 'Well . . . I must leave now. . .' and immediately drive the six hundred-kilometre return trip, to get back to his real world."[13]

MARY BORGSTROM (1916, Wynard, Saskatchewan) is three years younger than Lindoe. Like Lindoe, she knows what it's like to dig for local clays and to engage in what she describes as "an intimate love affair with the great out-of-doors and an insatiable curiosity about Mother Earth. . . ."[14] But there the similarities end. Borgstrom's clay art is considerably more primitive in its making and yet, in appearance, is as elegant and elemental as you can get. Mary Borgstrom is a prairie minimalist, a true believer in the adage of doing more with less. To this end, she has undergone such painstaking tasks as polishing the surfaces of her unglazed works by hand, using rocks.

By 1970, this rural homemaker, living in the Provost area, is well on her way to acquiring a national reputation for her low-fire, hand-burnished pots and, most remarkable of all, her shiny, smooth-surfaced spheres that are rich with planetary allusions. As one Montreal writer asked, "[is] Borgstrom working to express herself through the earth? Or is the earth working to express itself through Borgstrom?" [15] She begins the decade with a travelling one-person show of hand-built pieces, organized by Borgstrom's mentor-of-sorts: [16] the Visual Arts Branch of Alberta Culture. This is quickly followed by a one-person show (1971) at Montreal's Canadian Guild of Crafts, and her participation in such significant group exhibits as *Primitives Canada* (1973, Burnaby), *History of Ceramics in Alberta* (1975, Edmonton), *Faces of Canada* for Montreal's 1976 Summer Olympics and *Alberta Art* (1978, Hokkaido, Japan).

Due to the immense amount of time involved in making her work, and later because of health problems, Mary Borgstrom's oeuvre is small in number and short in time span (for instance, no more than a dozen spheres were made).[17] She is, nonetheless, an interesting figure in the history of Alberta clay. Borgstrom, the primitive, represents an approach to ceramics and art that is resolutely idiosyncratic and far removed from the art school/university route taken by many of today's practitioners. What training she did receive came through local workshops sponsored by Alberta Culture. Painter Les Graff, who for 31 years was the director of its Visual Arts Branch, considers Borgstrom to be the best example of what Alberta Culture did to bring the practice of art to Alberta artists in a grassroots fashion.[18]

One artist greatly influenced by Borgstrom's attitude and who similarly reaches into the earth for her subject matter is **ELKE BLODGETT** (1936, Leipzig, Germany). An assistant to Borgstrom early in her career (1975 and 1976) Blodgett learns that "you didn't need a fancy studio" [19] and that as a mother and homemaker, she could still be a potter "independent of guilds and universities." [20] The result is a twenty-five year career that changed direction in the mid-1990s due to pottery-related injuries. Blodgett describes her career as a "constant journey of discovery and chance happenings." [21]

Along the way, Blodgett developed distinctive, hand-built forms that, according to one reviewer, "seem to have sprung from the earth itself," [22] and, "would look at home as much in nature.... as in a living room or art gallery." [23] That the work can evoke these observations is attributed by the artist to two factors: the impact of her environment, first as a child in Germany's Heath country and later in Alberta amongst "the massive geological statements" [24] of the Rockies and the badlands; second, to the challenge of working with the accidental happenings of low-fire pottery. "To me, the great joy of working with clay and fire is watching the pots literally emerging from the ashes: cracked, crazed, beautiful or not, never perfect."[25]

Blodgett's art is often identified as raku yet she admits her personal, flamboyant work bears little resemblance to the serene Japanese tradition and its ties to the tea ceremony.[26] Instead, her primeval forms, as Bente Roed Cochran noted, "vociferously exclaim Elke Blodgett"[27] through their large sculptural shapes (some as high as five feet), their rough, cracked and pocked surfaces and the random splotches of glazed colour. She is best known for her large-scale, egg-shaped vessels, delicately balanced on a slender, pointed base. Open at the top, gaping even, these pots suggest any number of nature-related phenomena: germination, glacial scouring, eruption and erosion. Other shapes include globular pots, bowls, *moonrocks*, and the tall, pointed spirit houses which constitute her final body of work. Partly inspired by the monolithic prehistoric tombs of her childhood homeland, these large clay structures embody both the personal and the profound in Blodgett's life, motivated as always by her desire to see her work "remain a piece of the earth."[28]

In the 1970s, the theme of the land and nature will also be expressed with particular drama and imagination by several new names: John Chalke, Harlan House, Leslie (Les) Manning, Annemarie Schmid Esler and Charles (Chuck) Wissinger. In the process, they will contribute to altering the aesthetic of Alberta ceramics from the utilitarian-looking to the more idiosyncratically expressive, from the subdued to the more colourful and from the vessel-shaped work to more one-of-a-kind sculptural objects and assemblages. As described in the catalogue notes to the exhibit *Alberta Clay comes of age,* "The seventies were a time of ceramic adolescence when every new development and publication was rapidly assimilated by Alberta clay artists."[29]

Before moving to Ontario in 1973, ACA graduate (1969) **HARLAN HOUSE** (1943, Vancouver, British Columbia) produces innovative wall plates, bas relief murals and mixed media works, mostly in stoneware, dealing with "landscape as a theme, and as a metaphor for man's relationship to nature."[30] In some cases, his point of view is environmentally critical, as in his clay landscape murals, many of which appended with a long canvas highway falling to the floor. About these works, curator Bruce Ferguson observes: "Historically, landscape art provides a sense of the balance between man and Nature. House['s art] ... offers new reflections on that balance."[31] Some of his stoneware relief of that period also reckons with the idea of place, including *Alberta Coat of Arms* and *Alberta City Kit,* which appeared in the National Gallery's 1974 group show of Alberta artists: *For an Independent Hairy Hill.*

Another Alberta College of Art ceramics major (1966), **LESLIE (LES) MANNING** (1944, Provost, Alberta) also turns to the environment, but on a more modest scale with his "clayscapes" of laminated stoneware and porcelain. Beginning in 1976, Manning's fascination with the geological character of the mountains around Canmore/Banff with their ridges, faults and strata is first expressed in the layered clay bodies of vases and teapots, and later in non-functional, cylindrical pieces noted for their graceful curves and swelling contours. Not wishing to compete with the Rockies' monumentality, Manning says his only wish, both then and now, is to "capture a small slice of nature"[32] by using layers of different clays to show the surfaces and bands of sediment and snowpack that are the very matter of an alpine environment.

If the Rockies serve as source for Manning's own art, he in turn makes the Rockies, specifically the Banff School of Fine Arts, an important international centre for the study of ceramics by young, professional artists of post-graduate level. Program director of the Ceramic Studio from 1974–1995, Manning becomes (as John Potter noted), "Canada's unashamed hustler for the world of ceramics," participating in numerous conferences and exhibitions, conducting workshops and jurying and serving on the boards of many provincial, national and international ceramics organizations. He also is a co-founder of Canmore's Stonecrop Pottery co-op in 1974.

JOHN CHALKE's (1940, Gloucestershire, England) works of clay or, as he once called them, "plates too good to eat off,"[33] are often discussed in terms of their atypical glazes, radical surfaces and references to earlier pottery traditions. At their most tactile, though, the cracked, lumpy and blistered surfaces of some of his hand-shaped stoneware plates and vessels also suggest the terrestrial: parched earth, shifting soils, pitted stone and whatever else might be underfoot in the dusty Palliser Triangle. Elke Blodgett, for one, thinks: "He made some glazes that lived.... They [his large plates] were not frozen stiff into some strange dead thing, they are still moving and living."[34] His surfaces sometimes contain images built up with coloured glazes, stencils or small mould-made objects of animals, such as cows and fish, and conjure up the sensations of a blustery southern Albertan environment where he has lived since coming from England to teach at the University of Calgary in 1968.

There are even more direct and intentional allusions to the Albertan environment in the ceramic practice of **CHARLES (CHUCK) WISSINGER** (1945, Windber, United States). Not content to create a literal description of the landscape or its forms, Wissinger becomes best known in the late 1970s and early 1980s for his monolithic, free-standing, irregular, hoodoo-inspired forms, whose rawness and sheer "clayness" make them a presence to contend with. "One becomes conscious of the raw earth and the tenuous nature of the land itself,"[35] he writes in 1978, responding to his growing awareness of the environment he came to as a stranger.

Like the English-born and -educated Chalke, this Pennsylvania native is one of several influential outsiders to move to the province during the (Peter) Lougheed years of cultural expansion and opportunity. He arrives in 1974 to assume a position at Red Deer College as its first full-time ceramic instructor, and becomes, it might be said, the maestro behind the transformation of this small, central-Albertan city into a centre for clay art. Later reflecting on the particular aesthetic of the College's ceramic program, Wissinger observes, "Our work exhibits an overall rawness. It's not slick, it's not design-y. There's a palpable sense of the material."[36]

Leaning toward the sculptural side of ceramics, Wissinger couldn't have found a more "palpable" landscape than the prairie/foothill/badland environment of central Alberta. The wind-eroded badlands with their strong alien forms are especially well-suited to his interpretative eye and his sense that "time and space are revealed in cosmic proportion here, yielding insight into our place in the evolving continuum."[37]

Interested in the spiritual qualities of the landscape, his 1982–84 *Eolian Metamorph* series (meaning changed by wind) are described by the artist as being made for meditation.[38] An *Edmonton Journal* critic adds that seeing his piece *Eolian Metamorph X* "is to see Alberta past and present."[39] Ranging in height from 4 to 7 feet and as much as 5 feet in width, the obelisk-shaped pillars are salt fired, a technique favoured by the artist because it is "imbued with a primal nature, similar to the essence I am attempting to capture."

ANNEMARIE SCHMID ESLER (1937, Winnipeg, Manitoba) is the most postmodern and conceptual of the five. She is also a chameleon, in that change, sometimes very dramatic change (new ideas, new methods, new subject matter), is a constant in her art, stimulated by her travels, relationships and life experiences. But, as curator Valerie Greenfield outlines, the artist, from time to time, draws on nature and the land as a source of inspiration; it's a way, so to speak, of recharging her creative batteries.[40]

Two notable examples are the witty semi-surrealist *Turf Pieces* in which the sky will appear beneath the earth's surface (mid-1970s) and the monochromatically abstract-geometric wall sculptures inspired by a backpacking trip in the early 1980s on Vancouver Island. (In between would come the anthropomorphic *Bound Bird* series.) Both bodies of work are dramatically different from each other and underline a strong commitment to self-expression in whatever form it takes. Her idiosyncratic spirit or what Greenfield refers to as "[Schmid Esler's] pervasive romanticism,"[41] is further reinforced or "shaped by the grandeur of the natural environment."[42]

Nature as catalyst is similarly an important theme in **LYNDAL OSBORNE**'s (1940, Newcastle, Australia) practice. Already considered nationally an accomplished printmaker, it is her rural surroundings outside Edmonton that eventually spur her into collecting and then, more crucially, organizing nature's organic matter into some kind of poetic order, rich with metaphorical meaning. It's the natural vernacular that interests her, and with the seedpods, bird's nests, banana peels, tree branches, grasses and so on scavenged from her home and garden, from the river valleys and fields of the area, she creates printed images (lithographs) abundant in strong colour and design, and tactile sculptures and installations surprising for their botanical breath. In her work, she reveals the environment around Edmonton – with its long growing season and higher precipitation – to be a haven for the wild and the cultivated.

Osborne's scavenging and collecting abilities make her one of four Alberta artists featured in the 1988 exhibition *Surroundings* (Glenbow Museum). A little later, the *Edmonton Bullet* notes, "She draws her inspiration from a natural world that is neither pristine nor romantic. It's a world where objects erode, rot, shrivel, decay."[43] An example of this is her 1989 lithograph *Cocoon,* inspired by a coyote's decaying ribcage, which she finds half-buried in a field. According to Osborne, "Working directly with these materials has now become a very vital way for me to respond intuitively to what I see, and to understand the underlying organizing structure, origin, and natural evolutionary cycles."[44] In the exhibition *Of Mudlarkers and Measurers* (1997, Agnes Etherington Art Centre, Kingston), she displays 250 abandoned birds' nests alongside 65 small barn-board boxes with balls woven from copper wire. Comments the *Globe and Mail,* "This frenzy of collecting, recycling and reordering seems slightly loony, until one reflects that nature itself is constantly working similar metamorphoses."[45]

From 1988 on, the Australian-born artist will also focus more of her energies on her bound sculptural objects and arrangements, sometimes organized into groupings or bundles such as in the simple but elegant *Windbreak* (1992). Consisting of seven upright bundles of long willow branches bound into different shapes, *Windbreak,* with its poetic connection to a farmer's field, "speaks to us on a purely visual level, without the need for a common, spoken language."[46] Ditto for *Landmark,* another bundled arrangement featuring 19-foot rows of assembled dried grasses and plants mounted on steel plinths and exhibited at *In/Here/Out/There: Alberta Biennial of Contemporary Art, 1998* (Glenbow Museum, Edmonton Art Gallery). "*Landmark* is an organic wall constructed as a barrier against the advancing cold and isolation of a prairie winter, protecting the continuance of life,"[47] writes the artist, who also adds that, on a personal level, the arrangement "is able to bridge the memory of my native landscape in Australia in a present-day collaboration with the flatlands of Alberta."[48]

BILL MORTON's (1940, Didsbury, Alberta) intuitive art communicates largely on a visual level but using the textile medium, which has been compared to a universal language[49] familiar to people around the world. A self-described "country boy" from an Alberta farming community, Morton combines certain aspects of nature, such as "shifting light and reflections on the surface of moving water,"[50] with the ancient practice of Japanese silk dying. Primarily a creator of beautiful wall hangings, Morton's hand-painted artworks are typically saturated in layers of transparent colour that both obscure and reveal stencilled images of natural matter on the stubbly silk surface. The effect is a shimmering meditation both on the simple wonders of nature and the connection cloth has to ancient civilizations and traditions, a kind of silken yin and yang about nature and culture.[51]

Like a significant number of Alberta artists, Morton's sophisticated art is a reflection of his own roots as well as his travels and experiences abroad. Prior to 1983, Morton spends fourteen years in Kyoto, Japan, working in a design studio with Master Dyer Kunio Isa. Upon returning to Calgary, Morton then concentrates on making naturally dyed wall hangings plus the occasional kimono.

Sharing similar territory with Morton's silk art – at least in terms of nature being a subject of reverence – are **ANNE POPE**'s (1950, Red Deer, Alberta) mixed-media sculptures. Pope's work, too, is the product of a rural upbringing influenced by the artist's contact with the Inuit of the Northwest Territories, where she worked as a government agent. Particularly impressive are her large-scale outdoor works like *Broken Stairway* and *Circle of Silence.* Constructed on a wintry farmer's field near Red Deer in 1991, a total of nine works are made out of hundreds of hay bales stacked into monolithic shapes – a kind of prairie Stonehenge. The forms, such as a 24 foot enclosed circle and two towering stairways, emerge through what she speaks of as the experience of becoming "an integral part of the landscape,"[52] feeling its energy and sensing its material substance.

Pope is also attracted to stone (granite, sandstone, fieldstone, marble), cutting it into simple, clean shapes and allowing it to speak for itself as one of nature's enduring materials. This preference for simplicity is an aspect of all her mixed-media works, including a series of sculptural installations (1992) consisting of large quantities of grain in shallow steel bowls that make allusions to fertility and spiritual offering. This work is inspired by her childhood on a ranch, about which Pope writes, "Great reverence for the land, nature and its many harvests are the gifts of this heritage."[53]

Another aspect of Alberta's natural heritage present in its art, but more like a meandering undercurrent, is animal imagery. Historically, one need only think of an artist like Banff's Carl Rungius with his grand and noble depictions of mountain wildlife. Or, a little later, of Peace River's Euphemia McNaught, Medicine Hat's Luke Lindoe and pioneer Margaret Butok, Calgary's John Snow and Illingworth Kerr (who, it should be remembered, initially wanted be an animal painter and nothing else).[54]

Alas, as Kerr was to find out in 1924 upon his arrival at Ontario College of Art, animals have as much status in the serious art world as flying balloons. To quote curator Elizabeth Brown nearly sixty years later: "There is a feeling, held by many artists and critics that there is something over-sentimental or superficial about their portrayal."[55] In addition, not helping matters is the slick commercial world of animal illustration, commonly known as wildlife art, which sells what are essentially posters as "fine art prints" by the hundreds and even thousands.

Amidst all of this, then, what is a poor wolf to do? More to the point, what is an artist to do? In Kerr's own time, his animal work receives little attention. More recently, though, contemporary artists like Linda Carney, Maggie Dunbar, Maureen Enns, Alexandra Haeseker and Gary Olson depict animals – birds of prey, gorillas, bears, sheepdogs and cows respectively – but in less traditional compositions, giving these creatures a context linked with contemporary art practices since the 1970s. But on the periphery, there are artists of all kinds – from folk to western – for whom animals are a subject matter simply because of the kind of place Alberta is.

Only since the early 1990s have animals emerged as a theme worthy of serious exhibition. Alberta examples would include: *Animal Spirits, Animal Spirits Revisited* (Muttart Art Gallery, Calgary, 1994), *Arktypes: Romanticism in Animal Imagery* (Edmonton Art Gallery, 1995) and *Ark* (Illingworth Kerr Gallery, Calgary, 1995). Why this subject matter at this time? I think it's a many-sided phenomena but with a couple of key influences. One is the emergence of a new generation of First Nations artists who, like many of their elders, readily employ such imagery in compelling ways. Two Alberta examples are George Littlechild (Edmonton) and Roy Salopree (Meander River). In the latter case, animals, especially birds, are a central motif in his detailed pen and ink drawings of the mid-1980s. Winner of the Asum Mena scholarship (1985), this Meander River artist is described as exploring, "the relationship of these [natural] elements to humans," in the belief that, "we are a part of everything."[56]

In the work of Littlechild, animals are often symbols of personal and social themes like family history, Canadian history, the treatment of Aboriginal cultures and the environment. Commenting on his painting *Red Horse Boarding School* (1993) the Edmonton-born Littlechild writes, "In my picture the red horse is torn in half because Indian children coming to the [residential] schools were torn away from their culture, their language, their traditional ways and their families."[57]

Another reason for the increased respectability of animal subject matter is the emergence of the environmental movement and so-called New Age attitudes. Neo-romantic in their cultural impact, environmentalists and New Agers venerate nature and ennoble animals. Combine these two social movements with the enduring culture of animal husbandry on the Prairies, and you get a tremendous empathy for animals. Aspects of this attitude are reflected in the semi-mystical horses of the farm-raised Evelyn Kleis (Medicine Hat), or the whimsically benign animal portraits of Grant Leier. For Kleis, daughter of pioneer painter Margaret Butok, "The open space and the spirits of horses have provided rich nourishment for my soul."[58] And according to curator Denis Gautier-Villon of *Arktypes,* art such as Leier's "is an excellent vehicle for the expression of romantic themes since animals, in the popular imagination, embody many of the qualities considered romantic."[59]

On the reverse side of the coin, animal subject matter also finds a place within the more critical agenda of postmodern thinking. One example is the captured and tranquilized wildlife seen in Carroll (Moppett) Taylor-Lindoe's photo-based bookwork *Dreamland* (1990), exhibited in *Alberta Surveys: New Landscapes* (Edmonton Art Gallery, 1992). Curator Kitty Scott observes: "Frederic Jameson, a contemporary theorist, argues that we live in the postmodern era where nature has disappeared for good. In any case, we can no longer think of nature as a rarefied sanctuary synonymous with landscape."[60]

Conventional assumptions about the co-existence and symbiotic relationship between humans and animals were challenged early on in the contemporary era with the animal-centred artwork of Gary Olson, Harry Savage and Maureen Enns. A veteran printmaking instructor at the Alberta College of Art and Design, **GARY OLSON** (1946, Minneapolis, USA) is one of a small number of contemporary artists in the province with a history of spending a large portion of his practice on animal subject matter. (Other examples include dinosaur sculptor Brian Cooley and dinosaur painter Jan Sovak.) In his art, animals have a dual role as symbol and as form.

Once described stylistically as a post-pop realist,[61] Olson is best-known for his large-scale unsentimental portraits of cows. Beginning in the 1970s, this subject is used to tackle formal issues in contemporary art such as the "picture plane" and illusion, evolving to include magnification, foreshortening and other processes. The effect created is a kind of in-your-face realism, made even more relentless by his use of dramatic light and colour, and eye-boggling detail. Referring to his early depictions of the cow, writer Nancy Tousley observes: "His approach was straight ahead and blunt, not at all pastoral, and often confrontational."[62]

In 1984 Olson expands his subject matter to include wild animals from the nearby Rockies, and contends that "they are personal images with symbolic content that relate to my past and the environment in which I live."[63] In earlier works (mixed media on paper), the cow in its natural surroundings made reference to happy childhood summers spent on a farm and his adult years spent amidst the wide, open landscape surrounding his home in Cochrane, Alberta. More recently, his realist images have become vehicles for environmental commentary, especially concerning the skewed relationship between animals and society. In a series of paintings titled *The Tamed and*

Untamed (1987), he comments on the alienation between humans and the natural world. In another body of work, *Predator Competitor* (1994), Olson superimposes a target on the close-up image of a Rocky Mountain sheep: "The targets represent domination and control. They are surrogate male egos."[64]

Besides his animal-theme artwork, Olson is also known for his close-up self-portraits done in graphite (1976–1985). His face is pressed against what appears to be a sheet of glass but is in fact the flat picture plane. Considered a parody of abstract formalist art and reminiscent of American Chuck Close's art, these vivid "anti-high art"[65] images receive national attention in the late 1970s and early 1980s. Ten years later, he returns to these monumental portraits, this time portraying family members in acrylic and oil.

In the same year Gary Olson moves to Canada (1973), Harry Savage is finishing up a period of art making devoted to social issues like the Vietnam War and the environment. "In the late sixties I was angry about many things. I took a series of photographs of coyotes that had been trapped, raped, clubbed, run over by people on snowmobiles. My prints and posters were meant to grab people."[66] And grab they did, as in his ten-piece *Let It Be* poster series (1969), one of which, a print of a wolf, hangs in John Lennon's and Yoko Ono's Montreal hotel bedroom during their "bed-in" for peace in 1969.

A little later, a group of ten silk screens (1972–73) are made and described as graphic and provocative.[67] Known as the *Postage Stamp* series, Savage appropriates and enlarges the image of a Canadian stamp complete with its serrated edges and typeface, and places in the centre an image of a distressed animal or roadkill as photographed by the artist. In one work, the stamp features a deer, *One for Highway 16* (1972); in another, it's a bear behind zoo bars, *One to Look At* (1973). At the time, because of Edmonton's evolving institutional preference for apolitical modernism and pure abstract art, these socially aware prints marginalize the artist locally. But nationally and internationally, Savage's political and environmental art is timely and relevant, placing him within a strain of socially aware, anti-high art of the late 1960s, better known in the work of contemporaries like London's Greg Curnoe and Vancouver's Iain Baxter, who grew up in Calgary.

In Maureen Enns's western horse paintings (1981–1984), her attitude tilts towards irony rather than anger, and irony is a sentiment that will be increasingly evident in art of that period, becoming a buzzword of the 1980s art. In *The Bridal Path Series* (1983) and *Beauty Pageant* (1984), Enns paints the horse partly because such subject matter in contemporary art is usually dismissed as trivial, and because the western horse is pooh-poohed by many of the very people who think horses are important and meaningful. As the artist explains, "The Appaloosa is a very scruffy, macho horse, so is the [Indian] Paint. They are absolutely 'out' in the dressage circles I ride in. It's important to me to elevate them to an elegant realm."[68]

Enns's acrylics also suggest other meanings. About the travelling exhibition *Beauty Pageant,* Whyte Museum curator Elizabeth Brown comments on how these atypical portraits reflect the master-servant relationship between nature and civilized man: "The horse, no longer a symbol of power and freedom, has been given the role of a beast of burden or a pretty plaything."[69] This image of the subservient horse comes through loud and clear in Enns's work, as the title *Beauty Pageant* implies. In it, the horse is depicted in an artificial environment. which the artist compares to an empty stage.[70]

Like Gary Olson, Enns is also an artist of her time, interested in such formal issues as realism, abstraction, collage, decorative patterning, depth versus flatness, and so on. The results are unconventional animal portraits that evoke both contemporary painting concerns of the late 1970s and a very potent symbol of place. Like many Alberta artists, Enns has one foot planted firmly in the cosmopolitan art world and the other rooted in the western environment where land and heritage matter.

From the mid-1980s on, Enns draws upon a camel trip across the Australian desert (1986), an African elephant expedition (1989) and a three-year personal study of the grizzly bear (1991–93) as source material for her art. She describes her east African journey as the catalyst in sharpening her environmental concerns for a disappearing wilderness. Her subsequent *Grizzly Kingdom: An Artist's Encounter* includes nearly forty paintings and drawings, a film documentary and a co-authored book, dedicated to the grizzly bears of Alberta.[71] Created with the desire to champion what she views as a much-maligned animal,[72] Enns's colourful, accessible art is, according to co-author Debbie Thomas, unapologetically geared to the general public rather than to an academically informed art audience.[73] But even with the public, her fractured and collaged images are still a challenge, albeit for different reasons than subject matter. Witness the recollection of Banff warden Rick Kunelius: "Some park staff initially viewed Enns as 'a flaky woman who painted weird borders around otherwise realistic looking animals.' Wardens are not known for being art connoisseurs."[74] And neither are many in the public where the perception of artists as 'flakes' is a common stereotype. This anecdote underlines part of the reality of being a contemporary artist in Alberta: namely, you are really between a rock and a hard place. The rock being the general public's lack of knowledge about art and the hard place being the periphery that Alberta artists inhabit when dealing with subject matter that is close to home but is on the periphery of the wider art world.

HELEN MACKIE (1926, Tavistock, Ontario) is another artist who makes a career out of concentrating on what is meaningful in her own backyard. In fact, right from the start of her formal training as an artist in the early 1970s – when the preference in painting was for "arty, media-oriented abstract art"[75] – this former biochemist realized that her passion for plants and animals, landscape and local history would have to be pursued outside of the contemporary art world. Fortunately, while at the University of Calgary, she studied printmaking under the technical mastery and inspiration of J.K. Esler and Noboru Sawai. Especially important was Esler, who was less concerned about art-world ideology and styles than about encouraging artists to discover an individual voice.[76]

For Mackie, this idea translated into making prints – etching combined with block printing, or block prints – dwelling on the value of the handmade rather than on what is technically sophisticated in printmaking. Often comparing her prints to drawing, with line and mark-making used to convey energy, her animals are naturalistically portrayed without being fussy, illustrative or sentimentalized. Mackie's images are lucid yet personal, reaching beyond textbook biology with their vivid forms and strong contrasts, two qualities she finds already present in nature. "The natural forms are so expressionistic in themselves, you don't need to push them."[77]

Through wanting to know nature intimately, Mackie finds all life rife with symbolism and meaning. This adds another layer to her work, in which plant and animal life are sometimes arranged in horizontal bands across the paper to symbolize ideas about the sacredness of the environment and life's interconnectedness. Mackie's response to the natural world has a no-nonsense quality to it, informed by her rural upbringing and her father's involvement in scientific farming practices. This makes her art accessible to a wide public audience, engaging for its directness and symbolic insight. (Mackie is also a watercolourist of plant life and groundscapes.)

Environmental subject matter is front-and-centre for ROBBIN YAGER (1953, Kingston, Ontario), too. Although a generation younger than Mackie,

Yager's skill at mixed-media drawing, etching and painting infuses her art with an energy made all the more intense by her use of rich, dark colours and, in the case of her oil stick and pastel images, tactile surfaces. Nothing is very serene-looking in Yager's landscape-inspired images and, like Barbara Milne's work, her cogent images seem more a product of memories distilled than of specific places. Indeed, looking back at her decision in the early 80s to drop abstract minimalism, she writes "I began to work with landscape that was half internal, half external experience."[78]

A committed environmentalist who, along with other artists, is commissioned by the Western Canada Wilderness Committee to create art about the west coast's Carmanah Valley[79] (1989), Yager's images become more environmental in attitude at the end of the decade when she begins to juxtapose "two or three small images so that each portion derives meaning from its contrast and co-existence with the other."[80]

In one particularly striking series of multiple panels begun in the early 1990s, Yager creates vivid pictures around the theme of water, fire, earth and air. Describing these motifs as "psychic symbols from nature,"[81] she remarks they are being "tragically replaced by symbols manufactured and manipulated to influence our wants, and to fulfill an economic and material ideal.... Biophilia [literally the love of life] is a term that could represent my drive to create images."[82]

DARYL RYDMAN (1961, Edmonton, Alberta) also loves life, but his view is more typically postmodern. Hence his 1993 MA exhibition *Natural History,* in which, through the process of dealing with "his anxieties about the age-old fistfight between nature and culture,"[83] he does a number of things differently from the more senior Albertans discussed in this chapter. In a sense, Rydman is of a different generation whose developing outline is still somewhat blurry at the time of this writing. Let's just say Rydman takes a more critical view about how, for instance, the pristine forests of the Group of the Seven or the barrage of mass-media images from popular culture influence and shape our view of what is natural. He is, in other words, savvy about the visual culture of our society and responds to it by manipulating what it is already there. In the making of his art, he regularly appropriates and photocopies images from other sources like magazines and books.

Rather than depict or describe the natural world, there is actually very little of nature to be seen in a Rydman mixed-media artwork. At most, it could be a photograph of a brutally sheared pine tree merged with an image of the Catholic martyr St. Sebastian, or a Bambi-like deer figurine set on what appears to be a dark, glistening road, but is actually a wet card table. Strange images for a former Kananaskis parks interpreter. In his art, nature has gone missing, replaced by an environmental casualty like a clear-cut northern forest in Alberta (*Cutline 1,* 1993, mixed media on canvas) or a Disney-inspired example of the animal world (*Velvet Halo,* 1993, mixed media on masonite). His art is interpreted as moving "beyond the traditional views of nature."[84] According to the artist, his intent is "to engage in both the representation of nature and the nature of representation."[85] In regard to the latter, it is not a particularly new theme in the contemporary art world, but Rydman pushs the deconstructive envelope in Alberta with his potent high-tech melange of photocopies, photographs, acrylic paint and the occasional found object. Instead of being engaged with the making of an original work of art, Rydman's goal is "to take something fake and make it faker so that it becomes real."[86]

The representation of nature is also of great interest to **AMY GOGARTY** (1953, Abington, United States). Her found images, though, are of a more cultivated, scholarly type, like the kind seen in old encyclopedias or antiquarian books about the natural world. Linked to the nineteenth century, her multi-panel paintings evoke a precocious era when the observation and classification of nature was a hobby for many in the educated gentry. Conjure up an Audobon image and then think of Gogarty. This is possible because her artwork reproduces depictions she has found in nature guides, encyclopedias and out-of-print art history texts. A dedicated peruser of libraries and museums, she is like the naturalists she borrows from: intent on examining and dissecting how nature is organized and structured. But rather than stalking the flora and fauna of the wild, her prey is hand-made: pictures of the natural world produced in the good name of science and education.

Like Rydman, this more senior artist/writer and art instructor feels no compulsion to create original images, nor does she view nature as a citadel isolated from the impact of humankind. The dichotomy between nature and culture, science in particular, is a theme in her art, but instead of nature graphically portrayed as the victim, Gogarty's meticulously painted acrylics present what she terms as a "quiet, mute complaint."[87]

An example of this portrayal is *The Order of Passiformes* (*Such a Country*). Based on a series of bird pictures from a reprinted 1851 German encyclopedia, the seven square panels imitate "the way science dissects and orders the natural world into ostensibly self-evident categories."[88] Viewed together, the panels of redpoll, song thrush and vegetation suggest the perching birds are not lone individuals. "I thus assert a different perception of nature – as a seamless, indivisible web of mutually dependent life forms, rather than individual species."[89]

Considering Gogarty's imagery is borrowed from the cut-and-dry archival world of academia, her smooth-surfaced art is engagingly "both beautiful and evocative"[90] comments Nancy Tousley. Her pictures are even elegiac and otherworldly, a result perhaps of her attempt "to recreate the spellbinding attraction reading and illustrated books have held over me since childhood."[91] Since graduating with an MFA in painting from the University of Calgary in 1989, the artist has also applied her labour-intensive methods to exploring the history of women, the nature of illness, archaeology and the crafts, such as folk embroidery.

One artist who cuts her own swath through the genres of landscape and environmental art is **CARROLL (MOPPETT) TAYLOR-LINDOE** (1948, Calgary, Alberta). One of a small number of contemporary Alberta artists to attain a national reputation, her ongoing practice, which began to take shape in the early 1970s is still considered current and relevant because "[her] work continues to expand with such inventive and surprising verve that each new exhibition by this Calgary sculptor and painter becomes an event to anticipate."[92]

To varying degrees, the terra firma and natural world around Taylor-Lindoe have always figured in her oeuvre, although their presence has sometimes been superseded in favour of other concerns addressed in her work. Her art, at one point, is interpreted as "[conducting] a formal dialogue about space and perception."[93] In another instance, she is seen as "[positing] a new definition of sculpture,"[94] or a little later, "[dealing] with political issues – in particular the politics of representation,"[95] and so on. But whatever the artist's desire to tangle with contemporary-art concerns – and she does so rigorously – Taylor-Lindoe's response to the western environment is still one of the most original of the post-1970 period, both conceptually and formally. Her revisioning of the Alberta landscape through her charcoal drawings, polychrome wood sculptures, installations and paintings are as striking as Marion Nicoll's symbolic abstracts were for her time. And like Nicoll, Taylor-Lindoe has her own modus operandi, which she writes about in the 1987 exhibition for *Temporal Icons:* "I am rooted in the landscape. The artists, geologists, naturalists and palaeontologists who make up my family, approach the natural world with a form of inquiry that has added layers of meaning to what could have been a simple utopian view, helping us to transform it into something far more complex and real, but by no means less beautiful."[96]

Thus, Taylor-Lindoe does not fit comfortably into any of the romantic landscape traditions or practices that have circulated through the province. Although her artistic roots are in modernism, she is not shy about experimenting and reinterpreting its visual language. At one point in her career, John Bentley Mays suggests that Taylor-Lindoe has stumbled "upon a pile of rusting junk"[97] called "Western Art History."[98] More recently, David Garneau writes that she is in a struggle to distance herself from the art of a more particular past. "Imagine being raised among artists, as Carroll Moppett was, and having 'your vision' of the land pre-visioned, mediated by the vocabulary of the great/minor men of southern Alberta landscape painting. Carroll's landscape related paintings and *Palaeontology,* it seems to me, are attempts to re-describe, even recover 'her' land. Much of Moppett's work is a radical re-description of everything, inside and out, in order to symbolically wrest the world from its previous owners."[99]

The art Garneau is referring to is produced between the late 1980s up to the end of the century. Including paintings, drawings and installations, they are intended, according to the artist, "to destabilize conventional readings of familiar forms."[100] In her efforts to re-describe her environment and represent "a vision of the physical world that unites her perceptual and emotional responses,"[101] Taylor-Lindoe is remarkably fluid. Unlike many Alberta artists involved with landscape, nature and the environment, the artist has no singular signature style or format. Her oeuvre ranges from ceramics (late 60s to 1975) to constructivist sculpture and drawing (1975–85), and most recently painting, drawing, installation and photo-based art (1985–present). As well, she has staked out territory in both abstract and representational art, working on both sides of the fence when the need arises. One early instance is a large horizontal drawing (charcoal on canvas, 1985) entitled *Biography, Autobiography: I am Not I Any Longer When I See.* The piece features a conventional mountain panorama on the left, abstract and semi-abstract imagery in the middle, and ends on the right with a garden depicted in an expressionist and realist style. Curator Vincent Varga suggests, "In many ways [it] is an apt metaphor for the development and acceptance of modernism in the visual arts community in Alberta."[102]

Around the same time as *Biography, Autobiography,* Taylor-Lindoe is entering into a new phase of her practice that will also include the addition of text or writing on the artworks, installation and photo-based pieces. Some endeavours will address personal subject matter, her place as a woman within society and art history, or give a critical view of humankind's relationship with nature. In regard to the latter, she produces three photo installations: *Dreamland* (1990), *Paleontology* (1991) and *Geology Field Notes* (1995). All three environmental works appropriate and manipulate photographs taken for the purposes of scientific research with the intent of disrupting their intended meaning or purpose. In *Geology Field Notes,* Taylor-Lindoe incorporates the factual photographs of a geological survey into an installation work that, according to curator Richard Baillargeon, "[questions] the ways in which we see [the landscape], represent it to ourselves, and, in particular, appropriate it."[103]

In the artist's view, the kinds of images produced in the name of science and research too often amount to "the reduction of nature to a mechanism that serves the needs of man."[104] She turned to these unsentimental images of the mountains from northeastern British Columbia because Taylor-Lindoe wishes to see its nature valued "in its own right and exclusive of any use"[105] and to make a point about getting beyond the hermetic, navel-gazing art of the modern period "so perfectly expressed"[106] (she writes) by the "I am nature!"[107] proclamation of New York abstract expressionist Jackson Pollock. Living in vastness of the West, as Taylor-Lindoe does, makes her too humble for such ideas.

chapter five

A Place Called Alberta: Taking Photographs, Painting Pioneers, Carving Cowboys and Contemporary Responses to the Western Tradition

The Canadian literary critic Northrop Frye once proposed the question for Canadians regarding their identity. He said it is not "who are we?" but "where is here?" The answer might be as varied as the Canadian landscape. For some artists in Alberta, that answer has always encompassed more than just the province's physical terrain. It can also be engaged with the different cultures and histories in the region, perhaps confirming Frye's belief that "the centre of reality is wherever one happens to be, and its circumference is whatever one's imagination can make sense of."[1]

The attempt to make sense of "wherever one happens to be" has, in the post-1970 era, been a daunting and often undervalued activity in Canadian society, as the following observations attest:

> Global culture has increased the sense that real life takes place somewhere else, and that local creativity is second-rate.[2] ☙ Liam Lacey, 1991;

> With [English Canadians], the doctrine of universalism has succeeded to an awesome degree. As chroniclers like Northrop Frye have reported, we mistrust and fear the idea of local culture. As a theatre critic, I was often struck by the embarrassment of Canadians when confronted, for example, with a musical comedy set in their own city.[3] ❧ Ray Conologue, 1991;

> The problem of course is that there are authentic voices among the artists in this country, but there is an enormous fear in our critics, a curious reluctance to point out the authenticity in those voices and an undermining tendency to justify our best artists by using critical standards from somewhere else, nearly always the critics in this country extol Canadian imitations of American models.[4] ❧ Greg Curnoe, 1983.

To readers familiar with the Canadian cultural milieu, comments like these are nothing new. They reflect a bread-and-butter issue of cultural discourse in Canada in the twentieth century, and they have been digested vigorously in the fields of literature and the dramatic arts. At its most fundamental, for instance, it's not unusual to pick up a Canadian novel or play and find that it is set somewhere specific in Canada and represents characters and aspects connected to that locale.

In Canadian visual art, though, the idea of place, both in terms of its cultural and geographic definitions, has been, *nationally,* of limited interest since the advent of post-war modern art; a few exceptions include the ongoing tradition of so-called regional landscape and the nationally recognized art of Joyce Weiland, Joe Fafard, John Hartman, David Blackwood, John Boyle, Marlene Creates, David Thauberger, William Kurelek and Greg Curnoe. This state of sanctioned amnesia has sometimes been rationalized on the basis that place is too difficult to nail down in a country as fractured as Canada. As critic and curator Bruce Ferguson observes in 1991, "The 'where' and the 'who' of Canada are always at stake, always under interrogation, and always slipping away from any assured identity."[5]

For contemporary Canadian visual art today, place is a problem because of the impact of art-making concerns circulating in the larger art world. "How can we reconcile the importance of international discourse and the inevitable generalities that arise out of this vast territory with concerns that are localized and specific to particular communities of cultural producers?"[6]

asks the Toronto-based critic Monika Kim Gagnon. Thus, place (like much recent landscape) is a topic without a firm *place* in the more recent annals of Canadian art-making. In Alberta though (and certainly elsewhere) it does crop up – often in artwork that generally will never receive much serious critical and curatorial attention in the upper reaches of Canada's publicly funded art establishment. So why do cultural producers continue to pour energy into such endeavours? Perhaps it is a gut reaction to a sentiment so well-expressed in 1990 by the Welsh historian and travel writer, Jan Morris: "Canada is one country whose parts are greater than the whole, and its colossal scale is becoming increasingly irrelevant. The detail is what really counts now, and it is far more interesting, if only because it has had to survive against such overwhelming odds." The overwhelming odds[7] she refers to are the tendencies of this country's highly centralized cultural institutions to gloss over Canada's various places and regions.

An early post-1970 Alberta exhibition that had a strong connection to place but beat the odds because even the National Gallery of Canada managed to get involved by circulating it as part of its extension program is the 1973 *For an Independent Hairy Hill.* Alas, it will also be the last time the National Gallery ever shines the spotlight on a group of Alberta-based artists. (Until the end of the century only a small number individual Albertans will be invited to exhibit.)

Featuring paintings, ceramics, photographs, prints, drawings and weaving by 14 artists – including such notables as Harry Savage, Sylvain Voyer, John Hall, Wynona Yates, Harlan House, Norman Yates, Walter May, Tom Radford and Robert Sinclair – *Harry Hill* addresses the widespread disappearance of the small prairie town. Among the fifty pieces for the viewer to consider are photographs of abandoned buildings, a serigraph series about migration to the city, iconic drawings of the grain elevator, a painting of a Ukrainian graveyard and a three-panel acrylic of debris and garbage bags. (The show takes its name from the once-thriving village of Hairy Hill, northeast of Edmonton.) Immigrants move west to make of their lives what they choose,[8] yet, as Tom Radford writes for the travelling exhibition, they "ultimately had little control over how their society was to develop. No matter how distant the industrial East might have seemed from the West ... it was there that the fate of the West was being decided." Not all of the art in the Hairy Hill exhibition is as pointedly political as the title, but it is still described by a Montreal reviewer as, "an impressive show, which is both a moving social document and an aesthetic success."[9]

After *For an Independent Hairy Hill,* other like-minded projects will include *A Photographic Project: Alberta* (1980) and *A Sense of Prairie: Photographic Exhibition* (1984), as well as ones initiated by individual artists like Joane Cardinal-Schubert's *Canadian Heroes* (paintings, 1978), Orest Semchishen's *Byzantine Churches of Alberta* (black and white photographs, 1976) and Harry Savage's 1975–1978 "image collecting rampage around the province,"[10] which involved ten thousand photos taken by the artist.

Eventually, as the 1980s progress, the theme of place will be superseded by the more questioning and deconstructive attitude of postmodern thinking. "Identity," "the other," "difference," and "postcolonialism" will become the buzzwords of the day particularly as they apply to race, gender, sexual orientation, the dispossessed and the culturally marginalized. The social, cultural and historic landscape of Canada will be put under the microscope, so to speak, and analysed and dissected to discover what it can tell us about Canada, beyond the context of region or Canada as a bicultural nation.

This development will also influence the presentation of historical art and artifacts. From western Canada, for example, there is the travelling exhibition *The Urban Prairie*[11] (1993), which features historical depictions of urban and industrial life in the pioneering west. An eighty-year survey of photography, art and other material (like postcards), the exhibition questions the all-too-typical image of the Prairies as a largely rural/frontier entity. (Two Albertans included in this seminal show from Saskatoon are James McLaren Nicoll and Margaret Shelton.)

More contemporary is the 1994 exhibition *Search, Image and Identity: Voicing Our West*[12] in which the investigations of fourteen prairie artists into their personal identities underscore that being Canadian means that no two stories are the same.[13] More significantly, "[The art] signifies a marginalized regional community moving to distinguish itself from the traditional centre of power – eastern Canada, and all the history that region implies."

☙ Post-1970 Documentary Photography

Of all the visual arts, documentary photography can take substantial credit for making a sense of place and a sense of history a living, vivid theme in post-1970 Alberta. That it did so effectively recalls the activity of an earlier period, highlighted in the exhibition *Survey of Photography in Alberta (1885–1992).*[14] Starting with the late nineteenth- and early twentieth-century pictures of Boorne and May, Charles W. Mathers, Thomas Gushul and other early

Albertans, curator Harry Kiyooka demonstrates that this theme, including its colonizing aspects, is present in such photographs as *Birds Eye View of Banff* c.1886–1892 (Boorne and May), *Cree Indians near Edmonton* c.1893–1904 (Charles W. Mathers), *Group Portrait,* no date (Thomas Gushul) and *Chinese Bell Boys, Lake Louise* 1905 (Herbert W. Gleeson).

Fast-forward to the 1970s and early 1980s when, with institutional support, particularly from the Edmonton Art Gallery, the desire to record the different 'here's' of the province is enthusiastically undertaken. There seemed to be no place or community too remote, too isolated or too out-of-the-mainstream to attract the eager eye of a photographer. Wally Houn, for instance, trained his camera on the town of Hussar; Hugh Hohn on Hairy Hill and the suburbs of Edmonton; Harry Savage on the Saddle Lake reserve; George Webber on Hutterite communities and on the Lac Ste-Anne pilgrimage; Harry Palmer on Rosebud and Calgary; Douglas Curran on Metis settlements; Dario Argento on Calgary's Chinese community; Christine Tournauer on Native dancers; Jacques Rioux on the badlands and Calgary; Randall (Randy) Adams on outdoor folk art and rural graveyards; Sima Khorrami on the Hutterites and the invisible[15] (prisoners, the sick and the elderly); and Ernie Kroeger on Calgary's Broadview Road.

There is also the indefatigable **LAWRENCE CHRISMAS** (1941, Edmonton, Alberta) who, like Semchishen and his church project, devotes a substantial portion of his career to documenting a single subject: in Chrismas's case, the miners in Alberta and elsewhere in Canada. After twenty years and three books[16] on the topic, in 1998 Chrismas undertakes the costly proposition of self-publishing the book *Coal Dust Grains: Portraits of Canadian Coal Miners* (Cambria Publishing). Consisting of 280 photos and miners' stories in their own words, the book is one of seven publications shortlisted for the first annual Roloff Beny Photography Book Award in 1999. (Roloff Beny is a Medicine Hat-born photographer who achieved international recognition abroad.)

Although the above list of published or exhibited projects (including Chrismas's) is not a complete accounting, what much of this activity reveals is the complex and diverse nature of Alberta's social and historic landscape: a multi-layered set of observations underlining author Rudy Wiebe's own memories of his Crowsnest upbringing, "It was a cosmopolitan place, with the Mennonite church standing beside the Buddhist temple. That kind of cosmopolitanism is what gives Alberta its special flavour."[17]

In some ways, this flurry of documentary practice invites comparisons with the socially engaged photography of the 1930s when photographers such as Walker Evans and Dorothea Lange document Depression-era conditions in the United States. Forty years later, though, the photography scene in Alberta is somewhat more detached from the social issues of its time. Only a small number of photographers, such as Orest Semchisen, uses the camera as a vehicle for social commentary. Semchisen's low-key, untroubling black-and-white images of rural society seem to be quite unassuming, and yet they document a very subtle kind of resistance to mainstream culture.

"In our culture," he writes, "we are led to believe that the goal is to be slim, beautiful, rich, assertive, intelligent, popular etc., and many are struggling to achieve these objectives. Behind this facade is a large segment of humanity not scrambling for this idea." [18]

No less culturally detached are the countless pictures taken by the same photographer of Alberta's flatlands. Where many could never imagine photographing this terrain as they whiz by on their way to the Rockies, paying close attention to it becomes yet another form of resistance to standards about what constitutes beautiful landscape. As curator Elizabeth Kidd observes, "Semchishen finds a distinctiveness, a very particular sense of place ... that he describes as 'the presence of the prairie'." [19]

Of all of Alberta's post-1970 photographers – documentary or otherwise – **OREST SEMCHISHEN** (1932, Mundare, Alberta) is one of the better known nationally. He is called the "Atget of Alberta" [20] by photography dealer and writer Peter Duthie and "one of the best photographers in Canada" [21] by critic and curator Kate Davis – a statement that she admits is "very big ... but I stand by it." [22] Big indeed, but one that time has borne out, despite the fact that photography per se, especially the documentary genre, has fallen out of critical favour in Canada; usurped partly by the success of photo-based art in the 1980s and 90s.[23] Semchishen, however, is the proverbial outsider: a radiologist by profession who, in his spare time, diligently works at his art, "aware of but not interested in theoretical posturing." [24]

In 1994, the Canadian Museum of Contemporary Photography (CMPC) in Ottawa presents *Orest Semchishen: In Plain View/Voir Clair.* Consisting of an exhibition and catalogue, this major survey marks twenty-five years of unswerving commitment to recording what he terms, "the quieter segments of our society," [25] as in the people and places who will never rate a mention in our celebrity-drenched culture. To do this, Semchishen adopts an approach of being as "objective and unmanipulative" [26] as possible, "letting the subject reveal itself through my camera."[27] The result, according to many who write about his black-and-white work, is an "elegant matter-of-factness,"[28] a belief "in the eloquence of plain speaking through the language of photography,"[29] allowing "places and people to be seen as they are, without false sentimentality or idealization."[30]

An obsessive cataloguer of Alberta's diverse communities, the photographer's curiosity leads him to systemically document more than 250 of the province's Byzantine churches; follow three years in the life of Russian monk Reverend Seraphin (Westlock, Alberta); photograph members of the Japanese Buddhist community in Raymond, Alberta; record the subsistence culture of northern trappers; investigate the environment of Edmonton's Chinatown; knock on the doors of Cornation and other small burgs; and, as always, seek out the terrain of a "class of folk," according to the *Globe and Mail* critic Robert Everett-Green, "whose very name is a token of scorn" among many in the cultural and media elites – "the Prairie People."[31]

Raised in Mundare, an area of the province that attracted large numbers of Ukrainian immigrants, Semchishen's first and continuing series involves the Byzantine churches of his rural upbringing. It is a highly personal project based on his desire to document a disappearing building type that, in certain areas, is almost as much a prairie icon as the grain elevator. Working with larger cameras, like one with a 4 × 5 negative, the Edmonton doctor's images eventually catch the attention of photographer and instructor Hugh Hohn, and a little later on, the attention of the photo editor of the National Film Board's Still Photography Division, Ron Soloman, who buys a number of them on a cross-country tour in 1974. A year later Soloman gives Semchishen his first major solo exhibition, *Ukrainian Religious Architecture.*

The effect of receiving recognition from a national institution such as the NFB (predecessor of the CMCP) is an important incentive for Semchishen to continue this body of work.[32] In 1976 the Edmonton Art Gallery, which will undertake a major role in exhibiting the documentary form, organizes a three-year touring show *Byzantine Churches of Alberta.* Curated by Hugh Hohn, Semchishen's efforts to record faithfully what he sees fits comfortably within an Anglo-American aesthetic that critic Penny Cousineau defines as the prevailing aesthetic of the modern period.[33]

It appears to be a kind of photography minus the creative ego: black-and-white images made in the tradition of so-called pure or straight photography and one that is popular among many of Alberta's documentarians. It's the reason why some Alberta photography has a certain homogenous look to it. As well, as Nancy Tousley points out, this photographic attitude is not without its own inherent contrivances, such as the use of certain compositional devices: even lighting, a straightforward focus, etc. "The apparent open-faced simplicity of Semchishen's work is deceptive,"[34] she writes in reference to a ten year survey (1973–1983) of sixty-three silver gelatin prints.[35] "At a glance, the pictures look plain. Looking reveals their complexities."[36] Stating more often then not, as curator Martha Hanna observes of Semchishen's photos of Alberta's Japanese Buddhists, that, "family, tradition, nature and beauty are central" to Semchishen's small-c conservative view of Alberta.[37]

HUGH HOHN (1944, Tucson, United States) also explores the social environment of the province, but unlike Semchishen who studies his craft through workshops and courses as he pursues his projects, the American-trained photographer brings with him a high-profile background in documentary photography. His authoritative presence and enthusiasm for the medium create ripple effects wherever he goes. Described as the "guru of Alberta photography," the charismatic Hohn, according to Edward Cavell, didn't so much influence people with his own work as with his personality, knowledge and belief in the camera as a creative tool.[38]

A student of Ansel Adams and Minor White, Hohn spreads the gospel of fine-art photography in the 1970s through teaching, serving on juries, writing, curating and just plain ol' networking with other enthusiasts. Some of the notable Albertans who cross his path besides Semchishen include Wally Houn, Douglas Clark, Lawrence Chrismas, Mark Arneson and the inimitable Barbara Spohr who develops a more personal and idiosyncratic vision of the medium that is very different from Hohn's.

If there is any general philosophy to Hohn's own work during his 1967–1979 sojourn in Alberta, it can be best described as a detached, hands-off approach. Like Semchishen – whom Hohn describes as a "natural: not mired down in theory and aesthetics"[39] – he tries to capture the character of the place without imposing technique, past photographic styles or pictorial codes onto the subject.

He begins with *Alberta Landscapes* (a 1973 NFB exhibition), and follows it with the more documentary *Hairy Hill* (inspired by *For an Independent Hairy Hill*), *Suburban Landscapes* and *Edmonton Entrances*. These three later projects are displayed at the Edmonton Art Gallery where, under Terry Fenton's leadership, Hohn is hired as a freelance curator (1975–76) to "discover aspects of Alberta in photographs that were works of art in their own right."[40] Writing about Hohn's stark, pristine thirty-five millimetre black-and-white images of Edmonton's silent suburbs, Fenton noted, "[they] are in keeping with the spirit of Atget ... they capture the personality of the environment itself and for its own sake."[41]

In 1977, Hohn moves to Banff to teach at the Banff School of Fine Arts. A year later, he redesigns its photography program around a less structured studio model with more emphasis on image-making than technical matters. Established in 1950, the 1970s were a particularly bright time for the school's photography program, first under the direction of Robert Alexander, and then briefly under Hohn. Sadly, a devastating fire in 1979 destroyed its base of operations Crich Hall. While there, Hohn, with the assistance of Lorne Falk (then assistant curator of the school's Walter Phillips Gallery), also establishes a permanent collection of contemporary Canadian photography. Known as *The Banff Purchase,* a travelling exhibition and book is produced in which seven photographers are highlighted, including Orest Semchishen, the lone Albertan of the group.

One of Hohn's last projects dealing with the theme of place was a topographic study of the small towns of the Crowsnest Pass. Featuring black-and-white images of residential neighbourhoods and historic main streets, this body of work is his contribution to the exceptionally ambitious *A Photographic Project: Alberta 1980.* Shot during Alberta's 75th anniversary year, Hohn and nine other photographers, with the assistance of seven researchers, are each assigned to a community for nearly two weeks to "create statements about people and their environments."[42] Complementing their inquiry are images culled from a public submission campaign: *Get Clicking: People Pictures.* The project is modelled on the earlier documentary work undertaken by the photography section of the United States Government's Farm Security Administration of the 1930s.[43] And, while the project had none of the former's spirit of exposing Depression-era poverty as achieved through the work of such notable Americans as Walker Evans, Dorothea Lange, Ben Shahn and others, the Alberta version with its travelling exhibition, catalogue and archive formed a document of a region more socially and economically diverse than the prevailing national image of cowboys and well-heeled oil folk. Ditto for the 1979 book *Alberta/A Celebration,*[44] edited by filmmaker Tom Radford with text by author Rudy Wiebe and colour photography by Harry Savage. This publication presents a more congenial view of the province at a time in Canada's national affairs when "Alberta, and the West as a whole, became the bad boys of Confederation, needing a sharp rebuke."[45]

These two projects were part of a much larger trend in the province that historian Howard Palmer identified as "a growing historical consciousness,"[46] nourished in part by "a new surge of community museums, archives, historical societies, community reunions, recreated historic parks and literally hundreds of new local histories."

If there could be any criticism levelled at this type of thematic documentary exploration, photographer and writer Gail Fisher-Taylor sums up its shortcomings in reference to *A Photographic Project:* "In the exhibition there is only token urban documentation, very little activity, disproportionate happiness, and certainly not enough indication of the industrial boom and suburban sprawl that are so characteristic of Alberta in 1980."[47]

One exception to this type of representation is the work of **DOUGLAS CURRAN** (1952, Seaforth, Ontario). Of the ten photographers invited to participate in *A Photographic Project,* Curran is the newcomer from Ontario. Assigned to photograph the Cold Lake region in the northeast, the Toronto Ryerson graduate's view of its communities is that of an outsider, but an outsider with a keen inquiring mind. "What does a small Alberta town look like in 1980? The image which immediately comes to mind is one of comfort and warmth, familiar faces, and the lack of daily strife and pressure which are so evident in larger centres. The images still have some validity but many of Alberta's small towns no longer conform, strictly, to the rural stereotype."[48] And nowhere is this observation of Curran's more evident than in his assigned area where, in the midst of an oil boom, there are plenty of signs of development and change, including a tidy showroom of new Chevys, which, of course, he records.[49]

Although, like his older colleagues on the project, the photographer believes in letting the subject speak for itself; Curran's approach seems less formal, more immediate and, for that matter, less focused on the historical and the familiar: i.e. architecture and old-timers. (The same can be said about the project's younger Barbara Spohr and Mark Arneson, whose colour images of Paddle Prairie and Rocky Mountain House respectively are more spontaneous, expressive and with a slice-of-life feel.) Less of a documentary theorist than Hohn, or a historian/archivist like Semchishen, Curran's impulse is considered closer to that of a cultural anthropologist: more curious about people's behaviour, beliefs and customs.

This curiosity will play itself out in several projects, two of which are commissioned and sited specifically in the province: a black-and-white study of Alberta's Metis settlements[50] begun in 1981, and a colour documentation of Banff National Park[51] as a tourist destination (1985). Of the five years he spends among the Metis at the invitation of then Alberta Metis leader Elmer Ghostkeeper, Curran later remarks: "Photographing on the Metis Settlements forced me to search more deeply into the subtle aspects of habit and perception that define and create a culture."[52]

Considered pioneers in the area of self-government and land claims compensation,[53] the Metis leaders, during their negotiations with the Alberta government, use displays of Curran's work to articulate a view of their people as a distinct culture. It is a view that will prove to be of great interest not only to the politicians, but to Canadians in general. In 1983 and 1986 respectively, the National Film Board of Canada and the Edmonton Art Gallery organize travelling shows of the Metis portfolio. Both exhibits criss-cross the country for several years because of demand.

In 1990, a retrospective of twelve years of Curran's work is selected and displayed at the Alberta College of Art Gallery. Titled *Belief and Culture,* the exhibit includes fifty photographs from the Metis portfolio, the series *Moses Couldn't Draw A Crowd . . . Travelling Tent Preachers in Modern America,* and his most celebrated series *In Advance of the Landing: Folk Concepts of Outer Space.* This last work, which Curran undertakes early in his career, is an exploration of UFO seekers, homemade spaceships and other space enthusiasts. It earns him considerable attention, including coverage in *People* magazine and *Scientific America* and, as Justin Wonnacott points out, establishes a modus operandi for later work.[54] Summing up Curran's work, Wonnacott writes, "These are not just photographs of specific people and places; these are photographs of culture. Douglas Curran photographs ideas that transcend the specific time and place under investigation."[55]

DOUGLAS CLARK (1952–1999, Hamilton, Ontario) is another Ryerson graduate from Toronto whose sojourn in the province (1975–1982) has an impact on the exploration of place and history. He takes photographs, but also teaches, writes, and most importantly, curates and organizes exhibitions and projects encompassing these themes. While photography curator at the Edmonton Art Gallery from 1976–1979, he oversees exhibitions such as *Market: The Photographs of Orest Semchisen; William Tilland: The Landscape; Edward Curtis* and *The John Henry Hinton Photographs: China 1894–1914.* Then in 1979, he conceives and coordinates with Linda Wedman, *A Photographic Project: Alberta 1980*[56] and the accompanying book *Keepsake* (1981). His last major undertaking in the province (1984–1985) is the public art project *Gallery-In-Transit,* involving the display of Canadian photography in Edmonton, Winnipeg and Vancouver city buses. (Douglas Curran, Lauren Dale, Eleanor Lazare, Harry Savage and Orest Semschishen are some of the Alberta participants.) Call Douglas Clark an impresario during Alberta's golden age of documentary photography.

Impressed by Semchishen, influenced by Hohn, but clearly evolving his own ideas, during this period Clark adopts what he calls "a quasi-documentary approach."[57] Place and history are important topics, as in his pictures of the Edmonton Art Gallery[58] and Edmonton suburban architecture,[59] but as Clark the photographer moves into large-scale colour (20″ × 30″ or 30″ × 40″) around 1979, his notion of the two takes on a more idiosyncratic, less detached, slice-of-life flavour.

The results culminate in the 1981 exhibit *Timeline: Tales of Cold Waves*[60] in which banal and vernacular settings – a restaurant table, an entrance way, a kitchen windowsill, a department store coat rack – speak about the everyday places of our social landscape. Noted for their punchy colour and off-beat character, Clark describes these poetic close-up images as "[recording] the debris and the keepsakes, the marks we make, the evidence of our cares and our passing."[61]

By the end of 1980s, it is clear that fine-art photography, and particularly documentary photography, is under serious fire in Canada. Even in Alberta, where it has flourished with a significant but small group of serious practitioners, institutional support, artist-run gallery support (Centre Eye, Calgary, 1980–89), and the only privately owned photography gallery in Western Canada (Folio Gallery, Calgary, 1983–95), one has to go no further than the Banff Centre, previously a champion of the medium, to get an idea of the shift underway. Rather than acquiring pictures from Canadian photographers, as it had in 1979 for *The Banff Purchase,* in the 1980s the centre begins to collect work from what it calls "a new generation, who blur the distinctions between art and photography,"[62] work that especially reflects "conceptually oriented directions found in contemporary art."[63] Meaning, in plain language: photo-based art rather than traditional photography, summarized by Robert Fulford as "[art by] artists who regularly use photography but who are never described as photographers."[64] In the Banff Centre's case, this will entail artists like Ian Wallace, Roy Arden, Susan Schelle, Dominique Blain and others. These artists employ not only photographs, but slides, film, transparencies, video, text, installation and other media to produce a highly manipulated and theoretically aware art form, a favourite of many contemporary critics and curators in Canada. As a trend, it is almost the polar opposite to what many serious photographers in Alberta have aspired to and practiced. The following is a generalization, but just as most contemporary abstract art in Canada has become artistically "incorrect" in the eyes of the contemporary art mavens, so has documentary.

Still, within the confines of documentary work in Alberta, there are younger photographers – Randall (Randy) Adams, George Webber and **INGRID PLAUDIS** (1955, Red Deer, Alberta) – who are still interested in the tradition, but like Curran and Clark, are less willing to stand back and simply document what is. As Plaudis explains about her use of long exposures and hand-coloured images, "I think of photography not so much as a way of recording, but as interpretative."[65] Of the three artists, Plaudis became the most manipulative and adventuresome with the medium, yet remains keen on using Alberta as a subject matter. In a series of black and white portraits of her Red Deer friends, she presents a more urban image of prairie people.

After studying at the Emily Carr College of Art and Design in Vancouver, Plaudis is drawn back from the west coast in 1989 because of the land.[66] She undertakes a study of the rippling Drumheller badlands, *The Buffalo Jump Series* (1989–92), in which she hand-colours her black-and-white images with Marshall oils and pencils. Described as "a delicate balance of reality and fantasy"[67] by Diana Anderson, these photographs represent a very intuitive response to a place whose changing moods are interpreted and elaborated upon by the artist.

Drumheller's evocative terrain has an even more powerful effect on **GEORGE WEBBER**'s oeuvre (1952, Drumheller, Alberta). Born and raised in the area, Webber not only photographs its strange erosions – using infrared film to highlight its harsh textures and "feral quality"[68] – but also allows its melancholic desolation to influence his perception of the rest of the prairies and its inhabitants. Focusing on the shrinking and dying prairie towns rather than on the fewer but prosperous centres, Webber's photographs articulate what Tousley describes as "a sombre, gritty vision [of the] Alberta and

Saskatchewan prairies that casts an almost morbid, gothic atmosphere over the social landscape."[69] This comment is made in response to Webber's 1995 book and exhibition *Requiem: The Vanishing Face of the Canadian Prairie,*[70] where the artist's brooding and sometimes poignant black and white photographs present a sense of place far removed from the sweet prairie-boy charms of a W.O. Mitchell novel or a William Kurelek painting.

Webber's images of boarded-up businesses, junked cars and solitary farmhouses convey a sense of history that, in a Biblical-like view, is very fleeting. "In the prairies, all that is human is ephemeral. We arrive, we flourish and then we disappear. All within a hundred years."[71] Largely a self-developed photographer, Webber is initially inspired by the work of Henri Cartier-Bresson. As Peter Duthie suggests, his photographs are metaphors for "man's stoic struggle in life" comparable to a passion play, a drama where individuals are portrayed in often unpretentious surroundings, their presence defined with shadow and light.[72] Duthie cites Webber's Roman Catholic upbringing as his reference point for such themes, and for his interest in capturing individuals who are participants of a faith. Two inspired examples of this without so much of the gothic atmosphere of *Requiem* are Webber's portfolio of Hutterite children (1989), and his photographs of the First Nations, Metis and white pilgrims of Lac Sainte Anne in northern Alberta. Both projects attract recognition: a black-and-white image of a young Native boy shivering in the healing waters of Lac Sainte Anne captures the Grand Prize in *Faces of Canada* (1992),[73] and one of Webber's photographs of Hutterite children is included in the prestigious publication *American Photography* (1992).

RANDALL (RANDY) ADAMS (1951, Edmonton, Alberta) is another tireless explorer of the cultural and historical nooks and crannies that can be found between the western border of Alberta and the eastern border of Manitoba. In his extensive investigation of prairie decay, something he refers to as "checking the wreckage,"[74] he created *Icons for Our Modern Age* (1992),[75] an exhibition of twenty-five colour duraflex prints exposing grave markers from small and forgotten graveyards, including close-up shots of the Christ figure on worn and eroded tombstones. Curator Elizabeth Kidd says of these images; "they stand as visual metaphors for the changes that have taken place during their silent vigil over the years,"[76] a vigil that is remembered more permanently in a remarkable book by Adams entitled *Eternal Prairie: Exploring Rural Cemeteries of the West* featuring many of the same images from the earlier exhibition.[77]

In stark contrast to these haunting melancholic images is Adam's dispassionate documentation of what he describes as "the small gestures of life,"[78] consisting of whirligigs and windvanes, decorated pioneer artifacts and buildings, ornamental mailboxes and bird feeders, painted upright boulders and miniature shrines, outdoor sculptures and ironwork, all created and displayed in yards and fields across the prairies. One farm included in Adam's photographs is that of Harold Lorenson, who has painted every item on his property in a riot of colours, including the barb-wire around the chicken coop. In defence of such obsessive activity, Lorenson said: "Well, no one else 'round here's got anything like it."[79]

Travelling Alberta backroads in the 1980s, contracted by Alberta Culture to document local folk artists and motivated by the idea that "everything has a story: a deeper meaning,"[80] Adams brings forth to public attention some remarkable scavengers and fabricators, including Leonard Busenius and his *Happy Farm of Hay Lakes* – "Hung in trees around his house are ski boots, construction hats, hubs from wooden wheels, and electrical junction boxes, with a bird's nest in each,"[81] – and Dick Adkins, with his life-size plywood animal menagerie near Westlock, Alberta.[82]

Folk Art

Folk art has long inspired much discussion among critics and academics about how to identify and discuss such work, which is often made by artists who have little or no formal training and who are unaffected by mainstream art traditions or movements. As is pointed out, often such individuals create for their own enjoyment, as a means of self-expression, or as Nancy Tousley suggests, "a form of self determination."[83] Sometimes, though not always, this work is rudimentary in appearance and has more to do with intuition and memory than with the formal do's and don'ts of academic training or the art historical savvy of a professional art practice.

As with documentary photography, the early 1980s is an active period for researching and exhibiting Alberta folk art in the province. For the most part, however, this interest is mostly confined to the province, as most Canadian folk art exhibitions then criss-crossing the country do not include many Alberta artists.[84] This absence is not atypical as far as national institutions are concerned, but the degree to which Alberta artists are overlooked is breathtakingly evident, as in the 1983 exhibition *From the Heart: Folk Art in Canada* (National Museum of Man, Ottawa). Out of 279 pieces, the touring exhibition manages to rustle up *one single work* from Alberta.[85] This, in contrast to a healthy number of Alberta-based folk artists represented in *Playful Objects* (1980) and organized for the province's 75th anniversary. A travelling exhibition from Alberta Culture, *Playful Objects* suggests, as others will, that folk art in Alberta is far richer in numbers than many might assume. This becomes particularly apparent with a number of survey and solo exhibitions at commercial venues and public galleries, including the now-closed Beaver House Gallery[86] (operated by the Visual Arts Branch, Alberta Culture and Multiculturalism). Out of these collective and, in some cases, individual efforts, certain artists earn public recognition.

Starting with the inimitable painter and writer Irene McCaugherty of Fort Macleod, these individuals are not just retired farmers – although Martin Schatz and George Markel are – they are businessmen (Nigel Lawrence), homemakers (Irene McCaugherty and Doris Zaharichuk), geologists (James Reid) and tradespeople (Charlie Miller and Sid Kelsie). Nor do they all hail from isolated little burgs in the country; folk artist Doris Zaharichuk has lived in Edmonton since the 1950s. What many do seem to share, as discussed in the following section, is a very personal and keen sense of place and history, especially as it applies to their locale, and if their subject matter does come from elsewhere – say, straight out of their imagination, as is the case with Sid Kelsie and George Markel sculptures – they didn't "need anyone to tell them who they are."[87] Folk art exudes tremendous confidence in itself, it simply *is*, as the following recollections and descriptions attest.

IRENE MCCAUGHERTY (1914–1996, Hardieville, Alberta). It's been pointed out that "cowboys and Indians" in southern Alberta were facts of life in the childhood of McCaugherty. They were for her, then, neither a Hollywood invention nor the fiction of a dime-store novel. A longtime resident of the historic settlement Fort Macleod, the western life McCaugherty reflects on in her writing, photography and deeply charming watercolour and ink works is vivid, often humourous and populated by dozens if not hundreds of stick-like people, suggesting perhaps that isolation on the wide open prairie is all relative. Painted on paper cut into 8″ × 21½″ strips, the horizontal format of her art adds to their distinctiveness. McCaugherty's first serious crack at picture making begins in 1962 with a twenty-four-painting series entitled *Romance of the Land.*

"I had no formal art training, and I didn't know the rules of the art world, but I continued to enjoy my work. The buffalo picture was a challenge, as some of my buffalo ended up with horse heads or vice versa.... I took them to a Fort Macleod public school where I talked to the children about the historical content of the work. I couldn't teach them anything about art. I knew the paintings were muddy, but I had to tell my story of western Canada's history."[88]

HAZEL LITZGUS (1927, Lloydminister, Alberta) paints delicate watercolours of farm scenes from a prairie childhood. If history was once defined as the doings of great men and great empires, then Litzgus's attention to the small details of modest lives purpose a more populist view of history and place, that is without monuments or important names.

"My work has been variously described as 'primitive', 'naive', 'folk' and 'memory painting.' I have always had a head full of pictures complete in every detail and when someone or an event triggers a memory, a picture simply flips in place like a slide in a projector.... Sometimes a scent comes to me of wolf willow or a prairie slough or the call of a red-wing blackbird rings out and I am struck with such homesickness for that small shabby farm that fulfilled my every need for those childhood years. I know I can't return to that way of life, it doesn't exist anymore, but by painting it I can tell our story to generations to come."[89]

JAMES REID (1909–1987, Glasgow, Scotland) created large needlepoint embroideries of the mountain landscape and geology around his Canmore home in the Rockies. A trained geologist, friend of local trail-builder Lawrence Grassi and a surveyor of the Trans-Canada Highway, Reid defined the rocky stratified character of his place with strands of coloured wool thread, chosen by his spouse, Eileen.

"James Reid returned from [World War II] service overseas shell-shocked, and underwent therapy in the Westminister Hospital, London Ontario. It was during therapy that James was taught how to embroider. At first he balked. He called it 'knitting' which was only for women, and he was not going to do *that!* However, he did learn to embroider, and once he started he soon outgrew the standard kits and started to make his own designs."[90]

MARTIN SCHATZ (1911–1994, Foremost, Alberta) is a carver who created richly painted wood sculptures and whirligigs of rodeo scenes, farm animals and indigenous wildlife. A farmer in the Cowley area near the blustery Crowsnest, Schatz's art speaks volumes about the area's historical ties to ranching, its abundant wildlife, and, in his whiligigs, the constant westerly winds blowing from the nearby Rockies.

"When we was young kids, I seen a snake crawling around and it had a great lump in it and I was wondering what the heck was the matter with that snake. So we caught it and kind of tapped it on the back a little and it threw them all out ... the birds. They were all alive. We were just kids for sure but I still remember that. Maybe I'll make a snake next."[91]

DORIS ZAHARICHUK (1917, Willingdon, Alberta) is inspired by the "clear and shining stories"[92] of European homesteaders in east central Alberta. In her oil paintings, Zaharichuck tries to capture their rural bloc settlements, their cultural distinctiveness, their inability to speak English and the prejudice against them that kept them on the margins of western Canadian society for decades.[93] Her images touch on the cultural self-sufficiency of these people and their attachment to community: "I go back as far as I remember, how life used to be with housekeeping, harvest scenes, women working, church, children playing. We had it quite hard but people were satisfied. They were happy because everybody was the same, nobody was really better off."[94]

A farmboy from Vista, Manitoba, **CHARLIE MILLER** (1936) started painting in 1990. Trained as a millwright, welder and heavy-duty mechanic, he earned a living for more than thirty years in mining and the pulp-and-paper industry. Art was always one of his favourite subjects, and with early retirement and classes in oil painting, Miller began depicting – sometimes with a quirky eye – the deep wilderness and backcountry life seen from the back of a horse. Contemporary life and historic subject matter like the Frank Slide also caught his attention.

"In 1965, Charlie [Miller] and his wife Ethel moved to Hinton, Alberta. Shortly after arriving, they bought an acreage and two riding horses. Soon after the riding horses, he needed a few pack horses to enable him and Ethel to go out into the mountains on vacations. Each year part of their vacation was spent out in the mountains. With the horses, many miles were travelled in Jasper National Park and further to the north, in the remote Willmore Wilderness Park. Both being interested in photography, many mountain scenes were captured on film. Charlie now refers to many of them in his paintings.

Many funny and not-so-funny incidents happened to them that now come to life in his paintings."[95]

NIGEL LAWRENCE (1901–1990, Pine Lake, Alberta). Along the foothill ranches of southern Alberta and a few other rural areas like Pine Lake (Red Deer) existed "a transplanted British Victorian lifestyle,"[96] which is recollected in Lawrence's chalk and oil pastels. A member of the Pine Lake "aristocracy,"[97] Lawrence's west is not the wild west of popular imagination, nor what is often assumed about Alberta's ranching heritage. As historian David Breen notes: "The cattlemen left a legacy of gentility and social exclusiveness that has persisted to the present ... [contrary to the] stampede ethos that has imposed an ill-fitting American stereotype upon the ranch community at large."[98]

"In *The Exile,* Lawrence depicts his mother sitting side-saddle on a horse. She is dressed in English riding gear, and appears alone upon the open prairie. The men who settled the area were generally adventurers looking for new horizons and opportunities. Their wives were often gentle, refined women motivated by love, loyalty and courage."[99] "Born in Pine Lake at the turn of the century, Nigel and his brother, Pat, grew up canoeing, riding horses, hunting, and fishing. Those were also the days of lawn tennis, matronly chaperones and silver tea services."[100]

Western or Cowboy Art

Meanwhile, south of Calgary at the Stampede Ranch, working in the summer of 1946 is a young cowboy named **RICHARD (DICK) SCHAFER** (1922–2004, Cardston, Alberta). His employers are none other than the fabled creator of the Calgary Stampede, Guy Weadick, and world champion trick roper Florence LaDue, for whom Schafer breaks horses. This experience, along with his later escapades as a rodeo rider, ranch hand, sheep herder, hunter and guide, will provide Schafer with the material to eventually create table-top sculptures of cowboys that "ride" between folk art and the more polished efforts of western art.

It is when he retires in Medicine Hat that Schafer teaches himself to carve a 'mean' cowboy (in cedar if possible) and also to work in bronze. Shy about the art world, he prefers to exhibit his cowboys at rodeos and fairs,[101] where they can be judged as authentic. An exception to this will be the inclusion of his sturdy figures in the Alberta Pavillion at Vancouver's Expo '86 and in a larger show entitled *Rope-Burns & Saddle-Sores* (Medicine Hat Museum and Art Gallery, 1991).

There is a tendency, of course, at the end of the twentieth century to think of "westerning" [102] as being all hype and nostalgia, but as Schafer's work underlines, it's not Hollywood's *Urban Cowboy,* nor is it a way of life frozen airtight in some mythic past. As historian John Foster notes, "The cowboy, the rancher and the oilman ... they actually do exist here in Alberta. We need to accept these so-called Albertan myths before we can begin to understand our culture as a whole. Albertans are different from Torontonians. We will always be. Our reality, here in Canada, is regionality." [103]

However, Canadian western art, including what is found in Alberta, is largely overshadowed by its American counterpart and is barely acknowledged within Canadian art. As well, scholarship and study are virtually nil, [104] and on a cultural level there is even embarrassment about Alberta possessing a western heritage. Take, for instance, what political columnist and author Don Braid writes about Calgary's "spilt personality:" "For ten days every year we celebrate western culture – then spend the rest of the year trying to live it down." [105] Or political commentator Robert Mason Lee's query into the granting of federal funding for a canoe museum in 1994 when the Western Heritage Centre in Cochrane, Alberta, receives zilch: "Why does Ottawa consider a canoe more Canadian than a cowboy? Eh?" [106]

It is in the post-1970 period that the western genre begins to emerge with a larger body of committed practitioners and more exhibiting opportunities, partly encouraged by the "renaissance" and boom in American western art. Albertan painters and sculptors, however, generally prefer to speak about *their* west rather than someone else's (i.e. Hollywood's). A task, it should be noted, which is not a completely contemporary phenomena. Prior to 1970, a selection of artists in the western genre from Alberta include Nicholas de Grandmaison (1892–1978), Charlie Beil (1894–1976), Edward F.Hagell (1895–1964), Percy Plain (Two Gun) Woman (1895–1961), Gerald John (Jack) Fuller (1900–1986), Theodore M. Schintz (1904–1975), Harry O'Hanlan (1916–1996), Doug Stephens (1918–1972), Don Frache (1919–1994), Gerald Tailfeathers (1925–1975), Bert T. Smith (1929–), O.N. (Rick) Grandmaison (1932–1985), Malcolm J. (Mac) MacKenzie (1932–) and Don Brestler (1934–).

More recently there is the accomplished and distinctive **PATRICK DOUGLASS COX** (1953, Edmonton, Alberta). "While Cox has an affection for the history and the myths of the West, he has chosen to depict it from a personal rather than romantic point of reference,"[107] comments curator Christopher Jackson about the Gem, Alberta painter in *Looking West* (Glenbow Museum, 1994). Described as the "limner extraordinaire of people and places in southern Alberta,"[108] the formally trained realist represents in watercolour, egg tempera and acrylic the often drab routines of life on the dusty rangelands. Painted in cool, monochromatic colours, Cox's sober cowboys are a far cry from the dashing western heroes portrayed at the turn of the century by Frederic Remington or Charles M. Russell, when frontier life was still alive and well.

In Cox's art, the West is a changed entity. His ranchers wear running shoes instead of boots (*Longhorns,* 1995), baseball caps rather than Stetsons (*On the Ditch Bank,* 1995); and rest against small airplanes instead of horses (*The Pilot,* 1995). In their steadfast poses and weatherworn faces, the idea of the West still lives on, but it also appears to be an uneasy, uncertain place with its worn and dilapidated buildings and parched grasslands. These stark, almost photographic images have a psychological dimension that carry them far beyond conventional western art with its frontier ethos and idealized way-of-life.

American art scholar Patricia Janis Broder describes the prevailing view in western art as "Western purism ... the belief that the West is a simple place with simple values, and that Westerners, regardless of wealth or status, are basically just plain folks."[109] In the isolated reaches of Gem, Alberta, Cox would have us believe otherwise. Medicine Hat curator Allan Jensen believes that taking a personal rather than a historical or mythic point of view is characteristic of many of Alberta's western art practitioners, making this art different from the larger, more influential stream of American western art.[110]

Often a product of a ranching background, the large majority of these Albertans is either self-developed or trained in illustration – for example, Cox attended the Alberta College of Art and New York's Illustrators Workshop. This type of image making, though, has earned western art few friends in the mainstream Canadian art world. While the former values the metaphorical and conceptual, western art is often resolutely narrative, realistic down to the smallest detail. Nonetheless, the practice of western art has slowly developed its own exhibiting circuit, finding a few sympathetic ears amongst public institutions,[111] commercial galleries, provincial events[112] and cultural associations,[113] becoming a world unto its own.

In 1976, a few hours before he died, sculptor Charlie Beil was reported to be "refurbishing a chuckwagon and team"[114] at his home in Banff. That the Bavarian-born cowboy would be working on a Calgary Stampede trophy is poignant, considering that from 1938 to 1967, Beil's annual project was to cast bronze trophies for the rodeo winners. Using an ancient method known as "lost-wax," Beil was able to take work all the way from the mould stage to the bronze. A secretive man, he is reported to have never passed the technique along,[115] although in the area of western bronzes he did help to establish a precedent, making the western bronze a reality in the province.

After 1970, a considerable amount of western bronze is made in limited editions and in large-scale public artworks. Many of the latter are commemorative and heroic, confirming the well-entrenched, Euro-Canadian themes of progress, the march of civilization and the frontier spirit. Large-scale public pieces include: Malcolm (Mac) MacKenzie's *Men of Vision* (1979, Cochrane); Vilem Zach's *Our Land – Our Future: Alberta Farm Family* (1987, Calgary); Don Begg's *Sitting Eagle, 1874–1970* (1988, Calgary); and Rich Roenisch's *Bronc Twister* (1980, Calgary). Not surprisingly, the foothills area west and south of Calgary beomes a centre for the production of this type of western art. Other recognized sculptors include Medicine Hat's Jim Hauser and Coaldale's Cornelius (Corne) Martens.

There are also women who make western bronzes, stepping into an area traditionally viewed as the purvey of men. Part of a larger surge of female practitioners into the western genre, it can no longer be said, in Alberta at least, that they are "The Absent Other," as Susan P. Schoelwer termed the lack of women as either subjects in or makers of early American frontier art.[116] An example is the *Thoughts on Bronze* exhibition (1994), which featured the wildlife, horse, rodeo and ranch-life sculptures of Lynne Coleman, Peggy Dixon and Susan Reed. As members of the ranching community in the Pincher Creek area, their involvement in a type of art that Charles M. Russell once summed up by proclaiming: "The West is dead! You may lose a sweetheart ... but you won't forget her."[117] implies there still exists a West, which is lived and reflected upon by these women ranchers as well. Other recognized Alberta bronze artists are Cremona's Gina McDougall Cohoe and Bragg Creek's Linda S.Stewart.

Finally, not far from the ranch across The Great Coulee – that windy divide between the western idiom and its more urban-minded art-kin – exists a body of *contemporary* western artwork that is executed in a wider range of media including video, installations, ceramics and mixed media. Established in the 70s, this body of work is not well-known, western themes being generally absent from the larger sphere of twentieth century Canadian art. The most fertile period for such artistic output is the 1980s, when there is just enough craziness, boundary blurring and rule-breaking in the then-exploding contemporary art scene to make such subject matter possible. In the western US, there is also similar activity and, in a larger political context, there is the constant headline news about disagreements over resources between Alberta and the federal government. At the time, Alberta's oil wealth makes it a topic of national discussion. As author Andreas Schroeder observes about the period: "Thus Alberta, in Canadian shorthand, became a 'redneck' province of oilmen (read: roughnecks) and cowboys."[118] Into this swirling, highly charged context then comes a small group of contemporary practitioners ready to question, demythologize, play with and respond to the romance and the reality of the West.

Vern Hume works in video and installation art. A long-time member of Alberta's video community, Hume's *Boomtown* (1984) relates the story of an unskilled labourer and her disappointing attempts to find work. The twelve-minute colour work reveals the contradictions between reality and the mythic west with its promise of "wilderness surroundings, adventuresome heroes [and] black gold."[119]

A year later in *The Land of Milk and Honey* (1985), Hume trains his camera on the fascinating cultural and social interface between the cowboy life west of Calgary and the oil-fuelled economic hopes of the city. "The 14-minute colour tape reconstructs fragments of iconic prairie images: the oil derricks, the heroic cowboy, the pioneer, rolling landscapes and big skies."[120] Although seemingly worlds apart, the values and attitudes expressed by the video's rural and urban participants are strikingly similar, perhaps bringing into focus a question that has long haunted the political pundits. Here's how cultural geographer Mark Rasmussen put it a decade later in "Alberta Identity and the Second Pioneers."[121] "How can a place with Alberta's apparent cultural and natural diversity produce a society as relatively homogenous as this one? For example, what is it that has made Albertans so pervasively support one political party or move en bloc to another throughout its history?"

Rasmussen proposes that there are symbols and basic values that tie the earlier pioneers with the "massive second wave" – the professional, urban-minded immigrants of the boom-time era. Likewise, as *The Land of Milk and Honey* relates through interviews and personal reminiscences, "These individuals embody and sustain western myths through various lifestyles: rural, urban, corporate, tourist." [122]

More light-hearted and irreverent are John Will's videos of the time *Wherever the Four Winds Blow: The West* (1984) and *Trimmin' and Burnin'* (1984, 24 minutes). The first work toys with the cowboy image, while the latter juxtaposes the colourful language of ranchers near Longview, Alberta with the graphic business of dehorning, branding and castrating calves. Starring in *Wherever the Four Winds Blow* and in a subsequent photomural, *Urbane Cowboy* (1984), is Will's friend, Jack Anderson, who, in tongue-in-cheek fashion, dresses and performs the coveted role of the cowboy in both works. Alas, as Nancy Tousley notes, "cowboy Anderson is all dressed up with nowhere to go," [123] except to pose in front of the numerous Calgary businesses with "Western" in their names.

Two of Will's artworks are part of the *Third Annual Wild West Show* (1984) at the Alberta College of Art Gallery. Staged annually for three years during the Calgary Stampede, the exhibitions, according to curator Valerie Greenfield, highlight "The multitude of truths and illusions that fuse our Western sensibility." [124] This is contrary to the Stampede itself, which tends to present a nostalgic, even Americanized version of the Old West. "The Stampede has more basis in the Buffalo Bill's Wild West Shows and fictionalized accounts of life on the range than in fact," [125] writes curator Valerie Greenfield. "The reality of early ranching in Alberta had few romantic associations." [126]

Encompassing a wide range of media, the *Wild West Show* brings together many American and Canadian examples. Montana's Ken Little is invited to show his fibreglass animal sculptures whose "hides" are composed of actual boots and shoes. There is Vancouver's Alan Wood, who builds his own version of a corral right in the art college gallery. (Wood, a year later in the nearby foothills, will do a much grander outdoor version of ranch-style architecture in the *Ranch* project, later headlined in the Calgary Herald as, "*Ranch:* It's bright and it's fun but it's not brilliant." [127])

Altogether, eleven Albertans participate in the three *Wild West* shows, presenting artworks that, like the rest, upset the Western apple cart, filled as it too often is, with many competing imitations of Remington and Russell. Many of the sculptures, drawings, paintings and installations deal with issues of identity and belonging, as in Stephan Czernecki's pagan altar-piece, *Beefrodite* (1983); Myrna Harvey's feminist, mixed media velvet paintings *Bondage on the Prairies* (1983–84); Patrick Hurst's ornate porcelain clock sculptures decorated with angels and cowboys in the sparkling *Monument to Johnny West* series (1972–82); and Gordon Ferguson's humourous summation of the urban cowboy phenomena, *Buck*[128] (1982), featuring hundreds of miniature plastic cowboys riding a supermarket-style bucking horse. Contemporary Canadian art never looked so high-spirited, nor so non-academic.

chapter six

Upsetting the Chuckwagon: First Nations Responses

To understand what it means for First Nations artists like Joane Cardinal-Schubert, Jane Ash Poitras, George Littlechild and others to achieve recognition and even acclaim for their contemporary art, a historical context is provided in Sid Marty's deeply resonant book about place, *Leaning On the Wind: Under the Spell of the Great Chinook.* Quoted is Abee Carter Goodloe, a visitor from England who stops in Fort Macleod around 1896 and meets the local ranching establishment: "In the morning there is polo, and one sees young English fellows in patent-leather boots and baggy khaki riding trousers, for which they have sent all the way to England, dashing up and down and running the whole show." On the other hand, Goodloe continues, "The Indians standing around look like aliens, like visiting strangers. The Englishman doesn't insult or bully the Indian. He simply ignores him, and by pursuing a life as nearly as possible like the one he would lead in England, and by appropriating whatever suits his interest or fancy, he makes the Indian understand that it is *his* country. He impresses this fact upon [the Indian] even in his games."[1]

And, it must be said, in his art, especially once the placement of Plains people to the reservations was complete. When First Nations people later appear as subject matter in white man's art, they tend to be represented as a folkloric people in colourful costume from another era. Enter **JOANE CARDINAL-SCHUBERT** (1942, Red Deer, Alberta) who, in a most resolute fashion, upsets the "chuckwagon" view of western history with its romantic images of beautiful scenery, rugged cowboys, brave Indians and hardy ponies. Using western Canada, she manages to dump the myth-carrying four-wheel vehicle over and refills it with images more specific not only to her own heritage but Alberta's as well.

In her first solo exhibition, entitled *Canadian Heroes* (University of Calgary Art Gallery, 1978), Cardinal-Schubert paints a series of portraits on paper and canvas, as well as two mural-size oil paintings that convey something of the dramatic sweep of western Canadian history. Of this art, she writes: "It has become a habit of Canadians, whether unconscious or deliberate to adopt heroes of other countries. I would, therefore, like to present to you, the viewer, a few of your own heroes...."[2] Into the "Western Pantheon," she inserts the faces of Poundmaker, Crowfoot, Kootenay Brown, Big Bear, John Ware, Isabella Hardisty, Louis Riel and others, some who are First Nations and others who are not.

In these and earlier pieces, the mixed-media artist begins to distill a less complacent view of place and history, taking hold of subject matter that, at the time, had little artistic currency. Remarks Nancy Tousley on Cardinal-Schubert's two mural-size paintings, *The Great Canadian Dream-Treaty No.7* and *The Great Canadian Dream-Pray for me, Louis Riel:* "Cardinal-Schubert is dealing with meaningful subject matter.... What she attempts is a modern version of history painting.... [It is] a gutsy thing to try to breathe life back into what, in the development of modern painting, has become an anachronism."[3]

"I wanted to create a new image of being Indian from the inside, and escape the generic renditions used by so many artists. I wanted that image of Indian to reflect all the things I knew about my relatives,"[4] Cardinal-Schubert recollects. The product of both European and Aboriginal ancestry, an Alberta College of Art graduate (1968), Cardinal-Schubert is part of a wave of First Nations artists who, unlike many of their predecessors, receive a formal education in art. In addition, Blood women are noted as being skilled in the arts,[5] and this personal background will provide sustenance as well.

The artist once describes her practice as being akin to a revolving wheel, around which rotate many other spheres.[6] At its vortex is a lively engagement with matters pertaining to her own family, her identity and spirituality. More broadly, there is also the condition of First Nations people and the environment which concerns her. In response, an abundant array of paintings, drawings, sculptures, assemblages, installations and other mixed-media pieces will burst forth, Cardinal-Schubert being the type of artist who, as in her two- and three-dimensional *Warshirt* series, prefers to "work on several intellectual and aesthetic tracks at once."[7] Cardinal-Schubert will also be active as a writer and a curator, often organizing shows on behalf of artists of Native ancestry.

One enduring feature of the artist's formal research is the development of a symbolic vocabulary, inspired largely by Plains Indian graphic traditions and studied by the artist at Writing-On-Stone and other rock art sites in Alberta. Her symbolic version of the once-outlawed sweatlodge appears frequently in many richly coloured paintings and drawings (chalk, oils and acrylics), as well as in sculptural works such as the 1984 40-foot high *Homage to Smallboy.* Of the sweatlodge image, she observes, "It's a symbol of the universe and unification."[8]

Her artwork also includes simplified and lucid depictions of horses, birds, bears and bison (considered spiritual icons[9]) and symbolic references to the medicine wheel, the Sundance structure, ribstones, the powwow, the dream bed, and other aspects of "a vital, sophisticated culture."[10] Her interpretation of the Blackfoot warshirt (1986) also appears in a variety of media, such as the exquisite paper constructions[11] of the *Preservation of a Species* series, which toured nationally. The work is partly inspired by the warshirts she sees in the collection of Ottawa's Canadian Museum of Civilization: "I was shocked at how things closest to native people had become just another set of items to store [in museums]."[12] In another instance, the protective warshirt, worn in battle, is the central motif in an outdoor mural, *Preservation of a Species: My Mother's Vision,* unveiled on Calgary's busy 17th Avenue in 1992.

With these key pieces,[13] Cardinal-Schubert's national reputation for rendering what one Ottawa reviewer termed "exhortive, explicit and personal"[14] art begins to take stronger shape. It comes on the heels of her 1985 retrospective exhibition of works on paper and canvas, *This is my History* (Thunder Bay Art National Exhibition Centre and Centre for Indian Art). The following year she is a participant in Thunder Bay's travelling *Stardusters,* an important ground-breaking show of contemporary First Nations art. Curator Garry Mainprize describes her contribution in terms of using "symbolic vocabulary to bring Indian spiritual values and political issues together to make a contemporary artistic statement."[15] In a series of "biting installations"[16] and mixed-media works – usually prefaced with the title *Preservation of a Species* – Cardinal-Schubert creates an elaborate and dramatic body of work that, sometimes with irony and wit and sometimes with anger, juxtaposes autobiography, First Nations history and social issues on top of each other. An example is the room-size installation *The Lesson* (1989–93), which employs text-filled blackboards, chairs and other objects to conjure up the residential school experience.

Consisting of several components, some with subtitles such as *The Lesson* or *Spill, Deep Freeze, Art Tribe* and *Burial Platform, Preservation of a Species* in its various incarnations, will embark on a remarkable journey after first appearing in the 1986 *Stardusters* as a work-in-progress. With over fifteen showings in Canada, the United States and Europe, including her first Alberta retrospective in 1993,[17] these related works will be one of the most exhibited ongoing projects by an Alberta artist in the post-1970 era.

Contiguous to this three-dimensional work but critically overlooked are her paintings and drawings. Comparing her two-dimensional works to a "diarized account of her life,"[18] these works are less obviously polemical and inspired by experiences like her travels to Stonehenge – "part of my birthright is the English culture"[19] – her identification with Emily Carr and her exposure to a dream bed (a special site traditionally visited by young men seeking guidance from the spirit world) at Head Smashed-In Buffalo Jump. Also troubled by environmental destruction and committed to sharing "our world view with others,"[20] her paintings, with their mysterious landscapes and celestial skies and animal and human symbols, serve to convey the artist's spiritual feelings about nature, the cycles of life, the planet as a living organism and the interconnectedness of all. "My part in [the] preservation of a seemingly invisible culture – on the plains, for instance, we don't have totem poles – is as a receptor or translator, one who points out what there once was, what there still is, and the importance of this to us,"[21] observes Cardinal-Schubert.

If there is such a thing as the zeitgeist, then the 1980s are a particularly auspicious time for the critical recognition of contemporary art by Canadians of Native ancestry.[22] Auspicious, because, after years of indifference, there is an impetus among publicly funded Canadian art institutions to collect and mount exhibitions by "a new kind of Native artist ... an art-school educated, [contemporary artistic community] who has shifted away from tribal expression to a consciously individual and political point of view."[23] (*The Georgia Straight,* Vancouver, 1989.) According to another, critic/curator Scott Watson, this trend is indicative of how "The challenge to the monolithic European-based version of history now cuts across whole fields of inquiry into culture."[24]

By 1989 in Alberta, some of these 'new' Native voices, like the more senior Alex Janvier and Joane Cardinal-Schubert, are already well-established. But not far behind are younger practitioners like Faye HeavyShield, **GEORGE LITTLECHILD** (1958, Edmonton, Alberta), and **JANE ASH POITRAS** (1951, Fort Chipewyan, Alberta), who are also riding this wave to national recognition, propelled by their own artistic merit and its relevancy to Canadian current affairs: the Oka crisis, residential schools, Meech Lake and Native self-government.

In employing contemporary mainstream methods and styles, these artists challenge a common attitude in white society that to be an authentic purveyor of a Native point of view, one has to express him or herself using only traditional materials, iconography and subject matter.[25] But as Poitras asks in a 1993 letter to the *Globe and Mail,* "Why should we limit ourselves to only one way and one world when we can choose the unshackled freedom of both worlds and achieve satisfaction and success in them?[26]" Littlechild, who himself comes from a bi-racial family, echoes this sentiment with his own statement, saying, "We come from the spirit of two peoples."[27]

Adhering to no one overriding aesthetic or style – although collage is a favourite of both Ash Poitras and Littlechild – these Albertans reflect a range of artistic sensibilities, from the feisty, expressionistic mixed-media work of Poitras, to the boldly coloured painting/historical photo collages of Littlechild, to the lyrical and understated sculptural works of HeavyShield. Notably, early in their careers, each participates and wins awards in the important *Asum Mena* exhibitions of the 1980s, held annually by the now defunct Alberta Indian Arts and Crafts Society. (Poitras receives the society's first art scholarship, co-sponsored with Edmonton's Vik Gallery.)

Like Cardinal-Schubert, Poitras and Littlechild also recall, reclaim and re-represent elements of First Nations history, culture and spirituality by approaching it through their own personal links. Of Cree ancestry, both share the experience of being orphaned at a young age, raised in a supportive foster home in Edmonton and then, in young adulthood, learning the details about their birth families and their heritage.

Their art-making then reflects a personal journey of self-discovery and storytelling, aided by their own interpretations of local Aboriginal artistic traditions – the use of bright colour, Cree syllabics and symbols – and by their knowledge of modern art. Poitras, for example, is an admirer of the graffiti-like scribblings of American artist, Cy Twombly, while other contemporary Americans, such as Randy Lee White and Fritz Scholder have an impact on Littlechild.

Initially specializing in printmaking – intaglio and relief – Poitras's journey begins to take significant shape with two bodies of work: *Sweatlodge Etchings* and the *Sky Peoples' Village* paintings. Inspired by the ritual cleansing ceremony of the sweatlodge, a life-changing spiritual experience for the artist, the stark, evocative black-and-white etchings are made for the artist's graduating 1985 MFA exhibition at New York's Columbia University. Recalling the visionary atmosphere of the sweatlodge interior, the etchings earn the unusual opportunity of touring across Canada, thanks to the interest of the University of British Columbia's Museum of Anthropology. Soon after, *Sky Peoples' Village* (1985/86) also finds a ready venue in the aforementioned *Stardusters,* where the beautifully coloured, semi-abstract oil landscapes of a utopian Native homeland partly echo her condition as a new mother and, she says, "the idea of the home being sacred." [28]

From these early successes, less abstract, more representational art emerges, along with a switch from printmaking to painting and mixed-media pieces on canvas and paper. The mixed-media works employ text, photographs of family and friends, printed material including newspaper clippings and photocopies, and the works have an overlay of brightly hand-drawn motifs and Cree glyphs: buffalo, stick figures, bears, tipis, eagle feathers, shamans.

With these seminal works, Ash Poitras shifts into overdrive, creating the painter's equivalent of a rock video: dozens of fragmented images and motifs, collaged, colliding and intermingling with soundbites of text, slogans and information. Starting with the *Blackboard* series (1986 to the present) and following with the *Shaman Never Die* (1987–1993) triptychs, the artist's expressionistic inclinations towards the intuitive and emotional become, perhaps in keeping with broader art-making tendencies of the era, neo-expressionistic: more fervent and spontaneous, generating what critic Robert Enright later described as "in-your-face" [29] art.

Poitras's tone of voice also changes, becoming more critical, political and didactic, but tempered as well with irony and humour. First Nations history, both local and global, emerge in her work as a paramount concern, as is plainly evident in the double-edged tribute to her birthplace's bicentennial, *Fort Chipewyan Breakfast Club* (oil on canvas, 1988) and in *Who discovered the Americas?* (mixed-media paintings and installation, 1992) a continuation of her blackboard series. The pedagogical aid is used to recall the residential school system with its attempts to erase Native culture and language. "I can be a teacher now. I can write on the blackboard and no one will reprimand me." [30]

In addition, there is the topic of First Nations spirituality. References to its continued existence and practice, including her own, proliferate in Poitras's more visionary art, especially in *Sweatlodge Etchings,* the *Shaman Never Die* series and in more recent works like *Buffalo Rebirth* (1994) and *Tequilla Shamans* (1995). These references reinforce the central message of many like-minded contemporary artists that Native culture is alive and in the present. Spiritual icons from other cultures, such as the Christian crucifix, also appear. Unconcerned that her eclecticism might raise a few eyebrows, she confidently positions Native spirituality within a larger collective worldview, creating a place for it that is neither marginal nor cultish. "Non-Native beliefs can teach the Indian. Native beliefs can teach the non-Native world," [31] she says in response to her cross-cultural content. What stands out about the artist's "densely packed compositions" [32] is, as Ottawa critic Nancy Beale suggests, "a vision of reuniting the secular and the sacred, of showing how destructive it is to separate them like wheat and chaff." [33]

While the role of the shaman figures large in Poitras's art, it is the symbol of the horse that stirs George Littlechild. Flat and unmodelled, the horse is represented in a pictographic style. For Littlechild, this animal is a many-splendoured thing, becoming, as curator Janet Clark suggests, "[a marker for] the artist or a Plains Cree Indian, a spirit guide and ... a witness to the Plains Cree history that the artist narrates in his paintings." [34]

Littlechild's multimedia works are poignant commentaries on tribal history, such as *Too Proud to Die* (1991) with its mounted archival photographs of Louis Strawhat and Johnny and Fred Erminskin of Hobbema, Alberta, or *Give Thanks to the Grandmothers* (1991) featuring a picture of Littlechild's great-grandmother Peggy Louis Natuasis. [35] Almost "naive-looking" in appearance, with flat, simplified motifs and bold geometric shapes, his work combines impasto, collage, layered paint, heavy outlines, text, and mounted photographs retrieved from archival collections and sometimes hand-coloured. Curator Amir Ali Alibhai suggests that Littlechild's art is the result of "celebrating the beauty and the aesthetic sensibility of his people and their material culture." [36]

But in an era when many people's definition of serious art requires it to be sober and weighty-looking, Littlechild's buoyant art bumps up against these expectations, as demonstrated when he first exhibits in Europe. "The public and the critics were confused. In one of the most expensive streets of Europe, with twelve exclusive galleries, this 'exotic' Indian art was difficult to place. The colourful paintings are decorative and pleasing at first sight. However, the political message becomes clear from such titles as *Too Proud to Die* or *Almost Forgotten Chief.*" [37]

Formally trained with an art and design diploma from Red Deer College (1984) and a BFA from the Nova Scotia College of Art and Design (1988), Littlechild's "cultivated naivety" [38] first began to take shape in the mid-1980s with his pictographic symbols, his use of rich colours and the inclusion of political subject matter. In 1988, he expands his practice to include collage, using archival photographs and mixed media materials, like feathers, beads, buttons, fabric, gold foil and other smallish objects.

A practitioner of what Alberta filmmaker Loretta Tod describes as "decolonizing the archival photograph," [39] two of the artist's photo-based compositions are the ten-piece *Plains Cree Ancestral Blanket Series* (1989) and an eight-part suite *Sioux Warriors* (1989), based on the photographs of American Edward S. Curtis who, in an earlier time, wished to capture the "noble" race before their eventual extinction. In both cases, Littlechild creates a new context for the old, ethnographic photographs by placing them in surroundings that suggest other meanings. While often critical of the photographs themselves, this technique is always done with the intent of presenting the past and present of Native experience in a more telling, less stereotypical light.

Besides exhibiting his paintings, works on paper, and more recently, cibachromes, Littlechild's art also appears in a couple of book projects; *This Land Is My Land* (1992) as well as a collaborative endeavour entitled *In Honour of Our Grandmothers: Imprints in Cultural Survival* (1994). The former is reviewed in the *New York Times Book Review* with reviewer Carol Brightman commenting: "Like a sunflower in a garden of daisies, George Littlechild's book stands alone. Other books on the multicultural shelf, which is where *This Land Is My Land* takes its place, may be more gracefully written. But few children's books I've seen are illustrated with the imaginative power at the command of this Native artist."[40]

As with Cardinal-Schubert and Poitras, Littlechild also continues his project of reclamation through installation art. His first incursion is at the Surrey Art Gallery with *Dis-placed Indians: The Sixties Scoop* (1996). Utilizing text, audio and sculptural elements, Littlechild the researcher, historian and storyteller[41] presents the stories and perspectives of First Nations people who end up in foster homes as children, dislocated from their own culture and families. In a sense, the more politicized art of Littlechild, Poitras and Cardinal-Schubert sets a precedent for a type of art-making in Alberta that previously has seen only sporadic activity, with the exception of 'protest' art in the 1970s and feminist and environmental art in the 1980s. "My art is a social statement. It is issue-oriented art,"[42] remarks Poitras while Cardinal-Shubert elaborates, "If people think that emotion and caring about issues and people are political, then I can't stop dealing with that. It's too much of a reality for Native people. I don't want to do empty art."[43]

Calgary-born artist Andy Fabo views contemporary First Nations work as part of a larger movement over the last two decades to "disengage art from the stifling homogeneity of modernist concerns."[44] Quoting curator Carol Podedworny from the catalogue to *Rethinking History,* Fabo concludes, "Modernism as a methodology and set of criteria was detrimental to those who were not white, heterosexual, male Europeans."[45] These are forceful words that support the demands of Native artists on mainstream art institutions to "not display Native artwork simply as curiosity pieces."[46]

In the 1990s, some mainstream commentators and others still view contemporary First Nations art with scepticism, as is underlined by these observations in the the *Globe and Mail:* "This attention [to Poitras's work] has everything to do with the current struggle to accommodate Natives within the body politic,"[47] writes Kate Taylor. And from John Bentley Mays: "Most of those organizing uncritical anti-Columbus displays this year, I suspect, will soon slip quietly back to doing what they like better, which is mounting critical, questioning arrays of works by artists of European citizenship or descent."[48]

Some critics are more encouraging: "These paintings [by Poitras] can hardly be considered pretty by most standards, but are undoubtedly, powerful by any aesthetic yardstick,"[49] writes Elizabeth Beauchamp for the *Edmonton Journal.* And Robert Enright adds: "This is not a pleasant process for anyone –

makers and perceivers alike – but it strikes me as a necessary one. There is a good deal of deconstruction that remains to be done, as Joane Cardinal-Schubert's tributary installation points out."[50]

In turn, some practitioners have their own concerns about the blitzkrieg of attention. Consider, for instance, Joane Cardinal-Schubert's acerbic assessment in 1989: "We're always being discovered. Columbus discovered us and now the curators are discovering us."[51] Rarely had the country seen or experienced such a high-voltage mix of politics, history, culture and critique in its art. And contributing to this sturm und drang over the Canadian artscape were several important Alberta voices. Writing about Jane Ash Poitras, Annette Hurtig delivered perhaps the most insightful observation on this unsettling debate: "Any questioning of her work's status as contemporary art ultimately sheds as much light on the ideological orientation of the critic as it does on the work in question."[52]

chapter seven

A Place Called Alberta, Continued

CANADA HAS A PREOCCUPATION with how its culture measures up internationally. In most cultural fields and endeavours, recognition from abroad is the Holy Grail, lusted after and triumphantly savoured when achieved. But as political commentator Jeffrey Simspon points out: "Canadians sometimes overlook the domestic cultural space – within which the references are local, the collective memories are shared only by those who grew up with or learned them, the histories are unique, the tales reflect local mores and traditions. What was it that Northrop Frye once said about culture being rooted in 'place'?" [1,2]

Among the contemporary visual-arts community (and it's worth stating this again), there is an ambivalent relationship to the domestic cultural spaces of Canada, particularly to art whose references are local and, more importantly, whose overall content, choice of medium and presentation do not represent the cutting edge of contemporary art practice or the particular standards of the time that signal "here is a contemporary artwork." The following chapter is a continuation of the previous discussion about art that reflects a sense of place and/or a sense of history specific to Alberta and the Prairies. The art and artists touched upon are part of a kaleidoscopic sampling of work and projects that are steadfastly connected to here. In sometimes quite specific ways, they spring from the domestic cultural space, although their audience is not necessarily limited to this region. In some cases too, the artwork itself comfortably falls within the contemporary art practices of the time such as Nelson Henricks's video/installation about identity. In other instances, such as Marianna Savaryn's Byzantine-style icons painted for followers of Eastern Christianity, the art reflects a different wellspring but is made in the here-and-now.

In the 1982 exhibition *Canadian Contemporary Printmakers* at the Bronx Museum of the Arts, the source of **JOHN KENNETH (J.K.) ESLER**'s (1933–2001, Pilot Mound, Manitoba) art is described to the museum's metropolitan audience with the following words: "Esler needs to look no farther than his immediate environment to be completely captivated and inspired by the Rocky Mountain foothills location of his home studio ... that majestic view is overpowering, and he conveys all that power and excitement ... in his elegant, finely etched prints."[3]

This quote might create the impression that Esler was a landscape artist who rendered his images through the age-old technique of etching. This Manitoba-born artist, however, was anything but a traditionalist. A sixties radical drawn to experimentation, who, in fact, worked to turn printmaking on its pointy head, Esler responded to his time and place in a very personal yet contemporary fashion. He used content that was sometimes overtly social and political (as in the 1965 mixed-media relief about Alberta movie censorship in *Alberta: Great Society* [*Journey No. 2*]), environmentally aware (as in the 1972 etching *Conquered Mountain*), resolutely personal (as in his tree series of the mid-1970s), and sometimes art-related (as in the satirically titled 1973 print made from a crushed metal lunch box *#68 Lunch Kit* (*Relic of the 20th Century*). But whatever their content, his hybrid compositions all had the formal energy of a prairie dust devil, touching down, here and there, on various methods of image-making: employing abstraction as well as figuration, rendering geometric as well as organic forms, creating shallow space here but depth over there. Sometimes, he would juxtapose all of these aesthetic elements within a single image or series.

To be sure, Esler was a technical wizard, especially with tone and texture, but whose anything-goes approach to printmaking – he was a pioneer of the collograph – seems to have been partly honed by a spirit of independence and a sense of wit reminiscent of writer W.O. Mitchell. And while he readily acknowledged the prairie-boy environment he emanated from, it was rarely expressed with nostalgic image-making. Instead, within his abstracted landscape-based prints and constructivist-inspired compositions, he recollected it with irony and perhaps a grain of salt.

An exhibitor and prize-winner in a long list of national and international print shows, Esler's record exemplified the kind of outward-looking attitude so typical and so necessary for printmakers in the province. He had long been considered a key figure in Canadian print circles, and from 1968–1980 he served as professor of printmaking and drawing at the University of Calgary. By this time he was already a successful print artist widely collected by individuals and institutions, and he had founded two non-institutional workshops: Trojan Press (1978–81) and Studio JKE (1981–88). In 1994, seventy-seven of his works were displayed in *35 Years and 15 Minutes: Prints by John Kenneth Esler* (Nickle Arts Museum, Calgary), while the Triangle Gallery hosted a complimentary exhibit of twenty-one paintings.

K. GWEN FRANK (1960, Gravelbourg, Saskatchewan) was never a student of Ken Esler's, but this Calgary-trained printmaker and realist often thinks about the late artist's work, admiring "his enthusiasm for the natural environment, the way he plays with space, uses texture to express atmosphere and found new ways to express his ideas."[4] These qualities are common to her art (etching and aquatint prints, watercolour and pastels, and drawings), although it is plain to see that the two artists are of entirely different generations. For Esler, the language of his time was modernism, with its emphasis on abstraction; for Frank, it's late 1970s pluralism and its tolerance of realism and more humanistic content. Frank admires the American regionalist painters and Canadians William Kurelek and David Blackwood, as well as seventeenth-century Dutch genre art and its subject of everyday life and surroundings.

A lot has been made in the press about Frank's deep attachment to rural culture: how her pictures of social gatherings, animals and rural scenery are "pure Prairie,"[5] how her subtle use of colour gives the prints an old-fashioned quality; how she not only "[celebrates] a place for its own indigenous values,"[6] but also makes statements about its changing face. All of that is true, but as the *Edmonton Journal*'s Charles Mandel observed: "Don't let these seemingly ordinary celebrations of rural life fool you. More often than not Frank's work attains a highly charged atmosphere."[7] Or, as Frank once put it, "I explore a certain darkness, a richness of experience that may not be apparent to the casual observer. Oddity within the mundane."[8]

Thus, the place Frank seeks to describe – which, in more recent years has included a grassy Dutch island as well as her home environment – is almost one of pure imagination, more dreamed-about than seen, more sensed than actually touched, more implied than explained. The prairie is an enigmatic, magical place where an old farmhouse detached from the ground glides silently across the terrain (*Prairie Mobile Home,* 1988), where a macho pickup truck becomes a maternal symbol on a cold winter's day (*Umbilical,* 1992) and where *The Race* (1989) is between a bicycle rider and an approaching storm.

Far from being boring, life on the open plains for Frank is an ongoing drama with flashes of humour and mystery; a vivid daydream fortified by Frank's reliance on memory, her use of exaggerated perspectives and personal symbolism, and the development of a rich, deep aquatint in her intaglio, and dark textures in her other works. Herself once a Saskatchewan farmgirl, Frank blends together, in her art of the late 1980s and early 1990s, the sophisticated techniques of a European art tradition with the calling of a prairie soul. Or, as one European review – where Frank has exhibited her art extensively since the late 80s – noted: "The wisdom of nature is constantly present in her prints but she often combines this with the everyday life of ordinary people."[9]

Social interaction, family and community life, as well as events and places tied directly to their domestic cultural space is also evident in the fibre art of **JANE CAMERON** (1949–2000, High River, Alberta) and **LIV PEDERSEN** (1946, Copenhagen, Denmark) and the works on paper of **MARGARET SEELYE** (1915–1996, Massett, Queen Charlotte Islands, British Columbia). Their art exudes joy, pleasure, humour and even nostalgia.

Cameron and Pedersen design and create vivid tapestries – Cameron by embroidering wool and Pederson on a Dutch plank loom – that, due to their unique production techniques, have their own distinct texture and physicality. While Cameron's content is generally more symbolic or archetypical, Pedersen's unfolds like a story with figurative panels that read from left to right, as in a cartoon. Both artists present the figurative elements in their work – people, animals and environments – as rudimentary flat shapes, causing some observers to label their creations as folk art. And while on the surface, it might be possible to view them as such, the two are formally trained; Pederson received a painting diploma from the Alberta College of Art (1978), and Cameron, who has Down's Syndrome, spent most of the 1970s at Montreal's textile workshop, Le Fil d'Ariane. She also produces drawings in crayon, feltpen and tempera paint, and writes poetry, both of which sometimes accompany her fibre works.

On account of failing eyesight, Cameron had to give up making her embroidered wool wall hangings in the early 90s. In one of her last textile exhibitions (1990), she is described as a "phenomenon."[10] Her compositions of flowers, people and animals burst forth with the kind of directness and humanity reminiscent of what French artist Jean Dubuffet advocated in the post-war *art brut* movement. Throughout her career, she enjoyed numerous commissions and exhibitions in Canada, the United States and Europe, and in 1978 was the subject of a major study by psychologist Dr. Max Klager of Heidelberg University, titled (in English): "Symbolical Thinking in Images and Words of a Girl with Down's-Syndrome." Klager wrote about Cameron's 1989 show at Heidelberg's Textile Museum Max Berk: "Deeply moved we stand before an art that reveals the continuity of human feelings, thoughts and deeds."[11]

Like Gwen Frank and Cameron, Liv Pedersen creates images that are reconfigured from memory. And although there is a great deal of the real world in some of her work – as in her charming four-panel Stampede narratives *Stampede I, Stampede II* and *Prior to the Stampede* – she also depicts her fantasies and dreams in her wool and acrylic weavings. In 1985, Pedersen exhibited one of her four-panel pieces, *Day and Night,* in the third of four *Exceptional Pass* shows. Organized by the Whyte Museum of the Canadian Rockies in Banff, the exhibition series challenged artists and writers to share their imaginary musings about the Rockies. In Pedersen's work, that concept was expressed through the daytime frolic of a family camping trip, and in the last two panels, the night time reverie of trolls and other supernatural creatures.

Unlike Pederson and Cameron who trained at a young age, Margaret Seelye was seventy-two years old when she received her first formal instruction in monotype printmaking at Red Deer College's summer program series. Prior to that, the Red Deer native painted watercolours regularly for more than thirty-five years, earned a master's degree in art education (1971, U of A), and was honoured by the city of Red Deer (1979) and the Alberta government

(1980) for her contribution to arts development in her hometown. In the best sense of the word, Seelye is the proverbial self-developed artist. "The eternal student," observes *Alberta Culture*'s Les Graff. "But an artist in terms of the spirit of her involvement, an artist with regards to her wish to express herself, an artist by the quality of the work she produces." [12]

Graff's comments accompany *A Country School Christmas: Monoprints by Margaret Seelye,* an exhibition of eighteen engaging works that places the artist among a small number of practitioners who makes a single print or monotype by painting on a copper or zinc plate and then printing the image on paper. "The medium inspired me to draw stories," [13] Seelye says of her artwork with their sweet narratives like *Weiner Roast After Moonlight Skate I* (1991) and *Trimming The Christmas Tree I* (1991).

Drawing upon her memories as a rural school teacher, the exhibit – which is followed a year later by a showing of thirty-eight small watercolours called *Catch the Moments* – is important for shining a spotlight on the work of creative individuals who participate in an entirely different art scene that runs quietly parallel to the doings of professional artists with extensive academic training and exhibiting histories. And Seelye – through her long-time association with the Alberta Community Art Clubs Associations and other groups – was one of those individuals at the heart of that milieu based in small communities and rural areas.

ROBERT GUEST (1938, Beaverlodge, Alberta) also has a long history of involvement in the visual art activities of smaller centres: in his case, Beaverlodge, Grande Prairie and Grande Cache. Deeply attached to the backcountry of the fabled Peace River region, the veteran landscape painter hiked more than 340 kilometres of a forgotten but important trail over a period of seven years (1987–1993). Part of Alberta's prehistoric ice-free migration corridor of ten thousand years ago and used more recently as a packtrail by First Nations people and pioneers, Guest mapped, sketched and then painted the scenic *Hinton Trail* in a series of seventy-two crisp, 12 × 6–inch acrylics and a countless number of drawings.

In a country where the label "wilderness artist" gets freely bandied-about, especially in the competitive wildlife art market, Guest may be one of the few artists truly entitled to such a designation. A self-described "bush Canadian" [14] who grew up in Euphemia McNaught (Peace River) country, he writes this about the *Hinton Trail* project: "Much of the packtrail passes through remote and unsettled country, and it was not easy for me to reach some of the historic sites along the way. There were rivers to wade across and cliffs to climb, cold weather to contend with and a certain amount of travelling in the moonlight,"[15] which, it may be added, provided ample subject matter for his moonlit nocturnes and depictions of Eastern Slope river valleys.

A romantic at heart, Guest's visual journey takes the viewer through "all the moods, the textures, the colours, the [sublime] effects"[16] of the land, and past a fascinating array of abandoned cabins, defunct trading posts, forestry lookouts and old Native sites, including Sundance tipis, willow sweat lodges, spirit houses, wickiups and campsites. Descriptive but also interpretative, the wilderness in Guest's art is always but one step away from subsuming the human presence. There is implied in his art an intimation of the divine in nature.

That such an odyssey is possible in the fin de siecle of the twentieth century is due not only to his locale, but also to the initial training he received as an artist in the late 1950s (Banff School of Fine Arts) and early 1960s (Alberta College of Art), when landscape was still somewhat of a respectable topic in art academe. Also evident in Guest's work is the influence of the Group of Seven through his contact with Illingworth Kerr and his Beaverlodge neighbour, Euphemia McNaught. Other more unlikely influences are Jack Taylor's abstracted landscapes ("they're not pretty but they speak"[17]) and the figurative painter Ron Spickett ("he made us want to search and inquire"[18]).

In 1995, Edmonton's Lone Pine Publishing and the artist releases *Trail North: A Journey in Words and Pictures,* combining his paintings and drawings with his collection of stories and anecdotes about the trail. In his foreword to the book, Provincial Archivist Dr. David Leonard writes: "[this book] should be a standard for all lovers of Western Canadiana." Or, for those who still believe, as Guest does, "[around] every bend of the river, there is a painting."[19]

About the same time Guest is compiling his book, another type of investigation into place and history is underway further south by two younger practitioners: the Edmonton-based MONICA TAP (1962, Edmonton, Alberta) and Banff's MICHAEL CAMERON (1955, Banff, Alberta). At the time, they maintain there are still pictures to be made about Alberta's public and private spaces, as in Tap's *Public Interiors* (oils, 1991–94) and Cameron's portraits of three historic Banff homes: *Faith, Hope* and *Charity* (all later demolished). Cameron studied architecture at Ottawa's Carleton University before completing four years at the Ontario College of Art.

Tap believes there are clues to Alberta's heritage and culture to be found in its small towns, and she creates articulate studies in light and colour of such places as the *Fort Macleod Barbershop* and the empty barroom in *Brownvale, AB.* "I wanted to see if an interior sculpted by the hard prairie light could speak just as eloquently of the land and its inhabitants,"[20] comments the artist with an MFA (1994) from the Nova Scotia College of Art and Design.

A graduate of the Ontario College of Art and Design, Michael Cameron's series surface when it becomes publicly known that three heritage homes of 1913/1914 vintage and sitting side by side are slated for demolition. Working on the principle that art should be meaningful to the larger community, the artist presents a rare picture of Banff (in oil) resonant with a sense of its roots. This sentiment is also heightened by Cameron painting the house portraits on reclaimed doors and, in one instance, on the back of a large rug. Onto these mixed-media works, he also incorporates text expressing the thoughts and feelings of long-time residents from the neighbourhood. In 1996, they are exhibited at Banff's Whyte Museum as *The Future of Faith, Hope and Charity,* the poignant title taken from a local newspaper headline. Together, Tap's deserted interiors and Cameron's condemned houses evoke a sense that change is relentless, that their subjects are relics and that only small pockets of Alberta's prairie heritage are left.

A tendency to look back on what *was* is common in the work of many artists who reflect on place or whose art is the very definition of a tradition with inseparable links to a certain kind of cultural heritage. The imagery of **DEANNA A. LEMNA** (1940, Calgary, Alberta), **JAMES MARSHALL** (1939, Medicine Hat, Alberta), **MARIANNA SAVARYN** (1960, Toronto, Ontario) and **PETER SHOSTAK** (1943, Bonnyville, Alberta) is of a more conservative type but what gives their art its own vigour is how they have chosen to express their cultural and historical space: for Lemna, it is through her very unique clay-on-wood sculptures, for Marshall, it is murals made of carved brick, for Savaryn, with sparkling icons executed in the Byzantine style, and for Shostak, his story-telling paintings and serigraphs.

In some respects, Savaryn – an honors BA in fine art and art history (University of Toronto, 1984) – is an unlikely candidate to be a painter of icons: a strict religious art form first developed by Greek Orthodox monks as early as the fifth century. For one thing, she is a woman practicing what has been largely the preserve of men, for another she is young when she begins her training in a meticulous rule-bound art whose existence in the late twentieth century defies what critic David Garneau defines as our post-art age. In the past, art had a history, traditions and masters. Today art histories are dispersed, various and critical; traditions are parodied or fled from; and mastery is an elitist, masculinist scandal to be avoided writes Garneau.[21] Working in Savaryn's favour, though, is the Ukrainian cultural mileu present in her home base of Edmonton and beyond where there is a sizeable population able to identify such art and its role within Eastern Christianity. As well, there is artistic precedent for the making of such art in Alberta, including the important work of church artist Peter Lipinski (1888–1975), who, after arriving in Edmonton just prior to World War I, spent thirty-five years decorating the interiors of some forty-five Ukrainian churches in Alberta. Of his arresting achievement, historian Radomir Bilash wrote in 1988: "It is doubtful that anyone will ever surpass the contributions of Peter Lipinski to Ukrainian church art in North America."[22] Another contributing factor to the continuing presence of iconic art, according to Leysa Granger, was the desire of Ukrainian immigrants to Canada in the first half of the twentieth century to find meaning in their cultural heritage. "Icons have been an important catalyst in this search for an identity and its preservation."[23]

With fewer churches being built, Savaryn's audience is primarily a private one: egg tempera icons for priests, family and private collections. Her work also includes the *iconostasis* (a symbol-laden wall-size divider containing twenty-five icons) for Red Deer's St. Vladimir Ukrainian Catholic Church, and an icon in the collection of the Museum of Civilization (Ottawa/Hull). Her training in the fine details and rules of this art form began in 1989 at the Sacred Arts Academy (Ligonier, Pennsylvania), followed by further studies with master iconographer Fr. J. Mokrytsky in Woodstock, Ontario.

Interestingly, Savaryn has been quoted as saying "[I have found] greater freedom of self-expression in sacred art," a point of view that, despite sounding counter-intuitive, is somehow in tune with the mood of contemporary art and its love of contradiction and paradox. Also, if it is a post-art age that we live in, with an aversion to mastery, then the absence of an artist's signature on the front of Savaryn's icons is surely one way of denying the presence of a masterly hand. As *Ukrainian News* writer Shara Masiuk observed: "Marianna does not sign her work on the front as the process of transfiguration requires the artist to discretely disappear."[24] This is an unintended but perhaps perfect strategy for an artist in this post-art age.

Peter Shostak, on the other hand, is more than happy to sign his oil paintings and original serigraphs about Ukrainian pioneer life. He is also quite willing to "ignore the admonition 'you can't go home again.'"[25] Meaning back to rural Bonnyville, Alberta, where he began life as a Ukrainian-speaking farm kid; he then spent years as a University of Victoria instructor (1969–79) with a master's degree in art education. Spurred on by researching and collecting old photographs and anecdotes, it is the social history of the Ukrainian immigrant that has caught his attention over and over again, a history reflected in such descriptive works as: *What is the name of this town?* (1978), *I think spring is finally here* (1982), *Who is going to help Dad in the barn?* (1985), *Baba said we can grow these in our garden* (1988), and many others. Presented in a crisp, uncomplicated style, Shostak has sometimes been compared to the late William Kurelek, who wrote shortly before his death in 1977: "Despite the similarities in our style, he doesn't copy me at all ... His titles are very evocative – they have a loveable childlike humanity to them, derived straight from personal acquaintance with landscape, buildings and people."

In 1991, to honour the Ukrainian Centennial in Canada, Shostak tours a collection of fifty large oils through six Canadian cities, including Calgary, Edmonton and Red Deer. Entitled *For Our Children,* the paintings also appear in a coffee table style book of the same name. The exhibition is described in the *Edmonton Journal* as "an important documentation of Alberta history, it is an art show full of visual treasures which are sure to delight viewers of all ages."[26] And that is precisely where Shostak makes his impact: as a maker of accessible, somewhat naive-looking images that draw on the popular memories of early pioneer life.

As for Deanna Lemna and James Marshall, their connection to Alberta's past and present is in the medium of clay (Marshall also works in pen and ink). Neither Medicine Hat artist, though, works with their material in a conventional manner. Through a process of trial and error, they have each developed their own method of art making that relies more on a kind of homegrown ingenuity than on techniques acquired through training. "I thought I was doing an original thing," says Marshall of his brick relief sculptures. "In the early 70s I was carving bricks and the faces of anything made of clay, including huge pipes. Since then I've found there are two or three Americans sculpting bricks."[27]

Lemna also does relief sculpture – her largest being 4 feet long – but her version consists of carving and sculpting slabs of air-dry clay into detailed studies of prairie architecture, which are then painted with acrylics and bonded onto pieces of distressed wood (i.e. corral fencing) for display. Interested in "what we leave behind,"[28] the Calgary-born artist's high-relief scenes of rustic farmsteads, towering grain elevators, country churches and prairie main streets are seen by her as "an apt and moving metaphor for the people who built and occupied them."[29]

James Marshall had similar feelings, too, when in 1979, he and his partner Lorine Marshall, who is herself a weaver, set out on a three-year project to document as many details of the province's early architecture as they could, supplementing them with images of local scenery, people, flora and fauna.[30] From the 5,000 slides collected, Marshall produced a series of detailed pen and ink drawings that toured in 1984 as *Historic Alberta.* "Historic Alberta isn't buildings and vehicles abandoned in the countryside. It is alive and vital and very much part of the life of today and tomorrow,"[31] writes the artist.

Sensitive to the nuances of place, he articulately recorded not only the grand and the official – Edmonton's W.J. Magrath's mansion – but also the humble and the forgotten, like the now overgrown market gardens at the back of Lethbridge's Chinatown. Marshall later remarked about his undertaking, "Some of it is so subtle that it must be investigated on your hands and knees."[32]

Shortly after the completion of *Historic Alberta,* the artist turned back to an earlier idea: carving bricks and setting them in a mural. His first commission came from Medicine Hat's Saamis Rotary Club to create a giant centenary mural (1983) of the history of the Saamis people from whom the city gets its name.[33] By 1990, Marshall had twenty such murals under his belt, averaging 3,300 bricks each, many of them related to particular areas in Alberta. Notable examples are the outdoor murals of waterfowl and wildlife at Camrose's Bill Fowler Nature Centre, and the prehistoric and historic panels for Milk River's Town Hall.

In the early pages of the book *Art about Nature and the Environment,* the 1970s work of several now-senior clay artists such as John Chalke, Annemarie Schmid Esler and Chuck Wissinger is touched upon for its evocation of the Albertan terrain. This practice continues to surface from time to time in the ceramics of younger artists, three of whom were students of Red Deer College's Chuck Wissinger: **PAT MATHESON** (1954, Red Deer, Alberta), **SHIRLEY RIMER** (1950, Calgary, Alberta) and **LINDA STANIER** (1958, Lafayette, Indiana, United States). Another is Alberta College of Art graduate **JANET GRABNER** (1961, Calgary, Alberta). Together, their art represents only a slice of clay activity within the province, and individually, only a slice of what the Alberta landscape is. But through form, texture and colour, they – in the mid-1990s – each fashion their own response to the land based on memories, Alberta history and past travel experiences.

Two of them, Grabner and Matheson, look specifically to their locale – the exposed ancient sea bed and fossils of East Coulee (Grabner), the hoodoos, broad-shouldered valleys and skies of central Alberta (Matheson) – and then employ traditional pottery forms: the tray, teapot (Grabner) and the bowl (Matheson). Part vessel, part sculpture, these works represent the ease with which the two traditions have inhabitated the minds of some Alberta clay artists. Grabner's teapots and trays, made out of porcelain with surfaces suggestive of stratification and fossil life, trigger the imagination with their curved and pointed legs, handles and spouts. Are they the tentacles of an ancient squid-like form? Perhaps even the horns of an extinct herbivore? Who knows?

As for Matheson's irregular shallow bowl shapes, some that sit atop hoodoo-like pillars, strong allusions are made to the undulating valleys and depressions of glaciation, while his wall pieces give what seem to be a topographical view of the land, perhaps even a core sample. The artist considers the low-fire grainy surfaces of his mid-90s forms to be studies of light and atmospheric conditions and gives them suggestive titles: *Squall, First Light, Hues of Heaven* and so on. Associated with his interest in light, he has, in addition, added pieces of glass into the earthenware bodies, "capturing," he writes, "the reflection of the sky on the surface of a body of water while simultaneously hinting at the inner spirit or power of the earth."[34]

Matheson, whose work along with Stainer's is represented in an important survey of contemporary western Canadian ceramics, *Clay in Canada: North by NorthWest* (1995), later teams up with Linda Stanier and Shirley Rimer in 1997 for the touring show *Alberta Voices.* An exhibition specifically about place, Stanier and Rimer locate their voices in and around Alberta's oldest settled community: Fort Chipewyan (est. 1788 on Lake Athabasca), and in Red Deer's multicultural heritage, respectively.

Inspired by a 1994 field trip to Lake Athabasca, Stanier's freestanding multi-fired ceramic sculpture and paper-thin porcelain wall pieces are an elegant refrain about the region's particular geology, botany and human history. Situated in Alberta's northeastern corner, it is the only area in the province where the moody Canadian Shield visibly intrudes with its dark, rocky landscapes, deep cold waters and tapestries of moss and lichen. Stanier alludes to this special environment in the fissured surfaces of her irregular-shaped bowls and on the tops of small clay slabs imprinted with ghostly black-and-white photographs, featuring photographs of the Fort Chipewyan graveyard. Stanier's use of photography is consistent with her past interest in using other media with clay, coming from a desire to "evoke a feeling of place,"[35] as opposed to an actual representation of it.

In Shirley Rimer's *Alberta Voices,* the human history of the Red Deer region is what is vividly recalled. Consisting of seven artworks, each earthenware piece features a small, dressed clay figure atop a beautifully glazed half-globe shape. The half-globes possess a different colour and surface texture, each one representing a different cultural or ethnic group. Herself the daughter of refugee immigrants, Rimer uses her costumed figures as a way of celebrating what she calls the "richness of our Alberta heritage."[36] Groups represented include *Natives – the Original Peoples of Alberta, Hutterites – Isolationists,* and *Dutch – Good People to Cultivate.*

PIERRE OBERG's (1967, Westaskwin, Alberta) sense of place resides with the small family farm. Another graduate of Red Deer College, like Rimer, Matheson and Stainer, but with an MFA (sculpture, 1998) from the University of Calgary as well, Oberg is a fourth-generation farmer who operates an organic farm east of Red Deer in conjunction with his art practice. He creates lyrical assemblages made from materials (doors, pitchforks, spades, chairs, seeds, saws, etc.) found on the farms around him and has established a solid body of work in just a few short years. His art relates to his concerns about stewardship versus ownership, environmental degradation, isolation, the financial stress of farming and the history of rural prairie dwellers. His narrative assemblages with their weathered appearance often refer to an era before the urbanization of the Prairies.

One sculpture, entitled *Subsequent Encounters,* features a metal tractor wheel well, lying on a bed of prairie grass. At the bottom of the well is a glass sheet covering a layer of depleted alkaline soil with an Aboriginal hammer head lying in the centre. Karen Smith, writing for the *Whitehorse Star* on January 30, 1997, says of the work, "[Oberg] strives to reveal the reality behind the rural myth." This desire to be honest about the rewards and shortcomings of rural life is again demonstrated in the work *A Sense of Origin* (Art is Vital, Calgary, 1997). In this piece, the artist incorporates small archival and manipulated photographs, slides and historical texts from journals with found and fabricated objects that are decorative and yet convey multi-layered readings of Oberg's rural homeland.

Another artist who works sculpturally and makes strong references to a specific Albertan locale is Grande Prairie's **KEN HOUSEGO** (1949, Simcoe, Ontario). Unlike Oberg's found materials, however, Housego uses finished timber as the primary material from which to construct his pieces. His work has been included in such thematic exhibitions as *Western Canadian Icons* and *Visions of Alberta* (both organized by Calgary's Muttart Art Gallery in 1988) and more recently in *Symbols of Presence* (1999, the Prairie Art Gallery). Housego's mixed-media works are "symbolic, idealistic and fantastic representations of Peace River landscapes." [37]

More interpretative than descriptive, his response to place is based solely on his own personal experiences of it. In *Heart Land* (1990), for instance, his emotional attachment to the Peace region is boldly articulated in a larger-than-life heart, carved out of wood. Painted bright glossy red, the heart's rounded surface is dotted with small toy-like objects: a fox, a tree, a farmhouse and a goose, simple icons that mark the richness of the Peace for him.

Usually displayed on a wall, Housego's painted wooden constructions are often described as "delightfully humourous" [38] and "ultimately playful," [39] characteristics that might seem somewhat paradoxical considering he trained at the Nova Scotia College of Art and Design (1974) and Toronto's York University (1980). As the *Calgary Herald*'s Nancy Tousley observes: "There is something fresh and idiosyncratic about this work that belies the sophistication of Housego's lengthy education." [40] However, his education is not based solely in the institution and is supplemented by his own discovery of Nova Scotia folk art and influential exhibitions, such as *The Flowering of American Folk Art.* Add to this his youthful know-how as a whittler of boats, puppets and other wooden toys. To Housego, art-making becomes a "place where I exercise and play. For a moment in time, I am in that boat house [on Georgian Bay], a child again." [41]

An art instructor at Grande Prairie Regional College since 1983, the artist believes he is long past mimicking the look of folk art and is now "truly exploring my own prairie vernacular." [42] Shaped by memory and imagination, Housego's stylistic dialect distills his materials into clean, uncluttered sculptures that evoke what is personally familiar. There is, for instance, the toil of a friend recalled in *Homestead, Good Fare, Alberta* (wood, fabric, dye and oil paint, 1998) and the devastation of clear-cutting in *Plantation, North of Highway 40, Grande Cache, Alberta* (wood, dye and enamel, 1999).

❧ ❧ ❧

Since the arrival of more socially aware art practices – feminism, First Nations and other cultural studies – the themes of place and history have sometimes surfaced in a supporting-role. For instance, framed by the 1990s insatiable interest in identity, the influence of place is considered in the travelling exhibition *Search, Image and Identity: Voicing Our West,* where "memory, personal experience, corporeal and *geographic location* [my emphasis], and the psyche all weave into the make-up of our identities." (1994) [43]

In a more direct manner, there is also the 1998 Alberta Biennial of Contemporary Art, *In/Here/Out/There* (Glenbow Museum, Edmonton Art Gallery) which explores "the frontier in the context of Alberta, with references to its historical legacy in western Canada, as well as its effect on contemporary thought and culture." [44] Featuring twenty-six Albertans, place and history beat a strong pulse throughout the exhibition, as in the western comic-book-style paintings of David Garneau, the mixed-media and printed work of Sophia Isajiw examining the history of Ukrainian internment camps in Banff National Park,[45] and the unique video/car seat installation of Sharon Stevens, which traces the nomadic lives of early seismologists and their families who were employed to discover and map oil deposits across Alberta.[46]

As curator Elizabeth Kidd optimistically observes in another thematic exhibition, *Constructing Cultural Identity* (1991): "The postmodernist agenda has offered the possibility for artists to introduce personal or local themes into their work in the knowledge that these may be of interest not only locally but nationally and internationally as well." [47]

Four Albertan practitioners who weave place and history into their narratives about identity are **NELSON HENRICKS** (1963, Bow Island, Alberta), **ERNIE KROEGER** (1954, Winnipeg, Manitoba), **LEILA SUJIR** (1951, Hyderabad, India), and **ZOE WILLIAMS** (1956, Edmonton, Alberta). Williams explores the identity of pioneer women. For Sujir, it is the old-time cowboy and, more recently, people of colour living in Canada. Kroeger looks at the trials and tribulations of his refugee parents; while Henricks investigates his own identity as an outsider. About this kind of artwork and its relationship to the prairies, curator and critic David Wagner writes: "Alberta and Saskatchewan are unique in that they have no boundaries which are not man-made. Every other province and territory in the country has at least one border defined by a shoreline with the Atlantic, Pacific and Arctic Ocean, Hudson Bay or the

Gulf of St. Lawrence.... Our boundaries are the various roles and labels we define for ourselves or that are applied to us by others."[48]

In 1997, Wagner curates the group show *Inheritances: Some New Prairie Photography* (Southern Alberta Art Gallery) and includes Zoe Williams, whose wall hangings display old photographs that have been transferred onto the fabric. Embellished with text and embroidery, and replete with photographs from her family and others from the Glenbow Museum Archives, the pictures she chooses celebrate strong relationships between women: "My search for images and stories of everyday life of pioneer women has revealed how incomplete the stereotype of the downtrodden prairie woman is."[49] Williams's pictures of industrious women include the enterprising and progressive activities of the Famous Five and the Alberta Women's Institutes.

Ernie Kroeger also relies on his own personal background to broach a topic that in a modern-art context would have all but been dismissed as parochial and, worse, sentimental. He addresses the notion of the family and the influence it has had on his identity. "My parents experienced cultural displacement when they settled in Canada – the need to assimilate but also to maintain their cultural heritage. I experienced a similar spilt."[50] It is a story that, while personal, is also viewed by critic David Garneau as being emblematic: "they represent the first and second generation European-Canadians."[51]

Beginning with the exhibit *Photographs of Mom and Dad*[52] (1990), the artist and instructor enlarges his project about kinship and identity to include text, old family photos, memorabilia and documents. He continues this practice in the series *Family Stories,* exhibited in *Search, Image, Identity: Voicing Our West* (1994) and at the Canadian Museum of Contemporary Photography (Ottawa) later that same year in the exhibition *Alliances – The Family,* where he is given high marks by the *Globe and Mail* for "the most moving 'portrait' series."[53] In 1995, Kroeger's efforts receive further recognition when he is nominated for the Barbara Spohr Memorial Award by the Banff Centre. Based in Banff since the late 1980s, the Winnipeg-born artist has also made art related to the national park's identity, especially the Great Divide, a major watershed of North America. The divide also serves as the geographic border between Alberta and British Columbia, and Kroeger is one of several artists drawn to its potent physical reality and symbolic significance. His work *Water Maps* (1990–1998) – a series of archival maps collected and manipulated by the artist, juxtaposed with his black and white photographs of the high continental terrain – are included in the 1998 Alberta Biennial to show how the concept of borders, both real and imaginary, "have served as an important metaphor for the frontier [in the west]." [54]

Of all the artists presented in this chapter, the video work of Nelson Henricks and Leila Sujir is the most here and now. The place they reflect is a highly urbanized one, where postmodern concerns like identity and individuality are tangled up with the issues of race, history, family, memory and locale. Notably, the individuals portrayed in their videos are marginalized players in mainstream Alberta. Being on the margin is a condition familiar to Henricks and Sujir. Sujir remembers growing up in Calgary in the 1950s and 1960s as a person of Canadian and South Asian heritage: "People were having barbeques and we were vegetarians. It was hard. Ours is a story that's not supposed to exist in Alberta." [55]

Likewise, on another level, within the international art world, Alberta and other peripheral places like it have an identity problem in that they are largely invisible players. But as curator Katherine Ylitalo reminds us in her introduction to *Leila Sujir: Luminous Stories* (1999, Art Gallery of Peterborough), "[Montreal art critic Jean Tourangeau] places Sujir with a group of artists, Tomiyo Sasaki, Zak Kunak, and Daniele and Jacques Louis Nyst, who reject the code of universality and call for an understanding of regionalism." [56]

The contemporary sensibility of Sujir's and Henricks's work is heightened by the medium they use, with its potential for an abundance of imagery, sound and narrative. But rather than putting video's sensorial prowess to work for commercial or entertainment purposes, artists such as Sujir and Henricks bring a more personal, less generic point of view to this technology. They do it with "outsider" stories, presented in either a linear sequence of events, as in Sujir's and Vern Hume's *Buck* (1986), featuring an aging cowboy whose way of life is now lived by few but mythologized by many, or in a more circuitous manner like Henricks's *Legend* (1988), where the story is presented in a sequence of nine vignettes.

Henricks describes his work as a cross between a rock video and poetry. [57] A graduate of the Alberta College of Art, and a prominent figure in Calgary's alternative art community of the late 1980s, Henricks describes *Legend* – his first major work – as functioning on two levels: "One trying to determine an individual's identity, while the other attempts to locate a regional or national identity." [58] Playing himself, Henricks comes across as a young struggling artist veering between memories or flashbacks of a sweet prairie childhood and his "hip" life in the archetypal modern city. In a voice-over, he narrates powerful words about the only thing that he is certain of: "The name of her face was prairie. Prairie was her name. It was the same name as that untouched, unscarred space. It was that name of the space not taken up by the sky."[59] The artwork consists of two components, a twenty-five-minute video and an exhibition of display cases containing found objects, photocopies, postcards, colour prints and book works. *Legend* made its debut in the 1990 group show *Elemental Instincts: A Matter of Course* at Calgary's Nickle Arts Museum.

According to curator Donna McAlear, "Henricks simply describes *Legend* as an identity crisis.... Cultural identification symbols (driver's license, heroic rock musician, traditional scenes of pastoral landscape) are juxtaposed with those of private relevance (ancestral photographs, diaristic musings, the prairie region and family homestead).... Where and how does one locate oneself in a collusion between media images and everyday life?"[60]

Leila Sujir also brings a strong autobiographical and literary sensibility to her art, as in her well-known 1995 production *The Dreams of the Night Cleaners* (46 minutes, colour). Described as docu-fiction, *Dreams* weaves together like a fable the immigrant's dream of finding a better life despite the uneven playing field of Canadian society and its immigration policies. Drawing on her own Indian-born father's frustrated attempts to find a more prosperous life in Alberta as an airline pilot, Sujir, through the stories of several night-shift airport employees, casts light on a well-known phenomena in Canada: the highly qualified immigrant professional working as unskilled labour to make a living. This theme first came to life as a story of the same title, written by Sujir,[61] and it evolved into a film after Sujir's experiences on the project *Working Portraits*[62] (1992), a video installation in which the artist produced a composite of Calgary caretakers talking about their work, their hopes, dreams and disappointments. This work was presented as part of *Screens: Amantea, Aziz, Stone, Sujir* (Nickle Arts Museum).[63]

Curator Katherine Ylitalo writes: "[According to the artist], 'It is hard to construct an identity if you are not mirrored in a larger cultural context.' Her alternative to other forms of representation is to use the production itself like a mirror, so that [the caretakers] see themselves reflected in the video and then respond to those reflections. With [the caretakers'] choice of images, she builds portraits that are representative of them. Then she serves to make those portraits public."

Collaborating with others is also present in *India Hearts Beat* (1988, 13 minutes, colour), where the artist, her mother, Ruth Gorrick-Sujir, and friend, Rachna Joshi, produce a script about homesickness and cultural displacement. Employing performance and text, the tape is described as "a delicate exploration of Indian culture as it exists in these women's memories, where it is vivid, layered and intense."[64] This use of autobiography where the personal is deemed political, as well as Sujir's strong female-centred content, has garnered her a national and international reputation, particularly within feminist and post-colonial literary circles.

As her colleague, author Sarah Murphy, writes about Sujir's art: "[she makes] clear ... the need to acknowledge the hidden, to make the absent present, the invisible visible, in order to consciously change the order in which we live."[65] But Sujir's work is more than just an expression of the postmodern spirit of otherness. With their strong colours and sensuous textures, her installations and video projects are also visually tantalizing. According to Nancy Tousley, "The most stunning qualities of Leila Sujir's *The Dreams of the Night Cleaners* are the lushness and tactile layering of its images and sounds. These qualities are not always associated with video art, but they secure the success of this forty-six-minute television project, co-produced with the National Film Board and The Banff Centre for the Arts."[66]

Sujir is not afraid to create beautiful-looking work that makes use of special effects and her own aesthetic sensibilities, including rich fabrics, as she did in her 1991 video installation *My Two Grandmothers, Her Great Grandfather and Me.*[67] That Sujir should possess this bent for the optical, even the decorative, is perhaps attributable to her South Asian background with its rich material culture. She also shares a linkage with the larger Calgary visual art community: they are not artistic puritans, afraid of beauty lest it betray the content.

Of all the subjects that can possibly dwell in a work of art, why have place and history, or the domestic cultural space, been so pervasive in Alberta art of the last twenty-five years? In this era of globalization, why care about place or history, especially in a region that is politically so young? After all, doesn't *real* history reside in Europe, or in ancient civilizations like China and India? Was Elizabeth Bailey Price of the Alberta Women's Institute simply jumping the gun in the 1920s when she exhorted members to preserve their local history? "Don't let your community do away with the first house. Preserve the remnants of the old forts. You in the south follow the line of the first famous march of the North-West Mounted Police. You in the north follow

Mackenzie's trail. Already old Fort Edmonton has been torn down."[68] Where did Price think she was? Living on the Seine or the St. Lawrence? Not many of the big names in contemporary art internationally are concerned with place, why, then, are many Albertans?

Perhaps it is because Alberta artists somehow sense that beyond all the imported influences and traditions, the prairie west was and still is "radically and absolutely different from the East in every respect."[69] Different mainly due to what archivist and author Tony Rees underlines as the region's accelerated development: "What one sees begun in the last decades of the old century and continued through the first third of [the twentieth century] is not the creation of something new and indigenous to this particular place, but instead a severely compressed re-running of the same evolutionary pattern [of agrarian settlement and then industrial development] observed both in Eastern Canada and, beginning much earlier, in Europe."

In other words, what takes nearly 1,000 years in Europe and three centuries in eastern Canada to emerge, takes "perhaps only seventy-five or eighty years to run its full course in the prairie west," says Rees. And, like its history, the West's artistic development has also evolved on fast-forward. However, if there is one thing that *does* take time to develop is a sense of *confidence* concerning one's art. After all, the inherently unequal relationship between hinterland and metropolitan is still a thriving bit of business: undermining and frustrating for some on the margins, freeing for others, and, to those in the centre, a fait accompli. Toronto author John Ralston Saul provides a telling description of how this relationship operates in the arts in general: "Of course, cosmopolites who write from great cities are only mildly surprised by provincial effervescence. They know that they themselves are at the centre. They know their subjects count, because their subject is the centre. Everything else is secondary. It would be no good for an outsider to go back to the dictionaries and prove that it is they who are acting in a narrow, enclosed, provincial way, while we on the outside make the efforts of cosmopolites. 'Ambitious provincials,' they would think, 'always want in. But we don't want out.'"[70] (1986)

But what can be a negative has, in Alberta, also been turned by some artists into a positive thing: "For someone coming from Toronto, with its old, prosaic neuroses about being too square, too squat and too unlike New York, it is refreshing to know there are places that couldn't give a damn about being somewhere else."[71] In the many examples explored in this chapter and preceding ones, the above sentiment is all too true.

OPPORTUNITIES AND REORDERINGS

chapter eight

Standing on the Edge of a New Era

When I moved to Alberta in the seventies I despaired that I was coming to a cultural wasteland. Heading out from Toronto, I'd had to look up Edmonton on the map. I arrived expecting a metropolis set down in the prairies and found rolling wooded hills and farms, and just a few hours away, mountains, desert and tar sands. As the landscapes revealed themselves, constantly surprising me, so did the people. Alberta had a well-defined culture,[1] ❧ Juliet Kershaw, *Legacy*.

Calgary artists have felt, by and large, only the pressures of their own motivations to make art. Self-reliance has been not a choice but a necessity for survival, and the decision of artists to stay in Calgary has entailed a conscious commitment. Staking a claim in frontier territory has meant the cultivation of personal points of view. Coupled with this is the frontier's outward-looking attitude.[2] ❧ Nancy Tousley, *Canadian Art*.

Whether in Edmonton or Calgary, the above statements allude to the presence of a growing critical mass of individuals at least in those two centres that will make the post-1970 period an explosive one, not just for the visual arts but all arts activity in general. As well, as in many other parts of Canada and the western world, the 1970s mark a watershed in the visual-arts scene of Alberta. It isn't a sudden or abrupt demarcation, but by the end of the decade, new definitions and attitudes about art have emerged. Internationally, after a hundred of years or so of trailblazing, the avant-garde tendencies in visual art are forging a course no longer exclusively stylistic or overwhelmingly concerned with aesthetic issues as modern art had previously been. The spectrum of artistic mediums is broadened beyond the confines of painting and sculpture, and contemporary art makers begin to emphasize: content over style, process over product, popular culture over high art, the critical over the artful, the interdisciplinary over the single medium, appropriation over originality. Here's how Calgary art critic David Garneau will describe the end product of this many-tentacled development. "In this art world, objectivity [or the art object] is subordinate to ideas and the form of art is almost immaterial. They can range widely across disciplines because it's not discipline that holds contemporary art together as a class, but amenability to critical theory." [3]

To greater or lesser degrees, many of these postmodern tendencies will have an impact in Alberta as the contemporary period unfolds. But in the wild rose province, there is more give-and-take on this matter. In contrast to many artists elsewhere in the Canadian contemporary art world, who will cultivate more exclusively conceptual approaches, many Albertan creators will never forsake a fascination with their materials and their physicality, the history of their disciplines and the craft of making an art work. But interpretations of this situation will vary from what is showcased in major exhibitions of the post-1970 era.

"While a high degree of technical facility and craftsmanship is evident in Calgary, the content is not restricted to purely formal concerns. Representation, narrative, metaphor, and other literary associations co-exist with late modernist approaches," [4] writes Vincent Varga in *Aspects of Contemporary Painting in Alberta.*

"Although a few artists are actively engaged in a social critique of their art, on balance innovation is perceived as a matter of aesthetic shifts within art making, rather than in terms of broader cultural issues affecting content. A continuity of purpose, expressed in a preoccupation with formal change, underlies such apparently dissimilar artistic centres as Calgary and Edmonton, and has allowed for the development of a community of artists embracing plural options,"[5] state Diana Nimeroff and Jeffrey Spalding in *Survey Alberta.*

These options first appear in the 1960s and are aptly described by Terrence Heath, guest curator of *Western Untitled* (1976, Glenbow-Alberta Institute): "Since the mid-sixties the art scene has been bedlam. At the highly advertised level, movements seem to be rising and falling at a breathtaking rate – op art, kinetic art, pop art, funk, high realism, conceptual art.... Art history seemed to be in shambles.... What had been thought of as the great river of art [i.e. modern art] has become a delta of many streams." And from this delta is spawned a whole new generation of artists, many who were educated in the 1960s and early 1970s by the first generation of Albertan artists – Marion Nicoll, J.B. Taylor, Illingworth Kerr, Stanford Perrott and H.G. Glyde – as well as younger instructors such as Harry Kiyooka, Ronald Spickett, Harry Savage, Katie Ohe and Norman Yates. For younger artists, and even older graduates like Les Graff, these instructors are also role models of professional practice, independent thinking and determination.[6]

Of Ronald Spickett, for instance, Graff later said, "He had a professional stance, one of the first people I met who had that. He set up a studio alongside the students. He bought a whole gallon of turpentine, when most of us were buying much smaller quantities. We saw that and thought, 'Wow, this guy is really serious.'"[7]

With the expansion and creation of more post-secondary art programs, there are also many new instructors from out of province who will add different strains to the local art milieu. Overall, if they stay, their impact will be large, but will be tempered and influenced by the local environment in which they work and live. With their own art, these newcomers, too, will make a substantial contribution to the province's visual-art legacy.

Concurrent with the above and not to be forgotten is a large influx of touring exhibitions, highlighting art both new and historic from other centres in Canada and abroad. For Alberta and elsewhere, the 1960s/1970s are the heyday of the travelling show, with exhibitions coming from the extension programs of the National Gallery of Canada, and even from New York's Museum of Modern Art. Other important contributors are the Western Canada Art Circuit and the Western Association of Art Museums. Artist Ron Moppett, who was then curator of the Alberta College of Art Gallery (1969–1971), remembers that time as being so rich with touring exhibits that it was possible to have a different show every *two* weeks! Later in the 1990s, this kind of exposure to the broader art scene will be inconceivable with shrinking budgets and wilting provincial support for the arts overall.

In Edmonton, it is no different. Through the Edmonton Art Gallery (EAG), the University Art Gallery and Museum, and the Student Union Art Gallery, younger artists are exposed to the work of then-current American names, such as Jim Dine, Robert Rauschenberg, Claes Oldenburg, Tom Wesselmann, Roy Lichtenstein, Morris Louis and Kenneth Noland. Canadian names include Claude Breeze, Kenneth Lochhead, Roy Kiyooka, Yves Gaucher, Guido Molinari, Jack Bush, Claude Tousignant, Michael Morris, Gary Lee Nova and Jacques Hurtubise. Internationally, there is also Masuo Ikeda, Victor Vasarely and Six Young British Printmakers, as well as photography by such celebrated artists as Dorothea Lange, Robert Frank and Aaron Suskind.

If there is a certain zeitgeist in the air as many of Alberta's young artists begin to shape an art practice for themselves, two contemporary art exhibitions particularly ripe with newness are the travelling *Heart of London* (Edmonton Art Gallery and the Calgary Allied Arts Centre), and Edmonton Art Gallery's *Place and Process.* Making their debut in 1969, both exhibitions are hip and distinctly young in attitude. "Gallery rocks as show opens!"[8] declares a headline in the *Edmonton Journal* for the National Gallery's *Heart of London,* which highlights the artistic energies of London, Ontario – then, along with Vancouver, producing some of the most cutting-edge work in the country. "*Heart of London* was MTV compared to community cable,"[9] comments Ron Moppett, who himself, a few years later with John Hall, will push the same high art/low art envelope as the two travelling shows do by assembling 1,000 art and non-art objects for their nationally touring *Rose Museum.* A survey of the rose motif in western culture, *Rose Museum*[10] will deliberately mix aspects of high culture with low culture, including from the world of consumer goods a 4-cubic bag of Alberta Rose Peat Moss, a Red Rose Tea mobile and rose-patterned wallpaper'bars of soap.[11] Later reviewed in *Arts Canada,* two ceramic sculptures by the especially distinctive Calgary artist Patrick Hurst are singled out for their "beautifully decadent Rococo quality which is expressed particularly well in his larger work entitled *Calgary's Entry to the Rose Bowl Parade.*"[12]

"The level of pop culture was very high,"[13] John Hall observed many years later about their year-long project.[14] First exhibited in 1973 at the Glenbow-Alberta Institute, the *Rose Museum*'s compulsive and comprehensive attitude and love of detail foreshadow a taste for obsessive art-making in the city that will echo in the art of practitioners as diverse as Don Mabie, Mary Shannon Will, Alan Dunning, Chris Cran, Laura Vickerson and Greg Payce.

As for the Edmonton Art Gallery's *Place and Process,* the anti-modern attitude of 1960s avant-garde practice couldn't have been more starkly evident. Rather than being an exhibit of high art abstract painting and sculpture, artists such as Les Levine spread the contents of 250 jumbo boxes of corn flakes outside of the gallery's new building while Iain and Ingrid Baxter of the N.E. Thing Co. come up with the controversial but conceptual pièce de resistance *The Nothing Project.*

Also included in the exhibition is New York artist Dennis Oppenheim, who creates plaster casts of his footprints made from running a 220-yard dash across wet ground. In a similar vein, fellow American Robert Morris documents himself riding twelve successive horses back and forth over a white chalk line. Topping off this sixties tour de force is a two-day visit to Inuvik, where New Yorker Lawrence Weiner, Vancouver's N.E. Thing Co. and Harry Savage of Edmonton execute work specifically for that location. According to American art critic Lucy Lippard, one of the high points of the expedition is a spontaneous event staged by Savage involving local children and the inflation of huge lengths of plastic wiener casings. The participants, writes Lippard, "had a general field day while the RCMP watched suspiciously from a car."

Organized for the Edmonton Art Gallery by Willoughby Sharp of Kineticism Press (New York), *Place and Process* is a highly publicized show, serving to reinforce the gallery's growing reputation. As the *Edmonton Journal* art critic Virgil Hammock writes a few months later, "As international art magazines have been pointing out in the last year, Edmonton is not only ready to be part of the big picture – it already is. If you don't believe me, look in the new issues of *Arts Canada* or *Art Forum* for the feature articles on both Edmonton artists and the Edmonton Art Gallery.... In the last couple of weeks I have talked to two key people from the National Gallery who have said Edmonton is the most exciting centre in the country." [15]

Hammock is actually quite critical of *Place and Process*'s conceptual, site-specific art, but he did approve of then director William Kirby's curatorial attitude. "[Kirby's choices] show a fair cross section of our art on a national scale. Not what he might like to exist, but what actually is. It is not a gallery's job to dictate taste, but to present it." [16] This opinion would later not only be ignored at Edmonton institutions, but by other Canadian institutions as well.

Curiously, although the early 1970s are a stimulating time for the small but growing art scene in Alberta's two major cities, the pre-1970 period can't be forgotten despite a general tendency to consider it as being not worth much. In 1983, for instance, EAG curator Christopher Varley of *Winnipeg West: Painting and Sculpture in Western Canada, 1945–1970* writes, "As far as the rest of the world was concerned, Calgary and Edmonton were still in the cultural wilderness before 1970. Vancouver and Winnipeg exuded mellow sophistication by comparison. Alberta could claim no Carrs or FitzGeralds as native sons or daughters. Its most distinguished painters were conservative Englishmen who took a dim view of the sloppy liberties of modernist art."[17] *Winnipeg West* toured to six Canadian cities.

If there were any conservative Englishmen around, exhibitions from the 1960s of contemporary Albertans indicate that they are well-engrossed with the modern world. For instance, in the EAG's annual *All Alberta '69,* there is a range of sixties-style painting from the hard-edge, optical acrylics of Ihor Dmytruk to the new realism of John Hall.

Similarly, in the *Ninth Annual Calgary Graphics* show in 1968 (ACA Gallery), the abstract prints of Velma Foster and Alexandra Haeseker are right at home within international trends. Even the not-so-young artists who appear in the *All Alberta '69,* such as George Angliss, Lois Whitford, Douglas Haynes and Thelma Manarey, show that the dim view had long evaporated.

If there is any one development that towers above all others in the post-1970 period, it is the professionalization of the visual arts. This will take shape in many forms, from the building up of an infrastructure, including public art galleries throughout the province and the establishment of the Alberta Art Foundation, to the far-reaching notion that art can be a *real profession* in Alberta – a profession not just for a few who teach, but a way for many to earn a living or at least recognition.

Rather than being regarded as a vocation, there is now the tantalizing possibility that art can actually be a *career,* and all that that entails. But if an art practice is to become a career, there is also the expectation that any vestiges of regionalism within Alberta will of necessity be swept away because in an national or international context, there is no place for art deemed regional. "Perhaps the greatest difference between the current generation and their Albertan ancestors is one of *ambition* [my emphasis]. Earlier Alberta art was dominated by regionalism, which, it must be admitted, continues even among some present day artists who matured in the 1960s. Although it would be absurd to suggest that anyone aspires to minor status, many Alberta artists seem to have had a particularly modest view of their possible place in the history of art." [18]

If there is, as Karen Wilken terms it, a prevailing modest view, it may have to do with the fact that many creative Albertans prefer to concentrate on what is real and immediate in their own lives and community, regardless of whether it is condescendingly called regionalism or not. There is also, according to Joice Hall, an attitude among some senior artists that if you didn't rely on art as a career, then at least your art had a better chance of remaining *honest,* untainted by money and the pressures of the art world.[19]

Another graduate of the time, Don Mabie, believes that rather than it being a case of ambition, it had more to do with confidence: "With the explosion of the art world in the sixties, there was a feeling of possibility everywhere. Not only that, you had the attitude that you were just going to do your own thing, no matter what." [20] Personal freedom, then, is an impulse not to be denied and somehow out there, in that buoyant period, there will be a financial way to nurture one's practice.

Contrast this with Stan Perrott's observation that, for the older generation, "somehow we are not masters of our fate. We find we are in a circumstance [of building an art community], and you have to meet that circumstance. If your inner self was not fulfilled, it didn't seem to matter in those days." [21]

chapter nine

An Alternative Artscene Emerges

In the post-1970s artworld, new practices and new ways of making art are enlarging what is seen and exhibited in the province. The most significant of these, both in Alberta and in Canada, is the rise of intermedia or what later is called new media: video, performance, audio and electronic, and later digital-based presentations. The appearance of new media on the contemporary scene also signals the presence of an artistic underground with an appetite for more critical and experimental types of work that challenge aspects of Western society and its cherished art traditions. It establishes a level of practice less concerned with producing aesthetic art objects, and more interested in process and investigation however temporal.

From within this underground surfaces an influential entity more supportive of this experimentation: parallel galleries or artist-run centres (ARCs). The presence of this network of centres infuses the Canadian art scene with a rebellious spirit, born out of the experimentation of the 1960s. Taking its cues from international movements rather than regional ones, ARCs will fully embrace the earlier attitudes of dada and fluxus – earlier avant-garde movements from Europe – as well the more recent intrusions of conceptual art, and feminism. In fact, ARCs will be instrumental in supporting feminist art across the country in the 1980s and 1990s.

Often misunderstood and not well appreciated, even considered a fringe activity by some, the alternative art scene emerges at the beginning of 1970s as one of the newest and boldest developments in Alberta. And, like the province's unpredictable spring run-offs, it generally manages to hold its own, especially in Calgary. In the 1980s and 1990s, the influence of the ARCs swells, nurtured by the efforts of individuals as well as through collective effort.

One of the key individuals in breaking this new ground is **PAUL WOODROW**, whose thumbnail sketch of his own career up to 1992 provides insight into the alternative art scene as well: "Between the years 1970 and 1992 I have produced paintings, drawings, poetic objects, installations, prints, performance activities, social interventions, avant-garde music, parodies of popular culture, associated with other artists on collaborative work, produced videos and performed world beat music. The themes, styles and contexts of my work are extremely diverse, not for the sake of diversity alone, but as a symptom of a comprehensive attitude towards art-making."[1]

Thus, rather than embracing a particular style of art or a particular medium, Woodrow and his colleagues harbour a world view about art that can be unorthodox; treading into the realm of *anti-art.* Not surprisingly, Woodrow's influences include: "Fluxus, especially the work of Robert Filliou, Ben Vautier, Lamonte Young, Walter de Maria and John Cage. Another source of influence was conceptual art, through the work of Canadian artist Iain Baxter and the N.E.Thing Co. with whom I worked briefly as director of Special Projects."[2]

Important early examples of this alternative art scenes's evolution in Calgary include: WORKSHOP, a co-operative of artists and writers formed in 1971 that eventually spins off WORKSHOP II (1972); Dandelion Gallery and Workshop (1975) and *Dandelion* magazine (1975)[3]; the pioneering efforts of Woodrow and Clive Robertson via W.O.R.K.S (We Ourselves Roughly Know Something, 1972–74); and shortly after, with Don Mabie, Marcella Bienvenue, Leila Sujir and others, the establishment of the Parachute Centre for Cultural Affairs/Arton's (1975–78). This development, Sujir writes, "was perhaps before its time and thus didn't quite fit comfortably [in Calgary]."[4]

Earlier on in 1972, Robertson and Woodrow organized the first international performance festival in Canada, and the *1978 Canadian Video Open* remains a highlight in Parachute's history.

As well as these fringe activities, from 1976 to 1980, Brian Dyson programs over two dozen video/performance/installation works at the Alberta Collage of Art Gallery. Around the same time (1975), a couple of new artist-run centres appeared that, interestingly, were not adverse to showing more traditional mediums like painting and sculpture. These were the aforementioned Dandelion Gallery (now defunct) and the "dark horse"[5] Clouds 'n' Water Gallery, which eventually became Off Centre Centre (1980) and then the New Gallery (1988). Of all the centres to arise in Calgary, the impact of Off Centre Centre/New Gallery, especially under the direction of Don Mabie and Sandra (Tivy) Vida, made it one of the most important ARCs in the country.

Near the end of the 70s, two young aspiring interdisciplinary artists – Grant Poier and Stephen Peterson, along with artist/curator Charlie Fox – succeed in establishing the production house Centre Art Video (1980), later renamed EM/Media (1984). No wonder scholar and curator Denis Reid observes in *A Concise History of Canadian Painting:* "Calgary had a special character during the seventies that was enhanced by the innovative performance art as well as by the irreverence for artistic conventions of some of the printmakers [and painters.]"[6]

In Edmonton, the early history of the local avant-garde revolves largely around the efforts of the Edmonton Art Gallery under the leadership of William Kirby, and artists such as Harry Savage, Sylvain Voyer and ManWoman, who support and participate in avant-garde art activity. In 1973, Savage and Voyer form a loose partnership to establish an artist-run gallery "suited to the socio-political climate of the time."[7] Latitude 53 opens with the show *Sacramental Communion with Death,* an exhibition of prints and paintings by none other than ManWoman (born in 1938 as Patrick Kemball, a 1963 graduate of the ACA).

"A self-ordained priest of the 60s Order,"[8] ManWoman returns in 1974 with more paintings that depict: "skull telephones, dragon motorcycles, a chrome plated 'Jesus Christ's Original Lunch Bucket' and pamplets."[9] Not all of what Latitude 53 exhibits is so off-the-wall but this ARC's pluralistic programming, which included many Calgary artists, is remarkable. In its first decade, it features artists from both sides of what would later be regarded as a kind of Cold War in the Edmonton visual art scene (see next chapter).

With regard to video art in the capital city, its beginnings are more tentative. As Christine Conley observes about that earlier period in her 1986 catalogue *A Tale of Two Cities: Video Art in Alberta,* "Unlike Calgary, Edmonton has never had an identifiable community of video producers; the few artists who have been known to make tapes [early examples are John Freeman and Richard Titus] have done so independently."[10]

Curiously then, the earliest example of a post-secondary institution in Alberta offering video as a medium for fine-art students is in Edmonton at Grant MacEwan College. Established in 1982, video is incorporated by artist and instructor Cherie Moses as part of an intermedia course. Another turning point for video in Edmonton is the formation of FAVA (Film and Video Artists Society) and the North West Media Network Guild in 1983, and later, by the programming of Brian Donnelly, Liz Stobbe and Donna McAlear at Latitude 53. Eventually, the efforts of these individuals surface in 1990 with *Video From The North*[11] at the Glenbow Museum, along with the tapes of eleven artists including Moses, Lisa Trofymow and Colleen Finlayson.

Overall, the latter 1980s and early 1990s represent a high point for alternative art practices in Alberta. Not only is there serious attention paid to their efforts by the artist-run centres, but by public institutions as well.[12] From these exhibitions and other alternative-minded events, such as the *Art Rodeo* at a Calgary junkyard (renamed Graceland), the configuration of an Albertan community of video-art practitioners is becoming clearly evident.[13] Paradoxically, although the emergence of this community is a new and radical one for Alberta, many of the artists place themselves within a tradition of art-making that is not so novel anymore.

In her 1989 article "Calgary warms to local art," Nancy Tousley points out "[Mark] Dicey and [Colleen Kerr] are amazed at how many people think of their art as *new* [my emphasis] art. The act of taking random elements, whether it be Dicey's collages of organic and man-made garbage, or Kerr's theatrical mix of music, literature and art can be traced to the Dadaists, an early 1900s artistic movement which attacked conventional art."[14] Dadaists like the inimitable Marcel Duchamp (1887–1968), whose attitude about art rung bells not just within the alternative milieu but also more broadly among creative Albertans, especially in Calgary. This aspect is nicely explored in *A Duchampian Look at Glenbow's Art Collection* (1997)[15]. The contents of the exhibition encompass such work as Ken Elser's renowned 1973 intaglio print *Lunch Kit (Relic of the 20th Century)* – made from a squashed, corroded lunch kit – to Gordon Ferguson's more recent 1992 assemblage *Countersink*, consisting of two porcelain sinks attached to a metal pole. "I suppose the permission for this sort of work comes from Marcel Duchamp's assertion that the everyday object is more accurate as a meaningful experience in that it eliminates taste and imagination, both unquantifiable factors,"[16] comments Ferguson.

Another aspect about the alternative community is that instead of the modern-art paradigm of younger artists working in direct opposition to their elders, for instance, there seems to be in contemporary Alberta a propensity for the emerging to engage with the established and vice versa. An example of this cross-generational discourse is the 1988 *Media Blitz* in which more senior artists, Sandra (Tivy) Vida and Marcella Bienvenue, play a key role in pulling together the video, performance and film festival, showcasing work made by colleagues often ten to fifteen years younger in age. Writing about this multiple-age group, Vida remarks, "If there is a common thematic thread, aside from the literal references to place, it is the recurrence of several features noted by other writers as being distinctive of this region's output: personal history and memory, comments on mass media and culture, ironic humour."[17]

Humour is seen not only in some of the work presented by *Media Blitz* but also in the early Cherie Moses performance piece, *Brides and Opening Ceremonies* (1981, SUB Art Gallery, University of Alberta) with its installation of five fabric "bride bags" and five (live) grooms: "a work that parodies the wedding ritual and the social construction of the bride."[18] Another example of humour is the mass-media ritual of one TV-watching family in the fifteen-minute 1986 Marcella Bienvenue film *The Heart Is A Lonely Monitor*, which appeared in *Media Blitz* and also won the Alberta Motion Picture Industries Association Award for Innovation. Later, Bienvenue commented: "I think I'm monitoring the culture in my work,"[19] while Moses explains, "I have been exploring notions of stereotype and posturing in much of my work over the past few years."[20]

Both **CHERIE MOSES** (1949, Cleveland, United States) and **MARCELLA BIENVENUE** (1946, Stettler, Alberta) hold positions of distinction because of their early participation in Alberta's alternative art scene – both are also art pioneers from a feminist perspective in their respective cities – and have a solid record of practice in video, performance, installation, film (Bienvenue), photowork, mixed media and painting (Moses). "Edmonton has only one important artist working in alternative media,"[21] writes critic Liz Wylie in 1985 about Moses, while Nancy Tousley describes Bienvenue in 1986 as, "Calgary's only full-time performance artist."[22]

Interestingly, both artists have a background in printmaking: Moses completed an MFA in printmaking and mixed media at the University of Alberta (1979), and Bienvenue worked with photographic images in silkscreen and offset lithography before turning to performance art in 1980. Although the two disciplines, printmaking and time-based art such as video, may seem dramatically different, they actually share a tradition of being perceived as anti-elite art forms, and of having strong socially aware activist links with other practitioners nationally and internationally.

Initially a graduate in painting from the Alberta College of Art (1969), Bienvenue is best known for her performance work incorporating live spoken texts and choreographed movement, slide images and audio track. Central to her practice is the creation of personas, which she often acts out herself, "struggling," as the artist puts it, "to answer the questions I ask."[23] Questions about choice, and how an individual's identity is shaped in a mass-media-dominated society and where roles are, according to postmodern and feminist thinking, socially constructed (i.e. nurture rather than nature determines who we are).

Her investigations led her into the area of installation art, making her practice even more multidisciplinary, part of what she calls an "open approach to art-making."[24] In *MY POV* (point of view), for instance, created for the Glenbow Museum's adventuresome *New Alberta Art* program, the theme of identity is played out in an installation featuring a slide of Bienvenue's face projected on four female mannequins. Noted for its "elegance and high-tech eeriness,"[25] Tousley describes this 1990 work as being "an outgrowth of sets for performances in which she has developed these and other themes." The performances Tousley refers to are *Jane Doe* (1986, Calgary and Winnipeg) and *Central Nervous System* (1988, Vancouver and Calgary).

Accompanying the *MY POV* installation is a performance piece entitled *Phases of the Moon,* which reviewer Katherine Ylitalo described as "[continuing] the business of piecing together a persona,"[26] a persona speculating on "what choices does a woman make from the store offerings of consumable objects and images of romance?" Constructing "the event in a theatrical form of collage," Bienvenue interacts with a synthesizer, a TV, a typewriter, a telephone, a digital electronic sign and two projection screens. Ylitalo continues:

"her method of performing blends rehearsed acting and simple being in a manner that allows her vulnerability and intensity to shine through."

Cherie Moses also explores the themes of self, roles and identity – a major feminist concern not to be confused with the modernist notion of the (male) artist-hero. Her work, though, is more overtly feminist or concerned with gender, speared on by a "belief in the role that the artist plays in the presentation of important social issues."[27] An example of this is seen in *Placing the Talent* (1985), where Moses performs in front of a video camera as a fashion model. Only Moses's torso and the lower part of her face are visible as she rapidly goes through her poses under the demanding directions of four different photographers, whose male voices we hear. Writing about the five-minute colour video, Moses states: "The tape deconstructs the idealized image of fashion modelling/photographic modelling. It functions as an allegory for the confinement of the female within a culturally determined image."[28]

More recently, her twenty-four-minute colour video *Mubarakah* (1994) explores the theme of identity and displacement within the context of an unnamed woman of Arabic heritage trying to make sense of her adopted country: Canada. Hearing her inner thoughts in English, French and Arabic, we watch the young woman pace through the cool and lonely countryside of Alberta's parkland. As she walks, these thoughts indirectly piece together a portrait of the subject that oscillates between her feelings of pride and feelings of invisibility.

Moses also works with paint in an "austere and meticulous style"[29] and in the 1990s produces a series of works incorporating photo and laser copy transfers, and translations of her writings in Arabic script. With some exceptions, it's unorthodox for an artist long involved in alternative media to maintain a practice in painting, but then, Cherie Moses comes from Edmonton: a place, like Calgary, where it is possible to paint and still be critically accepted by your alternative peers locally. In other Canadian centres, there is the suspicion that despite her art's socio-political content she has to be tainted in some way by Edmonton's perceived preoccupation with formal issues and making precious art objects. Recalling her 1984 photoworks show *Imposed Image: Mother,*[30] Moses says, "The comment was to the effect that 'if you make something so very beautiful, how can it be political?'"[31]

Moses is not alone. Whatever side of the ideological fence Edmonton artists dwell on post-1970, there are certain consequences in terms of how their work is received, not just in Edmonton but elsewhere. What did this have to do with the art they produced? Not much. But since when has the art world, especially the publicly funded sector in Canada, been a generous, open-minded forum? Since when has work been evaluated on its own merits and within its proper context? An artist could be producing the strongest work of his or her career but if it is not in step with the prevailing curatorial and critical preferences, then tough luck.

Edmonton, you could say, became a textbook example of this phenomena and it is practically impossible to consider the careers of its post-1970 artists without taking into consideration that larger context. In 1984, Liz Wylie, in an important article for *Vanguard* magazine titled "The Underside of Edmonton," sums up what the city stood for at that time: "Generally speaking, the national image of art in Edmonton is that of elegant, abstract, late modernist sculpture and painting."[32] She then proceeds to discuss the careers of certain artists who did not fit the national image of Edmonton, who were in fact "the tip of the iceberg of underground art in the city," individuals such as Tommie Gallie, Jim Davies, Robert Iveson and, not surprisingly, Cherie Moses.

Moses also will address this issue in the same magazine but from a slightly different angle when she asks: "How is it that in a city of over a half a million people, so many artists wear the same shoes and walk in the same direction? Impressed by the phenomenon of media hype, the proponents of the myth that Edmonton is the centre of painting and/or sculpture in Canada have come to believe their own illusions. In a city where art has been for so long synonymous with abstract expressionist/colour field painting and constructed steel sculpture, it takes a monumental effort to dispel the notion that these are the only art activities here which are worthy of note."[33]

EDMONTON:

A MODERNIST CENTRE

chapter ten

Edmonton: The Making of a Centre

IN 1963, [Morris] Louis, [Kenneth] Noland and [Jules] Olitski were just beginning to win acceptance in New York, let alone in Canada. When their influence [as color field painters] was felt more quickly in the Canadian West than in the East, it was regarded with suspicion by many critics who felt that true Canadian originality must have its roots at least in abstract expressionism and preferably in the School of Paris. What made colour abstraction appear as such a unique phenomenon in the West was its peculiar tenacity,[1] ❧ Terry Fenton, *The National Gallery of Canada Journal,* 1976.

About fifteen years ago the full impact of New York art was felt in Canada. Particularly on the Prairies this was initially a very exciting and fruitful development. But how quickly the early excitement and the first stunning works gave way to doctrinaire opinions and imitations! What

> at first had been a positive direction became a feeling of having to look constantly over one's shoulder to see what the avant-garde in the eastern mecca were doing,[2] ❧ Terrence Heath, *Western Untitled*, 1976.

The two preceding opinions, both published in 1976, hint at a growing gulf early in Alberta's post-1970 scene concerning late modernist abstract painting – and its formalist agenda, in general – as a viable and relevant option amidst a growing field of other kinds of artistic expression. This gulf creates not only a deep, icy crevasse between the art-making sensibilities of Alberta's two largest centres, but also leaves an enduring and contentious legacy for Edmonton's visual-art community to end-of-the-century. Witness these later assessments made in the *Edmonton Journal* and the *Globe and Mail*, respectively:

> That the rest of the world had gone through several art movements since the hey-day of New York abstraction and was by 1980 rediscovering the representational image, seemed to be of little consequence in Edmonton. The tragedy was that a lot of good artists simply left town. Maybe the annual visitation and blessing of the pictures by doddering, once-eminent American art critics who specialize in New York-style abstraction just got to be more than some could handle,[3] ❧ Elizabeth Beauchamp, 1990.

> George Bures Miller, a multimedia and video artist who lives in Lethbridge and is currently showing in Belgium, France and Austria, said he found the painting program at the [U of A] so rigid that he dropped out in his third year.... He said his university experience left him questioning anyone who promotes art as a religion,[4] ❧ Charles Mandel, 1997.

The "religion" Bures Miller refers to is what will, in effect first put Emma Lake and Regina in the late 1950s, then Saskatoon in the 1960s, and lastly Edmonton in the 1970s, on the map of Canadian art. It will also mark the first time in Canada's cultural history that artwork from the prairie region beyond just a few stellar individuals will be deemed worthy enough of national attention – both positive and negative.

"By gaining national and international recognition for themselves [as abstract artists], they have opened people's eyes to the art of the Canadian West,"[5] curator Raymond Ouellet concludes in 1978. However, judging by the paucity of abstract art from the Prairies now on permanent display, for instance, in the National Gallery of Canada, this trend is short-lived.

But returning back to that earlier era before this vital period in prairie art is written off in the larger Canadian art scene: what an eye-opener it turned out to be! Beginning with such efforts as the National Gallery's *Five Painters from Regina: Bloore/Godwin/Lochhead/McKay/Morton* (1961) and New York's Clement Greenberg's much-quoted article "Painting and Sculpture in Prairie Canada Today" (*Canadian Art,* 1963), audiences outside of the region become acquainted for the first time with prairie practitioners, including a number of Albertans such as Ted Godwin, Douglas Haynes, Marion Nicoll, Ron Spickett, J.B. Taylor and Velma Foster, as well as landscapists including W.L. Stevenson. In his article, Greenberg, the connoisseur of post-war abstraction, actually tips his hat to Canadian landscape painters: "Landscape painting is where Canadian art continues, I feel (allowing for Borduas, Bush, McKay), to make its most distinctive contribution."[6]

Although Greenberg's views on art will come increasingly under attack in the national and international art world of the 1970s, and his name virtual poison in certain quarters, the first paragraph in his 1963 article still has a certain relevancy thirty years later: "When *Canadian Art* [magazine] asked me to do a report on the situation of painting and sculpture in Manitoba, Saskatchewan and Alberta, I was a bit taken aback. Didn't they know about that situation in Ottawa? Was that how difficult communication was between prairie Canada and the rest of the country? But then I remembered how little we in New York knew about the situation of American art outside of New York, and that reason was not geographical but simply the assumption that that *situation was not worth finding out about* [my emphasis].... The case, I concluded, must be more or less analogous in Canada. Montreal and Toronto as leading centres of art with Ottawa as a headquarters if not centre, and Vancouver in the role of San Francisco, took it for granted that prairie art was nothing but provincial – and were all the readier to do so because they themselves felt in a provincial relation, art-wise, to Paris and New York. For this reason I saw prairie art in Canada as being wrapped in double obscurity."

But in the 1970s, the obscurity facing western practitioners lessens with further shows outside of the region, like *Prairies: Western Canadian Paintings* organized by the Saidye Bronfman Centre in Montreal; *Abstraction West: Emma Lake and After* circulated by the National Gallery of Canada, and *Seven*

Prairie Painters as part of the Art Gallery of Ontario's programming. The preceding exhibitions all take place in public galleries but with the addition of an increasing amount of interest in prairie art from prominent commercial galleries concentrated in Toronto. Coverage in national and international art magazines also strengthens the position of prairie artists, with reviews sometimes coming from prominent figures such as Roald Nasgaard, a curator with the Art Gallery of Ontario. For *Prairie '74* and *Sculpture Alberta '74* (Edmonton Art Gallery), he writes, "it was artists working within advanced international modernist modes, especially painterly colour field painting, who stole the show."[7] In books on Canadian art that are published at the time, like J. Russell Harper's *Painting in Canada: A History* (2nd edition, 1977), readers learn that: "Western Canadian painters had by the 1950s become the running mates of the easterners."[8] And then a little later, Burnett/Schiff's *Contemporary Canadian Art* (1983) states, "Formalist painting has a particular strength in Alberta and Saskatchewan, and a similar situation exists in sculpture in those provinces."[9]

By and large, but not exclusively, the strongest spotlight on Alberta art in the early post-1970 era is on formalist abstract painting and sculpture, especially the type of abstraction that is primarily about the work itself or what is often referred to as its formal qualities. "In Alberta, Harold Feist, Doug Haynes and Ann Clarke are all commited to stripped-down, abstract images which emphasize stroke, texture and tone,"[10] explains curator Karen Wilken for the nine-city Canadian tour of *The Canadian Canvas: 1975–76.*

Any sort of similarity to the post-war New York School of abstract painting and sculpture and its various manifestations up to colour field also receive attention. For the exhibition *Abstraction West: Emma Lake and After,* curator Terry Fenton writes, "Haynes is something of a senior artist in Edmonton, and, like [Otto] Rogers in Saskatoon, has come to Olitski via [Adolph] Gottlieb and [Robert] Motherwell, two artists whose figure-ground concerns seem close to his own."[11]

Professionally informed and devoted to the by-then century-old tradition of modern art, both Terry Fenton, as director of the Edmonton Art Gallery, 1972–87, and Karen Wilken, as the EAG's chief curator, 1971–78, find themselves in a city where, although abstract art-making is already a fact, the potential of that practice has not yet been fully nurtured or vigorously documented, displayed and promoted. Overall, Edmonton, it seemed, could be part of the paradigm or the mainstream in which smaller centres absorb what the larger art centres think is important and progressive. And for that era, in many people's minds *and* eyes, it was abstract art almost exclusively.

"Unlike their predecessors – and like their colleagues everywhere else – many gifted Alberta painters and sculptors are committed to abstraction. While detractors sometimes deplore this fact as the result of presumed authoritarian formalism at the Edmonton Art Gallery, it would be more accurate to see it as a sign that Alberta is closer today to the mainstream and its preoccupations than it was at any time in the past,"[12] Wilken, *Painting in Alberta: An Historical Survey,* 1980.

That this particular idea of the mainstream was already being challenged in the 1970s by other approaches to art – even in the modern-art bastion of Regina with the populist funk ceramics of David Gilhooly, Victor Cicansky and Joe Fafard – did not seem to matter. These alternative modes are regarded as secondary flashes in the pan that will impress, attract attention and then fizzle-out. Furthermore, as Wilken herself points out: "Why abstraction should be labeled as New York and suspect, while work deriving patently from California funk should be acclaimed as grassroots regionalism, remains a mystery to me." (Wilken, *Canadian Canvas,* 1975)

An assistant director and curator at Regina's Norman MacKenzie Art Gallery (1965–71) prior to his EAG position, a friend of Greenberg and an Emma Lake participant in the 1960s, Terry Fenton had already witnessed a very fertile period in prairie art-making and is unafraid to state it. "I do think that the development of art in western Canada during the past two decades has been remarkable, but it has been largely overlooked by curators, critics, and historians elsewhere in this country. If I sound as though I think the best art produced in Canada during the past two decades came from the West, it is simply because, by and large, I believe it to be true – and as true today as it was ten years ago," Fenton, *Abstraction West: Emma Lake and After,* 1976.

Through his contact with a young New York artist named Michael Steiner, Fenton invites the then up-and-coming sculptor to appear at the Edmonton Art Gallery to jury an exhibition and lead a workshop. About that seminal workshop, EAG curator Russell Bingham later recalls, "[Steiner] encouraged local artists to be freer with materials and methods of paint application, and to take their art more seriously. After this, frequent visits from critics such as Clement Greenberg and Kenworth Moffat, as well as artists such as Walter Darby Bannard, Darryl Hughto and Stanley Boxer have helped reinforced this thinking."[13] While in Fenton's view: "[The two-week workshop] brought about the kind of dramatic development that Emma Lake had produced in Saskatchewan." [14] In others words, the coalescing of another centre for late-modernist artwork with like-minded counterparts working in Saskatoon, Toronto, New York City and London, England.

Like Clement Greenberg's earlier foray across the Prairies, the visit of this abstract sculptor in 1973 is part and parcel of a now well-petrified set of assumptions about late-modernist abstract art in Edmonton, beginning with the notion that the city was a vacuum waiting to be filled when, in fact, its potential for greater artistic diversity is about to be overshadowed by more substantial forces in favour of this dramatic development. These forces included institutions such as the Edmonton Art Gallery, eager to nurture a coherent scene that coalesces with its own views on art; commercial art galleries and corporate clients who supported the sophisticated New York–style abstract art; the painting and sculpture department of the University of Alberta where a number of key artists instructed; the media who provided numerous stories on Edmonton's abstract scene, including of all things, the conservative *Western Report*'s 1987 cover story entitled "Sculpture City: How Edmonton became the world's best in steel" [15]; and finally, a significant number of local artists who welcomed the attention and input because of their *genuine* interest in the practice. Painter Robert Scott, for instance, viewed [the Steiner juried] exhibition as the first step towards building a cohesive art scene in Alberta. "For Scott, personally, it was the first time someone actively punctured the wall of isolation here. Scott's eyes were opened to the fact that Alberta artists were judged by an outside eye and found good, in fact very good." [16]

But by the end of the 1970s, all the attention paid to the abstract scene in Edmonton and elsewhere on the Prairies, especially regarding colour field–inspired painting, is perhaps turning out to be too much of a good thing as certain assumptions are being created that others question, such as the Toronto-based David Burnett in a 1979 *Arts Canada* review. He begins: "It seems to me that an exhibition like *Seven Prairie Painters* [Art Gallery of Ontario] should be an opportunity to challenge the assumptions that the East may hold about the West, rather than affirm them. I do not mean to underrate exhibitions whose main function is to keep lines of communication open, but it is not useful if this is done at the expense of the individual artists. In this show the artists included are a grouping rather than a "group," and the choice of each artist, relatively speaking, seems to have been an arbitrary matter based on the generalized assumption that art in the West which traces its heritage from the foundation of colour field Painting through the Emma Lake and Edmonton Workshops [1973] must continue to affirm its collective roots."[17]

The net result of all of this tightly focused attention is that Edmonton is cast, nationally, in a very black-and-white light. The kind of light that leaves no room for either nuance or difference, and which, two decades later, can be said to have served nobody particularly well. As the long-time Toronto art critic John Bentley Mays noted in his 1993 talk in Calgary on abstraction, the 1970s and early 1980s were elsewhere a period of intense opposition to late-modernist art, and that in the long run the Edmonton group, as he referred to them, had probably been "short-changed"[18] of meaningful, long-term national recognition. In an article written a few months earlier, he noted, "At the same time, the NGC [National Gallery of Canada] will continue largely to ignore certain contemporary artists – I am thinking here of the best Alberta abstract painters and sculptors – whose serious work has too long been a target of routine scorn by the Canadian curatorial elite."[19]

In a sense, it could be argued that the routine scorn later facing many of these artists revolves around being in the wrong place at the wrong time. The wrong time because the tides of critical attention were turning against the kind of work the Edmonton modernists were becoming renowned for, and the wrong place in that Edmonton is an easy target for criticism due to its location in the hinterland of the larger art world.

However, from Scott's point of view, working on the periphery of the art world was never a problem: "This provincial setting, being on the edge, combined with travel, surprisingly had its advantages. I like the perspective. One could be informed yet not overwhelmed by antiquity, an affliction which I feel many European artists suffered from. Nor was one distracted by the annual wave of the new, which rose and rushed through the American centres of art only to crash at the end of each season. Here, one could be informed, stimulated, active, and above all, focused."[20]

But even for those who were sincerely interested in these developments in Edmonton and elsewhere on the Prairies, the idea that something serious in art could be actually taking place in the hinterland was still met with skepticism. For evidence of such attitudes, one need look no further than the 1983 CBC documentary film, blatantly titled *Art! In Edmonton?*

Let's continue to examine a series of assumptions that possibly short-changed what these abstract artists in Edmonton accomplished for themselves: The first assumption is that abstract art made its first solid steps as a practice in Edmonton with the arrival of Karen Wilken (1971) and Terry Fenton (1972). This is most definitely not the case. Being the *lingua franca* of contemporary art in the western world, serious abstraction of many kinds is well underway in Edmonton by the end of the 60s. In a 1970 review entitled "Impasto Prairie Spacescapes," the earlier abstract paintings of Douglas Haynes are said to be "more about the space that is here in the Prairies than an impression of fields and grain elevators."[21] While in a very different style, Ihor Dmytruk's untitled acrylics are described as "fine hard-edge optical paintings."[22] Similarly, sculptor Ron Kostyniuk is acknowledged as "a structuralist artist who relies on utilizing actual space rather than the implied space of a painting."[23] Then there is then-newcomer Ann Clarke, a promising young British artist whose "drawings make me wish that we could see her paintings. They are what I would call painterly and cry for larger scale,"[24] and the tight abstracts of David Cantine, "who goes to the opposite extreme by exhibiting a number of almost pocket-size paintings."[25] Also, working from the University of Alberta, Jonathan Knowlton is said to be "deeply involved in painting hard-edged acrylic abstractions, trying to synthesize organic and geometric forms."[26]

And last but not least, there is painter Norman Yates's room-size installation of ceiling-to-floor aluminum strips entitled *Kinetic Foil* (1969), which is nothing if not abstract. Exhibited at the U of A's Students' Union Art Gallery, Yates says he wishes to maintain "the rich medium of painting" but also "pursue his art beyond the limits of the canvas."[27]

In addition to the practice of abstract art, Edmonton is also well-connected to the goings-on of abstract artists in other centres. The Toronto-based colour field artist Jack Bush, for instance, is known to local audiences through a 1970 EAG exhibition of his 1960s work, as is Kenneth Noland and Morris Louis. Abstract painter Graham Peacock, who arrives in 1969 to teach at the university, remembers Edmonton as being "well connected with the main world influences."[28]

Thus, before the arrival of Wilken and Fenton, Edmonton already has a community of advanced modernist practitioners and a record of exhibiting such art. Abstraction is nothing new, nor is it the simple result of "a branch-plant culture transfer from New York to neighbouring Saskatchewan via the Emma Lake summer workshop,"[29] as one Ontario writer tried to explain it in *Arts Canada* in 1971. In fact, from 1955 to 1970, only two Edmontonians, Thelma Manarey and Velma Foster, are participants at Emma Lake[30] and neither would qualify as *agents provocateur* for a branch-plant culture.

If there *was* anything new about the tenure of Wilken and Fenton, it was the institution's tight focus on modern art beginning with *Masters of the Sixties,* featuring the work of Milton Avery, Walter Darby Bannard, Jack Bush, Helen Frankenthaler, Jules Olitski, Lawrence Poons and Frank Stella.

A decade later, Alberta Culture's the *Visual Arts Newsletter* reports, "Talk to any curators and gallery owners across Canada about the art scene in Alberta and at least half of them will refer to Terry Fenton, director of the Edmonton Art Gallery for twelve years. They cite Fenton as a person who has wielded considerable power, a person with a definite critical view (favouring formalist art) who has greatly influenced Edmonton artists." [31]

Another common assumption is that the University of Alberta serves as the breeding ground for these artists in Edmonton. Not exactly true in its full dimensions. Many of the city's better-known practitioners, painters especially, cut their artistic teeth at Calgary's Alberta College of Art, including Douglas Haynes, Giuseppe Albi, Bruce Dunbar, Robert Scott and Terrence Keller. Keller, for instance, attends the College from 1969 to 1973 where instructors Harold Feist and Ranjan Sen are "particularly influential in the shaping of Keller's attitude toward painting in that both stressed the importance of visual values over theory." [32] The college, however, is not completely copasetic with this practice. Keller remembers being in conflict with many of the instructors because they considered abstract art as being too American and are more regional in their tastes. Robert Scott has a similar experience at ACA and remembers the study of abstraction going only as far as Picasso. Graduating in 1969, Scott credits English artist and instructor John Hooper as being the most receptive to his interests.

Other well-known figures like Philip Darrah, Graham Peacock, Ann Clarke and Peter Hide are trained in Great Britain. The notion that the U of A is responsible for every high modernist walking the streets of Edmonton is somewhat overblown. In fact, it is not until the mid-1970s that the city, in the words of Bingham, "took over as the place to be." [33] By then, several of the ACA graduates (Haynes plus Scott and Keller as sessionals) and their British colleagues (Darrah, Peacock and Hide) are teaching at the University where their impact, coupled with the curatorial interest of the EAG, will have a major influence on a younger generation.

A third falsehood is that during Fenton's years as director, the EAG programmed *nothing* but abstract art. In fact, the gallery also had a strong interest in photography (including Albertan), prairie landscape and historic Canadian art. To its credit, and to some Calgarians discomfiture, the EAG organized a major travelling retrospective of Illingworth Kerr, *Harvest of the Spirit,* 1985. And after Fenton's departure, other retrospectives of Calgary artists followed, like *John Snow: Four Decades* (1990), *W.L .Stevenson: Painter of Darkness, Painter of Light* (1992) and *Alberta Society of Artists: Sixty Years* (1991).[34]

As for abstract art or modernism in general, there are plenty of shows of this ilk – well over seventy during Fenton's tenure and more to follow – plus a healthy record of collecting such work. It seems no rock is left unturned when it comes to modern art; no angle left unexplored. From the EAG's modernist concrete environs emerge thematic shows of locally produced art,[35] historic exhibits,[36] international homages,[37] solo presentations of Edmonton artists,[38] comparative exhibitions,[39] collection shows,[40] and of course, exhibitions of the art of one of Canada's most famous late modernists: Jack Bush.[41]

For a certain sector of the Canadian art scene, through the 1970s and for a good chunk of the 1980s, the Edmonton Art Gallery is regarded as a stellar place for abstraction and late modernist art. But the economic recession in Alberta will bring this period to a close, in addition to which the Canada Council pulls the revenue carpet out from underneath the gallery's feet. (As the later EAG director Alf Bogusky notes, "In the mid-eighties, changes to Canada Council funding were designed purposely to broaden the range of contemporary art exhibited in major public galleries. Until that point, block funding without peer review allowed directors and curators to program to their individual taste – which in Edmonton up to that time had run to abstract art."[42])

Thus, up and until that time, a pluralistic view of recent art was not a strength of the Edmonton Art Gallery. This bias had the effect of creating a lost generation of practitioners who had neither the attention nor the privilege of sustained exhibiting in the capital's prime venue. It also had the effect of narrowing the public's scope on contemporary art during a time when the field was broadening in so many directions, including video art, installation, representational painting, activist and feminist art. In Edmonton art critic Virgil Hammock's earlier opinion, the agenda of a publicly funded art gallery should be to present a balanced cross-section of the art of the times, but this attitude was nowhere to be seen in the overall collective ambition to create an Edmonton school.

❧ ❧ ❧

A fourth assumption concerning the development of late modernism in the province is that opposition to or criticism of its formalist ideology originates from outside of the province because Alberta, in its isolation, lacks a critical discourse. Not true. In response to Clement Greenberg's "Painting and Sculpture in Prairie Canada Today" (1963), the following issue of *Canadian Art* is showered with letters to the editor from Albertans critical of his viewpoint. Interestingly, all of the letters come from Calgary artists – Marion Nicoll, George Wood, Frank Palmer, Stanford Perrott – who have their own modernist inclinations. Ron Spickett's letter in particular illustrates a type of response that will become common in the following decades towards those critics or artists who are perceived to be art missionaries: "Why *Canadian Art* found it necessary to call upon the missionary from the land of the gods to examine the error of our ways and our lack of light, and why the apostles from the same place visit the natives and leave the New York gospel, is an unhappy but loaded question. Luckily, I 'missed his message when it came.'"[43]

Resistance is also evident in Edmonton right to the end of the century. Many artists not committed to a late-modernist agenda continue with their practice in the city nonetheless. As well, it is possible to be exposed to different approaches of art-making through the activity of the U of A's printmaking division and the fine art program at Grant MacEwan Community College. Also, the city's small-gallery circuit, including some commercial spaces, regularly presents other kinds of contemporary art. On the public circuit, there is Latitude 53 (est. 1973), SUB Art Gallery (closed in 1982), Beaver House (closed in 1987), Fab Gallery (est. 1987), Harcourt House Gallery (est. 1988) and the Ring House Gallery (closed in 1985), whose notable director, the late Helen Collinson, spoke about programming interdisciplinary art in response to the formalism of the EAG.[44] From this mix there emerges loose coalitions of local artists who collaborate to produce shows in whatever donated/cheap and suitable space can be secured.

Finally, there is the EAG itself, which beginning with the appointment of director Roger H. Boulet in 1987, sets out to diversify its contemporary art programming, making it more responsive to "to the complexity of the regional and national art scene."[45] According to local art critic Elizabeth Beauchamp, the changing of the guard is not, however, a casual affair. "Under [Boulet's] leadership the EAG continued to show the best of the modernist painters and sculptors for which the gallery was known, but it also began to mount Post-modern exhibitions with increasing consistency. For example, the "feminist show" *Dangerous Goods* was the first ever at the EAG to deal exclusively with that topic. And it caused consternation to many of the EAG faithful – in 1990! It did finally open, however, to a rare, standing room–only first-night crowd. While many welcomed Boulet's broad vision for its relevance to contemporary art-making, others saw the new-look EAG as being too populist."[46] This division continues to the end of the century. Five years later, the *Edmonton Journal* art critic Charles Mandel reports, "Many other Edmonton artists complain about the [modernist] ECAS [Edmonton Contemporary Artists' Society], but few will air their grievances in public. [Allen] Ball said people are reluctant to talk about ECAS members because of their high standing both within the city's small gallery circuit and at the University of Alberta."[47]

As an aside, the optics on the Edmonton art scene also have an impact on artist grants obtained from the Canada Council. At an infamous meeting[48] in 1991 with the Edmonton visual-art community, council representatives reveal that "the agenda of the Council is to support innovation and Edmonton – because of its formalist label – is not viewed nationally as a community of innovators."[49] This explains in part why Edmonton has such a low rate of grant recipients from the council during this period.

Assumption number five: In 1991, John Bentley Mays writes, "Before I went out West, everyone was telling me that the story of Edmonton abstraction was just about over."[50] But as he soon finds out, this is not the case. Despite being marginalized to the far end of Canada's visual art universe, these artists and their late-modernist abstract practices continue unabated in Edmonton to the end of the century. Since 1993, however, the rallying point is now the Edmonton Contemporary Artists' Society (ECAS) and its annual exhibition, which includes – to a lesser extent – landscape and figuration. Asked to define what sets the group apart from the prevailing winds of post-modernism, landscape painter Hillary Prince makes this observation in the society's quarterly newsletter, the *Edmonton Review:* "Public shows these days tend to be preoccupied with placing art into some kind of cultural or social context. I felt that it was important to show that good art cuts across styles and genres, that it expresses a kind of nonverbal aesthetic experience that is common to all art in all times and all cultures." (Spring, 1994)

In 1997, ECAS president Mitchel Smith states, "What it's about is maintaining a particular standard of quality. I think that's what links the members. I don't have a problem with saying it's elitist. ECAS doesn't lower the denominator to appeal to a larger section."[51]

Ironically then, what was once promoted as the international style has now become a regional art form with pockets of practice – or resistance, some would say – on the Prairies and elsewhere. Critical theorist, Caterina Pizanias,[52] who made a study of the overlooked role of environmental influences on Edmonton's modernist community, offers this opinion: "In some ways at least, the fall was a 'fortunate' one. Relieved of the pressures of keeping up with New York, the reluctantly dispossessed Edmonton abstractionists began experimenting with less derivative styles.... These new paintings looked quite different from what was being produced elsewhere on the continent."[53]

In other words, re-positioned as they now are on the margins, these Edmonton-based artists find their artwork looking more and more distinctive, distinguished by their apartness and particularity. Some recent developments in contemporary art, like the use of metaphor and external references, have also rubbed off giving some of these practitioners the freedom to abandon the self-referential and a strictly art for art's sake attitude. Thus, Edmonton's abstract painting is no longer simply a tale about "close-valued, subtle colour compositions and heavy, textural surfaces,"[54] nor is its steel sculpture only a matter of "relationships between forms and considerations such as surface qualities, issues related to scale, viewing parameters etc."[55] A new examination of this Edmonton-based phenomena art is long overdue.

In contemporary Alberta, there has been some very innovative abstract artwork made in the 1990s, but with perhaps the exception of Graham Peacock's arresting forms, not much of it is related to the Edmonton scene as it was or is still practiced on the Prairies. More surprisingly, a good deal of it comes out of southern Alberta and Calgary in particular, which, generally speaking, has had a stronger history of representational art. Nonetheless, there they are: the eye-bending stripes and whorls of Chris Cran's abstracts, the systematic coloured-pattern pieces of Arlene Stamp, the iconic gold leaf, formica and wood paintings of Christian Eckart, the playful geometric sponge compositions of Damian Moppett, the strange photographic/photocopy paintings of Martin Bennett, and the elegant but elaborately shredded, layered, pasted and compressed paper abstractions of Angela Inglis.

As the EAG's 1997 *Disrepresentation*[56] survey shows, there is clearly a very open-ended exploration of abstraction taking place in Alberta with a lot of energy emanating from the south. It is post-formalist in attitude, often obsessively labour-intensive, conceptual, detached, and unlike the efforts of its northern neighbour, less interested in the hands-on, subjective gesture of the artist. The romance of paint and brush has been replaced by the fastidious addition of industrial materials and technological applications. Or, as *Canadian Art* describes it: "Self-referentiality, opticality and spirituality confront incursions of irony from a younger generation of artists."[57]

chapter eleven

Navigating the Modernist Artstream

THE VIABILITY OF FAITH in the pure elements of painting was made clear in the choice of works in Robert Scott's latest show.... The aesthetics of abstraction have a tenacious hold for Edmonton artists because they imply limitless possibilities.... In Scott's case, art talking about art is still a conversation worth eavesdropping on, ❧ Lelde Muehlenbachs, *Artpost*, Summer 1989.

Painting

Robert Scott, Douglas Haynes, Graham Peacock and Terrence Keller all engage in the serious conversation about paint and picture making, first undertaken by the abstract expressionists (1940s–1950s) and then the colour field painters (mid-50s–1960s). In the eyes of Haynes, a child of the Dirty 30s and an art student of the 50s, working abstractly is all he ever wanted to do. "In art school we had to paint still life and interiors. And then I'd pick up an art journal and see a Jackson Pollock – there was the adventure!"[1]

By the time the Edmonton scene coalesces in the 70s, this adventure had been further pursued by New Yorkers Jules Olitski and Larry Poons, two influential late colour field painters with a preference for less staining and more tactile fields of monochromatic colour on a canvas. (Olitski used a spray gun while Poons threw buckets of paint at the top of hanging canvases for a cascading effect.) According to curator and critic Liz Wylie, the Edmonton participants "could be considered a 'third generation' in this high modernist dynasty, as could their counterparts working in Toronto, New York, or London, England. One factor which unites these artists is a strong interest in the painting's surface, something [earlier colour field] painters in the 1960s were trying to get away from."[2]

American critic and curator, Kenworth Moffat, suggests the third wave actually "looks past – or through – the second generation [to the first].... The new, third generation has brought back the textural effects of abstract expressionism along with its free swinging drawing style, and it has combined these features with the lessons learned from the 'colour field' generation."[3]

In Douglas Haynes's meditative *Toledo Series* of the late 1980s, colour is both subject matter and a means of expression: "The pictures seem to happen as we look at them, their glowing blocks of colour, as compelling as any image of a Mannerist saint, momentarily floating to the surface of the palpable darkness they inhabit, trailing halos of light."[4] Graham Peacock's works of the early 1990s are aggressive object-paintings: "As an artist, Peacock is not intimidated by the communicative force of colour. He relishes its obtrusiveness and insistent domination. Peacock was obviously meant to live modern times to play with high-tech fluorescent hues."[5] Terrence Keller's *November Pewter* (1988) juxtaposes areas of "thick texture with stained surfaces," creating "a physical entity, not just coloured air."[6] And then there is paint manipulator extraordinaire, Robert Scott, who can "make you feel like you're being swept away in a sea of paint."[7] Scott's method is to build up "the layers of paint, adding water, and pushing the coloured acrylic around with his hands, a long-handled brush, sticks, sponges or flat boards."[8] Shiny, reflective grains of black copper slag are then sometimes added to "clarify the drawing or to veil the surface."[9]

From the purely optical, these abstractionists each manage to take a detour away from the stained flatness of earlier colour field. Aiding this process is, of course, the ongoing transformation in acrylic-paint technology. First used by their predecessors in the colour field genre, the humble medium enters a new era in the 1970s, bolstered first by the introduction of gel and from there, a widening number of additives to make every kind of paint colour under the sun.[10] In *November Pewter,* for example, "Keller has used a highly reflective metallic pigment with the paint. Mixed in with the thick, semi-transparent gel overlay, it created the effect of light subtly shifting and changing over top of the thinly painted ground."[11]

Also important in the evolution of this late modernist practice are artist workshops, beginning with the Steiner session of 1973 at The Edmonton Art Gallery (described in the preceding chapter), and through more recent gatherings such as the annual Triangle Artists' Workshop in Pines Plains, New York. Started in 1982, a veritable who's who from Edmonton attend the first summer: Keller, Peacock, Scott and sculptors Catherine Burgess, Clay Ellis, Ken Macklin and Vesna Makale, with Peter Hide and Terry Fenton acting as two of the workshop leaders. "The Triangle," writes Russell Bingham, "refers to the three geographic points, Edmonton, New York and London, centres of what was perceived to be the most vital art-making activity."[12]

If art for the sake of art is still then, a viable option for this group, it is also on many occasions not the only thing that matters. According to Roger Boulet, "most discussions [of abstract painting and sculpture] seem to stress the technical advances," or, stress its place within the modernist canon. The curator of *Graham Peacock: Paint, Process and Spirit* (1988), Boulet proposes that, "the spiritual is a far greater realm ... because art is essentially spiritual, in as much as its process is fundamentally expressive.... When we were discussing his work, Peacock told me that he wanted his painting 'to be uplifting, joyous and inspiring.' He feels no need to explore social issues. By its very nature, his painting and process are to him a celebration of life, of creation, an affirmation of the freedom and the boundless creativity of the human spirit."[13]

Thus, persistent throughout this apparently non-objective art is a strong current of romantic energy where a work is defined as "an expression of feeling and personality ... essentially the product of an independent vision."[14] Roll this attitude into the avant-garde advances of the twentieth century and what emerges is "abstraction's visual purity – the absence of signs of anecdotal life – often accompanied by notions of spirituality and lofty idealism. During the first third of the century it was the chosen style of utopian social movements; in the post-war years, in the United States, abstraction was considered a vehicle for personal liberation."[15]

For Robert Scott: "Abstraction provides me with the most direct route to seeing. I work from an inner source; my statement would be compromised by illustrating the outer world."[16] For Doug Haynes, in reference to his stately *Toledo Series:* "I try to go for content through feelings and avoid narrative."[17] This also goes for his earlier work, in which long-time colleague Les Graff describes the painter's preoccupation with a central abstract image in his painting as a "link with himself, a conduit for feelings. All of this is too important for Doug to be satisfied with the content of formality."[18] Caterina Pizanias, in her study of Haynes, goes even further, suggesting that his inclination to make art is also influenced by his prairie background. "Douglas Haynes's inherited artistic disposition does not begin with Matisse and end with Jack Bush; it goes further back and is always tempered by his prairie roots. The prairie has been the clearing house, the unconscious and subversive source of his success. Haynes does make use of the grammar of modernism, but in order to tell his own story, by-passing the limits set by Greenbergian modernism."[19]

Meanwhile, Terrence Keller thinks of each piece as conveying a mood – an atmosphere that carries the work beyond the realm of pure painting.[20] Picking up on this aspect, Elizabeth Beauchamp observes of his 1988 one-person show at the Edmonton Art Gallery: "The musical term 'variations on a theme' seems somehow apropos to Terrence Keller's current work where the paintings brim with movement so refined that it's not merely gestural, it's dance-like."[21]

DOUGLAS HAYNES (1936, Regina, Saskatchewan) is the most senior of the Edmonton modernists, with an active exhibition record that stretches back to the early 1960s to his first one-person show at the city's Studio 60 (1960) and subsequent inclusion in the National Gallery of Canada's Fifth (1963) and Sixth (1965) Biennial exhibitions. Notably, though, Haynes thinks, "it has only been since 1977 when I started the spilt diamond series that I became a painter."[22] The split-diamond series brings him to national attention, making him, according to Karen Wilken, one of the boldest and most inventive colourists in Canada. "These pictures are particularly noteworthy," she continues, "because Haynes's local reputation was established in the 60s by richly textured, tasteful and polite monochrome canvases; his new paintings are neither tasteful nor polite, but intense and vigorous."[23] Speaking about the individual character of each picture, Haynes is later quoted, "I would keep working on them until they achieved a personality, often going through three or four until one felt right. This portrait idea carried on more or less until I ran into Cubism."[24] The spilt-diamond images lead to his first one-person show in Toronto in 1978, a 1983 survey at Regina's Norman MacKenzie Art Gallery,[25] and subsequent exposure in two national publications: *The Best Contemporary Canadian Art* (1987) and *Hidden Values: Contemporary Canadian Art in Corporate Collections* (1994).

Presenting a broader interpretation of his newer, more colourful pictures, curators Norman Zepp and Michael Parke-Taylor of the Regina survey wrote: "[Haynes's] entire career is the presence of an image which gives a sense of purpose, and reason for the act of painting, which keeps his work, unlike that of many of his contemporaries, from becoming a mere colourist exercise in the manipulation and application of paint."[26]

But the diamond motif and its numerous variations are eventually put aside in lieu of new investigations, propelled above all by a love of art, both modern and historic. As Peggy McDougall explains in *Douglas Haynes: Recent Paintings* (1988): "His travels influence him a great deal. If he sees a Matisse in Leningrad or a Goya in Madrid, he will subconsciously extract something of its feeling: a year or two down the road it will emerge in his work."[27] Haynes writes of the same subject, "The artists that become favourites are the ones that inspire me to get into the studio and start painting – to compete."[28]

Haynes's agenda is ambitious, befitting a man who is a bold member of "a generation for whom a serious art career was hardly a viable choice"[29] in Alberta when he started out. But by 1985, Haynes is ready to exhibit a new series inspired by the cubism of Picasso and Braque. Writing for *Cubism Revisited: The Paintings of Douglas Haynes* (EAG), curator Russell Bingham notes "Even though historical references in [recent] art have become fashionable, this is unexpected. [Something as dated as] Cubism appears totally foreign to the modern idea of [innovative] art-making but Haynes has managed to pull something new out of it." In these works, Haynes refashions the language of cubism and its fragmented compositions to suit modern painting techniques, materials and concerns. Reviewing Haynes's rendezvous with these two masters of the early twentieth century, Liz Wylie comments in *Canadian Art,* "It would be misleading to suggest Haynes is doing pastiches of cubist painting ... [the] new pictures are quirky but startlingly successful ... [they] have a great variety in composition, a wonderfully serious mood and some lovely surface effects."[30]

Haynes will continue with the cubist-geometric effect for a few more years after his well-received show at the Edmonton Art Gallery. The paintings, though, do not remain the same, instead becoming almost animate. They are vibrant coloured expressions of cubist ideas, with the planar shapes – which are scraped on or off the canvas – floating free of any overall composition. Colour and form seem to take their place on the canvas of their own free will. They allude to dances and battles, candies and storms, honky tonks and jives.[31] Beginning with *Zydeco* (1987), "whose colours are reminiscent of Matisse's Dance,"[32] the new series is exhibited the following year at Alberta House, London, England, earning the recommendation "for connoisseurs of international abstract painting"[33] from the *New Manchester Guardian.*

Haynes's next artistic encounter is with sixteenth-century Spanish master El Greco – "the painter of nervous dramas lit by flickering light"[34] – and his thirteen works for the Toledo Cathedral. More or less directly inspired or more accurately, provoked[35] by *El Espolio: The Disrobing of Christ,* and *Los Apostolados* – twelve half-length portraits of the apostles – Haynes works for nearly three years on *The Toledo Series.* Exhibited first at the Edmonton Art Gallery in 1991 and then toured across the country, the large acrylics with their planar shapes of strong colour freely hovering above a dark background "seem to be a hybrid of non-objective painting and painting that makes use of subject matter,"[36] comments painter Harold Feist in a review for *Canadian Art.*

A year later, still inspired by El Greco's expressionistic handling of light and colour, the long-time University of Alberta art professor (1970–1995) unveils two 21 × 9-foot canvases for Edmonton's new City Hall. *To Morning Light* and *Promise of Dusk* (1992) are described in the *Edmonton Journal* this way: "Jewel tones shimmer and float in front of a richly coloured background. Touches of gold flicker like cherubs against renaissance skies. Light radiates out from the painting and spreads through the air."[37] The latter element perhaps being a nod to the city where he has developed as an artist for more than thirty years. Haynes says, "The whole idea of rising from dark to light is what a city is all about. It's about aspirations that are pretty universal."[38] These aspirations include both the artist's wish to make masterful art and Edmonton's own progressive sense that it is more than a northern burg on the margins.

Like his three other colleagues, the late 70s – specifically 1978 – is an important juncture for **ROBERT SCOTT** (1941, Melfort, Saskatchewan) who, only a few years earlier (1976), completed a master's in visual arts at the

University of Alberta. (Doug Haynes acted as his advisor.) Rather than moving along with the general trend in formalist picture-making, "which emphasized the character of the [paint] material over the evidence of the hand," [39] Scott takes a different course: raking his fingers through one layer of paint to expose underlying layers. In other words, a sophisticated brand of finger painting that emphasizes drawing and surface effect. Of this method, Scott later writes: "While many artists in the 70s believed Pollock had taken drawing as far as it could be taken or felt that Pollock had painted them into a corner, and were looking elsewhere, I felt quite differently. I was still looking at Pollock. I felt he taught me that I must re-invent drawing for myself and had set about the task." [40]

The result of this mission, Terry Fenton later observes, "[is an] art conscious of the past. It recalls, resurrects, and even reconstructs. It looks old but new.... It seems to ruminate over expressionism in all painting, but especially in the painting of Jackson Pollock and Vincent van Gogh. By choice or by chance, Scott is appended to their 'family tree.'" [41] Reviewing Scott's first Edmonton Art Gallery solo exhibit (1978) of these literally hands-on paintings, one reviewer comments, "the rhythms of the jagged markings in *Spring Rhythms Return* give the mood of young growth, sunshine and green living things. *At War With the Angels* is dramatic with patterning and violent with colour, evoking aggressive emotions." [42]

Through the 80s and early 90s, Scott experiments with and enlarges his method by using his whole arm and shoulder instead of just his hand and wrist, and by employing tools from brooms to scrapers. Eventually, other materials such as recycled paper, lumps of dry paint and copper slag are added to the mix of acrylic and gel, prompting one writer to remark: "Scott's paintings are physical, and if they have a theme, it's called energy." [43]

Scott's art quickly attracts the attention of the corporate art sector – Cineplex Odeon, Shell Canada, Gulf Canada and so on – as well as some public art galleries. His distinctive practice is also highlighted in such group exhibitions as *Certain Traditions: Recent British and Canadian Art* (1978), *Aspects of Contemporary Painting in Alberta* (1987), *Survey Alberta '88* and Barcelona's *Casa de Caratat* (1987). There are another two solo exhibitions at the Edmonton Art Gallery, as well. The third one in 1993 is a touring exhibition that features acrylic on canvas as well as smaller acrylics on paper. Co-curator Elizabeth Kidd notes: "During the past ten years, most of Scott's paintings have increased in scale dramatically. They are expansive surfaces of texture and colour that feel more like murals or immovable fields of paint then the framed, detachable canvases they really are. Reminiscent of Paleolithic cave walls, it is not by accident that two of Scott's most recent paintings are named *Lascaux* and *Cave Mission.* In these, the built-up layers of paint resemble encrusted ancient walls that protect their history under rough surfaces and calligraphic markings."[44]

While it is rare for an Edmonton-based artist to be reviewed or discussed in a national publication, this survey of work from 1987–1993 does manage to appear in the *Globe and Mail.* Describing the practitioner as a "virtuoso ... holding something like ducal status" among Edmonton's abstractionists, John Bentley Mays goes on to say, "This important show comes as proof of Robert Scott's nearness to a culminating moment in Canadian abstract art – if he can ever free himself from the lingering provincial taste for the purely aesthetic – and the drawing-near of his own most fruitful moment as a painter of existence."[45]

Scott's long-time studio mate, **TERRENCE KELLER** (1947, Edmonton, Alberta), also has his first solo debut at the Edmonton Art Gallery in 1978. The year before, he shows in *New Abstract Art* and *Acrylic on Canvas* that include Scott, Henrick Bres, Richard Chenier, Ann Clarke, Philip Darrah, Douglas Haynes and Graham Peacock. All are based in Edmonton and appear in both exhibitions, with the addition of Bruce Dunbar, Bryan Nemish, Peter Van Santen and Nicolas Tyszka in *Acrylic on Canvas.* Clearly, something collective is afoot: a new generation of late-modernist painters whose aesthetic ambitions will put Edmonton on the map.

Not all of them, however, stay attached indefinitely. Eventually Bres and Nemish turn to landscape, while Clarke moves to Ontario. But Keller remains committed, feeling that the collective nature of the Edmonton art scene – as opposed to the idiosyncratic posturing of Calgary – is an extremely positive factor in his career.[46] As one reviewer reports, "[Scott] thrives on almost daily camaraderie from a circle of painter and sculptor friends whose criticism he welcomes. That the world has changed and become less accepting of Edmonton abstraction has made these artists even greater traditionalists, keepers of the painterly flame."[47] (1989)

In Keller's case, the flame becomes particularly bright after attending the inaugural Triangle Workshop (1982) in Pines Plains, New York. Loosening up his strategy of contrasting thick and thin paint surfaces on long, narrow canvases, Keller eventually develops a body of work that moves the eye with sweeping fields of stained colour and an overlay of thick gel-laden paint strokes. By the time of his second Edmonton Art Gallery exhibition in 1988, his pictures have become atmospheric, richer in reflective colour and tonal depth, restlessly energetic. Suggestive at times of landscape or of a voluminous curtain of rain, curator Bingham notes how his paintings "are more grandly conceived, bolder and clearer in their visual effect." [48] These canvases present an instinctive melding of colour field with the gesturally tactile: one generation's style with the tendencies of another. On a certain level, this practice involves a visual language that is foreign and esoteric to the uninitiated. But within this highly specialized art form and its philosophy of 'no post-modern agendas please, we're aesthetes,' Keller's standing is that of a "painter's painter. His cult-like following consists of a broad spectrum of artists – his public following is equally small, informed and passionate." [49]

Along with an active record of solo shows at commercial galleries, mostly in Edmonton and Calgary, Keller's work appears in numerous group shows throughout the 1980s – *Abstract Painting in Edmonton* (the Edmonton Art Gallery), *Aspects of Contemporary Painting in Alberta* (Glenbow Museum), *A Measure of Success* (Alberta College of Art Gallery), and he makes an annual appearance in The Edmonton Contemporary Artists' Society shows in the 1990s. Along with Robert Scott, Keller is one of a select group of North American artists invited to attend a Triangle Workshop in Barcelona (1988).

If Terrence Keller is a painter's painter, then **GRAHAM PEACOCK** (1945, London, England) is either a painter's nightmare or a maverick. Devoid of "fine palette work and ascetic detachment," [50] deliberately marred by jarring colour and cracked paint, his un-framable object-paintings are, as Elizabeth Beauchamp remarks to her *Edmonton Journal* readers, "works you either love or hate. Random possibilities are pushed to their limits. Images of lava flows, imaginary planets, even photos of Earth taken from space come to mind. Although this adventure into unknown territory is rooted firmly in modernist abstraction, it all has a pop art, pop culture feel. It's modernism for the post-Warhol, music video generation." [51] These words are written in response to the 1992 *Colour and Dimension* exhibition at the University of Alberta's Fine Arts Building Gallery. The English-born artist is identified by Beauchamp as "one of the most radical" of the Edmonton abstractionists, a designation that was already well established in 1988 when one critic's response is:

"Peacock, like Frank Stella, shows just how far an artist can put himself out on a limb,"[52] and the Boston curator Kenworth Moffat (Museum of Fine Arts) remembers Peacock, in 1980, for "raking paint over heavy carpets at the time and trying other 'far out' ideas, the results of which were truly ugly and made it seem to most of the other [Emma Lake] participants that he was being experimental in a naive way."[53]

Six years later, though, Moffat is describing the U of A professor of fine art as "one of the best informed and most ambitious of the abstract painters under fifty. By ambitious here I mean the irresistible drive to create something dramatically his. To this end Peacock has taken [Larry] Poons as his model and from Poons comes his large-scale experimentalism."[54] What changed? From one corner, it appears that Graham Peacock has forgotten about what constitutes taste and quality, in late-modernist camp and goes for broke. Elizabeth Beauchamp sees it this way: "Although most of his modernist colleagues have retreated into a low-key, almost monkish examination of the slightest subtlety of tone and texture, Peacock insists on taking highly public, artistic risks."[55]

Peacock's risk-taking begins in 1982 with a series of bright ultramarine blue and white paintings entitled *Polo.* By pouring thick acrylic gel wet on wet, and then letting it dry, Peacock discovers he can create a cracking or crazing effect over the entire surface of the canvas, akin, say, to the parched surface of a dried-out prairie slough where the top layer of sickly green algae has shrunk, shrivelled and cracked to reveal the primeval layers below. In the case of the paintings, what the fissures reveal are the layer of colours beneath. Thus, without laying a finger, brush, trowel or palette knife on the surface, Peacock "had his own unique 'drawing' [that] was jagged, electric and had an intensity of detail new to abstract painting."[56] Also new is the artist's wholehearted embrace of brighter, more brilliant, saturated colours, including fluorescent hues. All of this is a far cry from the tasteful, more muted coloured canvases of his late colour field peers. As Muehlenbachs later notes about his polychromatic approach, where pools of colour are poured into canvas-lined troughs and interact with other pools of colour, "Colour-field is too mild a classification, it gives way to colour topography.... The beauty of Peacock's pictures lies in the fact they don't live up to conservative preconceptions."[57]

Peacock, with an active exhibition record in the 1970s, including participation in touring group shows like *Abstraction West, Emma Lake and After* (1976) and *Canada × Ten* (1974) and two one-person exhibitions at the Edmonton Art Gallery (1972/77), returns to the gallery in 1987 with a large, five-year survey: *Paint, Process and Spirit.* As Boulet, the curator, makes clear in the catalogue, there is as much method to his madness as there is chance, with the artist directing the process of paint application, the addition of collage elements, like chunks of old canvas and stryofoam, and then choosing, cutting, contouring and shaping the final work.

By 1990, Peacock's thick plastic paint configurations are highlighted as part of a new wave of abstract art called new acrylic painting or new new painting, of which its chronicler, Kenworth Moffat, writes, "The spell cast by Olitski was broken. In [Peacock's] fully developed pictures, the surfaces, alternating from matte to shiny and smooth to wrinkled, surge forward and recede backward while the outside shape displays the same organic, undulating movement. Often they seem like strange, biological growths clinging to and moving on the wall. Sometimes the outer picture shape resembles an insect or a functional object. At other times it has a distinctly human shape or clearly forms a giant human profile."[58] One of two Canadians[59] associated with this so-called post Olitski or post colour field movement, the artist finds his artwork much in demand for new new painting exhibitions – twenty to date – in the United States and Europe. As well, he appears in at least five different foreign catalogues and one book on the movement – published in France, Germany, Korea and United States – since 1990.

Commenting on this art, American critic Donald Kuspit emphasizes what he sees as its break with the purist, impersonal and relentlessly materialistic attitude of their predecessors, Jules Olitski and Larry Poons: "[The] new new painting is, however modernist – materialistically pure – in appearance, anti-modernist (and thus post-modernist) in purpose: it aims not at selflessness, but rather to evoke and renew a lost sense of self. It turns tangible material into intangible feeling, the materialistically neutral into the emotionally articulate – the fundamental transformation that makes painting convincing. And yet the new new painting is not nostalgic. It remains pure and abstract, and the self is more suggested than presented."[60] This can also be said of Terrence Keller, Robert Scott and Douglas Haynes, even though their art is more in keeping with what is expected of late modernism. No matter how formalist this Edmonton art appears, someone made it and, as a consequence, there are fingerprints left by that individual.

This brings us to the distinctly personal and sometimes politicized abstract painting of another Alberta College of Art graduate, **ALEXANDRE (ALEX)**

SIMEON JANVIER (1935, Le Goff Reserve, Cold Lake, Alberta). Janvier is born a year before Douglas Haynes, receives his fine arts diploma from the college two years after Haynes (1960), and he presents his first solo exhibition at Edmonton's Jacox Gallery the same year the latter is showing at the Edmonton Art Gallery's *Three Man Exhibition* (1964). One of the most consistent aspects about Alex Janvier's thirty-year plus career is how often his paintings and works on paper have appeared in group exhibitions of First Nations art: from the Glenbow Alberta Institute's touring *Contemporary Indian Artists* (1968) to the much-lauded Land, Spirit, Power: First Nations (1992) twenty-five years later at the National Gallery of Canada. Within this context, the artist has been accorded much esteem and attention.

A second-generation Alberta artist who is a student of Ken Sturdy, Ron (Gyo-Zo) Spickett, Marion Nicoll, Frank Palmer and Illingworth Kerr, Janvier finishes art school the same year (1960) Canadian Aboriginals are given the right to vote. Proud of being a modernist – a soulmate even of Russian avant-garde painter Wassily Kandinsky (1866–1944) – artist/curator Robert Houle cites Kandinsky's 1911 book, *On the Spiritual in Art,* as a major early influence on the artist with Janvier later describing himself as a "mental illusionist."[61] Janvier credits Spickett for putting him in touch with art's "spiritual track,"[62] and Kerr is remembered for encouraging the young artist to "relate the abstraction of the Indians and the Paris school."[63]

Throughout his career, Janvier has reached beyond the goal of depicting the physical world, instead concentrating on conveying an individual's inner and essential feelings. Like Kandinsky, the Cold Lake First Nations artist is a pioneer, and not just because he is a significant precursor – one of the so-called Aboriginal Group of Seven – to the explosion of contemporary First Nations art in the 1980s. Importantly, the *Calgary Herald*'s Nancy Tousley sees in his art "a unique synthesis of European and Native art,"[64] as original as Marion Nicoll's fusion of the personal with modernist principles.

Robert Houle recalls: "While I was an art-history student at McGill University, Janvier's work was a source of pride. It helped me when I found myself looking at ways to understand contemporary Native sensibilities."[65] In Houle's essay prepared for the touring exhibition *The Art of Alex Janvier: His First Thirty Years, 1960–1990,* he writes: "Although modernism required the 'other' deny ethnicity, gender, sexual preference and world view, and accept assimilation as a necessary element of contemporary art, modernism as a methodology and a set of criteria was not detrimental to Alex Janvier. As an aesthetic warrior with a knowledge of the pitfalls of modernism as an ideology, Janvier is not a surviving primitive but an artist who has established a visual language of contemporary Dene symbols and images."[66]

Sense of place also plays an important theme in Janvier's painting. In such works as *Alberta Rose* (1977, acrylic on canvas) and *Colony of Alberta* (1980, oil on linen), his fluid calligraphic line and symbolic use of colour allude, respectively, to the province's exploitation of the northern boreal forest – "a tender sweet flower and yet Alberta is not that at all"[67] – while the latter's colonial theme refers both to the Canada Council's attitude toward Alberta visual art and Alberta's own attitude towards its native populations.

In the 1970s, while he has achieved some notoriety nationally within the narrow confines of late-modernist practice, within Edmonton's abstract-art community, he remains an artistic outsider. In 1973, when Alfred Schmidt curates *Alex Janvier* for the Edmonton Art Gallery, the artist realizes that "it was going to be a tough slug."[68] One of the difficulties he faces is that his evolving style does not conform to either Greenbergian abstraction or other critically received forms of abstraction like minimalism. Instead, his aesthetic trailblazing is of more interest to architects, such as the late Peter Hemingway, than to the local art elite. He receives two very high-profile public commissions, for the County of Strathcona Building (1975) and the Muttart Conservatory (1976). While he is completing the Muttart mural, he is quoted in *Arts West* as saying that artists living in the west must seek independence: "They must break with the 'New York Big Brother' schools of art and re-discover the creative pioneer spirit. Yankee curators have always voiced the opinion that Western works are only 'regionalistic copies' of the Eastern U.S. art schools. The same themes reoccur, says Janvier, with different signatures."[69]

That Janvier never felt compelled to either adhere to or break with the fashions of New York is something he attributes to his Aboriginal ancestry, where traditional decorative motifs in beadwork and porcupine quills were often abstract in design. Drawing from these traditions, the artist finds influences outside of his Eurocentric art education. "Indian art just always seemed so modern to me. It was very natural to be an abstract artist: I was already there."[70] Nevertheless, to plug into the resources of his cultural heritage, he first had to overcome a long recovery from the undermining effects of ten years of residential schooling: "They said my grandparents were evil and pagan. When you get that kind of information pounded into your head ... you don't know who you are."[71]

He spends a number of years devoting his youthful energies to teaching and administration, and he acts as a cultural advisor for the Indians of Canada Pavilion at Expo 67 in Montreal. In 1971, Janvier becomes a full-time artist with the support of his spouse, Jacqueline Wolowski, and as a form of protest, signs his art with his treaty band number, 287, for most of the decade. But steadily, as the decade progresses, he becomes more self-confident: stressing the importance of individual independence and freedom of expression in his painting, receiving out-of-province recognition and developing a very refined and highly stylized voice.

His mature compositions, sometimes referred to as "classical Janvier's," tend to contain as much negative (unpainted) as positive space, and are often energized by coloured calligraphic lines that seem like they are in motion – a luminous convoluting nebula with figures and symbols snared in its galactic field. Curator Lee-Ann Martin writes, "A distinctive synthesis of design elements and colour define Janvier's complex symbology of this time ... dots and circles are points of reference, used as metaphors for the cycle of life, embodying the unity and connection of all living things ... colour invokes emotional qualities or states of being that the artist associates with his particular subject matter."[72] Also evident in some works, like the blue and green *True West* (1975), is the presence of semi-representational imagery: eagle, fish, buffalo and feather. By incorporating such symbols within the abstract elements of his compositions, Janvier again demonstrates his refusal to adhere to the conventions of late modernism.

Not deeming it necessary to work within an art centre in order to be a professional artist, he and his family return to the English Bay reserve in 1977. From the reserve, located 300 kilometres north of Edmonton in the vast boreal region of Alberta, Janvier continues to address the treatment of Aboriginal people and the environment, but with room for reflection on and a celebration of the richness of life within the Chipewyan tradition. With symbolic references to family, community, and to his travels throughout the world, his painting is included in several group exhibitions in Canada, the United States and England, including a touring show to Belgium and France in 1975, organized by the Alberta Art Foundation. Janvier also has two important one-person shows at Gallery Moos (Toronto) and the then-named National Museum of Man (Ottawa), followed in 1978 by an exhibit at Toronto's Royal Ontario Museum. He also receives another large commission, *The Seasons* (1978–81), for the National Museum of Man. (In 1993, the same institution, renamed the Canadian Museum of Civilization, gives Janvier another major commission: a round ceiling mural, *Morning Star,* for the Grand Hall.)

As with many Alberta artists, travel has a significant place in Janvier's artistic life, particularly his trip to Linkoping, Sweden, for a solo exhibition (1977) and a Canada Council–sponsored trip to China with artists Betty Goodwin and Chris Reed (1985). He describes this latter trip as a profoundly influential experience, and upon his return, his paintings, such as *Indian Pow Wow* (1986) and *Networking Curator* (1988), become looser in form and line, and are endowed with more vivid colour, seeming to leap across the canvas or paper.

In the late 1980s, spurred on by the Lubicon Cree land claims in northern Alberta, the Meech Lake Accord, and other matters of First Nations protest regarding the environment, such as the Old Man River dam, Janvier's painting undergoes another major change from the lyrically abstract to the more blatantly realistic. Executed with a confrontational attitude of telling it "like it is," this aesthetic shift is met with concern and apprehension in the Canadian art world. Robert Houle calls it a "perilous journey,"[73] in the *Land Spirit Power* exhibition catalogue; Diana Nimeroff explains this new turn "left some observers uncomfortable";[74] while art critic Nancy Tousley, reviewing his 1990 solo show in Calgary, comments, "Janvier appears to have gone pop – leaving behind the embodiment of Native culture in abstract forms for illustrating stories about Native culture in a style that often resembles poster forms of commercial graphic art."[75]

From another point of view, the paintings made during this period, like *Intertribal Indians Unlimited* (1990), take a deliberate stab at the stereotypes about Aboriginal people in Western popular culture, mixing these images with portrayals of what life was really like before and after the arrival of the white man. According to curator Lee-Ann Martin, these paintings are "a metaphor for the attitude of most Canadians toward Aboriginal peoples, that is, they appreciate the exotic and beautiful aspects of Native arts and culture while denying the realities of the past and present."[76]

A controversial mix of image and message, the contemporary art world has always had great difficulty with Aboriginal work that treads too closely to commercial graphic art or decoration. There is also a tendency to criticize imagery that seems to be more concerned about the statement (message) than the art (medium). While Picasso was able to get away with the political content in *Guernica* because of its dramatic, cubist-inspired form, the jury is still out on Janvier's newer hybrid of abstraction and symbolism. His end-of-century painting defies aesthetic categorization, and although he is thankful that he is able to ride the surging wave of new Aboriginal art-making, he also feels that his career spans a time *before* Aboriginal art was considered Canadian: "It was safer to slot me into Indian art."[77] Quoted in the *Calgary Herald* in 1992 – the same year the National Gallery of Canada bestows recognition on contemporary First Nations art in *Land Spirit Power* – he surmises, "I don't really make Indian art. What it may be is purely Canadian."[78]

☙ The Edmonton Printmakers

Simultaneously and yet distinctly separate from the efforts of a lone maverick like Janvier, there is coalescing around the energies of the University of Alberta's Division of Printmaking (est. 1966) a dedicated group of artists who navigate a different channel of modernism. "Characterized by [their] use of abstract imagery, photomechanical processes, subdued colours and the techniques of lithography and serigraphy,"[79] these printmakers will also find themselves out of sync with the city's dominant mode of late-modernist painting and sculpture. So much so that in 1988 when the Edmonton Art Gallery finally does acknowledge the presence of this community with the exhibition *Contemporary Edmonton Prints,* curator and print historian Bente Roed Cochran is compelled to write: "In spite of their international success, Edmonton print artists are not well-supported in the local art community. Few public and commercial galleries offer exhibition venues."[80]

Throughout the 1970s and 1980s, printmakers are continually in search of places to exhibit their work, to lecture and present their views. Some of this is achieved under the auspices of the Alberta Art Foundation, which, for instance, hosts an invitational show of Albertan work in London, Brussels and Paris (1975). But as is more often the case, print artists rely upon their own tireless networking abilities to gain recognition and exposure in the international printmaking community. (Read the resume of any recognized Edmonton printmaker and you will generally find that he or she has participated in an impressive array of invitational and juried shows in Canada and abroad.) To this end, the notoriety of the printmaking program at the U of A is of great value. To quote the Ottawa-based artist Jennifer Dickson in the catalogue for *Edmonton Prints: Brazil,* which travels to Brasilia and Sao Paulo in 1988: "Long before my first visit to the printmaking division in 1984, I knew it by repute. Walter Jule was animating the Print and Drawing Council of Canada, while the prints of faculty and students were winning major international awards in print biennales from Ljubljana [Yugoslavia] to Bradford [England] and Seoul.... Faculty members Walter Jule and Lyndal Osborne are artists at the leading edge of contemporary printmaking."[81]

American-born **WALTER JULE** (1940, Seattle, United States) and Australian-born **LYNDAL OSBORNE** (1940, Newcastle, Australia) begin teaching at the U of A's Department of Art and Design in 1971. Along with Roger Silvester, an Englishman who teaches at the university from 1969 to 1982, they are part of a large influx of university-trained art instructors from the United States and the Commonwealth who arrive in Alberta in the post-1970 period. (Osborne earns her MFA in 1971 at the University of Wisconsin; Jule earns his in 1966 at the University of Washington.) Before their arrival – as Bente Roed Cochrane documents in her indispensable book *Printmaking in Alberta 1945–1985* (University of Alberta Press) – the practice of making fine-art prints is not unknown in Edmonton but through the development of the Division of Printmaking what does emerge with its undergraduate and graduate program is a high-profile centre for making print art in the city. (The Edmonton print scene is further strengthened in 1982 when two of the division's print technicians, Marc Seigner and Robin Smith, establish SNAP, Society of Northern Alberta Print Artists, a non-profit graphic workshop for intaglio, relief and serigraphy.)

Artists to emerge from the department include: Liz Ingram (b. 1949), Margaret May (b. 1951), Janet Cardiff (b. 1957), Richard Yates (b. 1949), Cherie Moses (b. 1949), Marc Siegner (b. 1956), Darci Mallon (b. 1954), Karen Dugas (b. 1957) and Sean Caulfield (b.1967). Published works and exhibitions spearheaded by the department include: the *Commonwealth Print Portfolio* (1978); Walter Jule's impressive print periodical, *Print Voice* (1984 and 1990) and exchange exhibitions such as *Edmonton Prints: Brazil* (1988) and *Sightlines* (1997), an international symposium on printmaking and image culture which is accompanied with a book edited by Jule. The printmaking division also builds up a collection of more than 1,000 prints and drawings, dating from the sixteenth century right up to the present day. Housed in the Print Study Centre (est. 1996), the print collection hails from all over the world and, in Dickson's opinion, surpasses "the permanent collection of the National Gallery of Canada in both scope and depth."[82]

Within Canada's contemporary print scene, Edmonton is perhaps best known for its early use of photomechanical techniques or incorporating photographic images into the work. Introduced by Walter Jule,[83] this relatively new tool in printmaking gives many of the Edmonton prints, especially those of the 1970s, a distinctly photo-based appearance, a sharp divergence from the more traditional etchings, block prints and lithographs of earlier Alberta artists. This technique also foreshadows other kinds of photo-based art that become so critically popular in contemporary art of the late 1980s. Thus, spurred on by a spirit of experimentation, the artwork coming out of the division – which often looks like a hybrid of photography and drawing – couldn't help but appear contemporary for its time and place. In addition, Edmonton print artists of the day have a preference for large-scale prints, for combining printmaking techniques, and, in some cases, for layering multiple images or fragmented elements that shift between the representational and the abstract, giving much of their work a sense that more than one concept permeates each piece.

As art historian Marytka Kosinski explains, "Developing a print can require long periods of time, consequently allowing an artist to become intimate with his or her primary idea while remaining open to other possibilities. It gives one the opportunity to introduce other ideas, to transpose one notion into another."[84]

In general, prints produced by Edmonton artists in the 1970s are more sensory than factual works of art. They are fluid and ephemeral, transcending everyday reality and relating the interpretation of feelings, experiences and states of consciousness. The imagery is drawn from a diverse range of sources including architectural and interior scenes, the behaviour of minor phenomena, autobiography, nature, landscape, and more recently, figurative and body-related concerns. Kosinski also suggests Edmonton's northern reality plays a role in the unique flavour of these prints: "the vast space of the country, the cultural isolation and the emptiness. They are all responding to these circumstances consciously or subconsciously and these elements are reflected in their imagery as well as in their cultural/social activities."[85]

Although it is common to think of this community in terms of the production of fine-art prints, several of its participants pursue a multidisciplinary approach to their practice, the best-known example being Lyndal Osborne and her nature-inspired sculptures and installations. Other works include: Walter Jule's installations and poster art (*Walter Jule: Selected Posters 1970–93,* FAB Gallery, Edmonton), and **LIZ INGRAM**'s (1949, Buenos Aires, Argentina) large-scale charcoal studies of female nudes, exhibited in *Under the Skin* (FAB Gallery, U of A, 1993).

Attracting the attention of the *Edmonton Journal* art critic Charles Mandel, Ingram's nudes are described as being "extremely accomplished works. British artist Lucian Freud is clearly the influence for Ingram's drawings. As with his nudes, Ingram's are meticulously rendered. Her working of tones is nothing short of exquisite." [86] One of the early graduates of the department's master's program (the oldest in the country), Ingram (MVA, 1975) appears to have absorbed some of Osborne's and Jule's interest in conveying the more microcosmic aspects of the natural world and other ephemera. Combining methods like etching, aquatint and drypoint in a single print, the artist creates dense atmospheric images composed of darkness and light. The surface of things also draws her attention, as in the action of water on the half-submerged torso of a male figure.

A long-time instructor at the university and a full professor since 1991, Ingram and others associated with the Division of Printmaking – twenty-nine artists in all – have a major opportunity to display their particular aesthetic in *Lines of Sight: Ideas, Forms and Materialities* (1999), a travelling exhibition (London, Tokyo and Calgary) [87] that marks twenty-five years of activity at the school. Of the exhibition, Lawrence Smith of the British Museum observes, "On the whole these are big prints, and while they mix techniques which many would still argue should be kept separate ... they do in fact combine methods requiring long and exacting training.... Both size and materiality keep the printmaker rooted in the physical world." [88]

Although not associated with the University of Alberta, **DARCI MALLON** (1954, Edmonton, Alberta) also knows something about this hands-on physical world. An art instructor and printmaker working across town at Grant MacEwan Community College, Mallon, who has an MFA in painting from Toronto's York University (1980), develops a new series in 1990 where the images are composed of hundreds of thumb and hand prints applied by the artist. Taking what could be a child's technique for making art, Mallon's rudimentary pictures of a spike, a tack and a hook are made on layers of huge sheets of transparent mylar, which are then backlit for display in a darkened gallery. [89] She describes these illuminated, hanging "impressions" [90] as drawings, and uses the same method to create articulate images of gesturing hands for her one-person Edmonton Art Gallery exhibition, *Engrams* (1995). Simple and yet extremely complex in their making, detailed and yet remarkably direct in what is being depicted, these strange representations preserve the kind of movement and drama seen in her bold linocuts of the 1980s.

Stark, black-and-white linocuts, woodcuts and drypoint prints also figure prominently in the career of RICHARD YATES (1949, Edmonton, Alberta). Along with Mallon, Yates, who is a U of A printmaking graduate (1983), is one of the few artists out of Edmonton to have worked extensively in what is the oldest method of making a print: the so-called relief method. Pinpointed by Roger Boulet in 1993 as being at the forefront of Edmonton print art,[91] Yates's unique interpretations of the western landscape come from a very personal and symbolic perspective, and bring to mind the art of Barbara Milne and Robbin Yager. More abstract than the paintings of the two Calgarians, though, Yates's large-scale prints with their vivid clean lines and "glowing intensity"[92] rely on a strong sense of drawing that relate to his dreams and visits to Aboriginal sites in southern Alberta. In 1992, the artist enlarged his oeuvre (which includes painting and pastel works) in *Pond-around Ritual,* a three-part installation rich in metaphor about the Prairies, past and present.[93]

There is no question the post-1970 efforts of printmakers such as those based in Edmonton and elsewhere broaden the printmaking scene significantly throughout the province. But even with its best creative intentions, the critical reception to this multi-faceted medium at the end of the century is ambivalent. As print curator Michelle Grandbois explains in the *Sightlines* book: "After the great success prints had enjoyed in the sixties and seventies came the letdown of the eighties. There were still exceptional works being produced, but the art community's attitude towards printmaking was no longer a positive one. Some said that printmaking was too easy and too influenced by market demands.... Other voices denounced [printmakings'] arts and crafts nature, seeing it as a technical rather than a creative art."[94] Although this comment is made in reference to the Quebec art scene, Grandbois's observations could easily apply to printmaking in the rest of the country. Like painting in the seventies, the making of original prints is assigned to art-world purgatory in the 1980s. To aggravate matters more broadly, this shift coincides with the commercial marketing of the so-called limited edition print where a popular painter reproduces his or her paintings in the form of a print and then signs it and sells it as something special, i.e. a limited-edition print when in fact it is nothing more than a glorified poster. This marketing phenomenon is unrelated to the efforts of bonafide printmakers but it affects their reputation all the same.

Unlike painting, however, which made somewhat of a comeback in the early 1980s, printmaking is still searching for critical credibility, in Canada at least. According to curator Diana Nimeroff of the National Gallery, who addresses the whole thorny issue in an interview with Jennifer Dickson in *Sightlines:* "The print is, in one sense, very much at odds with the broad image culture. Broad image culture is the inheritor and elaborator of concepts first put forward by conceptual art, which shifted the focus away from the medium, away from technical virtuosity, and also away from the author: i.e. the artist as a holder of personal vision. On each one of these counts printmaking finds itself at odds. Therefore, from this point of view, the position of printmaking is marginal." [95]

Leaving Dickson to lament, "Ironically, contemporary Canadian printmakers have become well known abroad but are still largely ignored at home." [96] A situation that, as Edmonton's printmakers can attest, continues to be the case right up to the end of the century and beyond.

chapter twelve

Abstract Sculpture and a Dissenter

In 1985, CALGARY ART CRITIC NANCY TOUSLEY identifies Edmonton as being "known as the stronghold of sculpture in Alberta," [1] while director Terry Fenton, in reference to a stellar showing of eleven local sculptors at the Edmonton Art Gallery declares, "[The exhibition] shows why Edmonton has attracted the attention of serious sculptors and critics elsewhere in the world. It explains and justifies the [exhibition] title *Sculpture City.*" [2]

Four years later, though, in a large Alberta-wide exhibition in Calgary, guest curator Nicholas Roukes suggests the abundance of three-dimensional art in the province is actually "a pluralistic phenomena, identifiable by a rich diversity of artistic styles, individual goals and innovative studio practices." [3] While there certainly is the steely abstract sculpture of such Edmontonians as Peter Hide, Catherine Burgess and Alan Reynolds to consider, the *other* artists in Roukes's survey indicate a much broader story needs telling, including the one pertaining to those who work in metal but are unrelated to the Edmonton group – names such as Katie Ohe, Tony Bloom, Ian Cook, Ben McLeod and Roy Leadbeater.

So, how did Edmonton and a certain cadre of artists trump the field and become Sculpture City? According to the *Edmonton Journal*, "[The] seeming ever-presence of the steel sculptors comes from the fact that there are about a dozen professional artists working within this idiom and their work has been seen in many group shows in Edmonton, at the EAG and elsewhere."[4] In other words, they had the critical mass and an ample supply of exposure. This exposure earns them both praise – British sculptor Sir Anthony Caro refers to Edmonton steel sculpture as "probably the best in the world"[5] – and criticism – the *Ottawa Citizen* reports in 1995; "Like a remote South Pacific cargo cult, some sculptors in the west are still worshipping at the shrine of Clement Greenberg's aesthetic theories, producing assemblages of cold, unreferential steel."[6] In any case, just like the fate that befalls Edmonton's abstract painters, many of these committed modernists will find themselves in the last decade of the century exiled to the periphery of Canadian contemporary art.

There are a few exceptions. For instance, in *The Other Alberta Sculpture*[7] (1995), at Ottawa's Carleton University Art Gallery, Catherine Burgess and Isla Burns are singled-out by curator Michael Bell as being different from "the mainstream of Alberta metal sculpture.... One distinguishing characteristic of this *Other Sculpture* is its capacity to refer beyond itself – to offer the possibility of meaning – both for the artist and the viewer."[8] In other words, their abstract configurations are interpreted as being a rebuttal to the late-modernist stance that "Pure form is Good. Recognizable content is Bad."(Elizabeth Beauchamp)[9] But is it all that black and white? Caterina Pizanias, who made a study of this group and earned a master's degree for it suggests a different scenario:

> What is really happening in Edmonton? Since the economic collapse, a revised 'open' or 'blurred' modernism has been practiced by Edmonton's steel sculptors, creating a successful idiom to deal imaginatively with life in the city. These sculptors, by challenging the master narrative [the legacy of New York abstract art and Caro] and acknowledging (however consciously or unconsciously) the prairie's presence as the physical and cultural other, not only create an authentic voice, but also open the doors of heterogeneity of texts without a hierarchy.[10] ☙ *Of Earth and Steel: Taming the Prairie in Canada,* 1989.

Of course, things do not start there. The story of Edmonton Steel begins in the 1970s with the young Alan Reynolds and Catherine Burgess working in wood, a feature Terry Fenton suggests detached their art "from the overpowering influence of Anthony Caro's steel sculpture and influenced the subsequent development of sculpture in the city." [11] Then there is the arrival of Ken Macklin and Isla Burns, the first students in this emerging scene "to work consistently in steel." [12] Next comes the more senior British sculptor Peter Hide in 1977. Later acknowledged as "the chief engineer of Edmonton's abstract heavy-metal scene," [13] Hide is hired by then art and design department head Douglas Haynes to run its sculpture program at the University of Alberta. A former student of Caro's, Hide, who is now working professionally, remembers his years in London feeling "trapped between becoming a disciple of Caro on the one hand, and abandoning all sense of the sculptural object [i.e. conceptual art], as required by the nihilist school on the other." [14] His solution, according to Fenton, is to develop his art in a "post-Caro" [15] manner, something that "in combination with the work already being done in Edmonton, led to a kind of sculpture that was neither geometric and repetitive like minimal art, nor linear, space consuming and pictorial like Caro's." [16] Caterina Pizanias believes that this new work also reflects Hide's encounter with the prairie: "His sculpture has become more and more physical, less like Caro's, and much larger in scale. Though it is still a variation of his landmark monolith, it has lost the patina of learned modernism and has acquired the characteristics of Edmonton's context." [17]

As for the criticism that Hide is a bloodless formalist making cold, unreferential art, he identifies formalism more with *a style of art criticism* than the art itself. "I don't know of any artists who just make art to arrange shapes and forms as a pleasing end in themselves. I think it's a stick that's been used to beat us." [18] Similarly, the opinionated Al Reynolds believes, "It's always been assumed that we abstract sculptors are stupid and can't say anything but 'Yeah, well I just put that bit of steel with this bit of steel'. And that's not the case." [19]

The wunderkind of the Edmonton sculpture scene in its early days, (LESLIE) ALAN REYNOLDS (1947, Edmonton, Alberta) is an interesting example of how, both literally and figuratively, the sharp angular edges of youthful art making are eventually pared away by what curator Mark Joslin assesses to be "an even more urgent intent of using artwork as a vehicle of personal expression." [20] In Reynolds's case, his art becomes more sensitive to life experiences, such as the birth of his second son (*Womb Series*, 1982), more appreciative of artistic sources other than modernism (for instance, Indian, Chinese and Cambodian sculpture) and an expression of what in the late 1980s the artist describes as "an inventory of myself."[21] The Edmonton-born artist also practices what the *Globe and Mail* art critic John Bentley Mays views as "an absolute seriousness about material practice.... Not for Reynolds, Hide and company [are] the abstemious, calculating, hands-off strategies of much postmodern art today. When Edmonton abstractionists talk about work, they appear to mean it in the solidly satisfying sense of job – making things with your hands for a living – and not in the postmodern sense of a career. If you ever want to know exactly what I'm talking about, spend a couple of minutes watching Hide and his assistant making steel sculpture with the seriousness of a couple of bridge builders."[22]

In addition, local observers such as Helen Collinson and Lelde Muehlenbachs (respectively) describe Reynolds's career as a "changeable, quixotic and deft love affair with visual art,"[23] brimming with "many twists and turns."[24] These aspects of his art are given a full airing in the exhibit *Inner Motifs: Fifteen Years of Exploration* (EAG). Spanning 1974 to 1990, during this period Reynolds renders sculpture not only in steel (1978–), but in wood (1968–80), clay (1985, 1989/90, 1996) *and* clay and steel (1986–1990). Largely considered self-developed – though he does study at the U of A for a few years – Reynolds's initiation into what is loosely described as constructivist sculpture occurs through a process of looking and doing; he participates, for instance, in the 1973 Michael Steiner workshop, a highly touted event in the Edmonton story.

Reynolds's sculptural output is so promising that by 1977, three of his free-standing painted wood sculptures (constructed of plywood, two-by-fours, and smaller pieces of wood) are included in the prestigious *14 Canadians: A Critic's Choice* at the Hirshhorn Museum in Washington, D.C. He and abstract painter Bruce O'Neil are the only Albertans in the show, an event that even today would be a rare occurrence. Critic Andrew Hudson highlights Reynolds as "the one Canadian sculptor who is expressing in his work something truly his own."[25] Fame comes swiftly to the then thirty-year-old artist who, at least in his own hometown, brings an edgy, charged face to the generally circumspect modernist scene. As Karen Wilken observed about the artist's creative disposition, including his lively improvisational attitude: "[Reynolds is] perhaps the closest to [David] Smith in spirit of any of his generation."[26]

Although his planar, geometric work of the 70s is generally analyzed for its formal ambitions, there are those commentators who can't quite help but see other things. For instance, of Reynold's first solo exhibit at the EAG (1974), Marytka Kosinski writes: "Examination of these sculptures invokes associations difficult to define. They go beyond all the formal aspects of Reynolds's art. It is rather a feeling about impalpable and distant alliances between Reynolds' art and the real, utilitarian objects, found abandoned in the old Canadian farms, including the old homes and barns." [27] Two years later, a *Vancouver Sun* reviewer notes that his open box-shaped pieces "[from] a distance, assume a quasi-architectural aspect, suggesting perhaps a medieval town or, at the other extreme, a futuristic model for a mass housing project." [28] And even when Reynolds did venture into the late modernist realm of cutting and welding steel plate to make abstract sculpture (his first solo exhibit of such work was at Edmonton's the Downstairs Gallery, 1981), his art never becomes 100 percent formalist or preoccupied with only the form. Quite the contrary. As Joslin notes in the *Inner Motifs* catalogue, the first series [of *Folded Wing* sculptures] Reynolds identifies as being directly affected by his personal experience.[29] The artist also remembers that these pieces are deeply influenced by the viewing of Smith's early work in the exhibition *David Smith: The Formative Years,* curated by Wilken for EAG in 1981.

This mix of formal and referential considerations continues to be evident in Reynolds's art, which will include both large-scale and table-top examples. Nancy Tousley, in a 1986 review of his new steel sculpture, observes that: "Often the abstract works suggest images: landscape, architecture, figures." [30] By the end of the 1980s, his sculpture has become so strongly figurative that the successful pieces seem to have a life of their own. Visually, the forms are generally upright and vertical, a collage of both geometric and oddly-cut shapes juxtaposed and arranged into artworks that bandy and spar with the imagination. These variations in style prompt one critic to remark: "Reynolds' work has been accused over the years of selling out to elegance, seductive surface treatment, glitz and dominant pictorialism." [31] While all these charges have some weight, they are too narrow in focus, pertaining only to what many imagine welded-steel sculpture to be about: hard-nosed, hard-hearted and hard-hat heavy metal art. In Muehlenbachs's view, "[Reynolds] is a survivor whose art is marked by its elegance and heart." [32]

CATHERINE BURGESS (1953, Ponoka, Alberta) is also a survivor, and of all her Edmonton colleagues, she is the one who will weather the challenges of being an Edmonton modernist the best, maintaining a regional and national reputation throughout her career. (Although, at the time of this writing, she nor any of her colleagues have been included in the National Gallery of Canada's collection, nor has *Canadian Art* reviewed or devoted any substantial space to the "blurred modernism"[33] in Edmonton.) Her record of exhibitions, catalogues and articles is impressive, and her pristine art has even received consideration outside of the context of steel sculpture, included in such group exhibitions as *Multiple Associations: Five Alberta Artists*[34] (1988), *New Economy* (1994) and *Oldman River Expedition*[35] (1991). (Clay Ellis and Isla Burns have also had some cross-over success, while Blair Brennan, the "enfant terrible,"[36] left the genre completely in 1986.) Within a larger context, Burgess's succinct pieces illustrate that no matter how curators and/or critics may want to define, praise, or dismiss a particular genre, ultimately it is the individual artists who, over years of practice, make the art what it is. Thus, her oeuvre is a kind of bellwether, signalling how the Edmonton sculpture scene has never really stood still.

The reason Burgess has survived so well can be attributed to a couple of factors. One is the continuing distinctiveness of her art – an "idiosyncratic vision"[37] is how one Ottawa reviewer described the grace and simplicity of her art. The other is the artist's much-publicized departure from the formalist preoccupations of the local community. "In the medium of steel, Burgess's direction is the most individual in Edmonton right now and no one should take away from that accomplishment by criticizing the work as minor, stiff, political, feminist or what have you. It's all beside the point because she's opened not just one door but many."[38]

Doors that were pushed open gradually, through "the influences of travel, place and architecture; motherhood; working in isolation; long absences from the studio; a critical personal turning point; and psychoanalysis."[39] Discovered is the importance of personal or lived experience in the shaping her art. Connected to this is also the matter of Burgess's gender due to the overwhelmingly masculine connotations associated with steel sculpture. But Burgess will redefine this "heavy metal" preoccupation on her own terms. One example is the surprising series of small, linear bronze pieces displayed in *Sculpture City*. Of these pieces, Caterina Pizanias wrote, "Some people referred to these pieces as renditions of the prairie surface. The [pregnant] artist recalls that she was conscious of the small life growing inside her, which was making her introspective and eager to work with small pieces."[40]

Burgess was an undergraduate student at the University of Alberta when the sculpture department still had a conceptual art slant – before the arrival of Peter Hide. She developed her formalist orientation after graduating in 1975. First came a six-year period (1975–1981) of constructing abstract wood sculptures, during which time she gradually acquired all the right pedigree for Edmonton modernism. This included a six-month stint sharing a studio with Alan Reynolds (1975), four years as a preparator and registrar at the EAG (1975–79), an Emma Lake workshop with Anthony Caro (1977), the beginning of a part-time sessional position in Hide's sculpture department (1978–1985), solo exhibits at major public venues such as the Edmonton Art Gallery (1979) and the Mendel Art Gallery (1980) and participation in such catalogued group shows as *Alberta Works in Wood* (1979, A.C.A. Gallery) and *Alberta Now* (1980, EAG, juried). Of her later chunky, compact painted-wood sculptures, curator Wilken remarked: "It's hard to imagine that Burgess would be as good as she is if Alberta and Saskatchewan hadn't offered a particular kind of nourishment for sculptors since about 1972."[41]

After switching to scrap and discarded steel in 1981, her modernist pedigree continued to expand, with an invitation to Anthony Caro's Triangle Workshop (1982), a touring exhibit of her new metal work[42] curated by Terry Fenton and inclusion in such group shows as Edmonton's *Universiade Steel Sculpture Exhibition* 1983, Sun Life Building), *Edmonton Steel* (1983, Beaver House Art Gallery), the much-celebrated *Sculpture City* (1985, EAG) and the outdoor *Sculpture By Invitation* (1986, Law Courts Building). Burgess is also discussed (along with Alan Reynolds, Peter Hide, Ken Macklin and Clay Ellis) in Burnett/Schiff's *Contemporary Canadian Art* (1983, Hurtig Publishers).

But even with all of these accomplishments as a member of the collective, or what Fenton identifies as "the Edmonton style,"[43] by 1986 Burgess is able to say, "my work differs a good deal from that of a lot of my colleagues."[44] Aesthetically, she never becomes a maker of what many in the public view as raw, rusty, monumental hunks of steel welded into obtuse abstract shapes.[45] Instead, she emerges as a sculptor of some finesse: a collector and synthesizer of visual experiences, especially those derived from travel and looking at architecture, particularly Mayan (which affected the stacked shape of her later wood pieces), ancient Egyptians temples, and a little later, the designs of the Renaissance master, Andrea Palladio.

In *Multiple Associations: Five Alberta Artists,* her five low-to-the-ground steel structures with their careful arrangement of "flat planes, arches, spheres, rectangles, triangles and circles,"[46] writes curator Katherine Ylitalo, "acknowledge the historic and familiar objects which come into play in these sculptures. The works are called 'altarpieces', and they have a kinship with the hearth, centre of the home, and with the altar, centre of the temple."[47] Her inclination is toward simplified forms and a remarkable economy of means, in which a little seems to go a long way, a style that is in direct contrast to the tendency of many Edmonton sculptors to create clusters of steel elements welded together.

Burgess's individual characteristics become especially pronounced in her work of the late 1980s, when the architectural influences give way to other concerns. With a series of semi-abstract works in 1990, collectively entitled *Things As They Are,* Burgess fabricates low, table-like sculptures with small geometric objects welded to their smoothly polished steel surfaces. Heralded as "a new and important development"[48] by Elizabeth Kidd, then EAG curator, who describes the works as "still-lifes of the subconscious," in which the objects (circles, cylinders, squares, disks) are "associated with people and landmarks in her life." According to the artist, "They were about looking back to my past to seek understanding of self."[49]

Of this long-simmering move into personal narrative, the then thirty-seven-year-old sculptor says, "It was about the same time [1985] that I became a mother and I realized that I no longer wanted to be one of the boys. That was how I had functioned as a sculptor and that now seemed ridiculous. I wanted to make work that was more about me and allowed that me to be a female me."[50] (Interestingly, parenthood was also a significant marker for fellow Edmonton sculptors Alan Reynolds and Blair Brennan.)

Things As They Are continued as a body of work, but underwent some startling changes. By the time of her next exhibition in 1994, organized by Lethbridge's Southern Alberta Art Gallery, her work has transformed from pure sculpture, free-standing and self-contained, into installation pieces, where the viewer is free to walk around the sculptural elements. The tabletop element becomes a large, thin plate of steel hung on the wall, while the objects are enlarged and placed on the floor as a few simple, evocative shapes: steel bowls, coils of wires, boxes, thin steel bars. "In many ways they are meditations on the nature of form itself, and on the way meaning can inhabit form,"[51] explain the artists, describing the long rectangular plate in the background as "the storehouse of experience which we bring to each act of perception and understanding."

Rigorous looking yet strangely alluring, these more recent incarnations give the viewer an open invitation to create his or her own reading of *Things As They Are.* Beyond their non-decorative, modernist appearance, Burgess's spare installations are wedded to new goals. Curator Bruce Grenville describes them as "alternative notions of abstraction and lived experience." [52] At the same time, these installations suggest a strong connection to the prairie, with its deep, enigmatic space – alluded to by the horizontal steel plate – and its humble topography of stark elements, both natural and handmade. But however they are interpreted, on one level these works simply are what they are: strong sculptural shapes that demonstrate a truly distinctive voice among a community of sculptors who put Edmonton on the cultural map.

For **ISLA BURNS** (1952, Calcutta, India), **CLAY ELLIS** (1955, Medicine Hat, Alberta) and **KEN MACKLIN** (1952, Edmonton, Alberta), their involvement in sculpture is related not only to the flourishing of Edmonton Steel, but also to the city itself, which Burns refers to as a steel quarry [53] because of its heavy industry and metal fabrication. This combination of art and industry creates an opportunity for practitioners working in steel to make what Pizanias describes as "superphysical" [54] work. There is the material, the know-how, and according to Burns, herself a trained industrial welder, the spatial presence of the prairie. "The openness of the prairie invites and daunts the artist and we could carry on, all of us together, for the next forty years making those sort of [large] size pieces and still never fill up the prairie. There is a sort of invitation in a way." [55] And it is in this sense that she, Ellis and Macklin have distinguished themselves as makers of superphysical work: large in scale and ample in form. This is by no means the sum total of their individual oeuvres, but it is one factor that puts them in an arena apart from Burgess.

However, working on such a large scale has had its consequences. Right through to the end of the twentieth century, modernist sculpture remains largely incomprehensible to a vast segment of Canadian society, and when sited in public areas, provokes debate. All three artists have experienced this situation firsthand. Clay Ellis's massive hard-edge, outdoor piece in Red Deer is, "roundly hated by the citizenry and was repeatedly vandalized," [56] according to *Canadian Art,* while Isla Burn's 3400-kilogram, 7-metre-long *Caravel* is received with sceptical appraisal. "Passersby stop in their tracks at sight of [the] stainless steel creation at city hall," [57] reports *the Edmonton Journal,* and in the same paper there is an article about a commissioned Ken

Macklin being rejected by the Canadian Polish Congress after months of debate concerning its merit.[58]

But these setbacks do not impede these committed artists. Philip and Muriel Berman of Pennsylvania, identified as "tireless collectors of international sculpture,"[59] sponsor Macklin and Ellis, along with Peter Hide, to each produce an outdoor piece for their collection, "stipulating only that the work be large."[60] In 1995, the Berman's loan these sculptures, along with seventeen other steel and stone works collected from Britain and the United States, for display in the pastoral surroundings of Grounds for Sculpture – a sculpture park in Hamilton, New Jersey.

By the early 1990s, Burns, Ellis and Macklin have each developed a singular practice that neither seriously alters their allegiance to late modernism nor prevents them from making excursions into other, more referential areas. Their modernism had become just as blurred as Burgess's and Reynolds's – adding yet more shades of grey to the Edmonton steel scenario. In recognition of this, the Edmonton Art Gallery organizes *Three Alberta Sculptors: Ken Macklin, Isla Burns, Clay Ellis* in 1993. In support of the artists, Caterina Pizanias argues, "the work of these sculptors cannot be accommodated within either of the orthodox canons [modernism and postmodernism], their contributions cannot be reduced to either of the inherited schemata without doing disservice to it."[61]

With a diploma in sculpture (1974, Alberta College of Art) and a master's of visual art from the University of Alberta (1978), Isla Burns is considered to be a heavy-metal master of Edmonton steel. But instead of chanting the influences of Picasso-Gonzales-Smith-Steiner-Caro-Hide (the Edmonton "mantra,"[62] says Burns), the artist refers to the early impact of Calgary's Katie Ohe and European sculptors Lipchitz and Brancusi. Her sculptures are solid, muscular and powerful, and they are assembled from sliced, stacked and shaped steel forms. She seems to revel in the weight and materiality of industrial steel, while simultaneously exploiting its potential for complex configurations and even ornamentation – she is said to use her welding torch like a cake decorator. Through a process of adding and constructing, carving and grinding, she creates surprising arrangements that often feature welded clusters of small, angular and circular shapes. It can make for sensual, playful work that paradoxically remains "as earthbound as any sculpture could be."[63] Combined with her meticulous finishes that soften the recycled steel to an elegant glow, the artist transforms what can be viewed as a hard, uncompromising material into something malleable and alive with allusion.

It has been suggested that some of her smaller, tabletop pieces, organized around a low bowl or conical vase, "evoke abstracted still lifes"[64] or things that "you look into rather than look at."[65] In the 1990s, these smaller works are followed by a series of larger, altar-like pieces: squat steel tables laden with a clustering of cut-steel objects and crowned with a steel arch. Their titles – *Altar for Ganesh* (1993), *Altar for Kali* (1993) and so on – leave no doubt as to their subject matter. Based upon her "spiritual journey through life,"[66] these pieces are inspired by an eye-opening return visit to India, plus earlier exposure to the Bumper Corporation's collection of Hindu sculpture (on loan to the Edmonton Art Gallery in 1985).

Ken Macklin and Clay Ellis also find inspiration in the 1990s: the former pursuing the god of energy (weightlessness, expression and movement), the latter merging "bodyness" (bulging organic volumes) with divine abstraction. While the result is two very divergent voices, both sculptors, along with Burns, continue to share an interest in large-scale, superphysical works unlike anything that has come out of Edmonton before. Macklin, for instance, the most adamant as a modernist, is making sculpture interpreted as being "more reminiscent of the open harmony found in a prairie sky, field or even river than a crowded, industrial British city,"[67] while Lelde Muehlenbachs writes, "despite their scale, the pieces are light and airy – Macklin seems to joyously toss circles into the air with the ease of blown soap bubbles."[68] About Clay Ellis' stained steel sculptures, she comments, "compared to what we have some to expect of steel, these pieces appear ghost-like and give off a sense of menacing disorientation. Bizarre containers are suggested which are in part samovars, plants, vaginas, protruding lips, even rockets."[69]

Of all the sculptors associated with Edmonton steel, Ellis emerges as the most provocative and inventive. In a few short years, he goes from the intuitive and improvisational practice of constructing abstract sculpture out of scraps of steel, to modeling and casting entire preconceived works, first out of iron and bronze, and more recently out of industrial plastic. The rounded metal works, such as *Medicine Hat* (cast iron, 1994), are unmistakably sculptures and are linked to his less well-known excursions into clay. The works in colour-saturated polyurethane, meanwhile, imply other mediums entirely. Oval shaped, hung on the wall or suspended on a steel frame, these flattened, barely three-dimensional pieces look unmistakably like paintings – striped, hard-edge paintings reminiscent of Kenneth Noland in the heyday of 1960s abstract art. First exhibited in 1998 in the EAG group exhibition

Looks Like...,[70] Ellis turns the tables on the separate disciplines of abstract painting and sculpture by stating: "These sculptures are representations of paintings. Not specific paintings, but what we generally think paintings to be. Placing these 'signs of paintings' in a gallery underlines how much art loses its function in contemporary culture. They are no longer filled with cultural, allegorical, personal or historical meaning, but become neutralized objects of connoisseurship."[71]

In other words, the sort of objects that critics of the Edmonton school and late-modernist art had begun to openly reject 1980s. Thus, Ellis is less of a rebel than many might think. His dialogue and his loyalties continue to be concerned with abstraction. Although, like other contemporary artists who have carried on a dialogue with this practice through to the end of the century and beyond, Ellis, through these unusual and uncategorizable works, seeks to widen the horizon of abstract practice in Edmonton.

Together, the presence of Ellis, Burns and Macklin help to change the perception of Edmonton monolith sculpture as immovable, impenetrable and anonymous. Gone are the hard, angular edges of the previous decade, and the resolute posture of Edmonton steel formalism. Instead, glimmers of a broader artistic sensibility emerge.

Of the metal sculptors already discussed in this chapter, no other artist has more name recognition than **PETER HIDE** (1944, Surrey, England). Described earlier as the chief engineer of Edmonton's heavy-metal abstract scene, Hide has run the apprenticeship-based sculpture program at the University of Alberta since 1977, and he has come in contact with just about every local artist involved with the practice. A group photo taken by Eleanor Lazare for the EAG's seminal exhibition *Sculpture City*[72] (1985) shows Hide standing alongside nine other casually dressed sculptors. Of these nine associated with Edmonton steel, five have studied with Hide at the University – Macklin, Andrew Klimczak, Lyle Lis, Vesna Makale and Blair Brennan. (The others in the photo are Reynolds, Burgess, Burns and Ellis.)

In addition to his work at the U of A, Hide is a seminal figure at international artist workshops, most significantly the international Triangle sessions (Pine Plains, New York), founded by Anthony Caro and Robert Loder in 1982. Both in 1982 and again in 1985, Hide participates in the workshop as sculpture leader. (Ellis and Macklin are also present the first year, and Burns attends her first Triangle in 1984.) Then in 1986, Hide, Ellis and Burns travel to Norwich, England, for the Hardingham Sculpture Workshop, and the next year, along with Macklin, attend the overseas Triangle session in Barcelona, Spain. (The city's Museum of Contemporary Art has work of all four artists in its permanent collection.)

Hide is also a regular in Edmonton-based group exhibitions, such as the outdoor show *Sculpture by Invitation* (inaugurated in 1986) at Edmonton's Law Court Plaza and the annual Edmonton Contemporary Art Society show (inaugurated in 1993). Further afield, he exhibits, for instance, in *Hide & Ellis: Two Edmonton Sculptors* (1997) at Fort Lauderdale's Museum of Art. "Hide's work has a grand, heroic mode of address. Ellis, on the other hand, is distinctly non-heroic, intimate, even playful and humorous. Hide likes sharp angles and edges and usually offers a dense composite of geometric planes,"[73] observes curator Kenworth Moffat.

However, art, it seems, can't do without its heroes and villains, and depending on what side of the fence you are positioned on, Hide can be either. Despite his long presence on the Edmonton scene, and the recognition he continues to receive within the modernist community – London's Tate Gallery, for example, acquired another work in 1988 – by the end of the century Peter Hide has also been relegated to the margins of contemporary Canadian art. Described as grand, heroic, monolithic and masculine – Hide himself is personally referred to as man of steel – his work is generally greeted with disapproval from postmodernist circles. To make matters worse, there is a prevailing view that Edmonton steel has been his creation alone, while all the other artists have taken their cues from him.

But all this is a bit far-fetched. While there is no doubt that Hide's arrival as professional sculptor in 1977 helps galvanize the already-developing sculpture scene in Edmonton, the depth and breadth of work produced in the city, especially since the 1990s, attests to a much broader artistic input than can be attributed to one man alone. Rather than being at the apex of some imaginary ladder, Hide, from a modernist perspective, was more concerned with his own personal goal – to overcome what Terry Fenton once labelled, "The mark of Caro."

In his youth, Hide had been a graduate student at St. Martins School of Art (1964–67) and then an instructor at the school from 1971–78. Reflecting on his mindset of that time as a promising young artist, Hide writes in 1995: "Intuitively, I was groping towards a more personal sense of form, a heavy, robust, compressive type of sculpture."[74] According to Fenton, Hide was successful in this endeavour, creating a sculptural style that, "instead of spreading and sprawling, gathered together and compacted. It was monolithic instead of pictorial."[75] In other words, Hide found a style that wasn't anything like that of his former St. Martins instructor, Anthony Caro, whose "open collage-type sculpture, more optical than tactile, more pictorial than three-dimensional,"[76] was a high point of 1960s modernism.

Further discussing the development of his artistic sensibilities, Hide explains: "This style [Caro's] depended on a certain evenness of emphasis; you were not supposed to have focal points or a core.... The skill lay in ensuring that junctions [between different parts of the sculpture] did not form dominant clusters or focal points.

"Verticality, [work] too redolent of the human figure was eschewed; even the wavy spine of Alexander Calder's mobiles were frowned upon; anything, in fact, that suggested the image of the human figure or the organic geometry of plant, crystal or skeletal growth was avoided. An all over effect in some ways similar to that of Jackson Pollock's painting was sought.

"The 'untouched by human hands' approach of the sixties [Minimalism] was also something that I, like many young artists, felt was getting in the way. I was searching for a way of working with volume and weight in an animated and compressive way that showed my hand."[77]

That Hide would eventually develop a style different from the critically approved styles of his teachers is nothing new in the annals of art, but in his case, it had less to do with being a rebel than with his own personal inclinations. In his words: "I was never particularly comfortable with the delicate art of placement,"[78] he states, then continues with: "I'm very interested in Gothic architecture and sculpture, [as well as] baroque architecture, particularly Borromini. This period, just at the beginning of the baroque is the most sculptural; where building facades are moulded in curves and there's a great feeling of movement and weight."[79] Over time, these proclivities resulted in a type of constructed sculpture for Hide that wasn't "all that far removed from the traditional view of sculpture as monolith."[80] By adopting a strong vertical format, Hide believes he rediscovered the figure for abstract welded steel sculpture,[81] something he was already technically familiar with from life drawing classes taken during his training at Croydon College of Art (1961–64).

Hide's method of making art also sets him apart. Describing Hide as "a different kind of welder and assembler than the steel sculptors who came before him,"[82] Fenton observes, "He doesn't 'draw in space.' Instead, he tends to group plates of steel in long pleats and folds. The effect is one of a kind of stiffened, geometric drapery. This, too, looks back to sculpture of the past, especially to the elaborate and expressive drapery of Gothic carving (which often compensates for parts of the body)."

Although Hide comes to Canada with these ideas already present in his work, Edmonton, with enthusiastic institutional support and lack of an established sculpture tradition, gives the artist the opportunity to develop along his own path, and yet act as one of the main representatives of this practice. (In 1987, Hide is featured on the front cover of *Alberta Report* for the article "Sculpture City: How Edmonton became the world's best in steel.") Two exhibitions in particular track the development of his art in Edmonton: a ten-year-survey-show in 1986, *Peter Hide in Canada* (Edmonton Art Gallery) and *Peter Hide* (FAB Gallery, U of A, 1996). Russell Bingham describes Hide's work in the latter exhibition as, "Closer in temperament to David Smith, perhaps than to Anthony Caro," and goes on to suggest that, "[he] has reintroduced much of the drama and effect that had been distilled out of modernist sculpture in its shift to abstraction.... [Through strong contours and jutting angles, through pieces that lean and twist, Hide] often allows references to human posture or gesture to imbue feeling and mood, or impart a sense of liveliness and movement."[83] One example of this is *Radiant,* which to Bingham "resembles a walking figure with its swaying contrapposto and approximation of human proportions."

Included in the 1996 show is a new compositional form that Hide had been experimenting with since the late 1980s. "From the beginning, my sculptures have been sort of stiff and hieratic."[84] His solution was to explore "a horizontal wall format, because I wanted to develop something that was more fluid and expansive." One example of his use of this configuration is the dynamic, 24-foot-long *Malevich Extended,* which made its exhibition debut at the first *Alberta Biennial of Contemporary Art* (1996). Constructed from fragments of other "unresolved" sculptures, the low-to-the-ground work with its welded sections of cut-up metal shapes, including a slice cut off from a generator winding core, gives the impression of something on the move, despite its ponderous weight and massive size. *Malevich Extended* is the only so-called formalist work included in the Alberta Biennial, prompting *Canadian Art* critic Joan Richardson to comment: "The sculpture [displayed outdoors] created an extraordinary axis to Janet Cardiff and George Bures Miller's interactive installation, *The Dark Pool,* inside the gallery."[85]

The piece took five years to complete (1990–95). Hide notes: "Having more or less completed the piece I can see that it was probably inspired by the great processions of CN rollingstock that daily go past my studio to the marshalling yards nearby, but this piece is certainly not just a representation of this. I too have been deeply affected by the Italian Renaissance painter Andrea Mantegna's great horizontal paintings of processions and reclining gods." [86]

Thus, in Hide's work, art comes full circle: the past meets the present, art meets the industrial, civilization meets the frontier and, in a modest sense, the non-referential meets the referential. As for an explanation about this and Edmonton steel's changing face over the past decade, Hide concludes: "We are beyond the high modernist phase, pure abstraction is over. We are trying to body-out: to give our art more substance, tangibility and even sensuousness." [87]

Another Edmonton sculptor who presents in the first *Alberta Biennial of Contemporary Art* is Hide's former student, **BLAIR BRENNAN** (1959, Edmonton, Alberta). Displayed are two artworks: *66 Grimoires,* a shelf-load of everyday books clad in a variety of steel bindings, and the ritualistic *Perish Like the Word,* in which the word "abracadabra" was burned onto the gallery wall with branding irons. A decade earlier, Brennan had been positioned on "the leading edge of the third generation of metal sculptors in Edmonton." [88] He had established himself in such canonizing shows as *Edmonton Steel, Sculpture City* and the first outdoor *Sculpture by Invitation* show in 1986. His non-monolithic welded work is, however, unlike anything seen in the Edmonton Steel idiom, and for a while, his idiosyncratic sensibility seems more suited to Calgary's art than to Edmonton's. By 1988, though, his practice shifts into an entirely new area. His next two shows – *Three Things I Know About Magic* (solo exhibition for the Works Festival at Ordo Templi Orientus) and *Multiple Associations* (group exhibition, Glenbow Museum) – demonstrate that his days with Edmonton Steel have passed.

His departure from the fold is propelled by a year-long hiatus (1986) following the birth of his first daughter, a strong discourse with serious literature and the opportunity to create a site-specific piece for *Edmonton: 1987 Installations* (curated by Helen Collinson for Latitude 53). In his first and very striking mixed media installation, *It's Easier to Bleed than Sweat* (later exhibited in *Multiple Associations* and Wor*mwood),* the groundwork gets laid for the next decade of creative activity. Brennan, it seems, had found religion, or at least a reason to make art that involved more than just producing aesthetic objects. In the work that follows, he forges a path that is distinctly his own.

> He chose the space [for *Three Things I Know About Magic*], and an unorthodox space it was, the Ordo Templi Orientis [a centre of neo-pagan worship in Edmonton], and all at once he questioned the monopoly of Christianity as the correct way of worship, as well as the authority museums and art galleries have acquired in western society as the repositories of artistic perfection. ❧ Caterina Pizanias, *Canadian Issues,* Volume XIV, 1992

> There's a rude, punk brutality in the material he uses to illuminate his theme of Christian sacrifice [in *It's Easier to Bleed than Sweat*]. Pointed steel, broken glass and, in one work, the artist's own blood are arranged in obsessive patterns. ❧ Liam Lacey, the *Globe and Mail,* Dec.3, 1988

With a preference for using small, non-precious materials and objects, and an eye for creating simple but beautiful visual patterns out of these materials, Brennan is making blatantly metaphorical, intensely personal and spiritually-inspired art. It is a tall order for a young artist to fill, especially when much of the celebrated art of the post-1970s, modernist or otherwise, avoid matters of the soul, the sacred; and the mystical like a bad rash.

But then, there are always the exceptions, as demonstrated by the 1986 group exhibition *Resistance or Submission: Snatches of a Christian Conversation* (Walter Phillips Gallery, Banff) in which the curator Manon Blanchette notes: "Signs and allusions bearing religious overtones are found in the work of several contemporary artists. The point is not new. Yet the way artists express their concern for the sacred, as well as their interpretation of religious rites have undergone changes. A Barnett Newmann painting was heavy with religious overtones, but today a new kind of artist uses direct representation, borrowing images, mythic dimensions and ritual objects."[89]

In Brennan's case some of the objects spring from his own curiosity about ecstatic religious experience, such as the small steel crosses in *It's Easier to Bleed Than Sweat,* the metre-long crown of thorns in *Home of the Welder* (1988), the lit candles in *Victories Over Us/Defeat at Our Hands* (1991), the cross-shaped altars in *Magic/Magick/Miracles* (1993) and the tall red-glass votives in *ex voto* (1995). The installations, according to the artist, "deal with the many and multifaceted aspects of Christian religious experience. Issues such as faith, grace, sin and salvation figure prominently."[90] Into the mix is also an effort to bring out the relationship between magic and religion, between pagan and Christian rituals, between spiritual and scientific practices.

In the act of installing his new pieces, Brennan found the process of laying out in repeated patterns dozens and hundreds of found and fabricated items (such as the dead beetles and broken incandescent light bulbs) to be a ritual in itself, the likes of which had long been important in the work of such influential artists as Germany's Joseph Beuys (b.1921). Writing about this connection, Thomas Heyd notes: "Beuys, like Brennan, engaged in repetitive ritual action and used religious imagery, such as crosses, in his work."[91] This process is also explored in *Rituals/Systems: Ray Arnatt, Adrian Cooke, Robert Hicks, Lylian Klimek and Teresa Posyniak* (1986). Curated by Liz Wylie for Edmonton's Ring House Gallery, Wylie explains, "Each of the five artists in this exhibition has begun with an initial vision or conception of their [site specific] sculpture and then progressed through ritualistic processes to bring their visions into being."[92]

Eventually Brennan joins forces with the innovative contemporary dancer Brian Webb (1951, Drumheller, Alberta), a performer with his own company in Edmonton and a dancer-in-residence at Grant MacEwan College since 1979. Together they will create a multi-disciplinary collaboration of a kind rarely seen in Canada. The catalyst for this hybrid art and what would be a fruitful seven-year collaboration (1988–1995) is Webb's own reaction to *It's Easier to Bleed than Sweat* with its carpet of glittering broken glass: "It was seductive and scary. I wanted to dance on this glittering surface dominated by a steel shark, to roll in its dirtiness not minding the many cigarette butts, the broken glass, to accept its dare.... This sculpture was visceral and it was powerful but it was also strangely peaceful. A spiritual integrity dominated its physical outburst."[93]

Webb actually does get an opportunity to perform on a bed of broken glass, rolling shirtless and lifting gigantic letters made of iron, when the two collaborate on *Victories Over Us/Defeat at Our Hands.* (Commissioned for the Works Festival (1991), with Jamie Philp composing original music and sound collage.) Writer Mark Joslin elaborates on Webb's role: "Brennan has referred to Webb as a provider of ritual for his artifacts. Webb's performances shift from recognizable dance vocabulary to movement borrowed from everyday work and functional acts, to a complex physical lexicon of ritual."[94]

Later there is *Magic/Magick/Miracles*[95] (1993) in which "Webb evokes the simple rituals of childhood and bedtime prayer"[96] in a chalk circle. He then moves on to another circle where, with the aid of a professional nurse, he "performs a thoroughly contemporary adult ritual: blood testing."[97] The ritual is completed by Webb spilling drops of his blood onto glass slides and placing them not under the microscope but alongside the wishbones [displayed on metal shelves].[98] Pamela Anthony, who witnesses the event for the *Edmonton Journal,* comments, "the metaphor is obvious and striking. Faith in science is equivalent to 'wishing' when it comes to the nightmare lottery of 'good blood/bad blood' in this age of AIDS."[99]

Brennan and Webb collaborated on six performance installations, touring their work to Calgary, Ottawa, Montreal, Vancouver and Toronto. When presented in their hometown, these events nearly always attracted a sell-out crowd and helped to define an alternative art scene in Edmonton. Their postmodern, post-Bible Belt partnership is unique to Alberta and is as significant as the video/performance/installation collaborations of Calgarians John Will and Jack Anderson (*Icon* series, 1985–86). And yet these two oeuvres could not be more different, the former being romantic, subjective and serious, the latter satiric, chaotic and cheeky. On a certain level, it's tempting to see these works of art as being somewhat emblematic of their respective cities: Edmonton and Calgary. Brennan, who was influenced in the early 1980s by Calgary sculpture, including that of Walter May, Blake Senini and Gordon Ferguson, is also conscious of how, somewhere along Highway 2, the art-making sensibilities of one city give way to another.

For his 1995 solo exhibition *Similia Similibus Curentur* at Calgary's Illingworth Kerr Gallery, the artist writes, "I recollect keenly that this [Calgary] support and interest burgeoned when there was little interest in my work in my home city of Edmonton. This is not sour grapes. Nor is it an attempt to elevate Calgary over Edmonton. From Edmonton, I have always viewed Calgary as a place of exuberant experimentation in art."[100]

Said to possess "a cult following"[101] within his own city, and to have "lent [Edmonton's] artistic scene the attribute of unpredictability,"[102] Brennan's career represents an important juncture in Edmonton's own development in the post-1970 era. Partly through the notoriety of his installations, projects and collaborative performances, the optics on the Edmonton art scene slowly begin to change from the homogenous back to the heterogeneous. By the time of the first (1996) and second (1998) *Alberta Biennial of Contemporary Art,* it is clear that this attribute of unpredictability is shared by many younger artists, and by some senior practitioners (like Lyndal Osborne) who have managed to prevail.

This change is also noted in a 1996 *Canadian Art* review by curator and critic Bruce Grenville: "Conventional wisdom identifies Edmonton and its art community as a bastion of abstract painting and sculpture – community bloated on a heavy diet of Golden paints and Corten steel. Contrary to this orthodoxy, a leaner and meaner community has emerged that blends its knowledge of modernism with an acute grasp of contemporary discourse. This community had its most recent airing in the Edmonton survey exhibition *40 Degrees Celsius*, organized by the Aggregate Society, a local artists' collective."[103]

To a certain extent, a much earlier exhibition, *Points North* (1986, Southern Alberta Art Gallery) performed a similar function by including a very diverse selection of emerging young artists from Calgary and Edmonton, including Brennan. But if *Points North* was one of a number of important steps along the way to altering what was still in 1986 a pretty homogenous-looking city, Brennan's journey away from Edmonton modernist traditions gave some real substance to the changing optics.

CALGARY AND SOUTH: DIVERGING STREAMS

chapter thirteen

Different Countries: Calgary and Lethbridge

ONE OF THE FIRST DEFINING MOMENTS of the contemporary Calgary art scene is the unveiling of *Environment 70,* offering an early peak at what the watershed decade of the 1970s will have in store. Spearheaded by Les Graff of the province's Arts and Crafts Division of the Cultural Development Branch and displayed at the Edmonton Art Gallery, it is the second of three such Alberta-wide showcases. Calgary artist Ron Moppett, who is then twenty-five years old, remembers the three *Environments* (1969, 1970 and 1971) as, "A wonderful introduction [to Alberta art] ... there was a huge amount of work to be seen; it was a major occasion for local artists because there really wasn't a lot going on in terms of showing this [local] work."[1] Specifically, *Environment 70* features what is in fact fifty abbreviated one-person shows all rolled up in one, where as one reviewer, described it: "Potters, architects, weavers, sculptors, designers, painters, printmakers and constructionists of all kinds and ages had a place in this exhibit. No one person or particular medium seemed to have been given particular emphasis, but rather the space best suited to present ideas. Of the latter there were plenty. A sense of adventure in the context of thoroughly acquired skills often produced interlocking media – ceramic paintings, sculptured pottery, woven sculpture or welded three-dimensional landscapes. Strong sensations of material texture and reflected colour, often heraldically brilliant, pervaded and modulated the gallery space." [2]

Meanwhile, in the *Edmonton Journal* the headline for the exhibition reads "Like a store on sales day: an art grab bag." In the article that follows, art critic Virgil Hammock goes on to say, "Let me add quickly, however, that it is an extremely well-done sales floor.... A bizarre note in the exhibitions is the geographic breakdown of the artists. Of the forty-one, thirty-one live in Calgary, five in Edmonton and five elsewhere in the province. Granted there may be more recognized craftsmen in the South and crafts are a big part of this show, but I find it unusual that a city that cannot support a proper art gallery like Calgary is home to six times as many artists as Edmonton." [3]

Among the Calgarians included in *Environment 70* are Katie Ohe, Marion Nicoll, Harry Kiyooka, Kay Angliss, Harlan House, John Snow, George Wood, Annemarie Schmid Esler, and to anyone not familiar with the high-plains city, the concentration of Calgary practitioners would have seemed baffling, as it did to the Edmonton-based Hammock. It was true, Calgary did not (and continues to not have) a large civic art gallery the way Edmonton, Winnipeg, Saskatoon and others have, which is to say a non-profit publicly funded facility devoted to the research, collection and exhibition of art from the region and elsewhere. But despite this noticeable absence, it does not *negate* the city's "brief but deep-rooted tradition of art making" [4] *and*, as the post-1970 period was to enfold, its large and multifaceted community of practitioners. Nor would it prevent other kinds of public institutions and exhibiting venues such as commercial art galleries and non-profit spaces, including artist-run centres, from emerging. As newcomer and Vancouver native, Gregory Elgstrand, observed many years later in a letter to a Calgary weekly in 2002, "The quantity and diversity of our cultural institutions is one of the city's great strengths and one that has created cultural conditions that are remarkably *distinct* [my emphasis] from other metropolitan centres in Canada." [5]

Thus, in spite of the city's relative geographical isolation from larger art *meccas* (always more of a problem for outside observers than for a city's own inhabitants) and its modest base of private and public patrons, the making of art in the post-1970 period will be a willful and spirited activity. Enough so to make Calgary one of Canada's brightest, productive and wide-ranging art communities. This fact remains largely unknown, however, often obscured and undermined by the larger issue of what *kind* of a community Calgary is overall. The perception of the city, past and present, tends to be as follows:

> Edmontonians are cultured and Calgarians are cowboys, Citadel Theatre founder Joe Shocter said. "In Calgary you've got that mid-west syndrome of boots and hats and backyard barbecues."[6] ☙ *The Edmonton Journal,* 1989;
>
> Calgary was a club. Membership meant holding dear a few tenets: the mountains were beautiful and business was good . . . a handshake meant a deal, and art without a horse in it was pretentious.[7] ☙ Katherine Govier, *Between Men,* 1987;
>
> Indeed, it was startling to hear of how often Calgary is referred to among [Montreal's] francophones. On the morning show of the main radio station, Mix 96, the hosts laughingly report the forecast in Cowtown.[8] ☙ *Calgary Herald,* 1997;
>
> Calgary is everything that Montreal is not. It's a macho city of unbridled optimism, busting out of its seams, a black-and-white kind of place. Montreal is many shades of grey, feminine, language-oriented and down on its luck these days. . . . Catholic church spires pierce the sky in every direction in Montreal. They're scarce in Calgary, but sniff the cool, clear wind and you catch an evangelical whiff blowing in from the Bible Belt. Conformity is encouraged; gays, vegetarians and immigrant cab drivers often don't feel welcome here.[9] ☙ Southam Newspapers, 1997;
>
> As recently as the economic boom of the late 1970s and early 80s, a cup of yogurt was said to contain more culture than Calgary. Calgary's arts scene was viewed as second-rate and parochial.[10] ☙ *Calgary Herald,* 1996;
>
> Some serious image-bending is going down in Calgary this weekend. Normally, you think Calgary and you think broncos and pointy-toed boots and black stetsons and oil. But today and over the next two days,

> the writers in town are striving instead to cast Calgary as one of a handful of Canada's literary gathering points.[11] ❧ *Globe and Mail,* 1996;
>
> Calgary will continue to grow as a place product because it satisfies a big North American niche: a reasonably coherent suburb with the appearance, but not the texture, of a big city, decorated by a few cultural institutions that recall a previous life.[12] ❧ *Globe and Mail,* 2002.

Call Calgary the most cliché-ridden place in Canada with Alberta running a close second. Almost without exception, certain themes, whether they are accurate or not, get regurgitated again and again. Sometimes this image is enforced with the help of local boosters fixated on the city's Western heritage and little else. Alas, visual-art writing isn't always immune to this phenomenon either:

> Calgary. The city looks new: big glass towers with the names of oil companies on their doors, and sprawling sub-developments with chic neo-Black-Forest architecture. Of course, the resource industry, the *raison d'etre* for all this is a risky one, and bust follows boom here with alarming consequences, except maybe for artists looking for reasonable studio space. Without a market for contemporary art, Calgary's artists cluster around the art school and the university for economic survival, and perhaps for the same reason can afford to be both individualistic and generous to one another. Still, Calgary is not a centre for art-making.[13] ❧ *Canadian Biennial of Contemporary Art,* National Gallery of Canada, 1989;
>
> Putting together a survey show of contemporary visual art that reaches across media, generations, culture and gender is an ambitious undertaking in any part of the country. It is more ambitious in Alberta where some doubted there is enough variety of art to warrant such a grand enterprise. Alberta, after all, is known as a two-note province: There's the painting tradition in Calgary and there's the big, formalist steel sculpture in Edmonton.[14] ❧ *Globe and Mail,* 1996.

Although such two-note opinions about Calgary's art-making history continue to persist into the next century, the story is in fact quite different: layered, full of nuance, and difficult to sum up in a twenty-second sound bite.

Yes, there is a strong painting tradition in the city, but there is also a strong ceramic art scene. Calgary, more recently, is a hub for glass art, has a long and fruitful acquaintance with printmaking, is a place for striking sculpture, installation and media arts, and has room for just about everything else, including multi-, cross- and even anti-disciplinary practices.

This eclecticism is also reflected in other nearby communities, including Lethbridge and the Banff area, which through its artists and public institutions – Southern Alberta Art Gallery, University of Lethbridge Art Gallery, Whyte Museum of the Canadian Rockies, the Banff Centre and Walter Phillips Art Gallery – have enriched the scope of visual-art practice in the south. Calgary "knows" about Lethbridge and Banff and vice versa, whereas Edmonton, Red Deer, Medicine Hat, Fort McMurray and Grande Prairie are far away on its horizon. (In fact, post-1970, Lethbridge will become a recognized hothouse for not only cutting-edge art-making but also curatorial and directorship talent.)

Add to this shifting mix the contribution made by artists raised and/or trained in Alberta who live outside of the province but maintain connections through exhibiting and lecturing. Such artists include Evan Penny (Toronto), Elizabeth LeMoine (London, England), Gisele Amantea (Montreal), Takao Tanabe (Parksville, British Columbia), Tim Watkins (New York), Attila Richard Lukacs (New York) and Christian Eckart (New York). Memory is crucial to the community's sense of self, which is not confined by the city's boundaries.

Thus, throughout most of the post-1970 era, Calgary will live, breath and sometimes celebrate the diversities of its artists to a degree perhaps not found in many other Canadian cities. As curator Donna McAlear noted in 1988 after moving to the city in 1986, "I joined a thriving scene where a diversity of approach is operative among generations of art practitioners; a place where working cross-media is accepted and encouraged by artists, both emerging and established, thereby generating a self-determined and self-supporting environment."[15] The city, however, will also go through periods where support and recognition of locally made artwork, both historic and contemporary, is confined to smaller venues – artist-run centres, commercial galleries (some who have been stellar) and a few smaller public galleries – while larger, better-resourced institutions preoccupy themselves with other tasks that only from time to time with the occasional exhibition or retrospective will inform its own audiences about what thrives outside its very doors.

This situation extends as well as to the kind of art instruction provided in the post-secondary institutions, and it is notable that during the expansionary 1970s, when imported instructors with master's degrees are filling the staffing needs of the art college and the university, Calgarian Carroll (Moppett) Taylor-Lindoe remembers the period for its "denial of the place, an almost total obliviousness to the place." [16] Meaning that whatever art history Calgary or even Alberta might have, it is deemed to be of little consequence to anyone because of its peripheral and/or regional status. Of course, this condition of denial is not unique to Calgary alone; many communities across the country continue to experience a kind of collective amnesia about their own cultural resources because they are places too small or remote from the important centres.

But, in returning to the discussion about diversity, ultimately it all boils down to the artists themselves, and as veteran art critic Nancy Tousley observes midway through this period, "Art in Calgary has long been characterized by the individualism of her artists. Unlike Edmonton, the southern Alberta city has not produced an identifiable local school." [17] This attribute of the city's artistic community is sometimes explained by outsiders as an outgrowth of the city's western heritage and its position as Canada's economic and political "upstart." For instance, James Morris makes the following assessment of the city in *Pax Britannica* (Penguin Books, 1979), his three-volume history of the British Empire: "Calgary was not a substitute for older societies, but an alternative." [18] Or, on a more visceral level, editorial writer Sydney Sharpe has this reaction: "Calgary always gives me a jolt, an adrenalin rush, when I see that glorious mountain skyline jutting over the rolling grasslands. The mountains are just like Calgarians – defiant, forever reaching for the sky."[19]

But others relate the independence of Calgary's artists to the position of the community within the larger art world itself. Writing for the national publication, *Saturday Night,* Charles Foran surmises, "What may be true is that the larger and more 'important' the centre, the greater the pressure it places on those operating within it to espouse the correct views, toe the latest lines, or else risk being dropped from invitation lists and Rolodexes. People toiling elsewhere, be it central Ontario or Halifax or Calgary, are spared these thousand tiny trials of character, leaving them in a better frame of mind to paint what, and how, they want." [20]

Still, as the contemporary era begins to take shape in the 1970s, the lack of a major public art gallery signifies to many an art scene and a city in a state of stalled adolescence. "If the downtown vacuum [in Calgary] could be given some impetus as the Vancouver Art Gallery and the Edmonton Art Gallery seem to be doing in their centres, the benefits would not only be a more conducive environment for local artists, but a service responsible for introducing less familiar art from distant centres. The three galleries, two institutional and one private, have the potential but, for different reasons, are unable to sustain any momentum in the art community,"[21] Dennis Elliot writes for *Arts Canada* in 1972. Thus, if there were any strengths about the Calgary art community in the 1970s, they will lie with certain individuals and their collective efforts with others, rather than with any one institution per se. Curiously, this has continued to be a feature of the city to the end of the century. In this sense, Calgary has been unlike Edmonton, Vancouver or Toronto where, over the last thirty years, a few powerful and influential institutional players have acted as rallying points for the artists in their communities. According to artist and curator Ron Moppett, "There were never the power brokers, the kingmakers around to promote a party line nor a public art institution capable of monopolizing the attention of the community." Thus, he concludes, "Calgary had more time to reflect on its own history."[22]

Lacking a central clearing house, by the 1990s the exhibiting infrastructure in the city will become as diverse as the practice of the artists it supports, including not only larger institutional players,[23] but also smaller ones, like the commercial art galleries, the non-profit art galleries,[24] the artist-run centres[25] and the city's unique but short-lived network of corporate art galleries. (There was a time in the 1980s when it seemed like every "committed" corporate citizen had a public space or gallery for showing art. Important examples were Petro-Canada, Nova Corporation, Shell Canada and Gulf Canada. Sun Life Plaza was the only one that was still extant by the end of the downsizing 1990s.)

None of this, however, would have emerged were it not for the ground work done during the 1970s, when Edmonton (via the Edmonton Art Gallery) is getting most of the national attention and Calgary and its artists are still struggling with the thought of moving elsewhere. Why not move to Toronto, Vancouver or New York, where conditions are perceived to be more hospitable? For many, though, leaving isn't an option. Instead, these artists rely upon their own travels and informal networks of friends and contacts to keep up with developments in contemporary art. As painter John Hall recalls about his colleagues of the time, "There was a lot of savvy about what was going on."[26] So much savvy, in fact, that a decade later in 1986, Nancy Tousley is able to conclude about the city she covers, "Something vital and exciting is happening here … The recent return in the international art scene to an embrace of the image and the expression of intense personal experience has sanctioned Calgary artists to follow their natural bent." [27]

In this respect, one aspect of art–making that has a considerable amount of pull for some Calgary artists in the 1970s is representational art. Judging by the contents of such large group shows from the mid-1970s, such as *Prairies: Western Canadian Paintings* [28] (1974), *Western Untitled* [29] (1976), *8 Calgary Artists* [30] (1976), and *Albertawork* [31] (1977), art with a recognizable subject as opposed to pure abstraction seems to be pretty much a fait accompli among such contemporary names as Joice Hall, Gary Olson, John Will, John Hall, Alexandra Haeseker and William Parker. Embedded too in much of this art, according to *8 Calgary Artists* curator George Moppett, are: "Memories, dreams, obsessions, desires, needs, feelings, ideas, intuitions, discoveries, insights, realizations."

This interest in recognizable subjects continues throughout the 1980s for many Calgary practitioners, expressed in a variety of contemporary modes: from the crisp realism of a John Brocke to the more expressionistic abstracted figuration of Don Kottmann and the mixed-media painting of John Will where words and photographs are included.

Conversely, there are fewer examples of artists whose two-dimensional work is purely abstract. The kind of non-objective abstraction practiced by the Edmonton formalists never really takes hold in the south, and depending on what side of the fence you are on, this fact can look either progressive – as it does now – or hopelessly reactionary – as it did in the 1970s. Instead, many Calgary-based artists preferred to walk the line between objective and non-objective art, between abstraction and representation. Abstract or semi-abstract elements might be incorporated into the image, but overall there is still the suggestion that there is content and meaning above and beyond the work's formal aspects. For others, abstract elements will serve a decorative purpose, used for the sake of patterning as in Wendy Toogood's cloth constructions of the early 1980s, or as a form of mark-making as in Yolanda van Dyck's lyrical abstracts of the same period. Even significant examples of abstraction from southern Alberta present the viewer with "meaning expressed in abstract imagery," [32] as in Harry Kiyooka's memorable *Aegean Series* (1973–1977) or "rely on associative (or unidentifiable) imagery," [33] such as Bruce O'Neil's much-celebrated acrylics of the 1970s.

This idea of working abstractly but with a wider agenda is fleshed out even more in the 1980s and 1990s in works of art that are largely non-representational but embody a postmodern attitude. Analytical in their intent, these works are linked to contemporary concerns, such as: disrupting formalist approaches (Geoff Hunter), feminist writing and psychoanalytic theory (Mary Scott), the history and language of painting (Christian Eckart and post-1990 Chris Cran), the circumvention of artistic authorship (post-1985 Arlene Stamp), re-describing the masculine tradition of painting (Carroll Taylor-Lindoe), reinterpreting symbolically the tragedies of modern history (William MacDonnell), and printed information transformed into an artistic commodity (Angela Inglis).

Does this make for a kind of cool, more intellectual brand of abstraction? Yes, but in a manner that leaves a bounty of truly beautiful and sometimes strange-looking art. Behind all the pre-meditation and procedures are some very idiosyncratic minds at work, like the patterned fanaticism of Mary Shannon Will and her quirky geometric pictures, a case where careful methods engender madly obsessive compositions.

Another strain that finds some sympathy in post-1970 Calgary is collage and its three-dimensional counterpart, assemblage. This avant-garde technique takes its time reaching the art-making horizons of the city, but when it arrives, it is a breath of fresh air. The art it engenders looks very different from any other prairie art of the time. Early practitioners of the medium, who begin working with this technique in the mid to late 1960s, are George Milhalcheon (b.1924), with his hot-coloured canvas collages, whose shapes are cut out of pre-painted acrylic canvas and arranged on the painting's surface, and George Angliss (b.1921–1991), who constructs totally unique, surreal assemblages incorporating found and recycled materials from turn-of-the-century prairie homesteads.

Not far behind these two local pioneers is a whole generation of Calgary-based artists who are alert to the social and cultural upheavals of the 1960s. Influenced by the visual jetsam of popular culture, advertising, the mass media, and Pop Art's use of alternative materials in the style of early avant-garde artists like the European Dadaist's Kurt Schwitters and Marcel Duchamp, this upcoming generation takes to collage and assemblage like a mother tongue. More than a technique, it is part of an emerging experimental attitude, where "you didn't want to be weighed down by tradition,"[34] where open exploration of materials is key and where multi-layered meanings are possible. According to John Hall, "Collage, photography, material discontinuity and assemblage [become] reflections of a will to create an art that would be able to more accurately reflect the fractured and discontinuous experiences of life in the last half of the 20th century."[35] Thus, Calgary becomes postmodern before it even knows it.[36]

Early notables of collage practice include: painter Ron Moppett, who "uses collage as the structural net to catch such ambiguity and enigma, to hold a myriad of possible points of view, spaces, styles and, ultimately meanings"[37]; painter John Hall, who works with photographs and other images of daily familiarity[38]; mixed-media artist Don Mabie[39]; printmaker John Kenneth Esler and his printing plates using "metal, acid, rosin, shellac, toothpicks, leather, wood veneer, aluminium pie plates, flocked wall paper, and letraset"[40]; and ceramic artist Annemarie Schmid Esler. Utilizing the medium's additive nature and the freedom it allows to re-appropriate found and existing imagery and text, artists such as these challenge not only pictorial conventions but also the norms of mainstream society. James D. Brodie's social-commentary prints from the 1970s,[41] for instance, criticize the treatment of Aboriginal people, and Sandra (Tivy) Vida's witty colour Xerox collages from the early 1980s examine gender roles and stereotypes.[42]

By the early 80s, Calgary artists take even more avidly to the practice of assemblage, transforming "the discarded, over-looked or simply utilitarian"[43] into three-dimensional artworks. Sometimes realized on a scale writ large, the Graceland site (1986–1997) will be its wildest and most radical expression. Located in a former demolition yard or "seven scenic acres of junk on the south east outskirts of Calgary,"[44] Graceland is an open-air studio that Alberta College of Art graduate Bart Habermiller (b.1962), with the help of a loose collective of artists, will turn into a mecca for found art on the prairies. For a period of time, with the involvement of ACA instructors Walter May, Blake Senini, Gordon Ferguson and Iain Baxter, a number of workshops or daytrips also take place at Graceland.[45] Many of the artists who gather at Graceland represent a new generation of Calgary artists – Bart Habermiller, Colleen Kerr, Steve Heimbecker, Nelson Henricks, Stephen Peterson and Mark Dicey – who are already making a more committed leap into performance art, video, installation, audio art and assemblage. Beyond Graceland some artists also get to display their work in artist-run centres, public galleries and in the more adventuresome commercial operations.

For Mark Dicey, assemblage is a natural outgrowth of his own personal tendency to hoard discarded objects. His expressionist, three-dimensional, wall-mounted art of the late 1980s and early 1990s is part-and-parcel of an extremely busy cycle of work, which includes performance and installation as well as static work (painting and drawing). Dicey's assemblage *Marsh* (1988), for instance, is indicative of this new brand of art. *Marsh* is laden with environmental messages and warns about meddling with nature. As Dicey describes it, "A rusted metal coffee mug is lashed to water-bleached driftwood. Swirling muddy colours streaked with blood red paint constitute its base and are symbolic of a post-nuclear era."[46]

Colleen Kerr also brings enormous energy to this younger, highly motivated art scene. Along with Dicey and six others,[47] she participates in the important Nickle Arts Museum exhibit *Elemental Instincts: A Matter of Course*[48] (1988), where she presents three videos and a dozen wall-mounted assemblages, the latter resembling scientific specimens from the Victorian era. Neat and tidy and at times creepy, these modest works with their inscribed phrases such as Vigil, Death Came Knocking and Habeas Corpus, suggest a story or a scenario attached to what would otherwise be a display of mundane household items. Several years later, the multi-media artist's interest in marrying literary text with found objects is given new expression in a series of simple wooden boxes, exhibited in *Seleni* (1991, Muttart Art Gallery) and *Minor Details, Major Issues* (1993, Glenbow Museum).[49] Of these refined assemblages, which tease the voyeuristic tendencies in every viewer, curator Franklyn Heisler writes, "The work [in *Seleni*] is based on Kerr's ongoing interest in folk beliefs, ancient systems of mysticism like tarot cards and in the concepts of Jungian archetypical society."[50]

Although not completely absent from the Calgary and southern Alberta art scene, art theory plays a limited role in the making of art locally. As Nancy Tousley comments in a 1986 *Canadian Art* issue: "Artists in Calgary look generally with great suspicion upon art whose primary reason for being is political or theoretical. Rather, they tend to make art as a way of exploring, understanding and speaking to the world: often a very personal world that implies the macrocosm in its microcosmic view."[51] In the broader Canadian scene, however, as the title of one 1996 Toronto-produced book adamantly declares: *Theory Rules.* It rules because of its presence in many publicly funded art institutions including art schools, public galleries, artist-run centres and art publications.

Here's what *Theory Rules* had to say about this development in the post-1970 era: "The shifting or withering of boundaries between artistic practice and the academy may be glimpsed in any trip to the magazine store or gallery book shop. The circulation of theoretical work within such venues as the art gallery (evident in artists' statements and the growing importance of exhibition catalogues) and the art magazine has created new forms of support and sites of intervention for the professional academic. With the emergence of a broad interdisciplinary and international audience for cultural theory, the rates of change and commodity value of theoretical innovations have increased. In this respect, just as the domain of artistic production has grown noticeably more 'academic,' the field of cultural theory and analysis within the academy has come more and more to resemble the market for art, with similar cycles of fashionability and a comparable emphasis on currency and innovation. In grant applications, exhibition statements and catalogues, one increasingly finds artists using theoretical tropes as the most effective means for positioning their past and projected work."[52]

Meanwhile, Calgary art writers make these observations:

> What the keynote address [for Calgary's *International Ceramics* 1995], the panel on collecting, and Aaron Milrad's lecture did make clear is that situations facing contemporary producers in any medium are extremely complex. The art world is riven by competing forces, conspiratorial allegiances and legal quagmires. Anyone entering the battlefield is best forewarned to be informed and familiar with competing institutional and critical agendas. [53]
> ❧ Amy Gogarty, *Contact,* 1995;
>
> Most participants in art symposia have a shared knowledge of, and may even agree with, contemporary theory's axiomatic critiques (of racism, gender construction, sexism, language, power, institutions and metaphysics). While artworks are discussed, their meanings and roles as theoretical works are the primary subjects. As Diana Nemiroff, curator of contemporary art at the National Gallery, explained to printmaker Jennifer Dickson in the *Sightlines* book accompanying the printmaking symposium [in Edmonton]: "We pursue works by artists – not by medium in contemporary art – the lines between media are blurred. Our collecting is issue-driven. Ideas are paramount," [54] ❧ David Garneau. *Border Crossings* 1998.

Postmodern Canada has come a long way from the comfy ol' days when art discussions revolved around taste and connoisseurship, and when the modernist dicta of art for art's sake reduced everything to a discussion about form with little regard for artwork's broader relationship to society at large. "Like most artists trained in a modernist ideology, I was not taught to consider the moral questions; in fact, moral questioning was traditionally discounted as an impediment to creative freedom, and responsibility was somehow equated with censorship,"[55] Carroll Taylor-Lindoe remembers.

This is no longer the case. By the end of the century, many more artists in Calgary are willing to engage in cultural analysis and to address current social or political issues with contemporary materials and techniques. Individual examples include Rita McKeough's imaginative Calgary-specific installations and prints dealing with the urban consequences of boom and bust around her neighbourhood, and former Banff artist Barbara Todd's *Security Blankets,* started after the birth of her first son in 1986, during a period of high international tension in the arms race. According to Nancy Tousley, "[The works are] appliqued with business suits, war planes and a Fat Man bomb, and surrounded with a border of missiles. The very process of quilt-making became a metaphor. With her hands, she was sewing a blanket that protected her son by giving voice and reason to her fears."[56]

Artists also act collectively to make social comments. Early in the era, the interdisciplinary group W.O.R.K.S. (1972–75) uses cable TV for the production of alternative programming, such as *Live Lice,* a cable show of anti-commercials, cultural news and parodies of the mass media. And, more recently, the joint efforts of the artists working at Graceland often have socially critical messages. In her article "Some theoretical stuff about Graceland," Mary Anne Moser comments, "Because there are no walls, no judges, artwork at Graceland is peculiar; it has not been legitimated by a curatorial mandate.... This year's *Art Rodeo,* held on Saturday, August 25 [1990] included a visible representation of several prominent themes which address questions of historicity, culture, nature and our understanding of them."[57]

Of course, no discussion about the presence of contemporary theory and cultural issues in art would be adequate without talking about the role of curators and writers, because they, along with some artists, are by and large what constitute the professional academic. In the best of circumstances, they are not there to tell people how to think about art but to provide a critical perspective on what is being shown, a point Alberta College instructor Amy Gogarty outlined at *International Ceramics 1995* (Calgary): "Why be critical? is a question often heard at such gatherings. During this conference, one panellist suggested what ceramics did not need was a bunch of esoteric and arcane theory thrown at it.... The first assumption, that criticism implies arcane or esoteric theory imposed from outside, does not sustain examination. One of the many purposes of criticism (and there are many – another topic for discussion) is to contribute to a greater awareness of the conditions of art-making and works of art. Judgement is commonly misconstrued as the primary objective of criticism, yet analytical precision is more central to any bona fide critical stance. Analysis can focus on formal components and relationships; it can be interpretive, or it can seek to expand its subject by engaging it in imaginative discourse."[58]

In terms of southern Alberta and particularly Calgary, there certainly is a history of curators and writers treading the contentious waters of contemporary theory, but again, it has depended very much on individual inclination and interest rather than on institutional mandate. One notable exception to this is the visual-art programming of the Banff Centre and the Walter Phillips Gallery, which for many years has focused almost entirely on such concerns, viewing art as a practice rather than about making discrete art objects. As The Banff Centre's publication *Front* (March/April, 1992) relates: "After fifteen years of conscious development in the domain of contemporary arts, Banff has transformed itself from a conservative cultural finishing school into a post-modern pressure cooker with an international reputation for leading edge art and theory."

In Calgary, the net tends to get thrown more widely with divergent opinions like the one expressed in a exhibition brochure for *Patterned After: Ornament, Repetition and Pattern in 20th Century Art* (1997, Triangle Gallery of Visual Arts, Calgary): "It is apparent that today much of the critical community is dedicated to the support of art which addresses larger world issues, often with dour seriousness of intellectual purpose," writes the curator Jeffrey Spalding of the University of Lethbridge. "The timing then would seem rather inopportune to evolve an art which embraces the decorative impulse and the playful, joyful investigations of form."[59] Inopportune perhaps in some Canadian cities but in a place like Calgary, where there is less ideology and more art-making, it is part of a diverse current flowing through the region as a whole.

But if there was not so much formalized theory present in Calgary in the late decades of the twentieth century, there was plenty of NSCAD or "Calgary's other art school"[60]: the Nova Scotia College of Art and Design (NSCAD). Located in Halifax, this much-touted Atlantic institution will leave numerous traces of itself in the foothills, coulees and mountains of Alberta, and to a lesser extent, in the northern prairie around Edmonton and Grande Prairie.[61] Its influence will come in the form of more than a dozen artists[62] and instructors who either have trained at NSCAD or have taught at that institution, such as Eric Cameron, John Will, Glen MacKinnon and the late John Clark. Several will be native-born Albertans like Helen Sebelius, a 1978 graduate of the ACA. "In Calgary, I learned to 'make' art. What was primary was the 'doing' and not so much the thinking," while studying in Halifax from 1984 to 1988, "was like learning another language. I studied history, theory, had seminars and learned to vocalize and articulate about art. I already had developed a visual language so it was like the two things came together, it was quite lovely."[63]

Sebelius' experience broadened her artistic and her economic horizons, helping her to land a teaching position at the Alberta College of Art in 1987. Why she chose NSCAD rather than seek post-graduate degrees either at the University of Calgary or the University of Alberta is partly related to the college's once formidable reputation as the "contemporary art world's most improbable intellectual hot spot."[64] With its fertile environment for argument, debate and critical discourse, its ambitious visiting artist program and a flexible cross-disciplinary approach, the college in the earlier post-1970 period is a magnet for artists across the country. Dedicated to the rethinking of art, the school is also highly critical of modernism and particularly formalist art strategies. As its former director of the MFA program, Eric Cameron,[65] remembers, "[NSCAD] seized the opportunities of a particularly academic moment in art (such as conceptual art was). It was a situation where artists could carry their art in their suitcase – when it couldn't be completely carried in their head."[66]

Another NSCADian, Jeffrey Spalding, who later ends up at the University of Lethbridge, writes about that period under the leadership of then NSCAD president, Garry Neill Kennedy[67]: "A visiting artist/faculty member had to be dutiful and earnest with respect to teaching, yet their pedagogic skills were of less importance than the quality of art thoughts they might engender, presented in whatever stilted language. NSCAD banked on these teacherly qualities, mindful of all the complications and contradictions. It was disdainful of the craft of art delivered by professional teachers proficient at producing results by conveying technique and style. NSCAD of the day believed this older, failed model deluded students into thinking they were getting something – closing in on progress towards emerging as artists. Instead, it was felt that this type of training only served to keep students pre-occupied with art's traditional past, keeping them away from re-invigorating their studio practice and challenging art's role in society and their own cultural assumptions."[68]

But, as Cameron points out, "what went in" – the college had strong affinity with conceptual art from New York and other subsequent new developments in the 1970s – and "what came out"[69] was quite different. *The Oxford Companion to Twentieth Century Art* (1981) defines conceptual art as: "Artists in the conceptual field deliberately render their productions uninteresting, common-place or trivial from a visual point of view in order to divert attention to the 'idea' they express."[70] Art was no longer about self-expression or aesthetics, it was now about idea and process. And yet, in an almost perverse way, by focusing on the theoretical premise of the work and its intention, plenty of NSCADians were still able to bridge the conceptual and visual worlds. For instance, while the physical sources – a head of lettuce, a shoe, an ice tray and so on – of Eric Cameron's systematic *Thick Paintings* can be considered commonplace or trivial, the otherworldly results can hardly be described as uninteresting. And while Mary Scott may contend that she "never cared much about how [art] looks but I do care about what it means,"[71] she is noted nonetheless for her "striking originality,"[72] her work described as "art that speaks truly of the body and beauty."[73]

Was NSCAD itself a magic formula? In a sense, yes, because during a crucial period in Canadian contemporary art when the school "clearly stood for and emphasized an art whose stance is conceptual and critical,"[74] those two adjectives become key in what will be recognized and supported by many of Canada's publicly funded institutions including artist-run centres. NSCAD will help generate the Canadian wave away from the shoreline of late modernism at a time when contemporary art-making internationally is also doing the same thing.

In Spalding's opinion, the influence and impact of NSCAD has been a double-edged sword for regions such as Alberta: "Many NSCAD graduates have set up house in Alberta following stints at Lethbridge and Banff. They have the right style and look to win national grants as simultaneously making work pertinent to Canada Council style pre-occupations, with the added advantage of satisfying regional quotas to give grants throughout Canada – without national jurors having to compromise by recognizing idiosyncratic practice from a region. (The evident death knell for western Canadian modernist-formalist artists and curators.)"[75]

Of course, not all of southern Alberta's most well-known contemporary artists go to NSCAD – Instituto Allende, Mexico; Concordia University, Montreal; University of Calgary; Chicago Art Institute; and Emily Carr College of Art and Design, Vancouver, are other examples of schools that have figured prominently in the city's artistic make-up – but a sizable number have had some association with the Halifax-based institution. The NSCAD mafia is a phrase sometimes applied in Calgary and elsewhere. As Helen Sibelius recalls of her return to Calgary, "There were expectations: now what are you going to do with that knowledge? [The NSCAD mafia] was said occasionally with resentment because the school was seen as more 'weighty' and engaged."[76]

The Visual Blooming of Lethbridge

More engaged is also a description that can be applied to the art community of Lethbridge: a bright, independent star in the Canadian Milky Way. "Folks here seem more daring than in Calgary when it comes to matters of aesthetics. They seem more willing to accept the best from beyond their own horizons,"[77] comments one *Calgary Herald* columnist in 1986. While ten years later, *Border Crossings* contributor David Garneau, in reference to the first *Alberta Biennial of Contemporary Art* (1996) notes, "Diversity reigned when the doors opened [for the exhibition] and the presumed dominance of the two big cities was challenged by exceptional work from Lethbridge."[78]

In 1967, the year of Canada's centennial, the Heisler-born author Robert Kroetsch writes *Alberta,* a classic in Canadian travel writing. In this chronicle, which takes the reader on a journey around the province, Lethbridge is introduced as, "A city of over thirty-seven thousand, which in its size, atmosphere, and location has the makings of the most attractive university town in Alberta.... Reflecting the irrigated countryside for which it is centre, Lethbridge is a city of gardens and parks. Sick's Landscape Garden is a beautiful rock garden. Galt Gardens is gracious ... Indian Battle Park, on the Oldman River, marks the site of the last Indian battle fought on the North American continent ... But for me, and for thousands of visitors to come, the new [Japanese] garden, the Nikka Yuko Centennial Garden, is the rarest experience in the city."[79]

In a little over a decade other cultural gems added to the city, include the Southern Alberta Art Gallery and the nascent University of Lethbridge Art

Gallery and Collection. These are in addition to the earlier and still extant Bowman Arts Centre (founded in 1965 by the volunteer-driven Allied Arts Council) and the Sir Alexander Galt Museum and Archives (which moved from the Bowman into its present location in 1971).

For a city with a population of approximately 63,000 by the end of the century, this rapid convergence of programming, collecting and education is practically unequalled anywhere else on the Prairies. Add to this a healthy number of professional artists and no wonder Lethbridge has often caused outsiders to shake their heads in amazement, or to at least remark on the vitality of the place. As Robert Kroetsch observes, "a certain giddiness characterizes an Albertan, a certain confident heady willingness." [80] Ditto for the development of Lethbridge's visual-arts scene.

In the year 1908 when Lethbridge's Donald W. Buchanan is born, the CPR is in the midst of building a structure that is still an impressive sight. Straddling the deep, coulee-lined Oldman River valley, the High Level Bridge is a symbol of connection: connecting coal mines in the CPR empire, and connecting the region to the larger art world in the case of Buchanan. Once described as a renaissance man and world traveller, [81] Buchanan's publishing credits include a 1936 biography of Canadian expatriate painter, James Wilson Morrice, and Canada's first modern-art history, *The Growth of Canadian Painting* (1950). (He also writes occasional reviews for the family newspaper, the *Lethbridge Herald.*) During the war and shortly thereafter, he is editor of *Canadian Art* and then works for the National Gallery of Canada ,where he eventually serves as associate and acting director (1955–60). Before he dies in 1966, he is a trustee of the National Gallery and coordinator of a major international art exhibition for Expo 67. To his hometown, he and his brother Hugh will leave an important collection of Canadian art.

Buchanan was obviously very close to the centre of the Canadian art world of his time and, is notably the first of a number of significant curators, writers and gallery directors to emerge from the community. Call Lethbridge a breeding ground for not only artistic innovation but behind-the-scene talent like Bruce Ferguson, Allan MacKay, Alf Bogusky, Joan Stebbins, Jeffrey Spalding and Victoria Baster. Along with the Walter Phillips Gallery at the Banff Centre, the Southern Alberta Art Gallery in particular develops a durable reputation for being a hot spot for contemporary art exhibitions in the province and in Canada. With a tendency to be national in their focus rather than regional, SAAG's programming receives strong approval from the Canada

Council. Although fewer Albertans are seen here than in other Alberta art galleries, the ones who benefit from SAAG's attention tend to be those with a national reputation or the possibility of one. Their exhibition catalogues are highly regarded for their scholarship and presentation. In 1985, the *Lethbridge Herald* calls the city-funded gallery Lethbridge's "*best-kept secret.*"[82]

Just as significant is the University of Lethbridge Art Collection, which by the 1990s is the subject of many newspaper and magazine articles; described in the *Globe and Mail* as "Canada's best academic art collection."[83] On the whole, its collection represents a cultural vision that will register particularly large in the heart and mind of its long-time director, artist Jeffrey Spalding. From 1981, Spalding's work with the collection is comparable to other trail-blazing figures in the province and their respective institutions: Joe Schocter and Edmonton's Citadel Theatre; Michael Dobbin and PanCanadian play-Rites Festival; Ruth Carse and the Alberta Ballet Company; Brian Paisley and the Edmonton Fringe Festival; Eric Harvie and the Glenbow-Alberta Institute; Illingworth Kerr/Stanford Perrott and the Alberta College of Art; Mel Hurtig and Hurtig Publishers (now defunct) and Walter Kaasa/Horst Schmid and Alberta Culture (now Alberta Foundation for the Arts). By the end of century, the University of Lethbridge Art Collection will contain approximately 12,000 objects, valued at around $30 million. It is also a centre for Plains' Aboriginal and paleontological material.

The Glenbow Museum, the Edmonton Art Gallery and the former Alberta Art Foundation also have substantial collections, but whatever their merits and specialities, none seem to have quite the cachet of the U of L holdings, which, it must be admitted, knew how to blow its own horn under Spalding's direction. Fuelled by some remarkably diverse donations and a policy of using the holdings as a readily accessible teaching tool at the university, the gallery and collection transformed the visual arts into an adventure. Beginning in the late 1980s, the gallery mounts a series of large-scale exhibitions in Edmonton (thanks to the Works festival) and in Calgary that has heads turning in excitement. With manic energy, modest budgets and abundant good will, shows such as *Soup to Nuts: Pop Art and Its Legacy* bring to light the collection's acquisitions of artwork by British, American and Canadian painters. "The one modern movement wildly approved by a general audience,"[84] says Spalding about this pop art extravaganza. *Soup to Nuts* tours to Edmonton and Calgary and is then reconfigured for Spokane, Washington, as well as Tallahassee and Ocala in Florida.

Other shows include the 1988 hits, *Art of Our Century: A Primer of Early Modernism* (Calgary) and *A Contemporary Survey* (Edmonton), which tackles art from the 1960s to the present. Landscape and landscape-inspired art also receives its due in *Reflecting Paradise* (four cities in Korea, 1993 and Calgary, 1994), as does abstract art in *Abstraction: Which Way From Here?* (Calgary, 1993), while *Mysteries of the Flesh* (Calgary, 1995) highlights figurative art from the collection. Add to this *Camera/Work* (photo and photo-related art, Edmonton 1996), *Art at Work* (corporate gifts to the U of L collection, Edmonton 1997), and *Patterned After: Ornament, Repetition and Pattern in 20th Century Art* (Calgary, 1997), and you have some idea why heads turned, especially when every show was able to include Alberta artists, suggesting that artistic life on the margins has relevancy and meaning within the wider world.

Another tour de force, this time for Lethbridge alone, is *Bridge* with its exhibition logo incorporating the city's historic railway span. Mounted in the summer of 1989 with Cadillac-Fairview donating a space (and further assistance from Alberta Culture, Alberta Art Foundation and local businesses), the art gallery staff and an army of volunteers fill the company's vacant Eaton's building with fifty temporary galleries showcasing the U of L's collection and the Buchanan Bequest. More than 1,000 works are put on display, including exhibits of Canadian historical art (1770s to 1950s), Inuit and Native American art, western Canadian art (1960–1989), international modernism (Picasso, Matisse, Leger, Moore, Miro, Derain and so on), artifacts from Papua New Guinea and post-war avant-garde art (Warhol, Hockney, Dine, Riopelle, Stella, LeWitt, Holzer). Unlike so many blockbusters, *Bridge* is a rare example of a mega-exhibition totally generated from within Alberta itself. As well, for the U of L Art Gallery, the exhibition is a necessary step in making visible its holdings, as the regular gallery occupies a tiny 1,500-square-foot space in the university's School of Fine Arts facility. As Tim Nowlin, a former associate of the U of L Gallery, later recalled about the three-month event, "Lethbridge was stunned. It was the first time the community had seen the full range of the collection and was able to realize the extent to which it had grown."[85]

The miracle of Lethbridge is not entirely Spalding's doing. Over the years, colleagues such as collection founder Billy McCarroll, Victoria Baster and Adrian Cooke provide valuable assistance to the gallery. In 1983, the gallery receives an important gift from the internationally recognized photographer Dr. Roloff Beny, originally of Lethbridge. The Beny donation features a large selection of early twentieth-century masters such as Matisse, Picasso, Dufy and Chagall, and along with another anonymous gift of British pop art, an important impetus is provided for the budding collection. What is fortunate is that there was the means and the passionate interest of a few dedicated art lovers to take the ball and run with it. Of Robert Kroetsch's definition of an Albertan, these locals certainly have been the most "giddy" and possessed the most "confident heady willingness" to make things happen.

chapter fourteen

A Strong Spring Run-Off Begins

In 1980, THE UNIVERSITY OF ALBERTA PRESS released *Artists of Alberta*[1], the first book ever published on the subject. Compiled to celebrate the province's seventy-fifth anniversary, the 100-page hardcover is a timely glimpse into artwork of the last decade, in particular some of the professional artists whose names will resonate in the post-1970 era. Generally under the age of forty at the time, these practitioners are what is new about art in Alberta,[2] including those who have recently made Calgary their home after accepting positions as art instructors (Lylian Klimek, Clyde McConnell, William Laing, Ron Kostyniuk, Margaret May). Others, such as sculptor **KATIE OHE** (1937, Peers, Alberta), are longtime residents, absorbing Calgary's not-so-visible visual-art history. Born "in muskeg west of Edmonton"[3] to German immigrant parents, Ohe receives her formal training in the late 1950s and early 1960s under Luke Lindoe, Illingworth Kerr, Walter Drohan, her mentor, Marion Nicoll, and Arthur Lismer (Montreal School of Art and Design). Thus, well-versed in the history of place and the preceding generation of artists, she becomes a significant link between the historic and contemporary periods.

Because of her lengthy presence in the city as a working, exhibiting artist, Katie Ohe can rightfully be considered an elder of the Calgary arts scene. With a professional career spanning forty years, Ohe remains as artistically engaged at the end of the century as she is in the early 70s when she begins to create a distinctive body of kinetic sculpture, largely for public commission. This commitment is partly due to her constant contact with students and younger artists largely through teaching at the Alberta College of Art and Design.

Unfortunately, as Katherine Ylitalo points out, Ohe is not publicly well-known in Calgary – "*Zipper* is probably the most popular public sculpture on the University of Calgary campus, but the name of the artist is the least recognized"[4] – nor is she any more recognized in the larger Canadian art world. Despite being "one of the first artists to make modern sculpture in Alberta," Ylitalo believes Ohe's low art-world profile is attributable to a couple of factors: her long-term association with public art "at a time when the art world was supportive of the model of the artist who pursued an individual quest for style, not an involvement with sponsors," and the fact that, as Ylitalo writes, "Ohe did not feel she was prolific enough to feed an exhibition every two years because it often took between one and two years to complete a particular piece."[5] While both these reasons are contributing factors, Ohe worked in a genre – metal sculpture – that has long been considered a male practice, and unless she worked to deliberately "subvert" the form aesthetically or bring to it gender-specific themes and images, the critical art world would not have been interested. As art historian Maria Tippett observed about the feminist revolution in art in her book, *By A Lady:*

> First, [feminist art groups during the 1970s and early 1980s] believed that women's art was different from that produced by men. They argued, with a number of the country's public curators, that women's art was more textured and body-centred, closer to the life sources and frequently produced in series. Second, they believed that private and public, personal and political issues could not be separated: art was political and personal at the same time. Third, they felt women artists owed their allegiance to the feminist movement, not to the commercial gallery that marketed their work or the private collector who bought it.[6]

In 1975, before positions had hardened on what kind of art was proper or correct for a woman to make, Carol A. Philips of the Norman MacKenzie Art Gallery (Regina) included Katie Ohe in the all-women show entitled *Changes: 11 Artists Working on the Prairies.* "The restriction to painting and sculpture was purposely established to emphasize the reality, that art in the 'grand' tradition is being produced by women."[7] Besides Ohe, Philips chose from Alberta the "photo-realism"[8] of Dulcie Foo Fat, the abstract paintings of Ann Clarke and the "personal image and symbol"[9] paintings of Joice Hall and Alexandra Haeseker. These four artists, like Ohe, would also come to exist in an uncertain, somewhat marginal zone between the established (male) art world and the increasingly critical and theoretical agendas of feminist art practices.

Overall, there would have been few brownie points to be had for an artist like Ohe, who, while having made a viable career for herself in the arena of modern metal sculpture, linked her art with a tradition that dated back to before World War II. In 1990, Ohe wrote, "Some thirty years [ago], at the start of my professional career, I saw the works of Giacometti, Brancusi, Noguchi and others for the first time. Their work impressed me for they had a presence, a spirit and a magic – qualities I believe significant sculpture must possess and qualities I have been striving to embody in my own work."[10] Thus, although Ohe worked in metal and even produced welded abstract forms, her sculpture was totally unlike the welded steel of Edmonton with its more recent links to the post-war creations of David Smith and Anthony Caro. Ohe and Edmonton had both been spawned from the delta of modernist sculpture, but in the 1970s the latter worked at widening one particular stream that was already established, while Ohe evolved her own idiosyncratic course out of the older traditions of the medium: less monumental, less formal and less rigorously abstract. Always "driven"[11] by the idea or concept rather than by the materials and process, Ohe's desire to "use kinetics as a psychological and philosophical component"[12] is what largely precipitated her move into metal in the late 1960s and early 1970s. Beginning with welded and chromed steel and then shortly after, cast bronze, the artist, with the help of local industry and skilled tradesmen in Calgary and Italy, engineered and fabricated an impressive array of sculptures, some large enough to occupy a public space – *Zipper No.2,* 1979, Edmonton Centre; *Lotus 1,* Bethany Care Centre, 1983, Calgary – others small enough to fold and unfold by hand – *Family Box, Carpet* and *Kiss.*

"Moveable elements have often been a part of my sculpture, this movement, disciplined and significant, is often the heart of my sculpture. For me, the aesthetic experience is a spiritual experience of communion, of sharing, it is the essence of my work."[13] These elements of movement and communal experience can be seen in works such as *Mantova Arch* (1979–80, welded steel, chrome), with its hypnotic twisting and rotation "set into motion with the gentle push of a hand,"[14] or in the fluid animation of *Venetian Puddle* 1977–78, welded steel, chrome), inspired by the rippling effect of water. Of this body of work, which was eventually explored in careful detail in a 1991 retrospective entitled *Katie Ohe* (Illingworth Kerr Gallery, Calgary), Ylitalo comments, "These sculptures are so brilliantly engineered, so precise and polished, that they do not appear to be humanly made."[15]

The retrospective also highlighted a very different, more recent body of sculpture from the mid-1980s, involving the casting of recycled automotive pistons for their aluminium content. What emerged was a series of lightweight floor pieces with oscillating parts, such as *Guardians* (1988–89). They were more playful, more eccentric and more directly suggestive of the human form than anything previous. With their scored and pockmarked matte surfaces and stubby legs, these conical-shaped figures – called *Markers* in a 1989 Glenbow exhibition – looked altogether humanly made.

Ohe's source of inspiration for these works was her sketches of "seedpods, mice, hills, towers, minarets, rockets, robots and Japanese lanterns and clay tomb guardians of the Haniwa era."[16] In one sense, Ohe seemed to be responding to some of the artistic tendencies of the decade: producing expressive, figure-related symbolic art. The geometry, the purity and techno-shine of the 1970s were gone, and in its place evolved sculpture with a more organic, humanistic flavour.

In 1997, an even more soulful side of the artist was revealed in yet a newer body of work that Ohe calls her "prayers." Exhibited for the first time in an important show of contemporary Alberta sculpture entitled *Real Objects* (Edmonton Art Gallery), local reviewer Nora Abercrombie had this to say: "Katie Ohe's steel sculptures stand out. I never knew steel could be convinced to be so emotional, could exhibit delicacy or lyricism. I am rarely moved to touch steel sculpture but I badly wanted to touch these."[17] And why not? Attached at eye-level on a wall, these small intimate works, the length of a child's arm, are meant to draw the viewer into an act of contemplation. Rather than setting something into motion, a prayer in the form of a tiny bowl is retrieved from the work's cage-like linear structure. Sometimes, to get there one must reach through what looks to be a bird's beak, a symbol for the artist about hunger and need.

Almost weightless in appearance, these three-dimensional drawings in steel strands are certainly the most intuitive of Ohe's oeuvre. Like the other artworks in *Real Objects,* they each have "a strong individual character" [18] and are "at once assertive and open to many readings." [19] Curated by Denis Gautier, Ohe's inclusion with artists at least ten years younger (Blake Senini, Nicholas Wade, Sandra Bromley and Clay Ellis) speaks volumes not only about her currency but also her contribution to making the practice of sculpture a reality in Calgary.

Like Katie Ohe, **JOHN HALL** (1943, Edmonton, Alberta), while a student of the Alberta College of Art (1960–65), absorbed its strong work ethic and a conviction in art being a professional practice informed by independent thinking. His role models were college instructors Ron Spickett and Marion Nicoll, and he recalls "the school was never prepared to push a party line in the 1960s. They pushed technique and form more than concept. The requirement for students was to make art that was their own." [20] Over time, this is exactly what Hall will do with his innovative and hyper-real still-lifes executed in a post-pop realist style.

But in the Canadian contemporary art world of 1971, abstract art and modernist ideals still predominate and for the twenty-eight-year-old artist, it's not enough. Instead, he writes, "I aspire after an art that is concerned with seeing the world as it is. An art that is non-escapist, non-idealist and non-elitist. An art that sees as its goal the clear communication of the artist's perception of his environment."[21]

Hall prepared this statement for the Alberta-wide *Environment 71* exhibition, where he displays a new painting entitled *Pepsi* (1970); an acrylic depicting a crushed Pepsi can against a plant-festooned, wall-paper background. As the work of a younger generation coming to the forefront, how radically different *Pepsi* must have looked in comparison to the vast land and sky painting of fellow *Environment* exhibitor Illingworth (Buck) Kerr. Then 65, the former head of the college (1947–1967), is also blatantly clear about his direction. "At present I am a reactionary, turning back to landscape painting, being sentimental, romantic, regional – all the dirty words. I am not concerned about being a Canadian painter but the prairie country is not only my native land but my spiritual home and I accept its dictation."[22]

Different sentiments and different goals indeed! To which could also be added the matter of their artistic roots: Kerr inspired by the Group of Seven, Hall by the recent incantations of pop art. "[Pop artists] made it seem possible to make a picture that was representational without being reactionary."[23] Despite this gap, though, there are areas where these two artists of different generations intersect and, in the process, illuminate some of the threads particular not just to Hall's history but to his larger community, Calgary. First, as the 1974 *Alberta Realists* (Edmonton Art Gallery)[24] illustrates in its survey of realism, Hall is part of a diverse tradition of representational art in the city that, in the exhibition, encompasses not only the more contemporary, photorealist renderings of Dulcie Foo Fat (a student of Hall's) and Gary Olson, but also the more conservative and painterly tendencies of an older practitioner like Illingworth Kerr. Second, both generations, as embodied by Kerr and Hall respectively, have a keen interest in communicating their perceptions of their environments. For Kerr and others of his generation, this means focusing on the landscape, although not exclusively if one considers the more urban representations of James McLaren Nicoll and Janet Mitchell, and the more philosophically tinged depictions of the human condition by Maxwell Bates and H.G. Glyde. Hall, too, is captivated by his surroundings but they are totally of an indoor kind, or at least a product of contemporary consumer society.

Comparing him to an "urban archaeologist,"[25] fascinated not only with the kitsch and junk of a consumerist culture but also the more personally meaningful objects individuals keep, Nancy Tousley observed in 1982: "For more than ten years, John Hall's meticulously described realistic images were the result of his direct observation of reliefs or maquettes set up in the studio. Made of objects and materials he selected intuitively and deliberately arranged, these still-life constructions were then translated as objectively as possible into seamless images in acrylic paint on canvas."[26]

In the 1980s the maquette is replaced by photographs of the still life and by the end of the century, it is the digital camera and computer software used to create the image he wants to paint. He does this despite learning in his student days that the aid of a camera "was considered about the poorest way to make representational art."[27] But not for someone like Hall, who is totally attuned to the shining and seductive photographic imagery produced by the mass media and advertising. Increasingly, his paintings will come to resemble or maybe even outdo the slick, colour-saturated photographs of fashion and product advertising.

But beginnning in the late 1960s with the "highly refined renderings of urban debris [garbage and junk] tacked-up, strapped together and or hung suspended"[28] from the studio wall and then followed in the mid-70s with the provocative *Rose* series which, as one critic writes, "[consists of painted] floral arrangements for the end of the world and the death of civilization, apocalyptic shrines for the death of Western culture,"[29] by the end of the decade it is clear that Hall is staking out a territory that is essentially preoccupied with his social and cultural milieu. There is no political agenda attached but only that of an image-maker whose canvases are interpreted as being "about cultural decay, while others are about sadness, or desperation, or confidence."[30] And, somewhere in this mix is also a good dose of sexual innuendo making the later more explicit, erotic skinhead imagery of Attila Richard Lukacs, (also born in Edmonton), seem rather cloying.

For the most part, Hall's response to his time and place comes out of the context of his or his friends' domestic surroundings, and as still-lifes, they are hard to forget. His perspective is as atypical as Maxwell Bates's post-war depictions of struggling, disenchanted prairie folk and just as Bates's paintings do not evoke nostalgia, Hall's still-lifes, filled with the ephemera of daily life or the spoils of late-twentieth-century materialism can be edgy and unsettling. And, when direct references to Alberta do appear, as in *Cut* (1986), or more specifically in his Calgary Winter Olympic still-lifes – shown in *The Game's The Thing* at the Whyte Museum, Banff, 1988 – the paintings have all the air-brushed artifice of an ad campaign. One half of you wants to examine more closely what the jumble of sports equipment and Olympic tourist souvenirs allude to, while the other half wants to recoil at the excess.

Cut is a little different in mood but its modus operandi is similar to the Olympic series in that the power of the image supersedes all reality. Writing about *Cut* for *The Best Contemporary Canadian Art* (1987), Hall states, "In this picture, art, as represented by a fairly aggressively assembled pile of painting hardware [paintbrushes, palette knife, paint cans and so on], stands between the viewer and the landscape [picture in the background], eclipsing virtually all of the landscape. In the picture's close and dynamic cropping, the art objects symbolize the way art (culture) insists on determining the ways in which we perceive ourselves and our environment."[31] In an interview with *BorderCrossings* a few years later, he adds, "It seems to me that we find ourselves surrounded by a media cocoon and it conditions how we see reality."[32]

By the late 1970s, national recognition is starting to come Hall's way. Writes one prominent Toronto critic about that period, "[He] was stretching ironic, narrative pictures when [Toronto] Queen Street's chic new realists were still in training bras." [33] His first survey *John Hall: Paintings and Auxilary Works* 1969–1978,[34] is even exhibited at the National Gallery of Canada in 1979 which, in the thirty-year period covered by this book, will be only one of two solo exhibitions by an Alberta-based artist shown at this resolutely central Canadian institution.[35]

After the survey, he embarks on several new projects, *The Tourist Series,* which depicts a selection of tourist souvenirs collected from his year-long sabbatical in New York, and the supposedly playful but twisted *Toy Series,* where a toy or a group of toys are arranged on a mirror and painted larger-than-life. "[The toys] are suddenly no longer harmless children's playthings. They become signs of the adult world." [36] Going deepest into his own backyard are the *Still-life Portraits,* based on the belongings and personal knick-knacks given to him by friends.

Arranged and displayed on a table for the artist to photograph, the results were then meticulously translated into hyper-realistic, larger-than-life, high-gloss painted images. Commenting on this distinctive but voyeuristic approach to the portrayal of a living subject – such as Hall and friend Don Mabie in the "nostalgic" [37] *Phoenix* or himself and his wife Joice Hall in the "erotic" [38] *Indigo* – Hall concludes: "They're reflections of me and they're also reflections of the sitters.... So the paintings point to me, they point to the sitters and I think they point to our society in general, to the sorts of things we tend to value." [39] The portraits can also be interpreted to imply that reality is nothing more than about appearances, about display, about illusion, about surface and about imitation. What one sees or witnesses to is not necessarily even close to what is actually true.

Hall, though, is not trying to be a moralist. Rather, his pictures are, as Nancy Tousley articulates so well in 1982, "Charged with an emotional and intensely private symbolism, they were so personal as to seem eccentric, and as disturbingly ambivalent in meaning as Hall was reticent to discuss their emotive content.... If he is disinclined to speak directly about the meaning, as many realists are, meaning is nonetheless present and significant." [40]

But if Hall's art is viewed as eccentric, the artist himself is also described in a 1985 article in the *Globe and Mail*'s as being "something of an odd-man-out in Canadian art."[41] For one thing, he is a talent who stays in what is deemed from a Toronto perspective as the hinterland, and then there is his allegiance to realist painting that, although publicly popular in the post-1970 era, is critically unpopular in more so-called advanced art circles. His technical mastery too is at best a controversial attribute in postmodern Canada: "Essentially conservative, my paintings have always tended to celebrate clarity, craft, traditional values in art. . . . In their conservatism they strike me as being, quite possibly quintessentially Canadian. There is a pioneer pragmatism reflected in my work."[42]

These attitudes cement Hall's work firmly within the art community of Calgary, with its respect for the art object and its fascination for manipulating both art and non-art to tease out new subject matter, new sensations and new meanings. Rather than "objectness [being] subordinate to ideas"[43] and "the form of art [being] almost immaterial,"[44] many Calgary artists seek to strike a balance between the two. Couple this with a propensity for a pluralistic range of expression in the community, and John Hall is a strong example of how dominant these eccentric, idiosyncratic and highly personal voices have been.

In the 1990s, with a lot of time now spent in Mexico, Hall alters his subject matter somewhat by rendering a body of work based on his reading of the rich and baroque material culture of a cluttered Mexican market. Entitled *La Disposicion del Mercado* (Disposition of the Market), these florid paintings are highlighted in *Traza de Evidencia* (Trail of Evidence), a solo show curated by fellow Calgary artist Derek Michael Besant for Mexico City's prestigious Museo de Arte Moderno (1993). An edited version of the show is also exhibited in Toronto and Calgary, of which Gary Michael Dault, in examining the flood of things populating every square inch of the canvas, wrote: "This performance is the painter's work, a painterly validation of the artist's being in the world. In just such a sense is Hall the maker of an epic ongoing autobiography of taste and (subsequent) meaning. His tastes and his subsequent meaning. Not anybody else's."[45]

Finally, within the context of contemporary realism in western Canada, Hall is an important figurehead. As a practice, photorealism may be the only so-called school of painting said to exist in post-1970 Calgary. Exhibitions such as *Six Calgary Realists*[46] (1985, curated by Hall), *Aspects of Realism*[47] (1989), *Realism Revisited*[48] (1995); and *Sight Specific*[49] (1997) also suggest that this sharp-focused practice is thriving in the city with some realists – like Dulcie Foo Fat, Jim Tanner, Glen Semple and Keith Harder receiving instruction from Hall himself at the University of Calgary, where he taught from 1971 to 1998.

But as Nancy Tousley points out in a review of *Six Calgary Realists,* "Realism, as a catch-all term, often seems monolithic, especially when contrasted with the forms and schools of advanced modernist art. But realism holds its wide umbrella over a variety of approaches to descriptive painting and this show reflects the pluralism of its contemporary practice."[50] This continues to be true of Calgary into the next century.

RON MOPPETT (1945, Eastbourne, Sussex, England) is only a few years younger than John Hall. Raised in the town of Eastbourne, Moppett moves with his family to the arid high plains of Calgary in 1957. Ten years later, he graduates from the Alberta College of Art, and in the tradition of some of its graduates will have a lengthy relationship with the institution. This includes periods of teaching and significant stretches as curator of the Alberta College of Art (ACA) Gallery – renamed Illingworth Kerr Gallery in 1990.[51]

Moppett also has a fruitful relationship with John Hall. In the late 1960s and 1970s, their paths cross with a kind of synergy, recalling the earlier friendship of Maxwell Bates and John Snow. In 1968, for instance, while serving as curator of the ACA Gallery, Hall gives Moppett his first solo exhibition. Then, in 1975, the two young men together organize Marion Nicoll's first retrospective for the Edmonton Art Gallery. Projects of this type are usually not within the realm of interest for young, up-and-coming artists, but Hall and Moppett, both deeply affected by the commitment of the older generation, possess an almost ingrained sense of that earlier history. A few years later, Moppett, as curator of the ACA Gallery, curates the reputation-making *John Hall: Paintings and Auxiliary Works 1969–78,* which then goes on to the National Gallery of Canada.

Hall and Moppett also organize the celebrated *Rose Museum* (1973), which, in the style of a museum exhibit, showcases 1,000 "objets de rose,"[52] many of which the two had accumulated, quite by coincidence, for use in their own art. There is one object, for instance, featured in Moppett's semi-abstract canvas, *Alberta Rose Landscape* (early 1970s) and in Hall's *Doll* (1971), which depicts a kewpie doll flanked on each side by a plastic rose. Both paintings are acquired by the National Gallery of Canada.

The success of *Rose Museum,* however, didn't mark the end of the flower's iconic use or, more importantly, the dialogue the two artists continue throughout their earlier art careers. Other examples include Moppett's *Rose-Case* (1974), an early assemblage appropriated by Hall for a painting of the same name, and Hall's *Long Island Sunset* (1979), an object-based portrait of Moppett identified as a forerunner to Hall's *Portrait* series.[53] Produced during Hall's year-long sojourn in New York City, *Long Island Sunset* is answered in kind by Moppett's symbol-packed *Siren Song 1: Portrait of the Artist at Midnight* (1979) and *Siren Song 2: Journey From Nowhere to Nowhere* (1980). According to Nancy Tousley, each of the two large horizontal paintings refers to a 1979 trip Moppett makes to New York and his subsequent decision not to stay for a year but to return to his young family in Calgary.[54] Moppett described the works as being about "going from here, which a lot of people think of as nowhere, to New York, which is somewhere. Okay. But New York is nowhere too if you can't do what you want to do there."[55] During his stay in New York, Moppett felt impeded by a feeling of physical and psychological dislocation. In other words, without intending to sound trite, you can take the boy out of foothills but you can't take the place and all it represents out of the boy.

Moppett eventually did return to New York – by sending an exhibition to the 49th Parallel, Centre for Contemporary Canadian Art, then the most important venue for the showing of Canadian art in that city. Displayed in 1988, Nancy Tousley observes in the exhibition essay, "Working in a region (Western Canada), Moppett reflects the condition of the artist who feels good about where he is and yet cannot help but question where he is not. Moppett's answer to this conundrum charts the map of his personal world. Thus the first fixed point on his map is the artist's studio, isolated in its larger cultural setting."[56] Simply put, Moppett is a romantic, and "his art is a synthesis of his viewpoint of himself, the world around him, and the essential nature of art itself."[57] A task John Bentley Mays will identify as "an engaging, original meditation on one of modern art's oldest topics:"[58] namely the artist in his or her studio, where the work is an expression of one's outer and inner worlds, emotions, dreams, travels, experiences and ruminations on life issues like birth, aging and death.

But, during much of Moppett's career, a different set of expectations will become more dominant in postmodern Canada, including a demand for "meaningful representation"[59] or work that is about more than just self-expression. "The unrestrained expression of subjectivity is associated with a romanticism which seems like an entirely outdated aesthetic project, idealized and hermetic,"[60] declare Bruce Ferguson and Sandy Nairne in the aptly titled exhibition, *The Impossible Self* (Winnipeg Art Gallery, 1988). But over a decade earlier, there is Moppett, the young rising artist appropriating recognizable content from the world's greatest romantic: Vincent van Gogh. In a series of mixed-media collages, paintings, assemblages and sculptures from found objects, produced from 1976 to approximately 1981, Moppett makes so many references to the famous Dutch artist and his images that one curator comments it's "hard to see where imagery about van Gogh left off and Moppett began."[61] Surreal as it may seem, the artist even shows up at the art college one day made up as van Gogh with a beard and a bandaged ear. A black-and-white photograph is taken and incorporated into the mixed-media collage *Self Portrait with Bandaged Ear* (1978). Later references to his alter ego can also be seen in his brisk *Portrait* drawings (1982, ink on paper). These works raise all sorts of questions about Moppett's intentions, especially when he admits to not being a huge fan of the Dutch artist.[62] But there is no cheeky postmodern irony at work here, only an empathetic exploration of the myth of the artist from a place (Alberta) where such individuals are generally invisible, and exist in popular culture as clichés like van Gogh, the tormented genius.

Moppett's association with van Gogh can appear somewhat juvenile, but his contemporary attitude towards the art-making process, coupled with a preference for creating and appropriating a visual language of signs and symbols that can each mean one thing but also another, made his work particularly current, casting his lot in with the postmodernists. Multilayered in its meaning and connotation, this aspect is often achieved through the use of collage, a technique that Moppett had shown himself to be nothing short of masterful at. Ultimately, the real value of the van Gogh period, according to Tousley, is that "his total identification with the other artist enabled Moppett to find his own speech, as signs signifying van Gogh came to stand for himself and his own experience."[63]

The van Gogh work is highlighted in *Ron Moppett,* a 1982 exhibition organized by the Walter Phillips Gallery (the Banff Centre School of Fine Arts). Commenting on the series in a *Calgary Albertan* review, Brooks Joyner writes: "He has set out some hard and fast objectives for himself and his work. Probably the most defiant of these has been his calculation that one's art should be as much a personification of the man who creates it as it is a reflection of the nature and the space it occupies. He has been consistent."[64] In this sense, Moppett is well on his way to evolving into a painter's painter, becoming one of Calgary's most serious contenders for such a designation in the post-1970 period.

Veering away from Calgary's long, solid tradition of descriptive art, Moppett's more difficult art may not make him the most publicly well-known, but his reputation carries critical weight nonetheless. There is both substance and mystique (an aura) attached to his practice. Many years later, when Moppett wins one of the largest national awards for visual arts, the 1997 *Gershon Iskowitz Prize,* it seems like a totally logical choice that such a plum would be bestowed on him. (Another Calgary-based artist to win this prize is Eric Cameron in 1994, then head of the University of Calgary's art department.) The jury citation reads "Ron Moppett is a beautiful painter who distills shapes and forms in very complex ways. His contribution has been consistent and thoughtful and he is deserving of far greater recognition than he has received to date." [65]

His "strong personal vocabulary" [66] is also acknowledged in the citation, something that, in relation to Calgary's own art history, ties him to the legacy of Maxwell Bates and W.L. Stevenson and their modernist, outward-looking attitude, including their high regard for what is sometimes referred to as art for the sake of art. Certainly all three non-traditionalists are subjective, emotionally expressive, intuitive and painterly. Moppett, like Bates, can also be described as an "engaged" artist, in that beyond his art-making, he is involved in the larger community as a teacher, colleague, curator and role model. Another similarity might be, as Kathleen Snow once wrote of Bates's artwork, "his colour was compelling ... though he often went against all the rules of pictorial composition." [67] Ditto for Stevenson and Moppett. As well, there is Bates's continual interest in duality, [68] which in Moppett's art is expressed by the bringing of "opposite things together, or to make something that can be two things at once (painting and sculpture, interior and exterior, dark and light, profound and silly, representational and abstract, secular and sacred)." [69] And it seems more than a little coincidental that both artists appear in Robert Stacey's *The Hand Holding the Brush: Self Portraits by Canadian Artists* (London Regional Art Gallery, 1983. The other Albertan included in this exhibition and accompanying book is, not surprisingly, John Hall). However, the connection between Bates, Stevenson and Moppett is more like a strong echo than a case of direct influence.

The echo between W.L. Stevenson and Moppett is more one of instinct. As the late curator Mark Joslin notes about the earlier artist in a 1993 interview, coinciding with the Edmonton Art Gallery's *W.L. Stevenson: 1926–1966 Painter of Light/Painter of Darkness:* "It's very much a personal vision that uses images from here with a modernist vocabulary to talk very much about an existential awareness of life in Western Canada."[70] Moppett's vocabulary is, of course, a more postmodernist one in that he "lays claim to all of visual culture"[71] for his signs, symbols and motifs. Nonetheless, his is a like-minded quest: grounded in the experience of existence by the individual. Thus, as Nancy Tousley suggests, "One comes away from a Moppett painting knowing not a story about the artist but where he has been and how it felt to be there."[72]

Although Moppett never meets this first-generation artist who once said, "[My work] looks like Cezanne but is done like van Gogh,"[73] he does remember Stevenson's art from when he was a young student as "being different from a lot of stuff here – that English landscape tradition.... There was 'air' and 'temperature' in them [Stevenson's paintings]. A lot of English art is sort of postcard: get things in the right place, fill in the shapes. Unless, of course, you're talking about Constable or someone who is more appropriate to Stevenson. [His] stuff looks almost like they are cut-out sections. They'd go on if they could. They are different than that snapshot version."[74]

Moppett's compositions also have this sense to them, which, according to Burnett/Schiff, "strain the classical expectations that painting be balanced and unified."[75] Moppett, whether it is with one panel or many, creates a complex mix and range of images that pull the eye this way, that way and every way. As the mind races to keep up, there is a sense of abundance and generosity. He is an artist able to bring forth a panoply of ideas, sensations, materials, artistic styles, textures and juxtapositions. In a single work, the viewer can be jarred, humoured, soothed, challenged, confused and moved. Then again, Moppett can also be terse, presenting simplified images that, besides possessing a graceful economy, reflect certain moments in international contemporary art. His *Siren* series and other works of the late 1970s and early 1980s, for instance, bring to mind the reappearance of recognizable subject matter as in new image art of 1970s. (Although, as Mayo Graham pointed out in the 1982 *Curnoe/Ewen/Falk/Moppett* exhibition, he and the others were hardly newcomers to this practice.[76]) The crisper, more resolved work of the late 1980s and 1990s, which includes the lyrical use of commercial fabric for colour, image and space, and features an interest in ornament and pattern, is part of the reason for his inclusion in the 1997 survey *Patterned After*.[77] Thus, while the artist may be a romantic, he is no island unto himself.

The 1980s proved to be an important decade for solidifying Moppett's national reputation. Like John Hall and other emerging faces from the 1970s

– Annemarie Schmid Esler, Alexandra Haeseker, Derek Michael Besant, Carroll (Moppett) Taylor-Lindoe, Dulcie Foo Fat – he obtains representation in a prestigious Toronto gallery – in his case the Mira Godard Gallery. He also garners much attention from curators, appearing in many group exhibitions including *Seven Artists from Alberta: Art in this Region* (London, England; Bury, Lancashire and Paris, France).[78] Featuring John Hall, Don Kottmann, Carroll Taylor-Lindoe, Mary Scott, Jeffrey Spalding, John Will and Moppett, *Seven Artists* is like the post-war Calgary Group reincarnated. Just as the group's original founder, Jock Macdonald, felt that Cliff Robinson, H.B. Hill, Vivian and Luke Lindoe, Janet Mitchell, Marion Nicoll, Dorothy Willis, Wes Irwin, W.L. Stevenson and Maxwell Bates "represented the new and modern spirit of Alberta,"[79] so too did this more recent group embody something fresh and lively about their own eclectic times.

At the end of the decade, the Glenbow Museum organizes *Ron Moppett: Painting Nature with a Mirror 1974–1989.* Curated by Katherine Ylitalo, this forty-piece retrospective encompasses such key early works as *Rosecase* (1974), *Veiled Threats* (1974), *Fire 1* (1980–81), *Studio/Light 3* (1981) and the *Siren* series (1979–1980), as well as the darker, more expressionistic paintings of the early 1980s. "Almost claustrophobic in their introspection,"[80] the turmoil of these edgy pieces eventually gave way to a body of work that is variously described as "remarkably clear, buoyant and decisive,"[81] "brighter in colour, flatter in space, bolder and more simplified,"[82] and having a "clarity [that] stings like the sharpness of high altitude air."[83]

Focusing on this latter work produced since 1986, the retrospective is, in many ways, a mid-career survey of a maturing vision. At the centre of it is a growing trust in his own intuition and perhaps a little inspiration from role model Illingworth Kerr, a critically old-fashioned male painter "who was a wonderful example of someone who lived for painting."[84] One critic contextualizes the Moppett exhibition like this: "In this moment of growing pluralism, decentering and feminizing tendencies in the visual arts, a major retrospective exhibition of a 45-year-old male's paintings might seem archaic."[85]

Of his later, more open and refined compositions, which continue apace well into the 1990s, Moppett says, "[I have been] putting more air into the paintings";[86] "the most convenient analogy I've found [to describe my work] is the dream";[87] "the new paintings are really quite abstract … and more sculptural";[88] "my art is more emotional than it's usually thought of being";[89] and "they are more sublime in feeling, more optimistic than the earlier pictures."[90] These are general observations, however. Moppett's subject matter is "seldom totally penetrable by analysis,"[91] his art is not intended to be taken like that. His rich collections and arrangements of symbols, signs and motifs are gathered in a "more elliptical fashion."[92] Take, for instance, his discussion concerning *Blood/Light/Angel,* a 1986 oil on canvas with mixed media, considered by the artist to be a breakthrough because of the way it is composed like a vignette or a series of discrete sections. Here we see how picture-making for the artist "can function as a meditation"[93] instead of "being forced into the symbolic at the service of narrative [ie. a story line]."[94]

In his work of the 1990s, elements of the landscape are more present than ever before. There have always been hints or suggestions of this subject matter throughout his oeuvre, sometimes in larger passages that Tousley once described as "some of the most vivid ... in Moppett's paintings."[95] They are painted with such clarity and drama that the temptation is to swoon over their high romance and sublime nature. Rather than describing an actual place, these landscape images or vignettes of some larger world seem to be a product of the imagination, like the perfect moonscape of *Lunar Sand* (1996), the shimmering water of *Shadowland* (1995); and the fairytale mountainscape of *Everything is True* (1994). As images, they are idealized and even fantasized exotic representations in a period when "avant-garde practice has been particularly intent on returning art to the praxis of everyday life and ridding it of those sensuous qualities that are not directly tied to utilitarian purposes."[96]

Even less utilitarian than his depiction of landscapes is his habit of evoking himself within his works, an idiosyncrasy that comes off as being playful. In early collages, paintings and assemblages, he often symbolized himself with an h-shaped chair, something that still appears from time to time. Since then, his repertoire of personal signifiers has expanded to include a hand, a gnome woodcutter (à la the Seven Dwarfs), a stuffed teddy bear dressed in angel's clothing and other such whimsical figures. When asked what function a teddy-bear angel would have in a grand, mythic picture like *Oenone* (1987), Moppett's answer was decidedly un-romantic: "For the angelic image and then just sheer goofiness of it. It operates in much the same way as it does in other paintings. Up and down, high and low, silly and significant. In the face of the largeness of that space and the perceived importance of the painting in its size, there's this goofy bear at the end [of the painting]. Quite frankly, that's a very specific self-portrait.... I see myself as – not nothing – but just a funny little creature. And [the bear] is all dressed up [in angel's clothing] to be something else. So I guess it has something to do with ambition."[97]

To have such a modest view of oneself, almost to the point of parody, is startling, given painting's long association with the artist typecast as the serious all-consuming genius. However, such an attitude may also be a signpost of the postmodern condition: more tentative and less privileged. Whether he knows it or not, Moppett's efforts can be interpreted as a response to the marginalization of the artist and the medium of painting. He remains someone who lives to paint, doing it with skill and finesse. With his unorthodox use of fairy tale–like stand-ins, Moppett may be the closest thing in Canada to a contemporary version of a "fairy" painter, intent on creating his own abundant realm of existence: "All painting is fairy painting: materialized visions of immaterial entities that are possessed of some spirit or another. Even the starkest abstract painting maintains in its rectangle a rule of sorcery by which appearance trumps logic and imagination is common sense. We enjoy that, if we like painting."[98]

With a diploma in painting (1969) from the Alberta College of Art, followed by a four-month period of post-graduate study at Instituto Allende (San Miguel de Allende, Mexico), **DON MABIE** (1947, Calgary, Alberta) steers a course almost identical to his slightly older colleagues John Hall and Ron Moppett. He does not, however, become a painter, nor even an artiste as the profession continues to be understood among the general population. Truly a child of the 1960s, Mabie's practice has taken place largely in the alternative/counter-culture community that can be found in larger centres across Canada. Although there are many aspects to this milieu, including its links to early periods of radical art activity like Dada (1915–23), and more recently Fluxus (1960s), the making of art objects for commercial sale or display was and is not a priority. Its aspirations are more utopian, anti-elitist, anti-establishment and experimental. And Mabie, under his nom de plume, Chuck Stake, would – by the force of his irreverent personality, long-term commitment, networking and mixed-media approach – become one of its most high-profile representatives in the country.

Nominated in Calgary for a 1999 Govenor General's Award in Visual and Media Arts, the artist explained the motivation behind his participation in such alternative modes as correspondence mail art and artist trading cards: "They both emphasize certain principles which are important to me, such as:

a democratic exchange and interaction with others (artists and non-artists); open-ended creativity; a non-hierarchical, non-judgemental act that exists within, but more importantly outside of the existing high-art world – [they] are a true vernacular art form."[99]

In one sense, the artist may be a throwback to another era, but even in the 1990s, Mabie's 60s-styled cultural and aesthetic leanings have a certain relevance. His art is included, for instance, in exhibitions such as *A Duchampian Look at Glenbow's Art Collection* (1997) and *In/Here/Out/There: Alberta Biennial of Contemporary Art 1998.* In the former he is selected for his use of chance as a way to make art, the influence of neo-dada artists such as Robert Rauschenberg and Iain Baxter, and his own obsessive methods. "Out of curiosity, I sought out [Marcel] Duchamp and the genie was released from the bottle,"[100] he says in explaining his roots. For the biennial, he is there because "[May's mail art] opens the process of art making, encouraging a plurality of creators and myriad interpretations."[101] But by participating in such an institutionally driven undertaking, there is also, according to the artist, a twist. "The irony (I like irony) of finding correspondence/mail art situated in the Glenbow Museum [and later in the Edmonton Art Gallery] reminds me of one of the most ubiquitous statements that has floated around the correspondence/mail art network for decades: 'Mail it. Don't jail it! Keep art out of the museums.'"[102]

In the case of the *98 Biennial,* his contribution consists of casually collaged invitations and numerous responses in mixed-media works tacked to a wall. "Don's [project] is really about collapsing … borders,"[103] explains *Biennial* co-curator Catharine Mastin, "one can communicate [with mail art] across a wide geography. He invited artists from all over the world to [send] in their art [about the frontier]."[104]

With thirty years of experience under his belt, Mabie is more than qualified for the above task. Beginning his career as an international correspondence artist in Toronto – where, according to the *Toronto Star,* the artist "reached his audience without having to apply for permission [from art dealers or curators]."[105] By 1982, Chuck Stake Enterprizes (CSE) had "organized six major projects and seventeen mail exhibitions, run a radio show, and participated in more than sixty-eight international mail art shows organized by others."[106] Then he moves back to Calgary in 1974 with his partner, the notable Wendy Toogood, where a new base for counter-culture art will be built. "I got pretty tired of seeing colour field painting as being the 'thing' to do in Toronto.

When I returned to Calgary you could feel a scene being created. And, by then the art college was in a new building as well."[107]

Once in Calgary, large amounts of Mabie's time become entangled with the building of a fledgling artist-run network in Calgary and other collective activities. In these endeavours, he will work devotedly as an administrator, curator and all-around cultural foot soldier. For example, in 1974 he assists Ron Moppett and John Hall in the assembling of the *Rose Museum* exhibition; becomes a founding member of the Parachute Centre for Cultural Affairs in 1975; joins the board of the Clouds 'n' Water Gallery in 1978 and oversees its transformation into one the most exciting artist-run galleries in the country – the Off Centre Centre (renamed the New Gallery in 1988). At OCC, he also co-founds, with Mark Dicey and Sandra Tivy, the Canadian Correspondence Art Gallery (1985–87). When he resigns in 1988 from The New Gallery as administrator and vice-president of the board, *The Calgary Herald* described his contribution in the field of cultural activism as "incalculable."[108]

But what about his art? In this regard, Mabie has had a rather unorthodox career, especially for a former ACA graduate who remembers "sitting for hours on end at the college learning to draw a cube. You would never do that today!"[109] Mabie regards his art training as being conservative – with the exception of the radical Vancouver artist Terry Reid, who taught him in his last year at the college.[110] Nonetheless, even with a conservative art education, he does in a circuitous way become known for his drawing and graphic abilities. He is included in shows such as the *9th Annual Calgary Graphics Exhibition*[111] (Purchase Award, 1969), *Graphic 71*[112] (1971), and *On Paper*[113] (1976), serves on the executive board of the Print and Drawing Council of Canada (1975–77), and curates two important province-wide surveys of drawing and printmaking for Alberta's seventy-fifth anniversary (1980).[114] Of this particular talent he has, Mabie later writes: "Drawing has always been an obsession with me, it underlies everything I've done/do.... Drawing is a drug: it's addicting, it's enjoyable, it's relaxing, it's stimulating, it's entertaining, it kills time, it expands consciousness, it provides meaning."[115]

Thus, strip away all the radical, anti-high art-activity – which, besides his mail art, includes drawings, bookworks, rubber stamp and colour-copy works, bodyworks, button works with slogans, installations and performance, including collaboration with the Canadian/European group The Nomads[116] and the Calgary-based group The Skep(tic)ks[117] – and there is revealed a closet doodler. It may not be drawing in the conventional sense of sketching a figure or a landscape, but it is drawing nonetheless. His own brand of pen and ink, coloured pencil, and acrylic work fills and animates all of his two-dimensional efforts, be they small or large, serious or silly, framed or unframed, mailed or unmailed. (In 1994, Mabie moved onto a PowerMac computer to produce his work.)

About Mabie's celebrated (pre-computer) word pictures, often meticulously executed on white illustration board, Patrick Tivy once wrote,

> He has a style of drawing that is unique. He makes drawings of words, filling entire great sheets with doodle-style slogans and phrases. The coloured-ink drawings are truly beautiful, although not everyone is ready yet to see them as art. His father, Frank, for instance, recalls with fondness the portraits he used to do when he was a teenager. ❧ Patrick Tivy. "Wasn't that a party!" *Calgary Herald,* March 25, 1982.

But, as the son later points out, Dad is a sign painter whose careful execution of the letters instilled in him "a particular attitude towards words – they were almost physical 'things' that you could manipulate and play with." [118] Thus, rather than being only conveyors of meaning, the letters in and of themselves also have a visual presence, an attribute Mabie will exploit like no one else in Canadian art. Even when the inclusion of text becomes a popular strategy in the early 1980s among certain artists, Mabie's topical text-loaded art is in a class of its own, vividly "linguistic on one hand, pictorial on the other."[119]

Lettering by hand words, phrases and sentences, often in the 3-D block style so typical of the psychedelic poster art of the sixties, Mabie creates collage-like drawings of "packed, stacked and jumbled" [120] text, scavenged from newspapers, song lyrics, radio programs, magazines, conversations and other sources. Citing a fear of "empty spaces," [121] the artist also attaches stickers, stamps, postcards, decals, photos and other relevant ephemera to the drawing's surface. The result of all of this obsessive activity is a body of mind-boggling word pictures that suggest a world bursting with information. Mabie's insightful drawings sum up the double-edged quality of our media age with its capacity to make information both meaningful and meaningless.[122]

"Diaristic in content, Don's drawings chronicle our times – like fast moving mirrors or television screens controlled by remote control 'zappers,' they record in fragmented fashion the comic and tragic aspects of our world," [123] explains John Hall. In this sense, Mabie takes his place beside his older colleague, John Hall – of whom he did a word "portrait" in 1990–91.[124] Both operate in *raconteur*-like fashion, their pictorial narratives about certain individuals reflecting the surrounding cultural and social mileu. Ultimately their art comments on the contemporary condition as in the following example:

> In his latest work, *Finally: It's All Over,* Mabie covers more than eighteen different topics including his leaving The New Gallery, the opening of Canada's [new building] National Gallery, free trade, a Dylan concert at the Saddledome, income tax changes, his brother's death, global pollution, American artist Jackson Pollock, the drought, the Flames winning the Stanley Cup, the water shortage issue, the Gretzky trade, the Goods and Services Tax, the Alberta pulp mills controversy, recent changes in Eastern Europe politics, AIDS, Meech Lake, and the Lubicon land claims. We are left to figure out for ourselves what the connections are between the issues.[125]

Produced over a period of three years, the triptych *Finally: It's All Over* is the largest 'doodle' displayed in *Don Mabie; Drawings: 1978–1990.* Organized by Calgary's Muttart Art Gallery, the comprehensive survey is something of a first for Mabie, at least in terms of the recognition it gives him outside of the alternative art sphere. This effort is then followed in 1996 with *Don Mabie/Chuck Stake: Aspects of Practice: 1969–1996* at his old alma mater, Alberta College of Art and Design (Illingworth Kerr Gallery). Taking a holistic approach to his varied output, the retrospective features not only drawings but also examples of other two-dimensional work, such as his mail art and more recent *Computerworks,* as well as documentation and material related to his earliest performance, *Mural Performance* (1968), and his collaborations with the Nomads and the Skep(tic)ks.

Multi-disciplinary artist Grant Poier, who has participated in both collectives and has had a long relationship with Mabie through the local network of artist-run centres, had this to say about Mabie's allegiance to the 1960s: "Don's 'Bring Back the Sixties' refrain is not a jingle for the rewarmed nostalgia of today's retro trends. The current mass media focus claims to reflect a popular yearning for supposedly simpler times, but, more truthfully, it is just a new angle for vacuous advertising strategies. Aside from invoking this much-stereotyped era to provoke critics who like to argue, it all dissipated like curls of herb smoke; Don is perhaps suggesting we infuse the nineties with a sense of wonder, energy and adventure that characterized the sixties."[126]

This observation takes on particular potency with the unveiling of *Making it New! (the big sixties show)* at the Glenbow Museum in 1999.[127] Featuring alternative and experimental art produced in Canada during the 1960s by Joyce Wieland, Greg Curnoe, Gathie Falk, N.E.Thing Co and others, the exhibition – which includes documentation of Mabie's 1968 *Mural Performance,* plus a happening (improvisational music, performance and art-making installation)[128] orchestrated by Chuck Stake, writer/curator Dennis Slater and artist-friends – suggests the 60s weren't so much an era as a state of mind. For thirty years, Don Mabie, with a wry sense of humour and a keen awareness about the present as well as the past, has done the near-impossible: kept the 60s alive and meaningful.

chapter fifteen

Printed, Painted and Otherwise

> I'VE ALWAYS WORKED WITH MEDIA in fairly uninhibited ways: [my] early paintings based upon family and the past, utilized photography, burning of paper edges, layers of wax, smoke over drawings, erasure and subtractive grounds, and casting isolated shapes encasing images in resin. My experiments with watercolour and lithography have directly influenced my paintings, and vice versa. The shaped sections on paintings, and the free-standing pieces go back to my resin drawings and sculptures. [1]

In the above excerpt, the Dutch-born artist **ALEXANDRA (SANDY) HAESEKER** (1945, Breda, Holland) discusses her versatility with a variety of media not uncommon in the careers of many of Calgary's important printmakers of the 1970s and 1980s. Trained in Calgary prior to the 1970s, she is one of a small number to be formally instructed in the city before the boom in printmaking takes place in several Canadian centres across the country. [2]

While this group includes other notables such as the more senior John K. Esler and Harry Kiyooka, printmaking in Calgary during the 1960s is a small-scale activity with only a few practitioners and instructors. All of this will change with the rapid expansion of both the Alberta College of Art and University of Calgary in the 1970s and the inclusion of more printmakers in their faculties.[3] Born and generally trained abroad, this diverse group of artists becomes the new gang in town: their experimental approaches to printmaking and other media reinforcing "the prevailing ideology in the south [i.e. Calgary]," which, since the late 60s, has "consistently been more sympathetic to, and supportive of, a variety of styles."[4]

For example, early works displayed in *Calgary Printmakers* (the Edmonton Art Gallery, 1974) show a strong interest in figuration rather than pure abstraction. Of the fifty-five silk-screens, etchings, collographs, lithographs, woodcuts and mixed-media works, the vast majority is representational. Organized by the assistant curator Alfred Schmidt, the exhibition, in his opinion, "illustrates a freshness in content, a diversity in techniques, and above all, a respect for the craft of printmaking."[5] Thirty years later, the roster of *Calgary Printmakers* reads like a partial who's who of post-1970 printmakers, including artists like Derek Michael Besant, Jim Brodie, John K. Esler, Alexandra Haeseker, Harry Kiyooka, Noboru Sawai and John Will.

Amidst all of this talent, Alexandra Haeseker blossoms into the young, versatile star of Alberta printmaking: her art is included in numerous juried exhibitions in Canada and abroad, and, in addition to, she has several solo shows of her mixed-media paintings, watercolours and sculptures. She also has the good fortune of showing with the prestigious commercial gallery Marlborough Godard in Toronto and Montreal, and later with the Mira Godard Gallery in Toronto, prompting a critic to observe in *Artscanada,* "[She is] an artist the mass of Calgarians are unfamiliar with, though she is well known in the East."[6] Like Ron Moppett, John Hall, Dulcie Foo Fat and Annemarie Schmid Esler, Haeseker is part of the first serious march eastward by Alberta artists into high-profile Toronto galleries and, as a consequence, into the national conscience.

However, despite the merit of such art, the practice of printmaking will experience a boom-and-bust cycle in the post-1970 period. In 1974 Schmidt tells his audience in the catalogue for *Calgary Printmakers* that "Printmaking has come into new prominence in many areas in Canada."[7] By the mid-1980s the tables will have completely turned, especially in Canada with the collapse of the print market and its now unfashionable status in contemporary art circles. As such, many printmakers turn their focus to Europe and Asia where the multi-faceted medium is better understood and appreciated. Haeseker, for instance, while often better known for her painting, will participate in several international print exhibitions throughout the 1980s and 1990s: *Fourth Seoul International Print Biennale* (1983), *Twelfth International Print Biennale,* (Krakow, Poland, 1988), and the International Grafika Biennale (MECC Museum, Maastricht, Holland, 1993). To survive in Canada, where increasingly the institutional mantra for contemporary art is conceptual, installation-based and new media, printmaking goes global, and as print historian Bente Roed Cochran notes in 1999, "Since prints are multiples, printmakers have taken advantage of the relative ease of shipping prints and have participated vigorously in exhibitions not only in Canada but also abroad."[8] One Alberta printmaker, Noboru Sawai, participates in eighty print competitions between the years 1968 and 1995, which doesn't include his solo and group exhibitions!

Haeseker's contribution, however, is not just confined to her efforts as a printmaker. As well as lithography, she teaches drawing, painting, watercolour and art fundamentals, and while she does serve as the printmaking program chair at Alberta College of Art in the mid-1980s, her oeuvre at the time is primarily focused on painting. All of her solo exhibitions, including her 1992 retrospective: *Alexandra Haeseker: Twenty Years* (Illingworth Kerr Gallery, Alberta College of Art), will concentrate on her work as a painter. Thus, like many of her fellow printmakers, her practice is far broader than the term suggests, encompassing many different approaches that take place beyond the lithographic plate.

In regard to subject matter, Haeseker accomplishes for figurative art what Joice Hall, Dulcie Foo Fat and Maureen Enns do for landscape art, broadening the medium both stylistically and conceptually. Drawing from personal experience, Haeseker explores the themes of childhood, family history, companion animals and personal life. In a letter to John Hall she writes: "It's pretty obvious that the source of my images is almost always autobiographical, based on what is intimately available to me. My national heritage, do you think? – going back to that seventeenth-century painting tradition in Holland scrutinizing the immediate domestic surroundings."[9]

While these subjects sound harmless enough, Haeseker's depictions are unique for their time in Alberta. Works including *Baby on a Winged Chair* (1970, charcoal and acrylic on canvas) and *Girls and Boys Come Out to Play*

(1971, mixed media) resonate with a strangeness that is partly due to how the subjects are portrayed and to the fact that anything connected to domestic life is bound to be greeted also with suspicion in a pre-feminist artworld. According to editor Christopher Reed in *Not at Home: The Suppression of Domesticity in Modern Art and Architecture,* "The notion of domesticity, itself an invention of the modern age – the home, the family, privacy, comfort, as opposed to the workplace – has been challenged and ridiculed by modernist artists, architects and designers." [10]

But by the late 1960s, modernism's penultimate innovation, abstract art, no longer seems all that radical or even iconoclastic. In the presence of so much art about form and colour, a painting of a young girl in a Sunday dress holding a doll – *What Shall My Blue Eyes Go See,* 1970 – is bound to look different. Displayed within the context of a contemporary art exhibition such as the Edmonton Art Gallery's *All Alberta Show,*[11] this work will be unsettling and seem reactionary to those who consider abstraction to be the measure of all that is advanced in art. In this light then, Haeseker is a proto-feminist figure in the Alberta art community. As Lynn Smith points out in her essay "Unleashing Cerberus," "the artist, while not a card-carrying feminist, has done certain things in her career that qualify as a feminist act." [12]

By and large, Haeseker's art of the 1970s will garner positive critical response, largely due to her engagement with art-making concerns of the time: "My paintings from the 1970s function as both readable narrative subject (painted in a realistic way) against abstract grounds (applied in a manner of what most expressionist field painters were physically exploring at that time)." [13] Implicit within a Haeseker work of that time is the idea that the image is not to be taken at face value. A delicate, poignant air of mystery seems to pervade, growing stronger as the images become more dream-like and surreal, bearing a relationship to Jack Chambers's art, which she looks at in her formative years. Haeseker is particularly fascinated by "his earlier series, which use dislocated fragments of figures floating in the pictorial space – allusions to passing time and shifting states of being rather than motion." [14]

Of her early body of work, featuring people with no legs or lower torsos against an ambiguous background, the most provocative is perhaps her series based on nineteenth-century photographer Edward Muybridge's study of a young amputee climbing in and out of a chair. Writing for *Artscanada* in 1975, Hugh G. Anderson comments, "Her works seem to evoke a dream state – a child's dream, made of pastel colour, featuring wonders of young fantasy.

One particular piece, entitled *Catch Him, Crow, Carry Him, Kite* features a flying pig, a clown and, of course, the dreamer [the legless boy], all set into a vista of baby blanket clouds. Verbal description cannot touch it, but it is a gentle thrilling piece, creating the flight into the dream world."[15] In another 1975 review, entitled "Surge of Symbols" for the *Montreal Star,* Henry Lehman offers this observation: "Haeseker's sensibility, like the legless boy, hovers between two extremes – the symbolist visions of Blake and the modern atemporal world of modern art heralded by Picasso and Breton."[16]

In the early 1980s, a shift occurs in her style and approach to form as her imagery becomes literally more grounded and focused on the material world. As Nancy Tousley notes, "One observes her techniques becoming more refined over the years, her photo-based imagery more highly coloured, detailed and photographic in look."[17] Writing for the *Calgary Herald,* Tousley also comments on how the dreamy and mysterious imagery recedes in favour of more visually dramatic pictures. This time, she depicts pedigree show dogs royally ensconced in temporary but vividly coloured outdoor enclosures or shade tents. (Haeseker was seriously involved in showing her dogs to top honors in North American dog shows for many years. In the late seventies she started incorporating old English sheepdogs into her spatially ambiguous imagery.)

Expressing an affinity with contemporary artists such as William Wegman and Donald Roller Wilson who, the artist believes, "explore some of the absurdities and social clichés of our relationships with companion animals,"[18] Haeseker, through several series – *Enclosure, Watch Dog, Expedition,* and *Objects of Desire* – mines this most perfectionist of subcultures for new ways of making a picture. Of the *Expedition* series, for instance, which "might refer to the pause, the temporary campsite or shelter, set up in an undescribed journey,"[19] the eye swirls in an attempt to comprehend the hyper-real drapery surrounding the dutiful animal. It is a baroque collage of colourful tarps, wind socks and metallic safety blankets, almost like an abstract painting; her acrylic images intentionally challenge and play with the viewer's perception.

The dog-show portraits represent a rather unconventional piece of turf to touch down upon, and Haeseker returns to the theme several times, producing images on canvas and paper, in wood and as a public, outdoor mural in Calgary (1990). Like her earlier work, these pieces increasingly have a twist of the surreal and the absurd. By the time she develops the *Objects of Desire* series, the dog is no longer a well-groomed, passive figure on display, he is a wild thing with his head turned up, madly preoccupied, it seems, with his own thoughts and dreams.

In the 1990s Haeseker also begins her *Night Crawlers* series, depicting one or two insects on crinkled neon backgrounds. Working with larger-than-life plastic insects, these entomological scenarios are painted on fragmented corners of masonite. Colourful and completely staged, this quirky engagement – somewhat reminiscent of the peculiar fascination of seventeenth- century Dutch still-life for insects amongst over-ripe fruit and flowers – seems in keeping with Haeseker's own sense of uninhibited exploration of media and subject matter. *Night Crawlers* relates to her childhood in Indonesia, where she gathered specimens of live tropical insects for observation, and an early job she had with the Geological Survey of Canada, illustrating fossils with the aid of a microscope. These close-up images of life-like insects are ambiguously situated between the real and the unreal, a place always favoured by Haeseker in her art.

Not long after Alexandra Haeseker steps forth with a new body of visually punchier work – the dog-show enclosures – two of her colleagues, **WILLIAM LAING** (1944, Glasgow, Scotland) and **DEREK MICHAEL BESANT** (1950, Fort Macleod, Alberta) make their own move individually into more expressive art. Previously, Laing had printed spare evocative images incorporating a few objects like a chair placed in a minimal setting, while Besant's are enigmatic interiors where the perspective of a room is manipulated or distorted. Both artists unveil their new approach in 1985: the former in *Bill Laing: New Work,*[20] seventeen etchings and three mixed-media constructions; and the latter in *Derek Michael Besant: Diagrams,*[21] an exhibition of thirty charcoal drawings on board. Writing about the two Calgary exhibitions respectively, art critic Nancy Tousley comments:

> [Laing] sees this work as a return to his cultural roots and to the concerns with drawing and the figure that animated his work in the early 1970s, before he moved to Calgary and became immersed in the "overpowering" Alberta landscape.... *The Views From a Tearoom* grew out of Laing's travels in England and Scotland last year during a sabbatical from the University of Calgary. Laing sketched people in tearooms, restaurants and parks.[22]
>
> [Besant's new works] are a radical change of pace from his watercolours [of interiors] of the past several years, the thirty charcoal drawings

in *Diagrams* are big, straightforward and blunt.... In their stark X-ray vision, the *Diagrams* portray ordinary things in space – vases, bowls, a cup and saucer on a stack of books, canoes, ladders, umbrellas, lawn sprinklers and a ceiling fan – with a degree of poignancy and mystery." [23]

Clearly a new adventure is underway. In the process, their horizons expand from producing primarily works on paper – prints, drawings and watercolours (Besant) – to an assortment of two- and three-dimensional artworks involving different materials and media. For instance, working with the theme of still-life and domestic interiors, Laing exhibits in 1990 another series of mixed-media constructions that incorporate painting, assemblage and collage, while Besant's *Diagrams* (1985) and *Sites* (1986–87) are described as "complex compositions [from cut, folded and bent cardboard] that are at once relief sculptures, two-dimensional drawing, and architectural installation." [24]

In addition, both artists seem to indulge themselves more fully in the things they love and are fascinated with. For Besant, it is the everyday object, architecture and linear pattern, illusion and fragmentation, the extraordinary in the seemingly ordinary and the gathering and altering of found images. For Laing, on the other hand, solitude, identity and isolation are further developed as major themes and interlaced with subjects such as landscape and nature, pattern and decoration, "illusion and the mystery of space," [25] daily and interior life. As well, for both artists, enriching these proclivities is an active regimen of travel and contact with the work of other artists in Canada and abroad. "The British arts and crafts movement with artists like William Morris, Duncan Grant and Vanessa Bell, which integrated elements from non-traditional art forms like fabric, furniture and book design with traditional art forms like painting certainly influenced my thinking," says Laing.[26] "Several artists have used cardboard.... I saw Michael Heizer's *Dragged Mass Geometric* at the Whitney [in New York] in 1983 which was one very large cardboard construction piece, silk-screened with large blowups of geological material. Also architects like Frank Gehry have used cardboard and redefined it as a material," says Besant. [27]

A long-time drawing instructor at Calgary's Alberta College of Art and Design, drawing underpins much of Derek Besant's art,[28] including printmaking, which he developed an appeal for because of inherent "graphic qualities." [29] Its importance is evident even twenty years later, in shows like *Impressions* (Glenbow Museum, 1991) and *Drawing +* (Open Space, Victoria, 1994). In both Canadian shows, his art is infused with a vivid sense of line: the simple contour of a bowl in *Eden #2* (1991) or the dense outline of a woman's torso in *Mechanism Induced by Fear* (1993). It's not the fashion in recent art to speak about an artist's abilities in the area of drawing – one contemporary art critic describes drawing as "[a medium] much too problematically bound into romantic and patriarchal notions of authenticity and originality,"[30] – but Besant's apt focus on drawn elements makes such pronouncements seem puritanical. (During this period, Besant also enjoys many international exhibitions at Prague, Taipei, Brussels, Barcelona, Mexico, Berlin, Sao Paulo, San Antonio and elsewhere.)

Another strong thread in his oeuvre is a willingness to play around with his imagery and its meanings. Besant revels in making compositions that, in the words of Calgary architect Jeremy Sturgess, prompt the viewer to "do a double-take."[31] Thus, like many of his generation in Calgary's figurative art community, the role of perception, or how an image can be variously interpreted, remains a key concern.

Lethbridge critic Leslie Dawn elaborates on this aspect of Besant's art in his essay "Traces Among the Fragments" (Hamilton Art Gallery, 1990): "The role of the viewer also changes from delectation of formal ingenuity to an active participation in creating meaning. This is, however, always ambiguous and de-centred; there is no privileged, singular viewpoint. Rather, the work [such as *Decomposition*] presents us with a type of conceptual cubism, that is, with a series of fragmented, overlapping and multiple readings, and shifting planes of signification where closure is never a possibility."[32]

Besant also inspires a double-take reaction with his public-art commissions. Two of his best-known are in downtown Toronto: the outdoor *Flatiron Mural,* which dresses up the plain backside of a historic flatiron building (Berczy Park, 1980), and the indoor *Waterfall* mural, which covers a large vertical wall in the atrium of Scotia Plaza (1988).[33] Hugely ambitious in scale and concept, the murals are a potent mixture of realism and illusion. The earlier mural consists of a painted theatre curtain depicting a Victorian building facade, and the later one represents the Upper Falls of Johnston's Canyon in Banff National Park.

In her 1991 book, *Splitting Images: Contemporary Canadian Ironies,* author and theorist Linda Hutcheon considered the flatiron mural of forty-nine painted panels an "example of the witty and pleasurable ironies that do seem to work totally within the [apolitical] realm of the aesthetic … a postmodern version of a baroque trompe-l'oeil."[34]

Part of the murals' magic also lies in doing the incongruous outrageously, as he did with the sixty-nine panel, fifteen-storey-high *Waterfall:* "It's taking something that's actually life-size out of the natural environment of Alberta and transporting it to the man-made environment of Toronto,"[35] Besant explains. It can be interpreted broadly as a visual statement about the drama and romance of the Hinterland supplanting the human-made forms of the Metropolis.

Aspects of the landscape are present as well in Bill Laing's public mural, unveiled in Calgary in 1995. Commissioned by the Uptown 17 Business Revitalization Zone, *Inside Out* is the final work in a public art program (1989–1995) that had already seen the commissioning of outdoor murals on Calgary's 17th Avenue S.W. from Barbara Milne, John Snow, Maureen Enns, Gary Olson, Janet Mitchell, Joane Cardinal-Schubert, Carroll (Moppett) Taylor-Lindoe, Wade Stout, Fernando Spina and Alexandra Haeseker. A three-paneled painting of a floral couch whose middle section is subtly interrupted by a close-up image of a leafy tree, the large-scale mural had as much to say about Laing and his practice as almost any other work rendered-up to that time. And, unlike previous art, the mural is a large piece that jumped from the more intimate scale of his paintings and prints (silk screens, etchings and lithographs) to a much larger arena. Like a piece of camouflage, the seductive blend of bold organic forms and decorative pattern challenges the eye to make sense of the mural. Noticeable, too, are his fine craftsmanship and sense of beauty, which heighten the artwork's metaphorical subject matter alluding to the human experience of longing and belonging. Writes the late English artist Tim Mara: "[Laing] wants to locate, to know who he is and where he belongs. He wants to know where home is."[36]

Throughout his career, both the rural and urban landscape are a central feature of Laing's oeuvre.[37] In the early 70s, while a young man returning to Britain from Canada for further art studies, it is the citified landscape of London that catches his attention, represented in etchings and lithographs as a white featureless expanse interrupted by solitary individuals or their shadows. Once in Alberta, as a newly hired art instructor with an MFA from London's Royal College of Art, the minimal settings become more spatially panoramic, inhabited by solitary symbols of life: a bird, a fence, a chair, a tree, a horse and so on. In the mid-80s, Laing's sense of landscape shifts back to a more social milieu as found in *The Views of a Tearoom,* and other work set around the home and garden. In his innovative relief constructions, exhibited in the early 90s, there is a sense that the subjects – a specific place (*View/Berlin,* 1991), person (*Barbara,* 1992) and moment (*View/AM,* 1992) – are being recalled through the screened images, painted wooden cut-outs, and found objects displayed on small decorative shelves: "The objects I use are often symbols of myself, things which somehow relate to places and thoughts which have surrounded me from early childhood to the present."[38]

Laing is also engaged with the notion of identity, a concern that for many Canadian artists would generate dozens of exhibitions in the 1980s and 1990s, especially as it relates to gender, race, ethnicity and sexual orientation. But Laing's approach to identity is apolitical and highly poetic, shaped by his cultural roots in Britain and in Canada. From Canada, he draws upon the persistent theme of landscape and the isolation of the figure and object in an urban or rural setting: "Now that I am living in Alberta, I appreciate the vastness of the land, the isolation of man and the mystery of his objects within it."[39] From Britain comes the figurative tradition and its remarkable heritage of cultivation – of which gardens are particularly important – and the decorative arts: "On an intuitive level I find myself responding to particular colours, fabrics, textures and objects only to realize that they hold some kind of connection to my British sensibility."[40]

In Laing's art of the 1990s, his British sensibility is given full expression in artworks made graphically vivid by incorporating decorative motifs and elegant patterns, sometimes reminiscent of Paul Nash and designer William Morris of the English Arts and Crafts Movement. From reproductions of their work, Laing collages actual materials or silk-screens their patterns onto an object or print. This act of borrowing, which includes reproducing images that already exist in some other form, is in keeping with what Paul Woodrow describes in his essay on Laing as contemporary printmaking's "fortuitous yet profitable relationship with the camera."[41]

Another feature from this period is the use of garden imagery. In the mural *Inside Out,* for instance, the image of the leafy tree is taken from a photograph of a tree in Laing's backyard. An avid gardener himself, the garden is, in a sense, the artist's spiritual home, a place of nature but also of culture. Commenting on a particularly arresting series of double-panel silk-screens, Woodrow writes, "The divided images contrast a world of cultivation, represented by the figure of the gardener, with the beauty of uninhibited nature in all its complexity.... To Laing, the persona of the gardener is synonymous with that of the artist."[42]

In tending his art, Laing brings what is essentially a Romantic temperament to a body of work that is carefully conceived of and constructed. While not an art of wild emotional abandon, his is still permeated with mystery and solitude. Over the years, as Laing has taken more expressive liberties in his art-making, what moves him as an individual is revealed without removing its intimacy.

In 1977, in his article "Printmaking in Alberta," Brooks Joyner, curator of the University of Calgary Art Gallery, observed: "If one were to ask today where in Canada there might be found a watershed of outstanding productive printmakers the not surprising reply would be the province of Alberta.... The impression one has, even for a relative newcomer, is that printmaking in Alberta may rival if not exceed in experimentation and production, any other province in Canada."[43] The names of many Albertans appear in the Joyner piece, including Haeseker, Besant, Laing, Gary Olson, Lyndal Osborne, John K. Esler, Walter Jule, John Will and Noboru Sawai.

Both Sawai and Will at the time are printmaking instructors at the University of Calgary. In 1980, Will stops making prints while **NOBORU SAWAI** (1931, Takamatsu, Japan) will continue with the practice exclusively. For this Japanese-born artist, the 1970s are an especially stellar decade, a time to push both the technical and social boundaries in his art: "I have always preferred to not be able to feel the walls around me, be they physical, artistic or emotional. And the freedom to 'not do things the right way' has given me an opportunity to create a true synthesis between East and West, sake and scotch."[44]

On a technical level, Sawai achieves this by combining traditional Japanese relief woodcut with the opposing technique of European copper-plate etching. The incorporation of two or more print techniques in a single print is typical of printmaking's experimental attitude in the 1960s and 1970s. What is not so typical, though, was the difficult marriage between etching and woodcut as rendered by Sawai. Nonetheless, it is a leap also later taken by several of Sawai's students: Helen Mackie, Susan Ford and Kyra Fisher. Figuratively, Sawai blends together already-existing images from Western and Eastern art. In one instance, he etches a well-known scene from nineteenth-century European artist Gustave Courbet[45] and inserts into it a coloured woodcut copied from Eastern erotic art. (Japanese Ukiyo-e prints and Indian miniatures are two of his sources.) Sometimes Sawai reproduces the pictures exactly as they are, while other times he will alter and reassemble them. The effect is often whimsical and witty, as in *Our Western Heritage* in which "a portion of Courbet's *The Studio of the Painter* [is combined] with a startling insert from a highly detailed eighteenth-century Japanese marriage manual. Not content with the contrast between the formality of the French salon and the exposed genitalia in the Japanese woodblock, he slyly added, in one corner, a pair of copulating beavers." [46]

One of the few artists in Alberta publicly known for representing overt erotic content, Sawai's masterfully crafted images provoke much attention and discussion in the 1970s. On a couple of occasions, once in Calgary (1974) and again in Toyko (1979), his art is removed from exhibitions for offending viewer sensibilities. But as Stephen Hutchings notes in a 1980 review of Sawai's prints at the Peter Whyte Gallery (Banff): "Don't let the 'parental guidance' signs keep you away, for the Sawai show should not be missed. By understanding the sexual images as a necessary theme, we will be able to learn about the cultural differences between East and West." [47] These differences relate directly to Sawai's own life: "I too am a synthesis of two cultures, the East and the West. Not only are the materials different – the woodblock in Japan and the incised metal plate in European art – but the attitudes are so different. To the oriental artist, sex is part of the natural scenery.... Western artists treat sex in a sombre way: as a compulsion and a necessity but never a joy." [48]

Arriving in Calgary in 1971 to teach printmaking and drawing at the university, Sawai's art develops during a time when the socially permissive attitudes of the late sixties are altering and even blurring the distinctions between pornography and erotic art. Into these waters also flow the growing voices of the feminist movement and its own analysis of how woman are represented in Western art for the gaze and consumption of men. But like the Ukiyo-e prints, *Images of the Floating World,* that Sawai draws upon, his irreverent imagery and playful satire seem to float above this turbulent debate with only a few bumps here and there: "Although Sawai's sensitive and intimate expression of man's most basic passion will challenge some viewer's morality, they cannot be confused with the violence and degradation of pornography," [49] asserts curator Franklyn Heisler (Muttart Art Gallery) in a 1989 survey of fifteen prints made between 1974 and 1989.

In 1994, the University of Calgary's Nickle Arts Museum organizes *A Garden of Earthly Delights: 25 Years of Prints by Noboro Sawai.* The show features forty-one images ranging from the sexually explicit appropriations of the 1970s to the more subtle and less irreverent works derived from his imagination and memory. Curator Katherine Ylitalo writes: "Many aspects of these [later] prints are sensual: the soft richness of the woodblock colours, the bite, the etched lines, the liveliness of the drawing and the joyful bounty of the catch of fish [from his childhood island in Japan]."[50]

Credited by *Calgary Herald* art critic Nancy Tousley as being "one of the first truly postmodern artists in the city,"[51] Sawai's practice addressed cultural difference, gender, race, and art history many years before such issues became critically topical in Canada. As well, with the establishment of the Sawai Atelier in Vancouver in 1981, the first print studio in North America to specialize in traditional Japanese woodblock techniques, the now professor emeritus is considered one of a small number of important practitioners in Canada to have reinvested the oldest print technique with a new energy for contemporary art purposes.

The last printmaker to fill out this overview of significant new voices to emerge from the Calgary printmaking community in the 1970s is the irrepressible **JOHN WILL** (1939, Waterloo, Iowa). He is a master lithographer and etcher who produces a large and significant body of prints before and during his first decade as an instructor at the University of Calgary. As mentioned earlier, Will stopped making prints in 1980 to pursue more painting, photography and collaborative work in video and performance. As a result his printmaking period has receded into the background a bit. But it shouldn't be overlooked, because the prints in many ways set the tenor and tone for what is to follow. For instance, when Will is at the top of his form as a printmaker, there is never any question about his desire to make art that is about more than aesthetics and technique. "He moves quite defiantly into the sphere of social commentary, political and psychological anecdote and especially into the arena of satire about art and contemporary art institutions," observes Brooks Joyner of the *Albertan* in 1979. Alternatively, as Will writes several years after making his last prints, "Regardless of the medium, the one constant that seems to run through most of my work is its graphic nature. By graphic I mean it is informational and hopefully informative."[52]

By the end of the 1980s, Will will have almost cult-figure status within certain local art circles because of his own cheeky interventions into the work of art itself. In *Calgary Printmakers,* for instance, a photograph of the artist as a bearded, potbellied, surly-looking Mountie is incorporated into two of the four prints on display. In a group exhibition where still-life and abstract or semi-abstract art predominate, and where the show's overall sensibility is serious and taciturn, these witty portraits stand out in stark contrast. Notably, he is also the only artist in *Calgary Printmakers* who integrates text into the image: a feature that will become more and more prominent in his art after 1980. (About his post-1980 work, Will explains, "As compared to the prints ... the texts employed in [my] paintings did not just prop up or enhance the visual content, but, rather became the visual content – the texts were the subject matter."[53])

There is, of course, more to Will's humourous and multi-layered images than his own interventions. Others get involved as well, such as artist Jack Anderson[54] and Gordon Trick, who, in *Jumpin Jesus* (video, 1988) wears an absurd hairpiece in the shape of the Olympic rings while visiting various venues at the Calgary Winter Olympics. Behind much of this high-spirited role-playing and self-portraiture, Will will always stress that the "impetus for much of my work has been based on autobiography."[55] Nancy Tousley attributes this element to California painter and printmaker Ed Ruscha who "inspired Will to make art out of his daily life."[56]

In 1980, one of the Mountie images, *The End Is Near* (colour lithograph, 1973), reappears as the cover to the catalogue, *John Will: A Survey of Prints, 1967–1980.* Organized by the Glenbow Museum as a cross-Canada tour, curator Jeffrey Spalding elaborates on how Will's self-deprecating, anti-heroic stance as an artist breaks with the romantic tradition: "The entire viewpoint which is presented [by Will] stands in opposition to the notion of the artist as seer or cultural clairvoyant. The circumscribed world of the artist's influence and concern seems to be recognized as his own personal backyard: his dealings and experiences with colleagues, friends and acquaintances. Occasionally, by the device of role-playing, Will oversteps these bounds to adopt the character of another persona, but it is here that he becomes the target of his own sharpest barbs. Will is a most unlikely Mountie, sports hero or rock star, yet we all delight in his imaginative leap of fantasy and are slightly unnerved by his public disclosure. He pokes gentle fun at himself and only by example makes us aware of our own inflated aspirations and expectations."[57] And, as one reviewer from the *London Free Press* observes, "A lot of artists are taking themselves far too seriously these days. It's refreshing to find one who's as ready to laugh at himself as at us. Calgary artist John Will makes no pretence of being holier-than-thou in his satirical lithographs and engravings."[58]

But as time was to show, Will is preoccupied with fame and how being a famous artist is subtly shaped not just by one's art but by geographical location and the prevailing sensibilities of a few larger art centres. "Will's shifting identities are part of his self-aware position as an artist on the margins.... If Will's subject matter is the life of the artist, it's a story told by one who understands the game and sets it in a specific social and political landscape. One of the longest running themes in his work, the elusiveness of fame, marks his awareness of himself and the link between art and social context.... If he couldn't be famous, he decided he would pretend,"[59] ascertains Tousley.

In *I Love Me* (1987, Stride Gallery, Calgary) and *John Wall* (1992, Glenbow Museum), Will takes his pretend fame to new heights. Inspired by the proliferation of bumper stickers and their simple-minded, attention-getting messages, *I Love Me* (1986–87) consists of a dozen large vibrant oils on canvas, each with bumper stickers and Polaroids stuck to their surface. *I Love Me* addresses a wide-range of subject matter "from religion to politics, to travel, to art history, to a videotape I had made and the works are esoteric and multi-layered."[60] In this first solo show of painting, Will will also play unabashedly with his own version of fame and celebrity-hood. Using Polaroids of himself and ones he has taken of friends and public figures like John Cage, Nana Mouskouri and G. Gordon Liddy of Watergate, several of the bumper-sticker paintings provoke Colleen O'Neill to write: "When viewing these paintings one is reminded of Andy Warhol's *Interview* magazine, which present bona fide celebrities as well as the glamorous unknowns. Will's paintings present the unglamorous unknowns. He elevates the unknown to celebrity status, giving stature to those who will never be interviewed by *Interview*."[61]

In the *John Wall* installation, Will pushes the "fame game" even further by first mimicking the light-box photography of one of Canada's most internationally celebrated contemporary artists, Jeff Wall of Vancouver – "Wall's work is highly produced and technologically sophisticated, Will's on the other hand, poses as the poor cousin."[62] This work is then followed by a 60-foot-long floor-to-ceiling display of 200 small square paintings (acrylic, collage, Polaroid photographs, mixed media on canvas) whose surfaces are enlivened with text and graffiti. These number-coded canvases,[63] later entitled *Anything and Everything* (1989–91), are an anecdotal tour through the heartland of Will: his restless life and times, his relish for the trashy underside of North American popular culture, his skewering of art-world pretensions and yet again, more work mimicking artists with national reputations, this time colleagues from Calgary who have managed to hit the big time: Eric Cameron,

Mary Scott and Chris Cran. In terms of dealing with the theme of artistic fame and success, Will is among few in Canadian art. (A zany crescendo is reached in 1993 when Stride Gallery holds a "John Will look-alike" fundraising party with the artist only too pleased to tell the costumed participants how they "never looked better!"[64] *as* John Will.)

Commenting on *John Wall* for the *Calgary Herald,* Tousley sums it up this way: "Fanciful autobiography written from the margins of the mainstream art world has been the subject of John Will's paintings, prints and videos for some thirty years, and his own techniques just get richer and richer. *John Wall* the installation is like a big wrap-around cartoon."[65]

Another important theme in Will's wordy, text-based art is his predilection for the oddball, the bizarre, the forgotten and the tacky. A voyeur of roadside North America, especially its western interior, he seeks out (or in some cases, stumbles across) its kitsch, its low life, its curiosities and its subcultures – new age, UFOS, bikers, preachers. According to his friend, artist Chris Cran: "Several years ago I travelled by car with John and Mary Shannon Will down to Bald Knob, Arkansas. John wanted to visit what he referred to as his 'creative birthplace.' On this trip John insisted on staying at motels with names like the Bide A Wee While Inn, the Nighty Night Nook and the Wee Willie Winkie Motor Hotel. He just loved those names. Whenever he spotted another one he became extremely agitated. A great squeal of breaks and delight invariably meant we were stopped for at least half an hour with John out collecting business cards, postcards and whatever souvenirs the motel office had to offer for free. The drive down to Bald Knob, which could have been done in five days, took two and a half weeks as a result of his passion. While we actually were driving, however, John talked non-stop about new ideas for his paintings."[66]

This anecdote about the artist's time-consuming but purposeful meandering through obscure western locales brings to mind *Great Plains* author Ian Frazier's comment: "The great Plains are like a sheet Americans screened their dreams on for a while and then largely forgot about."[67] But not John Will, who with dual Canadian and American citizenship, has made these marginalized places his mecca. With his midwestern corn-belt background, it may simply be a case of 'it takes one to know one' or, as Peter White suggests, "Will's attitude may be related to a regionalist point of view in the sense that regionalism 'represents a theory of art based on the validity of intimate experiences as these relate to growing up in a place well known. It is ... a demand for personal knowledge' in which 'place and family are a source of insight and authenticity.'"[68] Either way, the artist manages to draw sustenance from this territory without condescension or cynicism.

In 1988, White organized *John Will: Triple Threat Artist* (Dunlop Art Gallery, Regina), a survey of paintings, video and hand-coloured photographs dating from 1980. "Will's point of view as an artist is that of the isolated, disenfranchised outsider," writes White. "He has a natural gift as an offbeat humorist in a field so bound by the seriousness of its own rhetoric that it has had little use for humour, not even as a critical tool or within the limitations of the genre."[69]

Two potent examples of Wall's 'natural gift' are found in *Atomic Haiku* (Truck Gallery, 1995) and the earlier *Long History,* which, after its first appearance at Calgary's Stride Gallery in 1986, finds a place in *Triple Threat.* Consisting of photographs either collected or taken by the artist, both series contain, according to Tousley, "a canny mixture of wonder and manipulative intent."[70] The wonder of these pieces resides in their unusual subject matter: close-up images of unexploded nuclear weapons (*Atomic Haiku*) and the panoramic commemorative photographs of yesteryear (*Long History*) in which "the majority of them were taken in the first quarter of the twentieth century [by commercial photographers] and, more often than not, are of conventioneers or the military."[71] In the case of *Atomic Haiku:* "I initially took my snapshots simply to record what I thought were curious objects in a curious museum: [the National Atomic Museum, Albuquerque, New Mexico]."[72]

As for the manipulative intent, it lies in Will's blatant tampering with the photographic image. The least autobiographical of his oeuvre, the punch behind these works is the written phrases Will creates or borrows, and then applies to each image. Sometimes the text the artist supplies is presented with a straight face: factual and informative. Other times it is more farcical or ironic, as in the piece *Shusen Haiku,* in which Will types across his black-and-white photograph of the Honest John missile:

Pretty butterflies
Be careful of pine needle points
in this gusty wind[73]

An important source of the humour of both series is Will's deft recognition of just how absurd life can be. For instance, in *Long History,* there is a 1918 commemorative panorama (Rockford, 1985) of more than 20,000 soldiers lined up in front of their Illinois camp! And although hardly innocuous, the nuclear weaponry in Will's documentary photographs has a "big-toys for big-boys" appearance. As the artist recalls, "The bombs and missiles on exhibit are, for the most part, obsolete, displayed and explained in a somewhat clinical way with no particular point of view."[74] That is, until Will laid his wily hand on them.

As an offbeat humourist, John Will has had a high profile within southern Alberta's contemporary art scene. Along with his contribution, there is now a well-established "tradition" of humour, wit and irony in the region that is present not for the sake of itself, but arises, often quite naturally, out of work about one's personal and social environment. A relatively recent development that is rather unique in Canada, this tradition of irreverence has been shaped not only by the precedent of Marcel Duchamp and sixties pop art with its ironic approach to art and life, but also by what has best been described as a "wry sense of the absurd."[75] This aspect was first explored in *Do You Take This Seriously?* (Glenbow Museum, 1984), an exhibition that despite its controversial title surveyed artwork from the Prairies that "draw on irony, wit and humour in their reflections upon city and country life, on leisure time activities and on political and artistic issues."[76] Not surprisingly, two of Will's prints were included in this twenty-two-person exhibition, which also featured such well-known observers of folk and locale as Saskatchewan's Joe Fafard, David Gilhooly and David Thauberger.

Among this gathering, however, Will was and is no sweet-tempered raconteur. Operating more like a prairie dust devil, it's the more edgier bits he prefers to stir up. At the end of the century, he may be a "middle-aged, middle-class, middle-Westerner,"[77] but this in no way inhibits his work from adopting in appearance some of the garishness he encounters. Born in 1939, Will is also a bit of granddaddy and an influence[78] in terms of maintaining a contemporary art practice that still finds a place for itself in exhibitions of current art. Examples include the first *Alberta Biennial of Contemporary Art* (Glenbow Museum and the Edmonton Art Gallery, 1996); *Beauty and the Banal* (The Edmonton Art Gallery, 1998), and further afield, *Concealing/Revealing: Voices from the Canadian Foothills* (Museum of Fine Arts, Tallahassee, Florida, 1997) where the multi-disciplinary Will is described by curator Roald Nasgaard as a "comic painter of high, sly seriousness."[79]

ALBERTA ART TO THE END OF CENTURY

chapter sixteen

A New Ceramic Scene Coalesces

Pottery, anywhere in the world, starts with clay. Clay of some sort can be found exposed in almost any river valley or roadside cut-bank in Alberta.... The geology is complex but the result is simple. Seams of virtually pure 'pottable' clay, as much as thirty feet thick, are unique to Alberta and Saskatchewan.... This availability and variety of clay has encouraged prehistoric, industrial and art pottery, unlike anywhere else in Canada.

Several stunning prehistoric pots have been reassembled for display in the Syncrude Gallery of Aboriginal Culture at the Provincial Museum of Alberta. The oldest piece dates back 1,200 years. Archaeologists have found tens of thousands of pottery fragments throughout southern and central Alberta. No prehistoric pots have been found intact – not surprising considering Alberta's demanding climate and the millions of bison and antelope hooves that once trampled Alberta grassland.[1] ❧ Tom McFall, 1999.

> The creative ceramic movement did not occur until after World War II. Ceramics had been viewed as a mere hobby – China painting. Potters made useful bowls and cups. Their only scope for artistic expression was in painting or glazing the finished object. Then in 1946, Luke Lindoe [founder of Medicine Hat's Plainsman Clays, 1964] became ceramic instructor at Calgary's Alberta College of Art and elevated ceramics from a common craft activity to the aesthetic level of sculpture and painting. Although he stayed for only eleven years, leaving to take on other clay-related challenges, he gave ceramics a technical and philosophical base and trained the first generation of ceramic artists that would spark creative ceramic development throughout Alberta. By the mid-60s it had outpaced all other developing craft disciplines and was competing with painting as a vehicle of self-expression.[2] ❧ Les Graff, 1999.

Dig beneath the surface of what McFall and Graff are saying and a couple of impressions emerge. The first is despite the lack of public awareness about it in the province, ceramics/pottery is "a logical art form for Alberta,"[3] a well-rooted cultural expression that, on an amateur and professional level, casts a lively presence over the provincial art scene.[4] The second is that right to the end of Alberta's first century and beyond, ceramic art is simply that plentiful and in many instances, that exemplary. As McFall, Executive Director of the Alberta Craft Council, explains, "Alberta pottery is not solely of local interest. Many Alberta potters are steadily building national and international reputations as practitioners, teachers and experts.... Pages would be required to list the exhibitions, awards and accolades of Alberta potters such as Carol and Richard Selfridge (Edmonton), John Chalke and Barbara Tipton (Calgary), Greg Payce (Calgary) and others."[5]

Thus, in 1992 when the Canadian Craft Museum opened its doors in Vancouver, there is a healthy representation of Albertan work. In *A Treasury of Canadian Craft: Inaugural Exhibition,* some of the province's top clay artists are selected – Sally Barbier, John Chalke, Greg Payce, Kirsten Abrahamson and Barbara Tipton.[6] Proposing that "craft, design and art represent an essential triangle of creativity," guest curator Sam Carter elaborated on the broader cultural context of craft-based art: "For much of this century the craftsperson has been respected by the world of art and design on ethical rather than aesthetic grounds. Hard-won skills, labour, a sense of tradition, and a proclivity to be self-sufficient are all admirable human values. "Art is wonderful, craft is admirable, and design is teachable," replied noted British potter, Michael Cardew, when asked the difference between art, craft and design. With today's more balanced recognition of craft, design and art, one may consider each of these aspects of creativity to be wonderful, admirable and teachable."[7]

In other words, toward the end of century, a more holistic attitude towards craft had emerged. Increasingly irrelevant is the notion that art is made of "art" materials like paint, has serious content and serves no utilitarian purpose, while craft is functional and made of "craft" materials. Fleshing out this picture is a statement by artist Greg Payce who appears in *Treasury* and later curates the Alberta section of *Clay in Canada: North by NorthWest* (NCECA Conference, Minneapolis): "It is an exciting time to be making ceramics. Historically, artists involved in making craft have had their work undervalued largely because intelligent craft criticism had been neither understood or practiced. Postmodern ideology (particularly feminism) has had a profound effect on cultural criticism. The playing field has been leveled, so to speak. Art/crafts hierarchies that have been with us since the Renaissance are suddenly no longer relevant. Craft has been emancipated."[8]

This new vision of a craft-based art is largely inspired by the pioneering efforts of artists based in several key centres: Britain, Japan, the United States and western Canada.[9] It didn't occur all at once, nor is the impact of these various makers the same – the Canadian examples are mostly regional while the others are international in the scope of their influence. Suffice it to say, though, that by the time the post-1970 period rolls around, ceramics and other craft-based art is winning new respect from the artworld and the public alike. Controversy rages too, as artists debate over and over again what makes something a piece of art as opposed to craft, the role of function, and whether ceramic sculpture is more important as art than a nicely made teacup. Over the following decades, these and other concerns, such as the relevance of fine-art criticism, provide plenty of discussion and debate for ceramic conferences and thematic exhibitions in the province.

Of the exhibition *Ceramics International 73*[10] (Calgary and Banff), exhibition juror Walter Drohan warns that, "With the traditional boundaries stripped away in the headlong rush for unique, uninhibited 'self-expression,' the ceramic art has lost many of its craftsmen and lies exposed to deprivations of any number of manipulators. Those who have no respect for the material or self-restraint will distort the process and the medium to a state of non-existence."[11]

Ten years later, Lorne Falk, curator of *The Ceramic Bridge: New Expressions from an Old Tradition* (Walter Phillips Gallery) – a group exhibition accompanying the Canadian Clay Conference 84 (Banff Centre School of Fine Arts) – muses, "The provocation is this: will ceramic artists forsake their roots in their desire to become accepted in contemporary visual art? Will a schism occur [between pottery and sculpture], fracturing the medium into an oppositional polarity? Can traditional and contemporary aesthetics continue to co-exist within one artistic milieu?"[12]

Another decade and many conferences after that, Calgary critic and artist Amy Gogarty reports from the Banff Centre's symposium "Reconsidering Function(s) in Artistic Practices" that "the accompanying exhibition, *clay between my fingers* (Walter Phillips Gallery), is a controversial one because of its postmodern attitude. Instead of featuring one-of-kind clay artworks, the four-person show[13] highlights installation art where clay is used like any other material to make work with social and cultural content.

> This possibility is what annoyed some participants in the symposium – some seemed to feel the exhibition was suggesting ceramists make work that avoided being called "ceramics" at all costs. [But] for a number of the participants, clay is the issue: beauty, uniqueness and personal expression are important components.[14]

Another important aspect about post-1970 ceramic development is the growth of a more substantive infrastructure responsive to ceramic activity.[15] In 1971, the non-profit Alberta Potters Association[16] (APA) is established to reinforce a sense of a wider community and host events like exhibitions, workshops and conferences. By 1973, the organization's newsletter will evolve into *Contact* magazine, a quarterly publication which, for many years, will be the country's only clay magazine with a national and later international readership.[17]

Two years after its formation, the APA co-hosts, along with the International Academy of Ceramics (IAC, Geneva, Switzerland) and the assistance of the province's Cultural Development Branch, the ambitious *Ceramics International 73:* an event that brings the world of clay to Alberta and Canada. The accompanying exhibition, grandly titled *Ceramic Art of the World 1973,* is juried by such luminaries as Walter Drohan (Calgary), Ruth Duckworth

(Chicago), Luke Lindoe (Medicine Hat), Maurice Savoie (Montreal), Kurt Spurey (Vienna) and Peter Voulkos (Berkeley, California). Commenting on the 1973 exhibition, which attracts 12,000 spectators and 1,500 entries from all over Europe, North America, Japan, South America and Australia, Edgar Pelichet, president of the IAC, writes:

> For the first time in Calgary, it is possible to compare the works of the two worlds and the organizers are to be thanked for this revelation. Finally, and more than ever, the ceramic works of art show a total lack of generalized tendencies. The freedom of the fine arts (this miracle is mostly due to Picasso) means that today's ceramics are characterized by a total individuality.[18]

Twenty-five years later, Leslie Manning, who served as president of Alberta Potters Association during those heady times, considers the event "to be a pivotal period, the broad spectrum of technical and aesthetic differences that were witnessed during this celebration influenced major changes in the ceramic discipline across the nation."[19] More specifically, "It was a license to be outrageous in Canada."[20]

Besides exposing Canadian studio potters and other audience to less well-known techniques, such as raku and porcelain, as well as to more flamboyant examples of ceramic sculpture, *Ceramic Art of the World 1973* is displayed in the Alberta College of Art's new building perched on a corner of the city's North Hill. It is the art school's first real home since its inception in 1926 as a department of the Provincial Institute of Technology and Art (now SAIT). Eight years of planning and construction have gone into structure under the stewardship of ACA heads Illingworth Kerr and then Stanford Perrott. One of only four art colleges in Canada, the new facility enables the Calgary-based institution to expand its programming to offer the students a unique, intensive, four-year studio-based curriculum under the instruction of professional artists. Eight specialized areas of study are offered: painting, sculpture, printmaking, visual communications, photography, textiles, jewellery and ceramics. Complementing the educational experience, the new building includes a 9,500-square-foot gallery, later renamed the Illingworth Kerr Gallery.[21]

In effect, the expansion turns ACA into a cultural powerhouse, and although it does not receive institutional autonomy from SAIT (Southern Institute of Technology) until 1985, the college becomes an important centre in

Canada for clay-art instruction. Its list of graduates from the late 1960s onward include: Leopold Foulem, Harlan House, Leslie Manning, Annemarie Schmid Esler, Kirsten Abrahamson, Evelyn Grant, Jim Etzkorn, Leigh Harrington and Garry Williams.

Overall, the early post-1970 period is an encouraging one for any artist wishing to specialize in clay at a post-secondary level. (Later, this era of opportunity will come to an end with the downsizing of institutional resources and, importantly, the ideological shift in the contemporary art world from the single discipline like painting or ceramics to more multi-disciplinary practices. The face of Canadian art will be drastically altered.) But to return: at the college level, there is Red Deer College's diploma program (est. 1974); a BFA and MFA program at the University of Calgary[22] (est. 1963 and phased out in 1990); a BFA with a concentration in ceramics at the University of Lethbridge (also phased out in 1990).[23] Another source of instruction is the University of Alberta's Faculty of Extension, which for several decades (1955 to 1999) offers non-credit courses and workshops. Also at the U of A, in the Faculty of Fine Arts, figurative clay sculpture is taught by instructor Neil Fiertel while at The Banff School of Fine Arts, post-graduate development is offered through the Ceramics department founded by Les Manning in 1973. (Later under the guise of its new name, the Banff Centre, single-discipline pursuits like ceramics, painting, weaving, printmaking and photography are largely replaced with a more multi-disciplinary, postmodern approach, and a preference for installation and new media.)[24]

Finally, another development post-1970 is the first real avid collecting of ceramics/pottery by, of all people, the Alberta government, or more specifically the Alberta Art Foundation. Established in 1972 under one of the first pieces of legislation passed by the new provincial government under the enlightened leadership of Peter Lougheed, the Foundation's mission is to foster an appreciation and awareness of Alberta art by purchasing, collecting and then providing access to such artwork through loans, displays and exhibitions. Sometimes compared to the Canada Council Art Bank, which coincidentally is established in Ottawa around the same time, the Foundation's genesis lay in the enthusiasm and vision of such individuals as Calgary lawyer Henry Beaumont, who, in 1969, drew up the first draft of what eventually became the Alberta Art Foundation Act.[25] Initially provided with an annual grant of $50,000 for the acquisition of art, in 1973 the AAF presented its first purchases of 150 works to audiences in Edmonton and Calgary.[26] Total attendance figures to this introduction of what would become by the end of the century the most pluralistic collection of Alberta art[27] anywhere are a very respectable 50,000. Later, in 1991, in a period of government restructuring, the foundation and its collection are folded into the new Alberta Foundation for the Arts (AFA), which by the late 1990s would include the largest and most extensive public holdings of Alberta ceramic art. And although the foundation acquired works in other media, such as painting, printmaking, new media (video), sculpture, photography, fibre and glass, the collection's early commitment to seriously acquire clay work is unique and exemplary for its time.

The 1970s are an ambitious time for the AAF, fueled by its desire to create a higher profile for historic and contemporary Alberta art. Early in its history, for instance, there are forays abroad; a travelling exhibition including works of fired clay from ten artists[28] that is shown in Europe for five months (1975), New York for six weeks, Montreal for the 1976 Summer Olympics and then, finally, in Edmonton and Calgary for the 1976 fall season.[29] According to the *Edmonton Journal,* this was "probably the first time any province has had a show of its art in Europe."[30]

Writing about the adventure, then AAF chairman W.B. McMullen recalls, "The most apparent comment about our art in Alberta is that it has a place in the mainstream of world art. The space, light and colour in Alberta art are different and these become more noticeable in a varied collection such as this and more so when hung in crowded metropolitan areas."[31]

The year 1975 also sees *The History of Ceramics in Alberta,* a survey of clay production in the province beginning with the early industrial and commercial ceramics of the Medicine Hat area (Medalta Potteries), and follows with the later output of what its curator Nancy Townshend refers to as the "artist-potters."[32] Featuring eighty-five works of pottery and ceramic sculpture, this Edmonton Art Gallery exhibition also has many new faces who are part of a more contemporary wave of artist-potters. Attracted by the teaching opportunities available during the great institutional expansion, several of them arrive in Alberta in the mid- to late-60s. Displayed in the exhibition are Albert Borch, Victor Brosz, John Chalke, Santo Mignosa, Charles Hilton, David Green, Neil Fiertal and Noboru Kubo. Also new to the artistic landscape are: Annemarie Schmid Esler, Les Manning, Mary Shannon Will, Patrick Hurst, Sam Uhlick, Tony Bloom, John Ikeda, Neil Liske, Pierre Guy, Mary Borgstrom, Gail Jensen Carney, Harlan House and Caroll (Moppett) Taylor-Lindoe.

In trying to determine what is different about this new wave of clay activity for this exhibition, Nancy Townshend examines what proceeds it: "A characteristically Albertan piece at this time [1960s] would have been gas-fired, earthy looking, functional, high fired reduced stoneware."[33] Larry Weaver, who arrived in 1968 to teach ceramics at the University of Lethbridge, describes the earlier artist-potter scene this way: "Technically, when I came to Alberta I didn't see much that was different from what I experienced in graduate school in Iowa. A lot of stoneware firing with some basic bodies being prepared by Plainsman; not a great deal of experimentation in terms of radically new thoughts in clay. There was a homogeneity in the approach to clay."[34]

But all of this changes in the 70s: "The ceramic scene in Alberta today is exciting and diversified," enthuses Townshend, "ranging from talented potters, ceramists, sculptural ceramists to clay glazers." And, as Les Graff later notes, "The base built by [the earlier] Alberta potters was added to and diversified. Ceramics moved away from the limited idea of the vessel metaphor."[35] This didn't mean the end of the older tradition; the vessel will continue as a source of inspiration, and is evident in the pottery of some of the younger artists in the EAG exhibit including John Ikeda and Sam Uhlick, but the tradition is being expanded. Clay practice is becoming more permissive, something becomes even more evident in the 1981 Edmonton exhibit, *Issues in Clay: Western Canadian Sculpture.* According to the *Edmonton Sun:* "These artists liberated clay from the vessel-confined, wheel-fashioned idiom and put clay on the wall, off the wall, within things, added kitschy items to it, and generally disturbed a good number of gentle folk."[36]

Artist Ricardo Gomez, writing for the exhibition catalogue, notes that the largest issue raised by the presence of this new wave of ceramic practice "is that the origins of the concerns and stylistic preferences are largely imported. That is, the bulk of aesthetic and material concerns represented arose from artist/teachers who had either come from or studied elsewhere, particularly the United States. The vast majority of sculptural work in western Canada reflects the intelligence and influences of these itinerants, both Canadian and otherwise."[37] Featuring thirteen artists, *Issues in Clay* exhibits Albertans Mary Shannon Will, Annemarie Schmid Esler, Charles Wissinger, Sally Barbier and John Chalke.

Two names integral to the new story of Alberta ceramics are **JOHN CHALKE** (1940, Gloucestershire, England) and **ANNEMARIE SCHMID ESLER** (1937,

Winnipeg, Manitoba). Each a maverick in his and her own right, their one-of-a-kind ceramic pieces are highly visible and inspired examples. Like other artistic disciplines in the 1970s, ceramics become infused with the eclectic tendencies then sweeping through many art communities in North America. Most affected by this trend in Alberta is perhaps Calgary, which is also a hub for ceramic activity. As writer David Lasker later comments in "Clay Comes of Age," a 1984 article for the general interest publication *Western Living,* "If no Albertans have attained the popularity of [Saskatchewan's Joe] Fafard, neither has a single style predominated in Alberta as Fafard's funk-derived realism has in Saskatchewan."[38] Instead, a chorus of singular voices emerges, each with a particular part to contribute, as Chalke does with his richly tactile, multiple-glazed pottery and Schmid Esler with her dramatic illusionistic sculptures, assemblages and installations.

Given the physical appearance of their art and differing attitudes towards clay as a material, it is tempting to think the two artists have little in common. Chalke, for instance, has a deep interest in clay composition, glaze development and kiln construction. (In 1969, he built the first high-temperature, wood-fired kiln in western Canada. In 1996, Steve Bousseau shoots *West of Shino,* a video about another kiln-building episode by Chalke and friends.) Schmid Esler, on the other hand, is unmoved by such earthly activity: "It's kind of a romantic notion to dig clay – OK on a holiday perhaps – but as far as working is concerned, I am interested in the piece I am working on and I just want the materials to be there as cheaply and efficiently as possible. I use commercial glazes too. They are foolproof."[39] (This casual attitude will become increasingly common among younger ceramicists.)

Both artists, though, do share concerns that place them on similar terrain. For instance, both artists treat their clay works with a painterly sensibility: "Esler is most accurately described as a painter/sculptor, for she fuses a lifelong interest in painting with the sculptural medium,"[40] and, "John brings to clay the sensitivity of the painter/sculptor."[41] This quality can be traced back, in part, to their schooling. Esler first studies pottery in 1962 with Ronald Burke at the Winnipeg Art School. She eventually specializes in that discipline in her final year with Walter Drohan, 1968, at the Alberta College of Art, but in the meantime, she majors in painting and drawing at the college. Chalke is self-taught in clay, but his formal training includes a art Teacher's Certificate from the Bath Academy of Art (1962), which also means instruction by the renowned abstract painter Howard Hodgkin.

Both artists also make work influenced by their perceptions of modern society. Of Esler, Randy Adams writes, "The same conscience that [first] led her to social work [in the early 60s] is embodied throughout her artwork. Her use of found objects – natural and manufactured – refashioned or recycled into temples of refuge [*Temple* series, 1983], cityscapes that speak about the destructive power of modern times [*City Scapes,* 1986–87], tableaus of bound crows [1980s] – all testify to her central concerns with social history."[42] And Amy Gogarty notes about Chalk's background: "While at art school [in Bath], Chalke found that he regretted the loss of prewar industries and village life – the coal fired bottle kilns, the pride of craftsmanship, and the connectedness to a more natural world, which accounts for his affinity for aberrant, willful surfaces and his regard for hand skills and traditions."[43]

With this affinity come numerous artworks from both artists reflecting a sense of place: "She began [in 1978] a series of teacups which, as vessels, could be seen containing the memories and reminders of older generations and communities of the abandoned farms and ranches of the prairies she had been fascinated with as a child,"[44] Val Greenfield writes about Esler. "Many of the newer works reflect a strong feeling of identification with the history and culture of the province that has become Mr. Chalke's home. A typical piece, entitled *Looking Horse Pass in 1880,* incorporates figures of horses and a map of Alberta in a richly detailed composition."[45] (Lambert and Himel on Chalke)

Schmid Esler and Chalke also share, along with many artists of their generation, an irreverent attitude towards materials and traditional forms, the distilling of personal experience for inclusion in their art, a regimen of travel and research – Japan is particularly important to Chalke – and an intuitive and experimental approach to their practice. Chalke has been viewed as "a collector of experiences … his work carries residual and overlaid memories of places and events: life layers of personal history,"[46] while Schmid Esler states: "[I] sometimes [feel] I'm a filter, and the residue which clings to it [is] my work."[47] And both artists are known for their keen wit and unorthodox interpretations, inclined to turn convention on its head and challenge the viewer's perceptions.

In her essay for *Vessels*, Patricia Ainslie describes Chalke's practice this way: "[Chalke] makes objects based on functional forms but their use is ambiguous or denied: plates and bowls are hung on the wall rather than laid on the table, a skillet has only vestiges of a handle, and surfaces are highly worked and textured."[48]

Esler's work, meanwhile, is described in *Down to Earth: Canadian Potters at Work:* "Annemarie Schmid Esler plays a trick with our eyes. Her sculptural clay forms deceive us. She takes advantage of the chameleon quality of clay and uses it in non-traditional, often surrealistic ways. Her recent series of 'crows in crates' requires close examination to discover that the crates are made from textured clay, not wood, and that the wounded crows are bandaged not with surgical tape, but with paper-thin slabs of clay." [49]

This sleight-of-hand act of replicating in clay a banal item like a crow decoy or a wooden crate is identified by *Calgary Herald* critic Nancy Tousley to be Schmid Esler's "most innovative handling of the medium." [50] First used in the elegant imaginary prairie-landscape series, *Turf Pieces* (1976–77), and then applied with even greater finesse in *The Bound Bird Series* (1980–83), this technique serves as "the building block" [51] for much of her future work: small assemblages, large sculptural tableaux, and installation pieces occupying both wall and floor.

Early on, Annemarie Schmidt Esler's work is best known for its fanciful allusions to gender. Beginning with a whimsical series of hand-built porcelain beds, rich with "references of immediate and monumental significance: love, sexual desire, birth, motherhood, the place of dreams, [and] the final resting place," [52] these tiny decorative sculptures are highlighted by art historian John Stocking as an expression of "the time-honoured themes and values of the traditional women's realm, both in terms of that reality and as an empathetic parody of it." [53]

These works are made in the early to mid-70s, during a time when the California pop/funk ceramics movement is a prevailing force, turning attention away from wheel and stoneware idioms toward hand-built, low-fire techniques. The old-fashioned beds with their fairy-tale demeanor have often been cited as being related to this influential vein of art. Stocking goes one step further, though, locating Esler within a small but distinct group of local artists: "During the early 1970s, a group of women artists in Calgary were producing small clay sculpture that lightened the heavy-handed irreverence of funk, bringing to it a sense of intimacy and delicacy absent in the original West Coast movement." [54]

This activity is featured in *Five Calgary Ceramists* [55] (Glenbow-Alberta Art Gallery, 1974), which not only features more traditional examples of vessel-shaped pottery from Kim Bruce and Ted Diakow, but also the playful forms of Schmid Esler, Gail Jensen Carney and Mary Shannon Will. Reproduced a few months later in the American publication *Ceramics Monthly,*[56] Jensen Carney's whimsical *Cabbages and Furrows Checker Set,* Shannon Will's brightly coloured organic forms, and Schmid Esler's erotically suggestive beds are so different in appearance, character and imagery from mainstream Alberta clay they can be considered proto-feminist. As such, these artists join an idiosyncratic stream of 1970s art-making in Alberta that, while not directly concerned with women's issues as they were then evolving, set a precedent for new types of female-centred subject matter and aesthetic approaches that lie outside of what was considered the norm. This group of artists also includes the painters Joice Hall, Dulcie Foo Fat, Maureen Enns and Alexandra Haeseker.

In 1980, Esler introduces what will become one of her best-known and most significant bodies of work: *The Bound Bird Series* (1980–83, 1985). First exhibited in two solo exhibitions (University of Lethbridge Art Gallery and the Walter Moos Gallery, Calgary), these bold assemblages are somewhat unique in the history of Alberta ceramic art for their psychological impact. "The silent, sentinel presence of bandaged birds ... has been disturbing to some viewers who find the works macabre or morose,"[57] reports Nancy Tousley. But to Esler who first cast the bird from a plastic crow decoy found in a Seattle hardware store, "The bird had a compelling, almost mystical presence that moved me very much, so I made more."[58]

Possessing neither the reassuring presence of a sturdy stoneware bowl nor the humour of a more contemporary clay form, these gothic sculptures with their striking clay birds, weathered cupboards and simulated slat boxes, chipped cups and saucers, light bulbs and other found objects, are later interpreted by curator Valerie Greenfield as "metaphors for the human condition."[59] In the biographical dictionary, *North American Women Artists of the Twentieth Century,* curator Patricia Ainslie writes about the work, "They evoke the ambience of rural homesteads while the silent, watchful crows convey the feeling of psychic or physical isolation of the prairies."[60]

These works have other, historical leanings as well. The series is partly inspired by the boxes of American surrealist Joseph Cornell, and they are described in *Clay Comes of Age* as "an obsession of white crows, black crows, tinted crows and bandaged crows combined, in the eccentric manner of a 1920s Dadaist construction, with unrelated objects: orange crates, twigs, shells, decals and light bulbs."[61] Nancy Tousley agrees, suggesting that the sculptures are "expressionist in feeling and a contemporary cousin of surrealism in its associations."[62]

In 1985, Esler begins to incorporate her birds with dramatic arrangements involving groupings of crows and volcanic rock boulders. Designed as installation pieces, the bird/rock-scapes provoke an entirely different reaction: "Unlike their predecessors, one is immediately struck by the absence of any pervasive feeling of despair, captivity or isolation. The bird images are no longer enclosed or guardians of fading remnants of the past. They are, rather, free, choosing to remain where they are roosting,"[63] writes Valerie Greenfield. Wrapped in black tape, the crows in the sprawling floor piece, *Black Birds on Rocks,* for example, "appear not as much wounded, but as spectral images, swathed in dark robes."[64]

Each bird work implies a scenario or an event that has already happened, or is about to take place. This ability of Schmid Esler's to move beyond metaphor and allegory toward narrative and story-telling is another unique aspect about her practice. In the modern period, one of the worst things that could be said about a work of art is that it is too literal, or that it has literary intentions. For Schmid Esler and her crows, this is not an issue because the works are in a different spirit. Given that both bird series are her most figurative and that they were made at a time when figurative art and the use of narrative is again finding critical acceptance in the contemporary art world, perhaps this achievement need not come as a surprise. But within the context of Canadian ceramic art, they are still special.

Schmid Esler, though, generally views her practice within the larger context of contemporary art: "I go to a lot of exhibitions and not just ceramics. I like to see work that has some life to it. There is a lot of dead boring work around, many things that are rehashed. I can't see working in a history in which [I am] not living."[65] (In recognition of her importance in the development of the local history of contemporary art, the late curator Mark Joslin includes her in the largely non-ceramic show, *Dreaming Before Nature: Eight Calgary Artists.*[66])

Still, it cannot be forgotten that at the heart of her oeuvre is the medium of clay itself. One of the best examples of Schmid Esler's ability to manipulate its unique qualities is her *Odyssey* installation. Displayed on freestanding steel shelves in 1990 at Lethbridge's Southern Alberta Art Gallery,[67] the porous weighty objects have all the luscious texture, thick glazes, gorgeous colours, rich tactility, compact simplicity of the best in clay art. The pyramidal objects are non-figurative and while their shapes bear little relationship to anything recognizable, John Stocking suggests, "[they] are mainly about their own odyssey, out of the volatile living reality of the studio experience into the fossilized formality of an embalmed abstract concept."[68] The 1990 work is the artist's seventh major sculpture series. Considering the variety, the level of technical ingenuity and the conceptual scope of her long practice, Schmid Esler's career is also an odyssey in the history of Canadian ceramics.

Of all the ceramic artists to emerge in the post-1970 era, John Chalke is Alberta's most celebrated export. The first-ever recipient in the Fine Crafts category of the Governor General's Awards in Visual and Media Arts (2000), Chalke's contribution to pottery has been recognized in nineteen books on ceramic art, in over fifty magazine and journal articles and in more than 200 solo and group exhibitions, both national and international. His work is also collected by many international institutions, including London's Victoria and Albert Museum,[69] and in 1996, Chalke serves as the exhibition judge for the twentieth anniversary of New Zealand's *Fletcher Challenge Ceramics Award.*[70]

"[Chalke] is a hard one to precisely put [one's] finger on,"[71] Fletcher awards director Moyra Elliot declares. It is a reaction not uncommon to Chalke's versatile ceramic style. As the artist himself once admitted about his work: "My ceramic pieces are at once paintings, drawings, graphics and clay manipulations."[72] His "glaze research is almost legendary,"[73] ranging "some twenty-five glazes [rather than] the three or four used by most ceramists."[74] His influences are equally varied, including Bernard Leach, Japanese master Furuta Oribe, early American and English slipware, French wood-fired country pots and Spode transfer wares.[75] He is also one of the first Albertans to work extensively in raku, a sixteenth-century Japanese firing technique. As Medicine Hat potter Arne Handley observes, "It has been acknowledged that he introduced a new ceramic vision to the Alberta area – which had previously seen only a more rigid Laubenthal/Lindoe influence – by encouraging the use of 'softer clay, a slower wheel and a wider aesthetic.'"[76]

But in keeping with his versatile artistic language, on top of his experimental innovations, Chalke has also rendered a substantial body of work within the parametres of the ceramic vessel tradition. His one-of-a-kind plates for the wall or pedestal, for instance, are among his most enduring bodies of work. With their irregular edges and rudimentary shapes, the stoneware plates are sculptural but not totally three-dimensional like Esler's crow, rock, and bed works. Thus, rather than completely disassociate himself from the vessel tradition, as so many younger clay artists did in the 1960s and 1970s,

Chalke takes traditional clay forms and makes them uniquely his own: "My work has always made reference to that world [of pots]; always pottery more than sculpture."[77] Even his radical work of the 1970s – rugged landscape-like pieces – which go well beyond the traditional context of ceramic containers[78] are still referred to as "plates" by the critic Brooks Joyner. He describes these works as "torn, twisted and metaphoric in character,"[79] made free-form rather than thrown on a wheel.

In this respect, Chalke proves himself to be an artist both within and ahead of his time. In the 1980s, when the vessel enjoys a revival amongst ceramics artists, Chalke's work leads the way in ushering in new styles and techniques. By 1996, to celebrate its twenty-fifth anniversary, the Alberta Potters Association chooses to celebrate with a juried exhibition: *Vessels in Celebration.* As the exhibit coordinator Ria Meloche proclaimed, "Today, the functional brown pot, the expressionistic pot, the message-bearing pot, the postmodern pot, and the beautiful pot all thrive."[80] In 1990, Chalke throws another curve and produces a series of ceramic sculptures: abstracted forms vaguely suggestive of small, everyday objects – the skillet, the mirror, the brush, the trowel found in the kitchen or the backyard. But like his plates, much of this more recent work continues to straddle both sculptural and vessel concerns, seen in his stunning, hand-built, multi-fired *Orange Clasp* cylinder (*Vessels in Celebration,*[81] 1996) and in his lyrical, pebble-glazed trough entitled *Blue Goose Thermal* (*Clay in Canada: North by NorthWest,*[82] 1993).

How Chalke manages to carve out new territory for himself with nothing more than the humble plate as his sculptural and pictorial surface is related to a time-consuming process he once referred to as "refire madness."[83] According to artist/critic Barbara Tipton, "Once the pots are in process, they are placed on a large table and drawing, changing, painting begins. In his questing to describe what he does, Chalke once referred to himself as a clay glazer.... [His] unorthodox mixtures of ceramic compounds create in turn, unorthodox surfaces, full of bumps, cracks, blisters. In fact, it is likely that his use of these atypical coatings is what first attracted so much attention to his work soon after his arrival to Calgary from England in 1968."[84]

This technique continues to attract attention throughout the 1980s and 1990s. In 1981, Chalke makes his solo debut in Toronto and is praised in the *Globe and Mail:* "His reputation as a master of glaze chemistry is justified by the plates and plaques in this show.... Sometimes the results may seem simple and spontaneous but most effects are carefully controlled and Mr. Chalke re-fires his pieces up to a dozen times until he is satisfied. Often only a tiny detail is added between firing – perhaps a line or a few dots – yet it contributes to the balance of the composition [on the plate]."[85]

Working with visual associations and sometimes anecdotes, Chalke conveys ideas through surface treatment, coloured glazes and, from time to time, the addition of small figurative clay objects and stenciled images. Sometimes irreverent titles such as *Getting Dark (Lightened)* and *Winifred, Well-known for Her Fearlessness, Would Spend Much of Her Weekends Diving into Large Pots of Flowers* play a role in giving his works meaning. But whatever the spirit they are made in, the exhibitions and awards continue to add up, including the 1992 Prix d'Excellence at the Fifth National Biennial of Ceramic Art, Trois Rivières, Quebec. Nancy Tousley describes the particular strength of his work this way: "The result is an art form that combines aspects of both painting and sculpture. But they are stated in terms that only clay and glaze materials can give."[86]

In addition to the continued development of his critically acclaimed ceramic art and his teaching, Chalke also devotes a large amount of time to producing functional, domestic pottery (stoneware), which Handley says "would look appropriate in a rural kitchen from the last century, the particular texture and colour having come about from being fired in a salt-vapoured kiln."[87] These works are not as publicly well-known, but have appeared in exhibitions like *Vessels: Hand and Spirit,* a 1998 group exhibition at Calgary's Muttart Art Gallery.[88] Featuring small handmade pots, this utilitarian work of Chalke and others is highlighted by curator Franklyn Heisler for "their potential to provide meaning, to seduce the senses, to offer comfort and to touch one's soul or spirit.... For many, hand-made pots hold a kind of mystique."[89]

Of all the ceramic artists in the post-1970 period, Chalke is Alberta's 'guru' of contemporary clay. With his national and international stature, his extensive knowledge of ceramic history and clay technology, his connections to the teaching and mentoring of the craft, and his own distinctive practice, which melds a contemporary sensibility with aspects of the traditional and the influences of far-away places, Chalke embodies all the fundamentals of a master craftsman and artist. Much of his art achieves an indescribable beauty. There is a mystery to his abstract plates and sculptural vessels that is reinforced by their aged appearance and the treatment of their surfaces, which "are reminders of the longevity of the earth, of its hidden secrets, only a few of which will ever come to light."[90]

In 1968, Chalke came to Alberta as a foreigner with the intention to stay for one year. While there, he discovered it was the only place he really wanted to be, in spite of its apparent lack of history, culture and "the glitter bop rock things I was used to."[91] The insistence of the landscape and climate[92] infiltrated his spirit and, in turn, his work: "I was very reluctant for many years to admit that they were there."[93] So Chalke becomes an Albertan artist, enriching the province's artistic history.

Function Versus the Fanciful

Another important aspect of the broadening clay scene in the post-1970 era is the appearance of pottery studios dedicated to the creation of functional and sculptural pieces. Often driven by individual practitioners, these early studios – Davnor Studios (Lethbridge), Pottery West Limited (Edmonton), Hobbit's Notch Pottery (Fort McMurray), Stonecrop Pottery (Canmore), Beaver Flats Pottery (Rocky Mountain House), Dirtworks (Lavoy and later, Bragg Creek), Wells Pottery & Sculpture (Glenevis and later, High River), Grassroots Studio (Medicine Hat) – contribute to a cottage-based enterprise in Alberta. In much of this activity, a grassroots flavour prevails, spurred on by the earlier work of William Morris and Bernard Leach and their convictions about the value of the handmade, functional article, as well as the cultural climate of the rebellious 1960s and the back-to-the-land movement of the 70s. Even in larger, more commercial ceramics studios, like J.B. Kalbfleisch Pottery (Calgary), there is a sense of the era's counterculture values: "There is a certain human and comfortable warmth that prevails when one's environment includes handmade items, exemplified by individually designed and produced functional decorative pottery,"[94] writes founder Jim Kalbfleisch for the 1980 edition of the *Alberta Potters Directory.*

Ideally, success in the industry is considered to be a combination of making highly functional work with commercial appeal, while also creating other, generally more time-consuming pieces that receive the attention of artists, dealers, curators and so on. For example, Edmonton's CAROL and RICHARD SELFRIDGE (1948, Belleville, Ontario; 1943, Seattle, United States) operate a successful enterprise of serious exhibiting while also making a living from it. "We've lived from our work for over twenty years. We sell in fine art galleries, sometimes at a considerable distance," while their functional work "is sold directly through their studio [Selfridge Pottery] to loyal followers."[95] Another example are Edmonton-born Sam Uhlick and his partner Antonia Huysman, who after "350 firings, two kilns and eighteen years of pottery making in Bonnie Doon" move their workshop and home to an acreage near Ardrossan in 1998: "We make a wide range of pottery including teapots, coffee pots (one of which is in the Maxwell House Collection), tableware, as well as many sizes of bowls, vases, square and rectangle molded plates."[96]

These artists represent a way of creative life in the province that more than any other practice freely blends commerce with the making of artworks. It's a connection, however, often viewed with suspicion and condescension in some quarters of the fine art world. But, as Toronto art critic John Bentley Mays suggests to delegates of the *Canadian Clay Conference 84* (Banff Centre): "Potting has always been, for thousands of years, the major metaphor of creation in the world – in whatever culture you find it. Anyone who can make one brilliant place setting after another place setting ... is in fact doing a visual service for culture, humanity and civilization that [New York art star] Julian Schnabel will never even touch." (A sentiment that, no doubt, rang a sympathetic chord for many of the participants.)

Best known for their highly recognizable majolica vessels that Richard Selfridge once defined as, "a marriage between pot and painting,"[97] Richard and Carol Selfridge, formally trained, have a flair for incorporating two-dimensional imagery – figurative, still-life, mythological and humourous – on terracotta forms – vases, amphora, teapots and so on – whose constructed shapes are curvaceous but also flattened on one side. "We are interested in painting flat things to look round and round things to look flat," explains Carol, "Our pots usually have an illusionistic pot 'front' side and the reverse side often becomes a shaped canvas for a figurative/narrative glaze painting."[98]

Some of the influences they cite for this approach include the way Picasso and Braque depicted flattened cubist vases in their paintings, and a flattened sculpture of New York art critic Clement Greenberg by Saskatchewan's remarkable Joe Fafard. "We were already interested in illusionistic pottery and that piece of Fafard's really stuck. It showed us that pots could be flat, too."[99]

Major pieces of their colourful *trompe l'oeil* majolica appear in ceramic exhibitions around the world. In 1994, for instance, a shapely teapot and a tilted jar with a top were selected for the Fourteenth International Biennial of Ceramic Art (Vallauris, France), while another teapot, which playfully integrates a painted image of the mythical figure of Leda and her long-necked swan, is selected to compete in the international *Fletcher Challenge 95, International Ceramic Award* in New Zealand.

Another aspect of the Selfridge aesthetic involves the making of functional and decorative wood-fired stoneware and porcelain pieces that are "according to Carol, most appreciated by other potters." [100] Featuring salt glaze and shino glaze work, these remarkably understated pots have a presence that, while not as flamboyant as the majolica, transcend the mundane with their elegant surfaces and restrained forms. The awareness that these are indeed objects made of clay is also far more immediate. Overall, between the majolica and the wood-fired pieces, the Selfridge's twenty-five year oeuvre reflects both the energy and the tension between clay as sculpture and clay as pottery.

In the ceramics of **SAM UHLICK** (1953, Edmonton, Alberta) there is no question where his production stoneware is positioned: his works are pottery through-and-through. Highlighted in a 1999 *AlbertaViews* article surveying the range of diversity of the province's contemporary scene, Les Graff opined: "In terms of functional ceramics it doesn't get any better than the work of the husband/wife partnership of Sam Uhlick and Antonia Huysman. Conceived and executed with care and attention to detail, the work is beautiful in its simplicity and consistent in its quality and detail." [101]

This is high praise for an artist who, during a turbulent era of experimentation and boundary-pushing in ceramics, chose to focus his energies on producing functional, domestic pottery. Inspired by the history of the Japanese tea bowl, his studies at NSCAD in Halifax and his travels to Japan, Korea, China and England, Uhlich "epitomizes the Yanagi-Leach tradition," says artist and scholar Ann Roberts, "He may live in Alberta but his forms are English and his glazes oriental." [102] These elements are beautifully demonstrated in works such as the substantial stoneware pitchers displayed in *Containment: The Space Within* (Canadian Clay and Glass Gallery, Waterloo, Ontario, 1994). "His jugs speak to us of timeless throwing rhythms and a constant regard for the melding of decoration with form." [103]

This adherence to traditional values, which in the artist's words "must have a liveliness and interest that goes beyond technical mastery," [104] has earned him a strong exhibition record that criss-crosses the globe: Tokyo, Taipei, Sydney, Trois-Rivières, San Angelo, Texas, Minneapolis, Toronto and Vallauris, France. In 1993, his apprenticeship at Wenford Bridge Pottery (England, 1977) is recognized by his inclusion in the exhibition *Michael Cardew and His Influence* (Beardsmore Gallery, London, England).

At the time Sam Uhlick receives his first formal instruction in two summer sessions (1971, 1972) at the Banff School of Fine Arts, **LESLIE MANNING** (1944, Provost, Alberta) is present at the school as its artist-in-residence. Two years later, Manning takes over as the institution's program director of the Ceramic Studio, a position he will hold for twenty years. During that time, he develops a unique body of work inspired by the Rockies' layered terrain and his interaction with the clay world as a juror, conference participant and member of numerous professional organizations. Over the course of his career, Manning is the first president of the Canadian Craft Council (1974–75), serves as a delegate at eighteen American NCECA Conferences (National Council for the Education of the Ceramic Arts), and receives the Fourth International Ceramic Symposium Award (Toronto) for his outstanding contribution to the field.

Closer to home, Manning is a participant in the Stonecrop Pottery Studio in Canmore. Originally located in a massive log building – bespeaking Canmore's heritage as a coal-mining community – Stonecrop is founded in 1974 as a co-op by Manning and three other versatile individuals: Bart Robinson (co-author of renowned *The Canadian Rockies Trail Guide*), Bonnie Lebowitz (one of the Banff Centre's first graduates from the full-time ceramics program), and Tony Bloom (founder and first editor of *Contact* magazine[105]). According to an article by Banff poet Jon Whyte in 1975, "Canmore coal is used in reduction firings. The shapes of the local terrain are reflected in pots, and local plants are impressed in the surfaces.... Stonecrop is a model for minimally contaminating industry and craft."[106]

Unique in the province, the intention of the group is to establish a high-profile clay studio where ceramic artists and other craftspeople from Canada and elsewhere[107] could work, display and interact with one another and the public. Central to the concept of Stonecrop is an emphasis on experimentation, or in Bloom's words, "An innovative approach whether in thrown work, sculpture, glazes, murals, design objects, production techniques, marketing or in related media including enameling, blown glass and bronze."[108]

Taking this concept to heart, **TONY BLOOM** (1947, Tokyo, Japan) will eventually work his way through many of the above disciplines, his loyalties and aesthetic tendencies dramatically different from that segment of the clay community espousing pottery as a way of life. Trained in physics with a background in percussion, Bloom, who gradually acquires the Stonecrop operation (1979),[109] has made functional and non-functional ceramic and bronze objects, produced numerous porcelain and stoneware murals for private and public commissions (H.G. Glyde Building at the Banff Centre and Calgary's ESSO Resources, TransCanada Pipelines, the CBC and ICG Resources), designed large-scale public sculpture in metal (*Oliver Convergence,* Edmonton and *Border Marker,* Lloydminster) and constructed ceramic musical instruments (flutes).

Bloom is an artist and designer first and foremost. If what he has in mind can be made in clay, he will use clay. If it needs to be made in some other material, he will look elsewhere. Not surprisingly, Bloom considers his art to be more about form or sculpture than the material. Often, there is an emphasis on clean geometrical shapes, coloured surfaces, and in certain instances, a futuristic look that is unusual for Alberta art of any kind. An example of this is *Double Box* (stoneware, 1984): a hard-edge rectangular box in three sections, covered with coloured diagonal stripes that is a precise, deliberately engineered work of art.

The inspirations for his varied oeuvre come from architecture, geology, the dynamics of physics (wavelengths) and rhythms. Paradoxically, another source for Bloom is the Neolithic past of Japanese pottery, specifically the Jomon and Haniwa period. In this vein, he has made deceptively simple cradles holding functional bowls with rounded bottoms. Made of metal, these small table-top pieces are quiet, elegant works, pointing to ceremonial and spiritual concerns, like in his cast bronze *Cradled Cauldron,* part of the 1985 travelling exhibition *Handspirits.*

Organized by the Alberta Crafts Council – another important promoter of ceramics since its formation in 1979 – the exhibition of fifty-four works by forty-eight Albertans, prompts one jury member, Colleen Lynch of St. John's, Newfoundland, to write, "I approached the jurying experience with no preconceived notion of what constituted 'Alberta crafts.' There is common ground – an obvious concern for technical proficiency, for example, and a large number of works containing recognizable imagery – but I was pleased to find that no stylistic school predominated. Rather than a homogeneous look we saw idiosyncratic approaches to problem solving."[110] Which, within the larger picture of Alberta, is where Tony Bloom and his clean angular creations are positioned.

The story of Alberta ceramics wouldn't be complete without acknowledging the contributions of MARY SHANNON WILL (1944, Ithaca, New York) and SALLY BARBIER (1949, Lafayette, Louisiana). Both clay graduates of American institutions, they arrive in Calgary (1971 and 1974 respectively) at a time when ceramic practice is in a state of flux. While California funk art and the gregarious work of Saskatchewan ceramic artist Joe Fafard has some influence in the province, others like Will are in a mood to refine.

Upon her arrival, Will takes up experimenting with low-fire, handbuilt, brightly coloured forms that recall hybrid plant and tuberous sea life. Of her influences, Will comments: "When a lot of people look at ceramics they have some awareness of the funk movement in ceramics in California in the sixties and seventies. I feel that work probably had some influence on me but I don't feel my work is that funky or that the colours are meant to be funk. I find most of the colour things that I do are beautiful. I don't think that funky was meant to be beautiful."[111]

This remark reflects a sentiment shared by many of her Calgary colleagues. The influence of funk with its coarse humour and deliberately rough appearance is somewhat limited. Far more relevant is a highly honed sense of beauty that Will's work increasingly will come to embody. Of her first solo exhibition in Calgary, organized by Brooks Joyner for the Nickle Arts Museum, the curator describes Will's work as "[appealing] to our sensory appetite."[112] He also makes reference to what would become an extremely important formal change in Will's sculptural approach: "Two years ago she was involved in the creation of more organic or biomorphic shapes and soft forms. That suggestive softness has given away now to very colourful juxtapositions of convex and concave forms and a surface consciousness that far exceeds her earlier experiments."[113] Or, as Will put it soon after, "Now the work is a lot more calculated and the surfaces are developing more as three-dimensional drawings."[114]

These developments are among the most exciting and profoundly breathtaking examples of ceramic sculpture in post-1970 Alberta. As a body of work (1978–1984), they are not publicly well-known, but they should be. Generally untitled, these small-scale porcelain objects with their polished decorative surfaces are so singular in their vision, so outstandingly distinctive, it is no wonder that the reviewer for the *Lethbridge Herald* enthused: "Will's pieces have a luminosity and a transparency that belies their humble clay insides."[115]

As clay sculptures, they are just plain unusual, consisting of simple but perfectly poised arrangements of precise three-dimensional shapes, whose surfaces are meticulously decorated with solid colours and an overlay of hundreds of tiny coloured dots, dashes, fine lines and other marks. "Animated," as Nancy Tousley later describes, "by the balance of their offbeat colours and the obsessive, contained energy of the patterns and marks."[116] Lethbridge's Victoria Baster explains in her 1985 catalogue essay for the artist, "To investigate colour selection, Mary Will sought methods which would eliminate personal choice. Choices of colour are relegated to some extrinsic circumstance; all the china paints in the studio, or all the reds. This establishes a given and effectively removes the question of colour from individual preferences."[117]

Why do it this way? According to Baster, it is a way of enlarging the choice of colour "beyond the known and the familiar,"[118] an opportunity to utilize chance in what otherwise is a very obsessive and time-consuming process of applying decoration. ("Though the scale of her work is small, it's not unusual for her to spend three years on a ceramic piece."[119]) Despite the attention paid to the procedure, however, Will does exercise her conscious taste in deciding what the final result will be. The fact, though, that she reaches beyond the conventional methods of relying on one's own intuition or personal preferences allies her loosely with a strain of contemporary art built on procedural art-making practices. (This approach is especially popular at the Nova Scotia College of Art and Design in the 1970s.[120])

Despite her decisive use of clay as a sculptural material, Mary Will, with her particular formal concerns, will eventually look at other media as well. Early on, for instance, she remarks, "One thing that does happen to me is that a lot of my friends aren't working in ceramics. Most of the people whose work I respect are not ceramists. That has been a big influence on me."[121] Hence, by the time of her 1985 Lethbridge exhibition, her output already has expanded to include a series of paintings, drawings, mixed media on paper and lithographs. "These works [begun in 1983] clearly have their sources in the ceramic pieces. Nevertheless, they reveal the remarkable way in which ideas evolved in one medium can take possession of other materials and advance into realms of new expressive effects."[122]

Nancy Tousley writes of the exhibition, "In her works on paper, the sleek sculptural [ceramic] forms become disks, triangles, bars, spirals and zig-zags built entirely on small dashes and dots.... The intensity of Will's visible labour builds the intensity of the images. They are lush, immediate and sensuously tactile."[123] In a later commentary, Tousley adds: "The simplest and most abstract of Will's images – the square, spiral and circle – are ancient symbols that have been meaningful to many ages and cultures.... As Will renders them in a magical series of six, small square canvases, they are vibrant, ready to lift off the surface of the painting to hang in the air."[124]

Jeffrey Spalding suggests there is a duality about Will's practice,[125] a set of contrasts: to be expressive and yet be totally in control, to work small and yet have enormous ambition, to engage in systems and yet insist on doing it all by hand, to produce wonder out of the strictest of forms and to be obsessively concerned with the formal and get away with it. Like many of her colleagues in Calgary, such as Chris Cran, Will is an artist who revels in dichotomies.

As a ceramic sculptor, Sally Barbier starts out on a somewhat similar trajectory as Mary Will. There is her penchant for arrangements of eccentric clay forms, a love of colour and pattern, and most of all, a commitment to clay as a sculptural material. For Will, it was initially the influence of University of Iowa ceramic sculptor Ron Brown who set her on this course. For Barbier, it was instructor Joe Bova, a figurative clay artist: "I immediately found [clay] to be an irresistible medium. It proved to be responsive to every movement of my hands and heart, the ideal vehicle to record an impulse."[126] Nonetheless, in the beginning, "It was important to make the clay anonymous.... Once I covered everything with acrylic and enamel paints, glitter and pieces of fabric ... [because] I was adamant about being a sculptor, not a craftsperson."[127]

Thus, in one of her first solo shows in Alberta (Ring House Gallery, Edmonton, 1980), her abstracted clay sculptures, inspired by the watery environment of her home state of Louisiana, are painted with acrylic rather than glazed. "[Barbier] is frank about her use of materials, stating that they are important only in explicitly conveying an image. 'I feel no reverence toward having a material remain true to itself.'"[128]

By the mid-80s, though, Nancy Tousley is reporting in the *Calgary Herald* that the Alberta College of Art instructor "no longer wants clay to look like something it clearly is not.... Where many ambitious ceramic artists have abandoned clay in recent years, attempting to shed the craft aspects of the medium, Barbier has accepted it, at the same time reviving her interest and resuscitating her forms."[129] Artist and critic Amy Gogarty later describes,

"Sally Barbier was first taught to break the rules, to challenge the purism of tradition, but her research into primitive technologies and historical ceramics has rekindled her interest in these areas."[130]

Also important to this change of attitude are her travels to other countries, including Japan, Korea, Thailand and Indonesia, where she is nourished by "the impulse that drives people to make objects, build architecture and invent rituals in the name of reaching beyond the 'here and now' to something the makers feel is larger and more central to the meaning of their lives."[131] (Her travels also take her to Mexico, an engaging place for several Alberta creators because of its different environment and overt religious and cultural practices.)

Underpinning the change, however, is Barbier's strengthening conviction that her "strong religious upbringing, and the Black culture [of the deep south]"[132] are central to her artistic imagination and sense of identity: "I grew up on a sugar-cane plantation ... the family church, the Assumption of the Blessed Virgin Mary (built in 1793) was the earliest church along Bayou Lafourche. Its wall and ceiling were covered with glorious murals of good and bad angels fighting."[133]

Eventually, Barbier will distill and incorporate these images and themes from her past more fully in wall relief and freestanding sculptures that "are best described as personal shrines laden with historic, metaphysical and religious symbols personifying humanity's search for spirituality."[134] Utilizing both white clays and a fine-particle red clay for texture and colour, the smoked, crackle-glazed or stained surfaces of the sculptures are covered with molded symbols, like praying figures, hearts, alligators, hands, ears and cups and saucers. Cross-cultural influences are also present. In her *New Works* show (1994, Muttart Art Gallery, Calgary), for instance, the fringe of tiny clay shapes hanging from her *Shrine Series* is identified as being inspired by Mexican *milagros:* a prayer token or charm placed by believers on altars.[135]

Although many of her later sculptures are pared down and semi-abstract, she continues to be influenced by architecture. In addition, according to Amy Gogarty, writing for the 1995 *Ground/Connection* exhibit (Minneapolis and Winnipeg): "Barbier has begun to include references to sea life and shell forms, the 'natural architecture' of animals. Occasionally an archway punctures the forms; a tiny staircase articulates a wavering edge [of the sculpture], suggesting surrealistic shifts in scale. A sense of guilty pleasure in defiantly breaking the rules of logic animates these dream-like assemblages."[136]

In a 1993 issue of *Contact*, Barbier writes: "My work now involves making pieces that are nostalgic,"[137] a brave admission for any artist lest he or she be accused of sentimentality. Barbier's low-fire earthenware is, within the context of a northern country like Canada, a rich and sometimes foreign recollection of symbol and shape. Calgary, though, has provided "a kind of safe haven in which one's personal creative heritage can be examined and explored in a safe, secure environment."[138] That this is possible without the artist/instructor feeling constrained about her religious content is put into a broader perspective by the following:

"Mid-century artists turned away from religion and toward modernist universalism. They kept beliefs pretty much to themselves, or abstracted them à la Barnett Newman and Mark Rothko. Until recently, the art world sanctioned little work with overt religious content unless it possessed a critical, subversive edge."[139]

But certainly not the kind of edge that Barbier will declare about her own art in the early 1990s. "It may sound pretentious but I expect people to get a spiritual experience from these works."[140] One of six women to appear in *Ground/Connection,* Barbier's memory-laden pieces are included in the 1995 show because of its theme of mentoring, what Amy Gogarty describes as "the invisible network of support women artists have developed over the last twenty years.... In choosing Sally Barbier, Trudy Golley honours a brief but significant moment when Sally taught her at the Alberta College of Art. Barbier's 'stubborn honesty' and emphasis on technical knowledge in the service of personal vision made a lasting impression."[141]

A full-time ceramics instructor at the Alberta College of Art (1978–1998) and a rotating chair of its ceramics department (1988–1995), Barbier brought a strong sculptural attitude to the school where previously the emphasis had been on wheel-thrown pottery. She also initiated a guest artist/instructor program in the early 1980s, where students would be introduced to a "significantly different approach to the medium than the (two-member) faculty could provide."[142] Under this annual program, the Calgary scene will be enriched with the presence of such professionals as Joan McNeil, Paul Rozman, Katherine Finnerty, Diane Sullivan, Katrina Rozman, Trudy Ellen Golley and Greg Payce (who joined Barbier on the faculty in 1989).

In 1998, the artist returned to the tropical lowlands of Louisiana after nearly twenty-five years on the high, dry plains of Alberta. Despite feeling her artwork "has never seemed to fit in any 'current' movement or genre,"[143] Barbier's focus on clay as a sculptural medium with attention paid to its wonderful intrinsic qualities, her investigation of cultural identity and personal experience, her sly melding of semi-abstract forms with biomorphic ones, the reoccurring themes of memory and spirituality, and the deliberate aging of the surface through primitive firing, link the artist with many contemporary art-making concerns at the end of the century. Furthermore, she comes from a generation where, as she remembers it: "Female ceramics students were encouraged to aspire towards technical assistantships with well-known male artists, rather than work as artists in their own right."[144] In the new story of Alberta ceramics, Sally Barbier is there on the front line as an artist and an example.

chapter seventeen

Feminist Influences in Post-1970 Art

> THE FEMINIST ART MOVEMENT, which began in the late sixties, generally paralleled developments in the larger women's movement: conscious-raising, agitation for equal representation and the creation of alternative galleries and publications. Feminist artists, curators and art historians challenged the assumptions of the "male-strom" art world while alternative approaches to art-making led to potent strategies for revealing and subverting the dominant ideology of a patriarchal culture. By and large, however, this activity appears to have bypassed Alberta where there are no women's co-operative galleries, no women's art publications and few women artists whose work is overtly feminist in intent or execution.[1]

Published in 1986, this statement by the Edmonton-based art writer, Christine Conley, tends to leave the lingering impression that women and art somehow don't mix in Alberta. Albeit unintentionally, what is left out is the important fact that women artists have been a major presence in the province, especially in the latter half of the twentieth century, playing a significant role in the Alberta story.

In another instance, writing for the broad and informative survey of Albertan women artists, *Women's Work: Art by Women in Glenbow's Collections* (1996) – which includes such early examples as Adeline Baxter's *Three Sisters,* (watercolour, Canmore, Alberta c. 1917), Florence Maude Mortimer's *David* (1915, gouache on ivory) and Sarah Mary Blake's *The Deer Horn Ranch on the North Fork of the Old Man River, Alberta* (1889, watercolour) – Glenbow curator Kirsten Evenden points out that:

> Since the Industrial Revolution, and until the rise of the modern women's movement, it was difficult for women to gain professional artistic recognition in western culture because the very definition of the "artist" implied that he was male. Powerful myths developed during this period about the role of the artist in society. The artist was a male genius, who stood on the margins of society, creating works for a discerning public.
>
> On the other hand, during the nineteenth century, etiquette books for women promoted an image of the "lady painter," one who was proficient at her art, but who aspired to no more than a certain amateurism – as opposed to undertaking art making as a professional career.[2]

But many Albertan women have pursued art as professionally as they can. Before 1970, Marion Nicoll, Euphemia McNaught, Annora Brown, Violet Owen, Elsie May Bulger (known as Alberta's Grandma Moses), Vivian Lindoe, Doris Zaharichuk, Velma Foster, Jane Van Alderwegen, Gail Lindoe, Barbara Harvey Leighton, Barbara Roe Hicklin, Sibyl Laubental, Ella May Walker, Janet Mitchell, Margaret Shelton, Jean LaPointe Mihalcheon, Irene McCaugherty, Katie Ohe, Isabel Levesque, Holly (Janet) Middleton, Kay Angliss, sisters Helen and Isabel Stadelbauer, Margaret Seelye and Thelma Manarey are busy at work.[3] However, the world around them is not so quick to catch on. Even into the 1960s it is still a novel idea in Alberta that a woman would commit herself heart and soul to art. Take, for example, this 1962 newspaper description of the promising young Calgary sculptor Katie Ohe: "Miss Ohe is a gentle doe-like girl who is probably one of the most dedicated artists in Calgary. She can become completely absorbed in her work ... to the extent that her surroundings almost cease to exist."[4]

Born in 1937 (Peers, Alberta), Ohe attributes her sense of commitment to the early influence of her instructor Marion Nicoll (1909–1985).[5] Certainly a feminist in the way she lived,[6] Nicoll is acknowledged in *Women's Work* not only for her mentorship of other artists but also for her progressive use of craft materials to "explore contemporary art concepts."[7] An example is a series of hanging batiks, made in 1956 by Nicoll, which is shown in *Women's Work.* Typically acknowledged as "the first artist in Alberta to seriously pursue abstract painting,"[8] it's no small irony that while Nicoll devotes herself to teaching the "lesser" arts of craft and design at the Provincial Institute of Technology and Design (later the Alberta College of Art and Design), the recognition she later receives is for her abstract oils on canvas.

Like Nicoll, Ohe will also be recognized for her mentorship (YMCA Women of Distinction Award, 1989) and for being one of the first artists in the province to seriously pursue abstract metal sculpture. Using words like "participatory,"[9] "modest" and "non-confrontational" in the 1970s, the artist produced a series of fluid, kinetic metal artworks far different in spirit from what later would be referred to as Edmonton steel. With its emphasis on brawny materials like scrap steel, Edmonton steel is perhaps a more monumental and masculine approach to sculpture, firmly committed to the modernist belief in art for the sake of art. But for Ohe, materials and form are never as important as the concept[10] or as critcial as her concern that her artwork be "people friendly."[11] Also, Ohe's sculpture is de-gendered[12] – it can't be identified by appearance as being made by a woman – and does not specifically address the social condition of women or make statements that would be considered feminist. Instead, Ohe's oeuvre, even at its most purely geometric, is more concerned with tactile experience. Her sculpture pulls the hand toward it. For all of the geometry, engineering, discipline and finish of late-modernist sculpture, Ohe's have a striking non-authoritarian presence. Her bobbing, folding, rotating and interconnected forms stand in stark contrast to the heavy-metal, hard-edged character of abstract metal sculpture, so critically popular in Canada through the 1970s and 1980s.

Like other proto-feminist practitioners in the province, such as Joice Hall, Dulcie Foo Fat, Alexandra Haeseker, Maureen Enns, Annemarie Schmid Esler, Sally Barbier, Carroll (Moppett) Taylor-Lindoe, Wendy Toogood and others, Ohe is part of a broader swelling of formally trained women active in the 1970s. In their midst is the breakdown of modernism and ever-increasing infusion of styles, materials, content and practices that give rise to a more eclectic art scene, and while these women do not take up the specific concerns of feminist artists elsewhere, they do become immersed in a changing mileu.

A mileu where, as the influential American critic and curator Lucy Lippard suggests, you really can't think of pluralism without feminism. In her essay "Sweeping Exchanges: The Contribution of Feminism to the Art of the Seventies,"[13] Lippard, who, like her polar opposite the late art critic Clement Greenberg, travels to Alberta several times, writes: "Feminist methods and theories have ... offered a socially concerned alternative to the increasingly mechanical evolution of art about art. The 1970s might not have been pluralist at all if women had not emerged during the decade to introduce the multicoloured threads of female experience into the male fabric of modern art."

Feminism also helped broaden the impact of that other post-1970 development – postmodernism. According to American Robert Atkins of Artspeak, "In opposition to the purity and exclusivity of modernism, feminism called for an expansive approach to art. The feminist use of narrative, autobiography, decoration, ritual, crafts-as-art and popular culture helped catalyse the development of postmodernism."[14]

David Garneau, then an Alberta-based artist and writer, sums it up this way: "It has been art history's habit to read individual works of art into a single progressive, universal and masculine narrative; a habit which makes learning and appropriating that history easy, but which has not accommodated voices and stories alternative to those who compose the master narrative. Recently, many women artists have found the courage to abandon masculinist art traditions and have endeavoured to represent and express their different histories and experiences."[15]

Part One

In terms of post-1970 Alberta art, one of the significant areas where the "multicoloured threads of female experience" initially makes its presence known is in the fibre arts. An early cause célèbre of the sisterhood, feminism champions marginalized practices such as quilting and needlework as legitimate art forms; and draws a strong link between gender and the historical bias against crafts. In *AlbertaViews,* writer Berenice Gargus states: "Art is rare, made for beauty, not usefulness. Quilts are common and evolved from necessity and practicality. But perhaps the real reason quilts aren't valued as art is that quilting is a medium created and perfected primarily by women and historically women have not been the smiths that forged masterpieces of art."[16]

By contrast, Kirsten Evenden notes for *Women's Work,* "Not all cultures view art by woman in a similar fashion.... The distinction between high art and craft is not made in traditional indigenous cultures. Instead, artistic work is divided according to gender, but the perceived economic and spiritual values given the objects can be similar." [17] Among others in the *Women's Work* exhibition that illustrate this important idea is Emma Brass's very fine *Quillwork Belt* (ca.1950s). Made of cotton, porcupine quills and buckskin, Brass trains with a quillwork society of the Siksika (Blackfoot) nation: "One earns the right to do quillwork by learning the techniques and then going through a number of important rituals." [18] Within the southern Albertan community, this practice carries status, and it is given a different reception than the earlier creative work of women working in a Eurocentric tradition.

Thus, one of the strategies in the women's art movement is to refocus the lens of art on what has been traditionally marginalized. "In any event, if we are interested in rewriting art history from a feminist perspective, the place to look is not in the back rooms of the Louvre but in the world of folk art, where despite its constraints, women have left a legacy of authentic experience waiting to be decoded." [19]

A contemporary art example of this legacy is the touring exhibition *The Dinner Party* (1974–78) by American artist Judy (Gerowitz) Chicago and her many volunteers. Perhaps the most famous and controversial piece of feminist art ever made, and in post-1970 Alberta, one of the best-attended exhibitions in the province (62,000 viewers), this collaborative work of thirty-nine dinner place settings is partly a homage to needlework, ceramics and that most ridiculed of female pastimes, china painting.

Displayed in 1982 in Calgary, the exhibition is not Chicago's only contact with Alberta. In 1980, the artist, at the request of director and curator Joan Borsa of the Student's Union Art Gallery (SUB), gives a presentation in Edmonton about this very work. According to Christine Conley, it is a controversial invitation. "Typically a large portion of the criticism was levelled at Borsa for inviting Chicago in the first place. In the polarization of attitudes that formed – for or against Chicago/feminism – there was little room for any feminist critique of the work, neither then nor two years later, when *The Dinner Party* was shown at the Glenbow Museum in Calgary." [20]

The 1980s as a whole are an important decade for female-centred art in Alberta, including the groundbreaking *Alberta Quilts* [21] (1984), *Alberta Needles* [22] (1988) and *Alberta Needles II: Quilts for the 1990s* (1990). The first exhibition focused on early and more recent quilting activity in the province with such examples as a circa 1909 red and white *Signature Quilt* by Calgary's Hillhurst Presbyterian Ladies' Aid, while the other two feature a stunning range of recently made quilts using traditional and contemporary designs. Some of the accomplished quilt artists included in the *Needles II* show are Judy Villet (Edmonton), Faye Kindt (Nanton), Sanna Kaiser (Ponoka), Chris Hale (Lethbridge), the Bow River Quilters (Calgary), Jayne Willoughby Scott (Sherwood Park) and others. A curated selection of this show also travels to Alberta House (London, England). Writing for the *Alberta Needles II* catalogue, Paula Gustafson traces the institutional acceptance of this kind of work to earlier exhibitions, like a 1971 show of antique quilts at New York's Whitney Museum. From there, "it took another ten years before newly made quilts were lifted from the ghetto of 'women's work' and happily hung on gallery walls." [23]

Around the same time as *Needles II,* a more radical response to the craft is also presented in *Redefined: The Quilt as Art,* a 1989 exhibition in Banff that features artists from Alberta (Richard and Patricia Green, Grant Leier, Barbara Todd and Wendy Toogood), British Columbia, Quebec, Ontario and Saskatchewan. One weekly newspaper magazine reports: "A heated debate broke out when traditionalists at the biannual *A Patch In Time* quiltmaking convention in Banff on the same weekend stopped in at *Redefined.* Some were enthusiastic, but others violently opposed." [24] The show is hosted by the Whyte Museum of the Canadian Rockies and later circulates to eight Canadian cities where "a current of feminism" [25] is said to pervade the concerns [26] of many of the eighteen quilts juried into the show. As curator Katherine Lipsett observes, "A variety of political and social issues are being explored here, just as they are being examined in other art forms."[27]

Considering that the late 1980s is a particularly politicized period in contemporary art (including such projects as the 1987 *NAMES Project Quilt,* devoted to the victims of AIDS), many of the pieces in *Redefined* certainly do make social statements with the most politically inclined being crafted by the then Banff-based artist **BARBARA TODD** (1952, Galt, Ontario.) [28] Her quilts address the controversial Star Wars weapons program and in *Redefined*, her crib-sized wall hanging [29] *Security Blanket – A Child's Quilt* (1988–89, wool and cotton) "displays the wide range of missiles presently available, while the accompanying drawing identifies each by name. The concept of a child's quilt containing such disturbing imagery, yet providing warmth and a feeling of security, creates a sharp contrast." [30]

Todd's work makes a strong break from the conventional tradition of quilts being decorative, colourful, commemorative and/or optimistic. With their sombre colours and masculine imagery, Todd's wall hangings are later highlighted in *Equinox* magazine for having "drawn the ire of traditional quilters for bringing dark, seemingly death-filled imagery to what they feel is a loving, positive endeavour. 'They see me as taking advantage of the marvellous tradition,' [Todd] says. 'It kind of makes me sad, because it's the rich tradition that I love so much.'" [31]

Begun in 1986 with woollen suiting fabric and traditional quilting techniques, Todd's *Security Blankets* – which incorporate a range of images including business suits, bombs, military aircraft and eventually more traditional quilting designs like flying geese – are her attempt, according to the artist, to bring "history (war, business, power) to the personal (the quilt). The quilts produced to date [1995], collectively referred to as *Security Blankets,* encourage an ironic reading ... pointing to the conflict between power, as exemplified by nuclear weaponry, and human values." [32]

In the same critical spirit, the artist also takes a political stance in her 1990 quilt entitled *Alberta*. Constructed of pastel pink and pastel grey woollen fabric, this subtle artwork juxtaposes the gentle plant life of the foothills with the aggressive presence of the cruise missile at the Cold Lake air force base. "[*Alberta*] is unlike most of my work in that it is pale and landscape based," [33] but still connected in spirit to the quilting efforts of earlier feminists such as Canada's remarkable Joyce Wieland (1931–1998). Comments Bridget Elliot, "Wieland's interest in patriotism and militarism provide important precedents for Barbara Todd's work." [34]

In late 1992, Lethbridge's Southern Alberta Art Gallery organizes a nine-city national tour of eight of the *Security Blankets* and related drawings. One of a small number of contemporary Albertans [35] with the stature and opportunity to tour their art nationally in the 1990s, Todd's contribution is described by Marni Jackson as, "[A] fine example of what Rozsika Parker wrote about in *The Subversive Stitch,* [her] quilts turn the traditionally submissive image of needlework – the picture of a silent woman with her head bent over the quilting frame into a form of patient subversion, a way of 'pointing out' the significant shapes in our cultural landscapes." [36]

In *Redefined: The Quilt as Art,* however, the Banff-based artist is not the only renegade with needle and thread to surface in the wild rose province. Less overtly feminist but notable for disrupting "the notion that quilting is an inherently feminine art form"[37] are the works of Canmore's Richard and Patricia Green, Grant Leier (formerly of Calgary) and Charon Hill. Collaborative efforts, their quilts differ from Todd's in their use of non-traditional methods and materials. Green, for instance, attaches metal numbers to his *Quilt by Number,* while miniature electric chili-pepper lights protrude from the metal grommets in Leier and Hill's *Electric Quilt – Hot Pepper Nights You Make Me Crazy.* Add to this Wendy Toogood's *Zig Zag* and *Hang* and quilting has never looked so unorthodox in Alberta.

Born in England and trained at the Alberta College of Art, **WENDY TOOGOOD** (1947, Bristol, England), according to Kathryn Burns, who curated her 1996 retrospective, Toogood "occupies a unique place in the fabric of Canadian art. Her remarkable synthesis of Mexican folk traditions, indigenous crafts and the spontaneity of children's art, as well as a grounding in the modernist tradition, assures her work a place of prominence."[38] A child of the rebellious 1960s, as early as 1973 the *Toronto Star* is describing Toogood's wall hangings, soft sculptures and etchings as not only the product "of a joyous imagination," but also the result of "a total lack of concern for what is artistically respectable."[39] Which, after earning a diploma in crafts (1969), means incorporating stitchery into her pop art–influenced practice. Recalling the general reaction to this choice, the artist is later quoted: "I was discouraged from pursuing quilting. It was claimed that I would not be accepted as a serious artist in galleries once I finished school. [But, especially in southern Alberta,] this has definitely not been the case."[40]

As Toogood shows in *Fibrations: A New Generation of Fibre in Alberta*[41] (1980), her hand-sewn work is a unique blending of craft techniques with the so-called higher concerns of fine art. "[Her art] is related more closely to drawing and painting than textiles,"[42] observes Nancy Tousley in the *Calgary Herald.* Toogood herself says: "I think of the cloth constructions as a lot of drawing with material and bias tape."[43] Thus, in exhibitions including *Alberta Work*[44] (1977) and *New Image Alberta*[45] (1982), Toogood's wallhangings and framed pieces find a place amongst displays of new paintings and other media. Made of cut-out shapes of fabric stitched to a cloth background, her work resonates with a "buoyancy of spirit," a phrase coined by the guest curator of *Alberta Work*, Alvin Balkind.[46] "In general," Balkind writes of the exhibition, "there appears to be a buoyancy of spirit, indeed an air of considerable excitement in the arts of Alberta, which was not that visible as recently as five years ago. It is as though the arts in the province were moving in a crescendo toward some sort of extraordinary realization, somewhere over the next hill."[47]

Balkind's remarks will turn out to be prophetic. In the decade to follow, Toogood and many others turn the 1980s into a brilliant period of visual-art activity in the province. The precedent of their art lays a foundation that, with the support of a growing visual-art infrastructure, enables contemporary art production to be exceptionally bountiful and diverse by the end of the century.

Five years after Balkind's exhibition, *Vanguard* reviewer Charlotte Townsend declares about *New Image Alberta:* "Too little is known elsewhere about art in Alberta.... The implication is that the old image of art in Alberta, landscape and post-painterly abstraction, needs updating."[48] Not long after that, Toogood reinforces this sentiment with her work *Strong Winds* (1985), a long, horizontal mural commissioned for the Alberta Pavilion at *Expo 86* in Vancouver. Writing about this symbolically charged abstract composition, she declares: "I wanted to offer viewers a new image of Alberta; a more youthful image, a more modern image, a projection of Alberta as a place where exciting things are happening."[49] Worked in the techniques of applique and quilting, the four-panel collage is one of series of commissions she completes for corporations and public institutions, including a ten-panel history for Edmonton's City Hall (1992).[50]

Strong Winds also signifies the end of a particular period in her art where swarms of tiny flying forms animate the design and "had become a trademark image or icon in my cloth constructions."[51] After 1985, new ideas about line, colour, texture, pattern and form emerge, beginning with a very hip series of abstract, non-objective works (1985–1989). Employing new wave materials – punk-style spandex, leopard-print ultra suede, metallic fabrics, neon and checkerboard vinyl – Toogood evokes the glitzy funky exuberance of the 1980s in works such as *Zig Zag* (1988) and *Check* (1987). Different again is her work *Wall* (1988), a precedent-setting grid of fifty-five small framed collages, of which she said: "I wanted to create a work about large and small, miniature and grand scale, a work within a work."[52]

Then in 1989, inspired by her travels in Central and South America, the artist embarks on a series of large, Mexican-cloth constructions (1989–93). Made to reflect her experiences and her "respect for the Latin American cultures,"[53] these works are very different in feeling from the purely formal designs of her abstract period. More representational with simplified human and animal figures, these narrative pieces "look directly to Central American folk art in both style and subject matter."[54]

These quilts also represent another type of link that Alberta-based artists have with Latin America. For instance, in the 1950s and 1960s, Mexico's post-graduate Instituto Allende (San Miguel de Allende) is a popular place for Calgary art-school alumni, Toogood included.[55] Notably, it is the exposure to Latin American culture early in her career that convinces the artist to blur the boundaries between art and craft in the first place.[56]

Latin America also influences Toogood's later rapport with her paintings, several of which are displayed alongside her cloth constructions in her 1996 retrospective at Calgary's Muttart Art Gallery.[57] These new paintings (1993–1995) touch on the Day of the Dead festival, dolls from her own folk-art collection, and such topical feminist-influenced art concerns as identity and multiculturalism. In addition, they have "in a more direct, immediate and expressive manner, an intensity of colour and pattern."[58] Sure enough, when it comes to vibrant imagery in Alberta, Toogood's work, whether in cloth or gouache, is some of the brightest and most graphic, a characteristic nurtured not only by her contact with other cultures but also by her long association with the fibre arts, both as an artist and an instructor at her alma mater.[59]

Along with Wendy Toogood, twenty-two other artists appear in *Fibrations: A New Generation of Fibre in Alberta* (1980). Some, like Jane Kidd (tapestry), would continue to work primarily within the context of the fibre arts, while others, such as Pat Strakowski and Sandra (Tivy) Vida, venture into other media like sculpture, painting (Strakowski), installation, video, and photo-based collage (Vida). Sculptor Lylian Klimek, meanwhile, incorporates fibre into her enigmatic sculptures and installation art, as in her evocative *Ancient Dreams,* a pyramid made of wood and covered with raw, carded wool. Whatever route these artists choose, they continue to support and broaden the issues raised by feminism and the women's art movement. By considering a selection of artwork made in the 1980s and 1990s in the province, we can see how some of these artists and others responded to such currents.

SANDRA VIDA (formerly Tivy; 1947, Calgary, Alberta) is a notable example of a practitioner with strong roots in feminist art-making, in community projects and in the development of artist-run initiatives. She spends fifteen years in the administration of Calgary's Off Centre Centre/the New Gallery, and takes part in numerous collaborative projects, including: *Mz. Frankenstein* (1992, Calgary), a work with Tanya Mars and Colleen Kerr "about the negative effects of the 'beauty myth' on women's lives,"[60] and the performance piece *Gorilla/Guerrilla* (1990), a collaboration with Scottish musician Watt McDonald, presented at the opening of the exhibition *Glasgow Girls: 1880–1920* (Kelvingrove Museum, Glasgow).

In her *Kitchen Freedom* installation (2000), Vida demonstrates her recurring concern "with the limitations of restricting roles and stereotypes, especially for women."[61] The work consists of four photo-based collages and a room-size installation filled with "40s and 50s kitchen objects and images of typical housewives. Alongside these are displayed subversive images from Celtic tradition suggesting contradictory ancient associations – woman as leader, sorceress, healer, warrior."[62] The piece also exhibits her inventive nature and accomplished technique. Of the four collages, done in part with the use of a colour copier, curator Christine Sowiak recognizes Vida as "a master of the collage … [making use] of the unlikely but telling juxtapositions of image and symbol, word and meaning."[63]

Vida finds her way into performance, collage installation, video and film after spending several years in fabric and clothing design, teaching batik, fabric dyeing and related fabric arts at the Alberta College of Art. The 1980 *Fibrations* show marks her entrance into the fine-art world. She presents a velvet helmet – *Mask for Keeping Secrets* – decorated in batik.

CARLA COSTUROS (1952, Edmonton, Alberta) has worked as a weaver, fibre instructor and women's activist. In her large-scale installations, she incorporates traditional textile designs and techniques with contemporary concerns. Her work *Overlay* (1996), for instance, is a mixed media, outdoor installation made with bedding plants, large boulders, water urns and pebbled pathways. Forty-two feet in diametre, *Overlay* is interpreted as an environmental meditation layered with symbolic references to mythology, language and humanizing the urban environment. Produced as an outdoor piece for *The Works: A Visual Arts Celebration* (1996, Edmonton), aligned with the festival's theme of *Designs on the City*, the *Edmonton Journal* celebrates *Overlay* as "a beautiful prayer garden [that] brings a stately calm to the centre of the city."[64]

The founder and former chair of Grant MacEwan College's Fibre Program (1981–1992) as well as a co-founder[65] of Edmonton's SubText (Subversive

Textiles Association of Artists, 1992–1996), Costuros has long stressed a role in art for concerns that are linked to contemporary society, women's issues, history, culture and the environment. Once saying the purpose of SubText was "to subvert the notion of what textiles can and can't be,"[66] Costuros and the collective organize a juried exhibition (Edmonton, 1994) of twenty Commonwealth artists whose use of handmade paper as a "vehicle of cultural commentary is both conventional and idiosyncratic."[67] Entitled *Paper Speak: A Global View,* this showcase of paper art was later seen in Victoria (XV Commonwealth Games Arts and Cultural Festival) and in Toronto (the Museum of Textiles). One of the pieces selected for the show is Costuros's *Vanishing Point,* a floor-and-wall piece made from abaca (banana plant fibre), hemp, recycled wood pulp and the pickings from a boreal forest floor. This environmental work was inspired by a trip to northern Alberta. Critic Charles Mandel writes: "This can be a lament for what is lost. [She] gives us a road stretching to infinity, with a paper highway showing the modern, built environment cutting through ancient landscapes."[68]

A graduate of both Okanagan College and the Alberta College of Art, **COLLEEN KERR** (1961, North Vancouver, British Columbia) is an integral member of the alternative art scene in Calgary during the 1980s and early 1990s. Along with artists Mark Dicey, Nelson Henricks, Steve Heimbecker, Vern Hume, Rob Milthorp, Bart Habermiller, Grant Poier, Leila Sujir, Sandra Vida and others, Kerr works to make art forms through video, installation and performance more visible in the city. For instance, she participates in such events as: *Media Blitz*[69] (1988), a festival of video, film and performance art; *Elemental Instincts,*[70] an exhibition of installation, video, performance and mixed media art; and *Camera Obscura,*[71] a video-art series broadcast on local cable.

In 1987, when Kerr is barely out of art school, she quickly gains critical attention. The National Gallery of Canada acquires her 1986 video production *A Pack of Lies.* Five minutes in length, the tape takes a deliberately absurdist approach to "how easily we create our reality and mythology based on what we reveal to others."[72] In 1988, Kerr allies herself with the feminist art movement in her video *Teabell Tolls.* This seventeen-minute colour video follows a young heroine, played by Kerr, on an allegorical journey to womanhood, making use of storytelling and sociological subject matter. Unlike her modernist predecessors, Kerr incorporates these two feminist/postmodern tendencies – along with a deep interest in systems of belief such as mythology, nature-based religion, Christianity, tarot and astrology – as part of an art practice "rooted," she says, "in literary and verbal forms."[73] Much of Kerr's video work of the period is developed from site-specific performances. In theatrical pieces such as *Niagara*[74] (1988), the costumed Kerr "examines an individual's need to define their uniqueness by facing death through perilous adventure,"[75] while in *The Journey*[76] (1989), themes relating to the creation of identity prevail.

Kerr's assemblages[77] also reflect feminist themes. Representing another side of her creative energies, in the early 1990s she constructs small, decorated boxes out of found materials, which according to curator Annette Hurtig, "bring to mind a time when women were excluded from the creation of art and meaning."[78] Usually made for the viewer to handle, these decorative containers and their arcane contents would have been relegated to "fancy work or craft ... [because] the term 'master craftsman' itself, excludes the female by way of designating excellence in terms of masculinity."[79]

TERESA POSYNIAK (1951, Regina, Saskatchewan) has likened her mixed-media work *Abyss* (1992) to a journey into the psychological drama of motherhood: exploring both its joy and its tribulations.[80] Begun before the birth of her children and continued through their early childhood, the piece recalls British artist Mary Kelly's *Post-Partum Document* 1973–1979, which taxonomically records Kelly's relationship with her son through diagrams, texts and child-related material. *Abyss* is a more recent example of the earlier feminist credo, "the personal is political." Its autobiographical stance is deemed to be, as critic David Garneau remarks, an alternative to the master narrative. Reviewing the piece at the Edmonton Art Gallery in 1992, Garneau writes of Posyniak's work: "Recently, many women artists have found the courage to abandon the masculinist art traditions and have endeavoured to represent and express their different histories and experiences."[81]

Posyniak has also worked as a sculptor and maker of large mixed-media installations, for which she earned a master's of fine arts from the University of Calgary in 1983. Attracted to the idea of creating stage-like structures that require the viewer to walk through it, the artist considers her MFA work, *Sanctuary,* to be "a visual construct for specific feelings I have about myself as an individual in isolation, and as part of society.... Like me, this sculpture grows, changes and adapts to diverse situations."[82] As such, *Sanctuary,* built in sections with an elevated wooden floor on one side and sheets of handmade felt and paper that serve as wall coverings and shelves, has continued to evolve. For instance, Posyniak reconstructs the piece between its inaugural show in Calgary and its following exhibition at Regina's Dunlop Art Gallery. "Since its conception two years ago ... dancers have danced on it, a poet has used it as a subject for a poem, many people, including 1,000 Alberta school children, have explored it.... Through it I explore feelings of vulnerability, fragility, strength and self-preservation." With *Sanctuary,* Posyniak takes a less clinical approach to art-making at a time when many feminists were dispassionately deconstructing the codes of gender.

A decade later, the artist again taps into her emotions to create *Lest We Forget,* a 1992 sculpture dedicated to slain women in Canada, including the fourteen engineering students murdered in 1989 at l'Ecole Polytechnique in Montreal. Made of wood and Styrofoam, and covered with silvery-bronze handmade paper, the 7-foot-high slab-like sculpture elicits much public and media attention for its intentional resemblance to a (male-centred) war memorial. Countering this, the artist points out that the sculpture's human scale, its personalized script and its fragile composition make it an entirely different kind of memorial from those erected to pay tribute to Canada's war dead.[83] Installed in the University of Calgary law school after funds are found by concerned citizens in the community, the artist and others view its placement within the institution as a strategic reminder of the inadequacies of the legal system to protect women against domestic violence.[84]

LYLIAN KLIMEK's (1942, Humboldt, Saskatchewan) sculptural installations of the early 1990s incorporate high-art materials such as bronze with those of domestic life – a box of soap, linoleum and an antique wringer washer. Casting in bronze such unlikely items as a cleaning rag and a man's shirt, the artist addresses not only her own situation of working with a material traditionally associated with the male artist, but also comments on the neglected territory of women's labours. "By 'preserving' these [domestic] activities in artifact form, she offered an ironically celebratory look at the heroics of everyday life,"[85] observes art critic Paula Gustafson in Vancouver's *Georgia Straight.*

An ex-sociologist with two master's degrees – one in sociology, the other in art – Klimek has an abiding interest in cultural studies with a focus on consumerism. In *Give Away,*[86] for instance, the notion of art as a precious commodity is turned on its head when eighty compact sculptures of clay, cast mud, concrete and wood are given away on opening night. Another concern for the artist, who has taught at the Alberta College of Art and Design since 1978, is the disregard for nature and ecology in our consumer-driven culture. "In Klimek's *Meadow* [1990] the viewer is bathed not by the rays of the sun but in black light; while all around, a field of flat cut-out representations of objects of human manufacture give off an unearthly but seductive greenish-yellow glow." [87]

Analytical rather than overtly emotional or expressive in her approach, Klimek invokes a subtle wit, a rich austere aesthetic and an imaginative handling of materials that continually surprises. These elements are evident in her earlier sculptures made of wood and covered with masses of shredded rubber – "the wonderful dark monoliths of Lylian Klimek are primitive, fearsome things" [88] – and evident in her later forays into the social complexities of contemporary material culture – "There is a light bulb, a flush toilet, a jet fighter and so on ... cut from masonite.... The illusion of depth [is created] by adding a light coating of mud and carefully shading the surface of the objects with greenish-yellow fluorescent paint." [89]

Once commenting that what links her work to other women artists is that it does not focus on purely formal concerns but has multiple meanings and associations,[90] Klimek is a leading figure in sculptural-installation art in Alberta. In 1987, for her solo exhibition at the Southern Alberta Art Gallery, art historian and critic Leslie Dawn relates her to a broader, international movement: "The field of sculptural inquiry is expanding dramatically in the current postmodern period. Among those contributing to this development are, for perhaps the first time in the history of the medium, a substantial number of women. Lylian Klimek shares with Louise Bourgeois, Eva Hesse and others an approach that sets them apart from late-modernist sculptors such as Richard Serra, Anthony Caro, Sol Lewitt or Donald Judd. While neither feminine not feminist in origin, their work can be viewed as unique and special." [91]

Made of papier mâché and decorated with paint, beads, feathers and other materials recalling earlier cultures, **PAT STRAKOWSKI**'s (1937, Calgary, Alberta) art has always possessed, at its core, a consciousness about gender. It is present in such early work as: *Mothers, Daughters, Traditions* (1979) – a collaged and assembled paper and fabric book made the same year she graduates from the Alberta College of Art (textiles) – and in later work like her well-known shamanistic sculptures called ancestral and guardian figures, such as *Sky Woman Touched by Earth Stone* (1995). About *Sky Woman* curator Elyse Eliot Los writes:

"Her concern is with interpreting the female form, not as an object of beauty, but as a 'substantial' woman – powerful and master of her own fate."[92]

Considering herself to be neither a folk artist nor a "naive" artist, Strakowski, who turns to art after raising three children, stands in a category of her own. Interested in mythology, anthropology and folklore, she creates her own narratives and legends using human and animal figures that are enthusiastically decorated and embellished: "My ideas come from things, events and places around me. I start by saying, 'What if...?'"[93] Described as "mythical and mystical personalities,"[94] some of these standing sculptures also engage in subverting traditional legends. "The typical male figures – the athletes and warriors are no longer heroic models. They seem to work co-operatively, not competitively," observes Elizabeth Beauchamp in the *Edmonton Journal*. "*Challenger For the Games* [1989], a St.George-like figure does stand on top of the dragon, but not in victory over the creature."[95]

Ranging in height from 6 inches to several feet, many of Strakowski's creations are playful and fantastical, reflecting her own belief that art can leap into the imagination. She admires the humour of American sculptor Marisol, the personal imagery of Mexico's Frida Kahlo, and the light-filled representations of Britain's David Hockney.[96] As for her use of papier mâché – a cheap, non-toxic and recycled material often associated with children's art – the artist is attracted to its long history in Asia as well as its presence in other cultures like Mexico. In 1994, Strakowski collaborates with ceramic artist Kirsten Abrahamson in a large mixed-media installation *Revival* (Muttart Art Gallery, Calgary). Inspired by their own research into Mexico's Day of the Dead, the effusive show featured scores of brightly coloured artificial flowers, memorial shrines, rows of electric light bulbs and numerous "impish"[97] skeletons and skulls. Of this ambitious, ornate creation, Strakowski, like many woman artists who emerge in the 1980s, acknowledges *Revival's* cross-cultural agenda: "In my background, I have many cultural influences. My mother is Italian Catholic, my father Eastern Orthodox. I was born in the States, lived in the East and came out West. In the shrines I made for *Revival*, I have tried to combine my own personal, cultural, social influences with those of the [living] person I'm making it for."[98]

One of a small number of non-commercial photographers in Alberta to work in colour in the early 1980s,[99] **BARBARA SPOHR** (1955–1987, New Westminister, British Columbia) brought an unusual spirit to the practice that included taking quirky portraits of her own feet, focusing attention on a lone cup of coffee or the stroke of a swimmer, and taking the time to fondly observe situations and places often unnoticed. Thoughtful consideration pervades her work, as demonstrated by a note she writes across the pink-coloured border of a photograph depicting a garden tended by an elderly neighbour: "Old age must give you patience to harvest just two radishes." [100]

This kind of informal, idiosyncratic approach is not new, but within the context of the Banff Centre's photography program, where she first seriously pursued the medium, Spohr is fresh: "She just jumped right into photography. All the things that normally inhibit other students were not a problem," [101] her close friend Allison Rossiter once observed. Working for the program in the mid-70s, the American photographer also admired the liberties Spohr took with the finished print: embellishing, for example, the photograph's border with paint, text, patterns and decorative designs to extend the image's meaning or essence.

"It is significant that in striving to set forth artistic preoccupations that lay outside the ken of an overwhelmingly male-dominated aesthetic, Barbara staked claim in what was then largely uncharted territory. This was the arena of the 'small' moments of life, of the personal and everyday, and of questions surrounding the body and issues of identity," writes Penny Cousineau for the 1993 retrospective, *Barbara Spohr: Apparent Reasons* (Whyte Museum of the Canadian Rockies, Banff). "Her work anticipated that of dozens of women working in photography today, including the Canadians Raymonde April, Angela Grauerholz and Susan McEachern." [102]

That Spohr accomplished all of this within her all-too-short span of life – she died at age thirty-two of Hodgkin's disease – is no doubt partly attributable to her own multidisciplinary background as an artist first and a photographer second. In 1973 she spent a year studying at the Alberta College of Art in Calgary, then several years in the painting and printmaking programs at The Banff Centre before enrolling in photography in 1977. By that time, Spohr had already begun to distinguish herself, becoming one of only two women [103] to participate in *A Photographic Project: Alberta 1980* – a province-wide documentary project involving ten photographers. She first made an impact with a set of very strong self-portraits, still-lifes, landscapes, cut flowers and flowering plants, and then with her much commented-upon portraits of her feet: "In one image, embroidered flowers on the toes of Spohr's cotton slippers are surrounded by a plush field of starburst moss." [104]

The artist also had a flair for dramatic light and saturated colour, making her subjects seem far larger than life. Referring to these qualities, Vancouver photographer and critic Roy Arden labelled her photographs as "confident and gorgeous." [105] Commenting on a later exhibition of her work (Coburg Gallery, Vancouver) in 1985, he also offers the opinion: "In the context of the ever encroaching and endlessly multiplying varieties of kitsch that threaten human dignity and sanity, it is important to allow ourselves the delight that Spohr's art offers."

In 1989, seven years after Judy Chicago's *Dinner Party* makes headlines in Calgary, **ELIZABETH MENZIES** (1954, Provost, Alberta) exhibits three place settings – *Maiden, Mother* and *Crone* – for the juried show *Tablescapes* (Folio Gallery, Calgary). Naming the entire work *Trinity* in reference to what is believed to be the three phases of a woman's life, the artist proposes a rationale for making such a statement in earthenware plates and goblets: "The making of clay vessels is one of the earliest forms of culture developed by women. The analogies between woman/container/vessel/body/bowl/receptacle/cup are well known and documented." [106]

Trinity is inspired by archaeological evidence of various forms of goddess-worship during prehistoric times. As Menzies queried, "Recorded *his*-story is only 3,000 years old. What came before that?" [107] She believes these earlier matriarchal societies present "a more encompassing view of the world," [108] and uses her ceramics background and her four years of experience working at the Calgary Sexual Assault Centre to create art linked to identity and the representation of women, both in the past and the present.

Besides *Trinity: Maiden, Mother and Crone,* her work takes a number of poetic forms, including an early series of hand-built, earthenware platters whose whimsical imagery and text are derived from fairy tales. Believing, as many second-generation feminists did, that gender identity is influenced more by nurture than by nature, the artist rewrites many of the traditional fairy tales – as in her gaily decorated *Humpty Dumpty Platter* – to make them, in her words, "nonsexist and nonviolent. Words have power and form as intense and clear as visual imagery." [109] In 1990, the platters receive a solo showing at the Franklin Silverstone Gallery in Montreal, followed by *Nursery Tales and Fairy Rhymes II* in 1993 at the Medicine Hat Museum and Art Gallery.

Returning to the image of women in earlier cultures as "voluptuous healers, fertility and mother earth goddesses,[110] Menzies next responds with a question: "Is Barbie our contemporary goddess?" [111] Producing a set of small, abstract ceramic sculptures entitled *Barbie Series,* she becomes concerned with juxtaposing notions about body image and beauty standards. The work consists of simple hand-built shapes that make reference to the iconic Barbie doll, Ken doll, vessels, and prehistoric mounds. Arranged on oval clay platforms, the sheer poise and crackle-finish of these symbolic forms endow the series with a presence that belies their modest size.

Displaying her work by performing like a model on a catwalk, artist **DEE FONTANS** (1958, East Orange, New Jersey, United States) is nothing if not defiantly cutting edge with her hula-hoop dresses and *Birthday Bras* from the series *Outing the Body.* Begun in the mid-1990s and consisting of a series of performances, accessories and fashion works, *Outing the Body* is Fontans's response to the fashion industry's preoccupation with emaciated young models and, as the artist views it, the industry's attempt to warp the image of the female body: "No matter how big the consumer voice, we're not all fifteen years old and we are not size three, yet these are the messages we're getting from fashion," the internationally recognized artist tells the *Calgary Herald* for its "Crimes of Fashion" article.[112]

One of the more flamboyant examples in Canada of artwork influenced by the long-standing feminist inquiry into how women are represented in art and popular culture, the *Body* project, for all of its avant-garde flavour, displays as much method and careful calculation as it does madness and innovation. Writes Diana Murray for Calgary's *Avenue* magazine: "Her quirky, dramatic clothing designs echo and exaggerate the contours of a woman's body and play with ideas of form and movement ... large hula hoop skirts bob and swing with movement from the hips." [113]

Fontans explains about her practice, "The Rubenesque body is not fashionable at this point in time...[but some of my designs] revel in every curve, bulge and bump. I model all the dresses as an art act and a statement about being forty, 155 pounds, and 5′5″ without shoes, being beautiful and comfortable with myself." [114]

"In many ways, [her] fashion and spectacle recall the art and the era of Dada," [115] comments art critic Monique Westra, "but, at the same time, in its streamlined contours and shiny synthetic fabrics, the fashion has a futuristic quality."

This characteristic is also reflected in her jewellery and accessories, including *Birthday Bras,* designed when she turned forty. (Fontans has a BFA in jewellery and metalsmithing from the State University of New York at New Paltz.) The hard, round bras combine "ready made objects such as aluminium steamers [used for cooking], bra straps, and fibre optics with traditional jewellery materials and techniques including gem setting, riveting and twenty-four karat gold leafing."[116] Like her sterling-silver eye goggles – one pair entitled *A Woman of Colour* that are included in the national exhibition *Identity*[117] – the *Birthday Bras* reconfigure what is utilitarian into a hybrid of sculpture and wearable art. The results can be humorous, underlining Fontans's flair for connecting what is a matter of social concern with the absurd. Within the context of *Outing the Body,* the Alberta College of Art and Design instructor has also created works for and about men.[118]

Part Two

In sketching out some of the activities of the nine artists featured in part one, certain concerns prevail: validating the female experience, whether shared or personal; examining the role of gender and the systems of belief that either hinder or respect women; fostering other forms of artistic expression as an alternative to such male-oriented practices as painting and sculpture; and scrutinizing, subverting and redefining the representation of women and their bodies in art, language, the media and popular culture. This latter concern falls under the broad umbrella of what is sometimes simply referred to in cultural studies as the body: an incredibly varied topic that one Montreal art critic, Marcus Miller, labels the engine in an article for the *Globe and Mail.* "[The Body's] growing spectre has been the theoretical and imaginative engine driving much of the progressive artistic and academic work over the past few decades. For a time it seemed as if hair, semen and blood had actually usurped oil paint and slide projectors as bona fide artist's materials, and it was hard to find a humanities thesis that didn't address the body in one form or another."[119]

Bombarded with such cultural preoccupations as body piercing, tattoos, botoxed visages, extreme sports, the iconic super-buffed physique, plastic surgery, fitness clubs, the consumption of health-conscious foods and the late twentieth-century obsession with thinness and flat tummies, the body looms large in the consciousness of contemporary Western society. The feminist response to such issues is analytical and critical, concerned with "forging a language in which the female self is defined from the inside, rather than [from an] outside view constructed by patriarchal society."[120] Body concerns and the political response to them will become so pervasive in contemporary art that in 1984, Edmonton curator Russell Bingham astutely observes, "[despite the] resurgence of interest in figure painting, for the most part this attention has involved concepts that have more to do with social issues than interest in the figure as a form.... 'Straight' figure painting that, to many viewers, may have looked out of place or irrelevant during the popular heyday of abstraction seems to look even more out of place today."[121]

But relevant or not, it shouldn't be forgotten that straight figure painting does continue to surface in the province, especially with the efforts of veteran artist **VIOLET OWEN** (1930, Edmonton, Alberta). One of Alberta's foremost portrayers of the female form, Owen works solely with artist and model Mimi Mah for fifteen years, "capturing," according to Edmonton critic Elizabeth Beauchamp, "the many facets of this single personality with utter clarity."[122] Expressionist in style with a strong aptitude for drawing and colour, Owen has been describing the human figure since 1949, building up a lifetime of body art in chalk, pencil and paint on paper, canvas and Plexiglas. (In the early 90s, the artist also adds painted unfired clay and mixed-media sculpture to her oeuvre about the figure.)

Nonetheless, the younger generations of women artists who rise to the forefront at the end of the century have little in common with the older conventions of figurative art. One effort by artist **MYRNA HARVEY** (1955, Blackie, Alberta), for instance, displayed in 1984,[123] employed old-fashioned constraining undergarments – girdle and garter belt – among other materials like hay, to evoke the condition of rural womanhood. Entitled *Bondage on the Prairies/High Noon* and *Bondage on the Prairies/Midnight,* these witty, tactile, mixed-media works on masonite emerged out of her own observations of growing up in the Albertan countryside.

Trained in the 1970s at the Alberta College of Art and the University of Calgary, Harvey recalls there were few women role models in the art world, either internationally or locally. By the time of her exhibition at the James Ulrich Gallery[124] in 1984, however, the situation has improved somewhat, aided by the presence of several well-recognized women practitioners in the city and an expanding art scene. Two years later, in her groundbreaking article – *Parallelogramme,* Toronto – about feminist art practice in Alberta's two largest centres, the Edmonton-based Christine Conley observes: "The Edmonton picture stands in stark contrast to the vital pluralism of Calgary, a city with five artist-run centres and four sizable public galleries. Though not exactly a hotbed of feminism, there does seem to have been more room for women artists to participate in Calgary and more support for work that is critical of the status quo. Artists such as Marcella Bienvenue, Mary Scott, Sandra Vida and Rita McKeough are able to work as an integral part of this system without having to establish a separate venue exclusive to women."[125]

One of the artist-run centres Conley refers to is Stride Gallery, established in 1985 by photographers Don Corman and Colleen O'Neill, and painter MARY SCOTT (1948, Calgary, Alberta).[126] A lively addition to the city, the energy and camaraderie of Stride is, on a number of levels, infectious. Scott will part company with her two colleagues a year later but this event will not dampen the spirits of either Scott or her colleagues. Stride becomes a hub for showing contemporary art, while Scott continues to present the work of other colleagues, such as Rita McKeough[127] and Winnipeg's Aganetha Dyck, the latter associated with the emergence of feminism in Canada, whose twenty-year survey later comes to the Glenbow Museum in 1996.[128]

From 1988–89, Scott establishes and directs << >>dl Gallery, and then in 1993 creates One White Wall at her Calgary home. Combining elements of a gallery, salon and outdoor garden, the site, according to artist/curator Diana Sherlock, "is an extension of Mary's work because, like her painting practice, oww *skews* gallery and social conventions."[129] Scott first began undermining painting and its conventions in the late 1970s. Later, the *Halifax Mail Star* describes Scott as being "mad at a language [painting] that speaks for men and silences women."[130]

In the process of challenging the medium, though, Scott earns enough acclaim to make her one of Alberta's key contemporary art figures. "The originality of her work is startling and it puts her in the front ranks of important younger painters in Canada,"[131] writes Nancy Tousley, 1981. And another writer states: "She is represented in museum collections and galleries across Canada, including the National Gallery in Ottawa and the Canada Council Art Bank. In 1986, she was represented in *Songs of Experience,* a group exhibition at The National Gallery of Canada, which featured avant-garde work by women in Canada."[132] (*Contemporary Canadian Artists,* 1997) Finally, from John Bentley Mays: "She is probably the most talked-about woman artist to have emerged west of Winnipeg since the mid-1980s. (You'll have to admit that artistic radicalism isn't exactly what springs to mind when you think about Alberta)."[133]

Scott attends the University of Calgary, earning a BFA with distinction in 1978, as well as the Nova Scotia College of Art and Design where she is awarded an MFA in 1980. She believes the influence of U of C instructor, John Will,[134] has the most impact on her future artistic behaviour, while NSCAD reinforces the importance of community support and involvement. Being exposed to the college's anti-modernist stance and its association with theoretical issues concerning authenticity and appropriation, conceptual art and process, also leaves an impression on her.[135]

Initially interested in systematically exploring the physical properties of paint, Scott begins to stir things up by eliminating the paintbrush in favour of a syringe used over and over again to apply fine strands of acrylic paint. What emerges from this intensive process-oriented task is a series of small-scale paintings that on first viewing are nothing if not eye-catching. Writing about Scott's first solo show in Alberta in 1981, Tousley remarks, "One of the many unusual aspects of her work is the breadth of its public appeal. Viewers of the Glenbow exhibition, whether or not they immediately understand the intellectual ideas that have generated the paintings are drawn to the works themselves by their strangeness and beauty as objects."[136]

Highly physical entities of colour, texture and depth, these thickly rendered paintings (1978–1982) are unforgettable. In their minute interweave is the suggestion of womanly activity: cake decoration, weaving and needlework. In one reference book, this "self-conscious craft approach"[137] is later described as instilling a "feminine identity within the patriarchal traditions of contemporary art," while Scott herself casually expresses to the *Regina Leader Post:* "I'm sure some people see my work in terms of craft, and say that it looks like needlepoint. [If they do], that's fine, too."[138]

Just as casual is her laissez-faire attitude towards the painting's image and its source. Not one to create an original picture upon which to syringe paint on, Scott instead uses pre-existing images such as photographs, postcards, other artists' unfinished work, kitschy reproductions and even once a set of commercial china dinnerware. This act of appropriating also includes taking bits of text from letters, her own prose and that of others, including Gertrude Stein's *The Making of Americans.* Using her paint-filled syringe as a writing tool, Scott then reproduces on the painting surface the borrowed words or phrases in longhand. This action might be repeated obsessively hundreds of times, as she does in the visually juicy, Stein-inspired work: *Once Tree It Away It Complete* (acrylic on plexiglass mounted on plywood, 1978–79).[139]

By adopting the images and words of other creators, Scott delves into the relatively new practice of appropriation, whose theoretical aim is to demystify the notion of originality and the romantic image of the artist-genius, and also to stimulate debate on such notions as authenticity and subjectivity. In her 1981 review, Tousley explains the significance of this postmodern tactic with regards to the artist: "[Scott's] work manifests a rejection of the cult of the artist as personality by placing its emphasis on ideas rather than the expression of a personal world view."[140]

Again Scott's casual[141] reply is, "I rarely care what the image looks like, I think only about what it means.... Artists show you a model of how they see and think. My model is not masterly."[142] In other words, her art embraces neither the craft of painting nor its thematic idioms. Especially in its modernist phase when avant-garde painting (and sculpture) are critically assumed to be the subjective activity of larger-than-life heroes including Picasso, Jackson Pollock, Willem de Kooning and Barnett Newman.

Still, Scott's involvement with this high-art medium is not typical of her generation, influenced as these young artists are by the post-1970 phenomena of feminist scholarship. Observes Vancouver critic and curator Robin Laurence, "Painting continues to be a conflicted activity for women. Loaded as it is with associations of masculine authority and feminine subjugation, the practice of painting has been abandoned or rejected by many feminist artists."[143]

Scott's shift from being an irreverent critic of high art painting to a full-blown feminist artist of the 1980s coalesces during a period when she serves as assistant head of visual arts (1982–84) at the Banff Centre School of Fine Arts. According to Tousley, in the early 1980s the artist devotes much energy to reading "feminist criticism, psychoanalysis [especially Jacques Lacan], theory and literature which examine how women perceive themselves and how their images are socially defined."[144] With this perspective in hand, a new body of work emerges: "the fabric paintings,"[145] which, among other things, will engage Scott with the body and the shaping of sexuality and identity. Her grounding in French feminist theory, "which sees sexual identity as rooted in language, and sexuality overall as an arbitrary structure rather than as a fixed biological position,"[146] will prompt her to greatly enlarge images of male and female bodies and juxtapose them with quotes that disrupt traditional representations of the body and sexuality, thus deflecting the exploitative gaze of the viewer or voyeur.

Continuing to work with the appropriated image and the appropriated word, Scott abandons the syringe for other approaches, like applying paint and large amounts of shellac with her fingers on unstretched canvas, and using Letraset and spray paint to convey text. Then, as if her sparring with the painting tradition couldn't get any more heated, the artist begins to tear and cut out areas of the unstretched canvas so that any possible association with fine art is all but nullified. In visual terms, it suggests to one writer, "a kind of woman's language rebelling against man's language," [147] while curator Sigrid Dahle opines, "Mary Scott doesn't paint pictures. She constructs texts." [148]

In this vein of tearing, shredding, cutting, unravelling and finally hanging her pieces unstretched, her most celebrated works emerge: the militantly flayed *Back* series, made with matted felt and layers of slathered shellac and rhoplex and the delicately frayed *Imago* series, featuring large pieces of silk unravelled in sections. Made concurrently between 1983–89, the *Back* and *Imago* series tour across the country in *Mary Scott,* guest curated by Bruce Grenville and Catherine Crowston for the Southern Alberta Art Gallery in 1989.

Back utilizes the erotic imagery of American photographer, Robert Mapplethorpe, while *Imago* juxtaposes *Penthouse* photographs and Leonardo da Vinci's drawings of genitalia, sexual intercourse and religious subjects. Of the types of Body concerns that emerge, Grenville proposes, "It is a recent body, a body of lived experiences, a body of moments which cannot be represented or figured symbolically. It is a body that can only be recognized in the process of its making – it is unravelled, it is sewn, it is flayed, it is read." [149] the *Globe and Mail* art critic, John Bentley Mays, adds in a subsequent review, "While Mapplethorpe is at pains to create the most luxuriously eroticized depiction of flesh possible, Scott snatches away the pleasure.... The series, *Back,* rejects the false, eternal prettiness of traditional erotic art." [150]

Mary Scott will be one of eight solo exhibits for this artist organized in the 1980s. Add to this her participation in two dozen different group exhibitions [151] across the country, including seven in 1988 alone, and it appears Scott decisively hit a critical nerve in the country. With other Canadians of that decade, she can be found in exhibitions as diverse as the feminist *She writes in White Ink* (Walter Phillips Gallery, the Banff Centre), the prestigious *Songs of Experience* and *Canadian Biennial of Contemporary Art* (both at the National Gallery of Canada, Ottawa), as well as such contemporary signifiers as *Active Surplus* (Power Plant, Toronto and 49th Parallel, New York) *The Body and Society* (Embassy Cultural House, London, Ontario), *Striving for Ideal*

Resolution (Nickle Arts Museum, Calgary) and *Identity/Identities* (Winnipeg Art Gallery). Scott also found a place in major group displays of Alberta artists: *Alberta Now* (Edmonton Art Gallery), *Seven Artists from Alberta: Art in this Region* (Canada House, London, England/Canadian Cultural Centre, Paris, France/Canadian Cultural Centre, Brussels, Belgium), *Aspects of Contemporary Painting in Alberta* (Glenbow Museum, Calgary), *Survey Alberta 88* (Alberta College of Art Gallery) and *Multiple Associations: Five Alberta Artists* (Glenbow Museum, Calgary).

Of the two types of shows, Canadian and Albertan, it is interesting to note how Scott is one thing in the former (rootless) and another (rooted) in the latter. Generally, in exhibitions where Scott is amongst other Canadians, not a word is devoted in the accompanying essays or printed matter about the context in which this artist develops. In other words, place is of no consequence in her life and thus, for all intents and purposes, the Calgary art scene is irrelevant. The exception is the *Canadian Biennial of Contemporary Art* (1989) in which Calgary is judged by curator Diana Nimeroff as "not a centre for art-making." She adds that if its artists "can afford to be both individualistic and generous to one another," it is due to the existence of the art college and the university, which "Calgary's artists cluster around [like refugees]."

By contrast, in several of the Albertan group shows, Scott's career is considered within the context of place and community. There is, for instance, Nancy Tousley's perceptive writing for *Seven Artists from Alberta: Art in this Region* (1984), in which she concludes, "Artists in Alberta have reached the understanding that, to take root and grow, art must germinate in both the private and communal ground of place. Although formal vocabularies of art can be assimilated from afar, the specificity of context, the issues which give meaning to content are largely non-transferable."[152] Or, as Glenbow curator Vincent Varga notes for *Aspects of Contemporary Painting in Alberta,* "The diversification of styles recently established in Edmonton are not new in Calgary, where painting has been characterized by a variety of approaches since the 1960s. Variation and experimentation established Calgary as a centre of visual art throughout Western Canada."[153]

The influences of community are often somewhat elusive, but according to the artist herself, Calgary is "one of the richest art communities going," due to its attitude and support structure. In Canada at large, especially in the publicly funded art sector, uber-seriousness is often the overriding attitude, while in Calgary it is possible to have fun and be rigorous at the same time.

Scott also identifies with the city's general lack of bias to the art that is made and its engagement with "critical thinking without being ideological." Calgary is a place where "a stunning variety of materials" are used and "obsessive" art-making is a characteristic. [154]

And in Calgary the practice of painting is still considered relevant, meaning the artist can call herself a painter without apology, even though what she does with the proverbial canvas, is – as it is so matter-of-factly explained in 1988 to Calgary's Glenbow audience – an "unexpected classification which immediately challenges and opens the definition of the field." [155] Written in reference to Scott's *Imagos* paintings on display in *Multiple Associations: Five Alberta Artists,* the series – whose title is a psychoanalytical term used to describe "a kind of subconscious expression" [156] – continues until the end of the decade.

In the early 1990s, Scott elaborates further on her interest in Jacques Lacan's rereading of Freud's theories about sexuality and the development of the psyche with a silk-fabric series whose title, in short form, *In You More Than You,*[157] is taken from his book *The Four Fundamental Concepts of Psycho-Analysis.* Then, in 1993, she dramatically shifts gears with *In Me More Than Me,*[158] a collection of semi-sculptural work that the Montreal critic and curator Renee Baert terms "quite literally a departure from and a return to the past." [159] Scott is now taking earlier paintings like the syringe works and recycling them into new pieces by wrapping and bundling them with thread, double-sided conservator's tape, clothing and other materials. Coming in varying sizes and shapes, these heavily swaddled and sometimes stacked bundles will once again prompt the comment that they "don't look anything like our preconceptions of what a painting is." [160] One Montreal writer, Nell Tenhaaf, will write about one particular grouping toured by the Edmonton Art Gallery in 1993: "Clearly we intuitively sense a link with the body, through the feeling of organic form pervading the works. They variously look like chromosomes, truncated torsos, bundled babies, piles of brains, or some less-than-humanoid, motile life-form."

In Me More Than Me evokes memories of an earlier Mary Scott, when, out of a desire to create a visual analogy of her own research and investigation into the medium of painting, she arrives at the syringe works: logically made, yes, but whose results are surprisingly over the top. Despite this characteristic, though, Scott's art continues to be a highly intellectualized response, informed by the feminist discourse in gender, art history and literature. No wonder Scott's theoretically demanding yet formally rich art practice can provoke a nervous buzz amongst her audience.

One exhibition where this buzz has particular resonance, and is in fact magnified exponentially by the contributions of other artists, is the 1990 *Dangerous Goods: Feminist Visual Art Practices.*[161] Presented by the artist-run Latitude 53 and the Edmonton Art Gallery, this event features Scott, veteran Edmonton artist Cherie Moses and five other Canadians,[162] and it generates a record turnout for its opening at the EAG. "Many saw [*Dangerous Goods*] as a long-overdue critical venture addressing a number of social issues and feminist ideas,"[163] records *Legacy* magazine writer Hajnalka Santa-Balazs, "Still ... others were upset and criticized the gallery for becoming too populist."

Curated by Bridget Elliot and Janice Williamson of the University of Alberta, *Dangerous Goods* is an important marker for feminist art production in Alberta and especially Edmonton. Up to that point, such activity in the province has largely been underground, programmed by artist-run centres and smaller institutions with a strong postmodern mandate like the Banff Centre's Walter Phillips Gallery. (In the mid-80s, for instance, the Phillips gallery[164] presents *Production and the Axis of Sexuality* (1984), *Avant-garde Film by Women: To Conceive a New Language of Desire* (1984) and *She Writes in White Ink* (1985), the latter featuring Janice Gurney, Mary Scott and Nancy Spero "within a theoretical framework inspired by French feminist Hélène Cixious."[165]) *Dangerous Goods,* situated as it is at the beginning of the century's last decade, turns out to be a highly public acknowledgement of not only just how much "the work of Canadian feminist visual artists has been a large and influential force,"[166] but also of how important artist-run venues – SUB Gallery, Ring House Gallery and Latitude 53, the collective Celebration of Women in the Arts[167] – have been to this effort.

Following *Dangerous Goods,* more recognition bubbles to the surface of Alberta contemporary art, seeming to spin-off artists, events and exhibitions at a dizzying pace. One of those artists is sculptor Wanda Ellerbeck, a native Calgarian, who describes herself in a 1990 *Artichoke* interview as a product of the 1980s when "the most important thing for me, just personally, was the discovery of feminism and feminism in art, and the unbelievable room I had to express myself and realizing that not only did I have that room but other women were having that room as well, meaning many voices were being heard. Instead of feminism being a one-definition word, it became very, very broad."[168]

In 1992, the Banff Centre's Walter Phillips Gallery organizes a group exhibition of lesbian and gay art, *Much Sense: Erotics and Life.*[169] Writing later about this controversial event – the province's then Deputy Premier, Ken Kowalski, calls for a withholding of public funding for such shows – multimedia artist Celine Godberson offers this perspective in her article "Pride Is a Gay Word:" "In the past, the feminist movement has placed emphasis on reacting to the victimization of women. Women were not allowed to be sexual: only sexualized. When victimization is the only representation and/or experience women have sexually, a great void exists. It is this void that our current acts of representing ourselves and our sexuality reacts against it … it is only by taking risks, by coming out and taking space that we become fully alive."[170]

This idea of taking space, of asserting a stereotype-free identity, also extends to the post-colonial arena where First Nations and artists of colour have been making their presence increasingly felt. In Alberta, one of the participants in this volatile area is writer and multimedia artist Leila Sujir, whose 1988 colour video *India Hearts Beat* (1988) explores the Calgarian's own "attempt to locate herself across boundaries of generation, nation, gender and race."[171] Later, in an article entitled "On Being female and (Half)Asian in an Art World Narrative," Sujir extrapolates on the linkage between feminism and those who "are reframing the larger cultural story … taking their place as authors and artists, remaking the stories, the images."[172]

Functioning like an umbrella, the feminist discourse also has room underneath its wide canopy for the participation of male artists, demonstrated locally in the 1993 exhibition *Body, Gender and Other Issues.* In it, David LaRiviere and Charles Malinsky present their figurative paintings, and Rob Milthorp displays his multimedia installation, *Long Man,* inspired by England's prehistoric and very phallic Cerne Abbas Giant. Writes Muttart Art Gallery curator, Franklyn Heisler: "The three artists in this exhibition acknowledge … the controlling attitudes and beliefs that exist in the dominant society and the need to reconsider them."[173]

In that same year, as well, the issue of violence against women is given a very public airing in a ten-year survey entitled *Rita McKeough, an Excavation* in which a new site-specific, multimedia installation, *Take It to the Teeth* (Glenbow Museum[174]) is presented. An artist, musician, carpenter, social activist and much else, McKeough had been highly praised in the late 1970s and early 1980s for her whimsical prints and drawings and impressive installations dealing with the destruction of old Calgary neighbourhoods.

She moves to Toronto in 1985 and, while her socially imaginative artwork takes on new topics such as environmental abuse, the idea of home remains a central theme with increasing concern for what is hidden inside, away from public view. *Take It to the Teeth* is McKeough's third installation[175] in Alberta on domestic violence, and like the previous two, becomes a significant marker in Alberta-based feminist art production. The Glenbow showing is also part of a larger collaborative effort, *Art in the March,* organized by five recent graduates[176] from the Alberta College of Art. According to Amy Gogarty, the event "grew out of the belief that art – in particular, feminist art – can integrate with and enhance political action."[177] *Art in the March* coincides with International Women's Day (IWD), an annual celebration staged March 8 to commemorate a successful factory strike by women in 1907. Designed to involve the visual-arts community, the *March* participants create personal banners for the IWD parade, while the New Gallery hosts an evening of feminist readings and performances.

The following year (1994), *Art in the March* expands enthusiastically into a month-long cultural festival called *Feminist Spin.* Involving mainstream art galleries, artist-run centres, media outlets, clubs, theatres and other venues, this multidisciplinary event overseen by *Art in the March*'s Joan Caplan and Mary Lou Riordon-Sello is an important signpost of the depth and diversity of feminist art practice present in the province. Among the *Spin* events are a project and exhibition inspired by the feminist concept of mentoring, *The ARTemesia Project Exhibition;* an evening of video by women of colour, *Works of Resistance;* solo shows by Albertans Mireille Perron, Colleen Philippi, Isla Burns, Bettina Grunwald and Debra Rushfeldt; and a multimedia collaboration about sexual fantasy by Lock Up Your Daughters. Although *Fantasmagoria: Sexing the Lesbian Imaginary* (the New Gallery) is militantly upfront about its same-sex content, the video and installation exhibition pass without much media coverage, a drastic change from the attention two years prior to the more obtuse *Much Sense: Erotics and Life* at the Walter Phillips Gallery.

Feminist Spin also hosts an afternoon forum featuring readings and performance pieces. One is given by the then Calgary-based, **FAYE HEAVYSHIELD** (1953, Standoff, Alberta), who at that point is attracting national attention for her powerful yet understated mixed-media art. (In the early 1990s, she is included in such exhibitions as *Land, Spirit, Power: First Nations at the National Gallery of Canada* [1992, Ottawa], *New Territories: 350/500 Years After* [1992,

Maison de la Culture, Montreal and Quebec City] and *Heart, Hoof, Horn* [1993, Glenbow Museum.])

Entitled *She: A Room Full of Women,* the work involves the presentation of four stories written and performed by HeavyShield who is also a committed writer. Each story begins with: "My name is She," and the artist wears a different pair of shoes for each telling. Caterina Pizanias, a witness to the event, writes: "All stories were of women, about identities, their bodies, sexualities, spirituality, hope, the going back and forth, the swaying between Native and non-Native, between man and woman because 'He is part of S/he.'" [178]

Raised on the Blood (Kainai) Reserve in southern Alberta, Faye HeavyShield, along with **LAURA-KEIR VICKERSON** (1959, Edmonton, Alberta), figures prominently in the last decade of Alberta's twentieth century. Both artists begin exhibiting in the 1980s and by the mid-90s have earned enough critical acclaim and public profile to see their art represented in a national and international context. (Vickerson, for instance, is included in the *Fifth International Istanbul Biennial* in 1997.) In fact, as the 1990s unfold, their art seems to glide almost effortlessly into the larger spectrum of Canadian contemporary art, and more specifically, the publicly funded, Canada Council–led sector where both have exhibited almost exclusively. Writing in 1995, Calgary critic Nancy Tousley notes: "Today, post-*Dinner Party* young women deal in a variety of complex ways with their understandings of gender and identity, major issues for artists of all sexes." [179] Of Vickerson's practice she adds, "Women's art and women's work as a subject for art, or a source of techniques and materials, have been absorbed into the mainstream." [180]

In other words, after more than two decades of theoretical and visual elaboration, approaches inspired by feminist discourses are now firmly embedded in the Canadian art-making landscape. While earlier efforts are sometimes criticized for being too heavy-handed or obtusely academic, feminist-influenced art of the 1990s presents audiences with a more fluid and nuanced range of responses, in content and in materials.

From Alberta, HeavyShield and Vickerson are an integral part of this acceptance and are moved by the personal as well as the broader issues of feminism. There is, for instance, Vickerson's interest in the floral world – gardening, flower shows and private and public gardens – and her effort through "numerous tiny gestures ... to invest [flower art] with personal value and a deep sense of caring." [181] Heavyshield's art, meanwhile, often reveals a strong connection to the profound landscape of her family's home. She has even attributed the subtle monochromatic colouration of her art to the "solitude and simplicity of the plains."[182] HeavyShield's sense of identity is also greatly affected by growing up on Canada's largest reserve and being surrounded, she writes, "by changes, some subtle, some extreme. These are just a few. I heard some stories from my grandmother and stories from the nuns at the Catholic boarding school. I spoke Blackfoot and learned English. We bought groceries in town, my father still hunted."[183]

But despite her first-hand experience as a reserve-raised, residentially schooled Aboriginal woman, no generalities can be made: "The personal has to come first. I've never wanted to speak for a race or a gender."[184] As such, HeavyShield's treatment of such issues is approached from her own experiences. In *Cradle,* for instance, she recalls the traumatic day when, as a six-year-old girl, she is enrolled in a residential school (St. Mary's), more than eighty kilometres away from her home. The work is a simplified version of a hand-held Aboriginal cradle, whose canvas interior is bereft of child and instead filled with the long, hardy stems of prairie grass. As a wall-hung sculpture, *Cradle* is accompanied with this spirited statement, composed by the artist: "For a world that continues to believe that the noble savage is still up for adoption: the cradle is empty. The aged child stands beside you, with teeth, with voice, with song."

Cradle[185] is not the only artwork where prairie grass – the dominant vegetation of HeavyShield's home – serves as an affirmation of what has been essential to the artist's own life. The material is also present in the impressive column-shaped *Worship* (1994), a 3-metre-high, freestanding pillar of dried grasses in steel mesh that celebrates the strength of her family's Aboriginal culture,[186] and in *Snake* (1992), where a Catholic rosary lays largely covered and entangled in bed of tenacious sweetgrass stalks.

The incorporation of Christian artifacts and other religious symbols and imagery is also a prominent feature in HeavyShield's art in the early to mid-90s. In group exhibitions including *Canada's First People* (1992)[187] and the *New Territories: 350/500 Years Later* (1992), as well as solo shows such as *Heart, Hoof, Horn* (1993) and *Into the Garden of Angels* (1994, The Power Plant, Toronto), the artist demonstrates a heightened ability for altering and reshaping things: in this case, the "signs" of Catholicism. Nancy Tousley refers to this practice as the "bumping together of two cultures,"[188] lucidly applied in such bone-coloured sculptural work as the floor-sited *Heart, Hoof, Horn:* "The three [gessoed plaster] forms ... evolved from drawings of the cowl that surrounded the faces of the Grey Nuns at St. Mary's.... A heart develops a cleft to become a hoof, the hoof splits and divides into [a head with] horns.... Often, the forms of HeavyShield's work, which always refer to the body, seem to undergo transformations that blend the human, animal and vegetable worlds."[189]

The artist also directs such transformations to the subject of women, as she did with another floor-sited work of that period, *Sisters* (1993). Consisting of six pairs of painted high-heeled shoes representing HeavyShield and her five sisters, each pair is elegantly altered with plaster and moulding compound so that their toes have a cloven hoof mark. Installed in a circle with the toes facing outward, the *Ottawa Citizen*'s Nancy Beale remarks about the objects, "They are so simple one is unprepared for the way they resonate with meaning and feeling."[190] To the artist, *Sisters* is a definitive piece, connected to a well-rooted sense of identity: "I think women are waiting for men to figure out who women are, because women are very strong and they already know who they are, they know what they can do."[191]

HeavyShield's discovery of her life's vocation comes during her years at the Alberta College of Art in the early 1980s.[192] There, in contact with instructors such as Walter May and Blake Senini, she ascertains that she has a preference for organic rather than geometric forms (she is already a mother of four at the time), an attraction to feeling the physical shape of the work in her hands and an awareness that certain tactile materials – wood and fabric – speak to her intuitively. A distinctively succinct style begins to take shape, the product of a process that HeavyShield describes as "paring down to the bare bones."[193] Through this action, the artist manages to reveal the fundamentals of her own life and, in doing so, speaks to the broader issues of race, gender and cultural difference. Her work quickly gains attention: in the 1989 column "The Female Gaze," Susan Crean writes, "[HeavyShield's] sculptures begin and end with startling understatement."[194]

Laura-Keir Vickerson's training as an artist begins in Edmonton about three years earlier (1977) than HeavyShield's and leads to a BFA from the University of Alberta (painting and printmaking, 1981) and an MFA from the University of Victoria (sculpture and installation, 1986). It is while on Canada's west coast for her last year of the master's program that Vickerson is highlighted in Christine Conley's article "In From The Cold: Feminism and Art in Edmonton" (*Parallelogramme,* February-March 1986). This notable article labels

Vickerson as "practising outside the approved formalist ethic," which in 1986 is still how artists of both genders in Edmonton are often evaluated. But Vickerson will elicit a different kind of response with her site-specific installations and sculptural mixed-media art in Victoria and Calgary, where she settles in 1989. Her spectacular use of materials and labour-intensive techniques, as well as the theatrical nature of her art, quickly gains public attention. The sheer ambition of some of her projects – her piece *Velvet*[195] involves two 130-foot flowered swaths – makes her a force to be reckoned with while her "unabashed ... expression of the feminine"[196] is refreshingly novel.

The feminine aspect of her work, for instance, is expressed in the form of a "mosaic of luxurious and lush flower petals dipped in wax"[197] (*Learning Spanish,*[198] 1993); "garments made ... of gauze, then coated with wax and adorned with dried waxed flowers" (*Armour/Amour,*[199] 1993); and "innumerable tiny rose petals [pinned] onto vast lengths of organza" (*Studies of Nature,*[200] 1994, *Fragile Heart,*[201] 1995, and *Velvet*). While evident in other examples of recent Canadian art – Joyce Weiland's embroidered quilts, the cosy kitchen-related paintings of Mary Pratt, the fluffy porcelain beds of Annemarie Schmid Esler, and the Victorian-style teapots and stacked cups of Evelyn Grant – the feminine has generally been all but absent as a characteristic in contemporary art. Even in much feminist-influenced work, anything that can be possibly interpreted or described as decorative, opulent, whimsical, delicate, tender, maternal, effeminate, pleasurable, fairy-like, sentimental or vulnerable is usually shunned in favour of the serious and the critical. As Nancy Tousley remarks in 1994, "[The feminine] is something we are still getting used to."[202]

But in Vickerson's work, it is front and centre. Her work *Studies of Nature,* for instance, consists of a two-part, site-specific work fashioned out of little more than thousands of slightly dried rose petals, dress pins and a supportive backing of whisper-thin cotton organza.[203] Created for Calgary's 1994 *Art Week* festival,[204] critic and artist Amy Gogarty describes how "an archaic and carnal sense of beauty imbues [the art], harkening back to a world of apparitions and fairy tales.... The application, petal by petal, recalls the luxurious flower carpets of Central America and customs such as well dressing in Britain.... [The act of] pinning is also emblematic of a particular kind of feminist practice."[205]

Vickerson likens the act of pinning to needlework and sewing and says it is intended "[to] invest 'women's work' with value and integrity."[206] Involving "numerous tiny gestures,"[207] this activity reaches a crescendo the following year with the making of *Velvet* (1995). The work takes six months for the artist and her host of volunteers to complete for the Illingworth Kerr Gallery, and when it is done Nancy Tousley is moved to write, "Those who witnessed this opulent spectacle, felt something close to amazement."[208] Consisting of two rose-pedalled wedding trains that cascade from the ceiling down the wall and then spread themselves casually like carpet-runners across the gallery's lengthy floor, this two-piece work of a half million petals pierces the decorum of the institutional space with its allusions to blood and its life-giving and life-threatening dimensions.

"Beauty, pleasure and pain are constants among Vickerson's subjects. She makes her appeal directly to the body through the senses of sight, touch and smell, and the effects of scale," interprets Tousley. "With its connotations of ceremony, ritual and fairy-tale – of the cathedral aisle, the couture runway, the beauty pageant and the strip joint – this very abstract work celebrates the feminine: fragility and vulnerability underpinned with fierce strength."[209]

Although the expression of the feminine is not the only way in which contemporary Albertans address the multi-faceted subject of women and their condition, around the time of Vickerson's *Velvet,* it is also very present in *Fabrications: Stitching Ourselves Together* (1998, Red Deer and District Museum). Popularly known as the "wedding dress exhibit" and generated out of the museum world rather than the contemporary art sphere, *Fabrications,* like *Velvet,* radiates with a sense of beauty, pleasure and personal pain. The show features twenty-three wedding dresses, sewn by Red Deer homemaker Lorraine Church over a forty-five-year period for friends, family and neighbours, and a narrative text by her daughter, sociologist Dr. Kathryn Church. "With the dresses the women were actually constructing the story of their lives and their lives as women," explains Kathryn Church, who gathered the dresses and interviewed their owners – some whose marriage had ended in divorce, the garment now signifying something else other than the happily-ever-after. Part social history, part celebration of Lorraine Church's dressmaking talents, and part a stitching together of a mother/daughter relationship, *Fabrications* lucidly conveys how the personal can indeed be political. Embedded in the narrative is a thoughtful exploration of a particular era and the tensions between feminist and traditional aspirations regarding the institution of marriage, as well as an evocation of place and the role of small prairie communities in shaping a female identity. Likely one of the most well-attended exhibition ever organized by an Alberta-based museum, *Fabrications* later embarks on a national tour with a stop at the Canadian Museum of Civilization (Hull, Quebec), where it is viewed by 88,000 visitors in the summer of 1999.[210] It is also the subject of a radio documentary on the CBC.[211]

It is interesting to note that after feeling the effects of nearly thirty years of feminism and its contribution to visual art in Alberta, the century ends with such significant signposts as *Velvet* and *Fabrications: Stitching Ourselves Together.* Both tie into the largely womanly world of needle and fibre,[212] and like their much earlier "sister" exhibit, *Fibrations: A New Generation of Fibre in Alberta* (1980), there is plenty of evidence to suggest that all kinds of new territory is still being staked-out and explored by Alberta artists.

Overall, feminist-influenced activity proves to be extremely rich for the province, and although it does not always receive the attention it warrants, either regionally and nationally, it is no small matter that some of the most nationally recognized names from post-1985 Alberta have emerged out of this new tradition.

chapter eighteen

A Changing Scenario: From Boom to Bust to New Developments in the Eighties

> UNDER THE VERY NOSES of the rest of Canadians, not to mention Alberta's own citizens, Alberta has been experiencing and supporting, for the past fifteen years, a remarkable cultural/literary "second generation" flowering – so rapid and so extensive, that even its own writers and artists haven't fully appreciated its magnitude. Had such a cultural/literary flowering occurred in central Canada, all Canadians would have been exhaustively informed about it years ago. The phenomenon would have been determined, announced, itemized, tracked, analyzed and thoroughly celebrated. Between the *Globe and Mail* and the CBC's central operations in Toronto alone, this would have been inevitable.[1]

Published in 1988, this blunt commentary from British Columbian novelist and past president of the Writers' Union, Andreas Schroeder, appears in the conclusion for *Word for Word,* which is described as "a masterful piece of work that should set the standard for future arts reports in the province,"[2] by the *Edmonton Journal.*

A few years later, in an interview with *Artichoke,* artist Ron Moppett makes similar observations: "I guess if anything, in Alberta, in Calgary, what I think happened in the 1980s, apart from nobody being interested in printmaking anymore, was that quite a sizable community became visible that was outside of the normal constructs represented by the university or the art school. I think that is very positive. When I look around openings now, as distinct from ten years ago; at that time if you were involved in the arts you could describe the arts community, the people who were making it, the people who were looking at it, you knew it. You can't do that anymore and that is very good."[3]

The enlargement, diversification and subsequent growing pains of Alberta's visual-arts community through the last two decades of the twentieth century are the focus of the last three chapters in this book. Included, as well, is a selective accounting of some of the key artists who emerge during this period and the context from which they come. Many are based in Calgary and Lethbridge, although others practice in Edmonton and smaller communities. Some, including Demmit's Peter von Tiesenhausen and Edmonton's Jane Ash Poitras, Isla Burns, Catherine Burgess and Blair Brennan, have already been accounted for in other chapters, as have Calgary's Mary Scott, Carroll (Moppett) Taylor-Lindoe, John Hall and Barbara Milne, and Lethbridge's Jeffrey Spalding. These last chapters deal with other artists who rise to prominence in Alberta as well as other art-related developments and setbacks.

Galleries Open, Galleries Close and New Initiatives during the Recession

In the same 1990 issue of *Artichoke* that the Ron Moppett interview appears in, there is also an assessment given of the last decade by Les Graff, then director of the Visual Arts Branch of Alberta Culture and Multiculturalism. He identifies two key events: the celebration of Alberta's seventy-fifth anniversary (1980) and, more depressingly, the deep economic recession that hits the province. Recalls Graff: "There were cutbacks all across the board, not just in government but with corporations and private support,"[4] such as that provided by two of Toronto's top commercial players – Gallery Moos and Mira Godard Gallery – who close their Calgary operations in 1983 after four heady years of showing both local and nationally recognized talent. Ironically, the *Calgary Herald* reports at the time: "The success in Toronto of recent exhibitions by artists Barbara Ballachey, Tak Tanabe, Ron Moppett, and Otto Rogers has shown a stronger market for these Western artists [in Toronto] than in Calgary."[5]

By contrast, in that same year Paul Kuhn Fine Arts and Folio Gallery bravely open their doors, while the Virginia Christopher Gallery (established 1981) relocates from an industrial park to closer downtown and the veteran Canadian Art Galleries (established 1945) renews itself with new ownership and a subsequent move. These private, Calgary-based initiatives will help make a difference in the city's contemporary art scene, post-recession. The next year, though, brings more bad news: the demise of the James Ulrich Gallery (established 1981). Along with the artist-run Off Centre Centre[6] (established 1975), Centre Art Video (established 1979) and the Burns Visual Arts Society (established 1979), the James Ulrich Gallery had been part of a lively centre for contemporary art activity on Stephen Avenue in the historic Neilson Block. the *Calgary Herald* cites a lack of support for contemporary art as the reason for closure, attributed to the "conservative attitudes of the community."[7]

But to counter this, a strong movement is already underway to change attitudes, or at least to heighten awareness about Alberta art, not just in Calgary but all over. In 1981, for instance, Edmonton's *The Works* festival[8] is established with the sponsorship of the Edmonton Downtown Business Association; in 1983, commercial galleries in Calgary begin the annual event *Artwalk;*[9] and in 1985, the Alberta Art Foundation starts up a travelling-exhibition program to bring recent art to smaller communities. Even in the face of a recession, which gets worse in 1986 with a precipitous drop in oil prices, a widespread effort is taking shape to spread the word about Alberta art.

According to Graff, another important development on the Alberta art scene in the 1980s is the effect international art trends have on the fortunes of the province's two large centres. "We had the trans-avant-garde movement internationally and I think many Calgary painters who were figurative to begin with had very little trouble moving into that arena.... But in Edmonton, they had been pushing a formalist thing for a long time and it was coming to an end internationally and there wasn't much sympathy or interest in it. So little by little Edmonton artists became unto themselves while the Calgary artists tended to branch out."[10]

Also significant during that decade is "the number of artists who opened doors on their own and established reputations for themselves elsewhere. I'm thinking of people like John Hall, Robert Scott, Ron and Carroll Moppett [Taylor-Lindoe], etc. It's given Alberta artists the highest profile they have ever known. Also because of the pluralism internationally, there is far more variety in Alberta than there has ever been.... Now the door is open to almost anything,"[11] Graff observes.

But Alberta itself is also out there opening doors, especially for its artists, by sending work abroad through overseas exhibitions, such as *Seven Artists from Alberta: Art in this Region* (1984). Featuring the heightened still-life realism of John Hall, the patterned quasi-abstract expressionism of Don Kottmann, the landscape-based architectonic constructions of Carroll Taylor-Lindoe, the semi-abstract/semi-representational symbolic layerings of Ron Moppett, the text and image appropriations of Mary Scott, the cool, deliberately banal representations of Jeffrey Spalding, and the satirical word paintings of John Will, this touring show[12] travels to non-profit Canadian cultural centres in London, Paris and Brussels, prompting the observation from its curator, Nancy Tousley: "The idea that significant art could only be made in a handful of major centres was challenged in [the United States] in the 1960s, and continues to be, as regions of strong and well-defined character have produced strong art to express themselves. While this situation has no direct parallel in Canada, where patterns of regional development have been different, the growing strength of art in Alberta and in her neighbour province, Saskatchewan, is not a dissimilar phenomenon."[13]

A few years later, more anecdotal evidence of the growing strength of Alberta art surfaces. In 1987, *Visual Arts Newsletter* (Alberta Culture) reports that "[1987] must be one of the most successful seasons on record [for Albertan's exhibiting internationally]."[14] Among the many shows listed are *Derek Besant* at the Canada House Cultural Centre Gallery (London); *Ron Moppett* at Manhattan's 49th Parallel; *Jane Ash Poitras, Alex Janvier, Norval Morrisseau and Joane Cardinal-Schubert* at the Southwest Museum (Los Angeles), and *Clay Ellis, Isla Burns, Peter Hide and Lyle Lis* at the Sainsbury Centre for Visual Arts (University of East Anglia, England).

The Door Half-Shut: The Canada Council

Within Canada as a whole, though, things are actually far more uncertain as larger public institutions grapple with the loss of their annual block grant from the Canada Council.[15] The annual grants are rescinded in 1985 in the interest of making it possible for all of the country's publicly funded, non-profit galleries, large or small, public or artist-run, to have equal access to exhibition funds. But for all of its egalitarian intentions, this radical policy shift has some unsettling results right across the country. At the Glenbow Museum, for instance, the upcoming exhibition, *On Edge* is cancelled after receiving $2,000 from the council for curatorial research but no further monies for presentation and circulation. Designed to be an out-of-province touring survey of contemporary Alberta art, a rare event in Canada, curator Vincent Varga observes: "One of the problems is there is no continuity between [council] juries. One jury will give you research money to do a show, and when you apply again for implementation, the next jury can turn you down. I would rather go to Reno." [16]

For Alberta institutions, more worrisome than the cumbersome three-step grant application process is the thought of seeing their exhibition funding being determined by juries organized by a central-Canadian institution like the Canada Council. How would regionally important exhibitions be assessed by juries asked to consider funding excellence but from some so-called national context? As the Edmonton-born playwright and *Saturday Night* writer Frank Moher points out, "What's excellent in my community – that which touches the heart, which challenges, which is socially useful and moves the art form within a local context – may not be excellent in yours. I suspect my definition of 'excellence' reflects the place I live in." [17] Or as Newfoundlander Patrick O'Flaherty, a former board member of the Canada Council, states, "Artistic excellence is determined by judgment, not measurement, and it often comes down to who does the judging . . . and I for one am not prepared to presume where excellence resides in this country." [18]

In the 1986 article "Policy Changes Shake Art Institutions," Alf Bogusky, the recent director of Southern Alberta Art Gallery, elaborates on the possibility of the Canada Council becoming the country's chief curator for the publicly funded sector: "What I think you're going to see is homogenization of programming across the country and you know who is going to get the shows? It will be people who have a profile on Queen Street [Toronto] or who otherwise have a certain visibility within the network." [19]

A decade later, this concern is underlined even more starkly by Jeffrey Spalding, the driving force behind the University of Lethbridge's art collection, "The Canada Council gunboat parks in the harbour and enforces a blockade until finally the gallery is starved out of being denied programme funds to present its view of the world. Gallery boards tire of their peripheral status, want in on the action, and replace their directors and curators with hip curators from outside the province. They quickly enforce this hegemony of what is 'relevant' and what is not and turn the province's exhibition resources towards recognizing these principal interests." In regards to Alberta, where non-profit, publicly funded galleries can turn to the Alberta Foundation for the Arts for some programming monies, Spalding nevertheless concluded: "The entire art scene of the province of the past decade: what has been shown, what has been bought, promoted, who has been hired as teachers and curators, all of this and its concomitant inverse, has been thus irrevocably altered."[20]

The impact of the new council policy, for instance, leaves the Edmonton Art Gallery with substantially fewer programming resources in 1985 than it had enjoyed in previous years. This sets in motion the eventual departure of Director Terry Fenton (1986), and the marginalization of modernist abstract art from the contemporary scene in Canada. As the *Globe and Mail* critic John Bentley Mays later confirms in 1991: "Before I went out West, everyone was telling me that the story of Edmonton abstraction was just about over,"[21] a statement that provokes cheers in some quarters and dismay in others because of the subtle but important role played by Ottawa-appointed juries doling out exhibition grants.

Concerns about the distribution of individual grants to artists also arise in the 1980s. "In fact," reports the *Edmonton Journal* in 1991, "the Canada Council itself is concerned about the issue of Alberta funding and would like to see more applications from this province, and from Edmonton, in particular, which lags behind Calgary in winning council money."[22] But even with Calgary's successes factored into the equation, the amount of money given to Alberta artists is low – receiving only 7 percent of the visual-arts monies available in 1991[23] – and remains so right through to the end of the century. For the whole of the 1990s, 7 percent is the average.[24]

In 1998 and 1999, the Canada Council administers the one-time-only Millennium Arts Fund, a $10 million-dollar program in support of innovative work in all of the arts. Again, there are concerns about its distribution outside of central Canada. According to Tom McFall, "[The fund] had little impact in western Canada, and next to none in Alberta."[25] Responding as the executive director of the Alberta Crafts Council, McFall concludes about the program: "There is a common and quite justifiable belief throughout the Alberta arts scene, that central Canadian biases are alive and well. And numbers, such as the Millennium Fund results, seem to prove this.... The root of the problem is the inherent creativity and diversity of Alberta culture ... extraordinary to the point that a conservative central Canadian arts establishment can't believe (or even understand) what happens here."[26]

At best, then, it can be said Alberta has a love-hate relationship with the Canada Council. While there is much gratitude for the council's important work, there are questions about whether there are certain patterns detectable in the exercise of grant giving, especially for exhibitions organized by the non-profit sector: patterns connected to particular kinds of post-1970 art-making (such as installation, photo-based and new media) that are critically favoured in larger centres of the country. The Canada Council does keep statistics on how its exhibition funding is dispersed by province – statistics which drop considerably outside of the Toronto-Montreal-Vancouver axis – but concerns like these can always be dismissed by waving the flag of artistic merit. In principle, as a measuring stick, merit is a fine concept but relying on it as the be-all and end-all suggests that it need never be informed, contextualized or even compromised by the history and/or idiosyncrasies of places or regions not as conversant or committed to the critical consensus of larger centres. Admittedly, some of this important background could and should be brought by the individual juror to the assessment process but this is not necessarily a given when the issue of jury representation is examined.

During the 1990s, the percentage of participants from Alberta who served on the council's various juries, selection committees and advisory bodies connected to the visual arts (excluding architecture) ranged from a high of 10 percent in 1991–92 to a low of 3 percent in 1998–99. These numbers may be broken down further. Of forty-five assessors over the course of the decade who served on the annual jury for the Chalmers Funds for the Crafts, two were from Alberta. Even more eye-opening are the numbers for the photography juries: out of ninety-five peer assessors used from 1990 to 2000, only three hailed from Alberta. And then, of fifty-five assessors used to award funding to independent curators and critics, there was only one lone Albertan.[27] To be fair, the numbers were slightly better in regards to the key area of exhibition assistance: 15 out of 114 peer curators were Albertan.

But complicating the matter is that certain peers were used not just once but twice or even three times in either the same category or in a different capacity, making the actual number of Alberta-based jurors who attended

Canada Council juries over this ten-year period actually quite tiny. Needless to say, whatever the jury, whatever the selection committee or advisory body, the important centres of Montreal, Vancouver and Toronto were well-represented almost without exception throughout all of the 1980s and 1990s. Does it matter? If it doesn't, then it is even more inexplicable why peer representation from the Prairies, Atlantic Canada and elsewhere has not been given the same consideration.

Thus, for all the critical and institutional dialogue about "the canon," "hegemony," "decentering," "the other" and so on, the tearing down of hierarchies in the Canadian art world has only gone so far. While the roles of gender, race, ethnicity and sexual preference have all been conspicuously examined both artistically and critically, the differences between region and centre have not really been part of this exchange. This is a curious phenomena given that it has been heartily debated and analysed in *other* areas of national life. Witness, for instance, the *Globe and Mail*'s John Ibbitson's end-of-century summation about the economic interface between Ontario and the West: "Ontarians are imperialists. The province's founding fathers dreamed of a nation that would stretch to the Pacific, dominated by Ontario industry and settlers. Westerners rightly chafe at their colonial status: for much of this nation's history, Ontario treated them like colonies, forcing upon them the national policy of high tariffs and Bay Street capital that stunted their growth."[28]

Or, as Canadian historians H. Graham Rawlinson and J.L. Granatstein observed in *The Canadian 100: The 100 Most Influential Canadians of the 20th Century*, "To be born and raised in central Canada conferred an advantage."[29]

Given that on a political and economic level Canada is often analyzed as a colonial construction, it might be asked if on a cultural level our national institutions are complicit with this behaviour: using such terms as merit and excellence to unintentionally exclude art that is excellent in its own right but does not conform to what is considered important in larger centres. Curator Diana Nimeroff of the National Gallery of Canada often cites her curatorial focus as being related to "[Art] that seems of particular importance today."[30] On the other hand, in a series of letters to Nimeroff, Regina artist Vic Cicansky makes a strong argument that federal tax dollars should be used to "represent the diversity of art that exists in the country."[31] But right to the bitter end of the last century, any such recognition of this idea within the larger Canadian art sphere (based as it mostly is in Central Canada) is purely accidental.

ꕥ An Independent Alberta College of Art

During the post-boom of the 1980s, three exhibitions are presented over a ten-month period at the Alberta College of Art Gallery to "celebrate the coming of age of [the art school] ... [and] the establishment on July 1, 1985 of an independent Alberta College of Art."[32] Previously the largest department of the Southern Alberta Institute of Technology, the dream of functioning as an autonomous institution under the direction of its own Board of Governors and administration had long been waiting to come to fruition.[33] Finally, after a turbulent period of protest and agitation (1982–83), Canada's second largest art college is standing on its own feet with the fruits of its remarkable history on public display. Respectively titled *Founders of the Alberta College of Art, A Measure of Success: Graduates of the Alberta College of Art 1963–1973;* and *A Measure of Success: Graduates of the Alberta College of Art 1974–1984,* the three exhibitions provide a selective but wide-ranging survey of 125 of the institution's instructors and graduates in all media. Within that selection can be found many of the names associated with the early development of Alberta art – A.C. Leighton, H.G. Glyde, Luke Lindoe, Marion Nicoll, Walter Phillips and so on – as well as those deeply connected to its more contemporary period: Katie Ohe, Slyvain Voyer, Douglas Haynes, John Hall, Leslie Manning, Annemarie Schmid Esler, Amy Gogarty, Chris Cran.

Val Greenfield, curator of this ambitious undertaking, notes, "While these works were set in a peer context, it could be readily observed that the term does not necessarily equate similarity of style, content or direction. Over the years ACA students and instructors have been characterized by a spirit of independence, both within the college itself and externally, in the national development of artistic movements.... In direct contrast to the type of group style and philosophy that has identified other art colleges in this country, aesthetic choice and idiosyncratic practice remain paramount at the Alberta College of Art."[34]

The college, nonetheless, does have a history of employing its own graduates to teach at the school. But by the time Greenfield organizes the sixty-year showcase this practice has given way to a broader mix of instructors and students from across the country and beyond. It seems, then, that if the eclecticism of the post-1970 Calgary art community can be explained, it might partly be traced back to the art college. Notably, in that same landmark year of 1985, in Edmonton, there is *Sculpture City,*[35] where the applause for Edmonton steel abstraction is about to reach its pinnacle. By contrast that same year, there is also *Five Sculptors from Southern Alberta*[36] at Banff's Whyte Museum of the Canadian Rockies. Organized by curator Monique Westra, she suggests the artwork of the five underlines a new development in Albertan sculpture: "By freely manipulating synthetic, industrial and natural materials, both crafted and readymade, artists in the 1980s are asserting the primacy of the message over the medium as they assume the roles of prophets, social commentators, raconteurs, satirists and image makers."[37]

Two of the sculptors present in *Five Alberta Sculptors* are **BLAKE SENINI** (1954 Nanaimo, British Columbia) and **GORDON FERGUSON** (1953, High River, Alberta). Both instructors at ACA, they, along with fellow sculptor and instructor **WALTER (WALLY) MAY** (1950, Edmonton, Alberta), eventually earn the name the Gang of Three. Hired between 1981 and 1982, their dissimilar art becomes a signpost for a different kind of sculpture in the province. Of the three, only Ferguson is an ACA alumnus (1976), though like many other graduates he pursues further study elsewhere (Missoula, Montana) before he is hired to teach at the college.

For the exhibition *The Gang of Three* (Ace Art & Plug/In Inc., Winnipeg, 1987), curator Eleanor Bond writes, "Calgary art production can best be described as individualistic, pluralistic, post-modern and eccentric.... Generally speaking, the work produced in Calgary is very well-crafted and technically accomplished, with considerable emphasis on the object, its form and its materials. These concerns are evident in the work of [the three artists] who see these as a valuable legacy of their formalist backgrounds. Yet, common to [their] work is a pervasive wit and sense of personality, and a use of materials and forms that consciously contradict and parody formalist and traditional sculpture. Their stance is non-monumental and non-architectural, and an inter-connectedness with drawing has been a striking feature of all their work in recent years."[38]

The roles played by the Gang of Three within this divergent art community are varied and often subtly stated. Throughout the 80s, for instance, it can be said that Blake Senini is primarily a raconteur, his exuberant images – drawn on shaped plaster or wood – conveying anecdotal and ecologically concerned content related to his youth on the west coast and the world currently around him. Wally May, on the other hand, is a more philosophical type who uses his art – made of conduit, sheet metal, aluminium wire, tree roots, warped boards and colourful stains or paint – to address what is interpreted as "the shifting practice of sculpture, form as metaphor, [and] the distinctions between functional and non-functional, industrial and natural, illusion and reality."[39]

As for Gordon Ferguson, he establishes himself as an unconventional physicist grappling with the forces of nature: energy, matter, transmission or transformation. Matter-of-fact titles such as *Spin* (1984), *Current* (1984), *Fuel* (1987) and *Tap* (1986) all hint at the kinetic forces of the world, while the pieces themselves employ a "wonky"[40] elegance to make the connections between the viewer and the larger universe. With a preference for using hardware and building supplies, the artist utilizes handmade materials to address what contemporary society thinks it has safely distanced itself from – nature.

In Ferguson's first installation of note, *Function, Motion and Kitchen* (1982, Off Centre Centre, Calgary), a topsy-turvy, domestic-like environment is created with black plastic plumbers' pipe and discarded kitchenware covered in tar. Comparing the sections of black pipe attached to the floor, wall and ceiling to "the way a cartoonist draws with a thick black pen,"[41] the artist remarked, "It's like trying to snap an instance in time or make it stand still for a spilt second."[42]

In 1985, Ferguson confines himself to a small studio space and begins a series of neo-primitive androgynous figures, cementing his reputation in Alberta's new sculpture scene in the process. Made at a time when national and international art is dominated by figurative concerns, Ferguson's response is to make some of the most distinctive busts and full figures in Canada. In large works, including *Bentboy* (1984), *Fuel, Cake Top* (1986), *Tap* (1986) and the much-photographed *Red Head* (1986), the themes of energy and transformation continue, as does his proclivity for letting tactile materials such as electrical wire, strips of black tire rubber and gnarly tree roots fulfil both a formal and metaphorical function. "Ferguson's heads seem to speak of the realization that mental energy is, after all, electrical energy. Thus, the human consciousness is the site of both the natural and organic, and the technological and cultural. It is here, then, that we create an awareness of these oppositions and simultaneously reconcile them,"[43] comments critic Leslie Dawn in the 1988 catalogue: *Gordon Ferguson: Sense Your Place.*

Organized by Lethbridge's Southern Alberta Art Gallery – the only public institution in the province to organize a solo exhibition for each of the Gang of Three[44] during this important moment in Alberta sculpture – the nine-piece installation together creates an arresting image of "the forces which we cannot see but which affect us."[45]

A modified version of the aptly titled *Sense Your Place* is presented later that year in *Multiple Associations: Five Alberta Artists.* Presented by the Glenbow Museum, this show follows in the footsteps of several other exhibitions attempting to account for some of the keen passions and contemporary names associated with current three-dimensional art in the province.[46] Along with Ferguson, *Multiple Associations* includes Edmonton sculptors Blair Brennan and Catherine Burgess, Lethbridge's Carl Granzow and Calgary's Mary Scott. In describing what such a diverse group of the 1980s could possibly have in common, Katherine Ylitalo writes, "Through the layering of different materials, methods, forms and even the titles, these pieces have the potential to evoke a multitude of associations."[47] Picking up on this theme, so different from the late-modernist dicta of responding to only the formal qualities of the work, the *Globe and Mail* review had this to say about Ferguson's installation and the overall image it engendered: "[*Sense*] seems the most distinctively Albertan of the lot – both in its stark architectural qualities, and its theme of transformations of energy between organic and non-organic materials, a significant part of life where fossil fuels are so economically important."[48]

Of the *Gang of Three,* Walter May's practice[49] is the lengthiest, reaching back to the early 1970s when he is included in *Survey of Canadian Art Now* (Vancouver Art Gallery, 1972), *For an Independent Hairy Hill* (the one and only time the National Gallery of Canada ever organizes a show of Alberta art, 1973); and *Sculpture on the Prairies* (Winnipeg Art Gallery, 1977). Thus, by the time the Edmonton-born artist establishes himself as a significant presence in contemporary Alberta sculptor with his 1984 ground-breaking exhibit at Paul Kuhn Fine Arts, he is able to display a clever marriage between abstraction and figuration.

May's ability to employ both the abstract and the figurative in his art dates back to his wood sculptures of the 1970s, which are resolutely abstract and minimally spare in appearance but have a manner that defies much of the formal seriousness of the time. In his choice of materials, for instance, he prefers to find substandard industrial materials like wood beams, boards and veneer that are warped: "[Warped pieces of] wood seems to be in transition, back to being alive, back to being a tree. The idea that it has been manufactured and people have spent a great deal of money to make it functional and, then, all on its own, it manages to thwart that human interference [suggests] that it's not just a substance.... It's a substance with character."[50]

May will exploit this expressive trait to create his body of vertical works in the 80s. As Nancy Tousley describes this transition, "the lovable wonkiness of his earlier sculpture is turned into a kind of figurative gesture.... [These] spirited sculptures dance the eye around."[51] With titles like *Drummer, Guard* and *Lookout,* May's newer sculptures reveal his interest in primitive art, specifically Cree Manitokan figures.[52] Distinctively lanky and linear, warped and bent, stained and painted, the artworks appear like drawings in space rather than as sculptures with substantial mass and weight. Over succeeding years, he broadens the scope of these figures. By including such materials as copper pipe, roots, conduit, re-bar, lava rock, nylon rope and galvanized sheet metal, May adds a further dimension to their elegant yet eccentric forms. In many sculptures, the melding of the industrial with the natural is deliberate, suggesting multiple levels of meaning. In the opinion of reviewer Manon Blanchette, "The wood evokes natural energy; the machined metal reminds us of humanity's power over things and their functions."[53] Blanchette also found May's sculptures "unpretentious," an attribute echoed later in Eleanor Bond's observation: "Part of the magic of his work is that he can imbue such non-monumental and potentially unassuming pieces with so much power and presence."[54]

In 1989, May's oeuvre undergoes another substantial change. Instead of assembling pieces that are a hybrid of drawing and three-dimensional art, he turns to what he called "restoration" – the modification of abandoned objects found locally. For instance, he replaces a cauldron's missing handle with a bronze one to create the piece *Empty,* and for the piece *Full,* he reinterprets a desiccated tree trunk by plugging its knots with old wooden handles and filling the cracks with aluminium and wax. First presented at Calgary's Paul Kuhn Fine Arts, a review in *Artichoke* magazine opines: "May's new work is closer to traditional notions of sculpture being a volume in space.... Several of the new works, like the mighty cast-iron cauldron *Empty* and the thick-waisted tree trunk *Full,* occupy space rather than play with it."[55]

In another example of what May calls restoration, an old steel ball and a steel brick have a simple metal handle attached to their surface and are displayed on a set of small, sandstone shelves (*Wisdom and Folly*). More subdued and contemplative, many of the new works refer to a "certain kind of history ... rooted in the 'pioneer' era when certain articles and materials like sandstone facing, cast iron objects, and hand-turned tools were part of the vernacular."[56] But rather than treating his found items as artifacts, where the expectation is that they are a representation of history, May transforms the results of his scavenging into subjective objects, trimming them of their nostalgic value and altering their meaning.

May's restorations continue into the next decade, beginning with a room-size installation titled *Low Table, High Chairs* (1989–1990). Displayed at Calgary's Triangle Gallery, Mercer Union (Toronto) and the Edmonton Art Gallery, the eccentric multi-piece work resonates with the spirit of Marcel Duchamp's ready-mades, its low steel table and forty metal stools all modified to display a found metal object, placed either on the top of each stool or beneath the table. Calling the installation "a work in progress," Edmonton Art Gallery curator Elizabeth Kidd writes, "[May] also examines the different ways that sculpture can be looked at and understood: as real objects in a real space or as concepts in a transcendental space, as autonomous and self-referential space or dependent on their context for meaning. This exhibition marks the culmination of a number of directions that May has been pursuing for the past fifteen years, during which he explored different sculptural traditions that developed in Europe in the early part of this century."[57]

According to the artist: "There are [on the stools] vessels without handles in some cases, there are thick vessels made of heavy steel. It's difficult to imagine what might have been poured out of these. I'm not sure if these particular things should be called jugs. Are they called cans? Pitchers? Pitchers with spouts? In terms of trying to define or even understand these things you may be more tempted to look for other meanings that are perhaps more symbolic or metaphorical or whatever."[58] Thus, the mind is intended to be teased by what May presents and although his methods will continue to evolve and change, this engagement continues right to end of century and beyond.

At this juncture, a link can be made between the Gang of Three and what is known as New British Sculpture.[59] The work of these diverse artists casts a particular light on the practice of sculpture during the 1980s. As Manon Blanchette, curator of the exhibition *British Now: Sculpture and Other Drawings* (Musée d'art Contemporain de Montréal, 1989) opines, "For those who experience it, the British sculpture of the past decade evokes an atmosphere, a place or a dimension that is strange. The origins and nature of the objects are familiar and yet the unconventional treatment they are given reveals another world to us. The familiar and the unfamiliar are combined."

To varying degrees, the above observations can also be applied to the Gang of Three, but while May and Ferguson employ discarded and found objects to achieve these ends, Blake Senini uses other methods: "We can wonder for example if Senini is painter or a sculptor,"[60] writes Manon Blanchette; "For three weeks the gallery [with Senini's installation] was a magical/menacing world,"[61] says Marla Strong; "Senini created an intensely provocative altered state: drawing on the walls, painting on the floor, installing sculptures that were like dynamic 3-D paintings on the move, with some suspended in mid-flight from the ceiling,"[62] writes Eleanor Bond.

Notably, like Walter May, the British Columbia–born artist registers a major change of direction in his art in 1984. Previously, he concentrated on abstract sculptures made from laminated plywood and creosote-covered timbers that were, he recalls, "All about the formalist dictum, how things are put together … you could not put any emotive qualities in the work, any personal whim, humour or wit."[63] Eventually dissatisfied with these results, he develops a more personalized[64] approach that springs forth from his drawing. Colourful, graphic works emerge rich in narrative and anecdotal images. In the process of translating two dimensions into three dimensions, Senini fabricates two-sided upright sculpture from plaster or wood that is unlike anything else seen in the country. For the group exhibition, *WallSpace: New Sculpture by Six Calgary Artists* (Glenbow Museum, Calgary), curator Katherine Ylitalo explains: "Wooden constructions are cut out and carved, and he then draws on the surfaces vigorously using ink and applying oil paint with his hands.… *Lyell Island* [for instance] is loaded with narrative meaning. On one side is a single tree on an island. On the other, a menacing monster opens its jaws that resemble a chain saw. Through these Janus-faced sculptures, Senini conveys multiple meanings."[65]

And according to Eleanor Bond, "A sense of vengeance and parody is evident in the form and executions of Senini's work, in the delight with the loaded imagery and metaphorical bombardment, and in the personal and provocatively imaginative content."[66]

Fun and as irreverent as these works are, by the end of decade Senini will exchange the pictorial images and blatant use of narrative for a more spare, cooler and enigmatic art that Nancy Tousley describes as being "less humourously bantering in tone and, richer to boot … [as] forms and images are now coming out of the process of putting materials together."[67] This change may have come in part from the influence of new British sculpture. Curator Tim Long – *Simone: Blake Senini* (1996, MacKenzie Art Gallery, Regina) – notes that contact with the British sculptor Anish Kapoor in 1988 "impressed

[Senini] with an approach which did not purge narrative from the sculpture, but rather stripped away any narrative element that was not inherent to the sensuous materials and minimalist shapes of the work itself."[68]

Working with a whole new set of materials including cast polyester resin, Senini's sculptural works of the 1990s impress with their monumental simplicity, echoes of the spiritual, engagement with such ineffable matter as light, and with the presence of paradox and contradiction. In *Ashes to Ashes* (1993), a large collection of human-scale angel wings, each one cast in a rugged grey cement, defy heavenly ascent as they lie in a heap on the floor. In the glowing *Shape of the Light* (1996), a wide arched tombstone-like form made of a translucent resin shell is simultaneously a solid object and a shape of light – inspired by a reflection Senini saw on an interior wall at his home. As Long perceptively observes, "Senini's art has become a sculpture of presence ... (where) solids become voids, and voids become solid ... heavy objects become light; light objects heavy."[69]

This idea of sculpting space and light as well as architectural features into independent forms remains a central feature of Senini's work into the new century. In 2000, he is invited by the newly renamed Art Gallery of Calgary[70] to translate features of its historical quarters into an installation of resin works. As with much of his other art, including the narrative-driven work of the 1980s, the four pieces he produces are an act of memory but their translucency alluding to more ethereal matters. Thus, of the so-called Gang of Three, the gregarious Blake Senini becomes the most surprising, his objects "constructed to tickle the eye and the mind" as one Toronto critic so perceptively put it when reviewing his contribution, *Ether* (2000) to the *Alberta Biennial of Contemporary Art 2000.*[71]

Installation Art in Alberta

It's everywhere and it's nowhere: everywhere in the sense that installation art prevails like no other medium in the publicly subsidized sector of the contemporary art world,[72] nowhere in that it defies traditional art forms by not being necessarily a collectable art object. While some of this ephemeral art does get collected and installed on a more permanent basis, for the most part it is neither for sale nor is it permanent. And, while it can be said that painters, sculptors, photographers and the like have the capacity to make a living with their more saleable, collectable art, installation artists will "make art history [but] need a day job."[73] No wonder, then, that this medium is sometimes referred to as state art. "For the past twenty-five years the single most critical, daring and consistent source of funds for such advanced work ... has been the federal government through the National Endowment for the Arts,"[74] writes Hugh M. Davies, director of San Diego's Museum of Contemporary Art which, since the 1960s, has enthusiastically supported installation art.

Admired for its spatial ambitions, its subversion of fine-art conventions, its conceptual and experimental vigour, and its ability to utilize any material and/or medium, including new technology like video and digital presentation, installation art arguably sits at the apex of contemporary art practice in the late twentieth century. For the artistically pure of heart, it also projects a suitably anti-materialist, anti-commercial, anti-bourgeois attitude: "Artists who work in unconventional media such as installation function as the aesthetic explorers of their generation, and they operate in territory well beyond the conventional supply lines and safety nets of galleries and collectors. Whatever aesthetic bounty experimental artists bag rarely translates into trophy art to hang above the mantel that is likely to turn a handy profit."[75] (On the other hand, through no fault of its own, installation art also has a certain snob appeal among the more theoretically inclined postmodern crowd. Ironically, like its polar opposite, abstract painting and sculpture, installation is also as poorly understood and appreciated by the general public and the mainstream media.)

Created for an interior space or an outdoor setting, site-specific installation art is a significant step away from the creation of singular art objects. Within a defined area that has been customized by the artist, installation involves considering the relationships between a number of elements that contribute to the sum of the work.[76] Commonly thought to be the most advanced practice and subsequently the domain of privileged art centres such as New York and Toronto, in the annals of contemporary art in Alberta there are enough examples to suggest that this is not always the case.

In 1969, for instance, Norman Yates hangs his work *Hanging Foil* across a corridor near the Student's Union Gallery at the University of Alberta. Described as an interactive work, the viewer becomes part of the composition as he or she moves through the rows of foil strips that "seem to take on life [through] movement and sound."[77] Then, in 1973 the experimental Calgary group W.O.R.K.S (We Ourselves Roughly Know Something) is formed by newcomers Clive Robertson and Paul Woodrow. Dedicated to interdisciplinary work – otherwise called "synaesthetic" activity – in the spring of 1973

W.O.R.K.S appropriates a six-block section of downtown Calgary into a public art gallery, theatre and concert space called the *Something Gallery*.[78] This conceptual installation "encompassed all sound, movement, light conditions, traffic, people, buildings and their infinite combinations.... We are not announcing the opening of *Something* but merely recognizing its existence – (likewise it cannot close)."[79] A work totally in the mind of the beholder, Carol Hogg of the *Calgary Herald* sums up the deliberately ephemeral *Something* as a strong anti-object statement, "especially appropriate in an age overwhelmed with affluence, materialism and the profit motive."[80]

One artist who combines aesthetic exploration with the socially aware is **RITA MCKEOUGH** (1951, Antigonish, Nova Scotia). Yet another Alberta printmaker who moves comfortably between graphic and non-graphic areas, the Calgary-raised artist, instructor, carpenter, musician and performer constructed, in the early 1980s, some of the most significant and ambitious installation art in the province. Critic Joan Borsa describes her work as, "complex, labour-intensive installations that come off as playful, accessible experiences."[81]

Involving the use of narrative, humour and anthropomorphism, McKeough's earliest installation is *The Artificial Marsh* (Dandelion Gallery, 1977). Said to be the fanciful creation of the Twelve Brothers, a group of imaginary sheep aided by McKeough, the *Calgary Herald* describes the straw-strewn gallery with floating artificial *marsh* mallows as the first piece of large-scale "environment sculpture" to be created in the city.[82] Like her highly touted lithographs, etchings and drawings[83] about, among other things, a lost mitten and the hapless adventures of a thinking, feeling tennis ball, *Marsh* underlines the artist's strategy of devising fictional scenarios and environments to convey poignant tales with humanist values.

Eventually, though, a scenario will develop that has a strong socio/political focus, connected to Calgary and McKeough's own experience with the city after returning from the Nova Scotia College of Art and Design with an MFA.[84] Encompassing three works, *Defunct* (ACA Art Gallery, 1981), *Destruck* (University of Lethbridge Art Gallery, 1983) and *Urban Scrounger* (Off Centre Centre, 1984), the artist presents three different installations about the boom-time destruction of inner-city neighbourhoods that is unique, challenging and a large leap beyond the methods of protest used by preservationists. "This is the power of art," states architectural critic Stephanie White. "Being exposed to the passionate statements of Rita McKeough makes one realize how very few artists there are today who seem inclined to seize that power and run with it."[85]

Beginning with drawings of old historic homes that are subsequently torn up into pieces or boarded up with actual bits of plywood, the first large-scale work *Defunct* is a soundscape (recorded sounds of jackhammers, saws and pile drivers), a process piece[86] and a room-size installation where small-scale replicas of homes, built in the ACA Art Gallery, can speak in their own defence via planted audiotapes. Similar to the kind of wooden structures with which McKeough was familiar in Calgary's pre-World War One neighborhoods, the four homes are constructed by McKeough and volunteers with heartbreaking fidelity, and then over a period of two weeks are boarded up, vandalized and torn down one by one.

"She was horrified by the violence of the destruction, asserting that the death of the houses meant the extinction of personal memory and collective community history,"[87] recollects director/curator Linda Milrod, who in 1985 brought the artist to Saskatoon's Mendel Art Gallery to create an installation (*Afterland Plaza*) dealing with another kind of violence: environmental degradation in the form of uranium-mining pollution in Saskatchewan.

By 1985, McKeough is living in Toronto but without severing ties to the west. At Edmonton's Latitude 53 Gallery, she joins two other Calgary-based artists, Marcella Bienvenue and Mary Scott, for the exhibition, *Politically Speaking* where, with a feminist perspective, they present the notion of art being a social practice.[88]

For McKeough, the theme of home is still present but takes on new associations. Because of Edmonton's geographic proximity to the Cold Lake air force base and its testing of cruise missiles, McKeough constructs a fallout-like shelter, *Wake an Other*, which simulates a domestic retreat for eating and sleeping. The home will also become an important metaphor in her increasingly feminist-inspired art with the notion of it being a place of sanctuary as well as a place of domestic abuse.

Another impressive installation and mixed-media artist who, like McKeough, moves around the country but continues to return on occasion to captivate local audiences is **GISELE AMANTEA** (1953, Calgary, Alberta). With a background in ceramics, Amantea steers the material of clay down new avenues in the province by first combining or melding ceramic objects with small pieces of wood furniture (shelves, tables) that were then obsessively decorated and embellished. Nancy Tousley said they are "some of the most original and engaging ceramic sculpture in the province."[89] Later, the high-art/low art boundaries are blurred by including pre-made hobby-art figurines and other mass-produced ceramic kitsch into sophisticated large-scale installations. That she manages to do this with insight and charm, without being condescending about hobby art, speaks volumes: "[She]has explored the complicated terrain of women's work within the domestic crafts,"[90] writes Jamelie Hassan.

Her unapologetic attention to decoration inspires a strong response among Alberta viewers and critics. Of her installation *Antidotes for Madness,* Nancy Tousley writes, "[The work's] boldly conceived atmosphere invites the contemplation of decoration and its visual and spiritual rewards,"[91] while two years later Liam Lacey says of the artist, "Her work is partly about fun ... her efforts in dredging out worn-out symbols of love, death, joy and desire provide some startling results, and make one wonder why the domestic and the sentimental have always been the most abhorred of emotions in modern painting."[92]

In 1988,[93] 1990 and 1992,[94] the then Regina-based artist presents in Alberta some of her most obsessively made and lavish wall pieces and sculptural installations. One exhibition in particular, *Gisele Amantea: Recent Work,* exhibited at the Walter Phillips Gallery (the Banff Centre, 1990) summarizes her engagement with things that post-war modernism would have disavowed but feminism embraces. These include signs of domesticity, cultural traditions and the feminine: anything traditionally associated with women's creative work. "The exhibition [*Recent Art*] was breathtaking – not only for its vibrant physical richness and invention, but also for the generosity of its warm and human embrace,"[95] comments Nancy Tousley for *Canadian Art.*

Amantea's works often make reference to popular landmarks – sacred shrines, grottos, nature dioramas and roadside attractions – as being the source of her inspiration including *Blue Wall* (1987), *Heaven* (from *Antidotes for Madness,* 1987), *White Folly* (1988),[96] *Aporia* (1989) and *Sanctuary* (1990). Especially pertinent to Alberta and its self-image is the irreverent yet wondrous *Sanctuary*, created for the Walter Phillips show and later toured nationally. Drawing on her own recollections of family trips to Banff, the artist creates a site for the post-romantic contemplation of nature. It includes a 12 × 16-foot room containing a bench and a beautiful diorama of Moraine Lake, an icon of Banff National Park. (Ironically, the Moraine Lake image is one of only a handful of instances at the end of the century where something painted[97] of the Rockies appears in the pointedly avant-garde gallery.) Outside the room on the floor is a small forest of miniature pine trees made out of greenware clay, originally intended to be used as Christmas ornaments.

"The installation represents the seductive appeal of tourist traps ... but at the same time laments the rendering of nature as property and image,"[98] writes curator Daina Augatis. Likewise, the *Globe and Mail's* Kate Taylor comments, "One could quickly summarize (and dismiss) it as a rather emphatic statement about the ways in which our urban society packages and commodifies nature. But what makes the work intriguing and gives the visitor pause for thought is the artist's attitude to her inventive range of materials."[99]

Two other Alberta-based artists who are in the installation game early but embody a cooler and more cerebral attitude than either the baroque kitsch transformations of Amantea or the dramatic, fictional scenarios of McKeough are Lethbridge's **CARL GRANZOW** (1943, Chicago, United States) and Calgary's **RAY ARNATT** (1934, Nuneham Courtenay, Oxon, England). Majoring in sculpture in their respective homelands – Granzow with an MFA from Arizona State University (1974) and Arnatt with a silver medal for sculpture from the Royal College of Art (London, 1961) – both artists bring to Canada a keen regard for such non-art subjects as mathematics (Arnatt), the cycles of nature (Granzow), prehistory, cosmology (Granzow), binary structures (Arnatt), technology (Granzow) and physics. At one time or another, these science-related subjects will inform their installations and other mixed-media sculpture, and make them unique in the province.

Of his work *Proposition of Potential* (the Nickle Arts Museum, 1983), Arnatt writes, "When I read about the great scientific paradox between the general theory of relativity and the quantum theory, in which, at one extreme of observation, the behaviour of large objects, such as rocks, planets and stars is predictable, and at the other observable extreme the behaviour of atoms – and in particular their sub-nuclear particles – to act randomly, I am drawn to a parallel recognition of the paradoxes and contradictions which occur in my own work as an artist."[100] Granzow, meanwhile, researches an MA thesis in art education about, "An Exploration of Selected Synergetic Interactions between Technology and Art Experience.[101]

In a way, their art has less to do with aesthetics than with philosophical and scientific ideas and their application. As curator Liz Wylie notes about Arnatt's 300 gessoed-panel *Holon,* exhibited as part of the exhibition

Ritual Systems: An Exhibition of Site-Specific Installations by Five Alberta Sculptors (Ring House Gallery, Edmonton, 1986), "Not an 'expressive' artist in the general sense of that term, Arnatt uses colour, for instance, only as a code to differentiate shapes and lines as wires are colour-coded in electronic equipment." [102]

Nonetheless, within the parametres of their formally spare and non-monumental art, which seeks to activate the space around it rather than dominate it, other aspects of artistic practice are conveyed. In *Spinoff* (Winnipeg Art Gallery, 1986), for instance, Arnatt reconciles the tensions, opposites and ambiguities of the modular work by transforming them into "abstract poetry." [103] In Granzow's outdoor piece, *Case Sitting* (1985), the sight of more than a dozen solid steel briefcases positioned in rows across a prairie field makes for a humourous as well as a perceptual challenge: "I like the ambiguity of 'Is this real? Or is this art?'" [104]

An art instructor at the University of Lethbridge since 1979, where he initiates and manages the development of the Gushul Studio's Artist Residency Program (1986–1994) and serves as a director of 'Papokan,' the University of Lethbridge Sculpture Park, Granzow's interest in the cosmos and his facility for constructing kinetic light projectors eventually will turn him skyward in the latter 1980s, when the artist seeks to "build a place for communion with nature through technology." [105] In two major efforts, *Separation-Initiation-Return and with a Bang*[106] (1988) and *Tracking*[107] (1994), the themes of the universe and celestial phenomena are incorporated into large room-size works that make reference to the cycles of nature, and in *Tracking*, the Aboriginal presence in British Columbia's Lake Okanagan area and their knowledge of the heavens through pictographs. Made up of a group of sculptural components positioned on the floor, the latter installation includes a stack of antlers and thirteen hides as well as electro-mechanical devices designed to mimic and project on the walls the eclipse of the sun, the action of binary stars and a comet in orbit. Describing *Tracking* as a vehicle enabling the viewer to re-enter the history of the region, the artist considers the nine-piece work an "intuitive inquiry" [108] into the linkages between the cosmology of an earlier hunter/gatherer culture and the present.

As with Granzow, the abstract modular art of Ray Arnatt challenges many of the popular expectations about three-dimensional work. In fact, made with lightweight materials including gessoed balsa wood and thin mild-steel tubing, his installations and other mixed-media sculpture can be surprisingly flat and/or incredibly devoid of mass, as in the towering ladder-like *Duet* (1985, Jack Singer Concert Hall, Calgary). In the 1987 group exhibition *Wall/Space* (Glenbow Museum), curator Katherine Ylitalo suggested his wall-hung, low-relief works *Prairie Geometry* and *Winter Garland* question the boundaries between sculpture and painting. Arranged according to a methodology based on mathematical progressions, these pieces and others employ subtle, pale colours and subdued textures.

Arnatt's approach changes noticeably in the 1990s when he begins to incorporate the standing human figure and use casting processes to make such pieces as the wall-length installation, *Detritus.*[109] (1995, Muttart Art Gallery). Still fascinated by duality and paradox and defining himself as a "binary structuralist,"[110] his elegant, even classical work begins to address different concerns connected to the human condition and figurative art of the twentieth century.

The latter 1980s is the period when installation art really begins to flourish in Alberta. What makes the difference is the appearance of a sizable number of recent art graduates, primarily from the Alberta College of Art, coalescing around alternative practices like video and performance as well as more Duchampian projects involving found objects. Unlike Carl Granzow and Ray Arnatt, who were established artists with professorial positions in post-secondary institutions, or Rita McKeough and Gisele Amantea who graduate in the mid-70s, this emerging group allies itself almost exclusively with the non-profit, artist-run network of galleries in the province, such as the newly opened 2nd Story Gallery in Calgary.

Formed in 1983 and eventually renamed Truck, the presence of this gallery marks a new phase in the expanding story of artist-run spaces that includes in the 1970s Off Centre Centre, Centre Art Video/Em Media, and Edmonton's trailblazing Latitude 53, and in the 80s the Stride Gallery (1986), Graceland (1986–1997) and Edmonton's Harcourt House (1987).

In its early years, the upstart 2nd Story takes credit for hosting the first solo exhibition of such significant new painters as David Janzen, Geoff Hunter and Amy Gogarty (all ACA alumni) and, more crucially, for actively promoting installation. Describing the lack of young local artists involved in such a venture as distressing, 2nd Story's exhibition coordinator, Anne-Marie Larson comments: "In 1986, I identified two venues of expression that were not as prevalent here as on the east coast: installation art and political art.

One reason may be that the absence of overtly didactic art posturing to the left is an expected fall-out in a staunchly white-collar town."[111]

In response to this perceived problem, the following year the gallery hosts the juried exhibition *Place Settings* which is set in a modest 2,400-square-foot, one-story building formerly occupied by the St. John's Ambulance. Featuring site-specific environments created by Mark Dicey, Jim Goertz, Judy Cheung, Steve Heimbecker, Colleen Kerr and Jeff Viner, the six-week-long event, along with 2nd Story's previous promotions of performance art at the newly established outdoor venue, Graceland,[112] will help to propel into the public realm the names of a new generation with a decidedly interdisciplinary approach to art. Noting that nearly all of the artists in *Place Settings* are involved in performance art, the *Calgary Herald*'s Nancy Tousley rates the event as a solid artistic effort, and because of its variety, "a good introduction to anyone who might still be unfamiliar with installation art."[113]

Among the works presented in *Place Settings* is *Measurement/Filter* by **MARK DICEY** (1959, Calgary, Alberta) who, through performance and assemblage, transforms the building's kitchen into a disaster site. One of the most versatile artists to emerge in the province in the 1980s, Dicey, a 1983 ACA graduate, forges ahead with many solo and collaborative performances,[114] and solo and group exhibitions within the artist-run and public art gallery network. Because of his well-received expressionistic painting and lyrical aptitude for assemblage and mixed-media works, he also exhibits commercially from time to time: an unusual cross-over for one so closely identified with performance art.

Dicey's work is greatly inspired by existential literature, Joseph Beuys and Fluxus art, Marcel Duchamp, Meret Oppenheim and Jasper Johns, as well as the work of Alberta artists Don Mabie, Marcella Bienvenue and Ron Moppett. His focus is the experience of existence and the psychological and emotional aspect of being, preferring found experiences over preconceived ones. As such, his performances are always unrehearsed and an extension of his studio work and daily routine. He also collects and uses interchangeably in his art pedestrian materials and found objects, though he neither fetishizes them nor considers them precious or unique. One curator likens Dicey to being "the keeper of an urban curiosity shop."[115]

In two of the most significant public art gallery exhibitions – *Elemental Instincts: A Matter of Course* (1988, the Nickle Arts Museum, Calgary) and *Noise Under the Tongue* (1990, Walter Phillips Gallery, Banff Centre) – Dicey explores the social meaning of survival as it pertains to shelter and co-existence. As in all of his undertakings, he relates these themes back to basic human activity and his ongoing exploration of himself and his environment.[116] Sylvie Gilbert, curator of *Noise Under the Tongue* explains that the work also underlines Dicey's own desires to be a different type of artist: "In this new [anti-modernist] paradigm, the artists assembled here acknowledge themselves as subjects – not as solitary and heroic individuals at a comfortable distance at society but rather as active members of it, participating in its constitution.... The exhibition presents artists who question their culture by investigating different aspects that determine it."[117]

Similarly motivated by a desire to be engaged is **BART HABERMILLER** (1962, Regina, Saskatchewan), who graduates in sculpture from the Alberta College of Art (1986) three years after Dicey. Populist in spirit and increasingly involved in the community as an activist and a curator, Habermiller develops into one of the better-known figures of this anti-elitist, anti-high art generation. Part of his notoriety is connected to his pivotal association with Graceland (1986–1997), an alternative exhibition and studio space located on an industrial site in the eastern quarter of Calgary, and his "particularly western waste-not want-not philosophy, "[118] the latter becoming the foundation for some of the most memorable site-specific sculptural installations of the period. With most of his materials scrounged from the seven-acre junkyard that houses Graceland (once operated by Frank Landry and his Calgary Demolition Co.), these works will intersect with the recycled/found object transformations of Gordon Ferguson and Walter May.

It is Landry's widow, Grace Colton, who first invites the artist to make use of the piles of old building materials, furniture, fixtures and household items lying around the yard. Greatly repulsed by rampant materialism and consumer waste, Habermiller will make brave new metaphors with this collection of derelict and discarded items. The junkyard is fertile with artistic possibility, and with the participation of many of his colleagues,[119] Habermiller serendipitously converts the site into a hotbed of creative life and living – for a few years, he even lives on the property in a renovated grain bin. Functioning as a performance venue[120] and a make-shift outdoor studio for site-specific sculpture, Graceland attracts both local and national media, described as "a huge sandbox to play in"[121] and "art without gallery walls."[122]

The most celebrated event held at the site is the annual *Graceland Art Rodeo.* Presented irreverently as though it might rival the spectacle of the Calgary Stampede and its famous rodeo, the weekend art-blitz-cum-happening makes use of the property's rambling size for an ad-hoc sculpture park as well as a host of performance events that in 1989, for example, include a "ballet" performed by half-ton trucks and a 'Hawaiian sunset ceremony' where the tribal spirit of the place is celebrated through drumming.

Habermiller's own art thrives in this environment. His first solo show of small-scale sculpture is titled *Graceland* (1986, 2nd Story Gallery) and his first large-scale sculpture/audio installation is christened *Frank's Wild Years* (1987). Installed at Off Centre Centre with special regard for the ephemera Landry collected from the 50s and 60s, the 48-metre–long assemblage of household 'junk' reaching from the gallery floor up to the ceiling recalls "a [roller coaster], a garland, or the overflowing contents of a cornucopia."[123] Close up, "the density of the work's snaking body dissolves into literally thousands of individual objects, from smaller than a thimble to bigger than a breadbox in scale."[124] Cleverly lit and featuring a cacophony of deejay sounds blaring from six built-in radios, *Frank's Wild Years* melded social and environmental concerns together in a boisterous fashion, along with the particular history of one individual, Frank Landry, who "in his own eclectic way preserved a segment of our throw-away culture." (Tousley)

Other sculptural installations that follow include the Alberta-based works: *Our Home and Native Land* (*Elemental Instincts,* the Nickle Arts Museum, 1988), *Porch Climber II* (*My Country is Winter,* the New Gallery, 1988), *Firestone Falls* (*Recycled Art,* Triangle Gallery of Visual Arts, 1992), *Arcade* (*The End of Modernity,* Glenbow Museum, 1994) and *Coalbanks* (*Nature Redux,* Southern Alberta Art Gallery, 1996). Of the elemental *Our Home and Native Land,* which appears in the important generational group show, *Elemental Instincts,* curator Donna McAlear observes, "The impression [of the artwork] is of a swelling wave [of debris] with crushing weight and force. An authentic testimony to humanity's insatiable desire to consume, it overwhelms [the artwork's] wilderness facade."[125]

Of a much different character, that same year Habermiller produces the luminous *Porch Climber II* from thousands of window pane shards and broken bottles. Created for a 1988 Winter Olympic exhibition at the New Gallery and inspired by the icy, reflective nature of winter, the floor-to-ceiling work looks like a giant icicle lit from within. In this work, Habermiller's contribution is more lyrically expressed and connected to Quebec songwriter, Gilles Vigneault's own insightful sense of place: "Mon Pays C'est L'Hiver" (My Country is Winter).

Humour is present, too, in Habermiller's work, especially in his small-scale sculptures that seem to give the viewer a wry smile. In *Blahblahblah* (1988), for instance, a collection of old-fashioned black dial telephones are transformed into a series of eccentric gossipers with their receivers spewing out multiple strands of coloured electrician's wire; the phones an expression of the conversations transmitted. Similarly, for the 1986 *Graceland* Habermiller fashions eleven witty lights and lamps out of the scavenged remains of such items as a toy ship's metal hull and an electrical space heater's patterned grill.

The ability to combine and compose, to recast found, recycled; and ready-made objects into new and sometimes humorous or whimsical expression is also an important part of the sculptural installations of **TIM WATKINS** (1952, London, England) and the mixed-media works of **IAIN BAXTER** (1936, Middlesborough, England). English-born, both are raised and trained in Calgary, and then go on to practice elsewhere: Watkins establishes himself in New York in 1979 while Baxter flourishes in the expanding Vancouver art scene of the 60s and 70s.

The latter also maintains an important link with both the Banff School of Fine Arts and the Alberta College of Art. Although Baxter is never a student of the art college, as a self-developing artist in Calgary in the 1950s and a competitive skier (Alberta Junior Ski Team), he drops in on both schools regularly, establishing a rapport with Stan Perrott and Maxwell Bates, who both play a mentorship role in his career. As the artist fondly recalls, "Bates was like a Zen master with a gentle gruffness.... Perrott a wonderful watercolourist." [126]

Once described as a master conceptualist, a playful ironist and commentator on commodity culture,[127] Baxter has a crucial role in the shaping of a more experimental, counter-culture vision for art in Canada. For Baxter, this new vision takes place in counter-culture Vancouver and in collaboration with his then-partner Ingrid and their slyly named N.E.Thing Co. (1966–1978), which challenges and parodies the conventions of landscape painting and the precious status of one-of-a-kind art. The technological and commercial pressures altering the environment is another theme. One project, the critically acclaimed *Bagged Landscape with Water,* involves producing vacuum-formed art products for display on the wall. Playfully futuristic in attitude yet unsettling for what it implies about the ecological health of the environment, the series featured coloured vinyl bags filled with water and air, vacuum-formed into landscapes.

Back in Alberta from 1986 to 1988, Baxter – who once was a forestry major with a substantial background in biology and zoology – focuses on food, its commercialization and contemporary society's relationship to it. The result is the unbelievably absurdist work, *Food For Thought* (1987, Walter Phillips Gallery), a ten-piece installation, which in theatrical fashion makes use of common food products to create: a bronzed, jogging mannequin stuffed with wieners, a sky raining wiener bombs, hands emerging from a coffin of salt and so on.

Addressing the connection between advertising and obesity, there is also *Slobkebob,* which makes reference to the couch-potato phenomena of popular culture. Consisting of an upholstered chair, TV, sliced bread rug and large-cross kebob loaded with more bread, this chemically preserved piece appeared a year later in the 1988 Winter Olympic exhibition, *Survey Alberta 88* (Alberta College of Art). Concerning the showcase itself, the two jurors accurately describe the piece as a "ubiquitous" collage and assemblage "characterized by an obsession with unconventional formats and materials." [128]

A decade later, Baxter returns to the province for a Banff Centre residency that coincides with an important survey of his landscape art since 1965. Organized by the Walter Phillips Gallery, *Iain Baxter: Landscape Works* (1999) traces his broad interaction with the land through mixed-media sculpture, video, works on paper, installation, photography and landscape lushly painted on assorted household appliances, focusing on the "the play between the pastoral and the urban" that has been a constant in his work.[129] Commenting on Baxter's exuberant diversity, longevity and experimental approach, and the relative lack of critical attention given to the artist, art critic David Garneau concludes: "Iain Baxter's career is due for a reassessment." [130]

Tim Watkins's art is also featured during the heady, frantic days of the 1988 Olympics. Appearing in *My Country is Winter* with *Thin Ice,* his kinetic installation Is, like Habermiller's frosty totem, aglow with beauty and menace. The piece is a symbolic version of nuclear winter with small rudimentary satellites moving above the top of a large globe covered in fractured blue plexiglass.

Utilizing household wares and industrial materials, the New York–based artist, when in Alberta, will combine his interest of nature, technology and kinetics to create large-scale sculptural environments as striking as Gisele Amantea's. "In installation [art], objects talk about something bigger than they are," [131] Watkins once explained in reference to a meditative work in Lethbridge, whose main components consist of seven mechanical and illuminated lotus blossoms that slowly open and close. In addition, a watery pool (cut from a large satellite dish) holds three floating glass balls while grass grows from wall-mounted discs of peat moss. Titled *somewhere i have never travelled* after a poem by e.e.cummings, this artificial indoor landscape at the Southern Alberta Art Gallery (1989) underlines Watkins's belief that technology can be put to better use than simply running amok over nature. "I see these flowers as trying to work back to nature in a positive sense and using technology in a constructive way to show the beauty of nature." [132]

This optimistic attitude, such a contrast to what generally prevails in contemporary art in regard to environmental themes, would surface again in *Various Things That Move* (1994, Paul Kuhn Fine Arts, Calgary). Featuring a mechanical Garden of Eden with a constructed view of the world that includes forms like the steel-ribboned *Breathing Trees* and the reproductively suggestive *The Dance,* the installation, according to *Artichoke* reviewer Diane Dickert, "inspires hope of a possible accord." [133] Nancy Tousley suggests the work "points to the way our culture sees nature, as something exotic and 'out there', not where we live." [134]

One of the great ironies about the critical and curatorial marginalization of printmaking in Canada is that in Alberta, several of its most challenging artists emerge from a graphic-arts background. Scratch the surface of many of Alberta's most adventuresome artists – John Will, Rita McKeough, Lyndal Osborne and so on – and a substantial involvement with printmaking is revealed. To that list, add the names **ALAN DUNNING** (1950, Teddington, Middlesex, England) and **JANET CARDIFF** (1957, Wingham, Ontario). Both major in printmaking in the master's program at the University of Alberta,[135] and while later distinguishing themselves in other media (photography, installation, audiovisual, computer and digital art), the printing press, and its broader associations with the written language and modern communication, is a subtle echo behind much of what these two artists create. It is present in Dunning's attempts to disrupt and decentre authoritative speech and in Cardiff's multi-media, auditory work[136] with their layered narratives. As Cardiff notes about her use of narrative: "[They] counteract the position of objectivity (especially in contemporary storytelling media) by presenting women's stories and voices in a way that investigates and forefronts the complexities of women's relationships to each other and the world." [137]

These two multi-media artists will develop into two of Alberta's most successful contemporary practitioners of any medium. In 1994, the Calgary-based Dunning, for instance, is only the second Albertan[138] ever to be granted a one-person exhibition (*City of Lights/Ville de lumieres*) at the National Gallery of Canada. Cardiff, meanwhile, receives the much-publicized $50,000 Millennium Prize for her choral sound sculpture, *Forty-Part Motet* (National Gallery of Canada). In the same year, she and her husband/partner George Bures Miller represent Canada at the world's top art showcase: the 2001 Venice Biennale. The first Alberta-based artists ever to receive this Canadian-sponsored honour, their twelve-minute digital video installation *The Paradise Institute* goes on to win the Biennale's Special Award and the Benesse Prize, both firsts for Canadian artists.

The breakdown of conventional language structures and the creation of new ones are present in the work of both Dunning and Cardiff, a practice that situates them squarely within the amorphous and international circle of postmodern art. This activity is influenced by the so-called decentering or 'deconstructive' strategies of French philosopher, Jacques Derrida. From the Derridian perspective on language, there are no real hierarchies, no overriding themes, no privileged points of view, no stable meanings and no hard answers. Instead, the work or text – or even the world, for that matter – is considered to be in a state of constant flux, unhinged and fluid, an ever-changing play of meanings and appearances where no text or work is ever completely enduring or authoritative.

Subsequently, critics have remarked about Cardiff's and Dunning's work in the following ways:

> Cardiff's sounds and images connect in a nonlinear way, like a dream that makes no sense, an effect she sets out to create,[139] ☙ Michael Litvin, 1994;

> By never defining for us the story, [Cardiff's *The Whispering Room*] might tell, this haunting [audio] installation shines light into the gap that lies between differing viewpoints, and separates event from memory. The tall speakers take on the presence of bodies, each whispering a different version of an elusive truth,[140] ☙ Kate Taylor, 1992;

> For Dunning, official structures such as social and political language and architecture, are barriers to break down. His method is to collect and

> recompose information – images and words – into small bites, or more appropriately, now that he generates all his imagery on a Macintosh II computer, into infinitesimal bytes,[141] ☙ Nancy Tousley. 1991;

> ...the common link in *Still Wet* is the deliberate withholding or deferring of meaning. The artists [such as Dunning] employ strategies of disruption, dislocation, displacement, intervention, parody and disguise to subvert clear complete readings. To some extent these strategies may be seen as reactions to the valorised modernism and regionalism that have historically dominated artistic production in Alberta, [142] ☙ Leslie Dawn, 1986.

Creating art that puts the impetus on the viewer to decipher what its meanings might be is not just decentering, it is confronting, especially in a visually challenged society used to asking the artist: "What is it about?" But, as Dunning states, "[I am] not interested in making meaning." [143]

Also brought into question is the concept of what an artist does: in this case it is assumed to be more conceptual than self-expressive, disconnected from, as Dunning describes it, "the bravura tradition of invention." [144] Rather than adhering to the romantic model of the artist-genius, the maker of precious art objects rendered unique by the very hand of the Master, Dunning utilizes appropriation and other art-making strategies thought to distance the artist from the work.[145]

Some early examples of his hands-off technique are Dunning's graphically impressive charcoal drawings (1986–87) executed on folded brown Kraft paper. To create these artworks, Dunning imposed a systematic process that enabled him to remain unaware of what the drawing would look like until it was finished. Featured in *Scale: Drawings by Therese Bolliger, Alan Dunning and Tonie Leshyk,* curator Valerie Greenfield commented of the work, " [Their overly large] size alters the preconception of drawings as an individual work of art presenting instead almost an environment, an installation." [146]

Later describing his process-oriented work as open, Tousley observes: "Dunning collapses the author's role into the role of the reader and diminishes the omniscient, authoritative, authorial voice that knows in advance the text's outcome. Dunning knows in advance only the formal shape that the text will take, be it an installation or book." [147]

Dunning, who left Wales in 1980 to instruct at the Alberta College of Art, emerges by the early 1990s as a leading figure in Canadian installation art. Not only is he prolific, producing fifteen works and seven accompanying artist books between 1986–1994, he is astonishing as well: his site-specific manifestations a "spectacle of labour and visual stimuli, but with a twist."[148] Obsessive, encyclopedic, appropriated, and yet elegantly rendered with the most labour-intensive means. Physically, his installations take on an all-encompassing form, composed of large amounts of printed information applied in patterns to the walls, wrapping around the room. Containing repetitive units of found images, iconic symbols, half-tone reproductions of magazine photographs, photocopied text, Letraset typeface, and by 1990, computer-generated words and phrases, the flow of this information is always deliberately "undeterred by doorways and corners ... so that the entire room is encased."[149] Randomly appropriated from books, magazines, printed media and later from a computer used to manipulate material,[150] the information assembled for the seminal *Billy Bud's Stammer*[151] (1988) consists of 600 silkscreen images neatly displayed around-the-room in a hand-painted grid; *Greenhouse*[152] (1989) is composed of 50,000 photocopied disparate words, while in the script-to-visual *Elision*[153] (1992); dressmaker pins daintily secure 2,000 Letraset-like letters to the wall. No wonder one critic felt compelled to observe (while standing in the midst of one of these labour-intensive, panoramic collages): "[The work is] self-effacing, the artist seeks no authoritative voice, but disappears behind the work."[154] Perhaps best described as "babble" or "textual stew," these works suggest that Dunning's efforts might be a larger metaphor for the fragmentation of society and the diminishing of various hierarchies, including the charismatic, egocentric world of the celebrated male artist.

However, for all of its attempts at hastening the death of the author, Dunning's work includes highly traditional elements. The son of a printer and a translator, endowed with the notion of a job well done, the artist's affinity for labour-intensive, incremental action and small repetitive gestures – such as cutting, pasting, pinning and so on – reflects not only his regard for the craft traditions but also the belief that there is value in all types of work, no matter how lacking in societal status. The act of setting text on walls with his team of volunteers allies him (however momentarily) with the activity of a hands-on factory worker or, at the other end of the spectrum, a quilter. The making of art thus becomes neither a one-man show nor the expression of grand egocentric gestures, like those exhibited by such modern masters as Van Gogh, Picasso and Jackson Pollock. Instead, Dunning is a different kind of artist, not only through his conceptual concerns, but also through his methods, which honour the traditions of manual labour and co-operation.[155] Without being trivial, Dunning could be said to embody a new/old model of the artist.

By 1995, a major shift is underway in Dunning's practice that intersects more directly with cyberspace and the two new art kids on the block: virtual reality and the Internet. Invited to participate in *The Digital Village* at the Art Gallery (University of Maryland, College Park), Dunning labours on an interactive computer program that, among other things, incorporates the online suggestions of others in the design and construction of a virtual metropolis entitled *Lost Dimension: An Internet City.* At a moment in the twentieth century when innovative technology is posited to be at the centre of a new art frontier, an international event like *The Digital Village* gives the artist an opportunity to connect with this fast-developing field. Early in 1996, a large body of work entitled *Einstein's Brain* commences. Paul Woodrow, one of the artists who collaborates on the project, describes it as "an extension of the numerous immersive, site-specific and ephemeral installations [Dunning] has made since 1987."[156] With its manipulation of the real and the unreal, Dunning would also comment: "There are some ways in which we can trust our senses and others in which we can't."[157]

Throughout the latter 1990s, the Dunning/Woodrow virtual-reality adventure takes on several guises, including the time-based work *The Fall*[158] (1997), in which a gushing, digital waterfall and a human brain are projected opposite from each other. Explains Tousley: "When a viewer interacts by touching areas of the brain, images begin to emerge from the shifting flow, pointing to the fluid, contingent nature of perception, the faculty with which we navigate the world."[159]

Navigation and the manipulation of perception are themes also very much at the heart of Janet Cardiff's celebrated interactive audio walks (1991–). Made with the assistance of George Bures Miller,[160] these works often provoke strong responses from listeners:

> As in all Cardiff's pieces, reality and fiction are confounded, large holes of speculation left agape, our foothold never secure. And yet, when you experience [on a headset] one of her works, you go with it, body snatched by her seductive voice and dreamy pace,[161] ❧ Sarah Millroy, 1998;

Her fictious monologue [*Forest Walk*] was so startling that people left the walk feeling anxious and lost. Cardiff had figured out a way to jar her audience's sense of reality,[162] ☙ Sarah Borins, 2001.

A more surreal variation on the museum acoustic-guide tour, a Cardiff encounter can involve a thirteen-minute audio stroll through the tranquil grounds of a museum, accompanied by a running narrative that goes "a fire crackles, a helicopter hovers overhead, someone runs up from behind and continues, passing by. . . . "[163] or the piece might be a thirty-nine-minute scripted journey that begins inside a library, continues through a circuit of busy city streets as "here and there, a detective mystery leaks into the walk."[164] Recorded in biaural audio – which replicates, hyper-realistically, three-dimensional sound – these commissioned, time-based, site-specific tours, according to Glenn D. Lowry, director of New York's Museum of Modern Art "made [a] distinctive mark on the field of contemporary art practice in the second half of the 1990s."[165]

Not only did Cardiff leave her sonic "footprint" in such disparate locations as Humlebaek (Denmark), Munster (Germany), Rome, Sao Paulo (Brazil), Pittsburgh, London (England) and San Francisco, but at the prestigious New York institution itself, where, as Glenn Lowry recalls, "Donning a headset and Discman, participants were guided by Cardiff's suave and soothing voice, suggestive of dream-walking in an unusual and unconventional tour of our [MOMA's] collection."[166]

One of few artists based in Alberta to ever make a serious ripple within the competitive, art-choked confines of New York, Cardiff's use of auditory stimulation dates back to the mid-80s, first used in installation, as in the 1988 audiovisual work *Tabl'eau,*[167] and then on its own, beginning at The Banff Centre for the Arts where, during a residency, her digitally recorded, time-based *Forest Walk* (1991) emerged.

Writing in 1995 that, "Sound can hit the body like a blow or caress it like a kiss,"[168] central to her handling of sound is the layering of audio-based material that, while not logically sequential, is still story-like in impact. Her material can include snippets of stories – detective and science fiction are a favourite source – film clips, provocative dialogue – often delivered by the artist – music, and sound effects ranging from the banal to the sensational. This layering – as is often pointed out – harkens back to Cardiff's earlier work as a printmaker where, influenced by the more experimental photo-based work of the printmaking department at Edmonton's University of Alberta, her large-scale silkscreen images incorporated pictures taken from detective magazines, television and film noir movies: "Conceptually, I was doing the same thing in the eighties that I am now: mixing, layering ideas, making narrative juxtapositions – only I was doing it visually." [169]

Also characteristic of that period but more pertinent to her sound-based work of the nineties is the artist's acknowledged penchant for voyeurism.[170] Even in sound pieces that don't require the wearing of a headset, the viewer/listener is transformed into an interloper: hearing things that can be uplifting, as in the deconstructed choral work *Forty-Part Motet* where "you eavesdrop on each [singer] individually," [171] or as is more often the case, hearing things that have overtones of the sexual and the titillating, as in the acclaimed table/speaker installation, *To Touch* (1993). Starring an old wooden worktable that has been wired underneath, *To Touch* creates an interactive sound space that reacts to the movements of the listener. By touching different parts of the table, the room is filled with different sound bites of a couple whispering intimately: "I want you to touch me ... your skin's so soft ... Touch me, I want to hear the memories.... " [172]

According to the artist, this interest in the erotic, especially as it is expressed by a woman, "may also be a reaction to art history and to our culture's obsession with male desire. Think of analyzing Jackson Pollock – ideas of virility, and genius related to virility. In my pieces, it's the woman's voice that bosses you around, the voice of authority. You can be directed left or right. But also, there's an edge to it, a sense of insecurity and seduction, an enticement. I am quite interested in sexuality that has this edge of danger to it. I think a lot of people are." [173]

This kind of thinking about gender also extends to her time-based audio walks. In *The Missing Voice (Case Study B)*, for instance, Cardiff – playing the fictious role of "Janet" – describes how a character "grabs me from behind, his hand over my mouth. I bite his fingers and hit him in the ribs.... " [174]

With or without headsets, the whole notion of being made a witness or a third party to what is critically perceived as transgressive, is bound to provoke questions. Questions, for one, about why Cardiff goes to such lengths to implicate or corral the viewer. One idea proposed by Carolyn Christov-Bakargiev, who curates a major travelling survey[175] (2001) of the artist's work for New York and international audiences, is that while Cardiff is offering the viewer an "active experience," [176] she is also taking control: "This duality points to the underlying ambiguity of our technological society,"[177] where not only are we in constant flux between controlling and being controlled by technology, but where the difference between the real and the mediated experience is hopelessly blurred.

In the same year as the international survey, Cardiff and Miller orchestrate *The Paradise Institute,* their most immersive environment to date. Their intention, (as I interpret it), is to make the engagement with the filmic an all-enveloping experience. Not only is the viewer/listener required to wear a headset – as was not the case with their previous sensation, *The Dark Pool*[178] – but also to take a seat in the specially constructed movie theatre that is large enough to accommodate a small group of viewers at the back but is miniaturized in the front. "A film house that Lewis Carroll might have built,"[179]remarked one participant. Once seated, the viewer is exposed to a soundscape and a twelve-minute film that ends with a vividly staged house burning. Edmonton artist Lyndal Osborne, a print instructor at Cardiff's alma mater, later describes the experience as "mesmerizing, visually and aurally ... the most incredible experience of being totally in the minute; all of your senses were tingling."[180]

Not reticent about comparing the impact of their time-based work to entertainment,[181] the couple's open attitude to its cross-over potential is, in the context of advanced art-making in Canada, unusual and provocative. At the end of the twentieth century, their multi-layered synthesis of mediated sound and sight for an international audience proves to be, with "some lucky breaks,"[182] comments Cardiff, "the right art at the right time."[183]

During the period that Cardiff and Miller are getting it right, the couple lives in Lethbridge where, from 1988 to 2000, Cardiff teaches photography and new media in the university's art department. Referring to the community of 68,000 as a supportive place where "you can get a lot of work done,"[184] this sentiment is echoed as well by her fellow Lethbridge innovator and colleague **DAVID HOFFOS** (1966, Montreal, Quebec).[185]

"[As a teenager], I grew up in a big city [Sydney, Australia]," he recalls, "It's a tremendous relief to be away from all that [plus] the rent is cheaper."[186] A 1994 BFA graduate from the University of Lethbridge, Hoffos had already demonstrated an acumen for scrounged and cheaply assembled, time-based, viewer-activated work, that, while concerned with perception, illusion and simulation, was also fun to look at. In *Public*[187] (1992), for instance, which was installed in a Lethbridge storefront window, when pedestrians activated the electronic sensor at night, what suddenly appeared was a film loop of a

1950s family dinner scene projected onto a 3-D cut-out construction made of translucent mylar. The cut-out shapes made the figures look three-dimensional, turning the piece into a ghostly apparition in the darkness.

Fun is not an attribute normally associated with advanced art-making, but in Hoffos's case, it seems justifiably earned given the artist's experimentation with older forms of optical effects – phantasmagoria, kaleidoscope, zoatrope, stereoscope, magic lanterns – and their more popular cousin, film. As curator Katherine Ylitalo enthused a few years after the artist's graduation: "Seen in Alberta, Ontario and soon in Spain, his magical illusions/installations amaze and delight. As if in a time machine, we are transported to the early days of animation and cinematography. You can see how things work but gladly suspend disbelief." [188]

With an inclination for simulating the imagery, set designs and atmosphere of older movies – horror, sci-fi and romance – Hoffos generates, from the mid-1990s on, two distinctive types of time-based work. First, the smaller, self-contained pieces, including the enchanting time-lapse *Still Life with Rotting Fruit* (displayed at the *1996 Alberta Biennial*) and the nocturnal *Vanity*[189] (1997), utilize such things as a mirror reflection of a nursery in three dimensions, room-size installations of sound, music and video projections illuminating a miniaturized film set, freestanding cut-outs of spectators and strategically placed monitors. Second, as the artist grows more ambitious, wide-screen devices such as the self-invented 'telerama' (*Catastrophe,*[190] 1998) and cyclorama (*Another City,*[191] 1999) appear in his work.

Writes Nancy Tousley in her in-depth, aptly titled "David Hoffos: The Lethbridge Illusionist and His Cinema of Attractions:" "Each of these illusions speaks with its own rhetoric: the giant screen makes a sweeping public address, the miniature appeals to fantasy and to introspection, the near life-size cut-out figure projections boast of an out-and-out trick." [192]

Enticed to witness, for instance, the post-disaster remains of a suburban neighbourhood in miniature and other calamities in *Catastrophe,* or a futuristic metropolis where couples smooch and cars fly by as in *Another City,* the viewer is confronted with an ingenious handling of inexpensive materials and garage-sale electronics that with a healthy application of duct tape can best be described as home-tech.

Of this specialist in high artifice and mischievous play, where "every trick up his sleeve is aimed at constructing a medium-aware spectator," Tousley concludes, "Each of Hoffos's installations can be understood as an allegory of spectatorship, a contemporary kind of quest in which the spectator enters the spectacle, becomes enthralled by it, interacts with it, and is released from its spell. The goal of the quest is knowledge of our relationship to the world."[193]

ELIZABETH LEMOINE (1958, Toronto, Ontario) is also, in her own right, a specialist in the postmodern practice of high artifice. Her artifice, though, is not dependent on digital or electronically generated, time-based work as seen in the cases of Cardiff/Miller and Hoffos. With a strong affinity for sculpture, enriched by earlier employment in costumes and props – Stratford Festival, National Ballet of Canada, Canadian Opera Company – her study of jewellery and metalsmithing (Sheridan College, Mississauga, Ontario), and an honours diploma in sculpture and drawing (Alberta College of Art), LeMoine is one of the emerging stars of mixed-media art in the early 1990s, along with Faye HeavyShield. In addition, there is Peter von Tiesenhausen from northern Alberta, who is starting to explore site-specific installation with his large willow constructions. In a way, all three are outsiders to the Albertan scene: Heavyshield as First Nations (Kainai), von Tiesenhausen for being located in the real hinterland, and LeMoine for having a background as Toronto theatre artist. These identities influence the conceptual and aesthetic content of their art. For LeMoine, this initially entails a serious engagement with seventeenth- and eighteenth-century European enlightenment history and a sense of design derived from her work in the theatre. For instance, there is her stately, life-size plaster cast of a *Window, Hampton Court Palace*[194] (1989) and the stucco mouldings, laurel wreaths, plaster foliage and other decorative elements of *Salle de Guerre* (1990): the latter specially installed in a historic Calgary building dedicated to the memory of World War I. Located inside the neo-classical Muttart Art Gallery[195] (Calgary), the impressive *Salle de Geurre* "not only exposes the authority within the language of architecture," suggests curator Franklyn Heisler, "but also reveals the powerful presence and sense of authority objects themselves may have."[196]

Then, in the midst of pursuing a master's in fine art at Goldsmiths' College (1993–95, London, England), LeMoine dramatically downsizes the physical dimensions of her art and, with the encouragement of her instructors, moves away from big works about big issues like power and authority. This change leaves her Canadian audience surprised but intrigued about how she will tackle a different version of history: one connected with the personal, the everyday, and the particular.

"How is one to interpret these elaborate miniatures of seemingly irrelevant objects [i.e. a boat, a chair, a suitcase, a pencil and clothing] strewn about the exhibition space?" [197] asks one Calgary-based writer. While another one in Toronto comments: "It's as if the artist isn't quite sure whether she wants anyone to get a good look at her art . . . but once discovered, the discrete objects reveal themselves as utterly breathtaking." [198]

LeMoine herself states, "There are whole areas of experience that aren't addressed by most art. I model insignificant things, the kind of images you have at the back of your mind. Smallness can lead you into that overlooked mental space. . . . I used to make huge art [in Calgary]. I was trying to play the boys' game by the boys' rules, rules that were nothing to do with me."

None of the objects LeMoine fashions are perfect miniature reproductions though. Instead she transforms mundane objects, like a wine cork carved into a statue of the Virgin Mary, a clear plastic bag that serves as the fabric for a Barbie-sized Victorian dress and a wooden match that has been transformed into a tiny pencil. Many of her later pieces – dresses, bras, handbags – quietly celebrate "quasi-taboo areas of femininity; the things that feminism has told us we must discard." [199]

Around the same time, at a workshop in England's neo-gothic Braziers Park, the artist fashions tiny crowns out of candy wrappers and attaches them with wire to dozens of dried poppy heads still standing in the garden. According to a London-based writer, "Her point is not to reproduce the here and now, but to produce objects that look like memories feel: insubstantial, out of scale, brightly lit and slightly scary." [200]

Whether LeMoine's miniatures are created in response to a specific site or for a gallery exhibition, whether making them as one-of-a-kind objects or producing affordable multiples,[201] their impact is the same. As Amy Gogarty suggests, they enact art's power to produce meaning and context "with the most slender resources." [202] They are masterful works indeed.

GARRY WILLIAMS (1956–2005, Calgary, Alberta) also entered the field of installation art with a sculptural background; in his case, award-winning[203] ceramic figurative art that concentrated on personal, socio-cultural and environmental subjects. Two examples from this early period (1979–1988) include a realistic bust of a Chinese railway worker (*C.P.R. Coolie,* 1980) and a standing wolf figure symbolizing protection (*A Den of Points to Build On,* 1985). Totally different in style, both appear, respectively, as the cover art for the exhibition catalogues: *Alberta Clay Comes of Age*[204] (1980) and *Handspirits*[205] (1985).

With ceramics as the predominant element, Williams's installations are unique to the province. A graduate of the Alberta College of Art (1978, ceramics major) with an MFA (1990) from the Nova Scotia College of Art and Design, by the mid-1990s he has established himself at the forefront of his medium, straddling the ceramics/contemporary art divide like no one else.

A few years later, Williams is chosen as one of four artists[206] deemed postmodern enough in attitude to create a new work for the pro-installation exhibition *Clay Between My Fingers* (1993, Walter Phillips Gallery, Banff Centre). Of its deconstructive mission and its challenge to ceramic purity, critic and artist Amy Gogarty observes: "Common to all works in the gallery are the artists' use of space, the engagement with contemporary ideas that extend beyond issues specific to ceramics, and the use of memory, culture, history and a range of materials to make their point. All of which is to say that in this work, clay is a non-issue … [but] clay is [also] never apologized for – in Williams's work, particularly, it is an essential component to the meaning but it never confines or restricts the work."[207]

The installation Gogarty is referring to is the class-conscious *Gold Standard,* featuring his own replicas of eighteenth-century Wedgewood vases and Mexican earthenware. Like Williams's earlier *Same Song, Different Chorus,* the artist wants people to come into a particular space and walk around the environment he has created with these objects. Arranged within each installation is the noticeable presence of natural and living things: plucked stalks of Alberta rye fill sixty Mexican olla pots (*Gold Standard);* clay wall sconces are planted with hothouse flowers (*Same Song, Different Chorus*); as well as, in some instances, the unexpected inclusion of manufactured objects sucha as the electric razors that buzz from inside twelve large terracotta cone-shaped pots with beeswax tops (*Same Song, Different Chorus*). Of these unusual insertions: "I intend the work to metaphorically transcend the material's and/or object's most literal interpretations."[208]

Working to create more of an experience than a display of objects per se, artist and curator Les Manning suggests that while Williams's ceramics in an installation context may look radically new, there is actually a "natural affinity" between the two. Writing for the group exhibition, *Insideout,* he notes, "One way or another, ceramics have enveloped mankind for centuries as shelter and in art. Adobe architecture in life and sarcophagi in death are only the beginnings of the extended human experience with a clay environment."[209]

In Williams's environments, which have addressed ecological issues (*In the Same Breath, Same Song, Different Chorus, Cathedrals,*[210] *Genesis*[211]), the historic role of pottery as an economic and cultural signifier (*Gold Standard*), and male identity, there's no single meaning to a work. According to the artist, it's all very subjective, with specific objects and materials leading people to make their own connections. In addition to the conceptual, he seeks "a seductive, traditional artistic presentation that relies heavily on aesthetic pleasure."[212]

Thus, in *Cathedrals* (Southern Alberta Art Gallery, 1993), the arched windows and church-like setting of the second-floor gallery are elegantly echoed in the work's geometric arrangement. Muses John Stocking: "Cathedrals can be made of stone and glass; but the most beautiful cathedrals I have worshipped in were made of giant coastal redwood trees, which seemed to be holding up the vaulting of the open sky. The hand made terra-cotta pots in Garry Williams's installation, spaced in a pattern of random selection on the red and white stone grid, hold fragile little trees which could either become cathedrals, or much more likely, cardboard boxes and condominiums."[213]

Near the end of the decade, Williams returns to sculpting the figure, this time inspired by the tabletop porcelain figurines of eighteenth-century Europe. Originally made to represent and mythologize different aspects of life and classes of society, the artist revives this form of expression for the purpose of reinterpreting contemporary male roles. Fashioning his modern men out of porcelain, and purposely without clothes, their resemblance to the classical male nudes of antiquity is striking and ironic. First displayed in a courtyard setting[214] for the ceramic installation show *Insideout,* the twelve male statues and their poses speak symbolically of an age when masculinity is, as the artist characterizes it, in a state of flux. Even the "corporate warrior [who contemplates] strategies in brogues and socks"[215] comes with just one wing attached to his back and the uncertain title of *Fallen Angel.*

One of nine artists highlighted by Les Graff in a 1999 *AlbertaViews* article surveying the development of Alberta ceramics, post World War II, the artist/instructor is singled out for his move to installation and how "it has increased his range of materials and the complexity of the relationships among different pieces. [Williams's] use of myth, complex techniques and the sheer scale of his work make it fantastical."[216]

❧ ❧ ❧

Shelley Ouellet's life is a work of art. Philosophically a painter but technically a mixed-media installation artist, she lives and communicates as a creative person involved with the community she supports and believes in,[217] ❧ Anne Severson, 2000.

This selective survey of installation art in Alberta concludes with **SHELLEY OUELLET** (1964, Edmonton, Alberta) who graduates from the University of Calgary with a BFA in painting and printmaking (1991). A student of John Will, she emerges in the mid-1990s as a particularly fresh voice reflecting a set of tendencies common to a certain sector of the Alberta community: obsessive, materially rich, systematic, irreverent, hybridized, process-oriented, labour-intensive and inflected with humour.

In addition, Ouellet is as vital a connection to end-of-century Alberta as John Hall/Ron Moppett or Sylvain Voyer/Harry Savage were to their respective communities of Calgary and Edmonton at the beginning of the post-1970 period. Once makers of art-of-the-moment, their art-scene activism furthered an already established tradition[218] that Ouellet will continue to build on. As an example, from 1991–95 she serves as the director of the artist-run Stride Gallery, and in 1996 establishes the online vanitygallery.com, featuring Arlene Stamp, Chris Cran, Marc Hutchinson, Vera Gartley, herself and others. Aside from activism, there is also evident in Ouellet's practice a cross-generational desire "to extract [and] perhaps salvage from everyday life the material of art."[219] Hence Ouellet's totally artificial notion of nature (*Entomology*,[220] 1994), her Warholesque but digitalized nod to the omnipresent celebrity (*The Silver Screen* series,[221] 1996–1999), and her transformation of the nineteenth-century landscape into a pixilated field of luminescent bead craft (*Wish You Were Here,*[222] 2001–2002).

Oullete's attitude towards her rubbery, shiny and glittery art also sets her apart. Spurred on by the belief that art should be made for short attention spans and, above all, with "an awareness of spectacle,"[223] Ouellet's sense of showmanship will be highly foreign to a generation past. As well, despite being assembled with the help of sophisticated computer drawings and an army of well-organized volunteers (to string beads and so on), her finished product is also nothing short of gloriously absurd. In another context, one could consider her pieces the work of a hobbyist gone mad. For instance: her

8 × 8 × 14-foot suspended three-dimensional super-bug in *Entomology* is comprised of 10,000 dime-store rubber insects hung on strands of fishing line; *Rita Hayworth* of *The Silver Screen* series is a floor-to-ceiling pixilated image made of shimmering black-and-white sequins pinned to the wall in the thousands; and *Wish You Were Here (detail, Niagara Falls),* based on a 1857 painting of the spectacular site by American Frederic Edwin Church, is a monumental curtain of white, black and crystal beads suspended on 366 strands of silver wire.

Writing in 1996 as a participant of the first *Alberta Biennial of Contemporary Art,* where the glittering *Rita Hayworth* stole the show, Ouellet explained to the audience, "I combine toys, baubles, trinkets, sequins, pins, throw-ways, and anything I can amass a wealth of, with a mind-numbingly, labour-intensive process ... *Rita Hayworth* would have to be described as the evening wear line of my installations to date." [224]

Initially inspired by her own participation in the audience-interactive opening ceremonies for the 1988 Calgary Winter Olympics, of which she remembered "an incredible sense of magic was evoked from the images created by an audience of thousands wearing silly capes," [225] Ouellet's digital-art productions are planned and mapped out by computer and then created with dazzling, optical effects. In 1999, the Hollywood actress shows up again in the stellar Edmonton group show *Shiny* (Latitude 53), with the added razzle-dazzle of *9 Marilyns* (1999): pixilated representations of the Hollywood screen goddess, illuminated in Lite-Brite screens. Commenting on the "belligerent materiality, superficiality and wilful literalness" [226] of the exhibit's deliberately shiny artwork, essayist Maureen Fenniak says, "In *Shiny,* the artist's role as 'creator' of meaning is transformed into one of 'producer' of novel forms and indeterminable intent. The shiny object refuses to be pinned down, conceptually constrained, and so obstructs the quest for a deeper meaning than the surface reading." [227] In response, curator David LaRiviere asks, "The burning question is no longer 'what needs to be subverted [by contemporary art]?' but 'how can we reinvest the beleaguered shiny object with a genuine sense of wonder?'" [228]

Assisting Ouellet in this task are dozens of volunteers who are noted by name in the exhibition material. Their aid is solicited because of the magnitude of the task and, according to curator Katherine Ylitalo, because Ouellet is seeking an alternative to the paradigm of the male genius artist eschewing help or influence from others. As Ylitalo outlined in the seminal

Copy exhibition, "Knowledge, participation, anticipation and ownership are shared with a large circle of people. Ouellet's function as an artist is simply to develop the idea and to orchestrate the process."[229]

This sharing of authorship and mastery, which on the one hand is part of the larger feminist discourse in the Albertan community, is also linked by Ylitalo to the diminishment of such concepts as creativity and originality, first explored in Walter Benjamin's much-quoted article, "Art in the Age of Mechanical Reproduction" (1935). Stating that the discussion around the value of the original versus the replica has become more complex than in Benjamin's time, she suggests that the four artists in *Copy* offer a solution to the puzzle: "to copy a copy and make an original."[230] In other words, exploit and reconfigure what is already out there in our picture-full, image-saturated era. Something Ouellet has done in such projects as *The Silver Screen* series where, for instance, her images of Hayworth, Monroe, Brando, Harlow, Hepburn and LeMarr are taken from such popular-culture sources as magazines and advertising. Even the multicoloured superbug of *Entomology* is based on Ouellet's notion that nature lies somewhere between Godzilla movies and the nature worship of the Sierra Club.[231]

Nothing is drawn from real-life observation. Instead, everything is sourced from an already existing bank of images created and spewed out every day by films, art, photography, magazines, books, television and other media. By using computer technology to re-represent what has already been produced, Ouellet, in her practice of mixed-media installation, is indeed more of an image maker than a creator of an experiential environment. Her efforts, instead, intersect with many of the artists discussed in the upcoming chapter: Image Makers.

chapter nineteen

More on the Three-Dimensional Front

If THE PRECEDING TWO CHAPTERS are any testament to the abundance of the three-dimensional in contemporary Alberta, the following discussion on sculptural and ceramic-based art is yet further elaboration on what is a subtle but major shift during the post-1970 period. In no substantial way has this shift been acknowledged or accounted for, but – along with the development of an alternative art scene and the professionalization of the visual arts in the contemporary era – here is a many-tentacled story about how three-dimensional artmaking came into its own. It can no longer be considered the smaller or undeveloped sibling in the province.

Three sculptors – known and recognized in the communities of Lethbridge, Edmonton and Calgary, respectively – whose individual practices cover all or nearly all of the entire 30-year span of this book are ADRIAN COOKE (1948, Folkestone, Kent, England), TOMMIE GALLIE (1946, Halifax, Nova Scotia) and **RON KOSTYNIUK** (1941, Wakaw, Saskatchewan). Influenced by certain international art movements of the past (constructivism for Kostyniuk, post-minimalism for Cooke and Gallie), each one's art tends to stand on its own individual merit, apart from other sculptural activity in the province.

This autonomous attitude is especially evident in the constructed wood, Plexiglas and, more recently, aluminium reliefs of Ron Kostyniuk who, as the art critic/academic Virgil Hammock[1] observes, has developed a richer, more expansive response to the spare, abstract geometric tradition of constructivism.[2] This achievement, coupled with his exploration of regional subject matter (nature and the rural landscape), has not always engendered a receptive response. Hammock explains: "In the 60s and 70s, particularly in Alberta, a form of painterly modernism held sway, and more recently, post-modernism ruled the day. There was little appreciation of the jewel-like constructivist works of an artist like Ron. His [wall relief] works were dismissed by many artists and critics around him as being mere 'craft' or old hat and lacking in new ideas."[3]

Kostyniuk's first works in the constructivist idiom – a distinct and independent art form with a history reaching back to the first quarter of the twentieth century and the Russian avant-garde (Vladimir Tatlin) – date back to 1963, after he came in contact with Eli Bornstein ("Canada's best known contructivist artist"[4]) at the University of Saskatchewan in Saskatoon.[5] At the time, Kostyniuk was pursuing a career in biology and education; he earned a master's of science from the University of Wisconsin in 1970. The following year, though, he also obtained a master's of fine arts from Wisconsin[6] and, not long after that, a teaching position at University of Calgary's Department of Art (1971).

Thus, in the end it was art that prevailed as Kostyniuk's profession, especially the constructed relief, which will serve as a source of artistic expression and scholarly investigation. (An example of the latter is his monograph, *The Evolution of the Constructed Relief 1913–1979* and accompanying exhibition that tours across Canada in 1979.) In addition, a role will be found for his lifelong interest in the natural sciences; his painted geometric artworks described as "visual analogies to Nature's created forms."[7] Or, as writer/curator Kathryn Burns writes: "He sees the creation of his art as an extension of his technical understanding of his world transposed into coloured geometric form."[8]

Pauline Lindland, curator of the Petro-Canada Exhibition Gallery in Calgary, will later describe Kostyniuk's abstract efforts – with their hard edges, sharp colours and pristine finish – as "stunning metaphors of nature" that, in spite of their highly formal and rigorous appearance, rely on the artist's "intuitive sensibility."[9] Another observer will comment on how the reliefs, assembled from precisely cut-out shapes, "seem to jump off the wall to engage the viewer."[10]

Kostyniuk creates in series, each with a specific theme. In the early 1970s, for instance, the triangular *Winged Form Series* is inspired by wing of the moth and the butterfly. Midway through that decade, the mosaic-like *Crystalline Series* evolves from a childhood fascination for rock crystals. And – almost unavoidably for an artist raised in a small prairie community – at the beginning of the 1980s, the *Horizon Series* relates abstractly to the horizontal character of that environment.

Around the time Kostyniuk is appointed a full professor at the U of C in 1984, his artwork begins to change considerably in appearance and temperament. Featuring the incorporation of curvilinear shapes – inescapable references to architectural forms and the figure; more varied materials (including aluminium piping, wooden spheres and decorative metal screening); and, last but not least, a more flexible format that could be freestanding, involve negative space and be organized into sections, these developments are later summed up in his seminal *Neo-Constructions 1983–1991* exhibit at Calgary's Muttart Art Gallery. In Virgil Hammock's opinion, Kostyniuk had "succeeded in putting a personal face to his brand of constructivism."[11]

Evoking some of the zeitgeistal energy of postmodern industrial design and architecture, Kostyniuk's work is now more lighthearted and whimsical, with a strong sense of play. The references in the artwork can be surprisingly literal, as they are in his large-scale 1989 commission for Calgary's Amoco Building. Titled *Memories,* the free standing (90″ × 204″ × 24″) enamel-on-aluminium work contains several grain-elevator forms of differing sizes and simplification. A single outhouse also inhabits the right end of the brightly coloured structure that stretches across the floor like a freestanding altarpiece in several sections.

Group of Seven artist A.Y. Jackson once compared the towering structure of the grain elevator to the French cathedral. In 1997, with *The Saskatchewan Road Map Series,* Kostyniuk, too, draws a parallel between the physical and symbolic impact of the grain elevator on the Alberta landscape and that of the spired cathedrals on the European countryside. (A timely gesture, considering how the 1990s will be known as the decade when this distinctive sentinel is condemned to disappear from western Canada.) In works including *Dying Embers* (1998) and *Every Kingdom Had One* (1998), there is the suggestion of loss, of places devoid of these once-important markers of community.

Neo-Constructions, a hybrid sitting somewhere between a painting or a relief or a sculpture,[12] also addressed another enthusiasm of Kostyniuk's – art and modern architecture. Early on in this emerging body of work, there is the futuristic *Tatlin* triptych (1983) and the modernist *Pour Henri et Barbara,* (1986) with its elegant granite, marble and found stone shapes, part of the tribute to British sculptors Henry Moore and Barbara Hepworth. A year later comes the acknowledgement to the architectural legacies of Mies van der Rohe and the visionary Italian, Paolo Solari, in the symbolically rich *For Mies and Paolo.* Presented as a triptych that contains small freestanding models of simplified buildings and other forms, this relief appears in *Alberta Sculpture Survey 89* at Calgary's Triangle Gallery of Visual Arts. (This forty-two-piece survey, featuring thirty-nine artists from across Alberta in all media including ceramics and glass will be the only exhibition of its kind ever held in the province between 1970 and 2000. It reflected not only some of the diverse energies in three-dimensional art-making, but also the ambition of the two-year-old Triangle Gallery to act, within its confined space,[13] as the public art gallery Calgary never had – and, as it turned out, would not have in the twentieth century.)

Tommie Gallie and Adrian Cooke were also represented in Survey 89, with *Spilt Bow* (1988) and *Sentinel* (1985), respectively. Both are fabricated from wood and this material, more common to contemporary sculpture in the 1970s,[14] is one that both artists will employ steadily after postgraduate study in Edmonton (Gallie[15]) and New York (Cooke[16]). According to the Edmonton-based Gallie, who moves back and forth between the making of sculptural objects (freestanding and wall reliefs) and site-specific installations: "Wood has been my choice of material in most cases, as it's warm in both colour and connotation, as well as being flexible and easily manipulated."[17] In addition, as in his *Compression* pieces of the early 1980s, the wood is often worked in such a way that nails are not required.

This materialist focus would seem to put Gallie squarely in the modernist camp which, at a certain point in Edmonton's particular history, would seem to have been a good place to be artistically, but instead Gallie – along with others such as Cherie Moses, Jim Davies and good friend Robert Iveson – will find himself profiled by *Vanguard* magazine in 1984[18] as part of the "underside" of Edmonton's much-publicized, late-modernist art scene. Writing about Iveson and Gallie, Edmonton art critic/curator Liz Wylie commented: "Anywhere else their site-specific pieces (most often in wood) would not be thought of as far out of the ordinary. In Edmonton, however, they stand out like sore thumbs."[19] An ironic position for the two artists to be in, considering how deliberately inconspicuous their art is at the time. Their work, with its modest and carefully crafted references to the everyday world, is intended to blend in or complement its surroundings rather than intrude, challenge or stand provocatively apart.

In relation to Gallie, this more informal, give-and-take stance towards sculpture is derived from what curator Elizabeth Kidd emphasizes as "[an] interest in both the art process and the art object."[20] Or, as the sculptor explains it: "the making of art is much more enriching than just making [singular]objects."[21] This sentiment of Gallie's is thoroughly expressed in 1981, when wooden timbers and wooden dowelling are cut and wedged by him into the doors, room corners and niches of the Ring House Gallery, located in a historic Edwardian home on the campus of the University of Alberta. Titled *In Place,* this contemporary nod to the early Russian avant-garde, Tatlin and Rodchenko[22] will be Gallie's most publicly controversial project until a decade later, when the large-timbered *Hidden Charms* (1991) is installed as an abstract work of art above a new underground pedway.[23] (It's also the first site-specific work commissioned under Edmonton's "Per Cent for Art" program.)

Adds Kidd: "Tommie Gallie calls himself a post-minimalist. He is still interested in the intellectual investigation of such 1960s minimalist sculptors as Carl Andre and Donald Judd, who attempted to simplify the form of art object to its essential limits of space and material. Gallie, however, is less analytical in his approach and employs natural materials that are more connected to the senses than to the mind."[24]

This connection will be lyrically exploited in *Grace Under Pressure* (1988, Latitude 53), at the time the largest showing of Gallie's new work to date and one that would "mark the arrival of the artist into a fully realized sculptural attitude and style at mid-career."[25] On display are slender circular wall-mounted pieces like the aforementioned *Spilt Bow,* "the calmly balanced"[26] *Archer,* and *Down Bow,* whose "energy is just held in check."

Made from strips of laminated spruce and hemlock dowels that are bent, twisted and turned to create what Edmonton art critic Elizabeth Beauchamp compares to "fantastic musical instruments, mythical bows and arrows or whimsical drawings," these large wall pieces, like the exhibition title implied, test the physical limits of wood as well its intrinsic expressiveness. Subsequent to this important exhibition, the Edmonton Art Gallery accords Gallie his second solo exhibition,[27] *Pressure Points,* in 1992.

There, the focus is on the new wall-mounted pieces ("less curvilinear ... more compact, closed and architectonic in shape"[28]) and on an impressive sculptural installation: *Hit or Miss.* A daredevil act featuring sixteen long-handled axes supporting squared timbers of Douglas fir in a stacked arrangement on the floor, the deliberately low-tech *Hit or Miss,* with its "materials dear to the heart of the pioneering west"[29] and heightened allusion to risk-taking, represent a more conspicuous Gallie. It is similar to a phase in the 1970s when his art played more openly with the viewer and had the flavour of heavy industry.

Adrian Cooke, the third artist in this chapter on three-dimensional practice, is the most clearly rooted in a sense of place, or what the Banff poet and critic Jon Whyte once perceptively referred to as the "planar-prairie world"[30]: the architectural and agricultural forms (i.e. fence posts, sheds, snow fences) of southern Alberta.

"He makes use of whatever he finds visually exciting, especially in contrast with the grey/gold, bleak, yet cosmic southern Alberta landscape,"[31] explains Liz Wylie about the long-time Lethbridge resident (1971).[32] In the late 1970s, Cooke's freestanding folded-gate works – capable of being displayed in various positions and painted in high-gloss industrial colours (red, black and yellow) – are compared to such structures as the Texas gate, the railway baggage car and "the slate sides which fit into the loops of a stake back truck" (Whyte). A few years later, inspired by a visit to the newly reconstructed Egyptian Temple of Dendur at the Metropolitan Museum of Art in New York City, Cooke's prairie structures shift from the utilitarian to the spiritual or mystical, with larger installation pieces entitled *Prairie Keep* (1983[33]) and *Sentinel* (1985[34]).

Commenting on the 1983 work – a shiny, bright red canopy covering a black square-sided wood-slat structure with red carpet runners flowing from it across the floor – colleague Jeffrey Spalding asked: "A reliquary, a sanctuary, a representation of a Mormon temple in Cardston, Alberta? [*Prairie Keep*] is an exquisite example of an artist attempting to conflate the high polish and lofty aims of international modernism [i.e. minimalism], touched by the specifics of vernacular experience."[35]

In other words, Cooke is doing as he has always done: evoking the locale, but also relying on art history, travel and informal study abroad in the shaping of his art's minimal (plywood) forms and crisp appearances. In this regard, his sources can be surprising, as they were in slickly finished wood columnar pieces of the mid-1980s. Responding to the figures rendered in relief on classical Greek and Roman art, he introduced painted flames on some enamel and lacquered columns.[36]

In the 1990s, Cooke's art flourishes. Many of his sculptural pieces become less austere and more elaborately shaped, less hard-edged and geometrical and more textural, with the occasional inclusion of text like the prairie-appropriate *Utilitarian* (1991) and *Terminal* (1990/91).

In a metaphorical sense, the art of this period is also more evocative and imaginative. "These objects assume an aura, or iconographic presence. Clouds become threatening juggernauts, grain elevators are monolithic towers enshrouded by the endless sky. The moon hovers like a large halo, encapsulating its prey with a dominant light,"[37] explained the artist in *Explorations-Sculpture 95,* a group exhibition[38] guest-curated by sculptor Katie Ohe (a former instructor of Cooke's).

A more thorough showing of Cooke's development takes place in 1998 with *Adrian Cooke: Ingrained* (the Whyte Museum of the Canadian Rockies, Banff). Featuring a selection of paintings, carvings, sculptures and installation pieces, *Ingrained* plays beautifully on the rich textural qualities of wood as well as on that great prairie icon: the grain elevator. (Because of its overexposure in everything from calendars to advertising, that monumental form was something Cooke had long avoided. But in the later 1980s, spurred on by a particularly impressive example dominating the skyline at Bow Island, Alberta,[39] the image of the elevator did begin to appear as a semi-abstract element in his work.)

By the time of *Ingrained* a decade later, the grain elevator – now on its way to extinction – is almost a supernatural presence in such altar-like relief works as *Island* (1995). Comments Calgary critic Mark Walton: "[The exhibit] is not a ponderous examination of prairie icons; rather it's a lively reflection of the artist's urge to embellish, to make things and to creatively come to terms with world that surrounds him."

Another artist who is especially pertinent to the broad idiosyncratic range of sculpture in the province is the Calgary-trained[40] **EVAN PENNY** (1953, Elim, South Africa). Penny has been based in Toronto since 1980[41] but is a frequent exhibitor in Alberta. His contribution to the aforementioned *Alberta Sculpture Survey 89* (Triangle Gallery, Calgary) is a freestanding nude of coloured polyester resin titled *Janet* (1979–1980). It is an early, smaller-than-life-size work which, with the ghostly grey full-size *Norma* (1979–1980), marks the beginning of an outstanding practice in figurative sculpture.

What makes Penny exceptional in Canada? As has been observed many times, his art is capable of stopping viewers dead in their tracks. This is due not only to his sculptures' disarming verisimilitude but also because of the tension between the actual and the made, the real and the ideal.[42] "Human, all too human" is how one newspaper headline describes his figuration.[43] The detail in a Penny work is that fine-tuned, explaining why he is often labelled a hyper-realist. But this label falls far short of describing the intellectual/philosophical scope of his eclectic oeuvre which began, substantively, with the full-figure standing nudes – including the controversial and voluptuous *Ali*[44] (1983) where if "God is in the details, then Ali is on her way to canonization"[45] – and continued with such body-based art as the realist skin drawings of the 1990s and the photography-influenced head-and-shoulder portraits of the new century.

Penny always models his subjects (before the casting) first in clay, making what appears in flesh the "hard-won result of close observation."[46] This manner of working owes a great deal to the figurative instruction Penny received from Katie Ohe and Ole Holmsten at Alberta College of Art.[47] Initially, modelling puts him on the margins of contemporary art: aloof from the regional mode of welded abstract sculpture of Edmonton and Emma Lake, Saskatchewan,[48] the metaphorical found-object assemblages of Calgary, and further abroad – the earlier, more famous direct-to-body castings of super realist sculptors (American Duane Hanson) and, in another milieu – the installation art/social discourse preferences of Toronto.

But as Toronto critic Gary Michael Dault observed about the artist early on: "Evan Penny is building his career as an artist upon one central and absorbing problem: how to make it new when you're making figurative sculpture." (*Canadian Art,* Fall, 1986). Penny perseveres, though, at the modelling, despite the figure (the human subject) also being an aesthetic and political minefield in the post-1970 period. (Feminist investigations[49] into the representation of the female especially make such undertakings prone to criticism.) Eventually, Penny finds a place for his art in the burgeoning contemporary art discourse about the body[50] in the 1990s. And, in relation to a long southern Albertan tradition, he will match his colleague Calgary realist John Hall's passion for representation rather than duplication.

This point is important because: "It is, after all, Penny feels, in the manipulation of information that the presence of the artist is indelibly known."[51] Penny's presence is loud and clear, and not just because of his technical proficiency. His choice of subjects, especially as they appear in his earlier full-figure works, reflects something of his own sense of place and belonging. With their cropped hair and retro styling, they are the urbanized inhabitants of large communities, found in Toronto, Vancouver and elsewhere. Even the later all-blue, four-fifth size *Murray* (1995) – loosely based on Rodin's *John the Baptist* – conveys a punkish post-AIDS look. Interpreted by Penny in a matter-of-fact manner, these figures are counter-culture in comparison to the perfect-face-teeth-body paradigm of mainstream culture. More importantly to the artist, they represent an attempt to defuse the grander heroic tradition of figurative sculpture with a more personal, intimate approach.

These meticulously sculpted individuals, though, are still socially constructed or socially shaped subjects, and that issue is explored more fully in such pieces as the shadow groupings of the later 1980s, when gender stereotypes are deconstructed[52] and what it means to be an individual is re-examined. For instance, in *Male Shadow Grouping* (1985), a twentieth-century man is paired on a low pedestal with a classically inspired male of the same size. Cast in bronze, the latter has the ringlets of an ancient Greek; a right arm raised in a dignified Apollonian manner. Of the two, Penny observed: "together [they] seem to represent the war between what we are and what we want to be, between the non-heroic and the heroic, the figure grouping as a whole takes its place as a broader portrait of a single individual."[53]

In the late 1990s, the artist turns yet another conceptual corner when he merges sculpture with photography to explore the mediated experience. In two bodies of work – the monumental 5-foot-high busts of *L. Faux* (based on a real woman) and the one-and-a-half life-size *No One – In Particular* – photography acts as "the great mediator," influencing the making of their form and (once completed), their documentation. With *L. Faux,* this entails modelling an almost two-dimensional low-relief of the middle-aged woman's face (in epoxy resin, pigment and hair). While the (silicone, hair, fabric) *No Ones* are like photographic composites, their facial features are borrowed from more than one source. Exhibited with each of these wall-mounted busts is a colour photograph of the work in question. As sculptures, the head-and-shoulder portraits look like a photograph come to life. But even more real than the hyper-realistic bust is the documenting photograph itself. "The problem is to situate the work," remarked Penny, "in between the way we see each other in real time and space, and the way we've come to see each other in photographs."[54]

For these uncanny, almost surreal, works, Penny draws upon his accumulated experience in film make-up and special effects.[55] Inspiring as well are the larger-than-life creations of the Australian-born artist Ron Mueck. Another chapter is added to his continuing repartee with reality and illusion, and to his desire to carry on a meaningful relationship with the figurative tradition in sculpture. Of all those to emerge in this arena in post-1970 Canada, Evan Penny is one of the most fecund in his recognition of the rich history of figuration and its possibilities in a postmodern period.

There is no one in Canada who makes ceramic objects like **GREG PAYCE** (1956, Edmonton, Alberta). Sensuous, obsessive, curvilinear, rhythmic, playful, polymorphous and decorative, his wheel-thrown bowls, vases, plates, pitchers, garnitures (shelf works) and large-scale albarellos (apothecary jars) are as vivid to the eye as to the mind. Made of earthenware, they, too, can provoke surprise – as they did when David Ebony reviewed *Payce* (Nancy Margolis Gallery, 1997) for the important periodical *Art in America:* "It seems that Greg Payce, a young ceramist from Calgary, Canada quietly breezed into town, unheralded, for his New York solo debut. Those fortunate enough to see the show, however, have been much impressed by this amazing new talent ... What separates him from most other ceramists is his dynamic sense of sculpture. He conceptualizes his earthy medium to push it to new heights."[56]

While Payce does not actually consider his pots sculpture,[57] their fluid shapes and robust forms do convey attitude and style,[58] and, in more recent works, allude strongly to the figure. Sometimes, too, a touch of the surreal is present when, for instance, in the *Octopus Vase* (1990), the shape of its two handles mimics the curving tentacles of the mythic sea creature.

The potter also pushes ceramics by blending the present with a generous amount of the past; especially from the craft's own rich legacy. It's not an unusual approach – but Payce's composites do attract attention nonetheless. According to Nancy Tousley, "Payce draws on traditions from pre-Columbian pottery to Minoan vessels to Renaissance majolica plates and ideas generated in other arts from contemporary painting and printmaking to minimalist music. The synthesis is postmodern, without falling into the clichés endemic to current architecture."[59]

In addition, writes Tousley: "Payce has an invigorating flair for decorative surfaces and forms that makes the familiar vessel seem suddenly exotic."[60]

Payce is all "here-and-now" without overlooking or dismissing the one thing some contemporary art critics and non-craft curators overlook – or are suspicious of: craft, especially as it relates to the making of beautiful objects.

Critically, post-1970 is not a friendly time (especially in Canada) for any kind of medium where rigorous technique is needed and is above all apparent. But, according to artist/critic David Garneau, Payce – the master craftsman who also instructs[61] – circumvents this conundrum by making work that is: "suspended between art and craft ... [his] vessels participate in both but are beholden to neither: they are at once unrepentantly utilitarian pots and abstract, theoretical statements."[62] Continues Garneau, "The problem [with] bringing ceramics into postmodern times, [is that] many craftspeople made 'art' only by turning their back on craft. Greg Payce's strategy was to make playfully didactic work that also functioned within the tradition of beautiful and useful objects."[63]

That tradition, of course, is pottery; in particular, its most fundamental expression, the vessel. This utilitarian object was critically cast in the shadows in favour of more avant-garde ceramic sculpture and only made a comeback in the 1980s, albeit more as a visual statement and less concerned about functionality. Juror Matthew Kangas, writing for the *28th Ceramic National* (Everson Museum of Art, Syracuse, New York), described this revival as an "efflorescence" involving "the 'vessel as metaphor', to use Alice Westphal's term."[64]

Simply put, it is the (not-so-new) idea that vessels function symbolically as well as practically. In Payce's own words: "For millennia the traditions of pottery have flourished as a remarkable documentation of human cultural development. Pottery has inexorably linked many cultures in political, social, economic and artistic ways. Through diffusion and appropriation, it has served as a primary vehicle for the transfer of information between various cultures."[65]

According to the artist, one way this exchange has occurred is through decoration: a language in its own right, he says, albeit one that is more subjective than verbal or written. And while in Payce's art, "specific meaning is not necessarily intended,"[66] decoration can serve to document, celebrate, narrate, commemorate and "touch the inner self in the same way that a painting or sculpture can."[67]

Early in Payce's professional practice – which dates from 1987, when he graduated from the Nova Scotia College of Art and Design (NSCAD) with a master's of fine arts degree – the young Edmontonian distinguished himself with uniquely shaped pitchers in buttery majolica glazes (*Pitcher with Leaves,* 1987) and showy multicoloured platters with raised bosses (borders) inspired by fruit and vegetable shapes (*Carrot Plate,* 1987).

Around 1989, the flowing, stately elegance of ancient Minoan (Cretan) pottery supplants the earlier influences of English botanical ceramics and Italian Renaissance majolica in Payce's work. Sprayed and painted with delicate layers of terra sigilatta slip finish, these include tall, tapered vessels and squat, curvaceous teapots. Horizontal stripes become common. In the early 1990s, larger amphora-type vases are painted with Minoan motifs (the nautilus, the lotus flower and the octopus) juxtaposed in layers or behind a screen of painted horizontal bands.

By the mid-90s, the decorative impulse, so part and parcel of who Greg Payce is, reaches a new height of intensity with pots depicting bits of musical scores, silhouettes of Greek pottery and figures, classical columns, abstract geometric patterns and natural forms. "Though recognizable," writes curator Joan McNeil, "the imagery is often hybridized and sometimes spotted only after intent study. Such perceptual games are a key interest for Payce."[68]

In 1995, Lethbridge's Southern Alberta Art Gallery organizes the *Vase to Vase* exhibition, which hints at what is to come perceptually. (This is Payce's second solo presentation at a public gallery. In 1989, potter and curator Franklyn Heisler organized *Greg Payce – Recent Ceramics* at Calgary's Muttart Art Gallery.) Especially notable are the garnitures or sets of matching pots on shelves. The artist explains: "The images and forms operate in a more complex manner than those of the earlier decorated pottery forms. Inspired by late eighteenth century French Sèvres vase garnitures and historical Mediterranean apothecary jars (albarelli), the works utilize the negative spaces between pottery forms as windows and/or images."[69]

In one early example – the lusciously tri-coloured *Vase to Vase* (1995), the profiles of two male heads are visible in the negative space between the three neo-classical pots. Observes David Garneau: "As a set, the garniture is primarily a visual object, but when you pick up the pieces, the 'pictures' [i.e. the heads] vanish."[70]

Regarding the once-aristocratic garniture as a means to expand the use of decoration as language, Payce embarks on a five-year investigation of its sequential format to generate new perceptual material. At the heart of it: an illusion that can be found, virtually, in the negative space between the clay objects or on the shape/silhouette of the objects themselves. The latter kind – initially inspired by an impressive whirling clay figure he fashions in 1995 called *Dervish* – ranges in energy from the graceful, spinning *Han Maid Vase Pair* (1999) to the whirling, Rodin-inspired *Kiss* (2001).

In 2001, a major showing of the larger negative-space works (plus the positive piece *Kiss*) takes place in *Cineramics: Jeannie Mah – Greg Payce* (Art Gallery of Calgary[71]). The exhibition title is an allusion to how the cinema and its development have left visible marks on the pottery of Payce and Regina's Jeannie Mah. In content, it further elaborates on Payce's use of the garniture as a row of related objects to challenge the eye with what looks like a moving optical illusion. In dramatic wheel-thrown works such as the aging *Wane* (2000), the slithery *ssssss* (2000) and the monumental 7-foot *Al Barelli* (2001), his conceptually based art expanded the boundaries of ceramics into unexpected and innovative territory.[72]

The spirit of adventure so strongly embedded in Payce's practice can be attributed to his own particular educational background and working environment. According to Joan McNeil, the curator who included Payce in *A Question of Identity: Twelve Canadians* (1998, Canadian Clay and Glass Gallery, Waterloo, Ontario): "Payce questions the limits to which one can go within the standard craft conventions and techniques, thus he draws on his studies in printmaking, sculpture and art history as well as ceramics."[73] She adds: "The Calgary art community where Payce now works is an enlightened urban centre in which work that is experimental, intellectual or romantic flourishes. It is not surprising to find that Payce's level of sophistication is at home here."

In 1988, when Greg Payce moved to Calgary to instruct in ceramics at the Alberta College of Art, the deep recessionary mood that had gripped the city (and the province) for several years takes a brief respite for the xv Winter Olympics and the celebratory Olympic Arts Festival, an arts and culture extravaganza. A key component of the festival is a roster of art exhibitions which, accompanied with catalogues, leaves its own record of creative activity in the province since the oil boom. Three group exhibitions in particular are pertinent. They are *Survey Alberta 88* (Alberta College of Art Gallery), a juried exhibition featuring thirty-one artists from the province;[74] *Contemporary 88 Calgary,* a joint effort by three significant commercial galleries to highlight local contemporary art;[75] and *Restless Legacies: Contemporary Craft Practice in Canada* (PetroCanada Building). The latter is also adjudicated, and, as Paula Gustafson reported in the *Calgary Herald,* an impressive one-third of the artists selected is from the Calgary area. From the clay world, this includes John Chalke, Annemarie Schmid Esler, Franklyn Heisler and two former residents: Walter Dexter and **CHERI SYDOR** (1955, Mission, British Columbia).[76]

Responding to the title of this national craft exhibition, *Legacies* juror Lorne Falk explained: "Too many differences of opinion, intent and form characterize contemporary craft practice to presume one, centralized representation. It is this restlessness that inspired Rob Barnard, a potter who occasionally wears the hat of a critic, to remark that people used to ask, 'But is it art?' Now, more and more people are asking, 'But is it craft?'."[77]

The answer to this question, in the case of Cheri Sydor's three untitled stoneware and one porcelain (raku) pot, would have to be an unapologetic yes. Described as "the most elegant potter in Alberta,"[78] few studio ceramicists in the province can match the level of near-perfection in form and finish evident in a Sydor raku or stoneware (post-1986). In fact, her subtly coloured stoneware could be from another planet, so different it is from the more earthy functional ware of earlier Albertan pottery. Introducing her pottery in 1986, critic Nancy Tousley comments: "The new vessels have satiny black on their thicker [basket-shaped] bodies, and pink or gold lusters at the rim."[79] Made as one-of-a-kind pieces with light-reflective surfaces, Sydor's wheel-thrown pots are also unrelated to the more recent brightly coloured (commercial glazes), non-functional, hand-built sculpture of her own generation.[80]

Besides the stoneware on display at *Restless Legacies,* a shimmering porcelain vase (1987) represents Sydor's decade-long (1978–1988) foray into the perilous practice of raku, a 400-year-old Japanese process involving organic combustion and the element of chance. Sydor's delicate handling and atmospheric mineral colours establish her as one of the province's top specialists, with a growing list of museum purchases and invitations to national and international exhibitions. "Raku firing gives Sydor's pots the exquisite, iridescent finish of Tiffany glass [while] … the thin, fragile wall of an untitled porcelain bowl recently purchased by the Winnipeg Art Gallery evokes the shell of a sea urchin."[81]

A 1990 winner – as Greg Payce subsequently is in 1994 – of the prestigious Prix Pierre Legault at the *4th National Biennial of Ceramics* in Trois-Rivières, Quebec, Sydor's refined temperament recalls the exquisite style of the great modernist innovator, the Viennese-born Lucie Rie (1902–1995). Not surprisingly, in 2002, Sydor is included in a major international survey of Lucie Rie and Hans Coper at the Gardiner Museum of Ceramic Art, Toronto.[82] In Sydor's work, one can also see the local influence of artist/instructor Elizabeth Mould, whose graceful porcelain and stoneware ceramic plates convey a thoughtful and lyrical mood.[83]

More fundamental to Sydor is her early and steadfast commitment to the vessel form during the early 1980s, a period when its linkage to craft made it an ambivalent object for artists and others (i.e. curators and critics) wanting to place more emphasis on ceramic's non-functional side. (Sydor would later compare her plump, wide-mouthed stoneware bowls to baskets – another craft-based object.[84])

About her pottery's intrinsic content, she wrote in 1995: "I work towards a vision of beauty that exists in my mind … a place of peace, serenity and respite from this hectic world. In my mind's eye the pieces should have a rightness of scale, a purity of proportion and a suggestiveness of surface that makes one slow down and begin to wonder."[85]

The idea that the handmade pot or vessel can (in its own humble way) stimulate the senses, offer comfort and touch the soul – as suggested by Sydor's statement – is practically a mantra of the studio potter and its audience. Nourished by the arts and crafts movement of the nineteenth and early twentieth century, and by potter-guru Bernard Leach, it is more recently summarized by Franklyn Heisler,[86] curator of the 1998 group exhibition, *Vessels: Hand and Spirit:* "People who value pots … know how capable their wares are of transcending the mundane."[87]

It is just that aspect of transcendency that Heisler, the observant curator,[88] felt informed the beautifully crafted and functional pottery of the six vessel artists,[89] including the Calgary-based **JIM ETZKORN** (1948, Edmonton, Alberta). Displaying wheel-thrown and assembled pots of modest size and rich earthy glazes, Etzkorn defines the handmaking of objects as a humanistic enterprise. "We crave romance and seek relief from our preoccupation with technology."[90]

Trained at the Alberta College of Art (graduating in 1978) and at the Banff School of Fine Arts (1979–1984) during a time when – as Cheri Sydor discovers – non-functional sculpture is preferred,[91] and postmodernism is increasingly challenging aesthetics and object-making as a primary goal of art, Etzkorn, against the tide, adopts "a classical approach to ceramics."[92] He chooses to work with the vessel shape (bowl, urn, mug, teapot and so on), drawing on ancient forms for inspiration. These sources range from early Minoan vases and jugs to more rugged examples of Chinese and Japanese origin where contour (or swelling forms) is stressed over surface embellishment.

In a sense, form is everything to Etzkorn; his glazes once described as "often soothingly monochromatic, suggestive rather than narrative and never brittle."[93] As for the shaping of the pots, there will be (raku) urns gracefully balanced and teapots expressively rounded – the latter almost a record of the clay's swelling and wobbling on the potter's wheel. In some instances, indentations accentuating the clay's softness and plasticity are left. Etzkorn describes his quest as a synthesis of "Eastern contemplation and reflection with the freedom of Western romantic expression."[94] Thus, from the humble and the ceremonial emerge the distinctive and the idiosyncratic – as in his gesturally shaped porcelain teapots with a runny ash-type glaze.

In the 1990s, Etzkorn (like many other potters at the time) experiments with wood firing, which like raku introduces the element of chance in a manner sympathetic to Etzkorn's concentration on form. The result is stoneware pottery that strikes a "bold, open pose"[95] but is still calmly self-contained. In 1995, an early example of a wood-fired teapot is presented in the important survey *Clay in Canada: North by Northwest,* which is displayed in Minneapolis, Calgary and Edmonton. Etzkorn's inclusion – along with Edmonton's Sam Uhlick – gives substance to curator Greg Payce's[96] argument that "perpetuating hierarchies [between art and craft] within the field are irrelevant and a waste of energy. Diversity and controversy serve to strengthen and inform the discourse."[97]

It takes art to create a discourse, and a framework (i.e. exhibitions, workshops, criticism, instruction, publishing and the occasional conference) to help the discourse make sense. The art and the framework, though, are two different, time-consuming areas, and only certain artists concern themselves with both. In Alberta, three gifted ceramic artists who have worked fruitfully in both are **FRANKLYN HEISLER** (1949, Bridgewater, Nova Scotia), **EVELYN GRANT** (1953, St. Catharine's, Ontario) and **BARBARA TIPTON** (1942, Kankakee, Illinois). Their resumés are substantive, and, while this discussion is primarily concerned with their own art it is worth highlighting Franklyn Heisler's five years (1988–1993) as a multi-disciplinary curator at Calgary's Muttart Art Gallery; Evelyn Grant's direction of six biannual *International Ceramics* conferences in Calgary (1985–1997) and Barbara Tipton's work in an editorial capacity for eight years with *Ceramics Monthly* (1978–1986, Columbus, Ohio) and as editor/production manager of Alberta's own *Contact* magazine (1992–1999).

Heisler once stressed: "Although the making of ceramic objects have dominated my public life as an artist, my work in multi-media, installation and drawing have been equally important to me as has my work in movement and more recently rug hooking and writing and performing stories." [98] In 1992, Heisler also installs a welded steel and laminated plywood sculpture, *Dream Fragments,* on Calgary's busy 4th Street SW, after winning that year's competition for the area's Public Sculpture Project. In 2001, Evelyn Grant's *Counting Crows* is commissioned for the same outdoor program.[99]

An early postmodern presence on the Albertan ceramic scene, the NSCAD (BFA) and University of Regina (MFA) trained Heisler will eventually pursue a more critical-minded approach to clay concerns that puts him in a category of his own. Recognized in the 1970s as a bona fide member of the "upstart ceramic sculpture movement," [100] Heisler – along with other newcomers Sally Barbier and Mary Shannon Will – represents the cutting-edge of ceramic experimentation. With the addition of Annemarie Schmid Esler and Gisele Amantea, their presence on the scene signals "a formidable change from the Alberta ceramic tradition." [101] (See Chapter 16 for more on this era.)

This, according to Ricardo Gomez for the 1981 travelling survey [102] *Issues In Clay: Western Canadian Sculpture,* [103] which features Heisler, Charles (Chuck) Wissinger, Will, Schmid Esler, Barbier and John Chalke. "Reflecting on Alberta and clay," writes Gomez," one immediately thinks of the fine, strong lines of the crocks and stoppered bottles of the Medalta Potteries and of Luke Lindoe, Walter Drohan and other solid craftsmen doing what they do best." [104]

Doing what Heisler does best for *Issues in Clay* means *Variations* (1981):

an installation featuring small squares of flattened unfired clay pinned neatly to the wall in rows. This radical work, with its obvious references to the non-hierarchical grid of 1960s minimalism, placed ceramics in the broader context of international contemporary art and appropriated (ironically, I think) the vocabulary of a very lofty New York-based art movement that probably would not have had the time of day for an art form like ceramics.

To a large degree, Heisler in those days is a product of the NSCAD tradition, where "the emphasis in all fields is on intellectual rigour as well as craftsmanship." [105] But he also spends enough time further west (Calgary and Regina) to absorb some of the high spirits and witty play endemic to the era and to the region. Central to his play is the incorporation of kitschy figurines and mass-produced ceramic objects into sculptural arrangements (on the wall or on the table) that often comment on popular culture, popular taste and art in the middle-class home. "The works are created out of questions about values as we see them, as others see them," [106] Heisler notes about pieces that combine a well-crafted hand-thrown vase with a cheeky mouse figurine.

In 1988, three of Heisler's carefully arranged juxtapositions are juried into *Restless Legacies: Contemporary Craft Practice in Canada* (Olympic Arts Festival, Calgary, 1988). Working with a mixed-media agenda, the artist presents in two of the works his own version of a tableau where, in one instance, an altered wood table stand, a real tea cup and painted plywood cut-outs of plants are arranged to look like a pop-up still-life. This approach – mixed media and installation rather than the making of a single precious object – is distinctly postmodern and distinctly "Heislerian" as far as Canadian ceramics is concerned.

Near the end of Heisler's involvement with ceramics, he produces three maverick installations [107] that address the presence of ceramic objects in daily living, as well as other subject matter connected to the personal and everyday life. In the 1989 Glenbow work, *A Protestant Thought (Major Punishment for Minor Crime),* an audiotape of nursery rhymes envelops a make-believe living-room installation. With its allusions to child-parent relationships, memories of the past, dreams and the subconscious, the piece is "like a stage set," writes curator Patricia Ainslie She continues: "an intimate and contemplative place is established where the [commercially produced porcelain] bowl filled with water is set on the small table. The water, source of life, is precious." [108]

Notably, this installation – with its one small but metaphorical reference to ceramics – is created for the group exhibition *Vessels,* where the largely non-functional containers, above all, "act as metaphors, as vehicles for ideas."[109] Also featuring the multi-fired ceramics of John Chalke and the earthenware vases of Leigh Harrington, this exhibition underlines the strength of the vessel-form since its revival in the mid-1980s. Ceramic sculpture is no longer the cause celèbre. (Heisler himself had been thoroughly immersed in this cause, although he did acknowledge "the significance of ceramic objects as art, whether they were purely functional or sculptural in nature.")

Six years later, this re-engagement is accentuated with considerable passion and diversity in the large juried exhibition *Vessels in Celebration* (1996), where, regardless of whether the pottery in question is functional or non-functional, the vessel-form is treated as a multi-faceted vehicle. Commemorating twenty-five years of the Alberta Potters' Association, *Vessels in Celebration* is an important travelling showcase of deliberately humble – and remarkably imaginative – pottery-making from across the country.[110]

By the time this 32-artist commemoration makes its debut, Heisler, for health reasons, is no longer using clay. His unique and challenging vision – in ceramics but also contemporary art-making – is regretfully absent as it is from the other major survey of the 1990s: *Clay in Canada: North by North-West* (1995). Included in this survey of the four western provinces, though, are the sculptural ceramics of Evelyn Grant and Barbara Tipton, as well as works by Sally Barbier and Kirsten Abrahamson. This eclectic mix indicated that pottery and sculpture could share the ceramic stage at the end of the century, just as the two forms had done twenty years prior in the groundbreaking *The History of Ceramics in Alberta.*

At the time of that earlier exhibition in 1975, Evelyn Grant is pursuing a diploma in Ceramics from the Alberta College of Art, which she earns the following year.[111] Like many of her generation, Grant has a pragmatic, "nothing-is-sacred" approach to the rules and conventions of fine art ceramics.

Her preference is for low-fired clay – sometimes thrown on a wheel, but more often employing commercially available greenware – and casting from moulds. "Why do everything the hard way?"[112] the artist once quipped about her decorative and narrative pottery finished with glossy commercial glazes and lustres. What mattered more to Grant, according to the *Calgary Herald,* were the images and ideas.[113]

Inspired by the rich decorative heritage of the Victorian and Edwardian period, Grant's ceramics reflect a totally different aesthetic from what could be considered the norm in Albertan ceramics. "I love that whole Victorian thing: being rich and decadent – all that clutter and lace and romantic imagery."[114] She is also influenced by the sharp wit and unconventional style of Leopold Foulem, who instructs her at the Alberta College of Art. Grant develops a bent for embellishing everyday tableware. At one point in the 1980s, this involves a playful romp with miniature clay animals and toys arranged on top of teapots, tureens, butter dishes and clocks. For instance, on top of the baroque-style greenware clock, *Running Late* (1985), a sweet cherub looks at his watch, puts it up to his ear and then runs away. In the early 1990s, Grant captures the public's attention with her stacked arrangements, juxtaposing teacups, plates, teapots, vases and other ceramic objects.

One of these incongruous works, *Untitled Candelabra #1,* is described by S.V. Gersovitz when it appears in Montreal (Galerie Barbara Silverburg, 1992) with Greg Payce's art. "A large raven sits atop a teapot, which is in turn perched on an ornamental base. On the bird's back are two toads, bearing aloft two tea-cups which hold tapers. A third candle is supported on the teapot's spout. Improbable? Impossible? The final test is, 'Does it work?' And the answer is 'Yes.'"[115]

Another writer comments: "Despite looking like something out of the tipsy-topsy world of Alice in Wonderland, her stacked candleholders actually do hold candles and [some of] her teapots do pour tea."[116] Nancy Tousley concludes, in a review pertaining to Grant's "The Tea Pot Opera" (Provenance Gallery, Calgary), "If form is function, her forms function to charm, to cheer and amaze us going about the rituals of ordinary days."[117]

Grant's ceramics also make statements as the stacked teapots did in *Woman's Work* (earthenware, 1995), where the business of homemaking is illustrated on their white surface in black china painting. "My psychologist says it's because I'm piling things up, trying to do twelve jobs in my own life,"[118] reflects the artist about a condition common to working women everywhere. *Woman's Work* is Grant's contribution to *Clay in Canada: North by NorthWest.*

In contrast, *Rem(a)inder* (stoneware, 1995) by Barbara Tipton has the appearance of an ancient relic. Made to hang on the wall as a square clay tablet with a small, darkly coloured cup nestled on its curled shelf, *Rem(a)inder* alludes to two concerns of the artist. There is her longstanding interest in "conveying the abstract idea of containment while at the same time negating it in a physical sense,"[119] and – on a very different plane – a fascination with ancient sites of human habitation or worship. (For a period of time, she lived in Bath and London, England.) These two subjects, one contemporary and the other historic, will place Tipton in a category of her own almost from the time of her arrival in Canada in 1986.[120]

An exhibitor of one-of-a-kind functional and non-functional pieces since 1974, the American-trained artist had, in the 1980s, specialized in wheel-thrown porcelain plates embellished with an image. One series, *A Search for the Truth about Ceramics,* depicted, from a flattened perspective, teapots and cups, and/or a figure examining the pottery like a collector, a dealer or an art critic would. Witty and ironic, with an emphasis on the medium of drawing (done with slip or incised), these multi-layered plates address what Tipton will later articulate not long after settling in Calgary. "Must the contemporary vessel deny function in order to succeed as an artistic statement? " she writes in a piece for *Ceramics Monthly* "These are ongoing debates and developments in the ceramic (and art) world that amaze, intrigue and amuse me; they're in my head continually, so they naturally contribute to my imagery." [121]

Tipton refers to her plates as her porcelain drawings – a description that, at the time of her article, is in a state of transition because of an entirely new innovation she calls cup drawings. These cups and saucer forms that are first shaped on a potter's wheel and then thrown down almost immediately on a canvas-covered table to be stretched and flattened. This unusual technique accentuated the ductility of clay to a brazen degree. It also heightened, for Tipton, her relationship to drawing: "I think of these wall forms as drawings because they really look like the way I would draw a cup and saucer – tilting the perspective of the saucer so that it flattens on the picture plane. And I like thinking that I'm working three-dimensionally to depict two dimensions, instead of the reverse." [122]

Glazed together and often fired several times to create a variety of coarse and textured surfaces, these flattened and fluid objects become a signature of Tipton's oeuvre. Quirky and yet never pandering, battered and yet coolly elegant, as perverse as the *Cup Drawings* are, they are a thoughtful elaboration on fine art and ceramic concerns.

In the early 1990s, the artist also distinguishes herself with relief art inspired by ancient sites in Britain and her own personal roots. "I became absorbed with images of early English stone sculpture and architecture, and sought to realize them more fully in drawing." [123] Later, in stoneware, the result is wall-hung arrangements of small hand-constructed objects in the shape of robed figures, traditional pottery, boats and other items evoking what might have been recovered from old crypt. Featured in Ian Gregory's book, *Sculptural Ceramics* (A&C Black, London, 1992) and also *A Treasury of Canadian Craft* (Canadian Craft Museum, Vancouver, 1992), this work, with its sacred overtones, presents narrative possibilities without compromising the profound effect such places as Bath Abbey and Wells Cathedral has had on the artist.

In 1999, Tipton presents a five-day workshop, Building Ceramic Surfaces, as part of the ambitious *Series* program hosted and organized by Red Deer College. Established in 1975 by Alberta Culture – a government department that, during that period, is fast becoming the envy of the country because of its determination to make a difference culturally in the province – *Series* is, by the late 1980s, the largest residential adult summer art school in the country.[124] Offering a plethora of courses, from beginner to advanced, in many fine art and craft areas, the five-week program becomes an important venue for veteran artists like Tipton to share their technical and creative expertise.

In Medicine Hat that experience and knowledge would be disseminated, too, but on a smaller scale, with the establishment of the Medalta International Artist-in-Residence Program in 1998. Throughout a significant portion of the twentieth century, this southeastern Alberta city is the centre of Canada's clay industry. By 1929, 75 percent of all the pottery wares produced in Canada come from here, so the 1998 program is a fitting tribute to that history.

The Friends of Medalta Society,[125] a hardy group of volunteers dedicated to "the preservation and interpretation of Medicine Hat's clay products industry history, the people who create it and the products they make"[126] establishes the residency program, which invites guest artists[127] to instruct participants over a period of a month. The program is thus an important symbolic link between the past and the present windfall in ceramic art. As Alberta's first manufacturing industry, the making of commercial pottery (1912–1989) anticipated, in its own modest way, a time when the fashioning of three-dimensional objects would become not just an exception to the norm, but the norm itself, as it did by the end of the century.

chapter twenty

Image-Makers and Camelot "On Hold"

PAINTING HAS HAD A CONFLICTED JOURNEY over the last three decades of the twentieth century. Minimalist work coming out of New York in the late sixties heightened interest in three-dimensional art. Sculpture and installation gained critical attention and, along with photography, pushed aside painting, casting doubt on the validity of [this] entrenched art form. Many young artists simply ignored the prevailing winds and quietly pursued their own investigations, leading to a new plurality and giving rise to the term postmodernism. ❧ "Painting Problems: Abstract Expressionism and its legacy," *Gallery,* Southern Alberta Art Gallery, Lethbridge, Autumn 1999

If contemporary painting is largely beneath the art world's most sophisticated radar, that is not such a bad thing.... Painting can explore its own history unencumbered by the chatterings of the all-too-intelligent.

> It may be that the market which still supports painting, is today a space of relative freedom. If artists can sell their work, they can live to paint another day; and if artists can talk about painting without having to worry about critical decorum or correctness, they might say something very interesting. And that is exactly what is happening [in 2002]. ❧ Robert Linsley. "Who owns art history?" *Canadian Art,* Summer 2002

This last chapter is about image-making, particularly the work of the painters who appear in the 1980s and beyond. Also included are printmakers/painters (for instance, Margaret May, Ken Webb and Billy McCarroll) and an artist who uses paint to transform an object rather than create the illusion of one (Eric Cameron). Whatever these individuals do, they are (with the exception of Cameron) involved in the making of images that are two-dimensional. The images cover a range of personal, cultural, social and art-related subjects. In appearance, they can be representational, abstract or a fusion of the two.

It seems fitting to end this book with painting, the medium that opens this survey of Albertan contemporary art. The first chapter explored not only the marginalization of landscape art as a living, regional manifestation, but also the very medium (i.e. painting) in which it has primarily flourished. Both, but especially the medium of painting, have faced critical and curatorial indifference within Canada's publicly funded art sector. This phenomenon, of course, has varied in intensity, from institution to institution, centre to centre and region to region, but as the following example shows, it has played a role in the shaping of late-century Canadian art, as in the case of an important centre like Toronto. "Christina Ritchie, a contemporary curator at the Art Gallery of Ontario in Toronto, remembers how she and many of her colleagues scorned much of the painting they saw right through the late seventies, eighties and early nineties."[1]

The difficulty with this theoretical and trend-mongering squeamishness throughout the post-1970 period is that some of Alberta's most committed artists never gave up on painting. Even from distant Toronto, John Bentley Mays in 1996, declared: "[Alberta painters have] been fortunate, insofar as the current, corrosive distrust of painting appears to have skipped clear over their heads, from New York and Toronto right to Vancouver."[2]

However, with the exception of a small number of artists, much of the energy in this ridiculously diverse community has barely registered in the larger Canadian art sphere end of century. A few exceptions spring up here and there but are generally treated as isolated cases, as though being from Alberta is an anomaly in itself. In addition, with such curatorial and critically "sexy" acts as installation, photo-based art and new media flourishing in the country, why bother with the effort needed to dissect such diversity on canvas, panel or otherwise?

A glimpse into some of this accumulating energy is provided early-on in *Seven Artists from Alberta: Art in this Region.* Curated by Nancy Tousley, this 1984 travelling overseas showcase[3] – by a then-increasingly notable and diverse group of artists[4] from the southern part of the province – reveals that, aside from the commonality of "diaristic content,"[5] the differences, for instance, between a Jeffrey Spalding conceptual, process-oriented painting and the highly idiosyncratic expressionistic attack of a Don Kottmann couldn't have been more pronounced. (And then, of course, there are the paintbrush-free paintings of Mary Scott with their appropriated images, words and phrases borrowed from French feminism and other thinkers such as Jacques Lacan and Roland Barthes.)

Also significant for that era is the fact that Spalding's paintings are representational, depicting clean and precise domestic interiors, while Kottmann's images are abstract and gestural, recalling the all-over canvases of the abstract expressionists. Commenting on Kottmann's four acrylics, Tousley writes: "The textures, rhythms and colours relate to musical improvisation: each work has a tempo, temperature and mood of its own. Each is also a record of the painter's condition at a particular moment in time."[6]

DON KOTTMANN (1946, St. Louis, Missouri) says he was "raised on Beckmann"[7] (a renowned collection of German artist Max Beckmann's work resides in that city). Kottmann is an example of what can be called the other side of southern Alberta's artistic temperament. Edgy, intuitive, experiential and concerned with self-expression and/or the human condition, this attitude first made its mark locally with the expressionistic disquietude of W.L. Stevenson and Maxwell Bates (who studied with Beckmann in the post-war period). Later, it was illuminated by the jagged calligraphic and abstracted figuration of Ron (Gyo-Zo) Spickett and then absorbed, to varying degrees, by such dissimilar artists as Les Graff, Ron Moppett, Carroll (Moppett) Taylor-Lindoe, Mark Dicey, Bill Rodgers and Bev Tosh.

Arriving in Canada in 1974 to take up a post at the Alberta College of Art, Kottmann is largely an outsider to this particular history. He has, though, a significant-enough stake in painting as an avenue for emotional self-expression and creative ferment – for having, as he once put it, " its own independence"[8] – that, in Alberta at least, Kottmann becomes a strong representative of this type of art. And it really didn't matter if he carried this task out as an abstract painter, as he did until about 1983, or as a figurative artist into the 1990s. As Tousley observed in 1986 about his then figurative art depicting smoky tavern scenes and strippers in bars: "[Kottmann] talks of putting wounds on the surface of his canvases, of making them a part of life."[9] Vincent Varga explained: "[He] adopts a neo-expressionist approach that integrates psychological and emotional interpretation with vibrant colour, gestural marks, and loose brushwork."[10]

But in the more theoretical quarters of contemporary Canadian art, all of this painterly prowess – springing forth from the interior of its creator – and dicey subject matter (where women appear to be the object of the male gaze) does matter. In fact, it mattered a great deal, especially in the publicly funded, non-profit sector where, as critic Leslie Dawn recounts in his 1989 essay *Don Kottmann: An Expression of Faith – A Faith in Expression,* "[There] still exists the antagonism between what are loosely termed neo-expressionism and deconstruction [social or art-related analysis]. Both camps are openly hostile to each other and are attempting to occupy the same terrain."[11]

This terrain – in terms of critical and curatorial recognition – by the early 1990s has scant time for what is perceived and judged to be little more than a replay of the self-laden, male-centred art that abstract expressionism had sanctified two generations prior, and then had seen transformed into some of the most valuable blue-chip museum art ever.

In 1991, critic and artist David Garneau reflected on the new order: "Men making art within the current atmosphere of critique are often overwhelmed by the new possibilities and the impotency of the old roles.... As male artists we should examine things as they are, not as we mythify them to be.... To be shouting the loudest and occupying ever more space has become an embarrassment rather than a quality."[12]

Thus, in Kottmann's case, the times were not in his favour, whether or not he shouted the loudest. However, his presence in the image-making community in Calgary post-1980 is undeniable: increasingly viewed as a provocateur because of his artistically incorrect inclinations. With his large, psychedelically-tinged canvases, he is, in the parlance of an earlier era, so "out there" as to be larger-than-life. There is his pre-1983 body of hot, bright abstractions – first exhibited in the landmark *Don Kottmann: New Paintings* (1983, Off Centre Centre, Calgary) – that are described as a "magisterial series ... highly successful and undeniably beautiful."[13] While, more analytically, Tousley writes: " If what he does is expressionism, it's very different than the kind of expressionism practiced 30 to 40 years ago.... He negates the ideas of personal 'handwriting' and angst traditionally attached to abstract expressionist work."[14]

Then, after 1983, Kottmann's flamboyant new figurative work is interpreted as depicting "the collective psyche of the macho, beer-garden mentality" via huge primal heads (paintings and ceramic sculpture) and mythological females (dancing Hindu goddesses). There is also reaction to the fact that these explicit and theatrical figurative works appear just when neo-expressionism is the headline trend-setting art internationally and, more significantly, are interpreted to be a "head-on confrontation with current feminist theories and thought,"[15] as well as a reaffirmation of painting's value as a subjective act.

Painted in raw, bold, almost neon colours, these controversial images will later dominate the fifteen-year survey *Don Kottmann: Painting Drawing Sculpture* at the Alberta College of Art Gallery (1989). Comparing his work to reggae, where "[my] paintings are upbeat and pushy in colour and rhythm," the artist explained, "I think I see what's going on out there and what's going on with me and it disturbs me. It's like being in analysis under your own supervision."[16]

Shortly after, Kottmann gives up his figurative tendencies for more exploration of abstract art. Meanwhile, in the contemporary art world – after an era in which abstraction had been abandoned by many – this approach to image-making is undergoing a period of re-evaluation. In the midst of this new development, a few of Kottmann's memorable acrylics from the early 1980s find a receptive showcase when the University of Lethbridge Art Gallery and Art Collection presents over 350 paintings, prints, drawings and sculpture in *Abstraction: Which Way From Here?* (1993).[17] Displayed for a one-month period on two large vacant floors in Calgary's Canada Trust Tower as part of the city's annual Visual Arts Week,[18] the sprawling blockbuster, which attracts national coverage, represents an opportunity to see abstraction and its development from 1920 on, not as a model of linear progression but as a diverse and even unruly phenomenon.

According to *Artichoke,* the display of international and Canadian examples also speaks "about possibilities rather than exhaustion, its perspective is optimistic and celebratory: a stunning contrast to the heavy-handed themes and pessimistic content of many contemporary art shows of the 1990s."[19] An interview with Don Kottmann is also included in that magazine issue. His conclusion, after several visits to *Which Way From Here?* "Abstraction's moment should be a lot longer than we have given it."[20]

(As it turns out, the kind of abstraction that did resurface in the late 1980s and 1990s appeared with a cooler, more conceptual and depersonalized agenda: rooted in the minimalist and/or conceptual movements of the late 1960s instead of the subjective legacy of abstract expressionism.)

If the world of painting was transpiring to be a very different one post-1980 for Alberta-based painters, the same applies for contemporary printmakers, whose medium goes from being "of the moment" to "on the margins." Recent printmaking will have a peripheral status in much of the Canadian art world, largely due to the same set of "sins" posited for painting. These sins included being a medium (in a traditional and technical sense) and for having a strong rapport, in the modern period, with an aesthetic rather than a conceptual or political agenda.

As Diana Nimeroff, then curator of contemporary art at the National Gallery of Canada, informed Ottawa artist Jennifer Dickson about the institution's own bias: "We pursue works by artists – not by medium in contemporary art – the lines between media are blurred. Our collecting is issue-driven. Ideas are paramount."[21]

But despite this exclusion, printmaking, like painting, doesn't fade away after 1980. And in Alberta, there are still moments when it does receive serious attention. Instances include *Sightlines* – a five-day international symposium and exhibition series held in Edmonton[22] in 1997 – and the more modest-sized *Out of Print: New Wave in Contemporary Printmaking in Alberta* (Triangle Gallery, Calgary, 2000).[23] With one part of *Out of Print* devoted to a new wave of post-1980s artists, the other part to more senior figures in the community, this exhibition demonstrates that the medium is bound to remain a vital source of image-making in the new millennium. But it will be in *addition* to other kinds of art made by printmakers in Alberta.

Two of the veterans represented in *Out of Print* are **MARGARET MAY** (1951, Galahad, Alberta) and **KEN WEBB** (1950, Swalwell, Alberta). Singled out in the late 1970s and early 1980s for their artistry and technical savvy in the print media,[24] by the 1990s, May's and Webb's image-making branches out into painting for Webb and mixed-media pieces for May.

Says one art critic, "Webb's paintings recall the classical architectural heritage – a heritage we know by archaeological discoveries, surviving buildings and their influence on later styles. The geometry of his art responds to the rational structure of that heritage, just as his dark shadowy images reflect a past that we only dimly recognize as a source of our culture." [25]

As for May, "It's startling to see [May's new pieces] because almost nobody does it [i.e. combine a print technique with painting] ... the directness and immediacy of making the new work (as opposed to the distance and indirection of the printmaking processes) seems to have broadened the 39-year-old artist's horizons and brought her closer to her self as a sensual and emotional being in her work." [26]

Margaret May temporarily ceases making fine-art prints around 1987. By the following year, she has turned over a new leaf with a nine-piece series on plywood panel combining a print technique (lithography or silkscreen) with drawing and painting. Titled *Vignette Series,* it is first exhibited in *New Work: May, Besant, Parker, Sewell* (Alberta College of Art Gallery, 1988) where, according to Nancy Tousley, "printmaking techniques have become just another part of the artist's vocabulary but one which they have an affinity." [27]

Consisting of an image where a barely recognizable object or scene is on a darkened ground, May's mysterious vignettes are, in her own words, "evocative of such things as memory, longing, sexuality, joy, despair." [28] More are added to the series in 1989, and a new set (also on plywood) is completed that year. Titled *Vital Flame Series,* the five-piece work features tongued flame-shapes, which are interpreted to be variations on a theme symbolizing the inner spirit. Essayist Andre Jodoin describes the two opposite but related groupings, which are featured in the travelling *All and Nothing* (Southern Alberta Art Gallery, 1990), as "a portrait of the self.... In both, the self is referenced variously by verbal and visual images," [29] but not by a direct representation of May herself.

This evocation of the self-portrait – traditionally a depiction of the artist's physical likeness – and May's concern instead with constructing a metaphoric portrait of the inner self are viewed critically as an alternative to the romantic image of the artist as a heroic, self-made individual or "a coherent overall being." [30] By coincidence, it links May with postmodern thinking on the concept of the constructed and hybrid self and the related search for identity. By the end of the 1980s, the constructed self and identity are critically popular topics in visual-art practice. Identity art is especially prominent in the publicly funded sector of the contemporary Canadian art world. Generally interpreted to be anti-patriarchal and inclusionary, the identity buzzword goes hand-in-hand with the concept of "the other" (i.e. women, homosexuals, people of colour, First Nations and so on). Thus, May's art is in good critical company.

Vera Lemecha, who curates *Vita Peracta* at the Glenbow Museum in 1992, offers this interpretation. "Her works suggest the striving after the wholeness of the self and the frustration of its impossibility in the postmodern era.... May's works elicit an infinite process of self-discovery but never the whole self."[31] But more provocatively, in *Margaret May: Mind's Eye* at Calgary's Nickle Arts Museum, director Ann Davis places the artist in a more art historical context: "For some time Margaret May has been interested in mysticism, a spiritual approach to living.... In pursuing this interest, May is part of a definite but often misunderstood thrust in Western twentieth-century art. Kandinsky and Mondrian were early proponents of a mystical approach; in the United States Marsden Hartley and Georgia O'Keefe worked with the inexplicable, the divine ... in Canada Ozias Leduc and Lawren Harris were leaders in mystical thinking.... All probed anti-materialistic theories."[32]

While praised for her foray into mixed media, Mays returns to making fine-art prints (on fibrous or thick handmade paper) after travel to Italy in 1990 and 1993 provides her with a new body of black-and-white photographs.[33] This work, incorporated into two lithographic series, *Pilgrimage Suite* (1991) and *Night Journey* (1993), is seen to "mark inner journeys through dreamscapes and landscapes that resonate with strange familiarity for her.[34]"

In the same year as the *Mind's Eye* survey, May is selected to exhibit in the inaugural *Alberta Biennial of Contemporary Art 1996.*[35] Along with Jane Ash Poitras, John Will and Janet Cardiff, she is one four artists with a printmaking background to be displayed in this event, which is organized and hosted by the Edmonton Art Gallery and the Glenbow Museum. May presents two bodies of work, including the unusual and memorable *Volumes* (1995), a suite of cut-out objects whose super-smooth construction (gesso and acrylic on thick laminated medium density fibreboard) soothes the viewer's eye. Designed to hang on the wall, these ephemeral monochromatic presences with rounded edges are entirely imageless. They still convey – through their uncomplicated forms, their glowing, soft colours and titles *Inner Calm* and *Growth* – the artist's continuing quest to externalize and make concrete psychological material. As May comments about them: "The objects she made were not paintings and they were not sculptures and they were definitely not prints. She called these *Volumes.*" [36] They are also a fitting example of the *Globe and Mail* headline for this first *Biennial:* "Alberta looks beyond tradition." [37]

At the time Ken Webb turns to painting in 1984, he is a master printer and operator of an acclaimed one-man print shop: [38] Ken Webb Fine Art Printing (1981–1987). Specializing in etching and other intaglio techniques, it is one of three print shops to emerge in Calgary within a short period of time. In addition, there is the co-operative Station Studio (1977–), founded by Elizabeth Allen and Andie Wicherts, and Trojan Press (1978–1981) with John Kenneth Esler and Webb. As he had done previously at Trojan Press, Webb assistes other artists, including Don McVeigh and Jack Cowin in the production of fine-art prints.

He also makes his own etchings, and in 1983 one print in particular, *Classical Support,* provides some of the vocabulary for his future paintings on masonite. Inspired by a book on Greek temples, the stone columns depicted in the etching become part of what Webb describes in his black and dark-coloured acrylics – made textural with marble dust and sand – as a "classical fantasy." [39] They are spare, make-believe images that incorporate not only other iconic shapes (vases and arches) from the Classical period but also architectural configurations symbolizing Webb's native Canada. Thus, in *European Totems* (1986), "the columns of a Greek temple … inhabit the same image as the architectural elevation of a typical bungalow". [40]

A country boy's classical fantasy – inspired by a year spent in Europe [41] – could have been a corny idea. But, rather than acting as a tourist who seeks to express his or her impressions, Webb use this experience to "visualize his identity," [42] to acknowledge his own heritage as an artist. Characteristic of these shadowy hybrid pictures are dark tonal passages and diagrammatic drawing like that seen in architectural plans. Texturally, too, the fluted columns have actual ribs of raised paint, while the marbled surfaces are in low relief. Webb's background in etching also influences their look when incised white lines are drawn into the masonite's black ground. As Nancy Tousley perceptively observed, "his surfaces are equivalents of the materials and forms they depict." [43] Describing Webb's recognizable references to Western art history (vase, column and so on) as indicative of a postmodern approach, the artist also emphasized to the *Calgary Herald* critic the lasting impact of place and heritage by his suggestion that "living on the Prairies allows you to fantasize." [44]

❧ ❧ ❧

If large, impressive buildings and monumental sites signify the past, then the Prairies must be largely without a past, or, at the very least, deprived of the kind recognizable to most Canadians or Europeans. But what if the past, and its recall through history and/or memory, is embedded – as it often is on the Prairies – in the very landscape under one's feet? Or, even more challenging, if it's present in banal and unremarkable places not just on the prairies but on the very soil of Europe itself? For **WILLIAM MACDONNELL** (1943, Winnipeg, Manitoba), that's all the more reason to bear witness to places where something has happened. Taken to every "roadside cairn and old fort"[45] as a child, he now considers place – regardless of its sometimes mundane features – a powerful marker.

Since the mid-80s, MacDonnell has employed landscape (or urban scenery) in large, richly painted, sometimes pigment-dripping acrylics on canvas, to recall the darker side of modern history. In many instances, the sites are European, inconspicuous and unmarked: the forest where a disturbed patch of ground contains the remains of 4,500 Polish soldiers, murdered on the orders of Stalin, (*A Forest Near Smolensk* [*A Question of Aesthetics*], 1989); a decaying overgrown Berlin courtyard, once used by doomed Gestapo prisoners (*Gethsemane* [*For Dietrich Bonhoeffer*], 1994) and so on.

On a different continent, but no less haunting, is Vietnam, where the artist was startled to see bomb craters transformed by lush tropical growth into beautiful round ponds (*Cemetery In The Mekong Delta,* 1999). In 1994, MacDonnell was invited to join the Princess Patricia Canadian Light Infantry as a war artist for the United Nations peacekeeping efforts in the former Yugoslavia. From his "quiet and uneventful"[46] visit (albeit with military escort) came such depictions as *Tragedy on a Country Road* and *Mined Churchyard* where small details, like the road's cratered surface and red-and-white warning tape in the foreground of a church ruin, evoke unease.

Describing MacDonnell, a veteran art history and painting instructor at Calgary's Alberta College of Art and Design, as an anti-history painter, Nancy Tousley writes: "Stripped of the oppositional right/wrong rhetoric of heroic ideals, the secretive landscapes and scarred, sullen postwar urbanscapes he paints suggest the complexities and ironies behind simple equations of victor and vanquished or heroes and villains."[47]

As for MacDonnell's turbulently expressive style of painting: it's "faux-romanticism,"[48] comments Anne Severson, while Leslie Dawn suggests the artist undermines "Expressionism's ideology of the unique [random and spontaneous] brushstroke" by placing each one with "great deliberation, foresight and calculation."[49] Similarly, Tousley writes: "Fascinated by our continuing need for the romance of ruins and transcendent landscapes, he nonetheless sees romanticism as a lie and searches for new vocabulary to suit contemporary times."[50]

MacDonnell claims he is attracted to a mixture of what's beautiful and what's tragic, and he has stated that his works are not political statements per se. Ultimately, a painting is just that: a painting. His conviction is lucidly expressed in a body of dual-panelled paintings from the mid-1980s that juxtapose images from Canadian and European history and art history. Regarding this pairing, Dawn observes: "Painting in the postmodern era has come to embody a critical reflection on the practice of painting itself, and on its ability to represent events and/or to convey specific meaning."[51]

Obtaining an MFA (1979) from the Nova Scotia College of Art and Design (NSCAD), MacDonnell began his practice as many painters of his generation did: as an abstract painter. By 1980, he was introducing recognizable imagery into his art. Arriving in Calgary that year to take up a post at the art college, he found that representation already had a strong foothold in the community. Eventually, MacDonnell will appear with several other accomplished image-makers in the twenty-four artist survey *Aspects of Contemporary Painting in Alberta* (Glenbow Museum, 1987), where he is described as criss-crossing the terrain between late Modernism and its formal conventions, and the notion of image and content.[52]

By late 1987, when MacDonnell's work appears for a second time at the youthful Stride Gallery in Calgary,[53] certain symbolic motifs like the walled garden (symbolizing refuge, sanctuary, utopia); historic ruins; and angels (i.e. witnesses) have entered his vocabulary. Large monochromatic pink and blue-black borders bluntly frame his landscape images. Out of these evocative developments came the exhibition's memorable title: *A Conspiracy of Angels/The Romance of Ruins.* Used in the spirit of irony – a prevailing attitude of the 1980s – each motif could be read as "a complex, flexible and double-edged emblem."[54] Of MacDonnell's landscapes, Tousley later opined: "[He] strikes just the right tone, one that invokes the grand romantic tradition only to make the thought of it seem like a pathetic irony.... It is a singular achievement."[55]

In 1994, fourteen of MacDonnell's impressive paintings are exhibited in the plaintively titled *Dort? Ja, Ebendort* ("There? Yes, over there") at the Southern Alberta Art Gallery in Lethbridge, along with fourteen smaller studies. Many of these single-image works are derived from his experiences during a six-month sabbatical (1992–93) in Berlin. Infused with both irony and tragedy, the paintings "stem from an ongoing interest in the importance of a society's collective memory and, perhaps equally importantly, with a society's forgetfulness. The paintings are an attempt to links these thoughts and experiences to a sense of place."[56]

As a postmodernist, MacDonnell is not unique in addressing other kinds of history other than painting's own history. In fact, as the 1980s progressed, the subject of history – especially as a collection of facts pertaining to the doings of great men and powerful Western nations – comes under ever-increasing scrutiny as artists, writers, academics and others reassess its representation and role in the wider culture. In Canada, though, MacDonnell's attention to world affairs of the twentieth century, as well as his choice to pursue this goal through landscape imagery, will make him a singular figure.

If the re-representation of the past is one kind of post-1980 project, looking critically (or analytically) at the surrounding culture and the artist's role in the present is another. And how could it be otherwise, bombarded, as many artists are, by the imagery of the media, advertising, the cinema and an entirely new player: the expanding digital universe via the personal computer? Of course, the number one expectation about artists in Western society is that they create original (even disconcertingly foreign) things from an original perspective. But what if the very idea of artistic originality and mastery – long the Holy Grail of art history, modernism and the avant-garde – is up for re-evaluation in an already image/picture saturated society?

Of course, artistic originality is an issue not confined to just the visual-arts arena. In many cultural quarters, artists will ask (Canadian playwright, John MacLachlan Gray once did): "What's so creative about originality?

"The tricky thing about the words creativity and originality," writes Gray, "is that they imply an inside-to-outside continuum, when the process goes the other way: not generating ideas from within, but allowing ideas to penetrate from beyond our protective shell of desire and fear. Originality is not generation but observation. Creativity requires an openness to what's going on out there, even if it's not what you want to see; a ruthlessness; a what-the-hell attitude. Obsess over originality and your project is 'dead meat.'"[57]

Gray's assessment about living in a "derivative culture in which what we call original is usually a product of recollection and repackaging" is part and parcel of what in the deconstructing and decentering visual arts of the post-1970 period will be called appropriation. To appropriate is to borrow, to annex for one's own purposes. It's an approach or method of working that, paradoxically, while challenging modernism and its fixation on aesthetic invention will still manage to create something new or dare we say original, by transferring visual information from another place, time or person, to the (mediated) here and now.[58]

"For many artists today, appropriation comes as second nature"[59] – the most famous instigator being Andy Warhol, with his wholesale annexation of the Campbell's soup can and the Brillo box for his art. In Alberta, an early and witty example that challenged the meaning of originality is Sylvain Voyer's Art Recycling Depot. Located in Edmonton in the early 1970s, the depot provided a service to artists, collectors and art galleries where in Voyer's own words "creative, sensitive artists will attempt to alter and rejuvenate your tired art."[60] This service also extended to cheap mass reproductions. In one instance, Voyer inserted Vietnamese civilians into Picasso's famous *Guernica.* "Art can be updated, made more relevant and its meaning brought out again."[61]

Something of this Dada-esque spirit also underpins the efforts of two other earlier provocateurs: **WILLIAM (BILLY) J. MCCARROLL** (1937, Santa Barbara, California) and **ARLENE STAMP** (1938, London, Ontario). In 1987, both are participants in *Transference* (Walter Phillips Gallery, Banff Centre): an exhibition of six Alberta-based artists identified as being involved in various acts of appropriation.

For *Transference,* McCarroll presents boldly coloured prints and paintings of golf hero Sam Snead, derived directly from the 1953 how-to paperback *Sam Snead's Natural Golf.* Each image, though, is rendered in a different modernist style such as pop art, cubism, expressionism and colour-field abstraction. Curator Daina Augaitus observes about this work – made by an artist who trained in art and in competitive golf at approximately the same time in California – "By copying [since 1983] and recontextualizing the vernacular imagery of a 1950s graphic artist, the focus is as much on the artist's language and its formal qualities as it is on the content."[62]

Vincent Varga, who curates *Aspects of Contemporary Painting in Alberta* (Glenbow Museum, 1987), suggests on the other hand that "the real depth" of McCarroll's irreverent pictures "lies in its ironic metaphors."[63]

And Peter White, who curates a show of McCarroll's golf paintings in Regina, opines that "[a] wonderful and crucial irony of McCarroll's work" is that something as seemingly superficial as golf "turns out to be an excellent vehicle for the examination not only of many of life's most pressing issues but also those of art."[64]

One reviewer from Edmonton interprets the mock-heroic Snead pictures as satirizing "the hype and competition that sometimes turns the modern art scene into no more than a game,"[65] while Curator White goes on to connect McCarroll to "our collective cultural debt to [Walter] Benjamin, godfather of postmodernism. Whether it is called quotation or appropriation, Benjamin understood that in less than humanist times, [artistic self-expression] pales beside the critical, reflexive manipulation of already existing materials."[66]

A product of the late 1960s art world, with an interest in its variegated strands including pop, conceptual and process-oriented art, McCarroll is, until 1983, a painter of procedural geometric abstractions when the acquisition of a Snead paperback from friend John Will suggests the possibility of bringing together his two passions, golf and painting. "It seemed silly at first,"[67] he later told a newspaper reporter, but he finds the initial reception positive, the work appealing to the irreverent frame-of-mind so alive and well in certain of his Lethbridge and Calgary peers.

Beginning with the solo exhibit, *How to Play a Winning Game Your Natural Way: A Continuous Metaphor* (Off Centre Centre, Calgary, 1984) and followed up with two other versions exhibited in Regina[68] (1986) and Kelowna[69] (1987), the artist eventually moves away from the direct copy to more isolated iconic motifs, like the golf tee and Snead's famous fedora, boldly blown up. More lushly painted, with an increasing tendency towards abstraction, these striking oils on canvas – along with earlier acrylics and prints – are later highlighted in a ten-year (1983–1993[70]) travelling survey, *How to Play a Winning Game Your Natural Way: A Continuing Metaphor.*

Critic Jeffery Spalding argues that McCarroll is more of an assimilator than a purposeful Benjamin-inspired deconstructor of originality.[71] "McCarroll ... [doesn't] consider new creativity doomed or discredited.... Reflection upon 'pre-existing materials,' turning these towards unexpected, new use, is to embrace the classic role of the artist. [A pre-existing image] does not of necessity require a concomitant rejection of the concept of the self, individuality, originality, or authorship." Spalding adds: "All artists borrow, great artists steal, advised Picasso."[72]

As for McCarroll's choice of pictorial subject (i.e. golf) – which, in the more officious, institutionalized sector of the Canadian art world is totally unconventional – Spalding looks to the artist's admiration for west-coast funk art and other offbeat manifestations nurtured on the margins. Inspired by popular culture and locale, rather than modern art history as sanctioned by New York, Spalding points to Regina's anti-modernists David Gilhooly, David Thauberger, Joe Fafard, Vic Cicansky and others as a Canadian example of this energy.

Summing up their raison d'etre: "They were all concerned with establishing tolerance for personal, regional or idiosyncratic sensibilities."[73] The very thing that, from the 1980s on, the more powerful arbiters of contemporary Canadian art like The National Gallery of Canada would distance themselves from, but which artists such as McCarroll would continue to espouse through his art.

When Arlene Stamp exhibits three *Gladys* works in *Transference,* her 1982–1986 series is already a success: "among the remarkable achievements of contemporary Canadian painting,"[74] observes Marshal Webb in *Canadian Art.* Nancy Tousley concurs: "[Stamp's] appropriation of the oeuvre of a specific individual, Gladys M. Johnston (1906–1983), seems to be unique."[75] She adds, "So faithful does Stamp remain to the images of Johnston's small, thinly painted works on canvas board that one can indeed almost speak of Johnston's originals and Stamp's adaptations."

A native artist from Salmon Arm, British Columbia, Johnston – with flair and intuition – had painted the region's landscape and wildlife, folkloric scenes of pioneers and western adventure, and bursting florals set in vases. Stamp, on the other hand, having trained professionally in Calgary with additional workshops in Banff and Emma Lake, has a particular yearning that only an art-aware audience, familiar with contemporary developments, would have understood as being present. As she explains to Tousley: "I've always been an image painter, but I've never wanted to illustrate my own ideas or my own emotions. So these paintings are not [self] expressive in any sense. The images are not mine, the colour is not mine. It's in the painting, not the picture, that the content rests for me."[76] This comment is about her first showing of the *Gladys* work: ten Johnston images from colour photocopies of the originals, on a much larger scale, and in oil and wax on canvas.

As to why this should be the case, the conceptual painter later elaborated: "It has been my desire from the beginning not to assume special knowledge of what art should look like. One of the central issues of art-making today seems to me to revolve around finding ways of admitting one's own cultural bias. This imperative fits nicely with my own needs to circumvent authorship and to let the product somehow stand and reveal itself as all and only what it is."[77]

Although this self-denying stance to art-making is not novel in the context of the day, what is compelling is how such populist imagery, by an unheralded artist (Johnston), is writ large in conceptual terms using the medium of paint. In addition, there is the issue of how a colour photocopy is used to interpret or (in art world jargon, "mediate") the original, rendering a crucial distance between its originator and its admiring interceder.

As to whether this calculating/strategizing approach amounts to little more than a highly refined cover for stealing, Nancy Tousley opines: "When things don't work quite as well as they should, appropriation looks like a straight steal. When they do, some surprising syntheses are produced that, unlike appropriations which simply cannibalize, become collaborations with something new to say."[78]

Attracted to Johnston's intuitive ability and the lively character of her art, Stamp overall finds the *Gladys* oeuvre an expansive and heartening experience. *Gladys* is eventually replaced with an even more astringent concealment of her own artistic self. It begins in Calgary and is completed in Toronto, where she relocates in 1984. Starting with the strictly procedural, infinitely various *Red Works* (1987–1990) and followed by the grid-based but impishly irregular geometric *Tilings* (1991–1995), which are then succeeded by the computer-generated, kaleidoscopic-hued *Colour Chords* (1995), this last work – in addition to extrapolating on her play with grids and non-periodic patterns as seen in *Tilings* – includes exploring the relationship between recursive colour composition and musical scales.

Mathematical in their origins (Stamp also has a BA in mathematics), these intellectually driven, yet absurdly systematic works have impact even if the viewer doesn't have a clue about the thinking or the labour-intensive process behind their orchestration. The *Globe and Mail*'s Kate Taylor notes about the large, soft-coloured floor mat, *Plaza* (1991), which, like most of the

Tilings is made of vinyl household tiles: "It is a powerful piece that can be read at a whole variety of levels: a conceptual examination of visual systems, a tongue-in-cheek elevation of the classical kitchen floor to the level of art or simply a dynamic visual fact."[79]

This ability to create strong visual statements with the use of non-periodic patterning earns the image-maker two public art commissions in Toronto in 1993[80] and sets the stage for one of her most recognized collaborations – *Fictive Space: Judith Schwarz/Arlene Stamp* (1994). Designed for the Illingworth Kerr Gallery at the Calgary art college, the show features *Ready Set,* a large, irregular checkerboard black-and-white tile floor from Stamp and three large wall-mounted laser-cut steel sculptures (the two-part *Somersault* and *Floating X*) by Schwarz. In response, the American art critic Thomas McEvilley observes how bright, informed artists from smaller, distant centres (including Toronto) can "engage the larger issues of the moment as well as the inner details of their own emergence."[81]

McEvilley perceptively continues on to note that, unfortunately, what matters even more than such brightness from a marginal centre is the New York location of the influential art press. What this press covers "will eventually harden into art history"[82] and, since its discourse is largely focused on artists and issues important to the Big Apple, Stamp and Schwarz may remain outsiders because "neither seems burning to take her activity to New York."[83]

A year later, Stamp moves back to Calgary and, while she continues her exploration of making art using recursive systems, a more subjective theme imposes itself on her labours. The subject is Mary Smith, Stamp's elderly mother, who was born during World War I. Before Smith dies in 1997, Stamp records almost four-and-a-half hours of Smith's personal memories and then uses these "Mum Tapes" as the inspiration for some of her newest artwork. This includes the recursively coloured *Mary Smith;* a visual weave of popular song lyrics and Smith's own words on twenty-four panels of interwoven colour bands, and an installation recreating five domestic rooms of the kind Smith might have inhabited during different decades of her life.

Aptly titled *Mary is Here* (Glenbow Museum, 2000) and accompanied by audio recordings of Mary's recollections, this interactive work – which requires the viewer to visit each room – addresses any number of issues then pertinent to contemporary art practice in Canada. This includes the use of memory, the construction of identity, the role of the artist and the representation of women's history within the museum context.

Glenbow art curator Kirsten Evenden says: "Stamp considers her work in this installation as that of a kind of curator – one who mediates between Mary Smith and the institution where this project is presented."[84] It's considered mediation because it is Stamp who chooses furniture and artifacts from the museum's own collection for each period room to blend with personal objects belonging to her mother.

"The question of whether or not I can be considered to be a painter is an interesting one,"[85] Arlene Stamp in 1995 writes of her work, which by then has involved a wide gamut of materials: oil paint and wax on canvas; permanent marker and pigment on Plexiglas; permanent marker and carbon on paper; household tiles; glass mosaic; and various oil paint pigments with a relation to the colour or the word red. "From my point of view, it is not so difficult to use that word, because [my art largely] remains two-dimensional and because it could be seen to engage the issues of painting."

Arlene Stamp's public emergence into the Alberta art world in the 1980s – along with that of several other notable female artists – ensures the practice of painting will continue to have no shortage of women participants, even if painting is not the only thing these younger women do.

Their participation would have pleased Marion Nicoll, who passes away in Calgary in 1985 after almost six decades of making art. (Four years later, her former colleague at the "Tech," Illingworth Kerr, also dies. Thus, close two key pages in the first chapter of made-in-Alberta art.) Nicoll "felt that painting was the highest calling one could aspire,"[86] and that hand-in-hand with this vocation is the nurturing of a personal vision. Stamp, of course, does not share this attitude, but Nicoll's observation about what it means to have a painting practice would have rang a bell.

"You have to be an awfully practical person to be a painter. I've never been a romantic. You just work, that's all. And you hope,"[87] said Nicoll, who, along with her husband, Jim Nicoll, was the centre of Calgary's art world during the post-war period and beyond. "That is my Scottish-Presbyterian background," she explained. "It takes a lot of the zip out of life but it keeps you on an even keel."

A lack of the sentimental also runs deeply in Arlene Stamp's friend and colleague **CHRIS CRAN** (1949, Ocean Falls, British Columbia) who once compared his conceptually based practice to a "job"[88] and echoed Nicoll's view of art-making as being not very romantic. Raised in Salmon Arm and trained at Kootenay

School of Art in Nelson and the Alberta College of Art, Cran is the one who first brings Gladys Johnston to Stamp's attention. He too will be a participant in 1987's *Transference* at the Walter Phillips Gallery at the Banff Centre.

At the time of that landmark exhibition on appropriative art in Alberta, Cran is still working on his breakthrough series: *Self-Portrait Paintings (1984–1989).* Detailed and exacting in their execution, these faux-realist oils on canvas make painting look like more than just a job. Rather, it is a fictive place where all sorts of cheeky art world and societal commentary can reside, with a Cran look-alike often playing a central role in each image.

Most notorious and much to Cran's great personal delight is his satirical and over-the-top portrayal of what it might be like to be a bona fide "art star." In the context of the 1980s art boom and the academic discourse around art as a commodity, the shamelessly self-promotional *My Face in Your Home* (1986) and the brazen *Self-Portrait Accepting a Cheque for the Commission of This Painting* (1988) are iconic works. In these, and in other related images, Cran's look-alike in the painting is no suffering bohemian artist nor a pretend celebrity. Instead, Cran is smart, aware and totally at home in his dark suit apparel and straw panama hat (which he also wears in real life at the time).

But another role for the Cran look-alike is also that of the hapless nerd, starring in an even more perverse set of images such as the *Self-Portrait: Temptation of a Saint* and the wholesome but piggy-snout-nosed *Family.*

For the 1980s, Cran's dramatized subject matter and the spirit in which it is executed are – along with John Will's anecdotal life stories, Billy McCarroll's Sam Snead fixation and ManWoman's neo-pop mysticism[89] – about as irreverent as you will find in Canadian contemporary art of that period. If there is any spunk or "zip" (to borrow Marion Nicoll's word) to that body politic, these artists from southern Alberta and Cranbrook, British Columbia (ManWoman), with their collective joie de vivre, are deeply implicated. Though they are never a group per se, common amongst them is an outsider attitude: the recognition that place of practice can influence what one makes and have an impact upon attaining wider success elsewhere. To varying degrees, the conundrum of centre versus region can be read as subtext in their art.

This latter point – which is often politely ignored in Canadian art academia – is acknowledged in 1999, when Diana Nimeroff, curator of the National Gallery of Canada, tells the *New York Times:* "Those people who know [Chris Cran] really respect his work.... He's quite rigorous, very alive, very vital, not an academic artist at all. But Canada is very compartmentalized.

The scene is very small, very isolated. It's just the regionalism of the country. It doesn't mean they're not terrific."[90] This comment is in response to Cran's twenty-year retrospective, which is then passing through some of Canada's smaller institutions – but not any sizable public gallery like the NGC.

In the face of such a diminished view of Canada (all tiny and isolated), Cran's emergence then from the "distant hinterland" could appear to be a fluke when in fact, his art is nurtured in the sizable and supportive arts community of southern Alberta where, as even the *Times* writer understands, Cran hangs out "with nationally respected artists who also prefer to live off the beaten path."[91]

Still, in terms of national recognition, there are not a lot of artists from Alberta who have matched Chris Cran's success in post-1970 Canadian art. As David Garneau observed in a *BorderCrossings* review of the touring show *Chris Cran: Surveying the Damage 1977–1997:* "Among painters in western Canada, especially young male painters, [he] is a local hero. He is lauded as much for his well-crafted and inventive painting as for the fact that his critical, popular and modest commercial success came at home – even though, it is reliably speculated, he could have 'made it in New York,' like his friend, colleague and former Calgarian, Christian Eckart."[92]

In 1994, writing about Cran's *Heads* exhibition (which also tours to smaller public institutions across the country), Paul Woodrow notes in *Artichoke:* "Without doubt Cran is a serious artist ... who gives the most conservative city in the most conservative province in Canada a necessary injection of vital energy."[93]

Even more glowing, and from the same year, is John Bentley Mays's assessment for *The Globe and Mail:* "Cran is an intelligent artist ... laying the ground-work for an extraordinary career in Canadian painting."[94]

Cran's artistic beginnings actually stretch back to 1985, when his own brand of fictive imagery is revealed through the newly minted *Self-Portrait Paintings* in three separate group exhibitions. Featured in *A Measure of Success* (Alberta College of Art Gallery), *5 Plus 5* (Off Centre Centre) and *Points North* (Southern Alberta Art Gallery), these oils on canvas are rendered in an appealing, accessible style that – despite the literalness – is cognitively askew, even twisted, in its logic.

Their longish titles will give no reassurance. Instead, in matter-of-fact language, they often only describe the dysfunction at hand. In 1985 – a banner year – there is, for instance, *Self Portrait Just Two Maos Down From Guy With a Goddamned Tea Cosy On His Head, Self Portrait Watching a Man About to Shoot Himself In the Foot* and the unforgettably stylish (à la 1963 men's magazine) *Self Portrait With The Combat Nymphos of Saigon.*

Responding many years later to these incongruous paintings, where a pre-existing image (usually photo-based) from a magazine, ad or cartoon provided the scenario or pictorial content for a *Self-Portrait,* John Geiger writes for a *National Post* centre-spread on the artist: "Cran crossed the codes between realist imagery and cartoon subject matter. Although the paintings obeyed the visual canons of realism, they were cast into such a breathtakingly absurd context as to override the technique." [95]

If that weren't enough, there were also his artist statements to consider, like the one penned for the *Points North* exhibition: "Art is like mink," Cran rhapsodized in 1985. "If you feel it you know what all the fuss is about. The only real difference is that mink is dead." Thus, at a time when many a sincere, emotionally charged painter is caught up in the crashing wave of international neo-expressionism (late 1970s to mid 1980s), this ironic schmoozer is nowhere to be seen.

In all, some two dozen works comprise the *Self-Portrait* series. As a finale to this five-year "performance" on-canvas and off, in 1989 the Art Gallery of Windsor exhibits fourteen of the oil paintings in *Chris Cran: Loved by Millions* along with such fan club material as *The Handshake Tape* (1989, video, 58 minutes) and the docu-fiction *Loved by Millions* (1989, video). Put together with the help of fellow fame-game conspirators, Dennis Hrubizna (who plays the role of Cran's manager) and John Will (the director), the half-hour *Loved by Millions* documents the artist's bogus celebrity-style trip from Calgary to the Windsor exhibition.

In addressing Cran's series overall, David Garneau comments: "Many artists and critics loved [the self-portraits] because he came up with an elegant way to return to well-crafted, representational painting while incorporating recent critical theory (critiques of identity, masculinity, institutions, power, representations)." [96] In addition, there is also Cran's reproduction and adaptation of pre-existing photographic images from art and popular culture, as well as his passionate interest in the power of illusion or "tampering with people's perceptions." [97] Both characteristics are especially striking in *Self-Portrait as Max Beckmann,* where, in his finely tuned adaptation of a Beckmann self-portrait, Cran manages to blend his more youthful face seamlessly with that of the portly but suave modern master (1884–1950).

Tricky and disturbing at the same time, the construction of this 1986 image underlines how appropriative, especially illusionary tactics will continue to inform the next two bodies of work and still push his art into new pictorial terrain. First comes the semi-abstract/semi-representational *Stripe Paintings* (1989–1993) that, with their dazzling overlay of vertical stripes applied on top, employs enlarged half-tone photographic reproductions from art and the media. Then, following this series is the exceptionally various[98] *Abstract Paintings* (1993–1996), which are not sourced from photos, and at one point, concentrate on nothing more than the greatly enlarged monochromatic brush stroke made significant and palpably real. At times, this sensual, shimmering ridged creation of light and shadow veers into the holographic.

About his memorable *Stripe Paintings,* Cran proclaims in 1990: "I am interested in [the] simultaneous disintegration and recuperation of the image: image in the process of disappearing – image in the process of building.... This shift proposes that the eye is the first culprit in the process of the construction of meaning."[99]

In the later *Abstracts,* sustenance is drawn from the ideas and work of Edmonton's Brion Gyson and the American writer/painter, William S. Burroughs, "who felt that the viewer makes the work; that so long as there is a structure, the mind will fill out the rest and images will magically emerge."[100]

Thus, instead of deconstructing the fictive aspect of realism in the mass media and in representational art, (as he had already done in his *Self-Portraits*), in the *Stripe* (oil and acrylic) and *Abstract* (oil) works, art is a thing to be optically experienced. It's an occasion where the viewer has to move into, out of, and around the paintings to note their full optical effect. Technically remarkable and meticulous in their almost mechanical (impersonal) execution, both series hit the mark as far as some of the broader contemporary art discourse of the time. In Cran's favour, there is his: conceptual *modus operandi;* aforementioned engagement with the (appropriated) photographic image (*Stripe Paintings*); relationship to Germany's Gerhard Richter's own analysis of photography through painting; recontextualization of op art image-making and its polar opposite pop art; and for looks alone, its cool, anti-gestural, neo-geo, anti-self expressive stance.

Most of Cran's work just seems to click and yet be tantalizingly glamorous at the same time. The paintings get down to business without abandoning a deeply felt love of – and respect for – painting. But, like Arlene Stamp's work, Cran's paintings are a product of much different forces in contemporary art-making than personal expressiveness and the honing of a unique individual style.

In 1997, Chris Cran appears in *Concealing/Revealing: Voices from the Canadian Foothills* at the Museum of Fine Arts (Florida State University, Tallahassee) and Appleton Museum of Art (Ocala, Florida). Curated by Roald Nasgaard, former chief curator of the Art Gallery of Ontario (1975–1993), *Concealing/Revealing* brings together for the first time a particularly notable gathering of artists – Eric Cameron, Chris Cran, Jeffrey Spalding, Arlene Stamp, Nicholas Wade and John Will – whose individual practices have each been long exhibited and documented in southern Alberta and elsewhere.

According to Nasgaard in his introductory essay, although the exhibition is regionally based, the artwork in question is "rigorously non-regional," meaning it has developed "not out of grassroot loyalties but out of more universal tensions that bristle between personal concerns and the energies and/or strictures of current artistic languages."[101] Hence, the theme of *Concealing/Revealing* in which the featured artworks are generated from "strategies of concealment," or from tactics that "depersonalize the art-making process" or "dissociate the 'I' of the artist from the 'I' of the work."

Of the six artists featured in *Concealing/Revealing*, **ERIC CAMERON** (1935, Leicester, England) and Jeffrey Spalding are especially key to the exhibition's theme because of their unique involvement in 1970s post-conceptual[102] painting. Developed in reaction to the formalism of post-war abstraction and more recent colour field and hard-edge painting, (as championed by critic Clement Greenberg and practiced by a diverse range of artists including Helen Frankenthaler, Jules Olitski, Kenneth Noland, and Canada's Jack Bush), artists such as Cameron, on a completely different track from formalism, employed dispassionate procedural means to pursue goals more commonly associated with "minimalist and conceptual materialism of the late 1960s (Nasgaard)."[103]

In other words, a systematic procedure is used to produce the painting instead of relying on inspiration, intuition or subjective expression. It is idea-driven instead of a product of taste or the aesthetic manipulation of materials. In some respects, it is an art of visual indifference that engenders, nonetheless, some of the most compelling and physically beautiful works of post-1970 Canadian art – somewhere between, as Diana Nimeroff suggests, painting as high art and painting as work.[104]

In Canadian terms, post-conceptual painting develops largely in the "ruthlessly analytical atmosphere of the NSCAD,"[105] where a number of painters, either graduate students (such as Spalding) or instructor/administrators (such as Cameron and Garry Neill Kennedy), engage in methodically layering coats of paint on canvas or some other support. Later described by curator Cliff Eyland as "maybe a sneaky way to work with paint"[106] – especially when the medium is under attack from more vanguard elements of the art-making community (including feminists) in the 1970s – layer painting can be ridiculously rudimentary, yet rich in visual, art historical and intellectual meaning.

As a subset of post-conceptual art, layer painting is all about the application of paint fatalistically shaped by an attitude of que sera, sera. The favoured adjective describing this art's often demanding and laborious delivery is rigorous – a term that takes on an obsessive-compulsive dimension with Eric Cameron's *Thick Paintings*.

Begun modestly enough in 1979, the *Thick Paintings* (*to be continued*) are the product of a highly educated, even scholarly mind, which had already impressed others with the *Process Paintings* of the mid-1960s and video productions in the1970s. Featuring mundane items like a book of matches, a beer bottle and an egg painted daily with a half-coat of white gesso and then, after drying, a half-coat of grey acrylic, the *Thick Paintings* – by the time Cameron moves to Calgary in 1987 – have turned into a contemplative, ritualized practice of three hours a day involving twenty-seven objects. A brush entombed in the matter-of-factly titled *Brush Stroke,* for instance, is coated between 1979 and 1987 with 3,505 layers of gesso and acrylic, and weighs over ten kilograms at its conclusion. (Not surprisingly, the process would stop when the sheer weight of the object made it unstable to paint anymore.)

Variously described by critics as "plump, lumpish pale objects";[107] "wintry white paintings-in-the-round";[108] and "strangely organic forms with bumps, furls or delicate ridges,"[109] these curiously shaped, inexplicable forms are summed up in art historical terms by the artist himself as "an Ad Reinhardt wrapped around a Marcel Duchamp readymade."[110] Cameron also uses the term "material mysticism"[111] to describe his process: "As I have observed extraordinary transformations of shape and surface texture taking place under my hands – I have meditated on what was happening as I worked ... on the ascendancy of matter over mind, on the physical and psychological imprint of my own being with the developing mass of inert stuff; and on the possible implications of these things in the larger contexts of art in general and the world at large." [112]

As early as 1984 the Nickle Arts Museum presents an installation of the *Thick Paintings* entitled *Bent Axis Approach.* Then, after Cameron's westward relocation from Halifax, examples of his procedural efforts are quickly absorbed into such group exhibitions as *New Space* (1987, the Nickle Arts Museum), the juried survey *Alberta 88* (1988, Alberta College of Art Gallery) and *Essential Form* (1988, Walter Phillips Gallery). There is also a solo exhibition at Calgary's Stride Gallery in 1988: *In retrospect ... an installation by Eric Cameron with Thick Paintings.* It features six works displayed on white pedestals along with a much earlier, prescient piece, *Sellotape Painting* (1959), which was completed shortly after Cameron graduates from the University of London (Courtauld Institute). Donna McAlear surmises: "... as with all of Cameron's work, [*First Sellotape Painting*] cannot be taken at surface value; what is there is often not what we see, but what we don't see, not what we know, but what we don't know." [113] This comment about the relationship between the reality of appearance and the reality of that which is beyond appearance will reverberate even more poignantly when sixteen of the *Thick Paintings* are displayed in Cameron's next installation: the multi-media [114] *Divine Comedy.* The installation makes a six-city Canadian tour [115] from 1989 to 1991. The "paintings" are accompanied by slide projections of their earlier stages, a videotape interview with the artist, his book *Divine Comedy,* and the taped sounds of women's laughter. The banal object at the centre of each one of the *Thick Paintings* – including an egg, an ice tray, a chair, a lamp, a lobster, a mackerel and a paper bag – causes one critic to call them "the strangest works of art created during the last decade in Canada." [116]

They are also, in their three-dimensional solidity, some of the most secretive and repressed pieces ever realized: all those layers of paint employed in the service of entombment. Other-worldly and enigmatic, the modus operandi of *Thick Paintings* is critically interpreted, at one point, to be "a slow breaking of the shackles of common delusions – the paramount value of expression and originality in art, for example." [117] The artist himself regards them as "the objectification of the shell of numbness I have tried to avoid building up around myself. It follows that the life I have lived in my art may, in some ways – as with Oscar Wilde's portrait of Dorian Gray – have been more real than the life I have lived in the world." [118] This deeply subjective reading of a body of artwork produced under the most regimented and unsentimental conditions possible makes these concealed still-lifes a fascinating study in contrasts.

Undertaken by the artist as a life-long project, the *Thick Paintings* carries on as new objects are begun, like the fantastically rippled *Alice's Rose-is-a-rose-is-a-rose* (1996–2000, gesso and acrylic on a rose) and old ones concluded, like *Paper Bag* (1979–1995).

In 1994, Cameron receives the nationally prestigious Gershon Iskowitz Prize in recognition of his painting and his participation in the Canadian community.[119] As director of NSCAD's master of fine arts Program (Halifax) from 1976 through 1986, Cameron makes the acquaintance of such Alberta-bound graduate artists as Rita McKeough, Mary Scott, William MacDonnell and Jeffrey Spalding. Later, as head of the University of Calgary's art department – and thanks to his steady record of exhibiting locally – he establishes a presence in the Alberta art community that endures throughout the 1990s and beyond. For example, in 1996 Cameron is one of twenty-seven artists chosen to participate in Alberta's first *Biennial of Contemporary Art* (the Edmonton Art Gallery/Glenbow Museum).[120] The next year, in a *A 'Duchampian' Look at Glenbow's Art Collection,* Cameron's art is displayed among a diverse representation of Alberta-based artists who have been personally influenced by the iconoclastic Marcel Duchamp.

In that latter exhibition, "the idea that an artist is influenced not necessarily by creative thoughts, but by forces that occur without his or her knowledge"[121] finds its most canny and sensitive expression in Cameron's dove-white introverts.

Around the time Eric Cameron is planning a change of residence from Nova Scotia to Alberta, another British-born artist/instructor with Halifax/NSCAD connections,[122] **JOHN CLARK** (1943–1989, Howden, England), has already relocated from Britain[123] with his family to teach at the University of Lethbridge. The year is 1986, and, although his time in southern Alberta will be tragically shortened by cancer, Clark's representational imagery – and what he has to say about his approach to art – informs and illuminates this last section about image-makers who emerge in the 1980s and beyond.

What is relevant are Clark's attitude and his commitment to working within the parametres of only a few select areas: in his case, painting and drawing. Clark was something of an old-fashioned romantic, or at least an image-maker who didn't regard painting as a dead language. He believed meaningful, advanced art could be rendered out of the attitudes and values that once thrived in the western art world before the so-called postmodern "death of the author" and the demise of art for the sake of art. He cherished values from a time before "advanced art" is widened beyond such notions as self-expression, imaginative spontaneity, originality and just plain ol' inspiration.

Most of all, he feels that art does not have to be a mere extension of social theory and cultural studies, with its communitarian aspects examined and emphasized (and the art itself merely seen as an expression of its time and its society) and its individualistic legacy downgraded or dismissed as the work of too many white, male artists. In this paradigm, the messier aspects of art must be tamed for the good of the community – especially those efforts connected with the imaginative, the visionary and that always hard-to-define essence, the spiritual. Clark engaged with all of these things prior to – and even more so – after his arrival in Alberta.

Two years into Clark's Lethbridge experience, *Canadian Art* (Fall, 1988) quotes him as saying: "I work with images that often come from the imagination and all the things the imagination can unlock, which include possible narratives, memories and dreams." Even more daring of Clark – and certainly out of sync with the oft-repeated Canadian art critics' maxim that a contemporary artist's duty is to be rigorously non-regional – is his observation that "[since] I moved to Alberta, I've been using clearer, stronger colours because the light is particularly beautiful and clear.... I'm directly influenced by my environment and I welcome that."

As a newcomer to Alberta, Clark will not be unique in admitting such an influence on his art, but with a well-rounded background in European art history and personal contact with several of the international trends of the day, he could have remained comfortably aloof from the local environment. For instance, at one point in his youth, he paints well-received geometric abstractions. At another juncture, he connects for a short while with conceptually- and process-oriented art. By the time he teaches at the Nova Scotia College of Art and Design (NSCAD), his painting and drawing have an affinity for new imagepainting, especially that of Philip Guston, a former American abstract expressionist, whose radical, gestural, cartoonish imagery anticipates the 1980s return to recognizable figurative art and above all, paint-on-canvas art.

Of his monochromatic, simply composed "drawings in paint" whose expressive lines, strokes and marks render a telephone pole (*The Pole,* 1980) and a vacuum cleaner (*The Cleaner,* 1981) – the subjects of pure paint rather than of realism – Clark tells Halifax curator Ron Shuebrook in an earlier interview: "I want my paintings to be both overtly figurative and overtly abstract if such a thing is possible." [124]

Since he was a socially conscious individual, Clark's art can be interpreted as conveying an implicit concern for contemporary humanity, urban alienation and environmental issues. In his mature oeuvre, the artist also wanted his practice to remain "an existential activity, inseparable from his life." Writes Rosemary Pruess: "He resisted the literal and the illustrative in his painting, and sought a transformational art," one, it seemed, suffused with energy and a generosity of spirit. Irony, that buzzword of the 1980s, was alien to Clark as contemporary artist.

The contact the artist makes with the southern Alberta environment is unique and, in terms of post-1970 landscape-inspired art, almost without precedent in the province. His mythical figurative interventions such as *The Walker* (1987), *Swimmer in the Valley* (1988) and *The Dreamer and the Dream* (1988) anticipate those of Peter von Tiesenhausen in the 1990s. Further, the landscape can be an imaginary place, as in *Bird and Bridge* (1987), where a great raven-like bird clamps onto Lethbridge's striking High Level bridge.

Once in Lethbridge, Clark's subject matter deepened. Nature and the environment inspire him, but, more often than not, the imaginary prevails. The human and bird figures he draws, as well as his trees, are symbolic and sometimes otherworldly, highlighting his interest in the connection between contemporary humanity and the planet. Observable, too, in his art are unusual phenomena like the long sharp blades that dominate the foreground in *Scissors in the Sky* (1987) works. Similarly, in *The Night Paintings* (1988) a length of thick rope is strung across the heavens. The northern plains, as experienced by this artist, appear to be a place for conjecture and mystical yearning.

In a sense, Clark's response to this environment parallels the metaphysical view of some First Nations art towards nature and the land. A visible energy seems to flow through his Lethbridge oeuvre. The drawing is fluid, and the deep reds and vivid blacks are animate. "The sureness of his thinking/feeling hand" [125] is how critic Nancy Tousley describes this aspect of his art. She later adds that "[Clark's] concern for the human relationship to nature, time and the universe grows in mystery and power in the late works." [126]

John Clark: The Night Paintings at Banff's Whyte Museum (1989) is the artist's last solo exhibition before his death. Referring to the series as a distinct subgroup, curator Katherine Lipsett writes, "the stronger, bolder colours indicate a new sense of optimism" about humankind's kinship with nature. Inspired by his night drives across the prairie, the artist views "the night to be a vehicle through which the imagination flows freely."[127]

Shortly after Clark's death in September 1989, the University of Lethbridge Art Gallery organized a retrospective (1978–1989) of thirty-four paintings, drawings and experimental prints that travels for the next two years to six Canadian cities. Entitled *John Clark: A Tribute,* this effort to show Canadians a distinctly un-ironic, spiritually connected voice is followed in 1995 by another Lethbridge show, *Other Ramifications: Paintings and Drawings by John Clark* (Southern Alberta Art Gallery).[128] Writing in response to *A Tribute,* Nancy Tousley observes for *Canadian Art:* "[He] searched for a means to marry matter and spirit in images that embodied the humanizing qualities he missed in so much recent art."[129]

John Clark is not alone in his quest to reconnect painting more directly to life and personal experience. Among other new Alberta faces of that time, painter **DAVID JANZEN** (1959, Toronto, Ontario) is described in 1989 by Tousley as "committed to a rich tradition of painting tied directly to everyday things, views from the window of his tiny basement studio, neighbourhood sights and glimpses of nature seen in the urban environment."[130] Commenting on **JOHN BROCKE**'s (1953, Edmonton, Alberta) exquisite oil on linen, *John, Dovie, John* (1985), Christopher Hume of the *Toronto Star* observes how the three disabled subjects, seated in the light-filled kitchen of a Calgary group home, are "presented honestly and directly but with a strong sense of humanity."[131]

More descriptive and objective in their imagery than the older Clark, Janzen and Brocke are as much products of Alberta and its representational legacies (both regional and international) as Clark is of his. Both men study painting at the Alberta College of Art, and the two surface with a kind of brilliance that prompts Hume to ask: "Can there be any doubt that Calgary artist John Brocke is one of Canada's most extraordinary painters?"[132] and the *Globe and Mail*'s John Bentley Mays to enthuse that Janzen is "a wonderfully talented young Calgary painter."[133]

Mays adds a few years later in *Canadian Art* (Spring 1998): " Janzen belongs to the genealogy of Western painters – from Friedrich and Turner, Cezanne and de Chirico to Gerhard Richter – who've used landscape painting to probe, philosophically, the strange new world created by high technology. Any one of them would be worth five hours of thought, and more."[134]

This is high praise for an artist who, even by 2000 has never had a solo exhibition in a public institution or even a catalogue devoted solely to his art. Since graduating in 1983 and presenting what is still, in this writer's opinion, one of the best exhibitions (1985)[135] by an emerging painter in the Calgary area, Janzen appears in a modest number of group shows in public institutions[136] and several solo and group exhibitions in commercial and artist-run spaces. But, as far as being recognized in any larger (national) sphere for his post-Canadian landscape art, he remains admired, but generally not well-known, for his urban perspectives.

Unlike so much Canadian landscape still preoccupied with the countryside or the wilderness, David Janzen's carefully composed view of Canada is totally familiar, yet paradoxically alien to most. Here is an artist who, as he says, can paint with great regard "the ground [bristling] with poles, stacks, lamps, cable. Rooftop installations stand against a backdrop of weather, signifying settlement."[137]

In a Janzen oil on canvas, the viewer's eye is drawn either upwards towards a pristine vista containing such urban hardware as transmission towers, street lamps and telephone poles – totemic and isolated from their surroundings – or, downwards where, from the sterility of an aerial view, the landscape is managed by its division into grids. Of course, some viewers will wonder why such unsentimental subject matter, described in *Canadian Art* as "brave new terrain," is so compelling to the artist.[138] But Janzen believes he is conditioned to look at the transformed landscape,[139] attributing his receptivity to a childhood spent in park-rich Edmonton, where his father was the city's parks superintendent, in charge of civilizing the aspen-poplar prairie. More surprisingly, although his art is interpreted to be concerned with the less-than-benign effects of technology on the environment, these issues are raised only indirectly. "My depictions ... are not intended to be critiques of encroachment ... [but are instead] an effort to know it, to seek meaning in it and recognize its wonder."[140]

Janzen appears with several fellow Albertans[141] in *Transformations: Imaging Nature* in 1998. Displayed in Regina, curator George Moppett suggests Janzen's highly selective compositions "participate in a pictorial tradition that searches for the significance of the banal."[142] They are therefore similar to his earlier indoor still-lifes and collaged mixed-media works where, in the more successful images, sensitively rendered household objects "become sinister, humourous or personified."[143] This will be repeated in his later work when the focus changes to the larger-scale icons or objects of the urban environment. These include satellite dishes, storage tanks, transformers, earth-moving equipment and other infrastructure.

Notes Moppett about Janzen's ability to compose an evocative image: "In *Killarney Tower* (1996), an elaborate technological apparatus [a microwave tower], framed against the sublime beauty of a clear blue sky, presents an image charged with a sense of unease." [144] Speaking more specifically in reference to Janzen's controlled yet painterly style, Christine Sowiak, who curates *Blue* (The Nickle Arts Museum, 1999), elaborates: "The paintings are luscious and sensuous, finely crafted and meticulous, richly atmospheric." [145]

Thus, while formal and pictorial concerns still have a role, the symbolic, metaphorical, art historical and/or emotional content is more pertinent. In Janzen's case, not only is the "what" especially succinct and original, but as potentially mythologizing as the more traditional image of the country as a hinterland sanctuary. In Janzen's portrait, Canada and places like Alberta are a twenty-first century, high-tech landscape whose varied infrastructure is on the front line of all that progressiveness.

Familiar places and suburban scenery are two of the most visible features in the hyper-reality of John Brocke. That, and the jaw-dropping detail of his images. Painted on an epic scale – some Brocke canvases are 8 feet or more – his oil on linen works are reminiscent of old masterpieces painted to convey a detailed narrative for the erudite interpreter. But, as impressive as Brocke's devotion to accurate description is, he is no documentarist in the contemporary mode. Despite utilizing actual settings such as Calgary's Memorial Park for *Barb-Barbaros* (1985) or a dowdy rental apartment for *Basement Suite* (1986), the artist, according to Philip Ottenbrite, is after something else: "What we have come to expect from the realist mode is an opportunity to examine the tendencies of the artist as a voyeur. Brocke is not a voyeur, he is a creator, and his paintings are his inventions. He demonstrates not what he sees, but rather, what he visualizes." [146]

And what Brocke visualizes can sometimes be pretty strange or inexplicable, as it is in *Barb-Barbaros* where, to the right of a standing young woman dressed attractively in jeans, a bear lumbers casually through the trees. To the left, a man walks his dog towards her. Remarked Brocke about this scenario set in an old downtown park: "I realized intuitively that they [bear and man] all had to be there. I didn't know what the painting was about. Now I have a notion that it has something to do with adolescent female sexuality, that time frame and that striking awareness."[147]

But the visually incongruous – such as a bear in an urban park or a wolf howling on a deserted suburban street (*QOL/Voice,* 1987) – is not always present in a Brocke image. In his portrait of *Errol and Alice* (1983) or the aforementioned *John, Dovie, John,* nothing seems out of place: in the former a couple stands casually inside a steel-grey industrial elevator, in the latter three disabled adults serve as the subjects. Still, these two very singular paintings do have an impact, perhaps testifying to the "the spiritual presence [Brocke] feels in the physical world of everyday appearances"[148] and his realization of that in paint.

The *Globe and Mail*'s John Bentley Mays describes the artist's steadfast alliance to realism as "militant,"[149] while Brocke himself prefers to quote Philip Guston, who once said, "I do not see why the loss of faith in the known image should be celebrated as freedom. It is a loss from which we suffer and the pathos motivates modern poetry and painting at its heart."[150]

During a decade of painting (1982–1992), Brocke's art – or more specifically, the one or two canvases he produces a year – is never without comment or coverage. The opinions these works generate range from the general ("Brocke's vision is somewhat twisted, a trait common among other realist painters"[151]) to the specific ("[He] makes another sort of mythology.... His otherworldly narratives, with their hugeness and their meticulous detail, create an eerie drama."[152]). In addition, there is always something to be said about his technique of painting – working with opposing colour harmonies, and in almost a pointillist fashion, tiny strokes of thick pure pigment laid down "to catch the light and produce a depth of colour that is astonishing and mesmerizing."[153]

In 1992, after two years of work on one single oil painting, *Epoch* is unveiled at the Mira Godard Gallery in Toronto. Measuring 6 × 15½ feet, this strange and elegiac image is received, in one case, as "an ambitious and fully realized apocalyptic vision."[154] With a large bird above and a red helicopter hovering ominously nearby, four costumed men lead their horses through a blackened burnt forest. This medieval-like – yet entirely modern – pilgrimage (or flight) could be interpreted, on one level, as having links to contemporary issues revolving around ecology, high-tech surveillance, survivalist sects and the changing role of the male as provider and protector.

For Brocke personally, *Epoch* marks the end of an intense period of image-making. By coincidence, the title of the work also alludes to a fruitful period of new realist painting in Alberta that first develops momentum in the 1970s through the efforts of John Hall, Dulcie Foo Fat, Alexandra Haeseker, Gary Olson, Joice Hall and John McKee, and continues with great energy into the 1980s and beyond with a brief selective look at the following artists.

For **VIVIAN THIERFELDER** (1949, Edmonton, Alberta) of Spruce Grove, realism is in the service of elevating the floral still-life into the realm of the aesthetically excessive, the psychologically charged and the erotically ornate. "One could, faced with a Thierfelder painting, work up quite a sweat,"[155] remarks one Edmonton critic; while more generally for the artist: "It's a sensual, wonderful, joyous world we live in and I wish to share the exhilaration I feel."[156] This is not art for a puritanical disposition.

A BFA graduate from the University of Alberta, Thierfelder develops her large-scale, table-top still-lifes to great precision in the 1980s. With an orchestrated selection of photographs, objets d'art, ripe fruit, private mementos, swatches of fabric and flowers in full, lusty bloom, she is probably the only still-life realist[157] in Alberta who matches John Hall for that perceptual, over-the-top effect, which she achieves in watercolour applied opaquely. As with most realists, the process of painting is intensely absorbing and important for Thierfelder, but as gallery director Roger H. Boulet notes in her 1989 exhibition, *Vivian Thierfelder*, at The Edmonton Art Gallery, the image-maker's efforts do not stop there: "There is, in her work, a memory of the glories of past art, the very noble tradition of still-life that reached its zenith in the middle of the seventeenth century Holland. [Her] art is an affirmation that art has a memory, and can be concerned with its own past. In every still-life, there is something beyond the surface, beyond the objects, something a thinking person must inevitably bring to a work of art, unaware perhaps that it is the work of art that has provoked this consciousness."[158]

With the advent of postmodernism, the concept that art has a memory and can reflect on its own complicated past is a key feature in art of the 1980s and beyond. Certain types of art, though, have more critical and curatorial validity in the publicly funded sector of the contemporary Canadian art scene. These include the eternal Marcel Duchamp and the legacy of Dada, and more recent movements such as pop art, minimalism, process and conceptual art. If there is any interest in art's other pasts, such as the one pertaining to representation and realism in its many and various forms, it generally is exhibited in the for-profit sector (private or commercial art galleries) and the smaller public institutions.

In 1995, Calgary's Muttart Art Gallery organizes *Realism Revisited:* a bountiful cross-section of a dozen local artists committed to the art form's more contemporary expressions. These range from the more senior Joice Hall, and the somewhat younger Eve Koch and Marcia Perkins, to newcomers such as Marianna Gartner. Veteran artist John Hall is also part of the mix, his influence evident in the sparkling photo-like still-lifes by former student Glen Semple. Not all of *Realism Revisited* is of the photo-realist type, though. There is, for instance, Jean Pilch's exacting pastel pencil landscapes, Greg Edmonson's tonal photocopy-based face paintings and the almost painterly style of Marcia Perkins.

Perkins's brand of realism also appeared six years earlier in *Artist's Perspective* when John Hall – the city's most acclaimed realist and mentor to many[159] – is invited to curate a small selection for the Glenbow Museum's important *New Alberta Art* program (1988–1992). Of his selection Hall writes: "Much of contemporary art relies heavily on overt expression and/or inventive recycling of form for meaning. The art of [Alexandra] Haeseker, [Keith] Harder, [Eve] Koch, and Perkins presents a powerful alternative. With remarkable dedication to painting technique, they find meaning in the polite, gentle, thoughtful, and enthusiastic celebration of the ordinary."[160]

Art that is "polite, gentle, and enthusiastic about the ordinary" is – in the context of the ironic, critically edgy, theory-filled 1980s – definitely on the margins of contemporary art, in Canada and elsewhere. To favour the modestly quotidian and express it in a critically deemed conservative manner signifies that independent and alternative positions are being taken and sustained, as was true of the late **EVE KOCH** (1949–2001, Medicine Hat, Alberta). Noted for her innovative interpretation of photo-realism where, according to Hall, "the skin of paint becomes an almost transparent surface through which one views [her world],"[161] or from Koch's own perspective: "the paint itself is transformed into the image,"[162] Koch first garners attention with an important solo at Calgary's artist-run Stride Gallery in 1987. On display are fifteen acrylic works on paper and canvas that stand out for their use of the grid and their surrealist disposition. In *Blue Ribbon Interior* (1986), for instance, a cozy kitchen-table scenario is disrupted by the repeated forms of decaying fish heads rising through the checkered table surface. Queried reviewer

Christopher Jackson: "Is this a scene of domestic disruption, a metaphor for the breakdown of commonly held values?" [163]

In the essay for the Stride show, Donna McAlear observes how Koch's illusionistic paintings "embody a tightly sealed world," [164] where, at first glance, they "appear simple, placid and unassuming" before closer scrutiny reveals "a more complex and layered image." To attain this, Koch utilizes a process for which she coins the term "technique invisible." [165] According to McAlear: "The sanded matte finishes deny the artist's touch. Delicate brush strokes, marks from pencils, the collaging of paper-cut-outs and transfers, and the methodical layering of paint glazes are deliberately hidden under transparent coatings of gloss medium (often as many as 150 layers) to disguise the making of the painting, to further the illusion."

As a source of inspiration for this kind of beneath-the-surface refinement, Koch acknowledges the polished domestic interiors of the Old Dutch master, Jan Vermeer. His art and those of other classical realists have an impact, not only on the silken, luminous surfaces of her paintings but also on her more precise, serene imagery that emerges in the 1990s. "[My imagery] is more thoughtful, less confrontational, more poetic, less preachy, more feminine, less hard-edge," [166] Koch writes in 1997 about several years of imagery incorporating the full or partial female figure with still-life objects derived from her kitchen, bedroom and toilette. (In some instances, the figurative subject is Koch herself.)

Preferring to paint in a larger-than-life scale, and from close up, Koch's later acrylic on linen paintings heighten rather than exaggerate the realism at hand. This means, for instance, the skin is tactile but not microscopically pocked; a reflection in a mirror ephemeral but not sculptural. Most poignant are her depictions of the rough, worn hands and feet belonging to friend and sculptor Katie Ohe, as well as those of the toweled Koch posed in moments of quiet contemplation. The aim is not portraiture or anecdotal, instead, it seems to be reality itself that Koch wants to dwell on – including its socio-cultural connection to the colloquialism that "a woman's work never is done." By necessity, that reality is a personal one, related to her own surroundings, and yet, of all the new realist imagery to emerge in Alberta over a thirty-year period, Eve Koch's is perhaps the most introverted and discreet: a contrast to the gregariousness of a John Hall or a Glen Semple.

In the honing of her dispassionate art, Koch's intention is to absorb the viewer into the image at hand without any reference to her own presence in its making (hence its much worked-on and depersonalized surfaces). In this respect, she shares similar ground with those who labour intently on artworks that deliberately distance the maker from such concerns as self-expression or displays of authorship. Earlier in this chapter, Arlene Stamp talked about letting "the product stand and reveal itself as all and only what it is." Koch, working in the realist mode, was with Stamp in spirit.

From 1997 to 1999, Eve Koch is one of six[167] to tour her art in *Sight Specific.*[168] Koch is singled out in an *Edmonton Journal* review[169] for her exceptionally clear and sharp colours, as well for her "tricky perspectives," where the subject in *We Pine* (1997) or *Ivory Girl* (1997) is seen from straight above. Several of these figurative-cum-still-life paintings are shown shortly after her death, in an exhibit in New Mexico and then as part of a larger retrospective at the end of 2001. Organized by Calgary's Triangle Gallery of Visual Arts, *Con Memoriam: Eve Koch and J.K. Esler* encapsulated how these two neighbours, two founding members of the Triangle (and two victims of cancer in the same summer) left their mark in painting, locally (Koch) and printmaking, nationally (Esler).

Like Eve Koch, **MARCIA PERKINS** (1946, Washington, DC), also dispassionately renders the still-life, the figurative and the self-portrait. Sensitively described and coolly coloured, these works nonetheless possess only a little of the precise detail and refined polish of a photorealist work. Instead, a visible surface is present on her oil on canvas (or panel) art, and her realism more naturalistic than hard-edge photographic, itself connected to an interest in the appearance of things without any visual or perceptual heightening. In certain works, Perkins blends together into one image the still-life and self-portrait as she did for *Between Thinking and Spelling,* a 1990 solo exhibition[170] that featured some her most complex compositions. The artist likes to think of herself as an observer, and these hybrid works are preoccupied with the study of science, art and life (especially its physical anatomy).

In other works, the focus is largely on the artist as subject or on her haunting collection of symbolically important personal objects. About Perkins's self-portraits, the *Calgary Herald*'s Nancy Tousley is prompted to remark: "It's rarely easy to decipher character from a face, especially the way Perkins paints her own, head-on, with unflattering, merciless, almost clinical frankness."[171]

When Perkins returns to painting in 1986, it is her drawing skills that engender a sense of objectivity in her realism rather than the camera. Contrast this approach with a photorealist like Koch, who did "not bother with drawing except for a few thumbnail sketches to help decide the composition"[172] and had her photographs [which informed the paintings] taken by a professional photographer in the studio.

Before her relocation to the coast, Perkins was, according to David Garneau, "one of Calgary's very few serious artists who is committed to painting from life."[173] He adds further that "paintings from life are invested with the concentration of the gaze rather than the moment of the glance" – which is exactly what Perkins achieves in her realism. She has a gaze so penetrating that, on viewing her self-portraits, it is easy to wince while in front of her still-lifes: the reaction is closer to being mesmerized. "She describes objects a bit more lovingly than she does her own image, but with the same clear-eyed description."[174]

Perkins's still-lifes are essentially her knick-knacks set in careful arrangements: small bird and animal figurines, marbles, a miniature teapot, a tortoiseshell bread knife, mirrors, moulds for false teeth, a plaster ear, small slender bottles, anatomical illustrations and so on. This material is, of course, all just stuff, but as John Stocking asks in relation to another one-person exhibit, *Marcia Perkins* (1989):[175] "What is it about significant personal objects that intrigues us? Under Perkins's resolute concentration, the delights offered by optical and tactile sensations give way to a deeper consideration...."[176] In response, David Garneau looks to art-historical precedents. "While Perkins's work continues the tradition of homey Dutch still-life painting of the seventeenth century and [Giorgio] Morandi's repetitive but subtle compositions, her pictures are also related to the introspective self-portraiture of women like Christiane Pflug and Artemisia Gentileschi. Perkins's strange use of mirrors also resonates with Manet and Magritte."[177]

Besides the presence of the mirror as an object in her paintings, mirrors also serve as a tool in the construction of Perkins's self-portraits. The self-portrait is now sometimes regarded in certain contemporary art circles as an egocentric exercise; faulted for presenting an autonomous sense of self without any regard to how gender, cultural and social identity has shaped or impacted on that individual. But the route Perkins takes is not an emotive, confessional or even a confrontational one. Her examples appear to be more observational than about a revealing a discrete entity named Marcia Perkins as a forty-plus woman with thinning grey hair and a sagging posture. Aging is represented by the artist for the physical fact it is. Uninflected with the neo-expressionistic tendencies of 1980s figurative art, the self-portraits are unsparing in their allusion to mortality. Perkins spartan self-portraits are some of the most compelling images of an individual produced in post-1970 Alberta.

BEV TOSH (1948, New Plymouth, New Zealand) attracts attention for her strong, female-centred imagery represented in larger-than-life drawings or paintings, in series or in installation. Like the artist, who is herself a tall woman and familiar with the world from a vertical perspective, these artworks are characteristically long and narrow in scale. Her route to exploring a sense of self – which entails in one series figurative drawings and paintings related to rites of passage and being a woman – is framed both by an academic interest in psychology[178] and more broadly, by women artists transforming "the image of their sex from passive, submissive and sexually available, which male artists served up on their canvases, into a new, more realistic one of introspection, control and action."[179]

Executed in charcoal and/or oil, Tosh's calligraphic[180] female forms are described by Monique Westra as "[bespeaking] strength and solidity"; as "attenuated sentinels of solitude"; of "surging upward and expanding outward"; and as "[revealing] a range of emotions and states of being."[181] Intuitive and lucid, her semi-abstract gestural figuration recalls Winnipeg's Sheila Butler and Montreal's much-exhibited Betty Goodwin in which both artists have also depicted swimmers. An early exhibition, *Surface Tension* (Muttart Art Gallery, 1989), draws on Tosh's childhood contact with the ocean around New Zealand.

"I see the human body as a matrix of experience,"[182] she writes regarding her engagement with the female form to express her thoughts and emotions. Still, her art is not portraiture. "[But] since they are figures, there is always that element of autobiography ... [because] I am drawing from the inside out."[183]

By relying on what emerges subjectively (without a model) or from what Tosh calls "a mediated space within me,[184] Westra observes about the artist's drawing: "[Her] keen sense of the physicality of the body and her knowledge of its structure is expressed by carefully applied, broad brushstrokes that mould the forms, modulate tones, and articulate pose and presence. The black figural masses are never static or flat."[185] The figures are also sometimes quite ephemeral: instead of a brush, an eraser is employed to reveal a part of the draped figure from a charcoal-covered surface. Wiping off oil pigment in certain areas of the painted or gessoed surface can also liberate faces and hands. This reductive method, used to great effect, is a distinctive feature of Tosh's empathetic art.

In 1996, Tosh is moved to create an installation (three large paintings, a table of funerary foodstuffs and icon-style paintings on wood tablets) to address the issue of radioactive waste and the death of a Siberian friend and interpreter named Lidiya.[186] Entitled *Heavy Water,* the sombre devotional-style images make reference to an earlier Chernobyl-like accident in the late 1950s in the Ural Mountains and its likely contribution to Lidiya's death from cancer at 44. Neither biographical or strictly narrative, the paintings are rich in symbolism and in the psychology of gesture and posture (as evoked by the figures).

Near the end of the century, another project involving memory (which as a contemporary art theme in Canada had already stimulated a large outpouring of artworks in the country for a good decade) preoccupies Tosh. Inspired by her own mother's experiences as a war bride, the artist takes a dramatic step away from her intuitive gestural approach to produce "lush oversized portraits of WW II war brides; the most striking based on a photo of her mother."[187] Tosh spends two months in New Zealand searching for untold stories of war brides; the resulting body of work, *Herstory* is included in the *2002 ArtTalk* lecture series (Artcity, Calgary) on the theme of memory and identity.

Two other artists who emerge around the same time as Bev Tosh – but who are inclined to take a more imaginary route in their art – are **COLLEEN PHILIPPI** (1959, Winnipeg, Manitoba) and **MARIANNA GARTNER** (1963, Winnipeg, Manitoba). At one point, Gartner is painting "strange, morbid fantasies around babies and children,"[188] while "[in Philippi's] world, hey diddle diddle, the dish really did run away with the spoon."[189] Art relating to the imaginary, the exceptional, the abnormal, the illusionary, the dream-like (surreal) and what Philippi herself once summed up as "the secret stuff of life"[190] is the focus here because the invented worlds of these two women do resonate. For instance, Gartner's 1999 exhibition at Toronto's prestigious Sable-Castelli Gallery is deemed "weird enough to make some of his blue-chip artists wonder if veteran dealer, Jared Sable, who represents such comparatively restrained and tasteful painters as Betty Goodwin, Ric Evans and Tim

Zuck, had finally lost it."[191] And Philippi's mid-90s assemblages are described as "the work of a nursery school project on chaos theory."[192]

Both Gartner and Philippi have been consistently engaged in the territory of make-believe: stirring up associations with their visually complex imagery; tapping perhaps into the Freudian unconscious of the receptive viewer. As the *Edmonton Journal*'s Elizabeth Beauchamp opined about Philippi's speculative excursions: "it turns out to be a surreal place. Not in the musty sinister style of the 30s but with a more Monty Pythonesque surrealism of [the] weirdly coupled...."[193]

With a BFA and then a BA (classics major), both from the University of Alberta, it is perhaps not surprising that Colleen Philippi's art is packed with layers of meaning, symbols and literary allusions. In the 1990s, her wall-mounted assemblages are encrusted with collaged imagery, tiny childish objects and other quaint ephemera; as artworks they often contain tiny wooden doors that on opening reveal more treasure inside. Eerie and evocative enough to be showcased in a Victorian attic, they bring to mind the reclusive boxes of American surrealist Joseph Cornell. But they are also beautiful in a sort of pre-Raphaelite manner. Philippi's interest in the historical imagery of the medieval and early Renaissance periods give her painted assemblages a refined decorative presence atypical of assemblage construction in Alberta.

A participant in the excellent *Object Realities: Assemblages and Other Constructed Artworks* (1995)[194] and *A 'Duchampian' Look at the Glenbow's Art Collection* (1997),[195] Philippi considers the element of chance to be an important and necessary ingredient in the creation of her work: "I believe that Marcel Duchamp was right when he said that the artist is a 'mediumistic being' who does not know what she is doing or why."[196] Her work, nonetheless, is always done with finesse and attention to detail. She transforms a lot of unrelated bits, such as broken toys, cheap baubles, old pieces of games, busted dolls, crockery, utensils and cut-out pictures, into magical picturescapes that reveal something different on each viewing. One writer from Edmonton describes the artist's method as "rococo alchemy."[197] Imaginatively stirred by the subject of play (as a metaphor about life) and the memory of childhood, Philippi, conscious of the socio-cultural issue-oriented demands being placed on artists in the late 1980s, notes: "I don't use themes of angst, the environment, the holocaust.... I feel for me that play is an antidote to all these concerns ... to let loose, become less serious for a moment, makes us less egocentric." She adds in 1995 about her return to Alberta from Ottawa in 1990: "There's something about this city [Calgary] that lets you do whatever you like. It's a live-and-let-live town – at least visually speaking." [198]

Marianna Gartner receives her training at the University of Calgary with a major in painting and photography.[199] At one point, she is a student of the photorealist John Hall, and in her acrylics, the photographic is also evident, but impacts differently. Rather than acting as an informational aid in the creation of the painting, the "found" photographs she collects and uses are, in a sense, catalytic: appropriated and then reinterpreted with elements added and/or subtracted. For her 1994 *Myths and Images* exhibition,[200] Gartner's process is described thusly: "The photographic images [of obese clowns, snake girls, three-legged men etc.] are meticulously and literally translated to canvas, then rendered both decorative and iconic with the use of gold paint and the juxtaposition of ornamental and religious forms from both the West and the East." [201]

Her portraits also have a vintage sepia-toned appearance, unlike the brightly coloured and lively buzz of a Hall still-life. Gartner's attention to detail and technical craft is still there, but her culled and edited portraits of people, individuals and small animals (birds, monkeys and dogs) emanate from a different place and time, in contact with neither the contemporary nor the everyday. It is the old world, the turn-of-the-century and the vaguely remembered that fascinate Gartner. Curator Barry Lord – who includes Gartner in the prestigious London Life *Young Contemporaries, 1993* – draws attention to her central-European background and earlier use of her German-speaking family photographs to make a picture-from-a-picture.[202] She also has an interest in the socially grim figurative art of Europe during and after World War I, particularly Austria's Egon Schiele and Germany's Otto Dix. The American contemporary photographer Joel-Peter Witkin is another influence.

With the inspiration of sepia-toned and/or black-and-white photographs acquired from flea markets, junk shops and friends, Gartner has also delved into the world of circus-sideshow freaks, hermaphrodites and anonymous individuals who have, for one reason or another, become the subject of the artist's ruminations. Children hold a special fascination, but are sometimes treated in unexpected, disturbing ways. Thus, in *The Glad Season* (oil on canvas, 1995) a primly dressed young girl cradles an infant's skeleton rather than a doll. Her younger brother stands beside her, and above their shoulders Gartner has added a row of large flowers in full bloom, making for a very striking, albeit funereal, image. In tying the artistic imagination with the social, one reading might be: living in an age before antibiotics, will the two children survive into adulthood or be a casualty of illness and infectious disease?

"The mixed-up messages [Gartner's images] impart are both disturbing and funny, as in the childhood game of cards where you can put an old man's head on a bride's body."[203] More disconcertingly, there is a spooky immediacy to those frozen moments nearly 100 years ago when someone is told to hold still in front of a camera. (*Artichoke*).[204] Concerning much of her delicately twisted imagery, the artist believes "it's not for everyone's living room" but "back then, photography was a very serious undertaking. So you got a ghostly aura from those intense stares, something quite eerie." She adds, "a lot of my work deals with life and death, beauty and horror – simple contradiction."[205]

Because of her manipulation of the photograph and the reality it once documented, a small selection of Gartner's art is included in the insightful *The Camera Obscured* (Edmonton Art Gallery, 1996).[206] Featuring seven artists engaged in the critically popular practice of photo-based art, the travelling exhibition proposed about Gartner: "Belief in the myth that the old photo is a glimpse of the past is shaken by these dream-like paintings which combine formal portrait photos and the artist's own emotional responses to them."[207]

In the same year as *The Camera Obscured,* Gartner is commissioned by the Alberta Treasury Branch in Calgary to paint a large-scale mural for the dome of its 9th Avenue branch. Based again on old photographs of largely unknown individuals from different racial and ethnic backgrounds, this eight-paneled portrayal of early Alberta – with all its subjects' eyes focused directly down on the viewer beneath – is some of the most dramatic public art in the province. Serious and pensive, the subjects reflect little of the high-hopes optimism often associated with a frontier/pioneer environment; instead, uncertain aspirations pervade throughout.

The mountainous realm of the Bow Valley was once home to such historic notables as Catherine and Peter Whyte, Walter Phillips, Janet (Holly) Middleton, Byron Harmon, Charlie Biel and the de Grandmaison family, and a summer residence for Carl Rungius, Belmore Browne, H.G. Glyde and A.Y. Jackson. At the end of the twentieth century, a dose of new energy is present in the Banff-Canmore corridor, conveyed though the efforts of Barbara Todd, Allan Harding MacKay, Michael Cameron, Ernie Kroeger,

Dan Hudson and **STEPHEN HUTCHINGS** (1948, Halifax, Nova Scotia), a resident of Banff since 1979, who rounds out this selective survey of contemporary image-makers. Like many of the artists covered in this chapter who leave an impression at century's end, Hutchings begins attracting critical attention in the 1980s. Trained in Ontario as an art historian [208] and then as an artist,[209] he variously exhibits conceptual work utilizing photographs and text, environmental sculpture and multi-media installation before turning to photo-derived painting in the mid-1980s. Engaged with the postmodern idea of a picture made from a (pre-existing) picture, he renders striking large-scale paintings based on photographic images culled from the business pages of the *Globe and Mail* and a Geological Survey of Canada publication. The two series of oil on canvas are titled *Corporate Portraits (1986–88)* [210] and *Geological Portraits (1989–1990)*,[211] and, even in their monumentality or larger-than-life translation, these descriptive photo-like paintings suggest a linkage to some other source.

Having, as he says, "served his time with the avant-garde in the 70s and 80s" [212] and having made art about the state of modern society, Hutchings then begins to produce more monumental paintings, sourced entirely from that once-hallowed, but now most suspicious place of all (in contemporary art theory at least): "the inner creative spirit." [213] That's what Hutchings likes to call it, and for a while his key to this nebulous place where the imaginary, the emotive and the invented are generated is through drawing: "an act of the greatest intimacy."

A pencil doodle by the artist, lopsided and smudged, is how it starts in 1991. On the edge of his paper was "a rough, scratchy, grainy bush, perched, on a hillside and portrayed in strong silhouette. [It]seemed to be engaged in a struggle to maintain its equilibrium.... I felt an affinity to this small 4-inch-square drawing ... especially to its heroic stance, its roughness, and most of all its utter banality." [214] This banality later prompts essayist Lelde Muehlenbachs to comment: "Just as human existence is in limbo between heaven and earth, bushes persist in the middle ground of botanical hierarchy. They are neither as elite as vines nor as pedestrian as weeds. As the great equalizers in landscaping, bushes can be subservient to an aristocratic chateau as part of an elaborate garden, give a gentler face to suburbia, or simply mark property lines. Bushes can assume as many roles as we may think up." [215]

For Hutchings, bushes begin to represent "an inner state of mind, an emotion, a relationship." [216] Drawn in graphite, shaped with an eraser and then transferred to an oversized canvas, the artist concludes that "although the drawing was very intimate ... the painting should be a strong public declaration." Soon after, four such bush oils – each one 9 feet square – are exhibited at the Edmonton Art Gallery as part of their regional *Studio Watch* program.[217] The tonal, softly smudged works "looked like enlarged, aged, tinted photographs ... [were] it not for their scale and the transparent layers of oil paint, they could have also passed for old master drawings...." Nonetheless, "whether drawn or painted, the hand of the artist both is and isn't evident." More importantly: "The bushes that [he] renders have less to do with representation than with the artist's dredging of his psyche."[218]

Thus, the bush, with all of its subjective and personal connotations, supplants the nationalistic communal windswept pine of the Group of Seven, as epitomized by F.H. Varley's *Stormy Weather, Georgian Bay* (1920). The pine had been nothing if not symbolically ubiquitous in the creation of an officially sanctioned Canadian culture. Now something else is smoldering on the horizon, its darkened shape looming and soulful; a form largely alien. At times, when rendered a little less neatly, Hutchings' bushes have a distinctly western appearance, recalling the truculent misshapen willows of the foothills and coulees. Illingworth Kerr, who knew that type of gnarly willow by heart, would have related. What would have been more foreign to Kerr, and many artists of his generation, is that none of this art referencing the natural environment is derived from actual observation: including the *Hedge* paintings of 1994 and the entirely fabricated *Plant* paintings of 1995. In one large irony: "Banff slips out of focus for Hutchings when he closes his studio door. Thus, he liberates himself from an exterior environment that can be as suffocating as it is delightful."[219]

Similar to how Marianna Gartner's nostalgically flavoured practice has been received, Hutchings' art is interpreted as unsettling, even pessimistic. "[There] is something strangely unnatural about this nature-based world," remarks Montreal critic John K. Grande in a later review. "Indeed, if this is nature, it is a postmodern one."[220]

A link is seen between the pretences of romanticism and the grandly executed and dramatic look of a Hutchings canvas. According to curator Joseph Wyatt: "The bush gave visual expression to the transcendental philosophies that [the artist] studied in university ... they are surrounded by an aura of energy and electricity: the ether of the sublime."[221] Concurring with this connection, Robert Fulford writes: "Knowingly or not, artists since the romantic era have accepted the task of inventing nature ... whether it is J.M.W. Turner transforming the English hillsides into pre-impressionist dreams or Lawren Harris redefining the Rockies as new-abstract cones, the process and effect are in an important sense the same."[222]

"My reading of [these artworks]," continues Fulford, "is that they stand at the centre of renewed human concern for the natural world. We live in a time when 'the end of nature' and 'the death of nature' are phrases that appear as book titles or the headings on magazine articles ... most of us will scoff at that notion, but it hangs in the air around us."

Ditto for the "the death of the author," a postmodern literary term coined by Roland Barthes, which – by the time Hutchings is making these eloquent and sometimes moody registrations of self – has been translated throughout the much of the academic and institutional art world as signifying the "death of the artist" (but especially the painter). As an individual, *he* (because there is a specific gender attached) is now regarded as a misguided purveyor of such discredited modernist values as originality, authenticity, transcendence, autonomy, uniqueness and aesthetic quality. A variation on this issue would also surface in relation to Hutchings' art in the early 1990s. Writing for the *Globe and Mail,* John Bentley Mays opines: "[His] painting still evokes the specific melancholy felt by white, straight modern males, who, rightly or wrongly, feel their historic, cherished notions of male sexuality and heterosexual role play are under assault."[223] He continues: "In writing this out plain, I realize I have probably ensured Hutchings' everlasting exclusion from important museum shows in Canada...."

This is an overstatement, perhaps, but such is the discourse and the distemper of that time. As Toronto's Richard Rhodes remarks in 1991: "Criticism [today] downplays any sense of [the artist's] personal history and individuation. In one sense, it is embarrassed by artists and the heroic individualism that a more romantic brand of criticism once gloried in. Such ideas are anathema to the communitarian mentality now rooted in contemporary criticism."[224]

In spite of this, and because the Canadian art world is made up of several overlapping audiences, it is still possible for Hutchings' brand of subjectivity to attract serious consideration. There is a receptive place for his paintings in commercial art galleries and regional public art galleries. In 1995, for instance, the University of Waterloo Art Gallery mounts an Ontario tour of *The Recent Paintings of Stephen Hutchings*[225] and, in the following year, he is chosen to participate in the first-ever *Alberta Biennial of Contemporary Art.* (This exhibition is an ambitious moment in a decade better known for downsizing, stagnant public subsidies and anemic support from the corporate sector of which more is to follow in this final chapter.)

Migration is common among artists, and just as Stephen Hutchings ended up in the Bow Valley to raise a family and establish a successful publishing company, two young Albertans who leave the province and end-up florishing in a larger arena are **CHRISTIAN ECKART** (1959, Calgary, Alberta) and **ATTILA RICHARD LUKACS** (1962, Edmonton, Alberta).

"Each has found considerable critical and financial success since leaving Calgary,[226] Eckart in New York, and Lukacs in Berlin,"[227] observes David Garneau. "Judging by the enormous turnout for [them at the Illingworth Kerr Gallery, 1990] both the artists and their work are of interest to many people. The fact of these two artists, young men who have fulfilled the art school fantasy of making it big in New York and Europe, offers hope, or perhaps wish fulfillment for the students who saw them.... But," Garneau goes on to caution, "we live in a different time, a time that is not as appreciative of great white male narratives."

In the larger arena of the media, though, this issue has little resonance, especially with regards to the virtuosic Lukacs, a painter then best known for his portraits of virile young men and grim urban landscapes populated with Berlin skinheads in various states of dress and undress. About one public incident, the *Calgary Herald*'s Nancy Tousley observes: "The recent flap between Attila Richard Lukacs and Canada's national news magazine points to the undeniable power of the artist's male figures. *Maclean's* airbrushed the genitals of a naked skinhead out of a Lukacs painting, which was reproduced in an article that called the twenty-eight-year-old former Albertan the most renowned Canadian artist of the under-thirty generation."[228]

Locally, it is heady stuff, even if socially conservative Alberta is not the place Lukacs chooses to reside;[229] instead Vancouver is where he will first achieve national recognition as a "young romantic" painter.[230] Nonetheless, exhibitions and artist talks by Lukacs still occur in his home province, always well-attended, always well-covered. Not only do national publications like *Maclean's* and *Canadian Art* pay attention to Lukacs' rising star, so does the conservative *Alberta Report* which, in response to a Lukacs exhibition in Edmonton, runs the headline: "From dead modernism to a terrifying traditionalism: The paintings of Attila Richard Lukacs are perverse but defiantly realist."[231]

In effect, it is like a tightrope act for the artist: rendering subject matter that happens to intersect with such contemporary art topics as the body, sexuality and identity, yet representing it in a pictorially conservative style that doesn't mind quoting from European old master art. In a most un-Canadian way, there is nothing circumspect about a Lukacs work; making for a bold and disquieting mix between bad-boy genius and bad-boy same-sex consciousness.

From 1986–1993, Berlin serves as a base for Lukacs where, he says, a better artistic climate for painting exists than in paint-jittery Canada.[232] At the end of that seven-year sojourn, Montreal's prestigious Musée d'art contemporain organizes *Attila Richard Lukacs*.[233] Featuring six exceptionally large wall-size canvases from the *E-Werk* series, the exhibition travels to The Edmonton Art Gallery in 1995 where it is presented under a socially conscious agenda of "confronting stereotypes."[234]

As to why the nude or semi-nude male figure would so suggestively dominate many of his paintings of that period, Lukacs' reasoning is remarkably art historical: "I hate the term homoerotic. It's a nineteenth century or Victorian English term. As soon as you see a male nude in a painting, it's termed homoerotic, but when you see a female nude in a painting, it's never referred to as hetero-erotic.... What I'm trying to do now is deal with the male nude in the way classical nudes have always been dealt with – they don't have to have those sexual implications."[235]

But whatever reading is attached to his work, Lukacs' acclaim for his tough, profane imagery will be in stark contrast to the mystically inflected[236] abstract art of Christian Eckart.[237] "Unlike most artists of his generation," Eckart becomes known for addressing "the long-standing connection between the art object and the spiritual."[238] In the early years of his New York–based practice, this encompasses (as he conceives it) "meta-painting or painting about painting" that, according to Nancy Tousley, "questions [the medium's] ability to function in the late twentieth century as the site for an encounter with the divine [the spiritual]."[239] His gilded yet asymmetrical picture frames are an example of this concern where, as critic Anne Severson speculates, their empty, image-less interiors wait "to be filled with the spirit of the viewer."[240]

Later, circa 1994, the questioning subsides as the artist begins to design wall-mounted three-dimensional objects whose formal simplicity and lustrous surfaces are intended to evoke the luminous and the transcendental. Industrially fabricated and impeccable in their sleek craftsmanship, they have no purpose other than the very ambitious one of being awe-inspiring – capable of transporting the viewer into a contemplative metaphysical realm. Severson explains: "Many of his ... paintings technically aren't paintings at all. He doesn't use traditional pigment, a brush or canvas. Nor does he have a studio space. His non-traditional works are fashioned out of contemporary mass-produced materials such as Formica, aluminum, and acrylic urethane lacquer (similar to a car's finished surface). Under Eckart's personal supervision, the work is produced in industrial workshops within cycling distance of his New York residence." [241]

It is tempting to attribute Eckart's particular preoccupation with spirituality as being somehow indirectly connected to his upbringing in Alberta, where much is made in the media (often stereotypically) about the province's religious and even fundamentalist Christian character. But, as it turns out in his case, you can take the boy out of the vast prairie but you can't take its vast character out of the boy. "Growing up here is a major influence on why I do what I do and why I'm involved with subject of the sublime. The sense of scale in the land and the sky is directly related." [242] This link may be unexpected for an artist preferring to reside in an urban fortress, but given the deep indentations that place can make on one's identity, it is an entirely logical leap of imagination expressed in a paradoxically big-city techno-futuristic fashion.

With ten solo exhibitions in New York and regular showings in Paris, Belgium, Italy and Germany by century's end, Christian Eckart could have remained comfortably aloof from his roots. But in 1997, a large and representative selection of Eckart's fabricated paintings, entitled *Disturbing Abstraction: Christian Eckart,* is shown at Calgary's Nickle Arts Museum as part of a travelling exhibition that originates from London, Ontario.[243] The curator, Mark Cheetham, describes Eckart's efforts as "demanding and intellectual." The artist assumes his viewers "can recognize his historical allusions to the icon tradition in the *Eidolans* [series], for example, or to Renaissance art in the *Sacra Conversazione* [paintings]. Recent American monochromatic abstraction is a constant point of reference. But Eckart presents these traditions for us to consider in a contemporary world. Though he styles himself a contemporary icon painter, he is equally concerned with pop culture, industrial technologies, and with the present possibilities of abstract art." [244]

Referring to the art in the exhibition as "among the most beautiful things you are likely to see in a contemporary art gallery," and "magnificent specimens of industrially manufactured culture, but without the utility," David Garneau wonders whether such work may only "be symptomatic of an anxious yearning for an abstract absolute." In Garneau's opinion, the paintings are "most present as well-crafted things that are part of an art world discourse,"[245] including the mining of art history and such discredited modernist values like transcendence and the art object having universal meaning.

But however an Eckart or, for that matter, a Lukacs painting is interpreted, the work is still undeniably that of an 'artist', rendered in an era when the idea of such autonomous individuals (with all their questing) is theoretically perceived as quaint and outmoded. Also, on another level, their idealism is no match for the increasingly institutionalized character of contemporary art in Canada and elsewhere where, as art critic and author John Bentley Mays later observes about the post-1980 period: "For a great number of gallery-goers, the primary contact with advanced visual art took place in sedate settings resembling those of seminars or scholarly conferences – carefully distanced, disciplined, orderly. Much of the art of the last twenty years seemed to have been tailor-made, even when it wasn't, by tenure-track academics for colleagues."[246]

☙ Ambivalent and Even Unfriendly Times for the Visual Arts

Even more sobering is the observation by Richard Rhodes that "artists float in the background."[247] Commenting in 1990 on his then-situation as an art magazine editor in Toronto, Rhodes notes (as if all need reminding):

> [Artists] exist at the centre of whatever it is that we decide to call art. And yet with the institutional shifts and theoretical biases of today's art scene, the artist is often seen as only one of an interconnected series of producers important to art.

(The term producers includes curators, critics, art dealers, academics and, most of all, institutions that either exhibit, give out grants or train artists and other art professionals.)

> The art world now aligns, like the mainstream culture around it, with the paradigm of a service-oriented economy. With the expansion of institutionalized service to art and its audience, reality is increasingly

> defined in terms of managing the consumption of art.... It is the nature of our culture itself. And this, in itself, is not necessarily a bad thing. The service sector surrounding art is an undeniable support mechanism. But we should realize that this support infrastructure is not neutral, that it shapes how we think about both art and artists.

Rhodes, does, however, conclude on a hopeful note:

> We can welcome it, but we have to find a workable equilibrium. ❧ "Darker than Mid-Grey: The Institutionalization of Art, *Artichoke: Writings About the Visual Arts,* Calgary, Winter 1991

This workable equilibrium, sadly, appeared to be nowhere on the horizon in Canada at the end of the century. Further, (as a digression on Rhodes's assessment) "the support infrastructure" at a national and larger institutional level continued to be the least receptive to the diversity of what exists in the "regions." Despite all the well-intentioned discourse in the 1980s about difference, the other, the post-colonial, the particular, the specific, the marginal and so on, regionality is rarely recognized as being part of that discussion. In addition, as this writer states in the pages of *Artichoke: Writings about the Visual Arts* (Spring/Summer 1992): "If you are a formalist, a conventional landscape painter, a realist, a non-video, non-installation, non-photo/text-based artist, etc., you can pretty well forget about being a part of the officially recognized art pie." And what does become noticeable during this end-of-century period is the infrequency of non-thematic shows in the publicly funded art sector. Displays that are mounted simply to showcase an artist or an informal grouping of artists active in a certain place or at a certain time – regardless of whether or not a curatorial thesis can be used to string them together in a tidy thematic package[248] – are less evident. The retrospective approach, where money and energy are devoted to highlighting the career of a more senior artist, is also infrequently pursued, if only because many such individuals are deemed to be no longer in step with contemporary trends.

But the issue of curation and how inclusive it really is in the context of the Canadian scene is only a symptom of what goes astray in the post-1980 period. In fact, by the end of the 1980s, there is the emerging perception in some circles that while "pluralism has occurred in different countries ... it hasn't happened in Canada."[249] Canada, with its cultural infrastructure and centralized pecking order, continued to be essentially conservative and neo-colonial in its response to those pesky constituents out there who might have other ideas about what constitutes excellence. Those pesky constituents who might have, in fact, taken to heart the notion that any number of options are available, even ones leading to a kind of congenial chaotic dissonance.

"At one point there seemed to be a shared western civilization program we called modernism where you could have access to the same questions and rules whether you were working in Sao Paolo, Lethbridge or downtown New York. So it was possible to think that your behaviour [as an artist] could be justifiable in relation to the centre,"[250] recounts Jeffrey Spalding about the period he himself experienced as an artist and instructor. "As modernism began to fall away as the major mode of operation you could no longer say everybody is in possession of the same rules, so it [the art world] became more complicated. [Thus] it was a liberation for places that are on the fringe as it were."

After 1970, the proverbial apron strings did get loosened in Alberta and other fringe entities. It is a period in which it is a particularly buoyant time to train and develop professionally as an artist. Much of this book is dedicated to selectively chronicling this era in the province, its up and downs and, in particular, the efforts made by individuals and institutions to put Alberta-based visual art on the Canadian map. At certain junctures, the indifference and ignorance of Canada's centralized arts infrastructure have also been highlighted. And as the 1990s unfolded, the indifference of this unreliable and bureaucratically remote player continue, while the province's own support for the advancement of arts and culture began to scrape rock bottom.

From the so-called "Camelot" years of the Lougheed era (1970s to mid-1980s), a steady reversal of fortune had taken place. Where Alberta had once outshone most of Canada in its per-capita spending on the arts, by 1997–98 only Ontario is faring worse. Arts spending is $75 per capita for Manitoba and $63 each for Saskatchewan and British Columbia, in comparison to a paltry $44 per capita for the economically well-endowed province.[251]

Another disturbing issue is how the once high-profile ministry of Alberta Culture (with a designated minister) is no more. From 1975 to 1987, Alberta Culture, for better or worse, had symbolized the government's commitment to this highly productive sector. But as Michael Evans points out in his 2000 report – optimistically titled *Culture Steps Forward* – the 1987 reorganization of Alberta Culture into Alberta Culture and Multiculturalism was the beginning of a trend that within five years had all but buried the arts within a ministry charged with multiple portfolios including seniors, recreation, libraries, the Alberta Human Rights and Citizenship Commission, cultural facilities and historical resources.[252]

"The sector once serviced by an entire ministry looks today to the Cultural Facilities and Historical Resources Division and the Arts and Libraries Branch of Alberta Community Development for its champions within government,"[253] Evans reports. (The Arts and Libraries Branch provides grants and contract administration to the Alberta Foundation for the Arts, which is an agency formed in 1991 from the Alberta Arts Foundation to support and contribute to the development of the arts in Alberta.) Not only that, the monies distributed to all of the arts[254] through this labyrinthine arrangement remained solidly frozen at $16 million annually from 1991 to 2002. (A minor increase of $3 million did occur in 2003.) "A measure of how far the culture industries have fallen from the concerns of the present government is the fact that an articulated culture policy is conspicuously absent ... the few policy initiatives of the provincial government related to the artist tend to direct attention away from government and its capacity to promote the arts and culture (Evans)."[255]

In fact, so dramatic is the marginalization of the arts in the provincial government during the 1990s that in response, veteran Edmonton film producer and broadcaster Fil Fraser feels compelled to write a 226-page memoir entitled *Alberta's Camelot: Culture and the Arts in the Lougheed Years* (Lone Pine Publishing, Edmonton, 2003). He writes: "I will show you a different side of Peter Lougheed, premier of Alberta from 1971 to 1985. He is the man many Canadians think of as the blue-eyed sheik of Calgary, the man who fought Pierre Trudeau over the National Energy Program in the early 1980s. But from the time he swept into office in 1971 until his retirement party on October 11, 1985, Lougheed's Alberta experienced an unprecedented mushrooming of cultural and multicultural activity. With oil revenues flowing copiously, the province became a patron of the arts."[256]

Fraser's personal account – which is set largely in Edmonton and highlights some of that city's unique accomplishments within film, publishing and performing arts – does not extend to the visual arts. But if it had, his story would have probably had a different emphasis in which the southern portion of the province, especially places such as Calgary and Lethbridge, assume a much larger profile.

The 1990s thus presented a painful challenge to the arts. What did not cease, though, through all the uncertainty and downsizing, was the making of visual art; the organizing of exhibitions (most *without* catalogues to facilitate the dissemination of an artist's work); the opening of new (mostly commercial) art galleries; the start-up of new visual-art periodicals (with very modest budgets unlike the generously supported publications of central Canada); the honouring of a few senior artists through retrospectives; the creation of new events designed to reflect some of the contemporary art-making energies; and even the recognition of a few Alberta artists within a national context.

But with a more engaged partner at a provincial level, all of the above could have perhaps been much more. As it was, no substantial breakthrough – something to broaden public perception about the province beyond a few well-worn clichés – took place. Cracks certainly did appear in the proverbial glass ceiling, and certain individual artists did make headlines nationally and internationally, but with the province standing off to the side, it was like having a shoe drop off during a critical part of the climb.

One example: in the summer of 1995, Alberta Community Development ceases publishing a modestly produced black-and-white broadsheet that since 1978 had recorded and reflected on the visual-arts boom in the province. Titled Visual Arts Newsletter and after 1992 *Arts Bridge,* this publication had a wide distribution inside and outside of the province. It performed the simple but important function of letting people in the field know about other artistic activity in Alberta. Yes, there was the reportage of the local media, including CBC, ACCESS, the *Edmonton Journal,* the *Calgary Herald*[257] and others, but in terms of covering the breadth and scope of the province, there was really nothing like this so-called "arts rag" out of Edmonton. Reading it, one could get a sense of the arts activity happening not only in Edmonton and Calgary, but also in less well-publicized places such as Fort McMurray, Medicine Hat and Red Deer.

Even in the last issue of *Arts Bridge,* readers are informed that ceramist John Chalke has had a work acquired by the prestigious Victoria and Albert Museum in London, England; that Murray Gibson, an Alberta weaver then based in London, is one of only three artists from Canada invited to show at the *8th International Triennale of Tapestry* in Lodz, Poland; that photographer Ernie Kroeger is the winner of the 1995 Barbara Spohr Memorial Award at the Banff Centre for the Arts; that Catherine Burgess and Sandra Bromley will be installing a 40-tonne, 22-foot-high granite rock sculpture topped with a natural garden as part of *The Works Legacy Project* in Edmonton; and lastly, that sculptor Clay Ellis receives favourable reviews from the *New York Review of Art and Sculpture* for his solo exhibition in New York. On the same page where news about Clay Ellis appears is an especially poignant article titled *International Impressions.* In bold black ink it states: "More and more, Alberta is producing home grown, internationally recognized artists who've made it to the world stage without moving out of the province. They paint, sculpt, write, play music, act ... and the world is coming to them."[258] This is certainly a piece of good news, but in the future this news, despite all of its variety and energy, will be less readily heard or known about even within the very community that was covered.

But if the 1990s represented a serious downturn in provincial support – especially true of public art galleries that have little money to tour shows, produce catalogues, acquire art for collections or hire curators – there were some positive developments *unrelated* to the government. The most important of these is the gradual thawing of the Edmonton art scene and its re-emergence as a centre for more contemporary practices. Prior to and post-1970, there had always been a modest mix of both modernist and contemporary art, but, as artist Blair Brennan recounts about the 1980s and 1990s, artists of either disposition pay a price by remaining in the city.

Better Times Ahead for Edmonton

Brennan writes in hindsight about his community: "Nothing could overcome the rest of the country's indifference to Edmonton's brand of modernist art. By that time [circa 1980], the rest of the country (and the world) had gone post-modern so Edmonton's modernist artists did not, generally become nationally or internationally known. It may sound like paranoid ancient history now, but if you didn't make modernist art in Edmonton in the 70s and 80s, you were likely to be excluded from that powerful triumvirate (U of A, local commercial galleries, and the EAG). Without this important local support (artist-run centres alone can only do so much) it was extremely difficult for non-modernist artists to gain a local/regional reputation. Without a local reputation non-modernist artists failed to progress along the lines suggested by the Canada Council. These artists would leave or make do, but either way they did not become Edmonton's 'established' elite." ("Act Now for Free Information," Latitude 53 Society of Artists Newsletter, May 2000)

No wonder that Edmonton's artists (emerging or more established) secured so little Canada Council money, or invitations to exhibit elsewhere, in those intervening years. Despite this, though, the city never really sat still, and as I suggested in the chapters focused specifically on Edmonton, even those associated with the modernist camp had new areas to explore.

In fact, many moved on. From this group, coming on especially strong in the 1990s, were such sculptors as Clay Ellis, Catherine Burgess and Isla Burns, as well as painter Graham Peacock, with his wonderfully weird contributions to the advanced material manipulations of new new painting. (Even *Canadian Art,* rarely tainted with the presence of recent modernist art from the west in its pages, let down its central Canadian guard and in 2002 published an article featuring Graham's art.[259]) To this 90s list, add names such as David Cantine's slowly simmering thirty-year-plus study of the same composition; Lyndal Osborne's remarkable nature-based installations; Darci Mallon's bodily representations of illness and loss; and Blair Brennan's continuing formulation of ritualized actions to create striking works of art.

Aside from these more-established names adding to Edmonton's diversifying pulse, there were of course newcomers like the witty and culturally savvy Allen Ball from England and emerging artists whose names will first surface locally through exhibitions at art galleries or at such artist-organized events as Edmonton's *40°C* (1995), which jurors Blair Brennan and Simon Black compared to the *Great West Saddlery Shows* of the late 1980s. On occasion, the yearly visual-art festival *The Works* could also be insightful about the changing Edmonton scene when exhibits like *Sculpture – The Works: 2001*[260] and *Drawings-4: Bagan/Carson/Freeman/Stehelin*[261] are organized.

But most revealing of this thaw in the Edmonton art scene is its varied offerings on display in the *Alberta Biennial* exhibitions. Since its launch in 1996, the *Biennial* accomplishes something that had not been tried before: to survey selectively on a regular basis some of the best contemporary art activity in the province, bringing awareness of the work of many artists to a wider public. In the 2000 *Biennial,* there is even the appearance of Edmonton-based heritage artist, George Tosczak, with his delightful folk-art paintings of a rural Saskatchewan childhood.

But the *Alberta Biennials* is not notable just because of its indirect reflection of the changed Edmonton art scene or its banishment of the view that Alberta art is polarized between Calgary painting and Edmonton sculpture.[262] From day one it also receives national coverage. It showcases a wide range of art-making, from traditional painting, drawing, sculpture and photography to installation, new media and performance including healthy evidence of Lethbridge's contribution to installation and new media.

In addition, for those concerned with art as theory and art as an adjunct to cultural studies – an intellectual preoccupation of many teaching, curating and writing about contemporary Canadian Art – the Banff Centre's Sara Diamond could report in Toronto's *C* magazine: "As twentieth-century concerns about interior life, fragmentation, desire, abstraction and isolation continue to resonate in contemporary practice, [Catherine] Crowston and [Catharine] Mastin put forward strong evidence [in the 1998 *Biennial*] that postmodern art's theoretical concerns (from dialogues about gaps and transgressions, to post-colonial questions about ownership) also resonate strongly in the sometimes-assumed isolation of Alberta practice." [263]

Yes, even in "a province still immersed in its own mythology and romance," [264] as *C* reminds its readers, there is hope for Alberta. But who really wants to be culturally without mythology and romance? It's the very stuff that many writers, filmmakers and artists have used to inspire, inform, shape (or deconstruct in) their own work. The problem with Alberta's frontier mythology and pioneer romance is that it's not very fashionable or politically correct in a postmodern world. And, as the historian R. Douglas Francis reminds us in the opening pages of this book: "Throughout its history, the Canadian west has evoked strong images in the minds of those who visited, settled or sometimes simply wrote about the region. These people saw in the west what they wanted, or were conditioned by their cultural milieu, to see." Ditto for all the arbiters and gatekeepers of Canadian visual-art history and practice (including this writer).

Nevertheless, if more socially thematic concerns are addressed by the contents of the *1998 Alberta Biennial*, the body of work chosen for the 2002 edition is an entirely different matter. In a substantial review titled "A Bright Alberta Showcase," Winnipeg critic Robert Enright reports for the *Globe and Mail* that not only "the artists are stretching to make their art work in new ways ... irreverent play with conventional perception is one of the delights of this exhibition", the *Biennial* "is an essential show, and its essential characteristic is that it is constantly changing." [265]

Changing as the visual arts in Alberta have always changed, instinctively knowing that these visual arts need no discovering or encouraging statements about their future potential. As this chronicle about post-1970 contemporary art has attempted to show, it already has, on many levels, demonstrated its energy and promise.

ENDNOTES

chapter one

1. R. Douglas Francis. *Images of the West: Changing Perceptions of the Prairies, 1690–1960*, Saskatoon: Western Producer Prairie Books, 1989, p.231.

2. Ibid., p. 232.

3. Ibid., p.194.

4. "Dorothy Knowles: prairie passion." *Globe and Mail*, May 13, 1995.

5. Ibid.

6. Murray's book was published in 1999 by Dundurn Press. Other surveys included Richard Rhodes' *A First Book of Canadian Art*, Toronto: Owl Books, 2001 and Anne Newlands' *Canadian Art: From Its Beginnings to 2000*, Willowdale, Ontario: Firefly Books Ltd., 2000. In Newlands' book, prairie landscapes by Dorothy Knowles, Ivan Eyre and Takao Tanabe appear.

7. The exhibition was curated by Jetske Ironside for the Alberta Art Foundation. Outside of western Canada the exhibition travelled to St.Catherines, Downsview, Toronto, Sackville and Stratford.

8. Wylie's review appeared in the summer issue, p.92.

9. *The Cairn* is a publication of the Whyte Museum of the Canadian Rockies, Vol. XVII, No.3, Summer 1994, p.5.

10. Quote from exhibition catalogue *Twilight at Walden Pond: A short story about art on the edge of nowhere and everywhere.* Concealing/Revealing: Voices From the Canadian Foothills, Florida State University, Museum of Fine Arts, 1997, p.46. Curator: Roald Nasgaard.

11. Paula Gustafson. "Arts elders stand up for beleaguered landscapes." *Georgia Straight*, September 16–23, 1994, p. 45.

12. Quote from exhibition catalogue *The Culture of Nature*, Kamloops Art Gallery, 1996.

13. Quote from exhibition catalogue *Norman Yates: Toward Landscape*, Ring House Gallery, the University of Alberta, 1983, p.46.

14. John Bentley Mays. "Young painters prove you can't pin good art down." *Globe and Mail*, November 4, 1995, p.C5.

15. John Bentley Mays. "Driven to abstraction." *Globe and Mail*, Saturday, June 1996.

16. In 1967, Iain and Ingrid Baxter would go on to form the influential conceptual art practice: N.E. Thing Company in Vancouver.

17. At the time Holmes was quoted in *Globe and Mail*, November 1, 1991, he was the director of the VAG.

18. Terry Atkinson. Quote from exhibition catalogue *From the Lake to the Swamp. The Flat Side of the Landscape: The Emma Lake Artists' Workshops*, Saskatoon: Mendel Art Gallery, 1989, p.63.

19. Barry Lord. *The History of Painting in Canada*, Toronto: NC Press, 1974, p. 207.

20. John O'Brien. Introduction for The Flat Side of the Landscape ... Ibid., p. 14.

21. Interview with Harry Savage, November 20, 1995.

22. Quote from exhibition catalogue Robert Sinclair: An eight year survey, Aggregation Gallery, Toronto, 1976, unpaginated.

23. "Conference grapples with regionalism" *Calgary Herald*, April 24, 1988, p. A13.

24. Ibid.

25. "Art is more than a capital idea." *Lethbridge Herald,* July 21, 1984.

26. Alvin Balkind. Essay "The Triumph of the Egg," *Visions: Contemporary Art in Canada,* Vancouver: Douglas & McIntyre Ltd, 1983, p.29

27. "Vigourous regional voices drown out cries for national vision," *Globe and Mail,* December 30, 1989, p. C5.

28. Ibid.

29. "Group turned to symbolism of forests," *Globe and Mail,* October 14, 1995.

30. "Regrouping the Group," *Canadian Art,* Fall, 1995, p.73

31. Essay "Twilight at Walden Pond: A short story about art on the edge of nowhere and everywhere." Concealing/Revealing: Voices from the Canadian Foothills. Ibid.

32. John Allison Forbes. Catalogue essay *Robert Sinclair: An eight year survey,* Aggregation Gallery, Toronto, 1976 unpaginated.

33. Elizabeth Beauchamp. "Art of this Place…", *AlbertaViews,* Summer 1998, p.36

34. R.Douglas Francis. Images of the West…, Ibid., p.193.

35. Ibid., p.201.

chapter two

1. Christopher Varley. *Winnipeg West: Painting and Sculpture in Western Canada, 1945–1970,* Edmonton Art Gallery, 1983, p.19.

2. From Christopher Jackson's catalogue essay, *Marion Nicoll: Art and Influences,* Glenbow Museum, Calgary, 1986, p. 10.

3. Barry Lord. *The History of Painting in Canada,* Toronto: NC Press, 1974, p. 210.

4. Robert Fulford makes reference to this perception in "Regrouping the Group," *Canadian Art,* Fall, 1995, p. 73.

5. Quote from George Melnyk's essay for *Norman Yates: Painter of Land and Lights,* Edmonton Art Gallery, 1976, unpaginated. Thanks to Nancy Townshend for giving me this quote.

6. From exhibition brochure In Tribute to Rick Grandmaison, Masters Gallery, Calgary, 1987.

7. John Howse. "Artist creates own memorial in oils," *Calgary Herald,* December, 1985.

8. Interview with Sonia de Grandmaison, Nov. 20, 1995.

9. O.N. Grandmaison. Foreword to catalogue *Historic Ranches of Alberta: A Selection of Paintings of O.N.Grandmaison,* from the collection of Westburne International Industries Ltd. Calgary. No date.

10. Derek G.Whyte. "Grandmaison exhibition compelling." *Calgary Herald,* December 14, 1971.

11. Howse, ibid.

12. *In Tribute to Rick Grandmaison,* ibid.

13. Introduction to brochure Ken Christopher, Buschlen/Mowatt Fine Arts Ltd., Vancouver, 1988.

14. Russell Bingham uses this term in the exhibition catalogue *The Big Picture: Large Scale Landscape Painting of the Prairies,* The Edmonton Art Gallery, 1981, unpaginated.

15. Ibid.

16. Ibid.

17. Interview with John McKee, March 8, 1996.

18. Maggie Callahan. Essay for *Ken Christopher: Painting 1978–1980,* The Edmonton Art Gallery, 1981. Unpaginated brochure.

19. Quote from *The Big Picture,* ibid.

20. Ibid.

21. Ibid.

22. Quote from exhibition brochure, *John McKee: New Paintings,* Woltjen/Udell Gallery, Edmonton, 1990.

23. Robert Guest. Introductory essay to Isabel Perry's *Euphemia McNaught: Pioneer Artist of the Peace,* Edmonton: Reidmore Publishing, 1982, p. 22.

24. Maggie Callahan. Exhibition catalogue, *Harvest of the Spirit: Illingworth Kerr Retrospective,* Edmonton Art Gallery, 1985, p. 43.

25. Ibid., p. 43.

26. Ibid., p. 44.

27. Quote found in Terrence Heath's essay "A Sense of Place," *Visions: Contemporary Art in Canada,* Vancouver: Douglas and McIntyre Ltd., 1983, p. 46.

28. Marytka L.Kosinski. "Artists show nature without man and his problems," *Edmonton Journal,* February 8, 1975, p. 79.

29. William Duma. Artist statement, no date.

30. Geoffrey Simmins. Essay for *Lower Bow: A Celebration of Wilderness, Art and Fishing, Ted Godwin.* Calgary: Hard Art Moving and Storage Co. Ltd. 1991, p. 51.

31. William Withrow. *Contemporary Canadian Painting,* Toronto: McClelland and Stewart Ltd., 1972, p. 156.

32. Ibid., p. 156.

33. *Lower Bow: A Celebration of …* Ibid., p. 46.

34. *Contemporary Canadian …* Ibid., p.156.

35. Exhibited at the Nickle Arts Museum as *Ted Godwin: The Tartan Years, 1967–1976.* Curated by Ann Davis.

36. *Contemporary Canadian …* Ibid., p. 155.

37. Simmins, Ibid., p. 42.

38. Stan Rowe. *Home Place: Essays on Ecology,* Edmonton: NeWest Publishers Ltd., 1990, p. 36.

39. Maggie Callahan. "Harvest of the Spirit," *Update,* Edmonton Art Gallery, Vol.6, No. 2, (March/April 1985) p. 3.

40. Quote from Robert Amos's "Artist's landspaces exist in illusionistic space," *Times-Colonist,* Victoria, August 25, 1990.

41. Robert Amos, ibid.

42. John Allison Forbes. Essay for *Robert Sinclair: Time and place,* the Gallery/Stratford, Stratford, Ontario, 1976, unpaginated brochure.

43. Robert Swain. Catalogue Introduction, *Pertaining to Space: An Exhibition of Works by Robert Sinclair,* Art Gallery of Ontario, Toronto, 1976.

44. Robert Swain, ibid.

45. Anne Suche "Gallery: Robert Sinclair," *Western Living,* January 1986, p. 54.

46. Nancy Tousley, "Night Prairies: New drawings by Takao Tanabe," *Artscanada,* October/November 1979, p. 38.

47. Ibid.

48. Nancy E. Dillow. Exhibition catalogue, *Takao Tanabe, 1972–1976: The Land,* Norman Mackenzie Art Gallery, Regina, p. 9.

49. Tousley, "Night Prairies..." p. 38.

50. Nancy Tousley. "B.C. artist to receive honorary degree at U of L," *Calgary Herald,* Friday, October 13, 1995, p. D3.

51. Interview with Harry Savage, August 23, 1995.

52. Interview with Sylvain Voyer, October 10, 1995.

53. Marytka L.Kosinski. "Artists show nature without man and his problems," *Edmonton Journal,* 1975, p. 79.

54. Ibid.

55. Ibid.

56. Gordon Snyder. "Overview" in catalogue, *Frank Vervoort, 1930–1983: In Tribute,* Alberta College of Art Gallery, 1984, p. 15.

57. Christopher Varley, ibid., p. 25.

58. Kathleen Compton, "In Tribute" from Vervoort catalogue, ibid., p. 8.

59. Interview with Peter von Tieshausen, January 9, 1996.

60. Preface to *Dance with Minutiae...,* ibid., p. 6.

61. Artist statement from *Three Painters,* Southern Alberta Art Gallery, Lethbridge, 1976.

62. In a June 6, 1996, interview with the artist, Hall stated that her figurative art influences reach back to the naive art of Henri Rousseau and the symbolic art of Odilon Redon.

63. According to guest curator Monique Westra, "Foo Fat practices a Canadian version of New Realism." *Dance with Minutiae ...* Banff: Whyte Museum of the Canadian Rockies, 1988, p. 7.

64. Dulcie Foo Fat. Artist statement, 1993.

65. Christopher Hume. "Calgary artist closes in on the details of a vast land." *Sunday Star,* Toronto, April 11, 1982.

66. Information comes from Joice Hall's artist statement, *Three Painters,* ibid.

67. Curatorial statement by Carol A. Phillips in *Joice Hall: Celebration Landscapes, John Hall: Paintings,* Halifax: Dalhousie Art Gallery, July 1976.

68. Sandra Tivy. Catalogue essay, *Floating: Joice Hall,* Lethbridge: Southern Alberta Art Gallery, 1987.

69. Artist statement from catalogue *Enns, Evans and Ulrich,* Calgary: Glenbow-Alberta Institute, 1978.

70. Ibid.

71. Artist interview, Calgary, June 14, 1996.

72. Artist interview, ibid.

73. Interview with Les Graff, September 29, 1995.

74. Ibid.

75. Liz Bryan. *The Buffalo People: Prehistoric Archaeology on the Canadian Plains,* Edmonton: University of Alberta Press, 1991, p. 27.

76. Interview with Les Graff ... ibid.

77. John Bentley Mays. "Art history of Alberta tells story of isolation," *Globe and Mail,* August 6, 1980.

78–83. Interview with Les Graff ... ibid.

84. Robert Atkins. *Artspeak: A Guide to Contemporary Ideas, Movements, and Buzzwords,* New York: Abbeville Publishers, 1990, p. 36.

85. Exhibition. *Les Graff: Reality is Irrelevant, New Drawings and Paintings,* Virginia Christopher Galleries Ltd., 1995.

86. Artist statement from *Les Graff: Reality is Irrelevant.*

chapter three

1. The Baby Boom covers 1946/47 to 1964/65.

2. Lelde Muehlenbachs. Essay for *Daryl Rydman: Natural History,* Edmonton: FAB Gallery, 1993, unpublished.

3. Denise Oleksijczuk. Exhibition catalogue, *Lost Illusions: Recent Landscape Art,* Vancouver Art Gallery, 1991, p. 7.

4. Kay Larson. "What's Wrong with this Picture?," *Artnews,* New York, April 1996, p. 111.

5. Ibid.

6. Dorothy Labarge. "Landscape and Alberta," *Vanguard,* February 1983, p. 17.

7. Ibid.

8. Alice Saltiel Marshall. Comment found within "A Guided Tour of a Complex Context." Notes by Katherine Lipsett, Banff: Whyte Museum of the Canadian Rockies, April 1996, unpublished.

9. The other artists included were Laura Millard, Dan Hudson, David More, Peter von Tiesenhausen, Greg Murphy, Barbara Milne, Carol Perehudoff, Michael Cameron and Catherine Perhudoff.

10. Both the Oldman River Trip and the McIntyre Ranch were organized by Canadian Art Odysseys, a non-profit society.

11. The Cairn, ibid.

12. Letter from artist, dated July 27, 1995.

13. Ibid.

14. Liz Wylie. "Jim Corrigan" review. *Vanguard,* May 1985.

15. Examples would be Bate's *Prairie Woman* (1947) and *Prairie Life* (1947); Glyde's *The Exodus* (1941) and *Aftermath* (1952).

16. Quote from exhibition catalogue *Barbara Milne.* Southern Alberta Art Gallery, Lethbridge, 1988. Essay by Sandra (Tivy) Vida.

17. Artist statement sent to author, June 1995.

18. Nancy Tousley. "Local artist draws on moods of the seasons," *Calgary Herald,* September 1994.

19. This duality is suggested by Milne in an artist statement sent to author: July, 1995.

20. Patricia Ainslie. Exhibition pamphlet Visions of Nature: Barbara Milne and Jeffrey Spalding, Glenbow Museum, Calgary,1990.

21. The three exhibitions are: *The Romantic Landscape Now* (Artspace, Peterborough, Ontario, 1986); *Culture's Nature: Landscape in the Art of Gerald Ferguson, Douglas Kirton, Jeffrey Spalding and David Thauberger* (Dunlop Art Gallery, Regina, 1986); *Eye of Nature* (Walter Phillips Gallery, Banff Centre, 1989).

22. Margaret Hryniuk. "Landscape exhibit molded by cultural consciousness," the *Leader Post,* Regina, December 4, 1986.

23. Nancy Tousley. "Second look at nature reflects our lost ideals." *Calgary Herald,* Wednesday, August 16, 1989.

24. Nancy Tousley. "Landscapes mirror both a fascination and fear of nature," *Calgary Herald,* August 17, 1990.

25. Ibid.

26. Michael Jacobs. *A Guide to European Painting*, London: David and Charles Publishing Ltd. 1980, p. 206

27. Ibid.

28. Denise Oleksijczuk, ibid. p. 5.

29. Shirley Hard. Artist statement in exhibition hand-out, Canadian Art Galleries, Calgary, Sept.11-27, 1993.

30. Nancy Tousley. "Canvases teeter on edge" *Calgary Herald,* September 28, 1990, p. C2.

31. Ibid.

32. Ibid.

33. Artist interview, February 29, 1996.

34. David More. Artist's statement, July 27, 1995.

35. Exhibition organized and circulated by the Whyte Museum of the Canadian Rockies.

36. Katherine Lipsett, assistant curator of art. Exhibition statement for *David More: Forest-Fade to Silent,* The Whyte Museum of the Canadian Rockies, Banff, 1990.

37. Bob Weber. "Fade to Silent: When David More saw what acid rain had done to his beloved forests, he knew he had to act." The *Advocate,* Red Deer, July 27, 1991.

38. Katherine Lipsett. Ibid.

39. David More. Artist statement for *Perspective on Drawing,* Triangle Art Gallery, Calgary, December 18, 1995.

40. David More. Ibid.

41. Ibid.

42. Michael Bell. Curator's essay for *The Other Alberta Sculpture: Catherine Burgess, Isla Burns and Peter von Tiesenhausen,* Carleton University Art Gallery, Ottawa, 1995, p. 21.

43. Ibid.

44. Peter von Tisenhausen. Artist statement for *Peter von Tisenhausen: Projects,* Prairie Regional Art Gallery, Grande Prairie AB, 1994.

chapter four

1. Artist statement from *Come Walk with Me: A Luke Lindoe Retrospective,* Medicine Hat Museum and Art Gallery, 1992, p. 11.

2. Alison Appelbe. "Lindoe makes crusty exit from Hat art community," the *Medicine Hat News,* undated.

3. Artist statement from *Come Walk with Me…,* ibid, p. 11.

4. Ibid.

5. Artist interview, September 3, 1996.

6. Ibid.

7. Les Graff. "Turning Earth into Art: From clay quarry to museum shelf, a century of ceramic development," *AlbertaViews,* Summer 1999, p. 24.

8. Ibid.

9. Nancy Tousley. "Art," *Calgary Herald,* January 29, 1993.

10. *Come Walk with Me...,* ibid, p.70.

11. Ibid, p. 20.

12. Mike Murphy. "Luke Lindoe: Art Is Such A Response" *Artichoke: Writings About the Visual Arts,* Calgary, Spring 1993, p. 29.

13. "Luke and the Land," *Luke Lindoe Retrospective,* Calgary: the Nickel Arts Museum, University of Calgary, 1998, p. 8.

14. Artist statement from Alberta Art Foundation, *Biographical Sheet,* December 1980.

15. B. MacG. "Earth shapes" *Montreal Scene,* May 29, 1976.

16. Phone interview with Mary Borgstrom, October 7, 1996.

17. Ibid.

18. Interview with Les Graff, September 29, 1995.

19. Phone interview with Elke Blodgett, October 15, 1996.

20. Ibid.

21. Elke Blodgett, artist statement, September, 1995.

22. C.H. Moore. "Ambiguity, complexity of Blodgett pottery achieves 'brilliant success' at exhibit," *Alberta Gazette,* 1977.

23. Ibid.

24. Elke Blodgett, artist statement, ibid.

25. Ibid.

26. Phone interview with Elke Blodgett, ibid.

27. Bente Roed Cochran. "Through the fire…" *Edmonton Bullet,* Vol. 4 #10, January 1, 1987.

28. Florence McKie. "The Gentle Potter: Elke Blodgett," *Contact Magazine,* #39, 1979.

29. Catalogue essay (author not named) in *Alberta Clay Comes of Age,* Alberta Potters Association, 1986.

30. Gloria Hickey. Catalogue essay for *20/20 Hindsight, A Harlan House Retrospective: 1969–1989,* Toronto: The Koffler Gallery, 1990, p. 9.

31. Bruce Ferguson. Exhibition brochure for *A Prairie Sweet: Harlan House, Al Wilson & Robert Sinclair,* Glenbow Art Gallery, Calgary AB 1973.

32. Artist lecture, The Banff Centre Gallery, Calgary, September 1995.

33. Barbara Harmer Tipton. *John Chalke: Works on Clay,* Southern Alberta Art Gallery, Lethbridge September 5, 1987, unpaginated.

34. Interview with Elke Blodgett. "The Gentle Potter: Elke Blodgett" *Contact Magazine,* #39, 1979, p. 3–9.

35. Artist statement. *Chuck Wissinger-Ceramics,* Southern Alberta Art Gallery, Lethbridge, December 3–31, 1978.

36. *Ceramic Selects: A Retrospective Exhibition of 15 years of Red Deer College Ceramic Student works,* Beaver House Gallery, Edmonton: Apr. 27–June 1, 1990.

37. Bob Weber. "Chuck Wissinger's Sculptures of Time and Space," *Ceramics: Art and Perception,* Paddington, Australia: Issue 8, 1992, p. 26.

38. Statement from *Eolian Metamorph,* Gulf Canada Gallery, Calgary, September 17–October 8, 1986.

39. Vivienne Sosnowski. "Blandness of the title does grave injustice to splendid works," the *Edmonton Journal,* October, 1986.

40. Valerie Greenfield. Catalogue essay for *Annemarie Schmid Esler,* Alberta College of Art Gallery, Calgary, 1987, p. 21.

41. Ibid., p. 29.

42. Ibid.

43. Reg Silvester. "From a Private World," *Edmonton Bullet,* May 9, 1990, p. 11.

44. Lyndal Osborne. Artist statement, 1993.

45. Gillian MacKay, "Five-artist show engagingly eccentric," May 22, 1997.

46. Elizabeth Beauchamp, "Artist reveals inner world of the imagination" *Edmonton Journal,* July 31, 1992, p. C4.

47. Artist statement included in exhibition catalogue by curators Cathy Mastin (Glenbow Museum) and Catherine Crowston (Edmonton Art Gallery), p. 31.

48. Ibid.

49. Anne Severson. "The Rhythms of Life: For Jane Kidd and Bill Morton. The universality of textiles speaks a language that no other medium can offer" *Arts Bridge,* Edmonton: Issue 11, Summer 1995, p. 8.

50. Nancy Tousley. "Security Blanket a show standout" *Calgary Herald,* March 23, 1990.

51. Anne Severson. "Dyed silk leads artist to serenity." Anne Severson, now deceased, sent this clipping before her death to the author, without noting the name and date of publication.

52. Ann Pope. Artist statement, 1995.

53. Ibid.

54. Ronald Rees. *Land of Earth and Sky: Landscape Painting of Western Canada,* Western Producer Prairie Books, Saskatoon SK, 1984 p. 45.

55. Elizabeth Brown. Curators essay for *Realities Abstracted: Colleen Campbell and Maureen Enns,* Peter Whyte Gallery, Banff, 1983.

56. *Asum Mena* (1991) exhibition brochure. The Alberta Indian Arts and Crafts Society, Edmonton.

57. George Littlechild. *This Land is My Land,* Emeryville, California: Children's Book Press, 1993, p. 18.

58. Evelyn Kleis. Artist statement for *Animal Spirits,* Muttart Art Gallery, Calgary, 1994.

59. Exhibition brochure, *Arktypes: Romanticism in Animal Imagery,* Edmonton Art Gallery, 1995.

60. Curator's statement. *Outlook: The Magazine of Edmonton Art Gallery,* Volume III, Issue 2, June 1-August 31, 1992, p. 4.

61. Olson was included in a five-person exhibit curated by Shirley Madill. *Post-Pop Realism: The Winnipeg Perspective 1982,* Winnipeg Art Gallery, February 4 to March 13, 1982.

62. Nancy Tousley. "Artist loses touch with works' content" *Calgary Herald,* September 10, 1987.

63. Artist statement for *Predator Competitor,* Harcourt Art Gallery, Edmonton, November 1994.

64. Ibid.

65. Michael Parke-Taylor. *Gary Olson: Against the Picture Plane,* Norman MacKenzie Art Gallery, Regina, 1980.

66. Bente Roed Cochrane, ibid., p. 124.

67. Ibid., p.126.

68. Artist statement for *Beauty Pageant: Paintings by Maureen Enns.* Whyte Musuem of the Canadian Rockies, Banff, 1984.

69. Ibid. Essay by Elizabeth Brown.

70. Ibid. Artist's statement.

71. Debbie Thomas and Maureen Enns. *Grizzly Kingdom: An Artist's Encounter,* Detselig Enterprises Ltd., Calgary, 1995, unpaginated.

72. Ibid., p. 19.

73. Ibid., p. 20.

74. Ibid., p.12

75. Interview with artist, May 21, 1996.

76. Ibid.

77. Ibid.

78. Robbin Yager. Artist statement to writer, June 1995.

79. Yager's work is represented in *Carmanah: Visions of an Ancient Rainforest,* Western Canada Wilderness Committee, Summerwild Productions and Raincoast Books, Vancouver, 1989, p. 164.

80. Katherine Ylitalo. Curator's essay for *New Economy: Recent work by Jill Armstrong, Catherine Burgess, Roxanne Dunning, Dan Hudson, Margaret May, Darren Petersen and Robbin Yager,* Nickle Arts Museum, Calgary,1994.

81. RobbinYager, Artist statement…, ibid.

82. Ibid.

83. Lelde Muehlenbachs. "Daryl Rydman: Natural History," unpublished review, 1993.

84. Kitty Scott. Essay for *Alberta Survey: New Landscapes,* Edmonton Art Gallery, 1992, p. 4.

85. Daryl Rydman. Artist statement, unpublished.

86. Katherine Ylitalo. Curator's essay for *Copy, Calgary Herald,* Tuesday, February 28, 1995.

87. Interview with artist, August 19, 1996.

88. Amy Gogarty. Artist statement, May 1991.

89. Ibid.

90. Nancy Tousley. "Hot Dates: Art," *Calgary Herald,* October 2, 1992.

91. Amy Gogarty. Artist statemen, ibid.

92. Nancy Tousley. "Synthesis of experiences embraced," *Calgary Herald,* March 16, 1986, D6.

93. Nancy Tousley. "Challenging show needs long look," *Calgary Herald,* March 8, 1985, F6.

94. Manon Blanchette. Catalogue essay for *Convergence for Metamorphoses,* Walter Phillips Gallery, Banff Centre 1986.

95. Richard Baillargeon. Catalogue essay for *Configurations Changeantes,* Vox Populi, organizer of Le Mois de la Photo à Montréal, Montreal September 1995, p. 17.

96. Artist statement for *Temporal Icons* exhibition at Mercer Union and A.R.C., Toronto, 1987, p. 17.

97. John Bentley Mays. "Seven independent spirits from yonder by the sea," *Globe and Mail,* Thursday, June 18, 1985.

98. Ibid.

99. David Garneau. Catalogue essay for *Carroll Moppett,* Illingworth Kerr Gallery, Alberta College of Art, Calgary, 1992, p. 19.

100. Carroll Taylor-Lindoe. Artist statement to writer, September 22, 1995.

101. Tousley, "Challenging show needs long look," ibid.

102. Vincent Varga. Catalogue essay for *Aspects of Contemporary Painting in Alberta,* Calgary: Glenbow Museum, July 11–August 30, 1987, p. 46.

103. Richard Baillargeon. Catalogue essay, ibid.

104. Artist statement, ibid.

105. Artist statement, ibid.

106. Ibid.

107. Ibid.

chapter five

1. Joan Thomas. "How Canadian writing has evolved," *Globe and Mail,* August 12, 1995.

2. Liam Lacey. "People everywhere strive for protection from global culture," *Globe and Mail,* April 15, 1991.

3. Ray Conlogue. "No place like home: Ray Conlogue examines a philosophy of belonging." *Globe and Mail,* November 27, 1991.

4. Greg Curnoe. "A Bias of Communications: Visions Reviewed," *Vanguard,* December/January 1983/84.

5. Quote is found in *Other Frontiers* catalogue. Third Eye Centre, Glasgow, U.K., 1991, p. 14.

6. Ibid., p. 14.

7. Jan Morris. "Coming of age in troubled times," *Globe and Mail,* November 7, 1990.

8. Tom Radford. Essay "For an Independent Hairy Hill," in brochure published by National Gallery of Canada (1973). Exhibition organized by Myra Davies.

9. Virginia Nixon. "The National Gallery is bringing you Hairy Hill, Alberta." *Montreal Gazette,* February 16, 1974.

10. Reg Silvester. "Alberta/A Celebration," *Edmonton Journal*, October. 13, 1979, Section 1.

11. Exhibition organized and circulated by the Mendel Art Gallery, Saskatoon.

12. Exhibition organized and circulated by Photographers Gallery, Saskatoon. Show travelled to Banff's Whyte Museum.

13. Katherine Lipsett. "The Layering of Identity," *The Cairn,* Whyte Museum of the Canadian Rockies, Banff, Winter 1995, Vol. XIX, No. 2, p. 4.

14. Essay for *Survey of Photography in Alberta* (1885–1992), Triangle Gallery of Visual Arts, Calgary, 1993.

15. See exhibition brochure: *Confinement: Photographs by Sima Khorrami*, Edmonton Art Gallery, 1993. Essay by Elizabeth Kidd.

16. *Manalta Miners: A Tribute in portraits and words* (1989, Manalta Coal Ltd.); *Minto Miners: Photographs & Text* (1989, Village of Minto, New Brunswick) and *Alberta Miners: A Tribute* (1993, Cambria Publishing, Calgary).

17. Quote from Reg Silvester's article on "Alberta/A Celebration," *Edmonton Journal,* October 13, 1979.

18. Quote from *A Conscious Choice: Six Photographic Projects,* Muttart Art Gallery, Calgary, 1991.

19. Elizabeth Kidd. Essay for *Presence of the Prairie: Photographs by Orest Semchishen,* Edmonton Art Gallery, 1992.

20. Interview with Peter Duthie, October 18, 1996.

21. Kate Davis. "Profile: Orest Semchishen" *Photo Communique,* Winter 1986/87, p. 9.

22. Ibid.

23. For a fuller explanation of this see Robert Filford's "Photography and its discontents," *Canadian Art*, Spring 1995.

24. Martha Hanna. Essay for *Orest Semchishen: In Plain View/ Voir Clair,* Canadian Museum of Contemporary Photography, Ottawa, 1994, p. 35.

25. James Adams. "Semchishen's unpretentious images have underlying richness," *Edmonton Journal,* May 8, 1984.

26. Martha Hanna, ibid., p. 33.

27. Ibid.

28. James Adams. "Photos show community's incongruities," *Edmonton Journal,* March 16 1985.

29. Nancy Tousley. "Photos speak plainly," *Calgary Herald*, May 6, 1984.

30. Kate Davis. "Orest Semchishen: A Survey of Photographs: 1973–1983," *Update,* Edmonton Art Gallery, Volume 3, No. 2, March/April 1984.

31. Robert Everett-Green. "You won't catch me jeering at the elusive Prairie People." *Globe & Mail,* date unknown.

32. P. Scott Lawrence. "Orest Semchishen," *Look Again: A Guide to the Canadian Museum of Contemporary Photography,* Canadian Museum of Contemporary Photography, Ottawa, 1988.

33. Penny Cousineau. Essay for *Barbara Spohr: Apparent reasons,* Whyte Museum of the Canadian Rockies,1995, p. 76.

34. Nancy Tousley, ibid.

35. *Orest Semchisen A Survey of photographs: 1973-1983,* Edmonton Art Gallery, 1984.

36. Ibid.

37. Martha Hanna, ibid. p. 34.

38. Interview with Edward Cavell, October 23, 1996.

39. Interview with Hugh Hohn, October 30, 1996.

40. Terry Fenton. Essay for *Suburban Landscapes,* Edmonton Art Gallery, 1975.

41. Ibid.

42. Douglas Clark and Linda Wedman. Introduction to *Keepsake: Selections from the Archives of A Photographic Project: Alberta 1980,* Alberta Culture, Edmonton, 1981, p.11.

43. Terry Fenton. Essay for *Keepsake* ibid. p .14.

44. Tom Radford, Harry Savage and Rudy Wiebe. *Alberta/A Celebration* Edmonton: Hurtig Publishers, Edmonton, 1979.

45. J.F. Conway. *The West: The History of a Region in Confederation,* Toronto: James Lorimer & Company, 1983, p.206.

46. Howard Palmer with Tamara Palmer. *Alberta: A New History,* Edmonton: Hurtig Publishers, 1990, p. 341.

47. Gail Fisher Taylor. "A Photographic Project: Alberta 1980 and the Documentary Process," *Photo Communique,* Winter 1980/81.

48. Quote from *Keepsake,* ibid. p.54.

49. Image can be found in *Keepsake*, ibid. p. 59.

50. Commissioned by the Alberta Federation of Metis Settlements. Toured nationally by the Edmonton Art Gallery, 1986–89. Also travelled to Moscow and Leningrad in 1987.

51. Organized by the Walter Phillips Gallery, the Banff Centre, Curran's pictures were featured in a two-person exhibition with Michael Mitchell entitled *Structured Paradise: The National Parks Experience,* Walter Phillips Gallery, 1985.

52. Artist statement in *Belief and Culture: Photos by Douglas Curran,* Alberta College of Art Gallery, Calgary,1990, p. 12.

53. Howard Palmer with Tamara Palmer, ibid. p. 365.

54. Justin Wonnacott. Essay for *Belief and Culture: Photos by Douglas Curran,* Alberta College of Art Gallery, Calgary, 1990, p. 6.

55. Ibid.

56. *A Photographic Project* is an archival project in which 202 photographs from the collection is organized into a travelling exhibition. The photographers are Mark Arneson, Robert Brunelle, Douglas Curran, Lauren Dale, Hugh Hohn, Wally Houn, Orest Semshisen, Barb Spohr, Gabor Szilasi and Ronnie Tessler. On the other hand, *Get Clicking: People Pictures* sought submissions from the public.

57. Ibid.

58. *Gallery*, Edmonton Art Gallery, 1977.

59. *Urban Landscape,* Edmonton Art Gallery, 1978.

60. Exhibited at Edmonton Art Gallery, 1981 and Canadian Centre of Photography, Toronto, 1982.

61. "Marks We Make," *Vancouver,* November 1985, p. 102–104.

62. From Banff Centre press release, April 18, 1989.

63. Ibid.

64. Robert Fulford. "Photography and Its Discontents," *Canadian Art*, Spring, 1995, p. 58. This article is useful background on the differences between photography and photo-based art.

65. Susan Cockshutt. "Picture Perfect: photography and painting have many parallels for Ingrid Plaudis," *Red Deer Advocate,* 1990.

66. From brochure for A Change of Light: Photographs by Ingrid Plaudis, Red Deer and District Museum, 1992.

67. Ibid.

68. George Webber. "Portfolio: Badlands," *Camera Canada ,* Spring 1986, p. 14.

69. Nancy Tousley. "Soul of the Prairies," *Calgary Herald,* May 25, 1995.

70. Published by Folio Gallery Inc. Calgary.

71. Kim Heinrich. "Portrait of an Artist: George Webber," *Avenue,* Calgary, December 1995, p. 9.

72. Peter Duthie. "*George Webber,*" *CV Photo,* Montreal, Summer,1994, p. 39.

73. Consists of book and exhibition celebrating Canada's 125 anniversary.

74. Exhibition brochure for *Icons for Our Modern Age: Photographs by Randy Adams,* Edmonton Art Gallery, 1992. Essay by Elizabeth Kidd.

75. Ibid.

76. Ibid.

77. Fifth House Publishers, Calgary, 1999.

78. Randy Adams. "Small Gestures," *Arts Bridge,* Alberta Community Development, Edmonton, Issue 8, Fall 1994.

79. Ibid.

80. Ibid.

81. Randy Adams. "Down on the Happy Farm," *Arts Bridge,* Alberta Community Development, Edmonton, Issue 5, November 1993.

82. See Adam's article "Visitors & Picture Taking Welcome," *Arts Bridge,* Alberta Community Development, Edmonton, Issue 7, May 1994.

83. Nancy Tousley. Essay for *Welcome to Our World: Contemporary Canadian Folk Art,* McMicheal Canadian Art Collection, Kleinburg, Ontario, 1997, p. 37.

84. Mark Joslin. "An Innate Sense: The Intuitive Arts in Alberta," *Outlook,* Edmonton Art Gallery, Vol. III Issue 2, 1992, p. 6.

85. See p.192 of catalogue from National Museum of Man, Ottawa, 1983 for *Duck Whirligig* by Kost Pawlyk, Elk Point, Alberta.

86. *From the Heart,* 1981; *Heartfelt,* 1983 and *Heart to Heart,* 1985 are group shows of Alberta folk art curated by Ross Bradley for Beaver House, Alberta Culture, Edmonton.

87. Phylis Matousek. "Folk A.R.T.," *Edmonton Journal*, November 26, 1983.

88. Irene E.McCaugherty. *The Ladders We Climb,* self-published, Fort Macleod, 1994, p. 95.

89. Hazel Litzgus. Artist statement, August, 1995.

90. From unpublished notes prepared by Marijke Kerkhoven, Cultural History, Glenbow Museum September 19, 1989.

91. Stefan Czernecki and Timothy Rhodes. *Naive Art in the West,* Winnipeg Hyperion Press, 1991, p. 60.

92. Judith Kellock. "Paintings shows farm life," *Edmonton Sunday Sun,* August 21, 1988, p. S14.

93. Palmer with Tamara Palmer, ibid., p. 93.

94. Phone interview with artist, December 13, 1996.

95. Artist statement, undated.

96. Howard Palmer with Tamara Palmer ibid., p.55.

97. This term is used locally. The writer was introduced to it by Yvette Brideau and David More in August, 1994.

98. David H. Breen. *The Canadian Prairie West and Ranching Frontier, 1874–1924,* Toronto: University of Toronto Press, 1983, p. 98.

99. Barbara Milne. "Nigel Lawrence," *Visual Arts Newsletter,* Alberta Culture, Edmonton, Fall, 1981. Acknowledgements to Yvette Brideau for her research on Lawrence.

100. "Nigel Lawrence dead at 89," *Red Deer Advocate,* July 3, 1990.

101. Randy Adams. "Richard Schafer: Carving Memories," *Visual Arts Newsletter,* Issue 62, p. 5.

102. Historian Brian W. Dippie uses this term in the essay for "The Moving Finger Writes: Western Art and the Dynamics of Change." New Haven & London: *Discovered Lands, Invented Pasts: Transforming Visions of the American West,* Yale University Press, 1992, p. 90.

103. Brian Hutchinson. "Clues to Alberta," *Alberta Report,* July 31, 1989, p. 42.

104. Recent American examples on the topic of western art include: *The American West: The Modern Vision;* Boston: Little, Brown and Company, 1984; *The West as America: Reinterpreting Images of the Frontier, 1820–1920,* Washington & London: Smithsonian Institution Press, 1991; *The West of the Imagination,* New York: W.W. Norton & Company, 1986; and the aforementioned *Discovered Lands, Invented Pasts.*

105. Don Braid. "Stampede makes us friends and money," *Calgary Herald,* July 14, 1996.

106. *Globe and Mail,* August 6, 1994.

107. Brochure for *Patrick Douglass Cox: Looking West,* Glenbow Museum, Calgary, 1994.

108. Nancy Tousley. "Hot Dates: Art," *Calgary Herald,* November 24, 1995.

109. *The American West: The Modern Vision,* Ibid., p. 4.

110. Interview with writer, December 30, 1996.

111. Institutions such as the Glenbow Museum, Medicine Hat Museum and Art Gallery (i.e. *Not Just Another Horse Show:* 1983, 1984, 1986 and 1989) and more recently the Western Heritage Centre, Cochrane.

112. Events such as Calgary Stampede Western Art Show & Auction; Medicine Hat Stampede & Rodeo, National Finals Rodeo Western Art Show; Pincher Creek Cowboy Poetry Festival and the Stony Plain Cowboy Festival.

113. The Stockmen's Memorial Foundation, Calgary and the Open Range Art Association.

114. "Banff's cowboy artist has gone," *Banff Crag & Canyon,* Wed. August 4, 1976.

115. According to bronze artist and former Banff cowboy, Malcolm (Mac) MacKenzie in a phone interview, January 15, 1997.

116. See "The Absent Other," in Discovered Lands, Invented Pasts, ibid., p.135–165.

117. Quote from Brian W. Dippie's essay in *Discovered Lands, Invented Pasts,* ibid., p. 115.

118. A.P. Schroeder. *Word For Word: The Business of Writing in Alberta,* The Writers' Guild of Alberta, and Alberta Culture & Multiculturalism, 1988. p. 44.

119. See catalogue *Personal Territories: Vern Hume and Robert Milthorp,* Nickle Arts Museum, Calgary, 1990, p. 45.

120. Ibid., p.46

121. *Legacy,* Edmonton, Spring, 1996, p. 42.

122. *Personal Territories*, ibid., p. 46.

123. Nancy Tousley. "Wild west show has unlikely hero," *Calgary Herald* , June 29, 1984.

124. Valerie Greenfield. *Third Annual Wild West Show: A Visual Art Exhibition,* Alberta College of Art Gallery, Calgary, 1984, p. 5.

125. Ibid.

126. Ibid.

127. Review by Nancy Tousley, September 24, 1983.

128. There is one another Alberta artwork by the same name as Buck. Produced in 1986, *Buck* the video was made by Leila Sujir and Vern Hume of Calgary.

chapter six

1. Toronto: Harper Collins Publishers Ltd., 1995, p. 78.

2. Artist statement from *Cardinal-Schubert, Canadian Heroes,* Red Deer and District Museum, 1978.

3. Nancy Tousley. "Visual Arts," *Calgary Herald,* May 25, 1978, p. A19.

4. *Joane Cardinal-Schubert: Two Decades.* Muttart Public Art Gallery, Calgary, 1997, p. 27.

5. Donald Ward. *The People: A Historical Guide to the First Nations of Alberta, Saskatchewan and Manitoba.* Fifth House Publishers, Calgary and Saskatoon, 1995, p. 28.

6. Phone interview with artist, February 27, 1997.

7. Susan Crean. "Changing Directions: A New Perspective on Native Women's Art," *Canadian Art,* Winter 1989, p. 20.

8. Bob Weber. "Tracing a line between two worlds: Artist leans on native heritage," *Red Deer Advocate,* October 29, 1988.

9. Phone interview, ibid.

10. See Deborah Godin's essay in *Joane Cardinal-Schubert: This is my History* Thunder Bay National Exhibition Centre and Centre for Indian Art, 1985, p.5.

11. Susan Crean, ibid.

12. Henry Lehmann. "Artist's work hits us like a smack across the face," *Montreal Gazette,* late May, 1990.

13. Interview with artist, February 11, 1997.

14. Nancy Beale. "Five artists join past to present," *Ottawa Citizen,* April 19, 1990.

15. See Mainprize's essay for *Stardusters,* Thunder Bay Art National Exhibition Centre and Centre for Indian Art, 1996, p. 21.

16. Charles Mandel. "Medal in the mail fails to faze local artist," *Edmonton Journal,* December 17, 1993, p. D10.

17. *Passage to Origins I: Joane Cardinal-Schubert,* FAB Gallery, University of Alberta, Edmonton, December, 1993. Curated by Jetske Sybesma.

18. Interview with artist, February 11, 1997.

19. Artist statement for *New Beginnings,* Masters Gallery Ltd., Calgary, November, 1983.

20. See artist statement in *Passage to Origins I,* ibid.

21. Ibid.

22. Besides *Stardusters* (1986), other group shows of First Nations art across Canada included: *Cross Cultural Views* (Ottawa, 1986); *Revisions* (Banff, 1988); *Ode'Min* (Sudbury, 1988); *Crossing the Circle: Indian and Inuit Art From Canada* (Ottawa, 1988); *Changers: A Spiritual Renaissance* (Toronto, 1989); *Beyond History* (Vancouver, 1989); *Art for All* (Edmonton, 1989); *Diversities* (Calgary, 1989); *Seeing Red* (Kingston, 1990); *Strengthening the Spirit* (Ottawa, 1991); *Visions of Power: Contemporary Art by First Nations, Inuit and Japanese Canadians* (Toronto, 1991); *Indigena: Contemporary Native Perspectives* (Ottawa, 1992); *Land, Spirit, Power: First Nations at the National Gallery of Canada* (Ottawa,1992); *New Territories* (1992, Montreal); *Canada's First People: A Celebration of Contemporary Native Visual Arts* (Calgary/Edmonton, 1992); and *Contemporary Canadian Native Art* (Kamloops, 1993).

23. Laura Bushelkin. "Show of Native Art Not Limited by Traditional Images," *Georgia Strait,* June 16–23, 1989, p. 19.

24. Scott Watson. "Whose Nation? First Nations Art in the Past and Present," *Canadian Art,* Spring 1993, p. 36.

25. Deborah Doxtater gives an excellent analysis of how native art is perceived in her essay "Reconnecting the Past; An Indian Idea of History," *Revisions,* Walter Phillips Gallery 1992.

26. Letter was published in the *Globe and Mail,* February 24, 1993.

27. George Littlechild. *This Land Is My Land,* Emeryville Children's Book Press, California: 1993, p. 12.

28. Robert Enright interview with artist. *Border Crossings,* Fall 1992, p. 14.

29. Ibid.

30. Quote is found in Sherry Killam's "Jane Ash Poitras," *Western Living,* May 1991.

31. Robert Enright interview, ibid.

32. Quote from Gary Gee's "Artist explores spiritual ecology," the *Edmonton Sun,* May 18, 1989, p.39.

33. Nancy Beale. "The Storyteller: Cree artist presents modern picture about native peoples with startling clarity," the *Ottawa Citizen* , June 3, 1993.

34. Janet Clark. *George Littlechild: Red Horse/Red Indian,* Thunder Bay Art Gallery, 1990, p. 3.

35. Or there is the collective history recalled by *Columbus's Indians* (1992) or *Sioux Warrior #7* (1989); unfortunate histories like *She Was An Indian Princess … She Loved To Drink … She Died* (1988), an homage to the artist's mother Rachel Littlechild; or *An Endangered Species* (1993) with archival images of Cree Indian brothers Chief Jean Baptiste Erminskin and Chief Alexis Bobtail. He also addresses cross cultural histories in *Afro Native Love* (1992) and *Mixed Racial Marriage* (1989), featuring photos of Littlechild's family. In *Four Buffalo Spirits* (1989) and *Dancing Raven Spirit* (1990), he investigates spiritual memory, and addresses issues of his own autobiography with *Red Horse in a Sea of White Horses* (1989) and *Indian Artist Visits New York, New York* (1989).

36. Amir Ali Alibhai. *George Littlechild,* Surrey Art Gallery, Surrey BC, 1996, p.7.

37. Veronika Grahammer. "Most Forgotten Chief," *European Review of Native American Studies,* 6:1 1992, p. 54.

38. Janet Clark, ibid. p. 4.

39. Loretta Todd. Essay for *George Littlechild,* ibid. p. 32.

40. "Portrait of an Artist as a Descendant," November 14, 1993.

41. Amir Ali Alibhai's, ibid.p. 7.

42. Quote from Gary Gee's "Artist explores spiritual ecology," ibid.

43. Quote found in "The Sky is the Limit: Conversations with First Nations artists," *Border Crossings,* Fall 1992, p. 46.

44. "Rethinking History", *C Magazine,* Toronto, Summer 1992, p.38.

45. Ibid.

46. Laura Bushelkin. "Show of Native Art Not Limited," ibid.

47. Kate Taylor, May 8, 1992 edition.

48. John Bentley Mays, May 16, 1992 edition, p. C2.

49. The *Edmonton Journal,* April 12, 1990.

50. "The Sky is the Limit," ibid.

51. Laura Bushelkin. "Show of Native Art Not Limited," ibid.

52. "Jane Ash Poitras: Recycled Blackboards," *Canadian Art,* Fall, 1992.

chapter seven

1. Jeffrey Simpson. "Copps is firing her popgun at the wrong cultural targets," the *Globe and Mail,* February 14, 1997.

2. Ibid.

3. Karen Green. *Canadian Contemporary Printmakers,* Bronx Museum of the Arts, 1982, p. 25.

4. Phone interview with Gwen Franks, April 10, 1997.

5. Charles Mandel. "Magical and mundane meet in Prairie prints," the *Edmonton Journal,* March 24, 1995, p. E8.

6. Sherry Killam. "K. Gwen Frank," *Western Living Magazine,* July 1991, p.50.

7. Mandel, ibid.

8. Artist statement sent to writer, undated.

9. Remi De Cnodder. Translation of Epreuve Artiste, *Arts, Antiques, Auctions,* Brussels, October 1994, p. 70.

10. Unattributed comment found in exhibition brochure for *Jane Cameron,* Gulf Canada Gallery, Calgary, 1990.

11. Quote is from exhibition catalogue *Jane Francis Cameron.*

12. Quote found in exhibition brochure *A Country School Christmas: Monoprints by Margaret Seelye,* Red Deer and District Museum, 1992.

13. Randy Adams. "Satisfying a Deep Need: Margaret Seelye and the Alberta Community Art Clubs Association," *Arts Bridge,* Vol. 2 #1, Issue 3, May 1993.

14. Jack Danylchuk. "High-art romance on the Hinton Trail: a 12-year love affair," the *Edmonton Journal,* date unknown.

15. Robert Guest. *Trail North: A Journey in Words and Pictures,* Edmonton: Lone Pine Publishing, 1995, page 10.

16. Ibid., p. 11.

17. Interview with artist, May 6, 1995.

18. Ibid.

19. Ibid.

20. Artist statement, undated.

21. David Garneau. Review in *Fast Forward,* Calgary, May 1–8, 1997.

22. Radomir Bilash. "Peter Lipinski:Church Artist," *Alberta Past,*Volume 4, Issue 2, Dec. 1988.

23. Leysa Granger. "Notes on the Ukrainian Icon Tradition in Canada," *The Icon in Canada,* compiled and edited by Robert B. Klymasz. Canadian Museum of Civilization, Ottawa, 1996.

24. Shara Masiuk. "Theology in imagery and icons for education," *Ukrainian News,* November, 1994.

25. Phylis Matousek. "Peter Shostak is home again as artistic prophet with honor," the *Edmonton Journal,* November 18, 1981, p. D8.

26. "Preserving the past," ibid.

27. Randy Berting. "Artist sculpts life into brick," *Landmark,* October 1990, p. 70.

28. Interview with artist, October 27, 1995.

29. Artist statement, undated.

30. Project was commissioned by the Alberta Historical Resources Foundation.

31. Artist statement for catalogue *Historic Alberta,* the Alberta Historical Resources Foundation, Edmonton, AB.

32. "The historical drawings of Jim Marshall," *Alberta Magazine,* March/April 1982, p. 14.

33. Mural is located in the Medicine Hat City Hall.

34. Artist statement from the exhibit *Alberta Voices,* Alberta Craft Council, Edmonton AB, 1997.

35. Cathie Bartlett. "Four Artists in the Wilderness," *Environment Views,* Winter 1994.

36. Artist statement from *Alberta Voices.*

37. Interpretative material for *Symbols of Presence* written by Prairie Gallery director/curator Donna White.

38. Elizabeth Beauchamp. "Artists relate to expansive prairie vastness," the *Edmonton Journal* December 7, 1990.

39. Paula Gustafson. "Ken Housego – Sculpture 90," *Artichoke: Writings About the Visual Arts,* Fall 1990, p. 45.

40. "Stint in Nova Scotia gave artist metaphors," February 20, 1986, p. H4.

41. Artist statement "When I Grow Up," dated October 1998.

42. Letter to writer, dated February 14, 1998.

43. Monte Greenshields. Foreword to exhibition catalogue published by the Photographers Gallery, Saskatoon, SK.

44. From catalogue essay entitled *Curators' Statement,* by Catharine Mastin, senior curator of art, Glenbow Museum, and Catherine Crowston, senior curator, the Edmonton Art Gallery., p. 3.

45. Ibid., p. 7.

46. Ibid., p. 6.

47. Exhibition featuring the art of Jin-me Yoon, Bob Boyer and Liz Magor, Edmonton Art Gallery (1991).

48. Curator's statement for *Inheritance: Some New Prairie Photography,* Southern Alberta Art Gallery Lethbridge, AB. 1997.

49. Artist statement, May 1997.

50. Artist statement for *Family Stories,* Stride Gallery, Calgary, 1996.

51. "Sharable Truths: Ernie Kroeger's family album," *FastForward*, Calgary (Feb.8–14, 1996).

52. Floating Gallery, Winnipeg.

53. Ray Conlogue. "Family Viewing," *Globe and Mail,* 1994.

54. Catalogue essay entitled Curators' Statement, ibid., p. 7.

55. Ken McGoogan. "A video artist explores life," *Calgary Herald*, May 27, 1996, B4.

56. The essay is titled Leila Sujir: Luminous Stories, p. 5.

57. Nancy Tousley. "Artist comes home with success," *Calgary Herald,* December 21, 1994, D4.

58. See artist statement in *Je vais vous raconter une histoire de fantomes: videos de Nelson Henricks,* curated by Christine Ross for Oboro, Montreal, 1995, p. 31.

59. Excerpt is printed in catalogue for *Elemental Instincts: A matter of course,* curated by Donna McAlear, the Nickle Arts Museum, Calgary, 1988, p. 29.

60. See *Elemental Instincts: A matter of course,* ibid., p. 26.

61. Story published in *The Road Home: New Alberta Stories by Alberta Writers,* ed. Fred Stenson, Edmonton: Reidmore Books Inc., 1992.

62. Exhibited in *Screens: Amantea, Stone, Sujir,* Nickle Arts Museum, Calgary, 1992.

63. See catalogue for *Screens: Amantea, Aziz,* ibid., p. 29.

64. Marusia Bociurkiw. "India Hearts Beat," *Fuse,* August 1989, p. 33.

65. Essay for exhibition *A Dialogue: Reconstructing the Decorative.*

66. "Mixed Media: Leila Sujir," *Canadian Art,* Fall 1995, p. 111.

67. *Within a Room,* Muttart Art Gallery, Calgary, 1991.

68. Quote taken from "Elizabeth Bailey Price: A Brilliant and Unusual Woman," *Legacy,* May–July 1997, p. 37.

69. Following quotes by Rees are found in "Visions & Revisions: The future of the prairie west as history," prepared for the Annual Conference of the Historical Society of Alberta, June 1, 1996 (unpublished manuscript).

70. John Ralston Saul. *Globe & Mail,* May 17, 1986.

71. Stephen Godfrey. *Globe & Mail,* August 6, 1988.

chapter eight

1. Juliet Kershaw. "Why Save CKUA," August–October 1997, p. 30.

2. Nancy Tousley. "Roots, Rejections and Rewards in Calgary," *Canadian Art,* Fall 1986.

3. "Sightlined Impressions," *Border Crossings,* Winnipeg, February 1998, p. 54.

4. Introduction to catalogue produced by the Glenbow Museum, 1987, unpaginated.

5. Alberta College of Art Gallery, Calgary, 1988, p .3.

6. Nancy Tousley, ibid. p.74.

7. Nora Abercrombie. "On Being an Artist," *Arts Bridge,* Community Development, Edmonton, 1994.

8. March 21, 1969.

9. Interview with artist, September 25, 1997.

10. Exhibition travels to Burnaby Art Gallery, Charlottetown Confederation Centre and Hamilton Art Gallery. Catalogue is organized by Bruce Ferguson and designed by Chuck Stake.

11. Ibid.

12. Ibid

13. Ibid.

14. My thanks to John Hall who has a valuable archive of documentation about Calgary exhibitions.

15. "Arts criticism has its standards," November 28, 1969, p. 55.

16. "How they choose the paintings for the gallery," January 24, 1969.

17. Organized for the Edmonton Art Gallery.

18. Karen Wilkin. Catalogue essay for *Painting in Alberta: An Historical Survey,* Edmonton Art Gallery, 1980, unpaginated.

19. Interview with artist, Calgary, June 6, 1997.

20. Interview with artist, Calgary, September 19, 1997.

21. "Stan Perrott: Interview," *Glenbow,* Glenbow Museum, Calgary, July/August edition, 1987.

chapter nine

1. Paul Woodrow, Artist statement, undated.

2. Ibid.

3. My thanks to *Silver: 25 Years of Artist-Run Culture, The New Gallery's Retrospective Catalogue: 1975–2000* for this previously unknown aspect about Calgary's early alternative scene. See Melody Jacobson's essay "The Peaceful Coexistence of Tools and Flower-Weeds."

4. Leila Sujir. "Re:Placing the Lost Memory or Re:Presenting Ourselves," *Parallelogramme,* Toronto, Vol. 12, No. 2.

5. *Silver: 25 Years* ibid. See Don Mabie's essay: "Remembrance of Things Past (1975–87)," for why Clouds 'n' Water is the proverbial dark horse.

6. (Second Edition). Oxford University Press, Toronto, 1988, p. 354.

7. *Latitude 53: A Decade,* Latitude 53, Edmonton, 1983. Project Manager:Trudie Heiman, unpaginated.

8. Ibid.

9. Ibid.

10. Christine Conley. *A Tale of Two Cities: Video Art in Alberta*, Latitude 53, Edmonton, 1986, p.19.

11. Curated by Vera Lemecha for the Glenbow Museum's *New Alberta Art* series.

12. During that time, ARC productions included: Latitude 53's *New Video from the West;* Off Centre Centre's *The First Ten*; EM Media's *The Plains Travelling Film and Video Exhibition* and *Camera Obscura;* the New Gallery's *Media Blitz, Media Blitz 2* and *The Nomads: Winter Souvenir;* and 2nd Story Gallery's *Performance Focus* and *Dusk 'til Dawn.* Examples of public exhibitions are: Muttart Art Gallery's *Video West;* Southern Alberta Art Gallery's (Lethbridge) *Video at the S.A.A.G.;* the Nickle Arts Museum's *Interior Presence: projecting situations, Elemental Instincts: a matter of course* and *Personal Territories: Vern Hume and Robert Milthorp;* Glenbow Museum's *Video from the South* and *Video from the North;* and Ring House Gallery's (Edmonton) *A Tale of Two Cities: Video Art In Alberta.* As well, some Albertans – Leila Sujir, Colleen Kerr, Rob Milthorp, Vern Hume – find themselves included in the National Gallery's *Video by Artists* series. In 1989, Sujir and Hume also co-curate the nation-straddling *Film and Video from the Heart of the Heart of the Regions* (Glenbow Museum Theatre), one of the most comprehensive attempts to account for this activity in the country.

13 The video community included: Marcella Bienvenue, Grant Poier, Rita McKeough, Robert Milthorp, Don Mabie, Stephen Petersen, Bart Habermiller, Cherie Moses, John Will, Paul Woodrow, Leila Sujir, Vern Hume, Mark Dicey, Colleen Kerr, Brian Rusted, Moshe Ozeri, Charles Cousins, Lisa Trofimova, Sandra (Tivy) Vida, Steven Heimbecker, Celine Godberson, Nelson Henricks, and emerging in the 1990s, Mireille Perron, the performance group the Skep(tic)ks (1982), and Parole (Performance, Art, Readings, Opinions, Laughs, Experimentation, 1994).

14. Saturday, February 18, 1989, p. F2.

15. Predating *A Duchampian Look* by almost twenty years is the two-headed *Marcel Duchamp: Ready-mades* circulated by the National Gallery of Canada and *Marcel Duchamp: A European Investigation,* organized by Brian Dyson of the Alberta College of Art Gallery. Both exhibits are displayed at the gallery in 1979 with a joint catalogue.

16. Artist statement from *A Duchampian Look at the Glenbow's Art Collection,* Glenbow Museum, Calgary, 1997.

17. See introduction by Sandra Tivy in *Media Blitz,* the New Gallery, Calgary, 1988, p. 3.

18. Christine Conley. *"In from the Cold: Feminism and Art in Edmonton,"* *Parallelogramme,* Toronto, February/ March 1986, p.15.

19. Nancy Tousley. "Artist's work monitors culture," *Calgary Herald,* August. 3, 1986, F5.

20. Helen Collinson. "*Moses and Mother,*" the *Edmonton Bullet,* Vol. 2, #3, May 30, 1984.

21. Liz Wylie. "The Art Scene in Edmonton," *NeWest Review,* Edmonton, March 1985.

22. Nancy Tousley. "Artist's work monitors" ibid.

23. See artist statement for *My Pov,* Glenbow Museum (April 1990).

24. Artist statement, undated.

25. Nancy Tousley. "In the Frame," *Calgary Herald,* June 8, 1990, p. C8.

26. "Phases of the Moon," *Artichoke: writings about the visual arts,* Fall 1990, p.43.

27. Helen Collinson. "Moses and Mother," ibid.

28. Artist Statement, 1987.

29. Christine Conley. "In from the Cold: Feminism and Art in Edmonton," *Parallelogramme,* Toronto, Vol. 11, No. 3, p. 18.

30. Robert Vanderleelie Gallery, Edmonton.

31. Helen Collinson. "Moses and Mother," ibid.

32. Christine Conley. "The Underside," ibid.

33. Cherie Moses. "Latitude 53: A Decade," *Vanguard,* Vancouver, February 1984, p. 52.

chapter ten

1. Terry Fenton (Edmonton). "Abstraction West: Emma Lake and After," *The National Gallery of Canada Journal 11,* 1976. Reprint found in *The Flat Side of the Landscape: The Emma Lake Artists' Workshops,* Mendel Art Gallery, Saskatoon, 1989, p. 134–135.

2. Terrence Heath (Calgary), essay for *Western Untitled,* Glenbow-Alberta Institute, 1976.

3. Elizabeth Beauchamp, "Art scene stagnated in the 80s," *Edmonton Journal,* January 2, 1990.

4. Charles Mandel, "War of the art worlds," *Globe and Mail,* October 18, 1997.

5. Ouellet organizes *Seven Prairie Painters* for the Art Gallery of Ontario Extension Services in co-operation with Edmonton Art Gallery.

6. See "Painting and Sculpture in Prairie Canada Today," *Canadian Art,* Toronto, March/April 1963, p. 90-107.

7. December, 1974, Vol. XXXI, p. 107.

8. Toronto: University of Toronto Press, 1978, p. 314.

9. Edmonton: Hurtig Publishing, 1983, p. 219.

10. Catalogue published by Time Canada 1974, p. 32.

11. Reprint of exhibition essay can be found in *Flat Side of the Landscape,* ibid, p. 136.

12. Catalogue published by Edmonton Art Gallery, 1980, unpaginated.

13. Russell Bingham. "Abstract Painting in Edmonton," *Update,* Edmonton Art Gallery, Sept/Oct. 1986, p. 6.

14. *The Flat Side of Landscape,* ibid., p. 141–142.

15. Published in Edmonton, May 25, 1987, p. 54–58.

16. Kathleen Thurber. "Hand of an artist," Oct 6–20, 1993, p. 7.

17. Aug/Sept, 1979, Vol. XXXVI, p.47–48. Alberta artists included Douglas Haynes, Ann Clarke, Richard Chenier and Bruce O'Neil.

18. Notes of the Mays's talk by M.B. Laviolette.

19. "Rothko buy a good portent of things to come at NGC," July 17, 1993, p. C4.

20. *Recent Work by Robert Scott: 1987–1993.* Edmonton Art Gallery, 1993, p. 9.

21. Virgil Hammock. *Edmonton Journal,* March 20, 1970, p. 66.

22. Virgil Hammock. "Painting exhibition found confusing, old fashioned," *Edmonton Journal,* March 19, 1969.

23. Virgil Hammock. "Shall we keep Dmytruk?", *Edmonton Journal,* January 9, 1970, p. 53.

24. Virgil Hammock. "Art with something to say," *Edmonton Journal,* April 11, 1969, p. 53.

25. Virgil Hammock. "U of A staff exhibition opens in SUB art gallery," *Edmonton Journal,* May 15, 1969.

26. Phylis Matousek. "Knowlton travels many roads," *Edmonton Journal,* November 10, 1984.

27. Elizabeth Beauchamp. Catalogue essay for *Norman Yates: Toward Landscape.* Ring House Gallery, Edmonton, 1983, p. 37.

28. *Colour and Dimension: The recent paintings of Graham Peacock,* FAB Art Gallery, Art EVO Gallery and Edmonton Art Gallery, 1992, unpaginated. See Interview with Graham Peacock.

29. Barry Lord. "Sundogs in the Sky: Some artists and buildings in two prairie cities," Feb/March 1971, Vol. XXVIII, p. 28.

30. See *The Flat Side of the Landscape,* ibid. p.141–142.

31. Lois Hammond. "Close-Up: Terry Fenton," *Visual Arts Newsletter,* Alberta Culture, Edmonton, October 1984.

32. Quote from catalogue *Terrence Keller,* Edmonton Art Gallery, 1988, p. 4.

33. Russell Bingham. "Abstract Painting in Edmonton," ibid.

34. All three shows are curated by Mark Joslin.

35. *Abstract Works on Paper* (1975), *New Abstract Art* (1977), *Acrylic on Canvas* (1977), *The Threshold of Colour* (1982), *Studio Watch at the EAG* (1985), *Abstract Painting in Edmonton* (1986), *Sculpture City* (1985) and *Sculpture by Invitation* (1986).

36. *Sculpture in Steel* (1974), *The Fauve Heritage* (1977), *David Smith: The Formative Years* (1981) and *Hans Hofmann: 1880–1966* (1982).

37. *Masters of the Sixties* (1972), *Robert Motherwell: Selected Prints 1961–74* (1973), *Lawrence Poons* (1974), *Kenneth Noland* (1975), *Tim Scott* (1976), *Stanley Boxer* (1977), *Adolph Gottlieb: Pictographs* (1977), *Jules Olitski: Paintings of the 70s* (1979), and *Walter Darby Bannard: Paintings and Clay Reliefs* (1983).

38. L.A. Reynolds (1974), *Doug Haynes* (1976), *Peter Hide: Recent Sculpture* (1978), *Philip Darrah* (1977), *Richard Chenier* (1977), *Graham Peacock: Fans and Pillars* (1977), *Ann Clarke* (1977), *Terrence Keller: Recent Work* (1978), *Robert Scott* (1978), *Catherine Burgess: Recent Sculpture* (1979), *Alan Reynolds: New Sculpture* (1979), *Phillip Darrah: Recent Paintings* (1981), *Ken Macklin* (1981), *Peter Hide: Recent Sculpture* (1982), *Clay Ellis: New Sculpture* (1983), and *Vesna Makale: Welded Steel Sculpture* (1983).

39. *Chester-Bentham* (1973), *Canada × Ten* (1974), *The Canadian Canvas* (1975), *Certain Traditions: Recent British and Canadian Art* (1978), *The ABC of Sculpture* (1980), *Alberta Now* (1980), *Keller, Saito and Sutton* (1981), *New Small Sculpture* (1982), *Seven Sculptors Studio Exhibition* (1982), *Contemporary Canadian Art: The Current Generation* (1983).

40. *Sculpture from the Collection* (1977), *From the Permanent Collection: Sculpture* (1985), *The Vincent Melzac Collection: Abstraction and Scale* (1982) and *The Pyrch Collection: A Farewell Exhibition* (1983).

41. *Jack Bush: Recent Work on Paper* (1973), *Jack Bush: A Retrospective* (1977) *Jack Bush: A Selection of Paintings from Edmonton Collections* (1983), plus several acquisitions.

42. Quote found in Charles Mandel's "War of the art worlds," ibid.

43. See "Letters to the Editor," *Canadian Art*, May/June 1964, p. 196.

44. Interview with Helen Collinson, April 3, 1995.

45. Elizabeth Beauchamp. "Edmonton Art Gallery: One Step Forward, One Step Back?" *Artichoke*, (Spring/Summer 1992, p. 21.

46. Ibid.

47. See Charles Mandel's "War of the art worlds," ibid.

48. Lynne Van Luven. "Juries panned at final Canada Council session," *Edmonton Journal*, September 21, 1991.

49. Interview with Mallon, December 17, 1997.

50. John Bentley Mays. "Abstraction alive and well and living in Edmonton," *Globe and Mail*, June 29, 1991.

51. See Charles Mandel's "War of the art worlds," ibid.

52. Pizanias completed her PHD in philosophy with "The Social Construction of an Art World: A case study in the sociology of painting," University of Alberta, 1992.

53. "Re-viewing Modernist Practice and Criticism in the Canadian Prairies: A case study from Edmonton," *International Journal of Canadian Studies*, Winter/Hiver 1993, p. 147.

54. See "Abstract Painting in Edmonton," ibid.

55. Roger Boulet. "Man of steel seduces the eye with charm, whimsy," *Edmonton Journal*, March 5, 1993, p. F6.

56. Curated by Denis Gaultier. Artists included Angela Inglis, Damian Moppett, Martin Bennett (of Calgary), Jeffrey Spalding (Lethbridge) and Isla Burns, Dick Der and Monica Tap (of Edmonton)

57. Spring 1997, p. 25.

chapter eleven

1. Elizabeth Beauchamp. "Studio spawns other-worldly works," *Edmonton Journal*, April 20, 1992, p. B5. Note: Haynes graduated in 1958 from the Provincial Institute of Technology and Art, Calgary, now known as the Alberta College of Art and Design.

2. Liz Wylie. Essay for an exhibition by teaching staff of the Department of Art and Design, University of Alberta, Edmonton Art Gallery, 1985, p. 45.

3. *Moffett's Artletter*, Stanford, Connecticut, special supplement #2, March 1986, p. 3.

4. Karen Wilken. Catalogue essay for *Douglas Haynes: The Toledo series,* The Edmonton Art Gallery, 1991, p. 7.

5. Lelde Muehlenbachs. Catalogue essay for *Colour and Dimension: The recent paintings of Graham Peacock,* published in conjunction with FAB Gallery, the Art EVO Gallery and the Edmonton Art Gallery, 1992, unpaginated.

6. All preceding comments on Keller's work are found in the catalogue *Terrence Keller,* Edmonton Art Gallery, 1989, p. 10 and 11. Essay by Russell Bingham.

7. Lelde Muehlenbachs. "Scott's abstract excellence," *Pique,* Edmonton, September 30, 1993.

8. Elizabeth Kidd. Catalogue essay for *Recent Work by Robert Scott: 1987–1993,* Edmonton Art Gallery, 1994, p. 10.

9. Ibid.

10. Kenworth Moffat gives an informative description of acrylic paint development in *New New Painting,* Paris: Editions NEF Casterman, 1992.

11. *Terrence Keller,* see endnote 6.

12. Ibid., p. 8.

13. Roger Boulet. Catalogue essay for *Graham Peacock Paint, Process and Spirit,* Edmonton Art Gallery, 1988, unpaginated.

14. Michae Jacobs. *A Guide to European Painting,* London: David and Charles. Description found in chapter "Neo-Classicism and Romanticism," p. 194.

15. Mark Rosenthal. Catalogue essay for *Critiques of Pure Abstraction* by Independent Curators Incorporated, New York. Exhibition presented at the lllingworth Kerr Gallery, Alberta College of Art and Design, Calgary, 1995, unpaginated catalogue.

16. Elizabeth Kidd. *Recent Work by Robert Scott,* ibid., p.10.

17. Elizabeth Beauchamp. "Modernist follow El Greco's Path," *Edmonton Journal,* May 3, 1991.

18. "Doug Haynes: In search of the 'breathtakingly simple,'" *Visual Arts Newsletter,* February 1985, p.11.

19. Caterina Pizanias. "Re-viewing Modernist Practice and Criticism in the Canadian Prairies: A Case Study from Edmonton", *International Journal of Canadian Studies* (Winter/Hiver 1993) p.162.

20. Interview with Keller, July 3, 1995.

21. "Overtones of dance in paintings," *Edmonton Journal,* December 10, 1988.

22. "Doug Haynes: In search of", ibid.

23. *Painting in Alberta: A Historical Survey,* The Edmonton Art Gallery, 1980, unpaginated.

24. *The Toledo Series,* ibid., p. 4.

25. *Doug Haynes: Paintings in the Eighties.* Curated by Norman Zepp and Michael Parke-Taylor.

26. Ibid.

27. Essay for *Douglas Haynes: Recent Paintings,* 1988. Exhibition was organized for Alberta House, London, England.

28. "Douglas Haynes: Inspiration from Unexpected Sources," *Update,* Edmonton Art Gallery, March/April 1986, p.19.

29. Elizabeth Beauchamp. "Studio spawns other-worldly works," *Edmonton Journal,* April 20, 1992.

30. Summer 1995, p. 18.

31. *Douglas Haynes: Recent Paintings,* ibid.

32. Ibid.

33. Review by Tim Hilton, March, 1988.

34. *The Toledo Series,* ibid., p. 1.

35. Ibid.

36. "Focus: on Doug Haynes," Summer, 1991 ,p. 64.

37. Elizabeth Beauchamp." Studio spawns other-worldly works," ibid.

38. Ibid.

39. Russell Bingham. Catalogue essay for *Robert Scott: Paintings of the 80s,* Edmonton Art Gallery, 1986.

40. Ibid.

41. Essay for *Robert Scott's Paintings,* Gallery Moos, New York , 1987.

42. Jean Richards. "Scott's work 'talk' to viewer," *Edmonton Journal,* November 21, 1978, p. E3.

43. Lelde Muehlenbachs. "Scott's abstract excellence," *Pique,* Edmonton, September 30, 1993.

44. Elizabeth Kidd. *Recent Work by Robert Scott,* ibid., p. 10.

45. "Breakdown and breakthrough," October 14, 1993.

46. Interview with Keller, July 3, 1995.

47. Lelde Muehlenbachs. "Keller breaks formalist mold," *Edmonton Bullet,* January 1, 1989.

48. *Terrence Keller,* ibid., p. 14.

49. Lelde Muehlenbachs., ibid.

50. "Painter takes industrial approach to art," March 21, 1992, p. D6.

51. Ibid.

52. Lelde Muehlenbachs. "Edmonton," *Artpost,* Spring, 1988, p .28.

53. "The New Acrylic Painting," appears in *New New Painting,* Paris: Editions NEF Casterman, 1992, p. 41.

54. "Post-Color Field Painting," *Moffett's Artletter,* Stanford, CT, March 1986, p.6.

55. Elizabeth Beauchamp "Studio spawns" ibid.

56. "The New Acrylic Painting," ibid., p. 41.

57. Lelde Muehlenbachs. "Edmonton," ibid.

58. "The New Acrylic Painting," ibid., p. 40.

59. Toronto painter Joseph Drapell is the other Canadian.

60. "Excess and Intimacy: Painting beside and inside itself," *New New Painting,* Stanford CT: Fine Art 2000, 1996, unpaginated.

61. Robert Houle. Catalogue essay "*A Context for the Janvier Legacy,*" *The Art of Alex Janvier: His First Thirty Years, 1960–1990,* Thunder Bay Art Gallery, 1993, p. 53.

62. Interview with artist, February 17, 1998.

63. M.Sylvia Bough. "Northern Lights," *Edmonton Magazine,* January 1986, p. 25.

64. "Truly Canadian: Retrospective shows artist's Alberta roots," *Calgary Herald,* April 28, 1995, p. C1.

65. Ibid., p. 49.

66. Ibid., p. 59.

67. Interview with artist, ibid.

68. Interview with artist, ibid.

69. Anne Payne. "Janvier," March/April 1976, p. 20.

70. Interview with artist, ibid.

71. Nancy Tousley. "A voice for the Great Spirit," reprinted in *the Edmonton Journal,* October 11, 1992, p. D1.

72. "The Art of Alex Janvier: His first thirty years, 1960–1990," *The Art of Alex Janvier,* ibid., p. 37.

73. Robert Houle. Catalogue essay *A Context for the Janvier Legacy* ibid., p. 62.

74. "Alex Janvier," from *Land Spirit Power: First Nations at the National Gallery of Canada,* Ottawa, 1992, p. 162.

75. March 2, 1990.

76. "The Art of Alex Janvier" ibid., p. 43.

77. Interview with artist, ibid.

78. Nancy Tousley. "A voice for the Great Spirit," ibid.

79. Ibid.

80. Ibid.

81. *Edmonton Prints: Brazil* exhibition organized by SNAP (Society of Northern Alberta Print-Artists) Edmonton, 1988, unpaginated.

82. *Edmonton Prints: Brazil,* ibid. See Dickson's "Introductions."

83. Bente Roed Cochran. *Printmaking in Alberta: 1945–1985,* Edmonton: University of Alberta Press, 1989, p. 88.

84. According to the essay: "Introductions," Edmonton Prints: Brazil, Ibid.

85. Ibid.

86. October 15, 1993, p. C6.

87. Exhibited at London's Royal College of Art's Gulbenkian Galleries, Tokyo's Murashino University and Calgary's Alberta College of Art and Design. Co-curated by Desmond Rochfort and Ryoji Ikeda.

88. "Printmaking in Three Continents: A question of horizons," *Lines of Sight: Ideas, Forms and Materialities,* Edmonton: University of Alberta Press, 1999, p. 16.

89. Such work was displayed in 1992 at the Glenbow Museum under the exhibition title of *Observing Three Points.* Curated by Patricia Ainslie.

90. Ibid. See essay by Ainslie.

91. "Passionate, intense and very personal," *Edmonton Journal,* March 12, 1993.

92. Ibid.

93. Presented at Edmonton's Latitude 53, 1992, and Calgary's Nickle Art Museum with 45 prints, 1992.

94. "The Quebec Experience," *Sightlines: Printmaking and Image Culture,* University of Alberta Press, Edmonton, 1997, p.171. Edited by Walter Jule.

95. "Observations on the Contemporary Print in Canada," *Sightlines: Printmaking,* ibid., p.125.

96. Ibid., p. 127.

chapter twelve

1. "Exhibit samples sculpting efforts," *Calgary Herald,* November 1, 1985.

2. "Sculpture City: Introduction," *Update,* Edmonton Art Gallery, Sept/Oct 1985, p. 6.

3. Roukes's quote is from his essay for the brochure for *Alberta Sculpture Survey '89*, Triangle Art Gallery, Calgary.

4. Roger Boulet. "Man of steel seduces the eye with charm, whimsy," *Edmonton Journal*, March 5, 1993, p. F6.

5. Russell Bingham. "Art critics are remembered for their misjudgments (if at all)." letter to the editor, *Edmonton Journal*, March 20, 1993, p. A11.

6. Alan King. "Alberta sculptors come in from cultural cold," date unknown.

7. Peter von Tiesenhausen was the third artist in the exhibit. He is not part of the Edmonton steel sculpture scene.

8. Essay for *The Other Alberta Sculpture*, Carleton University Art Gallery, Ottawa ON, 1995, p. 1.

9. "Sculptor's inner strength matched by her steel," *Edmonton Journal*, November 12, 1990.

10. Caterina Pizanias. "Of Earth and Steel: Taming the prairie in Canada," *Canadian Issues*, Association for Canadian Studies, Montreal, Volume XI, 1989, p. 124.

11. "Sculpture City: Introduction," ibid.

12. Ibid.

13. John Bentley Mays. "Abstraction alive and well and living in Edmonton," *Globe and Mail*, June 29, 1991, p. C5.

14. Artist's statement, undated.

15. "Sculpture City: Introduction," ibid.

16. Ibid.

17. Caterina Pizanias. "Of Earth and Steel" ibid., p. 118.

18. Interview with artist, July 3, 1995.

19. Artist comment found in *Inner Motifs: Fifteen years of exploration, Leslie Alan Reynolds*, Edmonton Art Gallery, 1990, unpaginated.

20. Mark Joslin. Catalogue Essay for *Inner Motifs: Fifteen Years of Exploration, Leslie Alan Reynolds*, ibid., unpaginated.

21. Ibid., p. 12.

22. John Bentley Mays. "Abstraction alive and well and", ibid.

23. See *Inner Motifs: Fifteen Years*, ibid.

24. "Heavyweight: The twists and turns of Alan Reynolds," *The Edmonton Bullet*, October 10, 1990, p. 12.

25. See catalogue of same name, p. 18.

26. "At the Galleries," *Partisan Review 1*, Volume LVIII, No. 1, 1991, p. 146.

27. "Sculpture shows great feeling for form," *Edmonton Journal*, January 4, 1975.

28. Mary Fox. "Introverted – but friendly – sculptures," *Vancouver Sun*, 1976.

29. See *Inner Motifs: FifteenYears* ibid, p. 8.

30. "Steel Sculptor at best with his smaller works," *Calgary Herald*, April 25, 1986, p. F8.

31. "Heavyweight: The Twists", ibid.

32. Ibid.

33. Caterina Pizanias. "Of Earth and Steel", ibid.

34. Both exhibitions were in Calgary at the Glenbow Museum and Nickle Arts Museum, respectively. Katherine Ylitalo curated both shows.

35. Displayed at the Southern Alberta Art Gallery, Lethbridge. Organized by Canadian Art Odysseys Society.

36. "Blair Brennan: Eucharist Project," *Snap Newsletter,* Edmonton, December 1993, p. 1.

37. Alan King. "Alberta sculptors come in from the cultural cold," *Ottawa Citizen,* March 12, 1995.

38. "Gallery Watch," *Edmonton Bullet,* December 5–19, 1990.

39. Nancy Tousley. Essay for *Catherine Burgess,* Edmonton Art Gallery, 1990, p. 3. Exhibition curated by Elizabeth Kidd.

40. Caterina Pizanias. "Of Earth and Steel" ibid., p.119.

41. Essay for *Catherine Burgess: Recent Sculpture,* Mendel Art Gallery, Saskatoon, 1980, unpaginated.

42. *Catherine Burgess: Recent Sculpture.* Toured by Peter Whyte Gallery, Banff , 1982.

43. Ibid.,unpaginated.

44. Halyna Koba. "Horizontal Tendencies," *Visual Arts Newsletter,* Alberta Culture, April 1986, p. 12.

45. "Guerrilla criticism: Red Deer confronts modernism," *Canadian Art,* Spring 1985, p.14.

46. See catalogue for exhibition published by the Glenbow Museum, p. 11.

47. Ibid., p. 12.

48. "Three Dimensions: Betty Goodwin, Walter May, Catherine Burgess," *Outlook,* Edmonton Art Gallery, Summer 1990, p .4.

49. Artist statement, dated April 17, 1994.

50. Elizabeth Beauchamp. "Sculptor's inner strength matched by her steel," *Edmonton Journal,* November 12, 1990.

51. Artist statement, ibid.

52. Bruce Grenville. Essay for *Catherine Burgess: Things as they are,* Southern Alberta Art Gallery, Lethbridge, AB, 1994, p. 18.

53. Caterina Pizanias. "Of Earth and Steel", ibid., p. 118.

54. Ibid.

55. Ibid. p.117.

56. Spring 1985, p.14.

57. David Howell. "Abstract sculpture gets mixed reviews," October 1, 1992.

58. Charles Mandel. "Juried art contest: round three," *Edmonton Journal,* December 17, 1996.

59. Karen Wilken. Essay for *Grounds for Sculpture,* Hamilton New Jersey, 1995.

60. Ibid.

61. Caterina Pizanias. Catalogue essay, *Making their Mark in the Age of Theory, Three Alberta Sculptors: Ken Macklin, Isla Burns, Clay Ellis,* Edmonton Art Gallery, 1993, p. 2.

62. Phone interview with writer, April 28, 1998.

63. Nancy Tousley. "Strong new sculpture by Edmontonian," *Calgary Herald,* October 19, 1990, p. C6.

64. Kitty Scott. "Isla Burns," *Three Alberta Sculptors: Ken Macklin, Isla Burns, Clay Ellis,* Edmonton Art Gallery, 1993, p. 6.

65. Interview with artist, April 21, 1998.

66. Ibid.

67. Elizabeth Beauchamp. "For the love of art, not for money," *Edmonton Journal,* September 1991.

68. Lelde Muehlenbachs. "The Place of Sculpture", *Border Crossings,* Winnipeg, 1993, p. 47.

69. Ibid.

70. Curated by Denis Gaultier.

71. Artist statement from *Looks Like,* The Edmonton Art Gallery, 1998.

72. The Lazare photographs of the group were printed in the *EAG*'s *Update,* Sept/Oct. 1985, on the cover and page 9.

73. Quote is from the catalogue published by the Museum of Art, Fort Lauderdale, Florida, 1997, unpaginated.

74. Artist statement entitled Period of Working in England 1961–1977," August 1995.

75. "The Monolith and Peter Hide," *Vanguard,* Vancouver Art Gallery, May 1984, p. 15.

76. David Burnett & Marilyn Schiff. *Contemporary Canadian Art,* Edmonton Hurtig Publishers, Edmonton, 1983, p. 222.

77. Artist statement, see endnote 74, ibid.

78. Ibid.

79. Russell Bingham. "Interview: Peter Hide," the *Edmonton Review,* Summer 1994, p. 4.

80. Lelde Muehlenbachs. "Elegance welded in steel," *Edmonton Journal,* May 15, 1979.

81. Interview with artist, ibid.

82. "The Monolith and Peter Hide ... ibid.

83. From brochure for *Peter Hide's New Sculptures,* FAB Gallery, University of Alberta, Edmonton, 1996.

84. Russell Bingham. "Interview: Peter Hide," ibid.

85. "Alberta Biennial of Contemporary Art 1996," *Canadian Art,* Spring, 1997, p. 63.

86. Artist statement for *Alberta Biennial of Contemporary Art,* Edmonton Art Gallery and Glenbow Museum, 1996.

87. Interview with artist, ibid.

88. Phylis Matousek. "Sculpture with a difference," *Edmonton Journal,* June 23, 1984, p. D2.

89. See exhibition catalogue, p. 9.

90. Artist statement, February, 1990.

91. Essay for *Blair Brennan: Similia Similibus Curentur,* Illingworth Kerr Gallery, Calgary, 1995, p.10.

92. See Wylie essay in exhibition catalogue, p. 5.

93. "One of My Favourite Works of Art," *Outlook,* Edmonton Art Gallery, Summer, 1991.

94. Essay for *Facts* brochure published for *The Works* festival, 1991.

95. Work commissioned by Gallery 101 Artists' Centre, Ottawa, Ont.

96. Pamela Anthony. "Rituals riveting in magical show," *Edmonton Journal,* October 22, 1994, p. E3.

97–99. Ibid.

100. See "Not an Artist's Statement," in exhibition catalogue, p. 6.

101. "Blair Brennan Eucharist Project," *Snap Newsletter,* Society of Northern Alberta Print-Artists, Edmonton. December 1993, p. 1.

102. Ibid.

103. Summer 1996, p. 71.

chapter thirteen

1. Interview with artist, June 19, 1996.

2. Norman Yates. "Environment 70 in Alberta," *Arts Canada,* Vol. XXVII, No. 4, Aug 1970.

3. April 24, 1970.

4. Nancy Tousley. "Roots, Rejections and Rewards in Calgary," *Canadian Art,* Fall 1996, p. 72.

5. "City fails to recognize its galleries," *Fast Forward,* September, 2002.At the time of writing this letter, Elgstrand is the director/curator of the Art Gallery of Calgary (formerly Muttart Art Gallery).

6. Lynda Shorten. "City arts funding said left in the dust."

7. Quote taken from "City inspires portraits," *Calgary Herald,* December 7, 1997, p. C2.

8. Gloria Huang. "Young Calgarian afraid to speak in Montreal," October 20, 1997.

9. Yvonne Zacharis. "Montrealers warm to the city," reprinted in the *Calgary Herald,* October 12, 1997, p. A1.

10. "Herald writers check out health of city's culture," February 29, 1996.

11. Alanna Mitchell. "Cowboy town makes bid for literary glory," October 18, 1996, p. A2.

12. William Thorsell, "Calgary Zen: An absence makes a city," *Globe and Mail,* Toronto, May 6, 2002.

13. Diana Nimeroff, acting curator of Contemporary Canadian Art, Ottawa

12. Alanna Mitchell. "Alberta looks beyond tradition," November 9, 1996, p. E4.

13. Press release for *Elemental Instincts: A matter of course,* Nickle Arts Museum, University of Calgary, 1988.

14. Nancy Tousley. "Roots, Rejections and", ibid.

15. Ibid.

16. *Farewell the Trumpets: An imperial retreat,* London: Penguin Books, 1979, p. 414.

17. "The battle of alberta," *West Globe and Mail,* Febuary, 1990, p. 27.

18. "Past Master," Toronto, 1998.

19. "Twelfth Annual Calgary Graphics Show," Autumn 1972, p. 78–80.

20. Interview with artist, September 25, 1997.

23. Glenbow Museum, Nickle Arts Museum and Alberta College of Art Gallery/ Illingworth Kerr Gallery.

24. Calgary's Muttart Art Gallery and Triangle Gallery for the Visual Arts, Banff's Walter Phillips Gallery and Whyte Museum, and Lethbridge's Southern Alberta Art Gallery

25. Off Centre Centre/the New Gallery, Stride Gallery, Truck, and EM Media

26. Interview with artist, September 17, 1997.

27. Nancy Tousley. "Roots, Rejections," ibid., p.72.

28. Exhibition at the Saidye Bronfman Centre, Montreal. Manitoba section curated by William Kirby, Saskatchewan by Terrence Heath and Alberta by Terry Fenton and Ron Moppett.

29. Exhibition at Glenbow-Alberta Institute, Calgary. Curator: Terrence Heath.

30. Exhibition at Mendel Art Gallery, Saskatoon.

31. Exhibition at the Alberta College of Art Gallery, Calgary. Curator: Alvin Balkind.

32. Ron Moppett essay for *Harry Kiyooka: Paintings & Drawings 1953–1978,* Alberta College of Art Gallery, 1978, unpaginated.

33. Karen Wilken essay for *Certain Traditions: Recent British and Canadian Art,* Edmonton Art Gallery, 1978, p. 55.

34. Interview with artist Don Mabie, October 30, 1998.

35. Quote is from "Subject and Other Matters: Letters [between] John Hall and Alexandra Heaseker." *Alexandra Haeseker: Twenty Years,* Illingworth Kerr Gallery, Alberta College of Art, 1992, p. 17.

36. David Garneau and Vincent Varga in conversation with writer, November 12 and October 23, 1998.

37. Quote from Katherine Ylitalo essay for *Ron Moppett: Painting nature with a mirror 1974–1989,* Glenbow Museum, 1990, p. 9.

38. Quote from Shirley Madill's essay for *Post-Pop Realism: The Winnipeg perspective 1982,* The Winnipeg Art Gallery, 1982, p. 8.

39. Artist statement, dated January 9, 1995.

40. Susan Ford essay for *Thirty-Five Years and Fifteen Minutes: Prints by John Kenneth Esler,* Nickle Arts Museum, University of Calgary, 1994, p. 34.

41. Born in 1946, Hamilton, Ontario. Brodie was a printmaking instructor at Alberta College of Art, Calgary, 1973-82.

42. Collages were exhibited at the Peter Whyte Gallery, Banff, 1983.

43. Quote from Helga Pakasaar essay for *Object Lessons,* Walter Phillips Gallery, Banff Centre, 1987, unpaginated.

44. Mary Anne Moser essay for brochure "Some theoretical stuff about Graceland," for the Second Annual Graceland Art Rodeo, August, 1990.

45. Essay by Bart Habermiller. "Graceland/ Background," March 10, 1989.

46. Wendy Dudley, "Calgary warms to local art," *Calgary Herald,* February18, 1989, p. F2.

47. The other artists are Wanda Ellerbeck, Miriam Fabijan, Joyce Fraser, Bart Habermiller, Nelson Henricks and Stephen Peterson.

48. Curated by Donna McAlear.

49. Curated by Annette Hurtig, assistant curator, contemporary art, Glenbow Museum.

50. From *Colleen Kerr-Seleni,* Muttart Art Gallery, Volume 4, Issue 3, May/June 1991, unpaginated.

51. Nancy Tousley. "Roots, Rejections," ibid., p. 77.

52. Jody Berland, Will Straw, David Tomas. "Introduction: The art as theory/theory and art conference," *Theory Rules: Theory and art,* Toronto: YYZ Books, 1996, p. 5.

53. Amy Gogarty, "Why Be Critical?", *Contact,* Autumn 1995.

54. David Garneau, "Sightlined Impressions," *Border Crossings,* Winter 1998

55. Artist Statement from *Alberta Biennial of Contemporary Art 1996,* Glenbow Museum, Calgary and Edmonton Art Gallery.

56. "Night Watch," *Canadian Art,* Winter 1992, p. 45.

57. Mary Anne Moser. "Some theoretical stuff," ibid.

58. Amy Gogarty. "Why Be Critical? ", ibid, p. 11.

59. This quote and the following are found in Spalding's essay for the exhibition handout. Essay was produced by the Triangle Art Gallery, Calgary, 1997.

60. This phrase is used by artist/writer Anne Severson who is a MFA graduate from the University of Calgary.

61. Ken Housego of Grande Prairie and Tommie Gallie of Edmonton.

62. Susan Menzies, Helen Sebelius, Wanda Ellerbeck, Ken Housego, Greg Payce, Derek Dennett (BFA), Mary Scott, Jeffrey Spalding, William MacDonnell, Nicholas Wade, Garry Williams, Julie Duschenes, Robin Peck and Rita McKeough. My thanks to Helen Sebelius for helping to compile this list.

63. Following comments by Sibelius are from a November 23, 1998 interview.

64. Kenneth Baker. "Notes From NSCAD," *Canadian Art,* Winter 1985, p. 41.

65. Cameron ran the program form 1976 to 1986. Mary Scott, William MacDonnell, Rita McKeough and Helen Sibelius were MFA students during that time.

66. Interview, August 17, 1995, with revisions by phone Tuesday, December 1 and 4, 1998. My thanks to Eric Cameron for his input regarding the text on NSCAD.

67. Kennedy was president of the college from 1967 to 1990.

68. "NSCAD and Southern Alberta," December 8, 1998, unpublished. My thanks to Jeffrey Spalding for his in-depth analysis of NSCAD provided for this book.

69. Interview with artist, August 17 1995.

70. Edited by Harold Osborne. Oxford, London, Toronto and Melbourne: Oxford University Press, p. 123.

71. Interview with artist, July 10, 1997.

72. Nancy Tousley. "Striking originality animates the work of Calgary artist," *Calgary Herald* January 29, 1981.

73. John Bentley Mays. "Art that speaks truly of the body and beauty," *The Globe and Mail,* March 31, 1989.

74. Alvin Balkind's essay for "The Triumph of the Egg," from *Visions: Contemporary Art In Canada,* edited by Robert Bringhurst, Geoffrey James, Russell Keziere and Doris Shadbolt. Vancouver: Douglas and McIntyre, 1983, p. 29.

76. "NSCAD and Southern Alberta...," ibid.

77. Patrick Tivy. "Stunning art trove fills school," *Calgary Herald,* November 2 1986, p. E1.

78. "Post-ironic re-enchantments," Fall 1996, p. 65.

79. Published by MacMillan Canada, Toronto, 1968 and reissued in 1993 by NeWest Press, Edmonton. Quote and the following paragraph are found on page 153–54 in the NeWest Press edition.

80. Ibid, p. 53.

81. From brochure produced for *In the Public Trust,* Southern Alberta Art Gallery, 1996.

82. "Lethbridge gallery has national reputation," *Alberta Connections,* Alberta Community Development, Edmonton, Summer 1996, p. 5.

83. John Bentley Mays. "Curators shine in hard times," *Globe and Mail.* December 30, 1995, p. C6.

84. Quote from Jeffrey Spalding essay for "Little life on the Prairies: Pop art and the comfort and trauma of a mediated existence," *Soup to Nuts: Pop Art and Its Legacy,* Cheney Cowles Museum, Spokane, Washington, 1998, p. 25.

85. "Building the University of Lethbridge Art Collection," *NeWest Review*, Edmonton, June/July 1993, p. 21.

chapter fourteen

1. The book is complied by Suzanne Devonshire Baker.

2. Calgary-based artists in the book are Derek Michael Besant, Marcella Bienvenue, Jim Brodie, John Chalke, Peter Deacon, Maureen Enns, Annemarie Schmid Esler, John K. Esler, Norman Faulkner, Gordon Ferguson, Christina Greco, Alexandra Haeseker, John Hall, Joice Hall, Patrick Hurst, Lylian Klimek, Ron Kostyniuk, Don Kottman, William Laing, Don Mabie, Margaret May, Walter May, Clyde McConnell, Carroll Moppett, Ron Moppett, Gary Olson, Bruce O'Neil, Noboru Sawai, Wendy Toogood, and Katie Ohe.

3. Interview with artist, May 12, 1995.

4. From Katherine Ylitalo's catalogue essay *OheZen* for *Katie Ohe,* Illingworth Kerr Gallery, Calgary, 1991, p.39. Catalogue also includes "The Multilayering of Katie Ohe and Her Work: 1937–1981," by Nancy Townshend.

5. All above quotes from Ylitalo, ibid.

6. *By A Lady: Celebrating three centuries of art by Canadian women,* Toronto: Viking (Penguin Books), 1992, p. 168.

7. Quote from unpaginated essay: "11 Artists Working on the Prairies," by Carol A. Philips.

8. Ibid.

9. Ibid.

10. Letter to "Mr. Hardy," June 20, 1990, by Katie Ohe.

11. Phone interview with artist, January 15, 1999.

12. From Ylitalo's essay, *OheZen,* ibid., p. 36.

13. Artist statement from *Between Four: A quest for personal vision.* A traveling group exhibition, also featuring Barbara Roe Hicklin, Terry Gregoraschuk and Bill Morton, 1995-1996.

14. From Ylitalo's essay "OheZen," ibid., p. 36.

15. Ibid.

16. Ibid, p. 37.

17. "Visual Arts," *See Magazine,* Edmonton, November 27–December 3, 1997, p. 23.

18. From exhibition notes by curator Denis Gauthier.

19. Ibid.

20. Quote taken from Nancy Tousley's article, "Roots, Rejections and Rewards in Calgary," *Canadian Art,* Fall 1986.

21. From unpaginated brochure notes produced for the *Environment 71* exhibition organized by Cultural Development Branch of the Government of Alberta. Exhibited at Southern Alberta Jubilee Auditorium.

22. Ibid.

23. John Bentley Mays. "Hall's comfortable as the odd man out," *Globe and Mail,* May 18, 1985, p. E5.

24. Curated by Nancy Townshend for Edmonton Art Gallery, 1974.

25. Nancy Tousley. Catalogue essay for *John Hall's Still-life Portraits: Imitations of life.* Travelling exhibition organized by Agnes Etherington Art Centre, Queen's University, Kingston, 1989, p. 25.

26. Nancy Tousley. Catalogue essay for *John Hall: Tourist series/toy series,* Southern Alberta Art Gallery, Lethbridge, 1982.

27. Robert Enright. "Odd Man Out: Interview with John Hall," *BorderCrossings,* Winnipeg, Summer 1989, p. 8–19.

28. Nancy Tousley. *John Hall Still-life Portraits* ibid., p. 18.

29. John Bentley Mays. "Hall's comfortable," ibid.

30. From "Subject and Other Matters: Letters John Hall and Alexandra Haeseker," *Alexandra Haeseker: Twenty Years,* Illingworth Kerr Gallery, Alberta College of Art, 1992, p. 18.

31. Artist statement for Joan Murray's *The Best Contemporary Canadian Art,* Edmonton: Hurtig Publishers, 1987.

32. Robert Enright."Odd Man Out: Interview with John Hall," ibid.

33. John Bentley Mays. "*Hall's comfortable,*" ibid.

34. The survey is organized by the Alberta College of Art Gallery and displayed in Calgary in 1978.

35. The other artist is Alan Dunning of Calgary in 1994.

36. Nancy Tousley. Catalogue essay for *John Hall's Still-life Portraits,* ibid., p. 24.

37. Ibid., p. 35.

38. Ibid., p. 35.

39. Robert Enright. "Odd Man Out: Interview with John Hall," ibid.

40. Nancy Tousley. Catalogue essay for *John Hall: Tourist series/toy series,* ibid.

41. John Bentley Mays. "Hall's comfortable," ibid.

42. Artist statement from Joan Murray, ibid.

43. David Garneau. "Sightlined Impressions," *BorderCrossings,* ebruary 1998, p. 54.

44. Ibid.

45. "Ascending Pleasures," *BorderCrossings,* Winnipeg, Summer, 1994, p. 55–56.

46. Beaver House Gallery, Edmonton. Included a provincial tour.

47. The Triangle Art Gallery, Calgary.

48. Muttart Art Gallery, Calgary.

49. Provincial tour of Alberta and British Columbia.

50. "Exhibition reflects diversity of realism," *Calgary Herald,* January 4, 1985, p. F8.

51. Moppett taught painting, drawing and design at ACA from 1972–74, 1981–83, and in 1986. He was a curator from 1969–71, from 1975–78, and director/curator from 1988–2005.

52. "A rose is a rose is a museum," *Star Weekly,* Toronto, Dec. 22, 1973. Note: this clipping has no page number or author.

53. Nancy Tousley. Catalogue essay for *John Hall's Still-life Portraits,* Agnes Etherington Art Centre, Kingston ON, 1989, p. 21.

54. Nancy Tousley. Catalogue essay for *Ron Moppett's Sign Language, Ron Moppett,* Walter Phillips Gallery, the Banff Centre School of Fine Arts, 1982, p. 7.

55. Ibid.

56. Nancy Tousley. Essay for pamphlet, *Ron Moppett: Recent Work,* 49th Parallel, New York, 1988, unpaginated.

57. "Introduction" A persistence of vision," by Lorne Falk for *Ron Moppett,* Walter Phillips Gallery, the Banff School of Fine Arts, 1982, p. 4.

58. "The experience of seeing," *Globe and Mail,* September 24, 1985.

59. This term is used by Gary Michael Dault in "Reading Philip Monk: Analyzing a complex and controversial theory about Canadian art and artists" to describe the more pro-active, socially aware and relevant art being made by certain women artists. "Men, Monk insists, have given themselves over to a romantic yearning for aesthetic unity, to dreams of a fallen wholeness, to a longing for heroism; men he says, are basically expressionists." *Canadian Art* ,Winter 1984, p.71.

60. Ibid, p. 13.

61. Katherine Ylitalo. Catalogue essay for *The Artist, Le Flaneur, Ron Moppett: Painting nature with a mirror, 1974–1989,* Glenbow Museum, Calgary, 1990, p. 23.

62. Nancy Tousley. "Ron Moppett's Sign Language," ibid., p. 6.

63. Nancy Tousley. Essay for pamphlet *Ron Moppett: Recent work,* ibid.

64. "Moppett's art abandons formalism," *Sunday Albertan,* Calgary, April 13, 1980.

65. Nancy Tousley. "Prized Painter: Major national visual arts honor bestowed upon Calgary's Ron Moppett," *Calgary Herald,* May 10, 1997, p. 16.

66. Ibid.

67. Kathleen M. Snow. *Maxwell Bates, Biography of an Artist,* Calgary: University of Calgary Press, 1993, p. 60.

68. Ibid., p. 71.

69. Katherine Ylitalo. Catalogue essay for *Ron Moppett: Painting nature with a mirror 1974–1989,* Glenbow-Alberta Institute, 1990, p. 17.

70. "Past and Present: W. L. Stevenson," *Artichoke: Writings about the Visual Arts,* Spring 1993, p. 11.

71. Nancy Tousley. Essay pamphlet for *Ron Moppett: Recent Work,* ibid., unpaginated.

72. Nancy Tousley. Catalogue essay for "Ron Moppett's Sign Language,"ibid., p. 8.

73. Mark Joslin. Catalogue essay for *W. L. Stevenson: 1926–1966, Painter of Light/Painter of Darkness,* Edmonton Art Gallery (1995), p.7.

74. Ibid., p.18.

75. David Burnett and Marilyn Schiff. *Contemporary Canadian Art,* Edmonton: Hurtig Publishers, 1983, p. 283.

76. Norman Mackenzie Art Gallery, Regina, 1982, p. 6.

77. Exhibition at Triangle Gallery of Visual Arts, Calgary. Organized by the University of Lethbridge, 1997.

78. Organized by Canada House Cultural Centre Gallery, London and Alberta Culture, Edmonton. Curated by Nancy Tousley.

79. Kathleen M. Snow. *Maxwell Bates: Biography* ibid., p. 57.

80. Katherine Ylitalo. Catalogue essay for *Ron Moppett*, ibid., p. 13.

81. David Garneau. "Ron Moppett: Self in play," *Artichoke: Writings about the Visual Arts,* Summer 1990, p. 20.

82. Nancy Tousley. "Moppett's simpler, richer style shines through in latest show," *Calgary Herald,* November 16, 1988.

83. Katherine Ylitalo. Catalogue essay for *Ron Moppett* ibid., p. 13.

84. Interview with Ron Moppett, March 2, 1999.

85. David Garneau. "Ron Moppett ibid., p.19.

86. Nancy Tousley. "Painter adds air in studio," *Calgary Herald,* June 8, 1996.

87. Ibid.

88. Ibid.

89. Interview with Ron Moppett ibid.

90. Ibid.

91. Nancy Tousley. *Ron Moppett: Recent work* ibid., unpaginated.

92. Joan Murray. *The Best Contemporary Canadian Art, Edmonton:* Hurtig Publishers, 1987. See "Ron Moppett."

93. Ibid.

84. Ibid.

95. Nancy Tousley. Essay for pamphlet *Ron Moppett: Recent Work,* ibid.

96. Patrick Mahon. Catalogue essay for exhibition *A Critical Beauty,* Open Space Arts Society, Victoria, 1996, p .2.

97. Ibid.

98. Peter Schjeldahl. "Fairies Welcome: The Victorian uses of enchantment," *New Yorker,* November 9, 1998.

99. From artist statement accompanying nomination form for Governor General Award. Dated October 1999.

100. Quote taken from artist's statement dated July 1997.

101. Quote taken from "Curator's Statement" prepared by Catharine Mastin, senior curator of art, Glenbow and Catherine Crowston, senior curator, The Edmonton Art Gallery. Published in *In/Here/Out/There: Alberta Biennial of Contemporary Art 1998,* Glenbow Museum and the Edmonton Art Gallery, 1998, p. 8.

102. Artist statement from *Alberta Biennial 1998,* ibid., p. 25.

103. "An Interview with Catharine Mastin," *Artichoke: Writings about the visual arts,* (Fall/Winter 1998), p.15.

104. Ibid.

105. Sol Littman. "Correspondence artists don't need gallery," August 17, 1973.

106. Nancy Tousley. "Chuck Stake offers food for thought in mail art," *Calgary Herald,* March 25, 1982 , p. B20.

107. Interview with artist, September 17, 1997.

108. "*Art Briefs*: Mabie leaves gallery's helm," date unknown.

109. Interview with artist, ibid.

110. Ibid.

111. Alberta College of Art Gallery, 1969.

112. Gallery Moos, Toronto, Ont.

113. Gallery Moos, Toronto, Ont.

114. *Some drawings by some Albertans* and *Not Just Another Print Exhibition* were organized for Alberta Culture, Visual Arts Branch.

115. Artist Statement, September 1977, Calgary.

116. The Nomads in 1986 consisted of Germany's Jurgen O. Olbrich, Wolfgang Hainke and Ulf Rungenhagen; Holland's Arno Arts; London's Niall Monro; Zurich's M.Vanci Stirnemann. In 1987, Calgary's Grant Poier and Quebec's Alain-Martin Richard also joined the group. Activity continued until 1988.

117. Formed in 1992, the group's other members were Mark Dicey, Grant Poier, Cori Stent and the late Jeff Viner.

118. Artist Statement, January 9, 1988.

119. Brooks Joyner. "Don Mabie—an artistic enigma," *The Albertan,* October 8, 1977, p. 32.

120. Sandra Tivy. "Don Mabie," *Vanguard* magazine, Vancouver, November 1983, p. 38.

121. Term is taken from essay *Fear of Empty Spaces,* by Mary-Beth Laviolette. *Don Mabie: Drawings: 1978 to 1990,* Muttart Art Gallery, Calgary.

122. Ibid.

123. "Introduction," to *Don Mabie: Drawings: 1978 to 1990,* ibid.

124. Artwork can be seen on page 62 of *Don Mabie/Chuck Stake: Aspects of practice, 1969–1996,* Illingworth Kerr Gallery, Alberta College of Art and Design, Calgary (1996).

125. "See Beyond The Text," by Richard White, curator of *Don Mabie: Drawings: 1978 to 1990,* ibid.

126. "Don Mabie aka Chuck Stake: Life with lots of pockets," *Don Mabie/Chuck Stake: Aspects of Practice: 1969–1996,* ibid., p. 51.

127. Organized by the Art Gallery of Windsor. Curator: Robert McKaskell.

128. "Ride: A Happening. Somethin's happ'nin and it Ain't Quite Clear!" took place Thursday, April 22, 1999.

chapter fifteen

1. Quote from "Subject and Other Matters", *Alexandra Haeseker: Twenty Years,* Illingworth Kerr Gallery, Alberta College of Art, 1992. This quote appeared in a letter Haeseker wrote to John Hall.

2. BA (Art), U of C, 1963–66; Fine Arts Diploma, ACA, 1966–68 and MA (Art), U of C, 1970–72.

3. The year the following printmakers begin teaching in Calgary: John Will (1971, University of Calgary), Noboru Sawai (1971, University of Calgary), James Brodie (1973, Alberta College of Art), William Laing (1974, Alberta College of Art; 1977, University of Calgary), Stuart Parker (1974, Alberta College Art), Gary Olson (1975, Alberta College of Art) and Tomas Lax (1977, Alberta College of Art).

4. Bente Roed Cochran. *Printmaking in Alberta: 1945–1985,* Edmonton: University of Alberta Press, 1989, p. 42.

5. From brief introduction by Schmidt in *Calgary Printmakers,* Edmonton Art Gallery, 1974, unpaginated.

6. Hugh G. Anderson. "Derek Michael Besant and Alexandra Haeseker," March, p. 58.

7. From brief introduction by Schmidt, ibid.

8. Bente Roed Cochran, ibid.

9. *Alexandra Haeseker: Twenty Years* ibid.

10. Christopher Read, editor. *Not At Home: The Suppression of Domesticity in Modern Art and Architecture,* London UK: Thames and Hudson, 1996. Quote found on inside book jacket.

11. Exhibit takes place in 1971. Also displayed at the Glenbow Alberta Institute, Calgary.

12. *Alexandra Haeseker: Twenty Years …* ibid.

13. Ibid.

14. Ibid.

15. Hugh G. Anderson, ibid.

16. *Alexandra Haeseker: Twenty Years* ibid.

17. Nancy Tousley. "Haeseker celebrates 20 years of art."

18. "Subject and Other Matters", *Alexandra Haeseker: Twenty Years* ibid.

19. Ibid.

20. Paul Kuhn Fine Arts, Calgary.

21. The Nickle Arts Museum, University of Calgary.

22. "Etchings at core of strong exhibition," *Calgary Herald,* March 29, 1985.

23. "Besant's images straightforward and blunt," *Calgary Herald,* November 22, 1985.

24. From Leslie Dawn's essay "Traces Among The Fragments," for *Besant De-Composition,* Art Gallery of Hamilton, 1990, p. 6.

25. Quote found in 1992 interview with curator Richard White, *Bill Laing: Still-Lifes,* Muttart Art Gallery, Calgary, 1992.

26. Ibid.

27. From interview with Besant for *Besant: Sites,* Canada House Cultural Centre, London.

28. "The most important element in my drawing is concept" according to the artist in *Some Drawings by Some Albertans: A major survey of drawing in Alberta,* Alberta College of Art Gallery, 1980, p. 13. Curator: Don Mabie.

29. Bente Roed Cochran, ibid.

30. Robin Laurence. Catalogue essay "Drawing +" for *Drawing +,* Open Space, Victoria, 1994.

31. "Summary," *Derek Michael Besant/ Diagrams,* Nickle Arts Museum, Calgary, 1985, unpaginated.

32. *Besant De-Composition* ibid., p. 7.

33. The other three commissions are in Calgary (outdoor sculpture, Mount Royal College and an indoor piece for Calgary's plus fifteen walkways) and in New York (mural, Cineplex Odeon, World Wide Centre).

34. Linda Hutcheon. *Splitting Images: Contemporary Canadian ironies,* Toronto: Oxford University Press.

35. Nancy Tousley. "Falls transplanted to Toronto," *Calgary Herald,* May 31, 1989, p. B5.

36. Tim Mara. From essay *The Journey, William Laing,* The Nickle Arts Museum, The University of Calgary, 1997, p. 9.

37. In an interview with Laing on May 25, 1999, the artist emphasized this point, noting that his work is landscape-oriented.

38–40 Quote from 1992 interview with curator Richard White ibid.

41. Paul Woodrow. Catalogue essay for *William Laing: A Journey,* Nickle Arts Museum, University of Calgary, 1997, p. 16.

42. *William Laing: A Journey* ibid.

43. Brooks Joyner. "Printmaking in Alberta," *Artsmagazine,* March/April 1977, p. 10–12.

44. Noboru Sawai."Other Hands: Japan's unofficial ambassadors abroad," *Wingspan,* Vol. III No. 2, All Nipon: Toyko, February 1990, p.36.

45. Other artists he has appropriated include Botticelli, Goya, Hogarth, Daumier, Picasso and Tom Wesselman.

46. Sol Littman. "This erotic art's a must," *Toronto Star,* April 1, 1979.

47. Stephen Hutchings. "Sex isn't everything with this printmaker," *Crag & Canyon,* Banff, May 22, 1980, p. 6.

48. Sol Littman, ibid.

49. From exhibition statement for *The Floating World Of Prints: Noboru Sawai,* Muttart Art Gallery publication, September/October 1989, unpaginated.

50. *A Garden of Delights: 25 Years of Prints by Noboru Sawai,* Nickle Arts Museum, University of Calgary, 1994, p. 27.

51. Nancy Tousley, "Opposities explored in garden of delights," *Calgary Herald,* February 18, 1994, p. D1.

52. *John Will: Triple Threat Artist,* Dunlop Art Gallery, Regina, 1988 p. 14. Essay by artist is entitled "Triple Threat."

53. Quote is found in Will essay "Triple Threat," *John Will: Triple Threat Artist,* Dunlop Art Gallery, Regina, 1988, p.12. Curator is Peter White.

54. Will and Anderson's collaborations included *Icon I, Icon II, Icon III* and *Icon IV.* About this activity Will writes: "Our brief foray (6 works, 1985–86) into performance was precipitated by what Jack and I perceived in many instances as others' performance art as incompetence and/or inability to perform – in other words, no talent. We were loaded with no talent so we knew we could succeed, and we did! The audience loved us and the proof is all on the video tape." (May 1998 letter to writer.)

55. John Will: A survey of prints 1967–1980. Glenbow-Alberta Institute, Calgary, 1980, p. 6. Excerpt from a talk given by the artist.

56. Nancy Tousley. "Postcard from the Edge," *Canadian Art ,* Fall 1994, p. 97.

57. *John Will: A Survey of Prints* ibid., p. 3. From catalogue introduction, entitled "John's Willful Humour."

58. Doug Bale. "Calgary artist pokes fun at society," October 10, 1981.

59. Nancy Tousley. "Postcard from", ibid.

60. John Will. "Triple Threat." *John Will: Triple Threat* ibid., p. 12. The curator is Peter White.

61. Colleen O'Neill. Essay for *I Love Me,* Stride Gallery, Calgary, 1987, unpaginated.

62. Vera Lemecha. Essay for *John Wall,* Glenbow Museum, Calgary, 1992.

63. The 200 paintings are titled *Anything and Everything* and are in the collection of the Edmonton Art Gallery.

64. A description of the event is found in Mike Murphy's "A Night Calgary Will Never Forget," *Artichoke: Writings about the visual arts ,* Calgary, Summer 1993, p. 40–41.

65. "Artist plays the Name Game: John Will will use anybody's moniker to make a point," July 16, 1992, p. C1.

66. Quote is taken from Chris Cran's essay "Our Trip to Arkansas," *John Will: Atomic haiku,* Truck Gallery, Calgary, 1995, p. 7.

67. *Great Plains,* Farrar Straus Giroux, New York, 1989, p. 9.

68. Peter White. "Introduction" for *John Will: Triple Threat Artist* ibid., p. 9.

69. Ibid., p. 10.

70. Nancy Tousley's essay "John Will: On Photography," for *John Will: Triple Threat Artist* ibid., p. 22.

71. John Will. Essay "Triple Threat," for *John Will: Triple Threat Artist* ibid., p. 13.

72. John Will. Essay "Atomic [Editor's Note]" for *John Will: Atomic* [Editor's Note], Truck Gallery, Calgary, 1995, p. 10.

73. Ibid., p. 43.

74. Ibid., p. 10.

75. Eva Newman. Essay for *Do You Take This Seriously?,* Glenbow Museum, 1984, unpaginated brochure.

76. Ibid.

77. Nancy Tousley. "Postcard From the Edge" ibid.

78. Notably, Mary Scott and Rita McKeough were two of his students.

79. Roald Nasgaard. "Concealing/Revealing: Voices from the Canadian Foothills," *Concealing/Revealing,* Museum of Fine Arts of the School of Visual Arts and Dance at Florida State University and the Art Gallery, School of Fine Arts, University of Lethbridge, Alberta. p.11.

chapter sixteen

1. Tom McFall. "Fete of clay: made-in Alberta ceramics from functional to fine art," *Legacy,* November 1998 to January 1999.

2. Les Graff. "Turning Earth into Art: From clay quarry to museum shelf, a century of ceramic development," *Alberta Views,* Summer 1999.

3. Nancy Townshend. "Introduction," *The History of Ceramics in Alberta,* Edmonton Art Gallery (1975), unpaginated. Townshend was also the curator of this exhibition.

4. In a more commercial and industrial vein, domestic stoneware pottery did the same in the early half of the twentieth century, when it was copiously produced in Medicine Hat, including the now highly collectable Medalta pottery. Tracking this important industry in Alberta is Anne Hayward's *The Alberta Pottery Industry, 1912–1990: A Social and Economic History,* Canadian Museum of Civilization, Ottawa (2001).

5. Tom McFall. "Fete of clay" ibid., p. 15.

6. Other Albertan art in the exhibition include Wendy Toogood's applique fibre art, glass work by Jim Norton, Martha Henry and Darren James Peterson, tapestry by Jane Kidd and Murray Gibson, weaving by Lynn Kristmanson and C.B. Pinchin, jewellery by Dee Fontans and Charles Lewton-Brain, Henry Schlosser's wood art and metal work by Jackie Anderson, Jeff de Boer, Karen A. Cantine, Crys Harse and Donald Bednar.

7. "Preface," *A Treasury of Canadian Craft: Inaugural Exhibition,* Canadian Craft Museum, Vancouver, 1992, p. 9–10.

8. Published by Manitoba Crafts Council, Winnipeg, 1995.

9. British artists Bernard Leach, Hans Coper, Lucie Rie and Ruth Duckworth; America's Peter Voulkos, Richard Shaw, Ron Nagle, David Gilhooly and others; Japanese artists Shoji Hamada and philosopher Soetsu Yanagi; and western Canadian artists Sybil Laubental, Luke Lindoe, Joseph Fafard, Victor Cicansky, Marilyn Levine, Gathie Falk, Ricardo Gomez and so on.

10. The exhibition in Calgary and conference at the Banff School of Fine Arts was co-hosted by the Alberta Potters Association and the International Academy of Ceramics.

11. *Ceramic Art of the World 1973,* Alberta Potters Association, (1973), p. 4.

12. Catalogue produced by Walter Phillips Gallery (1984), unpaginated.

13. The four artists are Millie Chen, Jamelie Hassan, Baco Ohama and Garry Williams. The curator is Sylvie Gilbert.

14. "Reconsidering Function," *Contact,* Calgary, 1993/94, Winter, p. 22.

15. The APA is not the first example of a non-profit organization for potters in the province. It is preceded by the formation of the Edmonton Potter's Guild in 1952 with thirteen founding members. In 1953, the guild begins to offer classes with Sybil Laubental as its first instructor (1953–1957).

16. APA's first president is Victor Brosz, an instructor at the University of Calgary. According to Arne Handley, the signatories of APA's May 13, 1971 charter were Vic Brosz, Walter Drohan, Harlan House, Les Manning and John Porter.

17. Publication of *Contact* was suspended in 1999 by which time it was no longer under the auspices of the APA.

18. "Lessons From the Calgary Exhibition," *Ceramic Art of the World 1973,* Alberta Potters Association, (1973), p. 1.

19. "Twenty-Five Years: A Summary," *Vessels in Celebration,* Alberta Potters Association, Calgary, 1996, p. 37.

20. Telephone interview with Manning, October 13, 1999.

21. A history of the Alberta College of Art is available in Val Greenfield's "Introduction," *A Measure of Success: Graduates of the Alberta College of Art 1963–1984,* Alberta College of Art Gallery, 1985, p. 4–8.

22. "The entrance [to U of C's ceramics 1964-1990] is partially screened by a large commemorative placard listing the names of approximately ninety [U of C] graduates with BFA's specializing in ceramics … Too many important Albertans and Canadian artists are represented on this list to mention individually here," notes U of C art historian John Stocking about the posthumous exhibition.

23. Two important sources accessed for information on Alberta's ceramic history are: Nancy Townshend's *The History of Ceramics in Alberta,* 1975, published by the Edmonton Art Gallery and Francis Burke's *Alberta Clay comes of age,* 1984, published by the Alberta Potters Association.

24. Despite an illustrious history as a fine-arts school dating back to the thirties and a vibrant post-1970 period in the visual art – the H.G. Glyde Studio Building opened in 1976 – single-discipline pursuits such as ceramics, painting, printmaking and photography by the end of the century have a diminished presence at the institution. Overall, they represent an outmoded notion of art no longer in keeping with the centre's multidisciplinary postmodern sensibilities or its new objectives of being a techo/digital/new media institution.

25. Beaumont eventually served on the board of the AAF, 1976–79, and was its chairman, in his last year. Phone interview with Beaumont, October 28, 1999. My thanks to Nancy Townshend for pointing out Beaumont's role.

26. Other important contributors include Calgary MLA Dave Russell, who introduced Beaumont's Act as a Private Member's Bill; Dr. Horst A. Schmid, who as Lougheed's first Minister of Culture, shared Russell's conviction that the projected Act "would be an important legislation for the arts of Alberta" and oversaw the effort to make it a reality; and Les Graff, who as head of the province's Visual Arts Branch provided advice and services to the fledgling Foundation.

27. According to the AFA's Art Collection and Collection Programs brochure: "This provincial treasure of more than 6,000 works of art, valued at $8.2 million, represents the talents of more than 1,600 Alberta artists…." The brochure is undated but was printed in the late 90s.

28. The artists are Toru Hasegawa, Ed Drahanchuk, Jane Van Alderwegen, Annemarie Schmid Esler, Mary Shannon Will, Mary Borgstrom, John Chalke, Walter Drohan, Albert Borch and Luke Lindoe.

29. Harry Kiyooka, Terry Fenton and Slyvain Voyer selected the work for the show.

30. Catherine Carson. "Alberta art will be displayed in three European capitals," *Edmonton Journal,* August 2, 1975.

31. "Commentary," Alberta Art Foundation, 1976.

32. Nancy Townshend. "Introduction," *The History*, ibid.

33. Ibid.

34. Quote from Frances Burke's essay, "Alberta Clay Comes of Age," *Alberta Clay comes of age: Studio Ceramics in Alberta III 1964–1984,* Alberta Potters Association, (1986), p. 11.

35. Les Graff. "Turning Earth into Art", ibid.

36. Sam Middleton. "Clay breaks new ground," May 8, 1981. Show was at the Students' Union Art Gallery, U of A. Organized in conjunction with Latitude 53, curator Susan Abell Fridman, featured twelve artists including: Joe Fafard, Annemarie Schmid Esler, Sally Barbier, Mary Shannon Will, Victor Cicansky and Gathie Falk.

37. "Western Canadian Ceramic Sculpture: A ten year perspective," *Issues in Clay: Western Canadian Sculpture,* Latitude 53 Society of Artists, Edmonton, 1982, unpaginated. Exhibiton curator: Susan Abells Fridman.

38. David Lasker. "Clay Comes of Age," *Western Living,* November 1984, p. 63.

39. Judy Ross Thompson, David Allen, and Nina Czegledy-Nagy. *Down To Earth: Canadian potters at work,* Toronto: Nelson Canada Ltd., 1980.

40. Labarge, Dorothy. "Flights of Imagination, Pink cows and bananas at the surreal edge," *Interface,* August, 1981, C8.

41. Les Graff. "Turning Earth into Art" ibid., p.26.

42. Randy Adams. "Annemarie Schmid Esler: Yet another Canada Council Grant," *Arts Bridge,* December 1992. A publication of Alberta Culture and Multiculturalism.

43. Amy Gogarty. "Five Snapshots-in-Progress of John Chalke," *American Ceramics,* Winter 1993.

44. Val Greenfield. *Annemarie Schmid Esler: Fourteen Years,* Alberta College of Art Gallery, 1987.

45. Susan Himel and Elaine Lambert. "Potter's first show raises stir," *Globe and Mail,* July 16, 1981.

46. Patricia Ainslie. *Vessels,* Glenbow Museum, 1989. Exhibit included John Chalke, Leigh Harrington and Franklin Heisler.

47. Artist statement for *Pacific West Coast Series,* 1983, exhibited at Olga Korper Gallery, Toronto.

48. Patricia Ainslie, ibid.

49. Thompson, Allen, Czegledy-Nagy, … ibid.

50. Career cast in clay," *Calgary Herald,* November 5, 1987, p. F1.

51. Ibid.

52. Valerie Greenfield. *Annemarie Schmid Esler,* ibid., p. 7.

53. John Stocking. "Annemarie Schmid Esler: Firing the Blues Away," *Woman's Art Journal,* Vol. 13 (Spring/Summer), p.15–18.

54. Ibid.

55. Exhibition curated by Bruce Ferguson and Andrew Oko.

56. Columbus, Ohio, April 1975.

57. Nancy Tousley. "Ambiguous aura of bandaged bird sculptures disturbing," *Calgary Herald,* May 5, 1980.

58. Thompson, Allen, and Czegledy-Nagy ibid.

59. Valerie Greenfield. Catalogue essay for *Annemarie Schmid Esler: Fourteen Years* ibid., p. 13.

60. Edited by Jules Heller and Nancy G. Heller, New York and London: Garland Publishing, Inc. 1995, p. 494.

61. David Lasker. *Western Living* ibid.

62. Nancy Tousley. "Ambiguous aura of bandaged bird," ibid.

63. Valerie Greenfield, ibid., p. 21.

64. Ibid., p. 25.

65. Thomspon, Allen and Czegledy-Nagy ibid.

66. 1987, Edmonton Art Gallery.

67. Also exhibited in 1991 at Calgary's Triangle Gallery.

68. John Stocking, "Under the Volcano Again,", *Annemarie Schmid Esler,* Southern Alberta Art Gallery, Lethbridge, 1990.

69. Arne Handley. "Biography of John Chalke," from an Alberta Craft Council and Alberta Potter's Association application for a Bronfman Award for Excellence in the Arts, March 1994.

70. Fletcher Award is ranked as one of the top ceramic award exhibitions in the world, along with one in Faenza, Italy, and another in Mino, Japan.

71. Moyra Elliot. "John Chalke," *New Zealand Potter,* Auckland, New Zealand, April No. 1, 1996, p. 30.

72. "Moons of Ariosto: a reading of John Chalke," *Contact,* Calgary, Winter 1981) unpaginated.

73. Arne Handley. "Biography of John Chalke" ibid.

74. Bill Corbett. "Crafts World in Calgary," *Visual Arts Newsletter,* Alberta Culture and Multiculturalism, Edmonton, September 1990, p. 4.

75. Nancy Tousley. "Artist fires his work in rustic outbuilding," *Calgary Herald,* February 8, 1987.

76. Arne Handley. "Biography of John Chalke" ibid.

77. Artist statement drawn up in the 1990s.

78. "Impressions," *The Albertan,* date unknown, 1979.

79. Ibid.

80. From Glenbow Museum didactic material prepared by Ria Meloche.

81. A travelling exhibition sponsored by the Alberta Potters Association.

82. Displayed at Wyman Building, Minneapolis, Minnesota and the Nickle Arts Museum, Calgary. Co-sponsored by Manitoba, Saskatchewan and Alberta Craft Councils and BC Craft Associations.

83. Barbara Harmer Tipton. Essay for *John Chalke: Works on Clay,* Southern Alberta Art Gallery, Lethbridge, 1987, unpaginated.

84. Ibid.

85. Susan Himel and Elaine Lambert ibid.

86. "Ceramic artist's skills abundant," *Calgary Herald,* December 3, 1987.

87. Arne Handley. "Biography of John Chalke" ibid.

88. Other participants are: Jim Etzkorn, Bob Reimer, Sam Uhlick and Richard and Carol Selfridge.

89. "Vessels: Hand and Spirit," *Sightlines,* publication of the Muttart Art Gallery,Winter 1998.

90. Anne McPherson and Susan Jefferies. Essay for *White on White: Contemporary Canadian ceramics,* Canadian Clay and Glass Gallery, Waterloo, Ontario (1996).

91. Katherine Dickerson. "John Chalke: 1983 Bronfman Award Nominee."

92. Ibid.

93. Ibid.

94. Published by the Alberta Potters Association, Edmonton, p. 123.

95. Susan Cockshutt. "Marriages," *Alberta Craft Magazine,* Alberta Craft Council, Edmonton, May/June 1996, p.10–11.

96. Artist statement, dated 1994.

97. Susan Cockshutt. "Marriages," ibid.

98. Artist statement prepared for International Ceramics 1997 brochure. Leisure Learning Services, City of Calgary.

99. Elizabeth Beauchamp. "Life, art intertwine for city pottery duo," *Edmonton Journal,* February 18, 1989.

100. Ibid.

101. Les Graff. "Turning Earth into" ibid.

102. "Containment: The space within," *contact,* Calgary, Spring 1994, p. 7.

103. Ibid.

104 . *Alberta Clay Comes of Age,* ibid., p. 68.

105. Bloom was editor from 1973–77.

106. "Stonecrop: The home of gnomes and other strange folk," *Banff Crag and Canyon,* Banff, February 26, 1975, p. 7.

107. According to Bloom, sixty artists have spent time at Stonecrop since its founding. Interview with artist, January 5, 2000.

108. "Stonecrop: The home of gnomes" ibid., p. 7.

109. In 1979 Bloom bought out the other founders.

110. "Handspirits musings," *Handspirits,* Alberta Crafts Council, 1985, p. 5. Exhibition coordinator: Carol Sheehan.

111. Joan Murray. "Mary Shannon Will: Ceramic Sculptress," *Canada Crafts,* Toronto, November/December 1979, p. 18.

112. Brooks Joyner. "Curator's Message," *Mary Shannon Will: Sculptures,* Nickle Arts Museum, University of Calgary (1979).

113. Ibid.

114. Joan Murray. "Mary Shannon Will," ibid.

115. Leona Flim. "Bogusky makes his last appearance, "September 9, 1985.

116. "Mary Shannon Will's Drawings," *Calgary Herald*, July, 1987.

117. *Mary Shannon Will*, Southern Alberta Art Gallery, Lethbridge, 1985, unpaginated.

118. Published by the Southern Alberta Art Gallery, Lethbridge, 1985, unpaginated.

119. Nancy Tousley. "Bankview basement serves as flexible art studio," *Calgary Herald*, January 19, 1986, p. E3.

120. This observation is borrowed from Victora Baster's essay for *Mary Shannon Will*, Southern Alberta Art Gallery (1985), unpaginated.

121. Joan Murray. *Mary Shannon Will* ibid.

122. Victoria Baster. "Ceramics, Painting. Graphic Works," *Gallery*, Southern Alberta Art Gallery, Lethbridge (Sept/Oct 1985), unpaginated.

123. Nancy Tousley. "Will's works are eye dazzlers," *Calgary Herald*, March 27, 1992.

124. Ibid.

125. Jeffrey Spalding essay for *Mary Shannon Will*, Stride Gallery, Calgary, 1987, unpaginated.

126. Artist statement found in catalogue for *Ground/Connection: Trudy Ellen Golley, Sally Barbier, Grace Nickel, Therrese Chabot, Katrina Rozman, Joan McNeil.* Wyman Building, Minneapolis and St. Norbert Arts and Cultural Centre, Winnipeg, 1995, unpaginated. Essay by Amy Gogarty.

127. Nancy Tousley. "Artist directed by exotic past," *Calgary Herald*, October 26, 1986, p. E8.

128. Helen Collinson. Essay for *Sally Barbier*, unpaginated brochure.

129. "Other Climes: Barbier's works evoke the exotic," *Calgary Herald*, December 18, 1986, p. F1.

130. Essay for *Ground/Connection*, an exhibition project of Mentoring Artists for Women's Art. Displayed at Wyman Building, Minneapolis and St.Norbert Arts and Cultural Centre, Winnipeg, 1995 and 1996, unpaginated.

131. Artist statement, Calgary, 1995.

132. Allan Sheppard. "Sally Barbier, Art as memory," *Alberta Craft Magazine* November/December, p. 20.

133. Sally Barbier. "Memory Shrines," *Contact*, Calgary, Spring 1993, p. 32.

134. Mark Walton. "Sally Barbier: New Works," *Muttart Art Gallery Newsletter*, Calgary.

135. Ibid.

136. Essay for *Ground/Connection* ibid.

137. Sally Barbier. "Memory Shrines," ibid.

138. Allan Sheppard. "Sally Barbier", ibid.

139. Ann Wilson Lloyd. "In a New Millennium, Religion Shows Its Face." *New York Times*, January 23, 2000.

140. Mark Walton. "Sally Barbier", ibid.

141. Essay for *Ground/Connection* ibid.

142. Sally Barbier and Greg Payce. "Critical Philosophy of Alberta College of Art," *Contact* Calgary, p. 17.

143. Artist statement, Calgary, 1995.

144. Essay for *Ground/Connection* ibid.

chapter seventeen

1. Christine Conley. "In From the Cold: Feminism and art in Edmonton," *Parallelogramme,* Toronto; February/March issue, 1986.

2. Kirsten Evenden. Didactic notes for *Women's Work: Art by Women in Glenbow Collection*, Glenbow Museum, 1996. My thanks to K. Evenden for these notes.

3. This list is only a partial accounting and not intended to be comprehensive.

4. Linda Curtis. "Local artist work to grace church," *The Albertan,* Calgary, November 7, 1962. My thanks to Katherine Ylitalo for this quote.

5. Interview with Ohe, May 12, 1995.

6. This observation, made verbally on February 25, 2000, comes from artist Ron Moppett who knew Nicoll.

7. Kirsten Evenden. Didactic notes for *Women's Work,* ibid.

8. Ibid.

9. All three words from interview with Ohe, ibid.

10. Ibid.

11. Ibid.

12. This definition is borrowed from Robert Atkins, *Artspeak: A Guide to contemporary ideas, movements and buzzwords.* New York: Abbeville Press Publishers, 1990, p. 76.

13. *Art Journal,* Vol. 41, No. 1/2, 1980, p. 362.

14. *Artspeak: A Guide* ibid.

15. "Teresa Posyniak's Abyss," *Artichoke: Writings about the visual arts,* Calgary, Spring 1993, p. 33.

16. "Art Quilters: Taking our province's treasures off the bed and into the galleries," Calgary, March/Apr 2000, p. 17.

17. Kirsten Evenden, ibid.

18. Ibid.

19. Thelma McCormack. "In Her Place: Issues in feminist aesthetics," *Vanguard,* Vancouver, Summer 1987.

20. Christine Conley. "In From The Cold, ibid., p. 15.

21. Exhibition curators: Sandra Morton Weizman, Curator of Social History, Provincial Museum of Alberta Edmonton, and Elyse Eliot-Los, director/curator, Muttart Gallery, Calgary.

22. Both *Alberta Needles* are organized by the Quilters' Group of the Calgary Branch of the Alberta Handicrafts Guild for the Nickle Arts Museum, Calgary.

23. Paula Gustafson. *Alberta Needles II: Quilts for the 1990s,* Nickle Arts Museum, Calgary, 1990, p. 22.

24. David Burns. "Quilting breaks loose: A brand new art form, but cold comfort at night," *Alberta Report,* from August or September 1989.

25. Katherine Lipsett. "Exhibition Statement," *Redefined: The Quilt as Art,* Whyte Museum of the Canadian Rockies, Banff, 1989, p. 3.

26. Ibid.

27. Ibid.

28. Barbara Todd resided in Banff, Alberta, from 1981 to 1993 before moving to Montreal. Of her time in Alberta, she writes: "My twelve years there were the beginning of my serious career and I feel that I benefited greatly from the encouragement and contact with artists and galleries in Calgary, The Banff Centre and of course SAAG in Lethbridge." (Letter to author, dated October 18 1995.)

29. This quilt is presented within an installation (child's metal crib with bedding) created by Todd for *Redefined.*

30. Katherine Lipsett, "Exhibition Statement," 1989.

31. Alan Morantz. "Heavy Threads," *Equinox,* Ontario, January/February 1994, p. 39.

32. Artist's Statement about *Security Blankets,* 1988–1995.

33. Letter to author dated October 18, 1995.

34. Bridget Elliot. Catalogue essay, "Changing Differences: Quilting and moderism," *Redefined: The Quilt As Art,* Whyte Museum of the Canadian Rockies, 1989, p. 27.

35. Other artists include: John Hall, Mary Scott, Joane Cardinal-Schubert, Chris Cran.

36. Marni Jackson. Catalogue essay, "Uncoverings," *Barbara Todd: Security blankets,* Southern Alberta Art Gallery, Lethbridge (1993), p. 6.

37. Bridget Elliot. Catalogue essay, "Changing Differences," ibid., p. 26.

38. "Wendy Toogood: Cloth constructions and paintings (1971-1996)," *Muttart Public Art Gallery Newsletter,* Calgary, September/October 1996, p. 6–7.

39. Sol Littman. "Artist's soft wall-hangings show joyous imagination," July 3, 1973.

40. Kirsten Evenden. "Bridging the Gap Between Art and Life: Two quilts in Glenbow's collection," *Glenbow,* Glenbow Musuem, Calgary, Winter 1997, p. 9.

41. The juried exhibition was sponsored by the seventy-fifth Anniversary Commission and Alberta Culture Visual Arts. The co-coordinator/curator was Jane Thomas. It was seen at the SUB Gallery, U of A and the Nickle Arts Museum, Calgary.

42. "Cloth art comes alive on artist's studio walls," *Calgary Herald,* January 11, 1987.

43. Ibid.

44. A juried exhibition sponsored by the Alberta College of Art Gallery, Calgary. Part of the show is also displayed at the University of Calgary Art Gallery.

45. Exhibition was held at the Alberta College of Art Gallery. Curator is Valerie Greenfield.

46. At the time, Balkind is the chief curator of the Vancouver Art Gallery.

47. Alvin Balkind. Catalogue essay, "Random Thoughts on Trying to Judge the Entries to AlbertaWork," *AlbertaWork,* Alberta College of Art Gallery, Calgary, unpaginated.

48. "New Image Alberta," *Vanguard,* Vancouver Art Gallery, March 1983, p. 20.

49. Nancy Tousley. " Toogood's Strong Winds to blow over Expo," *Calgary Herald,* December 22, 1985, p. F3.

50. Toogood has completed commissions for Calgary's Harry Hays Federal Building, 1978; Nova Corporation 1987; and First Alberta Place (1988). Another is at Red Deer College, Red Deer (1986).

51. Artist statement: "The Abstract: Non objective works 1985–1989."

52. Ibid.

53. Artist statement: "The Mexican Cloth Constructions 1989–1993."

54. Ibid.

55. Other known Calgary artists who attended the school include: Ron Spickett, Roy Kiyooka, Bruce O'Neil, John Hall, Ron Moppett, Carroll (Moppett) Lindoe-Taylor and Toogood's husband, Don Mabie.

56. Kirsten Evenden. "Bridging the Gap", ibid.

57. The retrospective's title is *Wendy Toogood: Cloth Constructions and Paintings, 1971–1996.* The curator is Kathryn Burns.

58. Artist statement. "The Paintings 1993–1995."

59. Instructor in the textile department at ACA from 1976 to the present.

60. From artist statement produced by the New Gallery in April 1992.

61. "Artist's Statement," in brochure for *Sandra Vida: Kitchen Freedom,* Nickle Arts Museum, Calgary (2000) Curator: Christine Sowiak.

62. Ibid.

63. Ibid.

64. Charles Mandel. "The Works," *Edmonton Journal*, early July 1996.

65. Jill Fischer and Lainna Wolonski are the other two founders.

66. Helen Metella. "Exhibit offers subversive looks at paper," *Edmonton Journal,* July 4, 1994, p. B7.

67. From media release for *PaperSpeak: A Global View,* The Museum for Textiles, Toronto, dated October 26, 1994.

68. "PaperSpeak: A Global View," *PaperSpeak: A Global View,* Alberta Part Art Publications (1981) Society, Edmonton (1994) unpaginated.

69. Presented by New Gallery in collaboration with 2nd Story Gallery, EM/Media and the CalgarySociety of Independent Filmmakers.

70. Displayed at the Nickle Arts Museum.

71. Seen on Rogers Community 10, Calgary. Co-produced by Colleen Kerr and Nelson Henricks.

72. Artist's statement, undated.

73. Artist's statement, undated, but received by author in 1995.

74. Performed at the Nickle Arts Museum, Thursday, October 20, 1988 as part of *Elemental Instincts a Matter of Course* exhibition.

75. From the catalogue: *Elemental Instincts a Matter of Course,* the Nickle Arts Museum, Calgary, 1988, p. 39.

76. A performance/installation at the New Gallery, Calgary.

77. Two examples are Kerr's inclusion in: *Minor Details, Major Issues,* Glenbow Museum, 1993 and *Feminist Art From the Collection,* Glenbow Museum, 1994.

78. Annette Hurtig. Essay for *Minor Details, Major Issues: Colleen Kerr, Colleen Philippi, Linda Anderson Stewart,* Glenbow Museum, 1993.

79. Ibid.

80. David Garneau. "Teresa Posyniak: Abyss," *Extension,* Calgary, Winter 1992, p. 4.

81. David Garneau. "Teresa Posyniak's Abyss," *Artichoke: Writings about the visual arts,* Calgary, Spring 1993, p. 33.

82. "Teresa Posyniak: Artist's statement," *Beauparlant/Posyniak: A Collaboration,* Dunlop Art Gallery, Regina, 1984, unpaginated.

83. Teresa Posyniak. "The Building of 'Lest We Forget' – A Monument Dedicated to Murdered Women," undated.

84. Ibid.

85. "Feminism Enters the Foundry," May 19–26, 1995.

86. For description of work see catalogue *Out Side In: Iain Baxter, Lylian Klimek, William MacDonnell,* the Nickle Arts Museum, Calgary, 1988. Guest curator: Rob Milthorp.

87. Trevor M. Smith. Catalogue essay for "Endangered Memory," *Meadow: An Installation by Lylian Klimek,* Neutral Ground, 1990.

88. Vivienne Sosnowski McRoberts. "Alberta sculptors exhibit best works," *the Edmonton Journal,* March 1986.

89. Greg Beatty. "A strange stroll into artistic adventure," *The Leader Post,* Regina, June 21, 1990, p. C9.

90. Lylian Klimek. "Lylian Klimek," *Gallerie Annual,* 1988, p. 77.

91. Leslie Dawn. Catalogue essay for *Lylian Klimek: Sculpture,* Southern Alberta Art Gallery, Lethbridge, 1987, unpaginated.

92. "Alberta Fibrations, Changing Attitudes," *Muttart Public Art Gallery Newsletter,* November/December 1995, p. 2.

93. "Artist Statement," *Handspirits,* Alberta Crafts Council, Edmonton, 1985, p. 45. Travelling exhibition coordinated by Carol Sheehan.

94. From hand-out produced by the Alberta Foundation for the Arts and the Meeting Point Artist Association, 1994.

95. "Paper mache speaks pithy visual language," November 10, 1989, p. E10.

96. Interview with artist, Calgary. June 19, 1995.

97. Mark Walton. "Death Stalks the Muttart Art Gallery," *Artichoke: Writings for the visual arts,* Calgary, Fall/Winter, 1994.

98. Ibid., p. 36.

99. Edmonton photographer Douglas Clark and Mark Arneson are other examples.

100. The title of the photograph is *Old age must give you patience to harvest just two radishes,* 1985.

101. From an interview with Alison Rossiter in "Apparent reasons: The work of Barbara Spohr," *Artichoke: Writings about the visual arts,* Calgary, Spring 1994, p. 45.

102. Catalogue essay, "Barbara Spohr's Border Crossings," *Barbara Spohr: Apparent reasons,* Whyte Museum of the Canadian Rockies/Glenbow Museum, 1993, p. 75. Curator: Katherine Lipsett

103. Lauren Dale of Edmonton was the other photographer.

104. Roy Arden. "Barbara Spohr," *Vanguard,* Vancouver, October 1985, p. 42.

105. Ibid.

106. Artist statement for *Tablescapes,* Folio Gallery, Calgary, 1989.

107. Ibid.

108. Elizabeth Menzies. "In My Own Voice: Reflections on Process," *Contact*, Calgary, 1992/93 Winter, p. 21.

109. Ibid., p. 23.

110. Ibid., p.22.

111. Ibid., p.23.

112. Joanne Good. "Crimes of Fashion," *Calgary Herald,* December 31, 1999.

113. Diane Murray. "Body Beautiful," *Avenue,* Calgary, March 1997.

114. From the *Millennium in Motion* brochure published by AIDS Calgary, 1999.

115. "Dee Does Dada: Calgary artist dresses up her ideas in Stride exhibit," *Fast Forward,* Calgary, February 2000.

116. Artist Statement for *Outing the Body,* the Stride Gallery, Calgary, February 4–26, 2000.

117. A 1999 touring exhibition put together by the Metal Arts Guild of Ontario in collaboration with the Conseil des métiers d'art du Quebec.

118. Also exhibited as "OTB: Men Abreast," with the Stride Gallery show.

119. "Pain hurts: The biggest recent thing in cultural studies is the body. And when there is body, say the writers of this fine anthology, it will hurt," July 12 1999.

120. Nancy Tousley. "Show based on female experience," *Calgary Herald,* May 17, 1985, p. C5.

121. "Violet Owen." *Update,* Edmonton Art Gallery, March/April 1984, p. 10.

122. "Lone model inspires Violet Owen: Face affords artist wealth of portraits," *Edmonton Journal,* September 22, 1989, p. D10.

123. The exhibition was entitled Myrna Harvey and Susan Gorris and was displayed at the James Ulrich Gallery, Calgary.

124. Painter and instructor James Ulrich founded and operated the James Ulrich Gallery from 1981–1984, and then teamed up with artist, Peter Deacon to found and operate Deacon Ulrich Fine Arts, 1995–98. Ulrich has taught at the Alberta College of Art and Design since 1973.

125. Christine Conley. "In From the Cold: Feminism," ibid, p. 14.

126. Several years later, Scott would cite the example of Jim Ulrich's earlier gallery involvement (with the James Ulrich Gallery) as being the "model we (Don Corman, Colleen O'Neil and I) implicitly used when we opened Stride in the late 1980s."

127. McKeough also showed with Mary Scott and Marcella Bienvenue in *Politically Speaking,* an exhibition curated by Christine Conley for Latitude 53 Gallery, Edmonton (1986). The show was displayed two years later at Women in Focus, Vancouver and according to Conley "presents a feminist perspective on art as a social practice."

128. *Aganetha Dyck* was organized by the Winnipeg Art Gallery.

129. "Mary Scott: Readings in the Garden," *Mary Scott: In you more than you,* Stride Gallery, 1994 unpaginated.

130. Elissa Barnard. "Scott looks back in anger," *Halifax Mail Star,* October 7, 1986.

131. Nancy Tousley. "Striking originality animates the work of Calgary artist," *Calgary Herald,* January 29, 1981.

132. *Contemporary Canadian Artists,* Toronto: Gale Canada, 1997, p. 535.

133. John Bentley Mays. "Art that truly speaks of the body and beauty," *Globe and Mail,* March 31, 1989.

134. Interview with artist, August 1997.

135. Ibid.

136. Nancy Tousley. "Striking originality", ibid.

137. "Mary Scott," *Contemporary Canadian Artists,* Toronto: Gale Canada, (1997), p. 536. Author unattributed.

138. Meta Perry. "Artist 'paints' with syringe needle," February 18, 1986.

139. In the Glenbow Museum collection, the first and last words of every paragraph were written over and over again on the plexiglass surface until after 25 or so layers, the text became illegible and the painting was now an abstract of finely woven threads.

140. Nancy Tousley. "Striking originality", ibid.

141. Scott's casual attitude is described by the Calgary artist/critic Sandra (Tivy) Vida as an "amiable irreverence for artistic conventions" in her 1986 review of "Mary Scott" for *Vanguard* magazine, February/March 1986, p. 63.

142. *Striving for Ideal Resolution/Tendre vers une solution ideale,* the Nickle Arts Museum, Calgary (1988), p.13. Group exhibition curated by Donna McAlear.

143. Robin Laurence. "Enigma as a female form of expression," *Vancouver Sun,* undated, 1994.

144. "Scott's rug-size works take over living room," *Calgary Herald,* March 2 1986, p. E2.

145. Interview with artist, August 1997.

146. Sheila Butler. "Mary Scott," *Vanguard,* Vancouver, December 1987/January 1988, p. 31.

147. Elissa Barnard. "Scott looks back ," ibid.

148. Sigrid Dahle. Catalogue essay for *Mary Scott: Textu(r)al Strategies,* Gallery I.I.I., School of Art, University of Manitoba, Winnipeg (1987), p. 4.

149. Bruce Grenville. Catalogue essay for *Mary Scott,* Southern Alberta Art Gallery, Lethbridge, 1989, p. 7.

150. "Art that speaks truly of the body and beauty," March 31, 1989.

151. This number does not include her participation in two ACA faculty shows, 1984 and 1986.

152. Nancy Tousley. Catalogue essay for *Seven Artists from Alberta: Art in this region,* Canada House Cultural Centre Gallery, London and Alberta Culture, Edmonton.

153. Vince Varga. Catalogue essay for *Aspects of Contemporary Painting in Alberta,* Glenbow-Alberta Institute, 1987, p. 10.

154. All quotes in the paragraph come from an interview with the artist in August 1997 in Calgary.

155. Katherine Ylitalo. Catalogue essay for *Multiple Associations: Five Alberta artists,* Glenbow-Alberta Institute, 1988, p. 8.

156. Ibid. Ylitalo also explains that the term was first used by Freud and developed by Jacques Lacan.

157. The entire title of the series is *In you more than you schemas: diagrams: maps: knots: figures.*

158. The entire title is *In me more than me schemas, diagrams, maps, knots, figures: stuck.*

159. "Mary Scott: In me more than me," *Canadian Art,* Fall 1993, p. 85.

160. Robin Laurence. "Enigma as a," ibid.

161. See p.1 of the catalogue co-authored by Bridget Elliot and Janice Williamson for the Edmonton Art Gallery in 1990.

162. The other artists are Susan Day, Jamelie Hassan, Natalka Husar, Elizabeth MacKenzie and Sandra Meigs.

163. "Portrait of a Gallery: The Edmonton Art Gallery at 75," May–July 1999, p. 12.

164. The following three exhibitions are curated by the Gallery's assistant curator, Barbara Fischee.

165. Christine Conley. "In from the Cold," ibid., p.17–18.

166. Elizabeth Kidd. "Acknowledgements," *Dangerous Goods: Feminist Visual Art Practices.* The Edmonton Art Gallery and Latitude 53 (1990).

167. A more in-depth description of this activity in Edmonton is provided by Christine Conley in "In From the Cold," ibid, who is quoted on page 1 of Chapter 17.

168. Interview with Ellerbeck in "Post-Mortem on the eighties: A look at the past decade," *Artichoke: Writings about the visual arts,* Calgary Winter 1990, p. 23. Complied by Mary-Beth Laviolette. In 1991, Ellerbeck participated in the Glenbow Museum's *The Embodied Viewer,* curated by Vera Lemecha. Featuring eleven artists including Mary Scott, this exhibition is organized around the idea of the body.

169. The curator of the exhibition was Sylvie Gilbert. The artists were Robert Flack, Maurebb Connor and the Vancouver collective: Kiss & Tell.

170. Published in *Artichoke: Writings about the visual arts,* Calgary, Summer 1993 p. 18.

171. Christine Conley. Catalogue essay for *Regeneration,* Agnes Etherington Art Centre, Kingston, 1990, p. 6.

172. Published in *Artichoke: Writings about the visual arts,* Calgary, Fall/Winter 1992, p.19.

173. Catalogue essay for *Body, Gender and Other Issues,* Muttart Art Gallery, Calgary, September/October 1993, unpaginated.

174. The curator for both projects is Annette Hurtig.

175. The other two installations: *Retaining Wall,* Stride Gallery, Calgary (1986) and *Heave,* <<“ ”>>dl Gallery, Calgary, 1988.

176. Mary Lou Riordon-Sello, Joan Caplan, Lorrie Wagner, Susan Harrison, and Diana Zasadny.

177. “Art in the March: Celebrating our differences,” *Artichoke: Writings about the visual arts,* Calgary (Summer 1993).

178. “Feminist art: Issues and agendas,” *Artichoke: writings about the visual arts,* Calgary, Fall/Winter 1994, p. 22.

179. “Vibrant Velvet,” *Calgary Herald,* December 8, 1995.

180. Ibid.

181. Artist Statement by Laura Vickerson, undated.

182. Artist statement in *New Territories: 350/500 years later,* published by Ateliers Vision Planetaire, 1992, p. 111. Project Director and Curator, Pierre-Leon Tetreault.

183. Ibid.

184. Mike Murphy. “Intuition Before Order: A Conversation with Faye HeavyShield,” *Artichoke: Writings about the visual arts,* Calgary, Fall 1993, p. 55.

185. *Cradle* is one several works dealing the artist’s residential school experience, which also includes memories of sexual abuse that is evoked in a 1993 mixed-media piece, *Now I Lay Me Down.*

186. Exhibited as a site-specific work for *Into the Garden of Angels: Faye Heavyshield,* the Power Plant, Toronto 1994, the artist comments in the catalogue that *worship* celebrates “a way of seeing that was strengthened by my parents and grandparents, by the land and by my language.”

187. This travelling exhibition is sponsored by Syncrude Canada and produced by Alberta Part Art Publications, 1981, Society, Edmonton. The curator is Dana Williams.

188. “Double Meanings,” *Calgary Herald,* June 25, 1993.

189. Ibid.

190. “Artist creates from experience,” April 13, 1994.

191. Mike Murphy. “Intuition Before Order” ibid., p. 54.

192. HeavyShield attended ACA from 1980 to 1985 with a year off in between. She left just short of graduation. She also enrolled for one year in the fine arts program at the University of Calgary in 1986.

193. Unattributed. “Faye HeavyShield: Art is shaping memory,” *Fredericton Gleaner,* Fredericton, April 24, 1993.

194. “Changing Directions: A new perspective on native women’s art,” Winter 1989, p. 20.

195. Exhibited at the Illingworth Kerr Gallery, Alberta College of Art, Calgary, 1995; 284 William Avenue, Winnipeg, 1997, and 5th International Istanbul Biennial, Istanbul, Turkey, 1997.

196. Nancy Tousley. "Petals reflect feminine side of art," *Calgary Herald,* September 10, 1994, p. F1.

197. Ibid. This quotation and the two others in the sentence are from pages 9, 11 and 12 respectively.

198. Exhibited at the Edmonton Art Gallery, 1992.

199. Exhibited in *Seeing Through,* Window Project on the +15 of the Centre for Performing Arts, Calgary, 1994.

200. Exhibited in *Squint: Laura Vickerson, Gordon Ferguson, Walter May,* ArtWeek 94, Calgary, 1994.

201. Exhibited in *Rhythms,* Walter Phillips Gallery, the Banff Centre, 1994.

202. "Petals reflect feminine side of art," ibid.

203. Amy Gogarty. "Consuming Beauty: Laura Vickerson's Studies of Nature," *C,* Toronto, Spring 1995, p. 36.

204. Vickerson's installation was part of a three-person exhibition entitled *Squint* that included Walter May and Gordon Ferguson, 1994.

205. Amy Gogarty. "Consuming" ibid. p. 38.

206. Artist statement, undated.

207. Ibid.

208. "Mixed Media," *Canadian Art,* Spring 1996, p. 91.

209. Ibid.

210. Also exhibited at: Glenbow Museum, Calgary; Museum of Industry, Stellarton, Nova Scotia; Canadian Museum of Textiles, Toronto; St. Catherines' Museum, St. Catherine, Ontario; Thunder Bay Art Gallery, Thunder Bay, Ontario.

211. Documentary broadcast on CBC Radio's *Sunday Morning,* June 7, 1998.

212. This statement is made only in reference to the Western world (i.e. the Euro-American sphere) and does not acknowledge that in other parts of the globe, men as well, participate in the making of fibre and textiles.

chapter eighteen

1. A.P. Schroeder. *Word for Word: The Business of writing in Alberta,* 1988. Jointly published by the Writers' Guild of Alberta and Alberta Culture and Multiculturalism, Edmonton, 1988, p.40–41.

2. Alan Kellogg. "Report should be enshrined to set future standard," *the Edmonton Journal,* January 18, 1989, p. B6.

3. "Post-Mortem On The Eighties: A Look at the past decade," *Artichoke: Writings about the visual arts,* Calgary, February 1990, p. 19. Compiled by Mary-Beth Laviolette.

4. Ibid., p. 20.

5. Nancy Tousley. "Art Gallery forced to close outlet," June 8, 1983, p. C13.

6. Prior to 1980, Off Centre Centre was known as Clouds 'n Water Gallery.

7. Nancy Tousley. "Weak support dooms Ulrich Art Gallery," February 15, 1984.

8. The two original artistic directors of the non-profit *The Works* are Susan Abells and Linda Wedman. The ten-day event continues to this day.

9. The six galleries are Paul Kuhn Fine Arts, Virginia Christopher Galleries, Masters Gallery, Canadian Arts Galleries, Gainsborough Gallery and Kensington Fine Arts. The event continues today and includes the participation of artist-run and public art galleries.

10. "Post-Mortem on the Eighties," ibid.

11. Ibid., p.21.

12. Organized by the Canada House Cultural Centre Gallery, London and Alberta Culture, Edmonton.

13. Nancy Tousley. Essay for *Seven Artists from Alberta: Art in this region.* Published by Canada House Cultural Centre Gallery, London, June 1984, unpaginated.

14. Scot Morrison. "Reach for the Top: Alberta artists are making their mark internationally," *Visual Arts Newsletter,* Alberta Culture and Multiculturalism, Edmonton, June 1987, p. 5.

15. There were eighteen institutions receiving a yearly block grant including $105,000 for the Glenbow Museum and $190,000 for the Edmonton Art Gallery.

16. Mary-Beth Laviolette. "Policy Changes Shake Art Institutions," *Visual Arts Newsletter,* Alberta Culture and Multiculturalism, Edmonton, April 1996, p. 3.

17. Mary-Beth Laviolette. "Who is the Authority Now?", *Artichoke: Writings about the visual arts,* Calgary Spring/Summer 1992, p. 15.

18. "Impotence of arts overseers spawns Central Canada bias," *Globe and Mail,* August 26, 1985, p. 7.

19. Ibid.

20. Unpublished letter to Mary-Beth Laviolette, dated December 12, 1998.

21. Used as a quote in Chapter 10, this observation by Mays in "Abstraction alive and well and living in Edmonton," June 29, 1991 bears repeating.

22. Lynne Van Luven. "Canada Council comes to town," September 26 1991.

23. In 1991, Alberta artists received $292,029 through the Arts Award program, which had $4,363,391 to distribute.

24. In 1999, Alberta received $1,049,163 out of a total of $15,179,576 for visual-arts funding.

25. "So, why do we care?", *Alberta Craft Magazine,* Alberta Craft Council, Edmonton, March/April 2000, p. 1.

26. Ibid.

27. In 1995–96, there is no listing for this category.

28. "Ontario culture pioneering in style," *Globe and Mail,* March 10, 2001.

29. Published by Little, Brown and Company (Canada) Limited, Toronto, 1997. See p. 13.

30. Terrence Heath. "The Art of Regional Nationalism," *BorderCrossings,* Winnipeg, Issue #73, 2000, p. 13. In this pertinent article, Heath reports on artist Vic Cicansky's three-year correspondence with Diana Nimeroff, curator of contemporary art, about regional representation in the National Gallery of Canada's collection.

31. Ibid.

32. Valerie Greenfield. "Introduction," *A Measure of Success: Graduates of the Alberta College of Art 1963–1984,* Alberta College of Art Gallery, Calgary, 1985, p. 5.

33. For further information on the "dream," see *Seventy-five Years of Art: Alberta College of Art and Design, 1926–2001.* Editors: Christine Sammon and Mary-Beth Laviolette.

34. Ibid., p. 7.

35. Organized by the Edmonton Art Gallery. See Chapter 12.

36. The other three artists are Teresa Posyniak, Carl Granzow and Merv Krivoshein.

37. Quote taken from Nancy Tousley's "Exhibit samples sculpting efforts," *Calgary Herald,* November 1, 1985.

38. Eleanor Bond. "Gang of Three: New Sculpture from Calgary," Ace Art and Plug/In Inc., Winnipeg, 1987.

39. Elizabeth Kidd. "Walter May," *Walter May,* the Edmonton Art Gallery, 1990, p. 3.

40. Eleanor Bond. "Gang of Three," ibid.

41. Nancy Tousley. "Gordon Ferguson," *Vanguard,* Vancouver, May 1982, p. 45.

42. Mary-Beth Laviolette. "Calgary Sculpture: Oddly Out of the Ordinary," *Cityscope,* Calgary, May/June 1986, p. 46.

43. From *Gordon Ferguson: Sense Your Place,* Southern Alberta Art Gallery, Lethbridge, AB, 1988, unpaginated.

44. *Walter May: Recent Sculpture* is displayed in 1985 and *Blake Senini: Sculpture* in 1986.

45. Quote taken from "Preface," *Multiple Associations,* ibid.

46. These included exhibits at commercial spaces like Calgary's Canadian Art Galleries (*Gordon Ferguson: New Figures,* 1985) and Paul Kuhn Fine Arts (*Walter May: Recent Sculpture,* 1984), as well as public institutions such as the Glenbow Museum (*Wall/Space,* 1987), the Nickle Arts Museum (*Drawing Out the Form,* 1987), Muttart Art Gallery (*Hybrids: Painting and Sculpture, Part I and Part II,* 1988) and Edmonton's Ring House Gallery (*Rituals/Systems: An Exhibition of Site-Specific Installations by Five Alberta Sculptors,* 1986).

47. "Preface," *Multiple Associations: Five Alberta Artists,* Glenbow Museum, Calgary AB, 1988, p. 5.

48. Liam Lacey. "The medium is the message in Glenbow show," *Globe and Mail,* December 3, 1988, p. C4.

49. May earned a BFA from the University of Alberta, Edmonton in 1971 and was a special student in sculpture, University of Alberta from 1971–72.

50. Quote taken from "Walter May: Recent Sculpture," *Walter May: Recent Sculpture,* Southern Alberta Art Gallery, Lethbridge (1985). Essay by Mary-Beth Laviolette.

51. "Colorful sculptures full of surprises," *Calgary Herald,* September 14, 1984, p. F8.

52. Ibid.

53. "Walter May," Paul Kuhn Fine Arts, Calgary, *Vangaurd,* Vancouver, Summer, 1986, p. 42.

54. Eleanor Bond. "Gang of Three," ibid.

55. Mary-Beth Laviolette. "From Line to Form," *Artichoke: Writings about the visual arts,* Calgary, Fall 1989, p. 18.

56. Ibid.

57. Elizabeth Kidd. Essay for *Walter May,* the Edmonton Art Gallery, 1990.

58. "Walter May: Interview by John Chalke," *Walter May,* Mercer Union, Toronto, 1990, p. 4.

59. The title "new british sculpture' applied to artists Bill Woodrow, Richard Deacon Tony Cragg, Edward Allington, Anthony Gormley, Anish Kapoor, Alison Wilding and others. At various times, the work of several of these artists were exhibited in Alberta: Richard Deacon, Edward Allington and Tony Cragg were presented at Alberta College of Art Gallery in 1987 as part of *The Analytical Theatre: New Art From Britain;* Kapoor served as a visiting guest artist at the Alberta College of Art in 1988.

60. Manon Blanchette. "Five Sculptors from Southern Alberta," *Vanguard,* Vancouver, February 1986, p. 65.

61. Marla Strong. "Blake Senini," *Vanguard,* Vancouver, October 1986, p. 34.

62. Eleanor Bond. "Gang of Three," ibid.

63. Interview with artist in 1986 for *Blake Senini: Sculpture,* Southern Alberta Art Gallery, Lethbridge, 1986. Essay by Mary-Beth Laviolette.

64. Ibid.

65. *WallSpace: New sculpture by six Calgary artists,* Glenbow Museum, Calgary, 1987, unpaginated.

66. Eleanor Bond. "Gang of Three," ibid.

67. "Sculptor makes big changes in sixth solo," *Calgary Herald,* June 2, 1989.

68. *Simone: Blake Senini,* MacKenzie Art Gallery, 1996, p. 8.

69. Ibid., p. 7.

70. Formerly known as the Muttart Art Gallery and located in Memorial Park Library in Calgary, the public gallery moved into the historic downtown core in 1999.

71. Blake Gopnik. "Painting a picture of ceasefire between art's warring factions," *Globe and Mail,* July 3 2000.

72. David Hopkins, author of *After Modern Art: 1945–2000,* Oxford History of Art, Oxford University Press, 2000, titles the section on installation art as "Installation as a paradigm," p. 228.

73. Hugh M. Davies. "Introducing Installation: A Legacy from Lascaux to last week," *Blurring the Boundaries: Installation Art 1969–1996,* Museum of Contemporary Art, San Diego, 1997, p. 9.

74. Ibid., p.11.

75. Ibid., p.10.

76. My thanks to curator Helga Pakasaar for her "Thoughts on Installation," *Insideout: Four Canadian Ceramic Installations,* the George R. Gardiner Museum of Ceramic Art, Toronto, 1998, p. 7.

77. Elizabeth Beauchamp. Essay for "Extensions 1969–1972," *Norman Yates: Toward Landscape,* Ring House Gallery, Edmonton, 1983, p. 37.

78. This project was initiated by Clive and Su Robertson.

79. Clive Robertson and Paul Woodrow. *W.O.R.K.S.C.O.R.E.P.O.R.T.* Printed and bound by Beau Geste Press, England, 1975. All copyright remains with W.O.R.K.S. Calgary. Unpaginated.

80. Ibid. Hogg's reveiw is dated Friday, June 29, 1973.

81. "Rita McKeough: Some Voices Have Hearts," *Vanguard,* Vancouver, Summer 1986, p. 19.

82. Carol Hogg. "Visitors literally swamped by the art at Dandelion show," April 29, 1977.

83. McKeough's graphic art appeared in three of the Art Gallery of Brant's national Graphex exhibitions, Alberta Work ACA Gallery and the touring *Some Drawings by Some Albertans* between 1975 and 1980.

84. Rita McKeough earned her BFA in 1975 from the University of Calgary.

85. "Calgary Defunct: The art of Rita McKeough," *NeWest Review,* April 1983, p. 8.

86. A process piece is an artwork that continues to evolve as part of its exhibition.

87. *Afterland Plaza: An Installation by Rita McKeough,* Mendel Art Gallery, Saskatoon, 1986, p. 6.

88. The exhibition curator is Christine Conley.

89. Nancy Tousley. "Young Calgary sculptor presents most original, engaging pieces," *Calgary Herald,* May 13 1982.

90. Jamelie Hassan. Essay for Gisele Amantea, Southern Alberta Art Gallery, Lethbridge AB, 1988. Unpaginated.

91. Nancy Tousley. "Gisele Amantea: Antidotes for Madness," *Gisele Amantea: Antidotes for Madness,* Mendel Art Gallery, Saskatoon SK, 1987, unpaginated.

92. Liam Lacey. "Mining the sentimental for hints of the spiritual," *Globe and Mail,* March 14, 1989.

93. The exhibition *Gisele Amantea* was at the Southern Alberta Art Gallery. Curator: Joan Stebbins.

94. Amantea participated in *Screens* at the Nickle Arts Museum, Calgary. Curator: Katherine Ylitalo.

95. Spring 1991, p. 28.

96. *White Folly* was created for *Gisele Amantea* at Lethbridge's Southern Alberta Art Gallery, 1988.

97. The panoramic Rockies mural is painted by American Franz Spohn.

98. "Sanctuary: Protect and Ruin," *Gisele Amantea: Recent Work,* Walter Phillips Gallery, Banff Centre, 1991.

99. "Amantea explores the kitsch and the beauty of nature," December 20, 1991, p. C6.

100. From artist statement printed in Arnatt brochure, the Nickle Arts Museum, Calgary, 1983. Curator of *Proposition of Potential* is Karyn Elizabeth Allen.

101. This degree is awarded in 1974, the same year the artist completed his MFA.

102. Liz Wylie. Catalogue for *Ritual Systems* exhibit, p. 3.

103. From catalogue for *Illusion and Paradox, The Winnipeg Perspective 1986,* the Winnipeg Art Gallery, 1986, p. 6.

104. "Artist has made a good case," *Lethbridge Herald,* May 24, 1985.

105. From catalogue *Multiple Associations: Five Alberta Artists,* Glenbow Museum, Calgary, 1988, p. 9.

106. Installation was shown at the Boulder Art Center, Boulder, Colorado and at Calgary's Glenbow Museum in *Multiple Associations: Five Alberta Artists.* Curator is Katherine Ylitalo.

107. Exhibited at the Art Gallery of the South Okanagan, Penticton; the Kenderdine Art Gallery, University of Saskatchewan, Saskatoon; and the Southern Alberta Art Gallery, Lethbridge, Alberta.

108. Artist statement in *Carl Granzow: Tracking,* Art Gallery of the South Okanagan, Penticton, 1995, p. 7. Curator is Roger H. Boulet.

109. Created for *In Our Image: Bev Tosh, JoAnne Schachtel and Ray Arnatt.* Curator is Kathryn Burns.

110. From a talk given by the artist at the Nickle Arts Museum, November 22, 1995.

111. Curator's statement for *Place Setting,* 2nd Story Gallery, Calgary, 1987.

112. Those events are *The Night of the Living Junk Monkeys,* 1996 and *Dusk 'til Dawn,* 1997.

113. "Rooms transformed into environments," *Calgary Herald,* August 1 1987, p. E1.

114. One of Dicey's more frequent group collaborations is with *The Skep(tic)ks* ,1993, featuring Dicey, Cori Stent, Jeff Viner, Don Mabie and Grant Poier.

115. Jann L.M. Bailey. "Rehearsal for an exhibition: A copse, a corpse and a kaddish," *Diana Burgoyne, Mark Dicey and Steve Mennie: A copse, a corpse and a kaddish,* Kamloops Art Gallery (1992), unpaginated brochure.

116. Artist talk for *Surroundings,* Glenbow Museum, Calgary, December 4, 1988. Curator: Katherine Ylitalo.

117. "Noise Under the Tongue," *Noise Under the Tongue,* Walter Phillips Gallery, Banff Centre, 1990, p. 7.

118. Nancy Tousley. "Graceland hosts art rodeo," *Calgary Herald,* August 19, 1989.

119. Graceland participants include: Wendy Allen, Dino Baker, Alex Caldwell, David Clark, Fred Coates, Beth Harmer, Richard Issler, Mary Lammirato, Loyala Lewis, Jeff Norgren, Larry Petersen, Mike Ryan, Peter Stinson, Dawn Trueman, Jill Armstrong, Dean Bareham, Neil Callaghan, Natalie Clark, Christine Cook, Robert Hamilton, Harvey Issler, Joma, Letia Lewis, Trevor Mercer, Jim Norton, Dave Radcliff, Maxx C. Stevens, Carole Thorpe and Tim Westerbury. List courtesy of the Glenbow Museum.

120. Graceland's public premiere was a performance art festival, *Night of the Living Junk Monkeys,* 1986, organized by 2nd Story Gallery.

121. Debbie O'Rourke. "Bart Habermiller: A State of Grace in Calgary," *Espace,* Issue #35, Montreal, Spring 1996, p. 25–29.

122. Mary Anne Moser. "Graceland Art Rodeo," *Artichoke: Writings about the visual arts,* Fall 1990, p. 27.

123. "Society's junk moulded into social comment," *Calgary Herald,* April 26, 1987.

124. Ibid.

125. Catalogue published by the Nickle Arts Museum, Calgary, 1988, p. 22.

126. Interview with artist, March 24 2003, Banff.

127. David Garneau. "Natural Double Takes," *BorderCrossings,* Winnipeg, 1999, p. 52.

128. Diana Nimeroff and Jeffrey Spalding. "Jurors' Statement," *Survey Alberta 88,* p. 3.

129. Melanie Townsend. "In Praise of Baxter's Folly," *Iain Baxter: Landscape Works,* WPG Editions, Banff Centre. 1999, p.11. Townsend also curated the show.

130. "Natural Double Takes," *BorderCrossings,* Winnipeg, 1999, p. 52.

131. *Tim Watkins: Somewhere I have never travelled,* Southern Alberta Art Gallery, 1989, unpaginated. Essay by William Zimmer.

132. Nancy Tousley. "Show is natural mix," ibid.

133. "Tim Watkins: Various Things that Move," *Artichoke: writings about the visual arts,* Calgary, Fall/Winter 1994, p. 59.

134. Nancy Tousley. "The Dance explores our relationship with Nature/technology," *Calgary Herald,* July 29, 1994, p. D5.

135. Cardiff received her MVA in 1983. Dunning attended the programme 1975–77.

135. Cardiff's auditory work is achieved with the assistance of multimedia artist and spouse, George Bures Miller, b. 1960, Vegreville, Alberta.

136. Unpublished artist statement provided to the author in 1995.

137. John Hall was the first Albertan to have a solo exhibition at the NGC. Organized by the Alberta College of Art Gallery, the survey show was entitled *John Hall: Paintings and auxillary works, 1969–1978.* The curator was Ron Moppett.

138. Michelle Litvin. "On Exhibit: Hearing is believing," *Chicago Reader,* December 16, 1994.

139. Kate Taylor. "Art About," *Globe and Mail,* Toronto, July 17, 1992.

140. Nancy Tousley. "Alan Dunning," *Canadian Art,* Winter 1991.

141. Leslie Dawn. "Still Wet," *Vanguard,* April/May 1986.

143. Artist talk in Calgary, September 17, 1991.

144. Artist statement for *Translation,* Glenbow Museum, Calgary, 1991.

145. Quote from Dunning in Patricia Henderson's "Dunning turns Gallery into a Book," *Centre Letter,* Banff Centre June 16–23, 1988.

146. From curator Valerie Greenfield's essay for *Scale: Drawings by Therese Bolliger, Alan Dunning and Tonie Leshyk,* Alberta College of Art Gallery, Calgary, 1986, p. 5.

147. From essay *Reading Dunning, Elision,* Contemporary Art Gallery, Vancouver, 1992, p. 24. Curated by Keith Wallace. Also features an essay by Helga Pakasaar *Making Sense.*

148. Helga Pakasaar. *Making Sense,* Elision, Contemporary Art Gallery, Vancouver BC, 1992. Curated by Keith Wallace. Also includes an essay, *Reading Dunning,* by Nancy Tousley.

149. Ibid., p. 7.

150. From artist slide talk in Calgary, November 16, 1995.

151. Walter Phillips Gallery, Banff Centre. An artist's book was also produced.

152. Neutral Ground, Regina, Saskatchewan. Catalogue essay by Alan Brandoli.

153. Contemporary Art Gallery, Vancouver. Curator is Keith Wallace.

154. Leslie Dawn. "Stammering," *Vanguard,* Vancouver, September 1988, p. 34.

155. This interest in collaborative activity also figured importantly in the 1990s artwork of Shelley Ouelette and Laura Vickerson, also of Calgary.

156. "The Lost Dimension: An Internet city," *Mute #4,* Winter/Spring 1996.

157. Nancy Tousley. "Virtual Frontier," *Calgary Herald,* September 28, 1996, p. E15.

158. This project is exhibited during the 1997 ArtWeek, Calgary.

159. "Einstein's Brain: The fall," *Calgary Herald,* September 20, 1997.

160. Bures Miller is listed as providing technical, editing and vocal assistance.

161. Sarah Milroy. "The sights and sounds of art that's going places," *Globe and Mail,* Toronto, May 16, 1998.

162. Sara Borins. "Four Nights in Venice," *Saturday Night,* July 14, 2001.

163. From Kitty Scott's description of the *Louisiana Walk #14,* 1996 at the Louisiana Museum of Modern Art, Humlebaek, Denmark.

164. From Carol Peaker's *National Post,* Toronto description of the 1999 *The Missing Voice (Case Study B),* at Whitechapel Library, London, England. Reprinted in *Janet Cardiff: A survey of works including collaborations with Georges Bures Miller* by Carolyn Christov-Bakagiev for P.S.1 Contemporary Art Centre, Long Island, NY, 2001, p. 110.

165. "Foreword," *Janet Cardiff: A survey of works.* ibid, p. 9.

166. Ibid.

167. The installation is displayed at the Macdonald Stewart Art Centre, Guelph, 1988, Latitude 53, Edmonton, 1989, and Glenbow Museum, Calgary, 1989.

168. Artist statement in letter to author, dated July 27, 1995.

169. From an interview by curator Carolyn Christov-Bakargiev entitled "An Intimate Distance Riddled with Gaps: The Art of Janet Cardiff," *Janet Cardiff: A survey of,* ibid., p. 27.

170. Michelle Litvin. "On Exhibit: Hearing," ibid.

171. Essay by Carolyn Christov-Bakargiev for *Janet Cardiff: A survey of works,* ibid., p. 17.

172. Michelle Kowch. "Art With an Attitude," *The Endeavor,* Lethbridge, January 27, 1994.

173. From an interview with Carolyn Christov-Bakargiev, ibid., p. 22.

174. Ibid., p. 31.

175. **Janet Cardiff: A Survey of Works Including Collaborations with George Bures Miller,* P.S.1 Contemporary Art Center, Long Island, N.Y. Touring venues include Musée d'art contemporain de Montréal, Montreal and Palazzo delle Esposizioni, Rome.

176. Essay by Carolyn Christov-Bakargiev, ibid., p. 30.

177. Ibid.

178. Exhibited as *Black Pool* at the Walter Phillips Gallery, Banff Centre, 1995 and Front Gallery, Vancouver (1995). Later exhibited as *The Dark Pool* at the Alberta Biennial of Contemporary Art, 1996, the Edmonton Art Gallery and Glenbow Museum, Calgary.

179. Sara Borins. "Four Nights in Venice," *National Post,* Toronto, July 14, 2001, p. 26.

180. Juliet Kershaw. "Alberta artists scoop top art award," *Legacy,* Edmonton, Spring 2002, p. 44.

181. Sarah Milroy. "Janet Cardiff," *Globe and Mail,* Toronto, December 29, 2001, p. R2. The artist attributes the media attention to their work "because we're not just art. We really sort of bridge the entertainment industries."

182. Carol Peaker. "The voice of a friend," ibid.

183. Ibid.

184. Gail Helgason. "Artists say you can get there from Lethbridge," *Alberta Connections,* Alberta Community Development, Winter 1999.

185. Hoffos, who worked with the couple and who had Cardiff as an instructor for one course in photography, recalls their relationship in terms of "cross-fertilization," he coming up with the idea of the miniaturized set, they with the use of the motion sensor. (From phone call with author, May 8, 2002.)

186. Gail Helgason. "Artists say you can," ibid.

187. The work is displayed in an empty storefront window in Lethbridge and is sponsored by the Southern Alberta Art Gallery. A brochure with an essay by David Wagner is also produced.

188. "New Artists/New Works: Three small rooms and a TV," *Muttart Public Art Gallery Newsletter,* Calgary, Spring 1997.

189. Displayed at the Muttart Public Art Gallery, Calgary in New Artists/New Works: *Three small rooms and a TV:* David Hoffos, Andrea Inglis, Wright Simmonds and Kenneth Doren.

190. Displayed at the Illingworth Kerr Gallery, Alberta College of Art and Design.

191. Displayed at Southern Alberta Art Gallery, Lethbridge and TrepanierBaer Gallery, Calgary.

192. Published jointly by Illingworth Kerr Gallery, ACAD and Southern Alberta Art Gallery, Lethbridge, 2000 for *Catastrophe* exhibit and *Another City* exhibit.

193. Ibid.

194. This work is presented as part of the group exhibition, *Constructions,* Glenbow Museum, 1990. Also included are Sally Barbier, Bill Laing and Barbara Tipton.

195. From 1978 to 1999, the gallery is located on the second floor of the Memorial Park Library, a building connected to the park's commemoration of those who died in World War I.

196. "Installation As Art," *Muttart Art Gallery,* Muttart Art Gallery, Calgary, September/October 1990, unpaginated.

197. Caterina Pizanias. "Elizabeth LeMoine: some where else," *Some where else,* Neutral Ground, Regina, 1998, p. 9.

198. Deidre Hanna. "Minuscule rules in tiny, daring YYZ show," *Now* magazine, 1999.

199. Anna Murphy. "Dinky cars and hats and houses and handbags; they used to belong in the nursery, now you find them in art galleries," *Observer Life,* August 1998, p. 22.

200. Elisabeth Mahoney. "Size, Does It Matter," *Make: Magazine of Women's Art,* London, March–May 1999.

201. Anna Murphy. "Dinky cars and hats and houses," ibid.

202. Amy Gogarty. "Elizabeth LeMoine," ibid.

203. In 1984, Williams is the Canadian representative at *Rendez-Vous International Sculpture Symposium,* Saint Jean-Port Joli, Quebec. In 1987, the artist is granted the highest award at the *Trois Rivières National Biennial of Ceramics.*

204. A touring exhibition of studio ceramics, 1964-1984, organized by the Alberta Art Foundation and Alberta Potters Association.

205. A juried travelling exhibition presented by the Alberta Crafts Council.

206. The other three artists are Jamelie Hassan, Millie Chen and Baco Ohama, a graduate of the University of Calgary Ceramics program.

207. "Reconsidering Function," *Contact,* Calgary, 1993/94 Winter, p. 22.

208. Artist statement prepared for author, 1995.

209. *Insideout: Four Canadian Ceramic Installations,* The George R.Gardiner Museum of Ceramic Art, Toronto, 1998, p. 5.

210. Southern Alberta Art Gallery, 1993. Curator is Joan Stebbins.

211. *Cooled Matter: New Sculpture,* Columbus College of Art and Design, Columbus, Ohio, 1999. Essay by Mitchell Merback.

212. Artist statement prepared, ibid.

213. John Stocking. "The Wilderness and the Grid," *Cathedrals,* Southern Alberta Art Gallery, Lethbridge AB, 1993, unpaginated.

214. The George R.Gardiner Museum of Ceramic Art, Toronto.

215. Les Graff. "Turning Earth into Art," *AlbertaViews,* Calgary, Summer 1999, p. 25.

216. Ibid.

217. Anne Severson. "Hostess with the mostest," *FFWD,* Calgary, March 30-April 5, 2000.

218. This tradition dates back to the 1930s with A.C. Leighton and then H.G. Glyde establishing a place for visual arts at the Banff School of Fine Arts and the founding of the Alberta Society of Artists. In Calgary, it carries on with the founding in 1946 of the artist-run exhibition and cultural centre at Coste House, Allied Arts Centre.

219. Katherine Ylitalo. Curatorial statement for *Copy: Recent Work by Bennett, Ouellet, Rydman, Smith,* Nickle Arts Museum, 1995, p. 4.

220. First displayed at Truck Gallery, Calgary.

221. Her first project of this series, *Rita Hayworth,* was exhibited the first Alberta Biennial of Contemporary Art 1996, Edmonton Art Gallery and Glenbow Museum.

222. *Niagara* of this series was first exhibited in *Obsession,* The Works 2001, Edmonton. Curator: Catherine Crowston.

223. Artist Statement for Alberta Biennnial of Contemporary Art, 1996, Edmonton Art Gallery and Glenbow Museum, Calgary.

224. Ibid.

225. Ibid.

226. "The seduction of the shiny," *Shiny,* Latitude 53, Edmonton, 1999, p. 16.

227. Ibid.

228. "Shiny, shiny," curatorial essay for *Shiny,* p. 9.

229. Katherine Ylitalo. Curatorial essay for *Copy,* p. 16.

230. Ibid., p. 5.

231. Nancy Tousley. "10,000 miniature monsters," *Calgary Herald,* October 7, 1994.

chapter nineteen

1. In the late 1960s and early 1970s, Hammock served as the art critic for the *Edmonton Journal.* Later he served as Professor of Art at Mt. Allison University, Sackville, NB.

2. "Prairie Visions: The art of Ron Kostyniuk," *ArtFocus,* Fall 1992, p.14.

3. Ibid.

4. Ibid., p. 12.

5. Bornstein is the head of the Fine Arts Department. Kostyniuk attends lectures and some studio classes where he is introduced to the structuralists and the writings of Charles Biederman.

6. In 1969, the artist obtains his BFA from the University of Alberta, Edmonton.

7. Sheila Robertson. "Constructed reliefs contain nature analogies," *Star Phoenix,* Saskatoon, March 5, 1988.

8. "Ron Kostyniuk: The Saskatchewan road map series," *Artichoke: writings qbout the visual arts,* Calgary, Fall/Winter 2000, p. 8.

9. *Ron Kostyniuk: Recent Work.* Brochure published by the Petro-Canada Exhibition Gallery, Calgary 1985.

10. Sheila Robertson. "Constructed reliefs," ibid.

11. "Prairie Visions," ibid., p. 14.

12. Ibid., p. 15.

13. The gallery opens on September 15, 1988 in the southwest corner of the Municipal Building. It takes its name from the unique shape of the building.

14. For instance, in 1979 Cooke participates in the group exhibition, *Alberta Works in Wood,* Alberta College of Art Gallery, Calgary.

15. Gallie received a BFA from NSCAD, 1971 and an MFA from U of A, 1973.

16. Cooke is a sculpture major at ACA, 1967–1972 and does post-graduate work in sculpture, New York Studio School, NYC, 1972–73.

17. Artist statement sent to author, 1995.

18. Liz Wylie. "The Underside of Edmonton," May 1984.

19. Ibid., p.18.

20. Essay for *Pressure Points: Tommie Gallie,* Edmonton Art Gallery, 1992, unpaginated brochure.

21. From interview with curator Helen Collinson published in *In Place: Tommie Gallie,* Ring House Gallery, Edmonton, 1981, p. 26.

22. Ibid., p.24–25.

23. Neil Waugh. "Is it art or is it junk?", *Edmonton Sun,* May 22, 1991.

24. Essay for *Pressure Points: Tommie Gallie,* ibid.

25. Essay by Dan Bagan for brochure, *Tommie Gallie: Grace Under Pressure,* Latitude 53, Edmonton, 1988, unpaginated.

26. The next three quotes are from Elizabeth Beauchamp's "Gallie's exhibition a fitting tribute," *Edmonton Journal,* July 16, 1988.

27. The first solo exhibition is in 1975.

28. Essay for *Pressure Points: Tommie Gallie,* ibid. Curator is Elizabeth Kidd.

29. Elizabeth Beauchamp. "Pickaxes Save Art World," *Edmonton Journal,* May 27, 1992.

30. "Illusion and Simile in Western Sculpture," *Artmagazine,* 38/39, June 1978.

31. Essay for *Rituals/Systems: An Exhibition of Site-specific Installations by Five Alberta Sculptors,* Ring House Gallery, Edmonton, 1986, p. 3.

32. Since 1971, Cooke has worked at the University of Lethbridge as an art gallery technician and preparator.

33. First installed at the Southern Alberta Art Gallery, Lethbridge, 1983.

34. First installation in *Rituals/Systems: An Exhibition of Site-Specific Installations by Five Alberta Sculptors,* Ring House Gallery, Edmonton, 1986.

35. "Adrian Cooke-Prairie Keep," unpublished, 1991.

36. Unpublished statement, prepared by Valerie Cooke, c. 1986.

37. Artist statement, published in brochure form by the Triangle Gallery, 1995.

38. Displayed at the Triangle Gallery, the exhibition also showcased Catherine Ross, Rick Calkins, Steve Nunoda and Wright Simmonds.

39. Unpublished statement, ibid.

40. Penny studies at the Alberta College of Art, 1971–1975. He graduates with honours, fine art diploma (sculpture). He continues with another post-graduate year at the college, 1976–77. He then instructs at the college, 1978–79, and, 1982–83.

41. Because Penny has maintained a presence in Alberta through a steady record of exhibitions, the artist is suitable for this survey.

42. Nicholas Roukes. *Alberta Sculpture Survey 89,* Triangle Gallery, Calgary (1989). Roukes is the guest curator.

43. Gary Michael Dault. the *Globe and Mail,* Toronto, November 3, 2001, p. V2.

44. According to Nancy Tousley in "Sculptor shocks with realistic look at people," *Calgary Herald,* December 14, 1988, Ali's "florid representation raised feminist hackles."

45. Gary Michael Dault. "Evan Penny," *Canadian Art,* Toronto, Fall 1986, p. 58.

46. Nancy Tousley. "A new perspective: Sculptor Evan Penny plays with our perceptions of reality," *Calgary Herald*, January 26, 2002.

47. Interview with artist, Calgary, September 21, 1995. In the catalogue accompanying *Evan Penny: A sculpture survey*, Art Gallery of Algoma, Sault Ste. Marie, 1987, the artist dedicates the exhibition to Ole Holmsten and Katie Ohe "for whose formative influences I am indebted and forever grateful."

48. Interview with artist, Calgary, September 21, 1995. Penny tried his hand at abstract welded steel for two years, including a stint with Anthony Caro at Emma Lake, According to Penny, Caro told him he had more of an aptitude with the figure.

49. For a further description of the difficulties Penny has had in the area of representing female subjects, see: Nancy Tousley." Sculptor shocks with realistic look at people," *Calgary Herald*, December 14, 1988, p. C2.

50. An example of this is his participation in the group exhibition, *Loving the Alien*, Art Gallery of Mississauga, Ontario, 1997 and in the same year at Saskatoon's Kenderdine Gallery, *Extreme Close-up: The body in context.*

51. Gary Michael Dault. "Evan Penny," ibid., p. 62.

52. Michael Burtch. Catalogue essay for *Evan Penny: A Survey*, Art Gallery of Algoma, Sault Ste.Marie 1987, unpaginated.

53. Gary Michael Dault. "Evan Penny," ibid.

54. Nancy Tousley. "A new perspective," *Calgary Herald*, January 26, 2002, p. E8.

55. Penny has worked on many movies with such directors as David Cronenberg and Oliver Stone.

56. "David Ebony's Top Ten," *Art in America*, New York, 1998.

57. Artist talk, October 17 1998, Nickle Arts Museum.

58. Nancy Tousley. "Pottery challenges the eye," *Calgary Herald*, November 26, 1985.

59. "Artist is putting life into his pottery exhibition," *Calgary Herald*, May 26, 1989, p. H4.

60. Nancy Tousley. "Style from the Earth," *Calgary Herald*, May 1991.

61. Since 1988, Payce has been a faculty member of the Alberta College of Art and Design. He has also served as head of the ceramics program.

62. David Garneau. Catalogue essay, "Calm Suspense," *Greg Payce: Vase to Vase*, Southern Alberta Art Gallery, Lethbridge, 1995, p. 16.

63. Ibid., see p. 11.

64. "Abstract, Figurative and Narrative: American ceramics in the early 1990s," *The twenty-eighth Ceramic National: Clay, Color, Content*, Everson Museum of Art, Syracuse, New York, 1990, p. 9.

65. Artist Statement, undated.

66. Ibid.

67. Franklyn Heisler. "Greg Payce Ceramics," *Contact*, Calgary, Summer 1989, p. 28.

68. "Greg Payce, Prime Gallery, Toronto," *American Ceramics*, April 1997.

69. Artist statement, undated.

70. David Garneau. "Calm Suspense," ibid., p. 17.

71. Formerly the Muttart Art Gallery, the AGC occupies two heritage sandstone buildings in downtown Calgary. *Cineramics: Jeannie Mah and Greg Payce* was curated by Mary-Beth Laviolette.

72. "Cineramics: Jeannie Mah and Greg Payce," *Artichoke: Writings about the visual arts,* Special Edition No. 1, Canmore, AB/ Vancouver, Vol. 13, No. 4, p.8.

73. In 1977, Payce graduated with a bachelor of arts, major fine art, minor anthropology from the University of Alberta. In 1982–84, he did two sessions of ceramics at the Banff Centre. In 1984-85, he did course-work in Art History at the University of Victoria

74. Organized by Allan Harding MacKay. The jurors are Diana Nimeroff, The National Gallery of Canada, and Jeffrey Spalding, University of Lethbridge.

75. The galleries are Canadian Art Galleries, Virginia Christopher Galleries and Paul Kuhn Fine Arts.

76. Sydor returned to Calgary in the mid-1990s.

77. "Restless Legacies," *Restless Legacies: Contemporary Craft Practice in Canada,* Olympic Arts Festival, XV Olympic Winter Games Organizing Committee, Calgary, 1988, p. 31.

78. David Lasker. "Clay Comes of Age," *Western Living,* Vancouver, November 1984, p. 64.

79. "Elegant, fragile forms created in rustic studio," *Calgary Herald,* May 18, 1986, p. F2.

80. Sydor earns a BFA from the University of Calgary in 1980 with further study at the Banff School of Fine Arts in 1978 and 1981 and continues with Graduate level ceramics of the University of Calgary, 1982–1983.

81. David Lasker. "Clay Comes," ibid.

82. The exhibition's title is *Ceramic Modernism: Hans Coper, Lucie Rie and Their Legacy.* John Chalke also appeared in this exhibit.

83. Mould was a sessional instructor, ceramics department, University of Calgary. She was also the originator and co-ordinator of the City of Calgary sponsored ceramics seminars, which run from 1974–1982. The seminars are revived in 1987 under the leadership of Evelyn Grant for the city's Leisure Learning Services. They continue until 1997.

84. "Elegant, fragile forms.", ibid.

85. Unpublished artist statement, 1995.

86. Franklyn Heisler served as the curator of the Muttart Art Gallery, 1988–1993.

87. "Vessels: Hand and Spirit," *Sightlines,* Muttart Art Gallery, Calgary, Winter 1998.

88. The exhibition is presented at the Muttart Art Gallery in 1998.

89. The artists are Bob Reimer, John Chalke, Jim Etzkorn, Richard and Carol Selfridge, and Sam Uhlick.

90. Jennifer Poyen. "Jim Etzkorn," *Contact,* Calgary, Spring 1994, p. 20.

91. This aspect is noted by the potter in a talk given by Etzkorn, May 5, 1997 in Calgary.

92. Mark Walton. "Jim Etzkorn: New Works," *Muttart Art Gallery Newsletter,* Calgary, Winter issue, 1994, p. 5.

93. Jennifer Poyen. " Jim Etzkorn," ibid., p. 22.

94. Mark Walton. "Jim Etzkorn," ibid.

95. Jennifer Poyen. "Jim Etzkorn," ibid., p. 21.

96. Payce curated the Alberta section.

97. See unpaginated catalogue, *Clay in Canada: North by Northwest,* published by the Crafts Councils of Manitoba, Saskatchewan, Alberta and British Columbia, 1994.

98. Letter to writer, dated July 25, 1995.

99. The 4th Street SW program is run by the 4th Street Business Revitalization Zone with additional grants from the Alberta Foundation for the Arts and the Calgary Region Arts Foundation.

100. "Western Canadian Ceramic Sculpture: A Ten Year Perspective," *Issues in Clay: Western Canadian Sculpture,* Latitude 53 Society of Artists, Edmonton, 1981, p. 13.

101. Ibid.

102. This survey is seen in Edmonton, Calgary, Medicine Hat, Banff and Burnaby, BC.

103. The exhibition is presented by Latitude 53 Society of Artists, Edmonton. The curator is Susan Abells Fridman.

104. Ibid.

105. Untitled essay for *New Directions in Clay,* Peter Whyte Gallery, Banff, 1983, unpaginated.

106. Artist statement, 1986.

107. The three installations are displayed at the New Gallery, Calgary, 1988, Glenbow Museum, Calgary, 1989, and Neutral Ground, Regina 1991.

108. "Vessels," *Vessels,* Glenbow Museum, Calgary, 1989.

109. Ibid.

110. The exhibition traveled to Glenbow Museum, Calgary; Canadian Clay and Glass Gallery, Waterloo; Medicine Hat Museum and Art Gallery, Medicine Hat Museum; U of A Extension Gallery, Edmonton; Southern Alberta Art Gallery, Lethbridge and Red Deer and District Museum, Red Deer.

111. Tipton completes a BFA in ceramics from the Memphis Academy of Arts, Memphis, Tennessee, 1969 and Grant with a BFA in ceramics major from the University of Calgary, 1981.

112. Nancy Tousley. "Fanciful function informs ceramic artist's work," *Calgary Herald,* December 28, 1986, p. D7.

113. Ibid.

114. Ibid.

115. "Gregory Payce and Evelyn Grant," *Contact,* Calgary, Summer 1992, p. 5.

116. Mary-Beth Laviolette. "Evelyn Grant," *Avenue,* Calgary, April 1995, p. 9.

117. *Calgary Herald,* October 19, 1990.

118. Ibid.

119. Artist statement produced for writer, unpublished, 1995.

120. Tipton worked for eight years in an editorial capacity for *Ceramics Monthly,* Columbus, Ohio, 1978–1986.

121. "Symbolic Clay," *Ceramics Monthly,* Columbus, Ohio, December 1987, p. 31.

122. Ibid., p. 32.

123. Artist statement for *1990 Ceramic Invitational* brochure, published by Art Gallery, Brigham Young University, Provo, Utah.

124. "Series/Summerscapes," *Visual Arts Newsletter,* Alberta Culture and Multiculturalism, Edmonton, October 1988, p. 14.

125. Brick sculptor Jim Marshall, Medicine Hat, is a founding member.

126. "Spotlight," *Alberta Craft Magazine,* Alberta Craft Council, Edmonton, May/June 2000, p. 4.

127. In the first year of the program, Yasuo Terada from Japan was the guest artist. In 1999, Alan Lacovetsky, Winnipeg; Shirley Rimer, Red Deer and Robert Harrison, Helena, Montana appear and in 2000, it is Trudy Ellen Golley, Red Deer; Les Manning, Medicine Hat and Katrina Chaytor, Calgary.

chapter twenty

1. Blake Gopnik. "Perennial paint," *Globe and Mail,* May 15, 1999.

2. "Driven to abstraction," Saturday, June 1996.

3. Organized by London's Canada House Cultural Centre Gallery and Alberta Culture, this exhibition travelled to London, Brussels and Paris.

4. The artists in this exhibition are John Hall, Don Kottmann, Carroll (Moppett) Taylor-Lindoe, Ron Moppett, Mary Scott, Jeffrey Spalding and John Will.

5. See Tousley's essay Seven Artists from Alberta: Art in this region, Canada House Cultural Centre Gallery, London, 1984, unpaginated.

6. Ibid.

7. Nancy Tousley. "Artist relates work to life experiences," *Calgary Herald,* July 27, 1986, p. F5.

8. Nancy Tousley. "Exhibition prompts praise for city gallery," *Calgary Herald,* February 10, 1983, p. F5.

9. "Artist relates work to life" ibid.

10. "The Artists and their Works," *Aspects of Contemporary Painting in Alberta,* Glenbow Museum, 1987, p. 42.

11. Leslie Dawn. *Don Kottmann: Painting, Drawing, Sculpture Survey,* Alberta College of Art Gallery, Calgary 1989, p. 21.

12. "The Return of the Art Heroes," *Artichoke,* Calgary, Winter 1991, p. 35.

13. Leslie Dawn. *Don Kottmann: Painting, Drawing,* ibid.

14. Ibid.

15. Ibid., p. 23.

16. From Alberta College of Art Gallery press release, undated.

17. The curator is Jeffrey Spalding.

18. During the fall of 1993, the Glenbow Museum exhibited from The National Gallery of Canada: *The Crisis of Abstraction in Canada: The 1950s.* Curator: Denise Leclerc.

19. Mary-Beth Laviolette. "Head Over Heels in Abstraction," *Artichoke,* Calgary, Spring 1994, p. 24.

20. "An Interview with Don Kottmann on abstract art," ibid., p. 26.

21. "Observations on the Contemporary Print," *Sightlines: Printmaking and image culture,* Edmonton: University of Alberta Press, 1997. Edited by Walter Jule.

22. This event was organized by the Division of Printmaking, Department of Art and Design, University of Alberta, Edmonton.

23. The curators are Deborah Herringer and Carl Danker.

24. May considers herself primarily a lithographer with an emphasis on photo-based lithography, common to printmakers trained at the University of Alberta (see Chapter 11). Webb had little interest in experimental printmaking and honed his skills in etching.

25. David Burnett. "Webb," *Cineplex Odeon: The first ten years,* Cineplex Odeon Corporation, Toronto, 1989, p. 108.

26. Nancy Tousley. "New work mixes all and nothing," *Calgary Herald,* July 1990.

27. "Artists stretch printmaking into three dimensions," *Calgary Herald,* November 1988.

28. Artist statement for the brochure, *New Work: May, Besant, Parker, Sewell.*

29. *All and Nothing,* Southern Alberta Art Gallery, Lethbridge, 1990, p. 5.

30. Bruce Ferguson and Sandy Nairne. *The Impossible Self,* Winnipeg Art Gallery, 1988, p. 14.

31. Vera Lemecha. Essay for *Vita Peracta,* published in 1992.

32. "Foreword," *Margaret May: Mind's Eye,* Nickle Arts Museum, Calgary, 1996, p. 2.

33. May also went to Italy in 1995.

34. "Margaret May," *New Economy,* The Nickle Arts Museum, Calgary, 1994, unpaginated fold-out.

35. The curators are Bruce Grenville (EAG) and Catharine Mastin (Glenbow Museum).

36. Artist Statement, printed on a card as part of the Biennial documentation.

37. Alanna Mitchell reviewed this exhibition for the November 9, 1996 issue.

38. The print shop is in operation from 1981 to 1987. He printed etchings and aquatints of other artist's work. He worked with Margaret May in 1981.

39. Nancy Tousley. "Artist creates classical fantasy in paintings," *Calgary Herald,* May 25, 1986, p. E3.

40. Nancy Tousley. "Painter constructs classical fantasies on masonite," *Calgary Herald,* October 9, 1986, p. C2.

41. Nancy Tousley. "Artist creates classical," ibid.

42. *Ken Webb: Prints By/Printed By*, Muttart Art Gallery, Calgary, 1989.

43. Ibid.

44. Nancy Tousley. "Artist creates," ibid.

45. Nancy Tousley. "Historical irony fuels images in strong exhibit," *Calgary Herald,* January 17, 1989.

46. Nancy Toulsey. "Images of War: Alberta artists capture the horror and devastation of the Balkans," *Calgary Herald,* April 15, 1995, p. G1–G2. The other two artists who went with MacDonnell are Danielle Ethier and Bill Bewick.

47. Nancy Tousley. "Berlin experience inspires artist's work," *Calgary Herald,* February 3, 1995, p. D6.

48. Anne Severson. "Aftermath of Vietnam conflict captured on canvas," *FFWD,* Calgary, March 11–March 17, 1999, p. 20.

49. Leslie Dawn, "In the absence of the Monument," *William MacDonnell: Dort? Ja, Ebendort,* Southern Alberta Art Gallery, Lethbridge, 1994, p.16.

50. Nancy Tousley. "Focus on William MacDonnell," *Canadian Art,* Toronto, Winter 1989, p. 88.

51. "William MacDonnell: Dort? Ja, Ebendort," *Gallery,* Southern Alberta Art Gallery, Lethbridge, March/April/May 1994.

52. Vincent Varga. "The Artists and Their Works," *Aspects of Contemporary Painting in Alberta,* Glenbow Museum, 1987, p. 44.

53. Stride Gallery opened in 1986 under the leadership of Mary Scott, Don Corman and Colleen O'Neill. The gallery's inaugural show featured William MacDonnell.

54. Leslie Dawn. "In the absence of the Monument," ibid., p. 9.

55. Nancy Tousley. "Artist makes ugly subjects compelling," *Calgary Herald,* April 6, 1997.

56. Artist Statement for *William MacDonnell: Dort? Ja, Ebendort,* Southern Alberta Art Gallery, Lehtbridge, 1994, p. 1.

57. "What's so creative about originality?" *Globe and Mail,* Toronto, March 27, 2002.

58. Daina Augaitus. "Transference: An act of appropriation," *Transference,* Walter Phillips Gallery, Banff Centre, 1987, p. 26.Augaitus is the curator and at the beginning of her essay, a definition of appropriation is provided, which is absorbed into my text.

59. Arni Runar Haraldsson."Tracing Collage, Montage and Appropriation," *Transference,* Walter Phillips Gallery, Banff Centre, 1987, p. 7. The exhibition features Don Corman, Chris Cran, William J. McCarroll, Steve Peterson, Arlene Stamp and John Will.

60. See George Melnyk's "The Art Recycling Depot," *Quill & Quire*, Toronto, November 1975.

61. Ibid.

62. Daina Augaitus. "Transference," ibid., p. 28.

63. Vincent Varga. "The Artists and," ibid., p. 56.

64. Peter White. "Don't Forget: Keep your head down (an introduction)," *Billy J. McCarroll: How to play a winning game your natural way; the metaphor continues,* Dunlop Art Gallery, Regina, 1986, unpaginated. Peter White is also the curator of the show.

65. Elizabeth Beauchamp. "Sam in Orange: hole in one," *Edmonton Journal,* July 3, 1988.

66. Peter White. "Don't Forget: Keep Your," ibid.

67. Neil Godbout. "Passion for gold subject of paintings," *Kelowna Capital News,* Kelowna, BC, July 15, 1987.

68. Dunlop Art Gallery.

69. Kelowna Art Gallery.

70. Organized by the Sir Wilfred Grenfell College Art Gallery, Memorial University, Cornerbrook. The curator is Colleen O'Neill.

71. Spalding is actually quite critical of appropriation's popularity in the 1980s, calling it "a hopelessly middle-of-the-road approach." See "Appropriation: When does borrowing become stealing," *The Last Issue,* Calgary, August 1987, p. 20–28.

72. Jeffrey Spalding. "Taking Art to the Forefront: Billy McCarroll, Slammin' Sam, Appropriation and All That Jazz," *Billy J. McCarroll: How To play a Winning Game Your Natural Way: A Continuing Metaphor 1983–1993,* Sir Wilfred Grenfell College Art Gallery, Memorial University of Newfoundland, 1994, p. 13.

73. Ibid, p.9.

74. Marshall Webb. "Arlene Stamp, Paintings: The Gladys M. Johnston Series," Spring, 1985, p. 25.

75. Nancy Tousley. "Appropriated art still has voice of its own," *Calgary Herald* October 13, 1983, p. F8.

76. Ibid.

77. "Statement of Concerns and Interests as an Artist," August 4, 1995, unpublished.

78. "Appropriated art still," ibid.

79. "Vinyl tile enters the high-art arena," September 13, 1991.

80. One commission is three wall-mounted tile works for the Ernst and Young Lobby, Toronto-Dominion Centre and a glass mosaic tilework for Sheppard West Station, Toronto Transit Commission.

81. "Fictive Space: The collaboration of Judith Schwarz and Arlene Stamp," *Fictive space: Judith Schwarz/Arlene Stamp,* Illingworth Kerr Gallery, Alberta College of Art and Design, 1984, p. 9.

82. Ibid., p.17

83. Ibid., p.7

84. "Mary is here," *Mary is here, Arlene Stamp,* unpaginated brochure.

85. unpublished Artist Statement, 1995.

86. This observation was made by a former Nicoll student, Eileen Taylor who is paraphrased by Christopher Jackson in catalogue *Marion Nicoll: Art and Influences,* Glenbow Museum, Calgary, 1986, p. 35.

87. "Marion Nicoll 1909–1985," *Visual Arts Newsletter,* Alberta Culture and Multiculturalism, Edmonton, April 1985.

88. "Chris Cran: Portrait of the artist as an unromantic," *Herald Sunday, Calgary Herald,* May 14, 1989, p. 5.

89. Trained at the Alberta College of Art in the 1960s, ManWoman is based in Cranbrook.

90. Kathryn Shattuck. "Mixing Up Perceptions, On Canvas and Off, in Calgary," July 7, 1999.

91. Ibid.

92. "Painting the Fame Game," Winnipeg, January 1999, p. 56.

93. "From the Varnishing Point: The recent paintings of Chris Cran," Calgary, Spring 1994, p. 57.

94. "Brillant brushwork toys with photography," June 11, 1994, p. C5.

95. "Chris Cran," *National Post,* Toronto, July 7, 1999.

96. "Painting, the Fame Game," ibid.

97. Kathryn Shattuck, ibid.

98. This body of work consisted of four series: *Gesture, Screens, Clear* and *Silver.*

99. Artist statement sent to author.

100. "Chris Cran," *National Post,* ibid.

101. All quotes in this paragraph come from "Concealing/Revealing Voices from the Canadian Foothills," *Concealing/Revealing: Voices from the Canadian Foothills,* Museum of Fine Arts, Florida State University, 1997, p.10–11.

102. The writer is using Eric Cameron's term to describe what he and his colleagues were doing at NSCAD in the 1970s. From interview with artist, August 17, 1995.

103. "Concealing/Revealing," ibid., p. 11.

104. "Garry Neill Kennedy: Painting in the Conceptual Field," *Garry Neill Kennedy, Work of Four Decades,* National Gallery of Canada, Ottawa, 2000, p. 8.

105. Alison Gilmore. "A Sneaky Way to Work With Paint," *National Post,* Toronto, February 8, 2003.

106. Ibid.

107. John Bentley Mays. "Thick-skinned art strange but admirable," *Globe and Mail,* Toronto, January 13, 1990.

108. Nancy Tousley. "Divine Comedy," *Canadian Art,* Toronto, Spring 1991, p. 60.

109. Donna McAlear. "Eric Cameron, Still Life in Retrospect … to be continued," *Artichoke,* Calgary, Fall 1989, p. 21.

110. Artist Talk, Calgary, November 22. 1995.

111. Interview with artist, August 17, 1995, Calgary.

112. Artist statement sent to author in 1995, undated.

113. "Eric Cameron, Still Life in Retrospect … to be continued," *Artichoke,* Calgary, Fall 1989, p. 21.

114. Cameron's practice also includes video art, performance and collaborative projects.

115. *Divine Comedy* was a collaborative effort organized by the Winnipeg Art Gallery and the National Gallery of Canada. Shirley Madill was the curator.

116. John Bentley Mays. "Thick-skinned art strange," ibid.

117. Ibid.

118. Eric Cameron. "English Roots," *English Roots: Eric Cameron,* 2001, p. 125. This book accompanied the English Roots project, organized by the University of Lethbridge Art Gallery and presented as three installations in Great Britain, 2000.

119. Nancy Tousley. "Calgary painter a winner," *Calgary Herald,* September 13, 1994.

120. The curators were Bruce Grenville and Catharine Mastin.

121. Unpaginated didactic notes produced by Glenbow curator Kirsten Eveden for *A 'Duchampian' Look at the Glenbow's Art Collection,* 1997.

122. Cameron taught in Halifax from 1978–83.

123. From 1983–86, Cameron is head of the painting department at his alma matter, Hull College of Art, Yorkshire, England. He completes a national diploma in design, 1965, post-diploma in printmaking, 1966 and an MFA in painting from Indiana University, Bloomington, Indiana, 1968.

124. "An Interview," *John Clark,* Southern Alberta Art Gallery, Lethbridge, 1979, unpaginated brochure.

125. "John Clark 1943–1989," *Canadian Art,* Winter 1989, p. 96.

126. "Exhibitions pay tribute to painter," *Calgary Herald,* March 1990.

127. Both quotes from Lipsett's essay for *John Clark: The night paintings,* Whyte Museum of the Canadian Rockies, 1989. Unpaginated brochure.

128. Rosemary Pruess was the curator.

129. "John Clark, 1943–1989," ibid.

130. "Artist's concerns shadowed in work," *Calgary Herald,* April 29, 1989.

131. "Calgarians brighten dull summer season," June 21, 1985.

132. "Art, Christopher Hume," *Toronto Star,* June 2, 1989, p. D12.

133. "Dorothy Knowles: Prairie passion," (May 13, 1995).

134. "The paintings of David Janzen lift above the horizon and leave the land behind," p. 37.

135. *David Janzen: Paintings/Constructions,* 2nd Story Gallery, Calgary.

136. *Points North,* Southern Alberta Art Gallery, Lethbridge, 1985/86; *Hidden Values,* The Edmonton Art Gallery, 1994; *Reflecting Paradise,* ArtWeek Exhibition, Calgary, organized by U of L Art Gallery, 1994; *Alberta Biennial of Contemporary Art 1998,* Glenbow Museum and the Edmonton Art Gallery; T*ransformations: Imaging Nature,* Mendel Art Gallery, Saskatoon, 1998 and *Blue,* the Nickle Arts Museum, Calgary, 1999.

137. Artist statement for *Alberta Biennial of Contemporary Art 1998,* Glenbow Museum and the Edmonton Art Gallery. Curators: Catharine Mastin and Catherine Crowston.

138. "The paintings of David Janzen lift off," ibid.

139. Artist Statement for *Alberta Biennial,* ibid.

140. Ibid.

141. Also included Graham Fowler and Patrick Close from Saskatchewan.

142. *Transformations: Imaging nature*, Mendel Art Gallery, Saskatoon, 1998, p.2.

143. Artist statement for *David Janzen: Paintings/Constructions,* 2nd Story gallery, 1985, unpublished.

144. Ibid.

145. "Blue: Brett Eveson, David Janzen, Kevin Mazutenic, Guido Molinari, Anne Ramsden, James Slingerwood, Kelly Wood," p. 10.

146. "John Brocke," *John Brocke: Seven Paintings,* Mira Godard Gallery, Toronto, 1989, unpaginated catalogue.

147. Nancy Tousley. "Artist keeps faith with realism," *Calgary Herald,* March 30, 1986.

148. Nancy Tousley, "Display seems out of place," *Calgary Herald,* November 8, 1985.

149. "Independent spirits from yonder by the sea," June 13, 1985.

150. Nancy Tousley. "Artist keeps faith," ibid.

151. Linda Genereux. "Precisely the realist," *Metropolis,* Toronto, June 15, 1989.

152. Robert Fulford. "Reviews: People's Art," *Canadian Art,* Summer 1992, p. 59.

153. "John Brocke," *John Brocke: Seven paintings,* ibid.

154. Kate Taylor. "Art About," *Globe and Mail,* January 31, 1992.

155. Charles Mandel. "Working up a sweat," *See,* Edmonton, February, 1989.

156. Vivienne Sosnowski. "Alberta watercolorist better known elsewhere," *Edmonton Journal,* October 3, 1987.

157. Others hard at work in the still life genre include Edmonton's Robert Lemay and Susan Bruce and Glen Semple of Calgary.

158. *The Edmonton Art Gallery: Exhibitions,* Winter/Spring 1989, p. 9.

159. Hall also curated *Six Calgary Realists* in 1985 for Alberta Culture's Beaver House in Edmonton. The travelling exhibition displayed 17 works by John Brocke, Lynn Crouch, Keith Harder, Glen Semple, Wade Stout and Jim Tanner.

160. Hall's essay is published by the Glenbow-Alberta Institute in a card format.

161. John Hall. *Artist's Perspective,* Glenbow-Alberta Institute (1989).

162. Artist statement, unpublished.

163. Christopher Jackson. Review for "Eve Koch," *Vanguard,* Vancouver, December 1987/January 1988, p. 31.

164. Donna McAlear. Essay for *Eve Koch,* Stride Gallery, Calgary, 1987, unpaginated.

165. With a BFA in painting and lithography from the University of Calgary (1971) and an MFA in painting from the University of Cincinnati, Ohio (1973), Koch developed this technique for acrylic over a period of a dozen years.

166. Eve Koch. Unpublished letter to Janice Mackett, Calgary. Dated April 7, 1997.

167. The other artists are Lynne Crouch, Keith Harder, Glen Semple, Wade Stout and Jim Tanner.

168. Sponsored by Triangle Gallery of Visual Arts and the Alberta Foundation for the Arts. The curator is Mary-Beth Laviolette.

169. Charles Mandel. "Art that is real," April 13, 1998.

170. The exhibition was organized by the Prairie Gallery, Grande Prairie. Curator was Elizabeth Ginn.

171. Nancy Tousley. "Perkins facing herself in art," *The Calgary Herald,* August 8, 1990.

172. Eve Koch. Unpublished letter to Janice, ibid.

173. "Marcia Perkins' painted gaze," *FFWD,* Calgary, May 29-June 4, 1997.

174. Nancy Tousley. "Perkins facing herself," ibid.

175. The exhibition was at the Southern Alberta Art Gallery, Lethbridge. The curator was Joan Stebbins.

176. "Feeling, Meaning and Motif," Marcia Perkins, Southern Alberta Art Gallery, Lethbridge, 1989, unpaginated.

177. "Marcia Perkins's painted gaze," ibid.

178. Tosh has a bachelor of arts (psychology) from the University of Saskatchewan, 1968; a diploma with distinction (painting), Alberta College of Art, 1985 and a MFA (painting), University of Calgary, 1987.

179. *By A Lady: Celebrating three centuries of art by Canadian women,* Maria Tippett. Toronto: Viking, Penguin Books, 1992, p.168.

180. While living in Singapore, Tosh studied with a master brush painter in the 1970s.

181. All quotes in sentence from Monique Westra's "Bev Tosh: Body of Work," *Artichoke,* Calgary, Summer 2000.

182. Artist statement, unpublished.

183. Anne Severson. "Life. It's been an interesting journey," *Calgary ArtWalk Magazine,* ArtWalk Society of Calgary, 1999, p. 18.

184. Ibid., p. 19.

185. Monique Westra. "Bev Tosh: Body of Work," ibid., p. 27.

186. Tosh befriended the interpreter on a trip to Siberia where her husband worked for the oil industry.

187. Patricia Robertson. "Return of the Figure," *Galleries West,* Calgary, Fall 2002, p. 12.

188. Gillian MacKay. "Lacquered labels, found photos, terrifying tots," *Globe and Mail,* Toronto, February 27, 1999, p. C11.

189. Ken Schmaltz. "Colleen Philippi," *Avenue,* Calgary, October 1995, p. 6.

190. Ibid.

191. Gillian MacKay. "Lacquered labels," ibid.

192. Ken Schmaltz. "Colleen Philippi," ibid.

193. "Delicate exploration of artist's childhood," *Edmonton Journal,* August 17, 1990.

194. The Edmonton Art Gallery. Curator: Denis Gautier.

195. Glenbow Museum. Curator: Kirsten Eveden.

196. Artist Statement for *A 'Duchampian' Look at the Glenbow's Art Collection.*

197. Mary Howes. "A Child Again," *Edmonton Bullet,* August 1990.

198. Interview with artist.

199. She received a BFA in 1985 and pursued independent studies in photography at U of C in 1986.

200. Bau-Xi Gallery, Vancouver.

201. Robin Laurence. "An individual response to shifting identities," *Vancouver Sun,* October 8, 1994.

202. Catalogue published by London Regional Art and Historical Museum, London Ontario, p. 18. This exhibition travelled to Alberta in 1994 to the Illingworth Kerr Gallery.

203. Gillian MacKay. "Lacquered labels," ibid.

204. Paula Gustafson. "Bugs, Babies and Bones," Spring 1997, p. 39.

205. Nora Abercombie. "Prevue," *Vue Weekly,* Edmonton, November 14–20, p .21.

206. The curator was Denis Gaultier.

207. From exhibition didactic notes.

208. University of Toronto, 1971.

209. Ontario College of Art, Toronto, 1973.

210. These paintings are exhibited in the group show, *Heroics,* 1988, Walter Phillips Gallery, Banff Centre.

211. Exhibited at the Whyte Museum of the Canadian Rockies, Banff in 1990.

212. Lelde Muehlenbachs. "Experiencing the Bush," *Bush,* Southern Alberta Art Gallery, Lethbridge, 1992, p. 13.

213. This quote and the following from a 1995 artist statement sent to author.

214. Stephen Hutchings. "The Bush Series," *The Bush Series,* Mira Godard Gallery, Toronto and Altitude Publishing, Canmore Alberta, 1997, p. 5.

215. Lelde Muehlenbachs. "Experiencing the…" ibid.

216. This quote and the following from: Stephen Hutchings. "The Bush Series," *The Bush Series,* Mira Godard Gallery, Toronto and Altitude Publishing, Canmore AB, 1997, p.12

217. The year was 1991.

218. Lelde Muehlenbachs. "Experiencing," ibid.

219. Ibid., p. 17.

220. "Stephen Hutchings: Towards Arcadia," *Vie des Arts,* Montreal, Summer 2003, p. 77.

221. "The Recent Paintings of Stephen Hutchings," *Recent Paintings: Stephen Hutchings,* University of Waterloo Art Gallery, Waterloo Ontario, 1995, p. 11.

222. *Bush,* Southern Alberta Art Gallery, Lethbridge, 1992, p. 10.

223. "Celebrating some fine and private moments," November 25, 1993, p. A14.

224. "Darker than Mid-Grey: The institutionalization of art," *Artichoke,* Calgary, Winter 1991, p. 13.

225. The curator was Joseph Wyatt.

226. Lukacs was born in Edmonton but taken to Calgary at age one where he lived until moving to Vancouver as a young man.

227. *Artichoke: Writings about the visual arts,* Calgary, Winter 1991, p. 34–35.

228. "Skinheads mirror society," November, 1990.

229. Interview with artist in Calgary, November 23, 1995.

230. Lukacs graduated from Emily Carr College of Art in 1985. That same year, he also appeared in the highly acclaimed *Young Romantics* exhibition at the Vancouver Art Gallery, where a new generation of representational painters was identified.

231. The exhibition was at the Edmonton Art Gallery in 1995. The article by Kevin Michael Grace appeared in the July 10, 1995 issue.

232. Interview with artist in Calgary, ibid.

233. The curator was Paulette Gagnon.

234. The gallery press release, dated May 22, 1995 for Lukacs exhibition and others, is titled "Confronting Stereotypes."

235. Scott Watson. "Attila Richard Lukacs," *Canadian Art,* Toronto, Fall 1988, p. 88.

236. Christian Eckart is the name Christoph Spindler chose for himself at age 24. He legally renamed himself after a fourteenth-century Christian mystic known as Meister Eckart.

237. Eckart received his art training from the Alberta College of Art. He graduated in 1984.

238. "The Possibility of Grace," *Calgary Herald,* October 26, 2002, p. ES6.

239. Ibid.

240. "The Spirituality of Negative Space," *Where Calgary/Gallery Guide,* Winter 2000, p. GG11.

241. Ibid., p. GG10.

242. Nancy Tousley. "Artist probes the sublime," *Calgary Herald,* April 7, 1995, p. C5.

243. The John Labatt Visual Arts Centre originated the exhibition.

244. "Disturbing Abstraction: Christian Eckart," John Labatt Visual Arts Centre, London, Ontario, 1996.

245. "Christian Eckart's abstract disturbances," *FFWD,* Calgary, June 12–18, p. 17.

246. "C'est la vie: With its celebration of personal art making, Claude Gosselin's latest Biennale de Montreal offered a provocative departure from Big Show razzle-dazzle," *Canadian Art,* Spring 2003, p. 71.

247. "Darker Than Mid-Grey: The institutionalization," ibid, p. 11. This slightly abridged essay was originally produced for the Banff Centre's 1990 arts journalism program and was published as well in the centre's *Passages.* Rhodes had just terminated his job as the editor, publisher and designer of *C* magazine, Toronto.

248. One exception to this trend was the establishment of the *Alberta Biennial of Contemporary Art* in 1996.

246. Compiled by Mary-Beth Laviolette. "Post Mortem on the Eighties: A look at the past decade," *Artichoke: Writings about the Visual Arts,* Calgary, February 1990, p. 22.

250. Ibid.

251. "The History of the Culture Sector and the Alberta Government," excerpt from *Culture Steps Forward* by Michael Evans and published in a 2003 newsletter from the Visual Arts Association of Alberta, Edmonton.

252. Michael Evans. *Culture Steps Forward,* Chapel Rock Consulting Services Inc. for the Alberta Cultural Human Resources Steering Committee, Banff Centre Press, 2000, p. 63.

253. "The History of the Culture," ibid.

254. The word "arts" in this instance includes performing, literary and visual activity.

255. "The History of the Culture" ibid.

256. Ibid, p. 15.

257. This publication was especially important with the nationally known critic, Nancy Tousley, at the helm.

258. Ken Schmaltz. "International Impressions," *Arts Bridge,* Alberta Community Development, Edmonton, Summer 1995, p. 11.

259. Ken Carpenter. "With Honours in Prague: The new new painters in the Czech Republic," *Canadian Art,* Winter 2002.

260. The curator was sculpture Royden Mills. A catalogue was also produced.

261. The curators for this 2001 exhibition were Jim Davies and Les Graff.

262. Joan Richardson. "Alberta Biennial of Contemporary Art 1996," *Canadian Art,* Toronto, Spring 1997, p. 63.

263. November 1998–January 1999, p. 17.

264. Ibid.

265. July 6, 2002, p. R5.

INDEX